Clymer Collection Series

VINTAGE

SNOWMOBILES

VOLUME II

➤ POLARIS, 1973-1979

YAMAHA, 1975-1980

SKI-DOO, 1970-1979

The world's finest publisher of mechanical how-to manuals

Intertec Publishing

P.O. Box 12901, Overland Park, Kansas 66282-2901

The following books and guides are published by Intertec Publishing.

CLYMER SHOP MANUALS
Boat Motors and Drives
Motorcycles and ATVs
Snowmobiles
Personal Watercraft

**ABOS/INTERTEC BLUE BOOKS
AND TRADE-IN GUIDES**
Recreational Vehicles
Outdoor Power Equipment
Agricultural Tractors
Lawn and Garden Tractors
Motorcycles and ATVs
Snowmobiles and Personal Watercraft
Boats and Motors

AIRCRAFT BLUEBOOK-PRICE DIGEST
Airplanes
Helicopters

AC-U-KWIK DIRECTORIES
The Corporate Pilot's Airport/FBO Directory
International Manager's Edition
Jet Book

I&T SHOP SERVICE MANUALS
Tractors

INTERTEC SERVICE MANUALS
Snowmobiles
Outdoor Power Equipment
Personal Watercraft
Gasoline and Diesel Engines
Recreational Vehicles
Boat Motors and Drives
Motorcycles
Lawn and Garden Tractors

CONTENTS

QUICK REFERENCE DATA

IGNITION SPECIFICATIONS

1974 ENGINES

Engine Model	Static Timing (mm) BTDC	Static Timing Inches BTDC	Running Timing (mm) BTDC	Running Timing Inches BTDC
EC17PM	——	——	2.5	0.100
EC25PS	0.47	0.018	3.60	0.142
EC25PC	0.41	0.016	3.37	0.135
EC29PF	0.41	0.016	3.37	0.135
EC34PC	0.41	0.016	3.37	0.135
EC34PQ	0.33	0.012	2.75	0.110/6,000
EC40PM	0.47	0.018	3.60	0.142
EC44PQ	0.33	0.012	2.75	0.110/6,000
EC54PM	0.47	0.018	3.60	0.142/6,000

1975 ENGINES

Engine Model	Static Timing (mm) BTDC	Static Timing Inches BTDC	Running Timing (mm) BTDC	Running Timing Inches BTDC
EC17PM	2.5	0.100	——	——
EC25PS	0.47	0.018	3.60	0.142
EC25PC	0.27	0.012	2.3	0.100
EC25PT	——	——	2.15	0.089
EC34PC	0.27	0.012	2.3	0.100
EC34PT	——	——	2.05	0.089
EC34PQ	——	——	2.25	0.089
EC44PQ	——	——	2.25	0.089
EC44PT	——	——	2.25	0.089
EC51PT	——	——	2.05	0.089

IGNITION SPECIFICATIONS (continued)

1976 ENGINES

Engine Model	Static Timing (mm) BTDC	Static Timing Inches BTDC	Running Timing (mm) BTDC	Running Timing Inches BTDC
EC17PM	2.86	0.113	——	——
EC25PS	0.36	0.014	2.96	0.116
EC25PC	0.13	0.005	2.1	0.082
EC34PC	0.13	0.005	2.1	0.082
EC34PQ	——	——	2.1	0.083 ①
EC44PQ	——	——	2.1	0.083 ①
EC25PT-06	——	——	2.1	0.082 ①
EC34PT-05	——	——	2.1	0.082 ①
EC44PT-05	——	——	2.1	0.083 ①
EC25PT-05	——	——	2.1	0.082 ①
EC34PT-06	——	——	2.1	0.082 ①

① Running timing BTDC 5,000 rpm, lights off.

1977 ENGINES

Engine Model	Static Timing (mm) BTDC	Static Timing Inches BTDC	Static Timing Deg. BTDC	Running Timing (mm) BTDC	Running Timing Inches BTDC	Running Timing Deg. BTDC
EC25PS	0.36	0.014	8	2.96	0.116	23
EC25PC	0.13	0.005	5	2.1	0.082	20
EC25PM-01	0.13	0.005	5	2.1	0.082	20
EC25PT-07	——	——	——	1.70* ③	0.067* ①	18
EC34PM-03	0.13	0.005	5	2.1	0.082	20
EC34PQ	0.143	0.006	5	2.24	0.088	20
EC34PT-05	——	——	——	1.70* ③	0.067* ①	18
EC34PL-01	——	——	——	1.70* ③	0.067* ①	18
EC44PQ	0.143	0.006	5	2.24	0.088	20
EC44PT-05	——	——	——	1.83* ④	0.072* ②	18
EC44PT-06	——	——	——	1.83* ④	0.072* ②	18

* Timing specified at 5,000 rpm with lights on.
① Acceptable variance to 0.046 in. BTDC or 15°.
② Acceptable variance to 0.050 in. BTDC or 15°.
③ Acceptable variance to 1.18mm BTDC or 15°.
④ Acceptable variance to 1.27mm BTDC or 15°.

SPARK PLUG RECOMMENDATIONS — 1974

Engine Model	NGK	Champion	Plug Gap
EC17PM	B7ES	N3	0.015 in.
EC25PS	B7ES	N3	0.017-0.020 in.
EC25PC	B8ES	N2	0.017-0.020 in.
EC29PF	B7ES	N3	0.017-0.020 in.
EC34PC	B8ES	N2	0.017-0.020 in.
EC25PS	B7ES	N3	0.017-0.020 in.
EC40PM	B7ES	N3	0.017-0.020 in.
EC54PM	B8ES	N2	0.017-0.020 in.
EC34PQ	B7ES	N3	0.017-0.020 in.
EC44PQ	B7ES	N3	0.017-0.020 in.

SPARK PLUG RECOMMENDATIONS — 1975

Engine Model	NGK	Champion	Plug Gap
EC17PM	B7ES	N4	0.015 in.
EC25PS	B7ES	N3	0.020 in.
EC25PC	B8ES	N2	0.020 in.
EC25PT	B8ES	N2	0.020 in.
EC34PC	B8ES	N2	0.020 in.
EC34PT	B8ES	N2	0.020 in.
EC34PQ	B7ES	N3	0.020 in.
EC44PQ	B7ES	N3	0.020 in.
EC44PT	B10E	N57	0.020 in.
EC51PT	B8ES	N2	0.020 in.

SPARK PLUG RECOMMENDATIONS — 1976

Engine Model	NGK	Champion	Plug Gap
EC17PM	B7ES	N4	0.016 in.
EC25PS	B7ES	N4	0.020 in.
EC25PC	B8ES	N3	0.020 in.
EC34PC	B8ES	N3	0.020 in.
EC34PQ	B7ES	N4	0.020 in.
E44PQ	B7ES	N4	0.020 in.
EC25PT-06	B9ES	N2	0.020 in.
EC34PT-05	B9ES	N2	0.020 in.
EC44PT-05	B8ES	N3	0.020 in.
EC25PT-05	B10EV	N1 or N57G	0.020 in.
EC34PT-06	B10EV	N1 or N57G	0.020 in.

(continued)

SPARK PLUG RECOMMENDATIONS — 1977

Model Engine	Champion	NGK (Resistor)	Plug Gap
EC25PS	N3	BR8ES	0.020 in.
EC25PC	N2	BR9ES	0.020 in.
EC25PM-01	N2	BR8ES	0.020 in.
EC25PT-07	——	BR9ES	0.020 in.
EC34PM-03	N2	BR8ES	0.020 in.
EC34PQ	N3	BR8ES	0.020 in.
EC34PT-05	——	BR9ES	0.020 in.
EC34PL-01	——	BR9ES	0.020 in.
EC44PQ	N3	BR8ES	0.020 in.
EC44PT-05	——	BR9ES	0.020 in.
EC44PT-06	——	BR9ES	0.020 in.

Table 2   1978-1979 TUNE-UP SPECIFICATIONS

Engine Model	Static Timing (mm) BTDC	Inches BTDC	Deg. BTDC	Running Timing (mm) BTDC	Inches BTDC	Deg. BTDC
EC25PS*	0.360	0.014	8 ± 3	2.96	0.116	23 @ 2,000
EC25PC*	0.360	0.014	8 ± 3	2.96	0.116	23 @ 2,000
EC25PM-01*	0.048	0.002	3 ± 3	1.69	0.067	18 @ 2,000
EC34PM-03*	0.048	0.002	3 ± 3	1.69	0.067	18 @ 2,000
EC34PM-04*	0.048	0.002	3 ± 3	1.69	0.067	18 @ 2,000
EC44PM-01*	0.051	0.002	3 ± 3	1.83	0.072	18 @ 2,000
EC25PT-07	—	—	—	4.31**[1]	0.17**[1]	29 @ 3,000**[1]
EC34PT-05	—	—	—	4.31**[1]	0.17**[1]	29 @ 3,000**[1]
EC44PT-05	—	—	—	4.19**[2]	0.16**[2]	27.5 @ 3,000**[2]
EC34PL-02	—	—	—	5.05**[3]	0.198**[3]	31.5 @ 3,000**[3]
EC51PL-01	—	—	—	3.75**[4]	0.147**[4]	27 @ 3,000**[4]

*Point gap = 0.014 in. (0.35mm)
**Timing specified at 3,000 rpm
1. Acceptable variance = 4.02-4.59mm (0.158-0.180 in.); 28-30°
2. Acceptable variance = 3.76-4.65mm (0.148-0.183 in.); 26-29°
3. Acceptable variance = 4.60-5.52mm (0.181-0.217 in.); 30-33°
4. Acceptable variance = 3.48-4.02mm (0.137-0.158 in.); 26-28°

Table 3   1978-1979 SPARK PLUG TYPE

Engine	NGK	Champion (Gap = 0.020 in.)
EC25PS	BR8ES	N-3
EC25PC	BR9ES	N-2
EC25PM-01	BR8ES	N-3
EC34PM-03	BR8ES	N-3
EC34PM-04	BR9ES	N-2
EC44PM-01	BR8ES	N-3
EC25PT-07	BR9ES	N-2
EC34PT-05	BR9ES	N-2
EC44PT-05	BR9ES	N-2
EC34PL-02	BR9ES	N-2
EC51PL-01	BR9ES	N-2

- NOTES -

CHAPTER ONE

GENERAL INFORMATION

Snowmobiling has in recent years become one of the most popular outdoor winter recreational pastimes. It provides an opportunity for an entire family to experience the splendor of winter and enjoy a season previously regarded by as many as miserable.

As with all sophisticated machines, snowmobiles require specific periodic maintenance and repair to ensure their reliability and usefulness.

MANUAL ORGANIZATION

This manual gives periodic maintenance, tune-up, and general repair procedures for Polaris snowmobiles manufactured in 1974 and later.

The Supplement at the end of the book contains specific service information for 1978-1979 models. If a procedure is not mentioned in the Supplement, it remains the same as on earlier models.

This chapter provides general information and hints to make all snowmobile work easier and more rewarding. Additional sections cover snowmobile operation, safety, and survival techniques.

Chapter Two covers all tune-up and periodic maintenance required to keep your snowmobile in top running condition.

Chapter Three provides numerous methods and suggestions for finding and fixing troubles fast. The chapter also describes how a 2-cycle engine works, to help you analyze troubles logically. Troubleshooting procedures discuss typical symptoms and logical methods to pinpoint the trouble.

Subsequent chapters describe specific systems such as engine, fuel system, and electrical system. Each provides disassembly, repair, and assembly procedures in easy-to-follow, step-by-step form. If a repair is impractical for home mechanics, it is so indicated. Usually, such repairs are quicker and more economically done by a dealer or other competent snowmobile repair shop.

Some of the procedures in this manual specify special tools. In all cases, the tool is illustrated in actual use or alone.

The terms NOTE, CAUTION, and WARNING have specific meaning in this book. A NOTE provides additional information to make a step or procedure easier or clearer. Disregarding a NOTE could cause inconvenience, but would not cause damage or personal injury.

A CAUTION emphasizes areas where equipment damage could result. Disregarding a CAUTION could cause permanent mechanical damage; however, personal injury is unlikely.

A WARNING emphasizes areas where personal injury or death could result from negligence. Mechanical damage may also occur. WARNINGS are to be taken seriously. In some cases serious injury or death has been caused by mechanics disregarding similar warnings.

MACHINE IDENTIFICATION AND PARTS REPLACEMENT

Each snowmobile has a serial number applicable to the machine and a model and serial number for the engine.

See **Figure 1** for the location of the machine model and serial number on the right rear side of the tunnel. **Figure 2** illustrates the location of engine numbers.

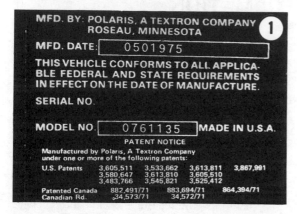

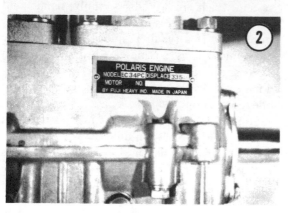

Write down all serial and model numbers applicable to your machine and carry the numbers with you. When you order parts from a dealer, always order by year and engine and machine numbers. If possible, compare old parts to the new ones before purchasing them.

If parts are not alike, have the parts manager explain the difference; the new part may be improved, but it could also be the wrong one.

OPERATION

Fuel Mixing

WARNING
Serious fire hazards always exist around gasoline. Do not allow any smoking in areas where fuel is mixed or when refueling your snowmobile.

Always use fresh fuel. Gasoline loses its potency after sitting for a period of time. Old fuel can cause engine failure and leave you stranded in severe weather.

Proper fuel mixing is very important for the life and efficiency of the engine. All engine lubrication is provided by the oil mixed with the gasoline. Always mix fuel in exact proportions. A "too-lean" mixture can cause serious and expensive damage. A "too-rich" mixture can cause poor performance and fouled spark plugs which can make an engine difficult or impossible to start.

Use a gasoline with an octane rating of 88 or higher. Use premium grade gasoline in all high-performance racing machines. Mix gasoline in a separate tank, not the snowmobile fuel tank. Use a tank with a larger volume than necessary to allow room for the fuel to agitate and mix completely.

Use Polaris Snowmobile Oil, or a good brand of 2-stroke oil, preferably one compounded for snowmobiles. Never use outboard motor oil, regular mineral oils, or automobile oil; they are almost certain to promote engine damage. All engines use a 20:1 ratio.

1. Pour half of the required gasoline into a clean container.

2. Add the required amount of oil and mix thoroughly.

3. Add remainder of gasoline and mix entire contents thoroughly.

4. Always use a funnel equipped with a fine screen when adding fuel to the snowmobile. Never add fuel when the engine is running.

Pre-Start Inspection

The few minutes necessary to prepare the snowmobile, as well as yourself, before starting it, may prevent a breakdown or an accident.

1. Check the cooling system. Ensure that the cooling fins are clean and free from obstructions.

2. Make sure the exhaust system and carburetors are securely fastened.

3. Check the operation of the throttle control. It should depress without excessive effort and return freely to idle. Ensure that the throttle safety switch is operating correctly. To adjust the throttle lever, see *Throttle Adjustment*, Chapter Two. To adjust the throttle safety switch, see *Throttle Safety Switch Adjustment*, Chapter Two.

4. Check the brake control. The brake should fully engage when the lever is depressed about ¾ in. and disengage freely when released. If more than ¾ in. of lever travel is required to engage the brake, or if the brake lever bottoms out on the handle control, adjust it as described in Chapter Two—*Brake Bleeding and Adjustment*.

5. Check the steering to ensure that the skis turn freely. If they turn with difficulty, remove ice or snow from around steering mechanism.

6. Check the fuel supply. Never take extended trips without a full fuel tank and a ready reserve for possible emergencies. For proper fuel mixture ratio, see *Fuel Mixing*, this chapter.

7. Check the toolbox. The tool kit and necessary spare parts should be carried at all times. In addition to the tools and equipment supplied with the machine, carry a spare drive belt and extra spark plugs.

8. Check to make sure the headlight, taillights, and brake light are working properly.

9. Make sure all nuts and bolts are tight. A loose nut or bolt could cause serious damage.

10. Clean the windshield with a clean damp cloth. *Do not* use gasoline, solvents, or abrasive cleaners.

11. Check track tension.

12. When the engine is started in extremely cold weather, prop up the back of the machine or tilt the machine to one side, and open the throttle slightly. Allow the track to turn several revolutions to allow the bearings, track, and drive belt to "warm up" before subjecting them to full load.

WARNING
Before starting the engine be sure that no bystanders are in front of or behind the snowmobile; a sudden lurch may cause serious injuries.

13. Start the engine and test operation of emergency kill switch and "tether" switch. Check that all lights are working.

Emergency Starting

Always carry a small tool kit with you. Carry an extra starting rope for emergency starting or use the recoil starter rope.

1. Remove the hood.

2. Unscrew the bolts and remove recoil starter (**Figure 3**).

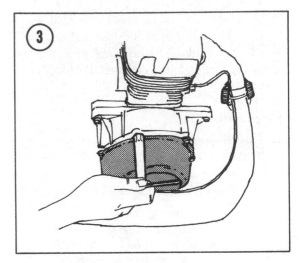

3. Wind rope around starter pulley and pull to crank engine (**Figure 4**).

Emergency Stopping

To stop the engine in case of an emergency, pull the tether string or switch the emergency kill switch to the STOP or OFF position.

Towing

When preparing for a long trip, pack extra equipment in a sled; don't try to haul it on the snowmobile. A sled is also ideal for transporting small children.

> **WARNING**
> *Never tow a sled with ropes or pull straps; always use a solid tow bar. Use of ropes or flexible straps could result in a tailgate accident, when the snowmobile is stopped, with subsequent serious injury.*

If it is necessary to tow a disabled snowmobile, securely fasten the disabled machine's skis to the hitch of the tow machine. Remove the drive belt from the disabled machine before towing.

Clearing the Track

If the snowmobile has been operated in deep or slushy snow, it is necessary to clear the track after stopping or the track may freeze, making starting the next time difficult.

> **WARNING**
> *Always be sure no one is behind the machine when clearing the track. Ice and rocks thrown from the track can cause serious injury.*

Tip the snowmobile on its side until the track clears the ground *completely*. Run the track at a moderate speed until all the ice and snow is thrown clear.

> **CAUTION**
> *If track does freeze, it must be broken loose manually. Attempting to force a frozen track with the engine running will burn and damage the drive belt.*

Proper Clothing

Warm and comfortable clothing are a must to provide protection from frostbite. Even mild temperatures can be very uncomfortable and dangerous when combined with a strong wind or when traveling at high speed. See **Table 1** for wind chill factors. Always dress according to what the wind chill factor is, not the temperature. Check with an authorized dealer for suggested types of snowmobile clothing.

> **WARNING**
> *To provide additional warmth as well as protection against head injury, always wear an approved helmet when snowmobiling.*

SERVICE HINTS

All procedures described in this book can be performed by anyone reasonably handy with tools. Special tools are required for some procedures; their operation is described and illustrated. These may be purchased at Polaris dealers. If you are on good terms with the dealer's service department, you may be able to borrow from them; however, it should be borne in mind that many of these tools will pay for themselves after the first or second use. If special tools are required, make arrangements to get them before starting. It is frustrating and sometimes expensive to get underway and then find that you are unable to finish up.

Service will be far easier if the machine is clean before beginning work. There are special cleaners for washing the engine related parts. Just brush or spray on the cleaning solution, let it stand, then rinse it away with a garden hose. Clean all oily or greasy parts with cleaning solvent as they are removed.

Never use gasoline as a cleaning agent, as it presents an extreme fire hazard. Be sure to work in a well-ventilated area when using cleaning solvent. Keep a fire extinguisher handy, just in case.

Observing the following practices will save time, effort, and frustration, as well as prevent possible expensive damage.

1. Tag all similar internal parts for location and mark all mating parts for position. Small parts such as bolts can be identified by placing them in plastic sandwich bags and sealing and labeling the bags with masking tape.

2. Frozen or very tight bolts and screws can

Table 1   WIND CHILL FACTORS

Estimated Wind Speed in MPH	Actual Thermometer Reading (° F)											
	50	40	30	20	10	0	—10	—20	—30	—40	—50	—60
	Equivalent Temperature (° F)											
Calm	50	40	30	20	10	0	—10	—20	—30	—40	—50	—60
5	48	37	27	16	6	—5	—15	—26	—36	—47	—57	—68
10	40	28	16	4	—9	—21	—33	—46	—58	—70	—83	—95
15	36	22	9	—5	—18	—36	—45	—58	—72	—85	—99	—112
20	32	18	4	—10	—25	—39	—53	—67	—82	—96	—110	—124
25	30	16	0	—15	—29	—44	—59	—74	—88	—104	—118	—133
30	28	13	—2	—18	—33	—48	—63	—79	—94	—109	—125	—140
35	27	11	—4	—20	—35	—49	—67	—82	—98	—113	—129	—145
40	26	10	—6	—21	—37	—53	—69	—85	—100	—116	—132	—148

*

Little Danger (for properly clothed person) | **Increasing Danger** | **Great Danger**

• Danger from freezing of exposed flesh •

*Wind speeds greater than 40 mph have little additional effect.

often be loosened by soaking with penetrating oil such as WD-40®, then sharply striking the bolt head a few times with a hammer and punch (or screwdriver for screws). A hammer-driven impact tool can also be very effective. However, make sure the tool is seated squarely on the bolt or nut before striking. Avoid heat unless absolutely necessary, since it may melt, warp, or remove the temper from many parts.

3. Avoid flames or sparks when working near flammable liquids such as gasoline. .

4. No parts, except those assembled with a press fit, require unusual force during assembly. If a part is hard to remove or install, find out why before proceeding.

5. Cover all openings after removing parts to keep dirt, small tools, etc., from falling in.

6. Clean all parts as you go along and keep them separated into sub-assemblies. The use of trays, jars, or cans will make reassembly much easier.

7. Make diagrams whenever similar-appearing parts are found. You may *think* you can remember where everything came from—but mistakes are costly. There is also the possibility you may be sidetracked and not return to work for days

or even weeks—in which interval carefully laid out parts may have become disturbed.

8. Wiring should be tagged with masking tape and marked as each wire is removed. Again, do not rely on memory alone.

9. When reassembling parts, be sure all shims and washers are replaced exactly as they came out. Whenever a rotating part butts against a stationary part, look for a shim or washer. Use new gaskets if there is any doubt about the condition of old ones. Generally, you should apply gasket cement to only one mating surface so the parts may be easily disassembled in the future. A thin coat of oil on gaskets helps them seal effectively.

10. Heavy grease can be used to hold small parts in place if they tend to fall out during assembly. However, keep grease and oil away from electrical and brake components.

11. High spots may be sanded off a piston with sandpaper, but emery cloth and oil do a much more professional job.

12. Carburetors are best cleaned by disassembling them and soaking the parts in a commercial carburetor cleaner. Never soak gaskets and rubber parts in these cleaners. Never use wire

to clean out jets and air passages; they are easily damaged. Use compressed air to blow out the carburetor only if the float has first been removed.

13. Take your time and do the job right. Do not forget that a newly rebuilt snowmobile engine must be broken in the same as a new one. Keep rpm within the limits given in your owner's manual when you get back on the snow.

14. Work safely in a good work area with adequate lighting and allow sufficient time for a repair task.

15. When assembling 2 parts, start all fasteners, then tighten evenly.

16. Before undertaking a job, read the entire section in this manual which pertains to it. Study the illustrations and text until you have a good idea of what is involved. Many procedures are complicated and errors can be distastrous. When you thoroughly understand what is to be done, follow the prescribed procedure step-by-step.

TOOLS

Every snowmobiler should carry a small tool kit to help make minor adjustments as well as perform emergency repairs.

A normal assortment of ordinary hand tools is required to perform the repair tasks outlined in this manual. The following list represents the minimum requirement:

a. American and metric combination wrenches
b. American and metric socket wrenches
c. Assorted screwdrivers (slot and Phillips type)
d. Pliers
e. Feeler gauges
f. Spark plug wrench
g. Small hammer
h. Plastic or rubber mallet
i. Parts cleaning brush

If purchasing tools, always buy quality tools. They cost more initially but in most cases will last a lifetime. Remember, the initial expense of new tools is easily offset by the money saved on 1 or 2 repair jobs.

Tune-up and troubleshooting require a few special tools. All of the following special tools are used in this manual; however, all tools are not necessary for all machines. Read the procedures applicable to your machine to determine what your special tool requirements are.

Ignition Gauge

This tool combines round wire spark plug gap gauges with narrow breaker point feeler gauges (**Figure 5**). The device costs about $3 at auto accessory stores.

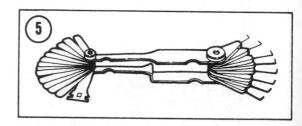

Impact Driver

The impact driver (**Figure 6**) might have been designed with the snowmobiler in mind. It makes removal of screws easy, and eliminates damaged screw slots. Good ones run about $12 at larger hardware stores.

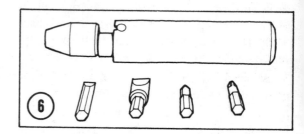

Hydrometer

The hydrometer measures state of charge of the battery and tells much about battery condition. See **Figure 7**. Such an instrument is available at any auto parts store and through most larger mail order outlets. Satisfactory ones cost as little as $3.

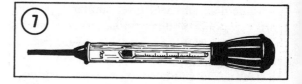

Multimeter (VOM)

A VOM is invaluable for electrical system troubleshooting and service. See **Figure 8**. A few of its functions may be duplicated by locally fabricated substitutes, but for the serious hobbyist, it is a must. Its uses are described in the applicable sections of this book. Prices start at around $10 at electronics hobbyist stores and mail order outlets.

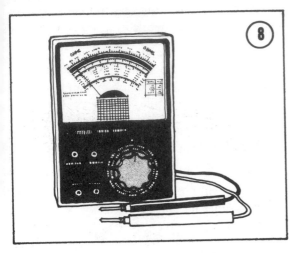

Timing Gauge

A timing gauge is used to precisely locate the position of the piston before top dead center to achieve the most accurate ignition timing. The instrument is screwed into the spark plug hole and indicates inches and/or millimeters.

The tool shown in **Figure 9** costs about $20

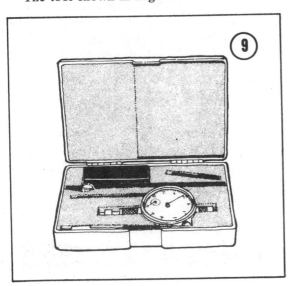

and is available from most dealers and mail order houses. Less expensive tools, which use a vernier scale instead of a dial indicator are also available.

Carburetor Synchronizer

A carburetor synchronizer is used on engines with multiple carburetors to fine tune the synchronization and idle speed. It is sometimes called an airflow meter.

The tool shown in **Figure 10** costs about $10-$15 at most dealers, auto parts stores, and mail order houses.

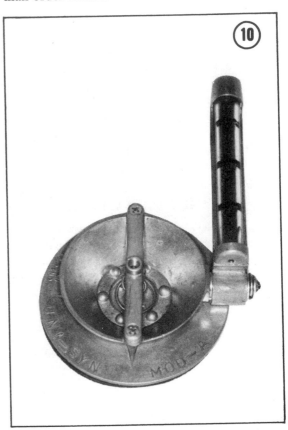

Compression Gauge

The compression gauge (**Figure 11**) measures the compression pressure built up in each cylinder. The results, when properly interpreted, indicate general piston, cylinder, ring and head gasket condition.

Gauges are available with or without the flexible hose. Prices start around $5 at most auto parts stores and mail order outlets.

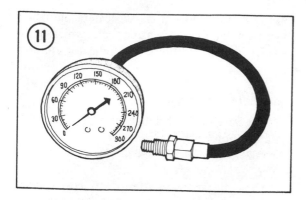

EXPENDABLE SUPPLIES

Certain expendable supplies are also required. These include grease, oil, gasket cement, wiping rags, cleaning solvent, and distilled water. Solvent is available at many service stations. Distilled water, required for the battery, is available at every supermarket. It is sold for use in steam irons, and is quite inexpensive. An increasing number of mechanics clean oily parts with a solution of common household detergent or laundry powder.

WORKING SAFELY

Professional mechanics can work for years without sustaining serious injury. If you observe a few rules of common sense and safety, you can enjoy many safe hours servicing your own machine. You can also hurt yourself or damage the machine if you ignore these rules.

1. Never use gasoline as a cleaning solvent.
2. Never smoke or use a torch in the area of flammable liquids, such as cleaning solvent in open containers.
3. Never smoke or use a torch in an area where batteries are charging. Highly explosive hydrogen gas is formed during the charging process.
4. If welding or brazing is required on the machine, remove the fuel tank to a safe distance, at least 50 feet away.
5. Be sure to use properly sized wrenches for nut and bolt turning.
6. If a nut is tight, think for a moment what would happen to your hand should the wrench slip. Be guided accordingly.
7. Keep your work area clean and uncluttered.

8. Wear safety goggles in all operations involving drilling, grinding, or use of a chisel.
9. Never use worn tools.
10. Keep a fire extinguisher handy. Be sure it is rated for gasoline and electrical fires.

SNOWMOBILING CODE OF ETHICS

When snowmobiling, always observe the following code of ethics as provided by the International Snowmobile Industry Association.

1. I will be a good sportsman. I recognize that people judge all snowmobile owners by my actions. I will use my influence with other snowmobile owners to promote sportsmanlike conduct.

2. I will not litter trails or camping areas. I will not pollute streams or lakes.

3. I will not damage living trees, shrubs, or other natural features.

4. I will respect other people's property and rights.

5. I will lend a helping hand when I see someone in distress.

6. I will make myself and my vehicle available to assist search and rescue parties.

7. I will not interfere with or harass hikers, skiers, snowshoers, ice fisherman, or other winter sportsmen. I will respect their rights to enjoy our recreation facilities.

8. I will learn and obey all federal, state, provincial, and local rules regulating the operation of snowmobiles in areas where I use my vehicle. I will inform public officials when using public lands.

9. I will not harrass wildlife. I will avoid areas posted for the protection and feeding of wildlife.

10. I will stay on marked trails or marked roads open to snowmobiles. I will avoid cross-country travel unless specifically authorized.

SNOWMOBILE SAFETY

General Tips

1. Read your owners manual and know your machine.

2. Check throttle and brake controls before starting the engine. Frozen controls can cause serious injury.

3. Know how to make an emergency stop.

4. Know all state, provincial, federal, and local laws concerning snowmobiling. Respect private property.

5. Never add fuel while smoking or when the engine is running. Always use fresh, correctly mixed fuel. Incorrect fuel mixtures can cause engine failure, and leave you stranded in severe weather.

6. Wear adequate clothing to avoid frostbite. Never wear loose scarves, belts, or laces that could catch in moving parts or on tree limbs.

7. Wear eye and head protection. Wear tinted goggles or face shields to guard against snow-blindness. Wear yellow eye protection only during white-outs or flat-light conditions.

8. Never allow anyone to operate the snow-mobile without proper instruction.

9. Use the "buddy system" for long trips. A snowmobile travels farther in 30 minutes than you can walk in a day.

10. Take along sufficient tools and spare parts for emergency field repairs.

11. Use a sled with a stiff tow bar for carrying extra supplies. Do not overload your snow-mobile.

12. Carry emergency survival supplies when going on long trips. Notify friends and relatives of your destination and expected arrival time.

13. Never attempt to repair your machine while the engine is running.

14. Check all machine components and hard-ware frequently, especially skis and steering.

15. Never lift the rear of machine to clear the track. Tip the machine on its side and be sure that no one is behind it.

16. Winch the snowmobile onto a tilt-bed trailer—never drive it on. Secure the machine firmly to the trailer and ensure that the trailer lights operate.

Operating Tips

1. Never operate the machine in crowded areas, or steer towards people.

2. Avoid avalanche areas and other unsafe terrain.

3. Cross highways (where permitted) at a 90-degree angle after stopping and looking in both directions. Post traffic guards if crossing in groups.

4. Do not ride the snowmobile on or near rail-road tracks. The snowmobile engine can drown out the sound of an approaching train. It is difficult to maneuver the snowmobile from between the tracks.

5. Do not ride the snowmobile on ski slopes or other areas with skiers.

6. Always check the thickness of the ice before riding on frozen lakes or rivers. Do not panic if you go through the ice—conserve energy.

7. Keep the headlight and taillight areas free of snow and never ride at night without lights.

8. Do not ride the snowmobile without shields, guards, and protective hoods in place.

9. Do not attempt to open new trails at night. Follow established trails; unseen barbed wire or guy wires may cause serious injury or death.

10. Always steer with both hands.

11. Be aware of terrain and avoid operating the snowmobile at excessive speed.

12. Do not panic if the throttle sticks. Pull the "tether" string or push emergency stop switch.

13. Drive more slowly when carrying a passenger, especially a child.

14. Always allow adequate stopping distance based on ground cover conditions. Ice requires a greater stopping distance to avoid skidding. Apply brakes gradually on ice.

15. Do not speed through wooded areas. Hidden obstructions, hanging limbs, unseen ditches, and even wild animals can cause accidents.

16. Do not tailgate. Rear end collisions can cause injury and machine damage.

17. Do not mix alcoholic beverages with snowmobiling.

18. Keep feet on footrests at all times. Do not permit feet to hang over sides or attempt to stabilize the machine with feet when making turns or in near-spill situations; broken limbs could result.

19. Do not stand on the seat; stunt, or show-off.

20. Do not jump the snowmobile. Injury or machine damage could result.

21. Always keep hands and feet out of the track area when the engine is running. Use extra care when freeing the snowmobile from deep snow.

22. Check the fuel supply regularly. Do not travel further than your fuel will permit you to return.

23. Whenever you leave your machine unattended, remove the "tether" switch and ignition key.

Preparing for a Trip

1. Check all bolts and fasteners for tightness. Do not operate your snowmobile unless it is in top operating condition.

2. Check weather forecasts before starting out on a trip. Cancel your plans if a storm is possible.

3. Study maps of the area before the trip and know where help is located. Note locations of phones, resorts, shelters, towns, farms, and ranches. Know where fuel is available. If possible use the buddy system.

4. Do not overload your snowmobile. Use a sled with a stiff towbar to haul extra supplies.

5. Do not risk a heart attack if your snowmobile gets stuck in deep snow. Carry a small block and tackle for such situations. Never allow anyone to manually pull on the skis while you attempt to drive the machine out.

6. Do not ride beyond one-half the round trip cruising range of your fuel supply. Keep in mind how far it is home.

7. Always carry emergency survival supplies when going on long trips or traveling in unknown territory. Notify friends and relatives of your destination and expected arrival time.

8. Carry adequate eating and cooking utensils

(small pans, kettle, plates, cups, etc.) on longer trips Carry matches in a waterproof container, candles for building a fire, and easy-to-pack food that will not be damaged by freezing. Carry dry food or space energy sticks for emergency rations.

9. Pack extra clothing, a tent, sleeping bag, hand axe, and compass. A first aid kit and snowshoes may also come in handy. Space age blankets (one side silverfoil) furnish warmth and can be used as heat reflectors or signalling devices for aerial search parties.

Emergency Survival Techniques

1. Do not panic in the event of an emergency. Relax, think the situation over, then decide on a course of action. You may be within a short distance of help. If possible, repair your snowmobile so you can drive to safety. Conserve your energy and stay warm.

2. Keep hands and feet active to promote circulation and avoid frostbite while servicing your machine.

3. Mentally retrace your route. Where was the last point where help could be located? Do not attempt to walk long distances in deep snow. Make yourself comfortable until help arrives.

4. If you are properly equipped for your trip, you can turn any undesirable area into a suitable campsite.

5. If necessary, build a small shelter with tree branches or evergreen boughs. Look for a cave or sheltered area against a hill or cliff. Even burrowing in the snow offers protection from the cold and wind.

6. Prepare a signal fire using evergreen boughs and snowmobile oil. If you cannot build a fire, make an "S-O-S" in the snow.

7. Use a policemen's whistle or beat cooking utensils to attract attention or frighten off wild animals.

8. When your camp is established, climb the nearest hill and determine your location. Observe landmarks on the way, so you can find your way back to the campsite. Do not rely on your footprints. They may be covered by blowing snow.

NOTE: If you own a 1978 or later model, first check the Supplement at the back of the book for any new service information.

CHAPTER TWO

2

PERIODIC MAINTENANCE
AND TUNE-UP

Regular maintenance is the best guarantee of a trouble-free, long-lasting snowmobile. An afternoon spent now, cleaning, inspecting, and adjusting, can prevent costly mechanical problems in the future and unexpected breakdowns on the trail.

The procedures presented in this chapter can be easily carried out by anyone with average mechanical skills. The operations are presented step-by-step and if they are followed it is difficult to go wrong.

SERVICE INTERVALS

Service frequency (see **Table 1**) depends on use but as a rule of thumb, the items that follow should be checked and corrected, if necessary, prior to a long ride or anticipated use of several hours. Though many of the items will not require actual service even after many hours, a systematic check is a good habit to develop. It can serve to warn of impending trouble and it will allow you to become familiar with the machine and gain a measure of confidence in the bargain. A day of riding is much more pleasant if you are not worrying about the condition of your machine.

FUEL FILTER

The manufacturer recommends that the in-line fuel filter be checked once a month, but there is no harm in checking it visually more often to be sure that it has not become clogged by dirty fuel. A typical filter installation is shown in **Figure 1**. If the filter is dirty, disconnect the lines from the filter body and plug the fuel line from the tank to prevent fuel from leaking into the machine.

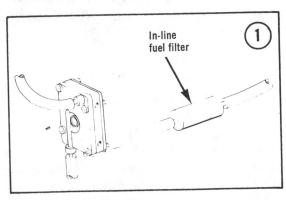

In-line fuel filter

If the filter is not damaged, it can be cleaned by flushing it with fresh gasoline, poured in through the arrow end (fuel pump end) of the filter. Cover both spigots and shake the filter to

Table 1   SERVICE INTERVALS

Daily
- Cooling fins
- Carburetor and exhaust systems
- Throttle system
- Brake system
- Steering system
- Fuel supply
- Taillight, brakelight, and headlight
- Emergency shut-off switch

Weekly
- Ski alignment
- Wear bar

40 Operating Hours
- Lubrication

Monthly
- In-line filter
- Chain tension
- Track tension and alignment

100 Operating Hours or End of Season
- Drive clutch/driven pulley service check
- Engine service check

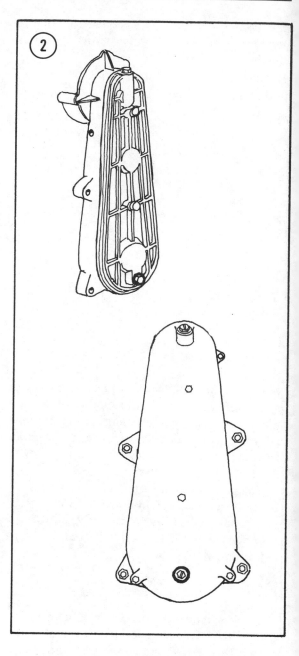

loosen particles. Then, shake out the gasoline and particles through the fuel tank end. Install the filter with the arrow pointing toward the fuel pump. Make sure the connections are tight and leak-free. If the filter case is damaged, replace it with a new filter, obtained from a Polaris dealer. If this is not convenient, a small automotive filter, the size of the original, may be substituted.

CHAINCASE OIL LEVEL

Check level of chaincase oil at intervals as specified in **Table 1**.

Remove the check plug (**Figure 2**) and check that the oil level is at the bottom of the access hole. Top up oil level if necessary. Use a syringe or oil suction device to remove old oil when changing oil or for machine storage preparation.

DRIVE BELT

Inspect the drive belt (**Figure 3**) for wear, cracking, stretching, or other damage or deteri-

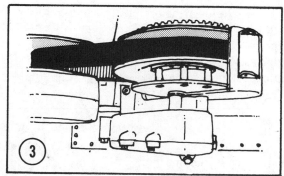

oration. If the belt is not in good condition, full power will not be transmitted from the drive clutch to the driven pulley.

1. Remove the clutch guard (**Figure 4**). Set the parking brake.

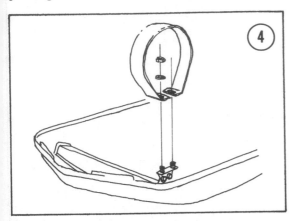

2. Push against the moveable sheave and rotate it clockwise until the sheaves are apart.

3. Hold the sheaves apart, pull the drive belt up, and roll it over the stationary sheave (**Figure 5**). When the belt is completely off the drive pulley, slowly release the moveable sheave. Then, remove the belt from the drive clutch.

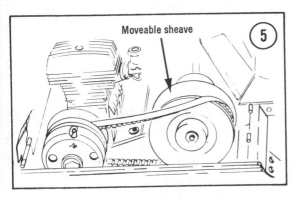

Moveable sheave

4. Install a new belt by reversing the removal procedure. Place it first around the clutch pulley, then, push the moveable sheave back as far as it will go and roll the belt over the stationary sheave. Reinstall the clutch guard and release the parking brake.

BRAKE

The brake system should be checked daily or each time the machine is ridden. Check for wear and damage to the lever, master cylinder, slave cylinder, hose, caliper, pads, and disc. Check also to see that the brake operates smoothly and releases completely when the lever is released.

WARNING
Never operate the snowmobile when there is any doubt about the condition of the brake system. Brake failure as well as an unexpected inadvertant stop could cause serious injury.

Bleeding

If the brake lever feels spongy, and the performance of the brake is not as it should be, it is likely that there is air in the hydraulic system. It can be removed very simply by bleeding the brake.

1. Check the master cylinder (**Figure 6**) to make sure the fluid level is within 1/8 in. from the top. If not, add automotive brake fluid (J1703) to correct the level.

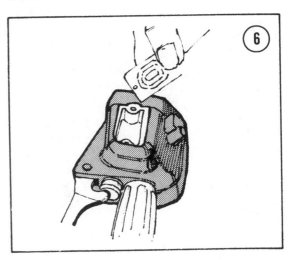

2. Install a length of tubing on the bleeder valve on the chaincase (**Figure 7**). The tubing should be long enough so that the other end can be put in a glass or clear plastic container, partially filled with fresh brake fluid—enough so that the open end of the tube is submerged.

3. Squeeze the brake lever and hold it. Open the bleeder valve 3/4 turn (**Figure 8**) and observe the fluid in the jar. If there is air in the system, bubbles will exit from the tube. Close the bleeder valve and release the lever.

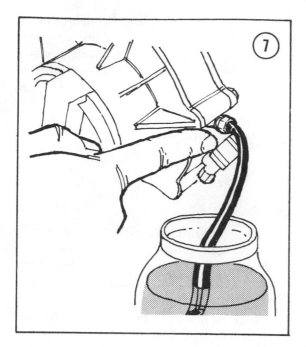

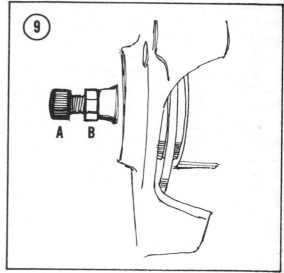

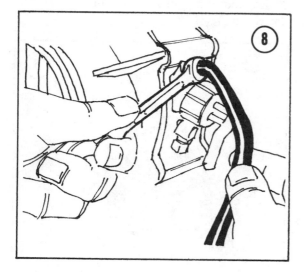

4. Squeeze the brake lever once again and open the bleeder valve. Wait, and then close the bleeder valve before releasing the lever. Continue to do this until the fluid exiting the tube is free of air bubbles. Periodically, check the master cylinder and top it up to replace the fluid that is expended during bleeding.

Adjustment

1. Loosen the locknut on the brake adjusting bolt (**Figure 9**) and run it up against the bolt head.

2. Screw in the bolt until the pads are locked against the disc.

3. Unscrew the bolt ¼ turn, hold it to prevent it from turning further, and tighten the locknut against the boss on the housing. When the adjusting bolt can be run all the way down, with the bolt head contacting the locknut with the locknut against the boss, the pads have reached their wear limit and should be replaced, as described in Chapter Seven, *Brake Pad Replacement*.

DRIVE CLUTCH AND DRIVEN PULLEY

The drive clutch and driven pulley need no maintenance other than disassembly and cleaning after 100 hours or at the end of the season. This work should be entrusted to a dealer. In addition, if premature belt failure or wear indicate misalignment of the drive clutch and driven pulley, the problem should be referred to a dealer because special tools are required.

TRACK TENSION

Correct track tension is important. If the track is loose, it will slap the tunnel and can ratchet on the drive sprockets. If it is too tight, the slide rails and rear idler will wear rapidly. Tension should be checked and corrected, if necessary, once a month.

1. Clean ice and snow from the track and from inside the skid frame. Raise the rear of the snowmobile so the track is off the ground and free to rotate.

2. Pull down on the track at midpoint (**Figure 10**) with moderate force and measure the distance. It should be ⅜-⅝ in. (10-14mm).

3. If adjustment is required, loosen the jam nuts on the track adjusting bolts (**Figure 11A**). If the distance is greater than ⅝ in. tighten the adjusting bolts and then lock them with the jam nuts to prevent them from turning further. If the distance is less than ⅜ in. the adjusting bolts must be loosened and the jam nuts tightened when the tension is correct.

TRACK ALIGNMENT

Track alignment is related to track tension and should be checked and adjusted at the time track tension is checked and adjusted. If the track is misaligned, the rear idler wheels, drive lugs, and track will wear rapidly.

1. Clean ice and snow from the track and from inside the skid frame. Raise the rear of the snowmobile so the track is free to rotate. The tips of the skis must be against a wall or other immovable barrier.

2. Start the engine and apply just enough throttle to turn the track several times. Then shut off the engine and allow the track to coast to a stop; do not stop it with the brake.

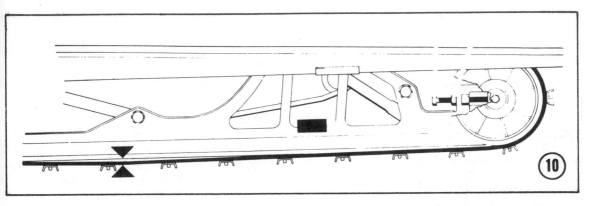

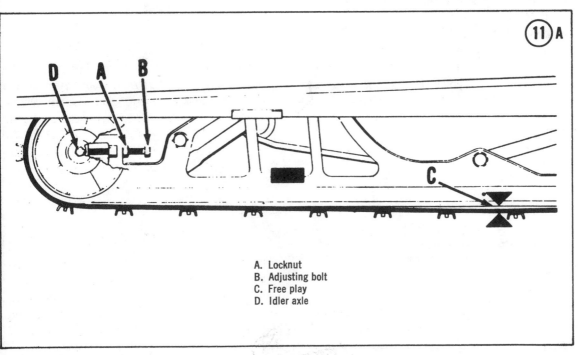

A. Locknut
B. Adjusting bolt
C. Free play
D. Idler axle

WARNING
Do not stand in front or to the rear of the snowmobile when the engine is running, and make certain hands, feet, and clothing are kept away from the track when it is turning.

3. After the track has stopped, check the alignment of the rear idler wheels and the track lugs (**Figure 11B**). If the idlers are centered between the lugs, the alignment is correct. However, if they are offset to one side or the other, alignment adjustment is required.

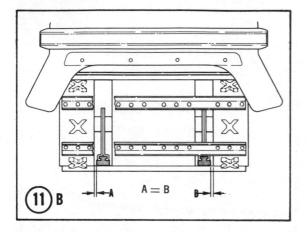

4. Loosen the jam nuts on the rear idler adjuster bolts. If the track is offset to the left, turn the left bolt clockwise or the right bolt counterclockwise. If the track is offset to the right, turn the right bolt clockwise or the left bolt counterclockwise. Also make certain the correct track tension is maintained during alignment correction. When the adjustment is correct, tighten

the jam nuts to prevent the adjuster bolts from turning further.

5. Test drive the snowmobile, then recheck the alignment as described above and make any corrections that are indicated.

Track Alignment and Tension—TC Models

1. Raise and support the rear of the machine. If the track is offset to the left, loosen the left tension bolts and turn the left adjustment bolt clockwise (**Figure 12**).

2. If the track is offset to the right, loosen the right tension bolts and turn the right adjuster bolt clockwise. When the alignment is correct, tighten the tension bolts securely.

3. Start the engine and slowly accelerate it until the track has made at least 3 revolutions. Observe the alignment of the track and correct it as described if it is not right.

4. Check the track tension by measuring the distance from the center of the idler wheel to the tunnel with the machine suspended. The distance should be 2 in. (50mm). If it is not correct, loosen the 4 track tension bolts and turn the 2 track adjustment bolts equally clockwise until the distance is correct (**Figure 12**). Tighten the track tension bolts.

SUSPENSION ADJUSTMENT

The suspension on all models but Colt can be adjusted to accomodate rider weight and driving conditions. This is described in Chapter Nine.

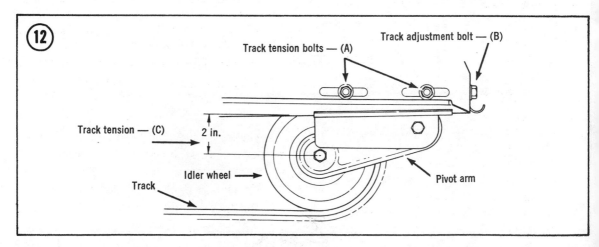

Track tension bolts — (A)
Track adjustment bolt — (B)
Track tension — (C)
2 in.
Idler wheel
Track
Pivot arm

TUNE-UP

A complete tune-up should be performed after every 100 hours of operation or at the end of the season. Expendable ignition parts (spark plugs for all models, plus points and condenser for models equipped with contact breaker ignition should be routinely replaced during the tune-up. Have the plugs on hand before you begin.

Always check the condition of spark plug wires, ignition wires, and fuel lines for splitting, loose connections, hardness, and other signs of deterioration. Check that all manifold nuts and carburetor nuts are tight and no crankcase leaks are present. A small air leak can make a good tune-up impossible as well as affect performance. A small air leak can also cause serious damage by allowing the engine to run on a "too-lean" fuel mixture.

The following list of general hints will help make a tune-up easier and more successful.

a. Always use good tools and tune-up equipment. The money saved from a few home tune-ups will more than pay for good tools; from that point you are money ahead. Refer to Chapter One for suitable types of tune-up/test equipment.

b. The purchase of a small set of ignition wrenches and 1 or 2 "screwholding" or magnetic screwdrivers will ease the work in replacing breaker points and help eliminate losing small screws.

c. Always purchase quality ignition components.

d. When using a feeler gauge to set breaker points, ensure that the blade is wiped clean before inserting it between the points.

e. Ensure that points are fully open when setting gap with a feeler gauge.

f. Be sure feeler gauge is not tilted or twisted when it is inserted between the contacts. Closely observe the points and withdraw the feeler gauge slowly and carefully. A slight resistance should be felt; however, the movable contact point must *not* "spring back", even slightly, when the feeler gauge blade is removed.

g. If breaker points are only slightly pitted they can be dressed lightly with a small ignition point file. *Do not* use sandpaper as it leaves a residue on the points.

h. After points have been installed, always ensure that they are properly aligned, or premature pitting and burning will result (see **Figure 13**). Only bend the *fixed* half of the points not the movable arm.

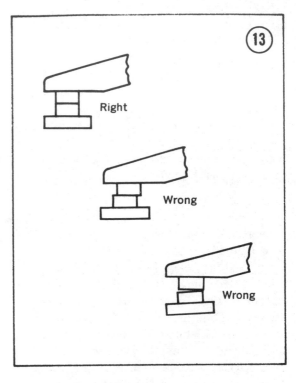

i. When point gap has been set, spring points open and insert a piece of clean paper or cardboard between the contacts. Wipe the contact a few times to remove any trace of oil or grease. A small amount of oil or grease on the contact surfaces will cause the points to prematurely burn or arc.

j. When connecting a timing light or timing tester always follow the manufacturer's instructions.

Because different systems in the engine interact, the procedures should be done in the following order:

1. Check and tighten cylinder head bolts.

2. Work on ignition system.

3. Adjust carburetor.

Cylinder Head Bolts

1. On fan-cooled models, remove the upper engine cooling cowl.

2. Refer to **Figure 14** and tighten the head bolts to the correct torque value, in the pattern shown.

Ignition System

With the exception of all Colt and Electra racing models, Polaris snowmobiles use electronic capacitor discharge ignition (CDI). The CDI is virtually trouble-free and should last the life of the machine without service or adjustment. Air gap and timing are preset and will not change. If trouble is suspected, the unit should be entrusted to a dealer; special skills and test equipment are required to correctly evaluate the condition of the CDI, and incorrect test connections could damage an otherwise good unit and render it unserviceable.

Spark Plugs

Spark plugs should be routinely replaced at each tune-up. In addition, they should be removed and inspected if poor performance indicates that the plugs may be dirty or faulty (see Chapter Three, *Troubleshooting*). In any case, the plugs should be compared to **Figure 15** to determine their suitability (heat range) and the condition of the engine. Recommended spark plugs are shown in **Table 2**.

Carefully pull the spark plug caps from the plugs by grasping the caps; do not pull on the spark plug wires. Clean the area around the base. Unscrew the plugs from the cylinder heads and compare them to **Figure 15**. If a change in heat range is indicated, it should be only one increment (see **Table 2**).

1. *Normal Condition*—If plugs have a light tan or gray-colored deposit and no abnormal gap wear or erosion, good engine, carburetion, and ignition conditions are indicated. The plug in use is of the proper heat range, and may be serviced and returned to use.

2. *Carbon Fouled*—Soft, dry sooty deposits are evidence of incomplete combustion and can usually be attributed to rich carburetion. This condition is also sometimes caused by weak

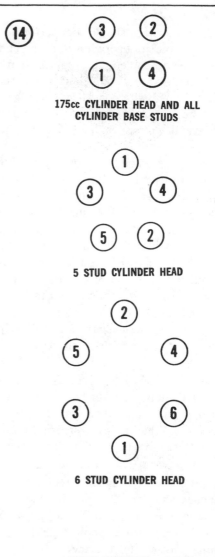

175cc CYLINDER HEAD AND ALL CYLINDER BASE STUDS

5 STUD CYLINDER HEAD

6 STUD CYLINDER HEAD

BOLT TORQUE — COLD

Engine	Cylinder Head
EC25PS	17-18 ft.-lb.
EC25PC	17-18 ft.-lb.
EC34PC	17-18 ft.-lb.
EC34PQ	17-18 ft.-lb.
EC44PQ	17-18 ft.-lb.
EC25PT-05	17-18 ft.-lb.
EC25PT-06	17-18 ft.-lb.
EC34PT-05	17-18 ft.-lb.
EC34PT-06	17-18 ft.-lb.
EC44PT-05	17-18 ft.-lb.
EC17PM	21-23 ft.-lb.

Normal plug appearance noted by the brown to grayish-tan deposits and slight electrode wear. This plug indicates the correct plug heat range and proper air fuel ratio.

Red, brown, yellow and white coatings caused by fuel and oil additives. These deposits are not harmful if they remain in a powdery form.

Carbon fouling distinguished by dry, fluffy black carbon deposits which may be caused by an over-rich air/fuel mixture, excessive hand choking, clogged air filter or excessive idling.

Shiny yellow glaze on insulator cone is caused when the powdery deposits from fuel and oil additives melt. Melting occurs during hard acceleration after prolonged idling. This glaze conducts electricity and shorts out the plug.

Oil fouling indicated by wet, oily deposits caused by oil pumping past worn rings or down the intake valve guides. A hotter plug temporarily reduces oil deposits, but a plug that is too hot leads to pre-ignition and possible engine damage.

Overheated plug indicated by burned or blistered insulator tip and badly worn electrodes. This condition may be caused by pre-ignition, cooling system defects, lean air/fuel ratios, low octane fuel or over advanced ignition timing.

Spark plug condition photos courtesy of AC Spark Plug Division, General Motors Corporation.

Table 2   SPARK PLUG RECOMMENDATIONS

SPARK PLUG RECOMMENDATIONS — 1974

Engine Model	NGK	AC	Champion	Plug Gap
EC17PM	B7ES	AC42XL	N3	0.015 in.
EC25PS	B7ES	AC42XL	N3	0.017-0.020 in.
EC25PC	B8ES	AC41XL	N2	0.017-0.020 in.
EC29PF	B7ES	AC42XL	N3	0.017-0.020 in.
EC34PC	B8ES	AC41XL	N2	0.017-0.020 in.
EC25PS	B7ES	AC42XL	N3	0.017-0.020 in.
EC40PM	B7ES	AC42XL	N3	0.017-0.020 in.
EC54PM	B8ES	AC41XL	N2	0.017-0.020 in.
EC34PQ	B7ES	AC42XL	N3	0.017-0.020 in.
EC44PQ	B7ES	AC42XL	N3	0.017-0.020 in.

SPARK PLUG RECOMMENDATIONS — 1975

Engine Model	NGK	AC	Champion	Plug Gap
EC17PM	B7ES	S43XL	N4	0.015 in.
EC25PS	B7ES	S42XL	N3	0.020 in.
EC25PC	B8ES	S41XL	N2	0.020 in.
EC25PT	B8ES	S41XL	N2	0.020 in.
EC34PC	B8ES	S41XL	N2	0.020 in.
EC34PT	B8ES	S41XL	N2	0.020 in.
EC34PQ	B7ES	S42XL	N3	0.020 in.
EC44PQ	B7ES	S42XL	N3	0.020 in.
EC44PT	B10E	S40XL	N57	0.020 in.
EC51PT	B8ES	S41XL	N2	0.020 in.

SPARK PLUG RECOMMENDATIONS — 1976

Engine Model	NGK	AC	Champion	Plug Gap
EC17PM	B7ES	S43XL	N4	0.016 in.
EC25PS	B7ES	S43XL	N4	0.020 in.
EC25PC	B8ES	S42XL	N3	0.020 in.
EC34PC	B8ES	S42XL	N3	0.020 in.
EC34PQ	B7ES	S43XL	N4	0.020 in.
E44PQ	B7ES	S43XL	N4	0.020 in.
EC25PT-06	B9ES	41XL	N2	0.020 in.
EC34PT-05	B9ES	41XL	N2	0.020 in.
EC44PT-05	B8ES	42XL	N3	0.020 in.
EC25PT-05	B10EV	N/A	N1 or N57G	0.020 in.
EC34PT-06	B10EV	N/A	N1 or N57G	0.020 in.

(continued)

Table 2   SPARK PLUG RECOMMENDATIONS (continued)

SPARK PLUG RECOMMENDATIONS — 1977				
Model Engine	NGK	Champion	NGK (Resistor)	Plug Gap
EC25PS	——	N3	BR8ES	0.020 in.
EC25PC	——	N2	BR9ES	0.020 in.
EC25PM-01	——	N2	BR8ES	0.020 in.
EC25PT-07	B9ES	——	BR9ES	0.020 in.
EC34PM-03	——	N2	BR8ES	0.020 in.
EC34PQ	——	N3	BR8ES	0.020 in.
EC34PT-05	B9ES	——	BR9ES	0.020 in.
EC34PL-01	B9ES	——	BR9ES	0.020 in.
EC44PQ	——	N3	BR8ES	0.020 in.
EC44PT-05	B9ES	——	BR9ES	0.020 in.
EC44PT-06	B9ES	——	BR9ES	0.020 in.

ignition, retarded timing, or low compression. Such a plug may usually be cleaned and returned to service, but the condition which causes fouling should be corrected.

3. *Oil Fouled*—This plug exhibits a black insulator tip, a damp oily film over the firing end, and a carbon layer over the entire nose. Electrodes will not be worn. Common causes for this condition are listed in **Table 3**.

Table 3   CAUSES OF FOULED PLUGS

• Improper fuel/oil mixture	• Weak ignition
• Wrong type of oil	• Excessive idling
• Idle speed too low	• Wrong spark plugs
• Clogged air silencer	(too cold)

Oil fouled spark plugs may be cleaned in a pinch, but it is better to replace them. It is important to correct the cause of fouling before the engine is returned to service.

4. *Gap Bridging*—Plugs with this condition exhibit gaps shorted out by combustion chamber deposits used between electrodes. On 2-stroke engines, any of the following may be the cause:

   a. Improper fuel/oil mixture

   b. Clogged exhaust

Be sure to locate and correct the cause of this spark plug condition. Such plugs must be replaced with new ones.

5. *Overheated*—Overheated spark plugs exhibit burned electrodes. The insulator tip will be light gray or even chalk white. The most common cause for this condition is using a spark plug of the wrong heat range (too hot). If it is known that the correct plug is used, other causes are: lean fuel mixture, engine overloading or lugging, loose carburetor mounting, or timing advanced too far. Always correct the fault before putting the snowmobile back into service. Such plugs cannot be salvaged; replace with new ones.

6. *Worn Out*—Corrosive gases formed by combustion and high voltage sparks have eroded the electrodes. Spark plugs in this condition require more voltage to fire under hard acceleration—often more than the ignition system can supply. Replace them with new spark plugs of the same heat range.

7. *Preignition*—If electrodes are melted, preignition is almost certainly the cause. Check for carburetor mounting or intake manifold leaks, also over-advanced ignition timing. It is also possible that a plug of the wrong heat range (too hot) is being used. Find the cause of preignition before placing the engine back into service.

The spark plugs recommended by the factory are usually the most suitable for your machine. If riding conditions are mild, it may be advisable to go to spark plugs one step hotter than normal.

Unusually severe riding conditions may require slightly colder plugs.

> CAUTION
>
> *Ensure that the spark plugs used have the correct thread reach. A thread reach too short will cause the exposed threads in the cylinder head to accumulate carbon, resulting in stripped cylinder head threads when the proper plug is installed. A thread reach too long will cause the exposed spark plug threads to accumulate carbon, resulting in stripped cylinder head threads when the plug is removed.*

It may take some experimentation to arrive at the proper plug heat range for your type of riding. As a general rule, use as cold a spark plug as possible without fouling. This will give the best performance.

Remove and clean spark plugs at least once a season. After cleaning, inspect them for worn or eroded electrodes. Replace them if in doubt about their condition. If the plugs are serviceable, file the center electrodes square, then adjust the gaps by bending the outer electrodes only. Measure the gap with a round wire spark plug gauge only; a flat gauge will yield an incorrect reading.

Set the gap on the new plugs by bending only the side electrode. Correct gap is also shown in **Table 2**. Screw the plugs into the cylinder heads using new washers. Tighten the plugs snugly but do not tighten so much that there is risk of damaging the threads in the heads. Reconnect the high-tension leads.

> NOTE: *On models with contact breaker ignition, do not install the spark plugs until the timing has been checked (see* Contact Breaker Ignition Timing *which follows).*

Contact Breaker Ignition Timing—175cc Single

The 175cc single cylinder engine is timed statically, using the running specification of 0.100 in. (2.5mm) BTDC. There is no mechanical advance in this ignition. The stator plate is not moveable and timing is altered by changing the point gap.

1. Remove the flywheel. Install a dial indicator or timing gauge in spark plug hole (**Figure 16**).

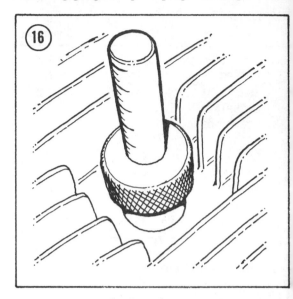

2. Connect one lead of a timing light to the red ignition lead and the other timing light lead to ground.

3. Rotate the crankshaft to locate TDC as indicated by the dial indicator or gauge. When you have found it, zero the indicator or make a note of the measurement on the gauge.

4. Rotate the crankshaft counterclockwise past the point where the lamp lights, then turn it clockwise until the lamp goes out. The indicator or gauge should indicate a difference of 0.100 in. (2.5mm) BTDC. If not, alter the timing by changing the point gap. Increase the gap to advance the timing, and decrease it to retard the timing. The final gap should be 0.011-0.017 in. (0.28-0.43mm).

Contact Breaker Ignition Timing—244cc Single

The 244cc single cylinder engine is timed statically, with static timing specifications, or statically with advance timing specifications with the advance mechanism locked in the fully advanced position. Timing is altered by movement of the stator plate.

1. Install a dial indicator or timing gauge in the spark plug hole (**Figure 16**). Set the point gap at 0.014 in. (36mm).

2. Connect one lead of a timing light to the red ignition lead and the other timing lead to ground.

3. Rotate the crankshaft to locate TDC as indicated by the dial indicator or gauge. When you have found it, zero the indicator or make a note of the measurement on the gauge.

4. Rotate the crankshaft counterclockwise past the point where the lamp lights, then turn it clockwise until the lamp goes out. The indicator or gauge should indicate a difference of 0.018 in. (0.47mm) static; or 0.142 in. (3.6mm) advanced. If the timing is incorrect, loosen the screws in the stator plate and rotate the stator clockwise to retard the timing, or counterclockwise to advance it. Tighten the stator screws and recheck the point gap. It should be 0.011-0.017 in. (0.28-0.43mm).

Contact Breaker Ignition Timing—2-Cylinder Engines

2-cylinder engines are timed statically, with static timing specifications, or statically with advance timing specifications with the advance mechanism locked in the fully advanced position. Timing is altered by movement of the stator plate.

1. Install a dial indicator or timing gauge in the spark plug hole of the No. 2 cylinder (clutch side of engine). Set the point gap at 0.014 in. (36mm). The white ignition lead identifies the No. 2 point set.

2. Connect one lead of the timing light to the white ignition lead and the other timing light lead to ground.

3. Rotate the crankshaft to locate TDC as indicated by the dial indicator or timing gauge. When you have found it, zero the indicator or make a note of the measurement on the gauge.

4. Rotate the crankshaft counterclockwise past the point where the lamp lights, then turn it clockwise until the lamp goes out. The indicator or gauge should indicate a difference of 0.012 in. (0.27mm) static; or 0.100 in. (2.5mm) advanced. If the timing is incorrect, loosen the screws in the stator plate and rotate the stator clockwise to retard the timing, or counterclockwise to advance it. Tighten the stator

screws and recheck the point gap. It should be 0.011-0.017 in. (0.28-0.43mm).

5. Move the indicator or gauge to the No. 1 cylinder. Connect the timing light to the No. 1 point set (red ignition lead) and TDC and the firing position as described above. The difference should be the same as for the No. 2 cylinder. If it is not, the No. 1 point set gap must be altered to change the timing.

6. If the timing is advanced, close the point gap, and if it is retarded, open the point gap. The point gap must be 0.011-0.017 in. (0.28-0.43mm). If the gap is greater than 0.017 in. (0.43mm), reduce the gap of the No. 2 point set by 0.001-0.002 in. (0.025-0.050mm). Then, retime the No. 2 cylinder as before, advancing the stator plate slightly (counterclockwise). Then recheck the timing and gap of the No. 1 cylinder point set.

If the gap is less than 0.011 in. (0.28mm), increase the gap of the No. 2 point set by 0.001-0.002 in. (0.025-0.050mm). Then retime the No. 2 cylinder as before, retarding the stator plate slightly (clockwise). Then recheck the timing and gap of the No. 1 cylinder point set.

CDI Ignition Timing—All Engines

Both spark plugs on CDI fire at the same time, so there is need to time only one cylinder. A strobe light is required for this task, and make certain it will withstand the high voltage of the CDI system.

1. *Remove the drive clutch from the engine.* The engine must be run at high speed during a timing check. Install a dial indicator or timing gauge in one of the spark plug holes. Rotate the crankshaft to locate TDC as indicated by the indicator or gauge. When you have found it, zero the indicator or make a note of the measurement on the gauge. Rotate the crankshaft counterclockwise past the appropriate timing mark (see **Table 4**) as indicated by the indicator or gauge, and then rotate it clockwise to obtain the correct setting shown in **Table 3**.

2. Check the alignment of the timing marks on the flywheel and blower housing (**Figure 17**). If they are aligned, proceed with the next step. If they do not align, scribe a new set of corre-

Table 4   IGNITION SPECIFICATIONS

1974 ENGINES				
Engine Model	Static Timing		Running Timing	
	(mm) BTDC	Inches BTDC	(mm) BTDC	Inches BTDC
EC17PM	—	—	2.5	0.100
EC25PS	0.47	0.018	3.60	0.142
EC25PC	0.41	0.016	3.37	0.135
EC29PF	0.41	0.016	3.37	0.135
EC34PC	0.41	0.016	3.37	0.135
EC34PQ	0.33	0.012	2.75	0.110/6,000
EC40PM	0.47	0.018	3.60	0.142
EC44PQ	0.33	0.012	2.75	0.110/6,000
EC54PM	0.47	0.018	3.60	0.142/6,000

1975 ENGINES				
Engine Model	Static Timing		Running Timing	
	(mm) BTDC	Inches BTDC	(mm) BTDC	Inches BTDC
EC17PM	2.5	0.100	—	—
EC25PS	0.47	0.018	3.60	0.142
EC25PC	0.27	0.012	2.3	0.100
EC25PT	—	—	2.15	0.089
EC34PC	0.27	0.012	2.3	0.100
EC34PT	—	—	2.05	0.089
EC34PQ	—	—	2.25	0.089
EC44PQ	—	—	2.25	0.089
EC44PT	—	—	2.25	0.089
EC51PT	—	—	2.05	0.089

Table 4   IGNITION SPECIFICATIONS (continued)

1976 ENGINES				
Engine Model	**Static Timing**		**Running Timing**	
	(mm) BTDC	Inches BTDC	(mm) BTDC	Inches BTDC
EC17PM	2.86	0.113	—	—
EC25PS	0.36	0.014	2.96	0.116
EC25PC	0.13	0.005	2.1	0.082
EC34PC	0.13	0.005	2.1	0.082
EC34PQ	—	—	2.1	0.083 ①
EC44PQ	—	—	2.1	0.083 ①
EC25PT-06	—	—	2.1	0.082 ①
EC34PT-05	—	—	2.1	0.082 ①
EC44PT-05	—	—	2.1	0.083 ①
EC25PT-05	—	—	2.1	0.082 ①
EC34PT-06	—	—	2.1	0.082 ①

① Running timing BTDC 5,000 rpm, lights off.

1977 ENGINES						
Engine Model	**Static Timing**			**Running Timing**		
	(mm) BTDC	Inches BTDC	Deg. BTDC	(mm) BTDC	Inches BTDC	Deg. BTDC
EC25PS	0.36	0.014	8	2.96	0.116	23
EC25PC	0.13	0.005	5	2.1	0.082	20
EC25PM-01	0.13	0.005	5	2.1	0.082	20
EC25PT-07	—	—	—	1.70* ③	0.067* ①	18
EC34PM-03	0.13	0.005	5	2.1	0.082	20
EC34PQ	0.143	0.006	5	2.24	0.088	20
EC34PT-05	—	—	—	1.70* ③	0.067* ①	18
EC34PL-01	—	—	—	1.70* ③	0.067* ①	18
EC44PQ	0.143	0.006	5	2.24	0.088	20
EC44PT-05	—	—	—	1.83* ④	0.072* ②	18
EC44PT-06	—	—	—	1.83* ④	0.072* ②	18

* Timing specified at 5,000 rpm with lights on.
① Acceptable variance to 0.046 in. BTDC or 15°. ③ Acceptable variance to 1.18mm BTDC or 15°.
② Acceptable variance to 0.050 in. BTDC or 15°. ④ Acceptable variance to 1.27mm BTDC or 15°.

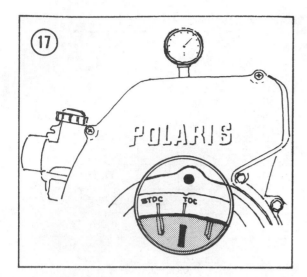

sponding marks on the flywheel and blower housing.

3. Remove the dial indicator or gauge from the cylinder and install a spark plug. Connect the positive and negative leads of a strobe timing light to the corresponding leads of a battery, and connect the trigger lead of the light to one of the spark plug leads.

4. Start the engine and slowly increase its speed to 6,000 rpm, while directing the timing light at the timing marks.

CAUTION
Do not run the engine at this speed for more than a few seconds at a time.

5. If the marks align, the timing is correct. If they do not, the stator plate must be rotated to correct the timing. If he flywheel mark passes the blower mark, the timing is retarded. Turn the stator counterclockwise to advance it. If the timing mark on the flywheel appears before the mark on the blower housing, the timing is advanced. Rotate the stator plate clockwise to retard it.

Carburetion

Polaris snowmobiles use Mikuni carburetors. The main jet is preset at the factory. Extremes of altitude may necessitate a change in main jet; this should be entrusted to a dealer. The adjustments covered here control idle speed and mixture.

WARNING
Carburetor adjustments must be made with the engine off to prevent inadvertant engagement of the drive clutch.

Starter (Choke) Adjustment

The starting (choke) system on Mikuni carburetors (**Figure 18**) is controlled by a starter plunger with separate metering of fuel/air mixture through independent jets. When the engine is started, the throttle valve must be closed or the starting mixture will be made too lean for engine starting.

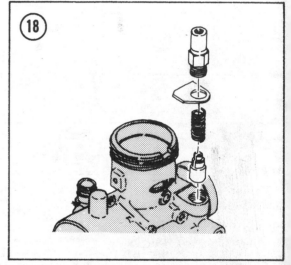

1. Place starter lever on instrument panel in the down position. Lever should have slight free play.

2. Look through starter plunger air hole (3 o'clock position in the carburetor bore). Check that starter plunger is all the way down in its bore (**Figure 19**).

3. To adjust the starter plunger perform the following:

    a. Loosen jam nut securing adjusting nut (**Figure 19**).

    b. Rotate adjusting nut clockwise to lower the starter plunger down in its bore. Tighten the jam nut.

NOTE: *If the starter plunger is not fully down in its bore, the carburetor will run rich and affect the entire engine performance level.*

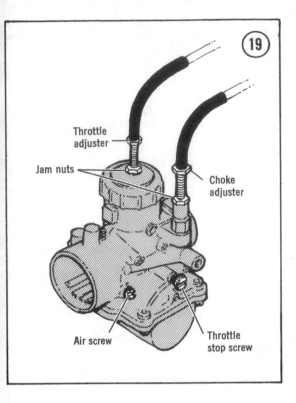

Throttle adjuster

Jam nuts

Choke adjuster

Air screw

Throttle stop screw

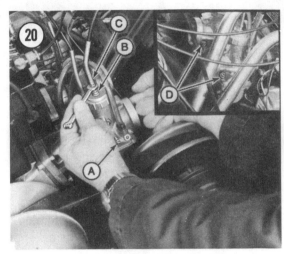

A. Throttle stop screw
B. Jam nut
C. Adjusting sleeve
D. Pilot air screw

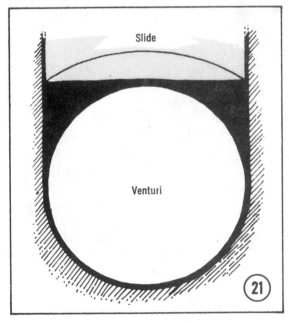

Slide

Venturi

Adjustment and Synchronization

This procedure includes throttle cable adjustments and idle speed adjustments for all models equipped with Mikuni carburetors.

On models equipped with 2 carburetors, a more precise synchronization can be achieved with an air flow meter described in Chapter One. If such a device is available, perform the following procedure as a preliminary adjustment and proceed to *Carburetor Air Flow Meter Synchronization* for the final fine tuning.

Refer to **Figure 20** for this procedure.

1. Remove the air intake silencer.

2. Use strong rubber band and clamp throttle lever to handlebar grip in the wide-open-throttle position.

3. Loosen the jam nut securing the adjusting sleeve. Feel inside the carburetor bore and turn the adjusting sleeve until the cutout portion of the throttle valve is flush with the inside of the carburetor bore.

4. Turn the adjusting sleeve counterclockwise several additional turns to position the backside of the throttle valve flush with the carburetor bore (**Figure 21**).

NOTE: *The additional turns on the adjusting sleeve should position the throttle valve flush with, or slightly above, the carburetor bore. If any part of the throttle slide protrudes into the carburetor bore, turn adjusting sleeve until throttle slide is flush.*

5. Rotate throttle stop screw counterclockwise until the tip is flush with inside of carburetor bore.

6. Remove rubber band clamp from handlebar and allow throttle to return to idle position.

7. Turn in throttle stop screw until tip just contacts throttle slide valve. Turn in stop screw 2 additional turns for a preliminary idle setting.

8. Slowly operate throttle lever on handlebar and observe that throttle valve begins to rise. On models with 2 carburetors, ensure that throttle valves move an equal amount together. Readjust throttle cables if necessary.

9. Slowly turn in pilot air screw until light seating is felt. *Do not* force it or the air screw may be damaged. Back out the pilot air screw 1 turn (½ turn for standard 250 Colt).

10. Install air intake silencer and start engine. Warm up engine to operating temperature and check that idle speed is 1,800 to 2,400 rpm. Adjust throttle stop screw as necessary for specified idle speed. On 2-carburetor models ensure that both throttle stop screws are adjusted an equal amount.

> NOTE: Do not *use pilot air screws to attempt to set engine idle speed. Pilot air screws must be set as specified above.*

Carburetor Air Flow Meter Synchronization

To obtain a precise synchronization of twin carburetor models, use an air flow meter device as described in Chapter One. Perform *Carburetor Adjustment and Synchronization* to obtain proper preliminary adjustments.

Refer to **Figure 22** for this procedure.

A. Idle adjusting screw
B. JDM-64-2 air flow meter
C. Tube in vertical position
D. Float
E. Air flow control

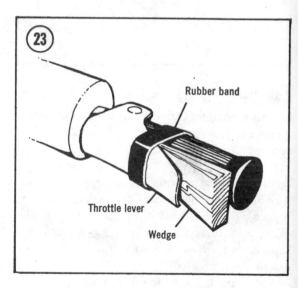

WARNING
The following procedure is performed with the engine running. Ensure that arms and clothing are clear of drive belt or serious injury may result.

1. Raise and support the rear of the snowmobile so track is clear of the ground.

2. Start the engine. Bind and wedge the throttle lever to maintain engine speed at 4,000 rpm (**Figure 23**).

3. Open the air flow control of air flow meter and place the meter over right carburetor throat. The tube on meter must be vertical.

4. Slowly close the air flow control until float in tube aligns with a graduated mark on tube.

5. Without changing the adjustment of the air flow control, place the air flow meter on the left carburetor. If the carburetors are equal, no adjustment is necessary.

6. If adjustment is necessary, loosen the jam nut on the carburetor with the lowest float level and turn the adjusting sleeve until the float level matches that of the other carburetor.

7. Return the engine to idle and repeat Steps 3, 4, and 5. Adjust the throttle stop screws as necessary for a balanced idle.

Carburetor Main Jet Selection

The main jet controls the fuel metering when the carburetor is operating in the ½ to full throttle range. Because temperature and altitude affect the air density, each snowmobile owner will have to perform the following trial and error method of jet selection to obtain peak engine efficiency and performance for his own particular area of operation.

CAUTION
Air intake silencer must be installed during the following procedure or a "too-lean" mixture may result. A "too-lean" fuel mixture can cause engine overheating and subsequent serious damage.

NOTE: *The snowmobile must be operated on a flat, well-packed area for best results.*

1. Operate the machine at wide open throttle for several minutes. If peak rpm cannot be achieved or the engine appears to be laboring, the main jet needs to be changed.
2. Make another trial run and shut off the ignition while the throttle is still wide open. Examine the exhaust and spark plugs to determine if the mixture is too rich or too lean. The mixture is too rich if exhaust manifold or spark plug insulator is dark brown or black. Refer to *Spark Plugs* in this chapter. Decrease the jet size if the mixture is too rich.

NOTE: *Change jet sizes one increment at a time and test after each change to obtain best results.*

If the manifold or spark plug insulator is a very light color, the mixture is too lean. Correct by increasing jet size.
3. If the state of fuel/air mixture cannot be determined by color of exhaust manifold or spark plug insulator, assume the mixture is too lean and increase jet size. If operation improves, continue increasing jet size until maximum performance is achieved. If operation gets worse decrease jet size until best results are obtained.

OFF-SEASON STORAGE

Proper storage techniques are essential to help maintain your snowmobile's life and usefulness. The off-season is also an excellent time to perform any maintenance and repair tasks that are necessary.

Placing in Storage

1. Use soap and water to thoroughly clean the exterior of your snowmobile. Use a hose to remove rocks, dirt, and debris from the track area. Clean all dirt and debris from the hood and console areas.

CAUTION
Do not spray water around the carburetor or engine. Be sure that you allow sufficient time for all components to dry.

2. Use a good automotive-type cleaner wax and polish the hood, pan, and tunnel. Use a suitable type of upholstery cleaner on the seat. Touch up any scratched or bare metal parts with paint. Paint or oil the skis to prevent rust.
3. Drain the fuel tank. Start the engine and run it at idle to burn off all fuel left in the carburetor. Check the fuel filter and replace it if it is contaminated.
4. Wrap up carburetor(s) and intake manifold in plastic and tape securely (**Figure 24**).

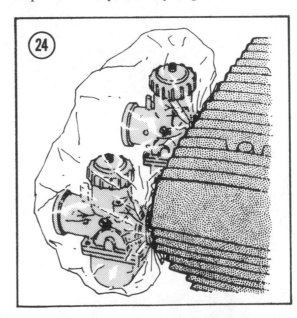

5. Remove the spark plugs and add a teaspoon of engine preserver or oil to each cylinder. Pull the engine over several times with the starter rope to spread the oil over the cylinder walls. Replace the spark plugs.

6. Remove the drive belt. Apply a film of light grease to drive and driven sheaves to prevent rust and corrosion.

7. Change the chaincase oil.

8. Raise the rear of snowmobile off the ground. Loosen the track adjusting screws to remove any tension on the track.

9. Carefully examine all components and assemblies. Make a note of immediate and future maintenance and repair items and order the necessary parts. Check and tighten all threaded fasteners.

10. Cover the snowmobile and store it inside if possible.

Removing From Storage

1. Check all threaded fasteners for tightness.

2. Completely remove grease from the drive and driven sheaves and then clean them with an acetone-type cleaner. Install the drive belt.

WARNING
Acetone-type cleaners are extremely volatile; keep flame, heat, and cigarettes away.

3. Fill the fuel tank with fresh gasoline/oil mixture. Refer to Chapter One.

4. Check the throttle and brake controls for proper operation and adjust them if necessary.

5. Adjust the track tension.

6. Familiarize yourself with all safety and operating instructions.

7. Start the engine and check the operation of the emergency stop switch and "tether" switch. Check that all lights and switches operate properly. Replace any burned out bulbs.

8. Start out slowly on short rides until you are sure your machine is operating correctly and is dependable.

TROUBLESHOOTING

Diagnosing snowmobile ills is relatively simple if you use orderly procedures and keep a few basic principles in mind.

Never assume anything. Do not overlook the obvious. If you are riding along and the snowmobile suddenly quits, check the easiest, most accessible problem spots first. Is there gasoline in the tank? Has a spark plug wire fallen off? Check the ignition switch. Maybe that last mogul caused you to accidentally switch the emergency switch to OFF or pull the emergency stop "tether" string.

If nothing obvious turns up in a cursory check, look a little further. Learning to recognize and describe symptoms will make repairs easier for you or a mechanic at the shop. Describe problems accurately and fully. Saying that "it won't run" isn't the same as saying "it quit at high speed and wouldn't start", or that "it sat in my garage for three months and then wouldn't start".

Gather as many symptoms together as possible to aid in diagnosis. Note whether the engine lost power gradually or all at once, what color smoke (if any) came from the exhaust, and so on. Remember that the more complicated a machine is, the easier it is to troubleshoot because symptoms point to specific problems.

You do not need any fancy equipment or complicated test gear to determine whether repairs can be attempted at home. A few simple checks could save a large repair bill and time lost while the snowmobile sits in a dealer's service department. On the other hand, be realistic and do not attempt repairs beyond your abilities. Service departments tend to charge heavily for putting together disassembled components that may have been abused. Some won't even take on such a job—so use common sense; don't get in over your head.

OPERATING REQUIREMENTS

An engine needs 3 basics to run properly; correct gas/air mixture, compression, and a spark at the right time. If one or more are missing, the engine will not run. The electrical system is the weakest link of the three. More problems result from electrical breakdowns than from any other source. Keep that in mind before you begin tampering with the carburetor adjustments.

If the snowmobile has been sitting for any length of time and refuses to start, check the battery (if the machine is so equipped) for a charged condition first, and then look to the gasoline delivery system. This includes the tank, fuel petcocks, lines, and carburetor. Rust may have formed in the tank, obstructing fuel flow. Gasoline deposits may have gummed up carburetor jets and air passages. Gasoline tends to lose its potency after standing for long periods. Condensation may contaminate it with water. Drain old gas and try starting with a fresh tankful.

Compression, or the lack of it, usually enters the picture only in the case of older machines. Worn or broken pistons, rings, and cylinder bores could prevent starting. Generally a gradual power loss and harder and harder starting will be readily apparent in this case.

PRINCIPLES OF 2-CYCLE ENGINES

The following is a general discussion of a typical 2-cycle piston-port engine.

Figures 1 through 4 illustrate operating principles of piston-port engines. During this discussion, assume that the crankshaft is rotating counterclockwise. In **Figure 1**, as the piston travels downward, a transfer port (A), between the crankcase and the cylinder, is uncovered. Exhaust gases leave the cylinder through the exhaust port (B), which is also opened by downward movement of the piston. A fresh fuel/air charge, which has previously been compressed slightly by the descending piston, travels from the crankcase (C) to the cylinder through transfer ports (A) as the ports open. Since the incoming charge is under pressure, it rushes into the cylinder quickly and helps to expel exhaust gases from the previous cycle.

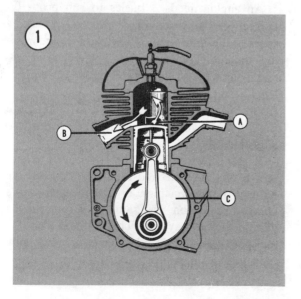

Figure 2 illustrates the next phase of the cycle. As the crankshaft continues to rotate, the piston moves upward, closing the exhaust and transfer ports. As the piston continues upward, the air/fuel mixture in the cylinder is compressed. Notice also that a low pressure area is created in the crankcase by the ascending piston at the same time. Further upward movement of the piston uncovers the intake port (D). A fresh fuel/air charge is then drawn into the crankcase through the intake port because of the low pressure created by upward piston movement.

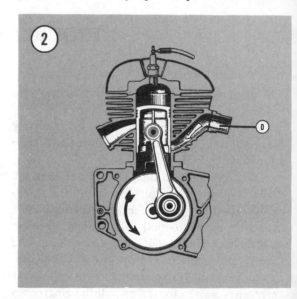

The third phase is shown in **Figure 3**. As the piston approaches top dead center, the spark plug fires, igniting the compressed mixture. The piston is then driven downward by the expanding gases.

When the top of the piston uncovers the exhaust port, the fourth phase begins, as shown in **Figure 4**. The exhaust gases leave the cylinder through the exhaust port. As the piston continues downward, the intake port is closed and the mixture in the crankcase is compressed in preparation for the next cycle. Every downward stroke of the piston is a power stroke.

ENGINE STARTING

An engine that refuses to start or is difficult to start can try the patience of anyone. More often than not, the problem is very minor and

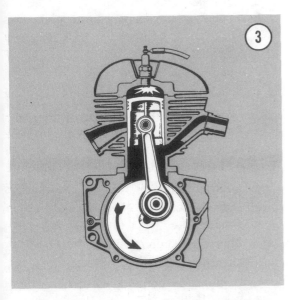

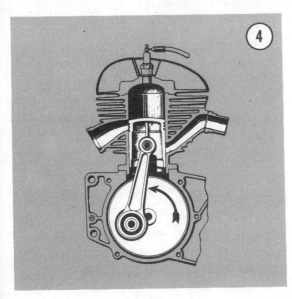

to a good grounding point on the engine. A large alligator clip makes an ideal clamp. Position the spark plug so you can observe the electrode.

3. Turn on the ignition and crank the engine over. A fat blue spark should be evident across the spark plug electrode.

WARNING

On machines equipped with CDI *(capacitor discharge ignition), do not hold spark plug, wire, or connector or a serious electrical shock may result.*

4. If the spark is good, check for one or more of the following possible malfunctions:

   a. Fouled or defective spark plugs

   b. Obstructed fuel filter or fuel line

   c. Defective fuel pump

   d. Leaking head gasket—perform compression test.

5. If spark is not good, check for one or more of the following:

   a. Burned, pitted, or improperly gapped breaker points

   b. Weak ignition coil or condenser

   c. Loose electrical connections

   d. Defective CDI components—have CDI system checked by an authorized dealer.

Engine Difficult to Start

Check for one or more of the following possible malfunctions:

   a. Fouled spark plugs

   b. Improperly adjusted choke

   c. Defective or improperly adjusted breaker points

   d. Contaminated fuel system

   e. Improperly adjusted carburetor

   f. Weak ignition coil

   g. Incorrect fuel mixture

   h. Crankcase drain plugs loose or missing

   i. Poor compression—perform compression test.

Engine Will Not Crank

Check for one or more of the following possible malfunctions:

can be found with a simple and logical troubleshooting approach.

The following items provide a beginning point from which to isolate an engine starting problem.

Engine Fails to Start

Perform the following spark test to determine if the ignition system is operating properly.

1. Remove a spark plug.

2. Connect the spark plug connector to the spark plug and clamp the base of the spark plug

a. Defective recoil starter

b. Seized piston

c. Seized crankshaft bearings

d. Broken connecting rod

Compression Test

Perform a compression test to determine condition of piston ring sealing qualities, piston wear, and condition of head gasket seal.

1. Remove the spark plugs. Insert a compression gauge in one spark plug hole (**Figure 5**). Refer to Chapter One for a suitable type of compression tester.

2. Crank the engine vigorously and record compression reading. Repeat for other cylinder. Compression readings should be from 120-175 psi (8.44-12.30 kg/cm²). Maximum allowable variation between cylinders is 10 psi (0.70 kg/cm²).

3. If compression is low or variance between cylinders is excessive, check for defective head gaskets, damaged cylinders and pistons, or stuck piston rings.

ENGINE PERFORMANCE

The following items are a starting point from which to isolate a performance malfunction. It is assumed that the engine runs but is not operating at peak efficiency.

The possible causes for each malfunction are listed in order of probability.

Engine Will Not Idle

a. Carburetor incorrectly adjusted

b. Fouled or improperly gapped spark plugs

c. Head gasket leaking—perform compression test.

d. Fuel mixture incorrect

e. Spark advance mechanism not retarding

f. Obstructed fuel pump impulse tube

g. Crankcase drain plugs loose or missing

Engine Misses at High Speed

a. Fouled or improperly gapped spark plugs

b. Defective or improperly gapped breaker points

c. Improper ignition timing

d. Defective fuel pump

e. Improper carburetor main jet selection

f. Weak ignition coil

g. Obstructed fuel pump impulse tube

h. Obstructed fuel filter

Engine Overheating

a. Too lean fuel mixture—incorrect carburetor adjustment or jet selection

b. Improper ignition timing

c. Incorrect spark plug heat range

d. Intake system or crankcase air leak

e. Cooling fan belt broken or slipping.

f. Cooling fan defective

g. Damaged or blocked cooling fins

Engine Smokes and Runs Rough

a. Carburetor adjusted incorrectly—mixture too rich

b. Incorrect fuel/oil mixture

c. Choke not operating properly

d. Obstructed muffler

e. Water or other contaminants in fuel

Engine Loses Power

a. Carburetor incorrectly adjusted

b. Engine overheating

c. Defective or improperly gapped breaker points

d. Improper ignition timing

e. Incorrectly gapped spark plugs

f. Weak ignition coil

g. Obstructed muffler

h. Dragging brake

Engine Lacks Acceleration

a. Carburetor mixture too lean

b. Defective fuel pump

c. Incorrect fuel/oil mixture

d. Defective or improperly gapped breaker points

e. Improper ignition timing

f. Dragging brake

ENGINE FAILURE ANALYSIS

Overheating is the major cause of serious and expensive engine failures. It is important that each snowmobile owner understand all the causes of engine overheating and take the necessary precautions to avoid expensive overheating damage. Proper preventive maintenance and careful attention to all potential problem areas can often prevent a serious malfunction.

Fuel

All Polaris snowmobile engines rely on a proper fuel/oil mixture for engine lubrication. Always use an approved oil and mix the fuel carefully as described in Chapter One.

Gasoline must be of sufficiently high octane (88 or higher) to avoid "knocking" and "detonation".

Fuel/Air Mixture

Fuel/air mixture is determined by main jet selection. Always adjust carburetors carefully and pay particular attention to avoid a "too-lean" mixture.

Heat

Excessive external heat on the engine can be caused by the following:

a. Hood louvers plugged with snow

b. Damaged or plugged cylinder and head cooling fins

c. Slipping or broken fan belt

d. Damaged cooling fan

e. Operating snowmobile in hot weather

f. Plugged or restricted exhaust system

See **Figures 6 and 7** for examples of cylinder and piston scuffing caused by excessive heat.

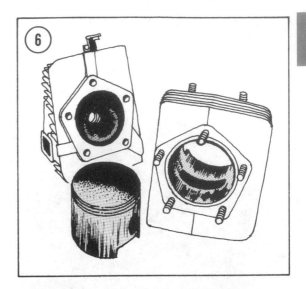

Dirt

Dirt is a potential problem for all snowmobiles. The air intake silencers on all models are not designed to filter incoming air. Avoid running snowmobiles in areas that are not completely snow-covered.

Ignition Timing

Ignition timing that is too far advanced can cause "knocking" or "detonation". Timing that is too retarded causes excessive heat build up in the cylinder exhaust port area.

Spark Plugs

Spark plugs must be of a correct heat range. Too hot a heat range can cause preignition and detonation which can ultimately result in piston burn-through as shown in **Figure 8**.

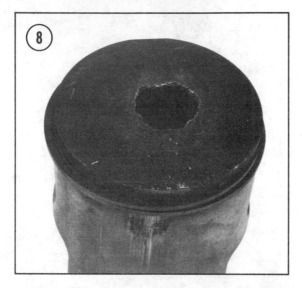

Refer to Chapter Two for recommended spark plugs.

Preignition

Preignition is caused by excessive heat in the combustion chamber due to a spark plug of improper heat range and/or too lean a fuel mixture. See **Figure 9** for an example of a melted and scuffed piston caused by preignition.

Detonation (Knocking)

Knocking is caused by a "too lean" fuel mixture and/or too low octane fuel.

ELECTRICAL SYSTEM

The following items provide a starting point from which to troubleshoot electrical system malfunctions. The possible causes for each mal-

function are listed in order of probability.

Ignition system malfunctions are outlined under *Engine Starting* and *Engine Performance*.

Lights Will Not Light

   a. Bulbs burned out
   b. Loose electrical connections
   c. Defective switch
   d. Defective lighting coil or alternator
   e. Defective voltage regulator
   f. Defective battery (electric-start models)

Bulbs Burn Out Rapidly

   a. Incorrect bulb type
   b. Defective voltage regulator

Lights Too Bright or Too Dim

   a. Defective voltage regulator
   b. Defective alternator

Discharged Battery (Electric-Start Models)

   a. Defective battery
   b. Low electrolyte level
   c. Dirty or loose electrical connections
   d. Defective voltage regulator
   e. Defective lighting coil
   f. Defective rectifier
   g. Defective circuit breaker

Cracked Battery Case

a. Discharged battery allowed to freeze
b. Improperly installed hold-down clamp
c. Improperly attached battery cables

Starter Motor Does Not Operate

a. Loose electrical connections
b. Discharged battery
c. Defective starter solenoid
d. Defective starter motor
e. Defective circuit breaker
f. Defective ignition switch

Poor Starter Performance

a. Commutator or brushes worn, dirty, or oil soaked
b. Binding armature
c. Weak brush springs
d. Armature open, shorted, or grounded

POWER TRAIN

The following items provide a starting point from which to troubleshoot power train malfunctions. The possible causes for each malfunction are listed in order of probability. Also refer to *Drive Belt Wear Analysis*.

Drive Belt Not Operating Smoothly in Drive Sheave

a. Face of drive sheave is rough, grooved, pitted, or scored.
b. Defective drive belt

Uneven Drive Belt Wear

a. Misaligned drive and driven sheaves
b. Loose engine mounts

Glazed Drive Belt

a. Excessive slippage
b. Oil or grease on sheave surfaces

Drive Belt Worn Narrow in One Place

a. Excessive slippage caused by stuck track

b. Too high engine idle speed.

Drive Belt Too Tight at Idle

a. Engine idle speed too fast
b. Distance between sheaves incorrect
c. Belt length incorrect

Drive Belt Edge Cord Failure

a. Misaligned sheaves
b. Loosen engine mounting bolts

Brake Not Holding Properly

a. Incorrect brake cable adjustment
b. Brake lining or pucks worn
c. Oil saturated brake lining or pucks
d. Sheared key on brake pulley or disc
e. Incorrect brake adjustment

Brake Not Releasing Properly

a. Weak or broken return spring
b. Bent or damaged brake lever
c. Incorrect brake adjustment

Leaking Chaincase

a. Gaskets on drive shaft bearing flanges or secondary shaft bearing flanges damaged
b. Damaged O-ring on drive shaft or secondary shaft
c. Cracked or broken chaincase

Rapid Chain and Sprocket Wear

a. Insufficient chaincase oil
b. Misaligned sprockets
c. Broken chain tension blocks

DRIVE BELT WEAR ANALYSIS

Frayed Edge

A rapidly wearing drive belt with a frayed edge cord indicates the drive belt is misaligned (see **Figure 10**). Also check for loose engine mounting bolts.

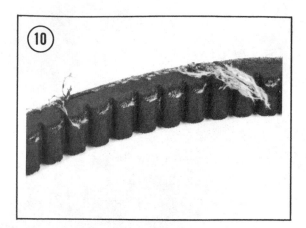

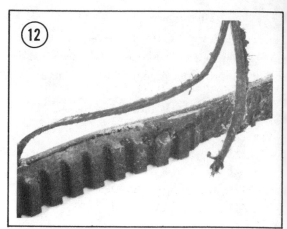

Worn Narrow in One Section

Excessive slippage due to a stuck track or too high an engine idle speed will cause the drive belt to be worn narrow in one section (see **Figure 11**).

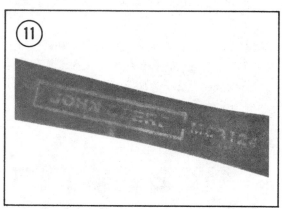

Belt Disintegration

Drive belt disintegration is usually caused by misalignment. Disintegration can also be caused by using an incorrect belt, or oil, or grease on sheave surfaces (see **Figure 12**).

Sheared Cogs

Sheared cogs as shown in **Figure 13** are usually caused by violent drive sheave engagement. This is an indication of a defective or improperly installed drive sheave.

SKIS AND STEERING

The following items provide a starting point from which to troubleshoot ski and steering

malfunctions. The possible causes for each malfunction are listed in order of probability.

Loose Steering

a. Loose steering post bushing
b. Loose steering post or steering column cap screw
c. Loose tie rod ends
d. Worn spindle bushings
e. Stripped spindle splines

Unequal Steering

a. Improperly adjusted tie rods
b. Improperly installed steering arms

Rapid Ski Wear

a. Skis misaligned
b. Worn out ski wear rods (skags)
c. Worn out spring wear plate

TRACK ASSEMBLY

The following items provide a starting point from which to troubleshoot track assembly malfunctions. The possible causes for each are listed in order of probability. Also refer to *Track Wear Analysis*.

Frayed Track Edge

Track misaligned

Track Grooved on Inner Surface

a. Track too tight

b. Frozen rear idler shaft bearing

Track Drive Ratcheting

Track too loose

Rear Idlers Turning on Shaft

Frozen rear idler shaft bearings

TRACK WEAR ANALYSIS

The majority of track failures and abnormal wear patterns are caused by negligence, abuse, and poor maintenance. The following items illustrate typical examples. In all cases, the damage could have been avoided by proper maintenance and good operator technique.

Obstruction Damage

Cuts, slashes, and gouges in the track surface are caused by hitting obstructions such as broken glass, sharp rocks, or buried steel (**Figure 14**).

Worn Grouser Bars

Excessively worn grouser bars are caused by snowmobile operation over rough and non-snow-covered terrain such as gravel roads and highway roadsides (**Figure 15**).

Lug Damage

Lug damage as shown in **Figure 16** is caused by lack of snow lubrication.

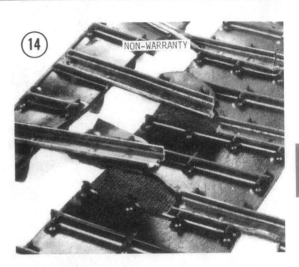

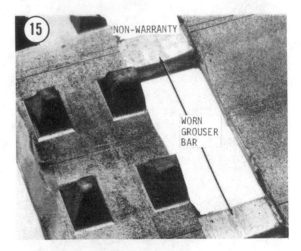

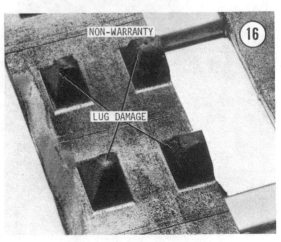

Ratcheting Damage

Insufficient track tension is a major cause of ratcheting damage to the top of the lugs (**Fig-**

uge 17). Ratcheting can also be caused by too great a load and constant "jack-rabbit" starts.

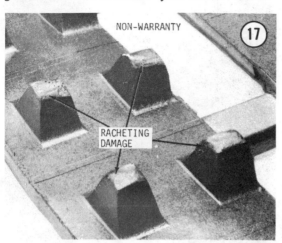

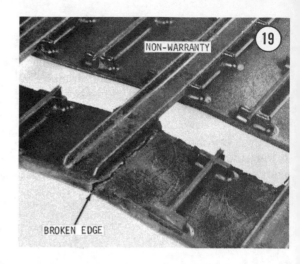

Over-Tension Damage

Excessive track tension can cause too much friction on the wear bars. This friction causes the wear bars to melt and adhere to the track grouser bars (see **Figure 18**). An indication of this condition is a "sticky" track that has a tendency to "lock up".

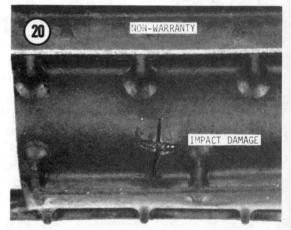

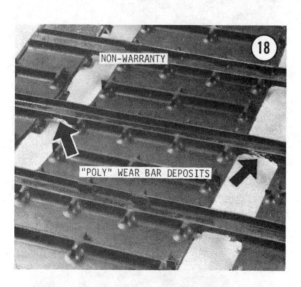

Loose Track Damage

A track adjusted too loosely can cause the outer edge to flex excessively. This results in the type of damage shown in **Figure 19**. Excessive weight can also contribute to the damage.

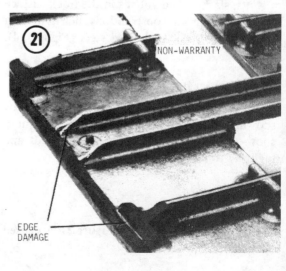

Impact Damage

Impact damage as shown in **Figure 20** causes the track rubber to open and expose the cord. This frequently happens in more than one place. Impact damage is usually caused by riding on rough or frozen ground or ice. Also, insufficient track tension can allow the track to pound against the track stabilizers inside the tunnel.

Edge Damage

Edge damage as shown in **Figure 21** is usually caused by tipping the snowmobile on its side to clear the track and allowing the track edge to contact an abrasive surface.

3

CHAPTER FOUR

ENGINE

All Polaris snowmobiles are powered with 2-stroke engines (1-, 2-, and 3-cylinder). Refer to Chapter Three for the *Principles of Operation* of 2-cycle piston-port engines.

All engines are equipped with ball-type main crankshaft bearings and needle bearings on both ends of the connecting rods.

It is recommended that lower end work be entrusted to a dealer; experience and special measuring equipment, along with a press, are required to service the lower end. Engine removal and upper end disassembly are covered to reduce the cost of lower end service.

An upper end overhaul is within the abilities of the average hobbyist mechanic equipped with a reasonable range of hand tools, and inside and outside micrometers. Before beginning work, read Chapter One, and particularly the headings *Service Hints, Tools, Expendable Supplies,* and *Working Safely*. The information they contain will contribute to the efficiency, effectiveness, and safety of your work.

Also, read the procedures in this chapter carefully and completely before picking up a wrench. It is also a good idea to physically compare the instructions with the actual machine beforehand to familiarize yourself with the procedure and the equipment.

A complete upper end overhaul can be performed without removing the engine from the machine; however, you may find it more convenient to have the engine on a workbench, and should a small part, tool, or dirt fall into the crankcase, it is more easily removed if the engine can be inverted. For these reasons, engine removal is described first.

The removal/installation procedures, as well as most service procedures, are virtually identical for all Polaris engines. Exceptions are noted where they apply.

When measuring wear surfaces for critical dimensions, be sure to consult the appropriate tables for your engine. This holds true also for critical torque values.

ENGINE REMOVAL/INSTALLATION

Air-Cooled Engines

With only a few exceptions, the engine removal procedure for air-cooled engines is virtually the same for all models. Each engine is shown with its related attachment and connection points along with hardware that should be removed (**Figures 1 through 8**). Study the general suggestions that follow, then select the appropriate removal illustration and proceed in the numbered sequence.

1. You may find it easier if you remove the hood before beginning work. First, disconnect

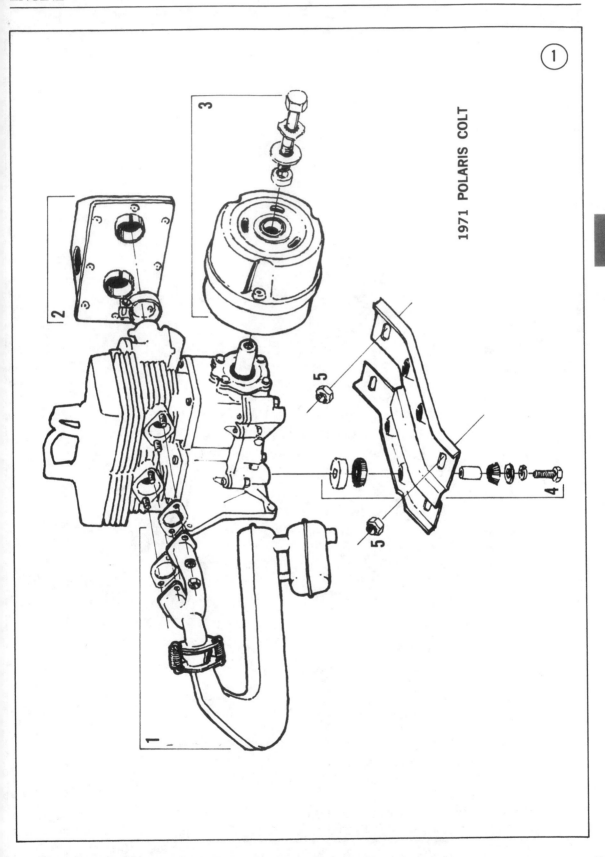

1971 POLARIS COLT

4

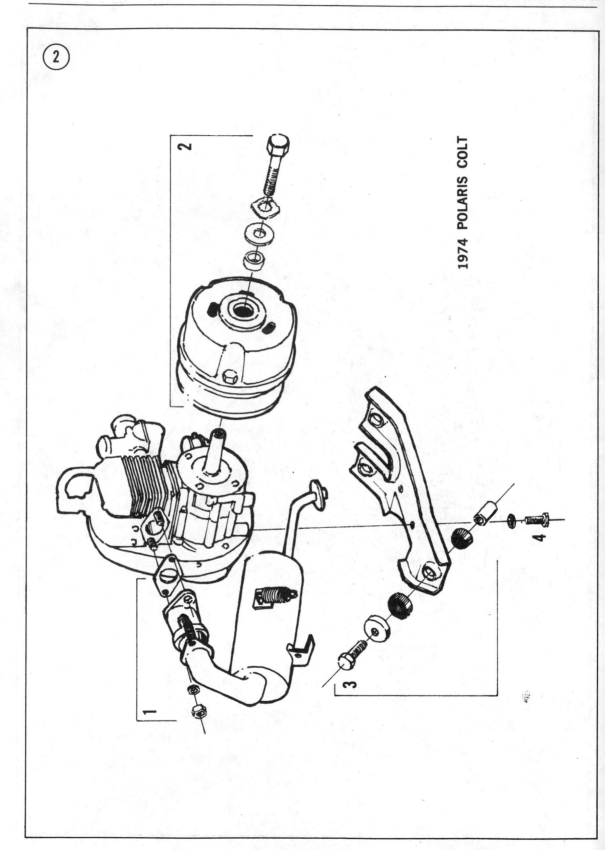

1974 POLARIS COLT

3 A

1974 POLARIS TX

4

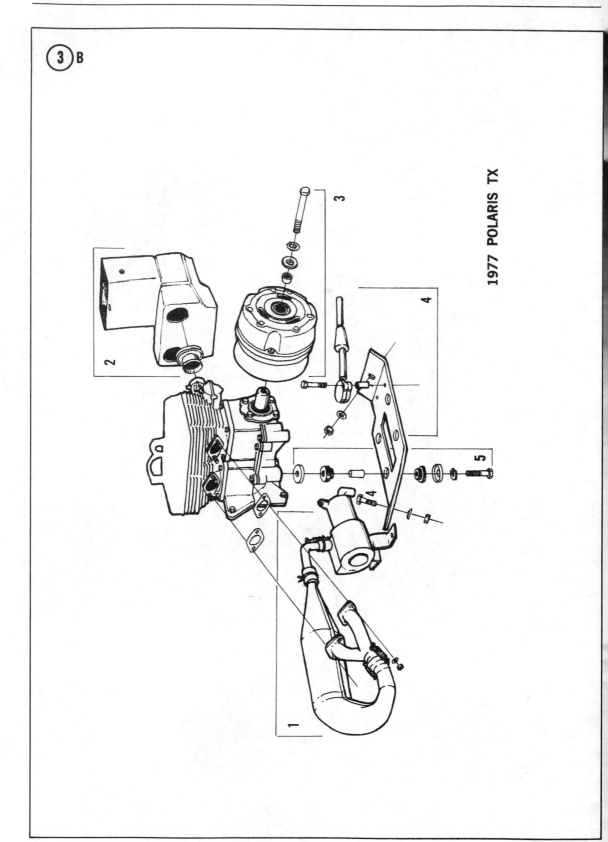

1977 POLARIS TX

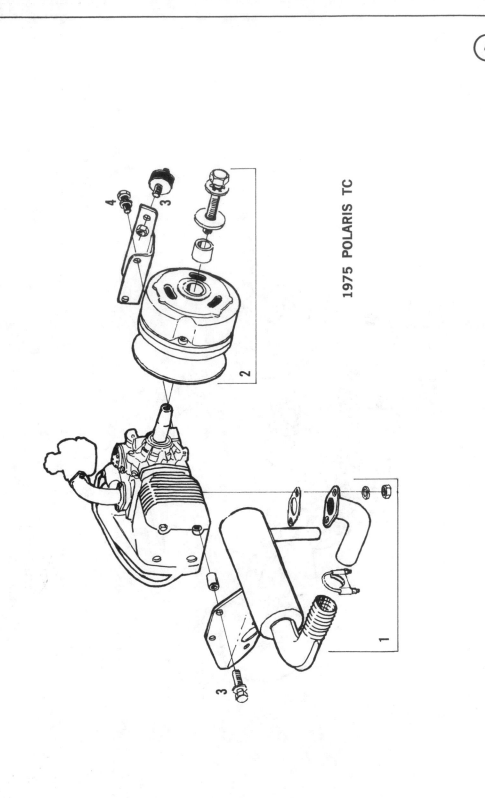

1975 POLARIS TC

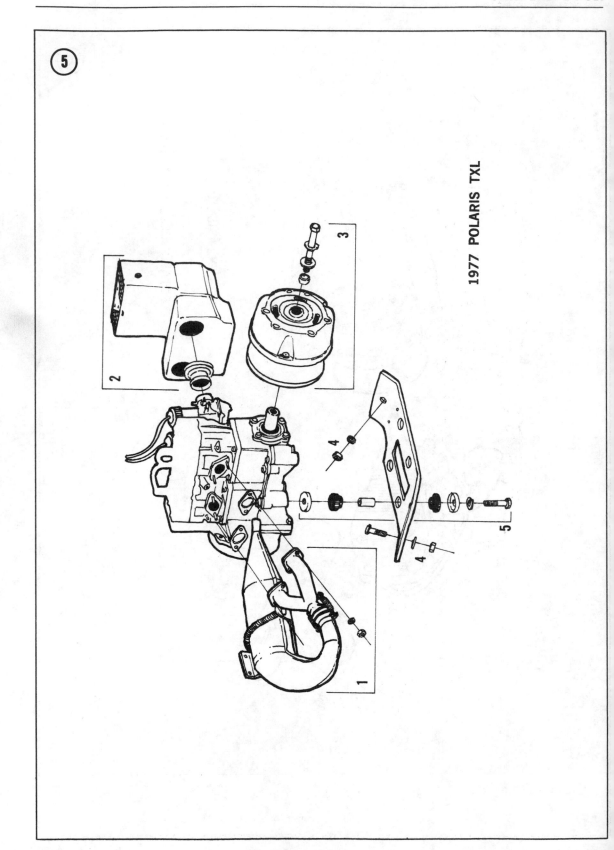

⑤

1977 POLARIS TXL

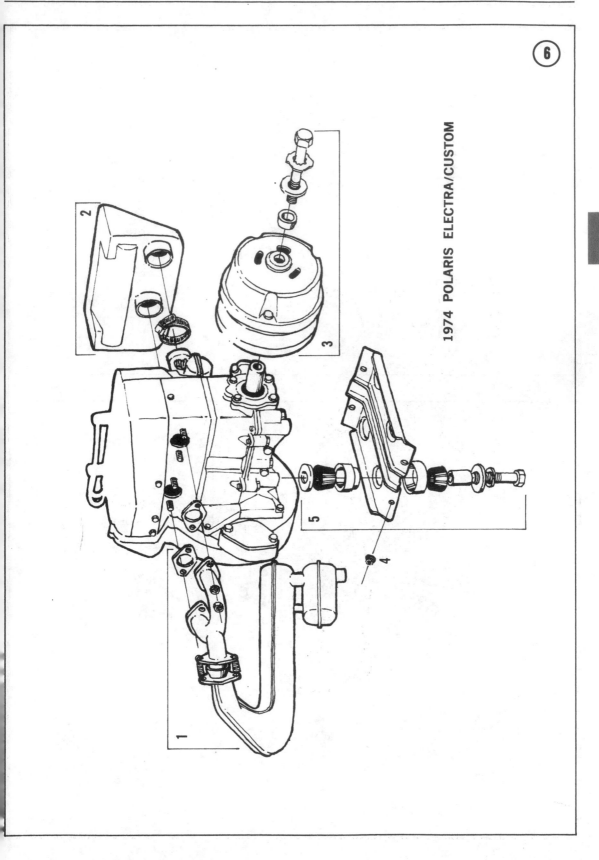

1974 POLARIS ELECTRA/CUSTOM

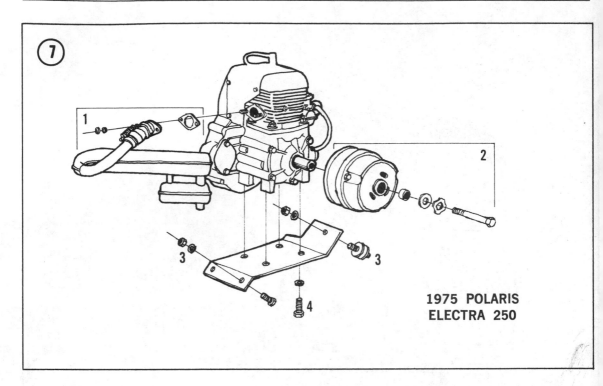

1975 POLARIS
ELECTRA 250

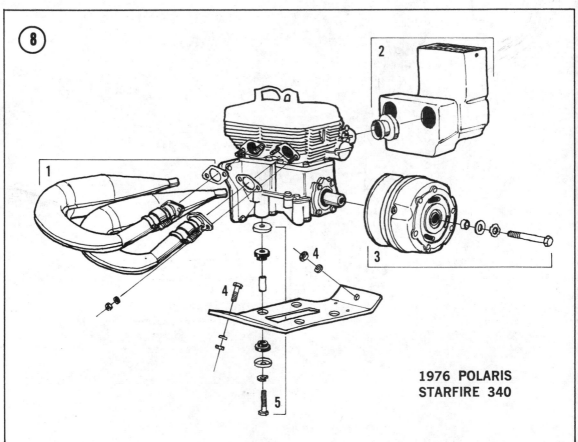

1976 POLARIS
STARFIRE 340

the headlight wiring. Then unscrew the hinge bolts, remove the hood, and set it out of the way.

2. Remove the recoil starter assembly and set it aside in the nose (**Figure 9**).

3. Unscrew the carburetor top, pull the slide assembly out with the cables attached, wrap it in a bag and hang it out of the way. Unscrew the choke assembly from the carburetor.

4. Disconnect the fuel line from the fuel tank and plug it.

5. Remove the clutch guard. Remove the drive belt.

6. Refer to the appropriate removal illustration and perform the steps in sequence.

7. Installation is the reverse of the above. Refer to **Table 1** for critical torque values.

Liquid-Cooled Engine

1. Lift the clutch guard and remove the drive belt.

2. Unscrew the exhaust manifold nuts and release the springs that attach the manifold to the expansion chamber. Remove the manifold and chamber; the resonator can be left in place.

3. Remove the recoil starter assembly and set it aside in the body.

4. Remove the radiator cap and the caps on the heat exchanger. Open the air vent on the top cylinder head plug, place a drip pan beneath the cylinder block drain plug, open the plug, and allow several minutes for the coolant to drain.

5. Disconnect the coolant lines, the temperature gauge sending unit, and the spark plug high-tension leads.

6. Disconnect the engine electrical connector.

7. Disconnect the fuel line from the fuel pump and plug it.

8. Disconnect the headlight harness and pull it out from between the engine and the engine plate.

9. Refer to **Figure 8** and perform the remaining steps in sequence.

10. Installation is the reverse of the above. Refer to **Table 1** for critical torque values.

UPPER END OVERHAUL

An orderly sequence should be followed to efficiently and correctly disassemble the engine upper end once the engine has been removed from the machine.

  a. Remove exterior components (cooling shroud, coil, CDI "black box," manifolds, carburetor, etc.).

  b. Remove spark plugs.

  c. Remove cylinder heads and gaskets.

  d. Remove cylinders.

  e. Remove pistons.

1. On fan-cooled engines, remove the front shroud (**Figure 10**). Remove the carburetor mounts and remove the rear shroud (**Figure 11**).

Table 1   ENGINE INSTALLATION TORQUES

Bolt Size	Description	Torque
$\frac{7}{16}$ in.	Engine mounting bolt	55-60 ft.-lb.
$\frac{7}{16}$ in.	Drive clutch bolt	40-45 ft.-lb.
$\frac{3}{8}$ in.	Engine mounting bolt	34-38 ft.-lb.
	Flywheel nut — 175cc	30-35 ft.-lb.
	Flywheel nut — all other	60-65 ft.-lb.

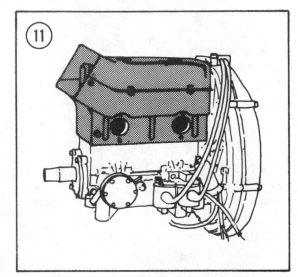

On liquid-cooled engines, remove the thermostat housing and the thermostat (**Figure 12**).

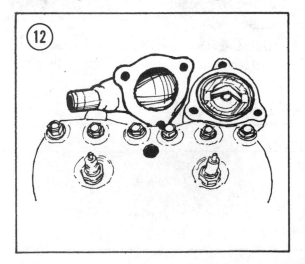

2. Remove the fuel pump and the ignition coils (**Figure 13**) or black box.

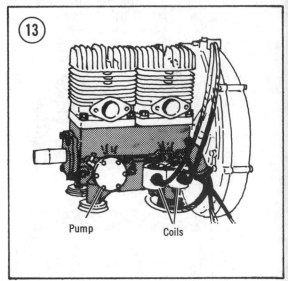

Pump   Coils

3. Remove the outer blower housing (**Figure 14**) and remove the starter cup and dust shield from the flywheel (**Figure 15**). On liquid-cooled engines, remove the water pump pulley (**Figure 16**).

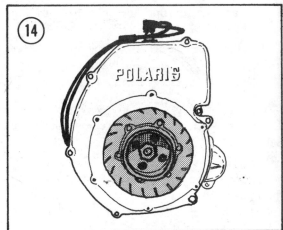

4. Unscrew the flywheel nut and install the puller (part No. 2870159) (**Figure 17**). Hold the flywheel with a strap wrench and tighten the puller bolt to break the flywheel loose. Remove it.

5. Unscrew the bolts that attach the inner blower housing to the crankcase (**Figure 18**) and remove it.

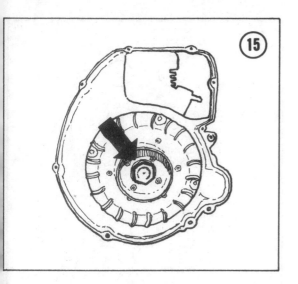

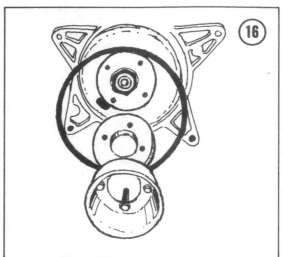

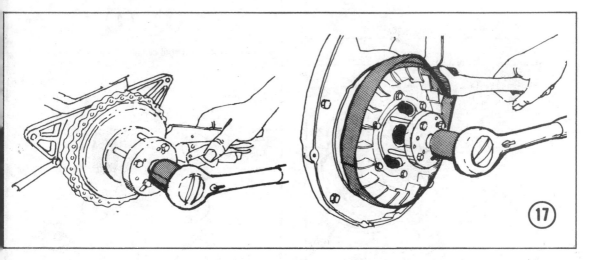

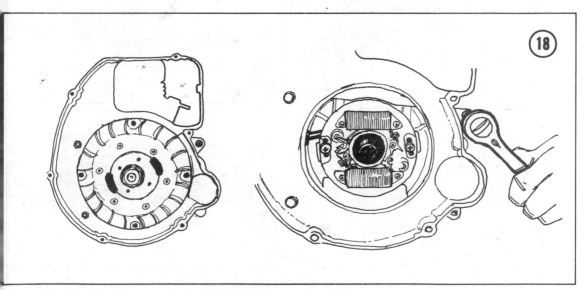

6. Make a reference mark on the stator with a chisel (**Figure 19**). Unscrew the 2 stator screws with an impact screwdriver (**Figure 20**) and remove the stator baseplate.

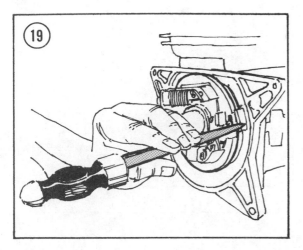

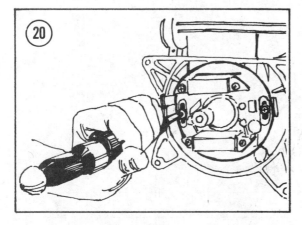

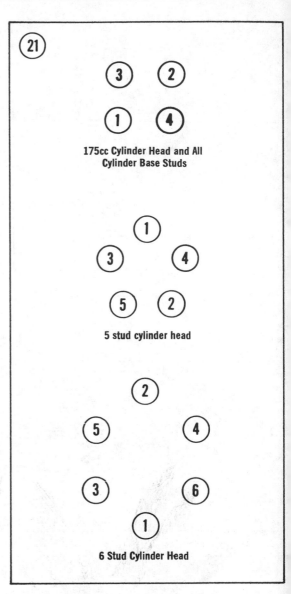

175cc Cylinder Head and All
Cylinder Base Studs

5 stud cylinder head

6 Stud Cylinder Head

7. Unscrew the cylinder head nuts progressively in the appropriate pattern shown in **Figure 21**. Begin with ¼ turn for each nut until all nuts have been loosened 2 full turns. While this may seem tedious, it will help prevent warping the cylinder head. When all the nuts have been loosened, unscrew them and remove the cylinder head. If the head does not release with upward pressure, tap lightly around the bottom of the head with a soft mallet. Remove the gasket.

> NOTE: *On fan-cooled engines, note the location of the special nuts that the shroud is bolted to.*

8. Unscrew the cylinder base nuts (**Figure 22**), collect the washers, and remove the cylinders

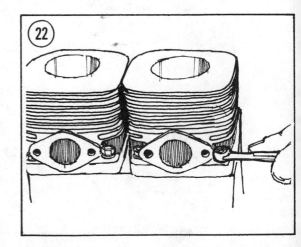

by lifting them straight up; don't rotate the cylinders as they are raised or you may damage otherwise good piston rings. When the cylinders have been removed, place a clean shop cloth in the top of each half of the crankcase to prevent small parts and foreign matter from falling into the crankcases.

9. Remove the circlips from both sides of each piston (**Figure 23**) and push the pin out. An extractor (**Figure 24**) is available through auto parts stores. In most cases, it will be necessary to remove the pins after wrapping the pistons with a cloth heated in boiling water.

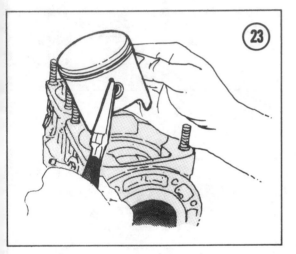

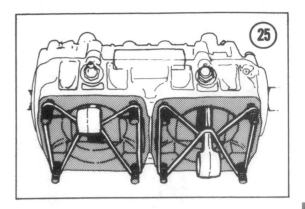

Cleaning

1. Scrape carbon from the combustion chamber in the head and the exhaust port in the cylinder, using a soft metal (aluminum) or wood scraper. Do not use a hard metal scraper; it will burr the surfaces and create hot spots.

2. Clean the head and cylinder with solvent and dry them with compressed air if possible.

3. Remove the rings from the piston and clean the dome with a soft scraper. Clean the ring grooves with a ring groove scraper or a piece of old piston ring (**Figure 26**). Clean the piston with solvent and dry it with compressed air.

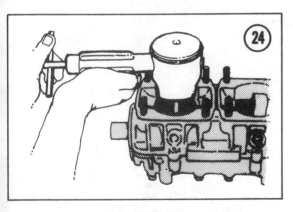

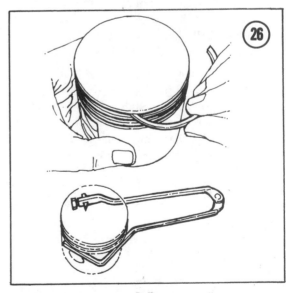

10. Remove the small end bearing from the connecting rod. For twin cylinder engines, keep the piston sets separated and do not mix the pieces.

11. Secure the connecting rods with rubber bands stretched over the cylinder base studs (**Figure 25**) to prevent the rods from striking the crankcase and damaging it.

CAUTION
Pistons fitted with keystone cross-section rings must not be cleaned with a ring groove scraper. Instead, use a piece of old ring.

Inspection

1. Check the flatness of the cylinder head on either a surface plate or a piece of glass (**Figure 27**). If the head does not make contact over the entire sealing surface, it must be trued. This is a job for a specialist.

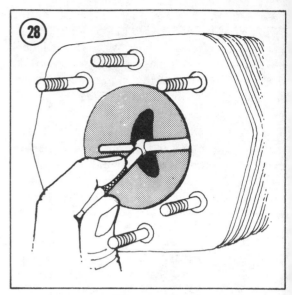

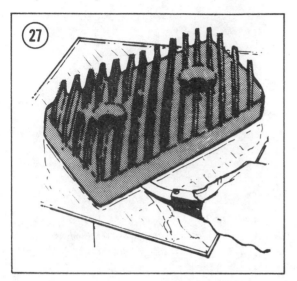

2. Check the cylinder and the piston for wear, galling, scuffing, or burning. Minor irregularities can be removed from the piston with crocus cloth and light oil. The cylinder may be cleaned up with a light honing, provided it is within specifications as described below.

3. Measure the cylinder bore with an inside micrometer or cylinder gauge. Measure ⅜ in. below the top of the cylinder, in two locations, 90° apart (**Figure 28**). If the 2 measurements differ by more than 0.002 in. (0.05mm), the cylinder is out of round beyond specification and must be bored or replaced. Measure again in 2 locations 90° apart just above the intake port. If these 2 measurements differ by more than 0.002 in. (0.05mm), the cylinder is out of specification and must be bored or replaced. Acceptable cylinder diameters are shown in **Table 2**.

4. Check piston skirt-to-cylinder clearance by first measuring the base of the cylinder bore, front to back (**Figure 29**). With an outside micrometer, measure the piston skirt, front and rear, about ¼ in. (6mm) from the bottom (**Figure 30**). Subtract the piston measurement

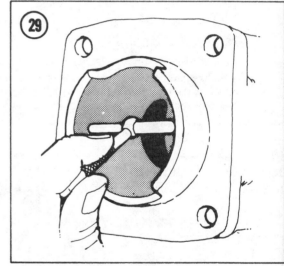

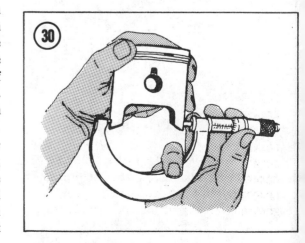

Table 2   CYLINDER DIAMETER ①

Engine Model	Standard Bore		Maximum Piston/Cylinder Clearance ±0.002 Inch
	Inch	mm	
EC17PM	2.4409	62	0.007
EC25PS	2.8346	72	0.009
EC25PT	2.1017	53.4	Dress with fine stone only*
EC25PC	2.1063	53.5	0.006
EC25PM-01	2.082	52.9	0.005
EC34PC	2.4409	62	0.007
EC34PM-03	2.432	61.78	0.006
EC34PQ	2.3622	60	0.0065
EC34PT	2.441	62	Dress with fine stone only*
EC34PL-01	2.432	61.78	0.005
EC44PQ	2.6673	67.75	0.008
EC44PT	2.6673	67.75	Dress with fine stone only*

* Chrome cylinders may be de-glazed and refinished using fine stones.
① If more than 0.020 in. material must be removed with a hone, to clean up the cylinder surface, the cylinder should be bored 0.020 in. oversize and an oversize piston and rings installed.

4

from the cylinder measurement to determine actual piston skirt-to-cylinder clearance. Refer to **Table 3** for acceptable clearances. If the bore

Table 3   PISTON/CYLINDER CLEARANCE

Engine Model	Piston Clearance	
	mm ±0.051	Inches ±0.002
EC25PS	0.228	0.009
EC25PC	0.152	0.006
EC25PM-01	0.127	0.005
EC25PT-07	——	——
EC34PM-03	0.152	0.006
EC34PQ	0.165	0.0065
EC34PT-05	——	——
EC34PL-01	0.127	0.005
EC44PQ	0.203	0.008
EC44PT-05	——	——
EC44PT-06	——	——

is acceptable, but the clearance is excessive, the piston must be replaced with a new unit that includes a matched pin and bearing, as well as rings.

5. Measure the piston ring end gap. Place a ring into the cylinder, ⅜ in. from the top. Use the piston to square the ring with the cylinder by pressing down on the ring with the skirt. Measure the gap as shown in **Figure 31**. Refer to **Table 4** for acceptable end gap. If the gap is too large for either ring, replace them as a set. Check new rings in the manner just described, and if the gap is too small, file material off the ends of the rings. See **Figure 32**.

6. Inspect the piston pin. Look for galling at the ends, an indication the pin is rotating in the piston.

7. Check the pin bores in the piston for signs of galling. If this is apparent, the piston, pin, and bearing must be replaced as a set.

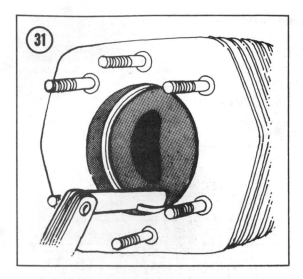

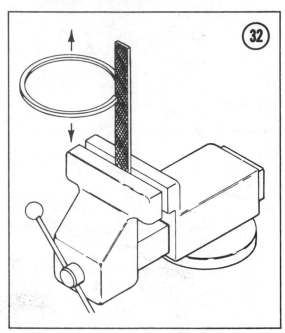

8. Set the bearing and pin in the small end of the connecting rod and check for rocking movement, back and forth and up and down. See **Figure 33**. If movement is apparent, recheck with a new pin and bearing. If movement is still apparent, the rod must be replaced. This is a job for a dealer.

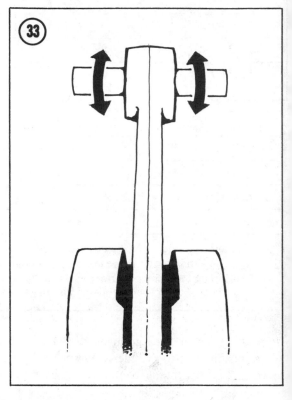

Assembly

1. Apply a thin coat of gasket sealer to both sides of new cylinder base gaskets and install them over the studs on crankcase (**Figure 34**).

Table 4   PISTON RING END GAP

Standard Bore	End Gap
2.082 in. (52.9mm)	0.031 in. (0.79mm)
2.1017 in. (53.4mm)	0.031 in. (0.79mm)
2.1063 in. (53.5mm)	0.031 in. (0.79mm)
2.3622 in. (60mm)	0.031 in. (0.79mm)
2.432 in. (61.78mm)	0.032 in. (0.81mm)
2.441 in. (62mm)	0.032 in. (0.81mm)
2.6673 in. (67.75mm)	0.033 in. (0.85mm)
2.8346 in. (72mm)	0.034 in. (0.86mm)

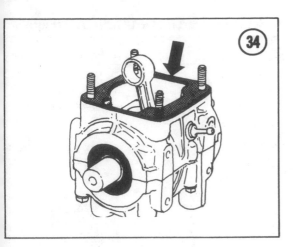

2. Oil the connecting rod big end bearing (**Figure 35**), the piston pin, and the piston pin needle bearing (**Figure 36**).

3. Install the pistons with the arrow on the piston crown facing the exhaust port. This is

essential so the ring end gaps will be correctly positioned and will not snag in the ports. See **Figure 37**. Install the piston pin clips, making sure that they are completely seated in their grooves with the open ends of the clips facing down (**Figure 38**).

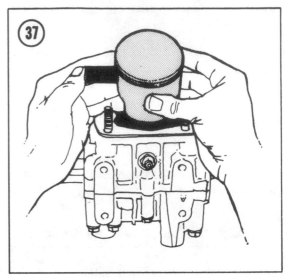

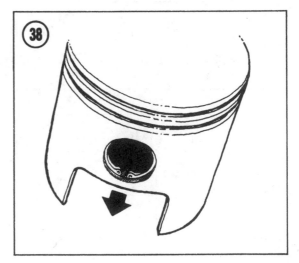

4. Coat the piston and the cylinder bore lightly with oil. Line up the piston ring ends with the locating pins in the ring grooves (**Figure 39**). Install a ring compressor or a large hose clamp to compress the rings.

5. Line up the cylinder with the piston, hold the piston to prevent it from rocking, and push the cylinder down over the piston. Some resistance will be felt but if binding is experienced,

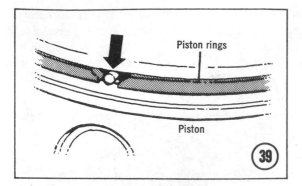

Piston rings

Piston

(39)

remove the cylinder and locate and correct the problem before proceeding; don't force the cylinder down over the piston.

6. When the cylinder is in place, screw on and tighten the cylinder base nuts to the torque shown in **Table 5** in a crisscross pattern. See **Figure 40**.

Table 5   CYLINDER BASE NUT TORQUE

Engine	Cylinder Base Studs
EC25PS	24-28 ft.-lb. (3.3-3.9 mkg)
All twin cylinder	24-28 ft.-lb. (3.3-3.9 mkg)

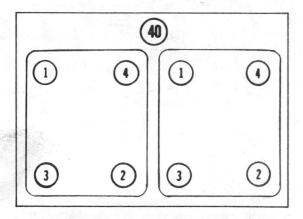

(40)

7. Set new head gaskets in place, then install the cylinder heads. Tighten the cylinder head nuts (see **Table 6**) in the appropriate pattern shown in **Figure 41**.

8. On liquid-cooled engines, install the water pump drive pulley and tighten the nut to 60

Table 6   CYLINDER HEAD NUT TORQUE

Engine	Cylinder Head
EC25PS	17-18 ft.-lb. (2.3-2.5 mkg)
All twin cylinder	17-18 ft.-lb. (2.3-2.5 mkg)
EC34PL-01 (liquid cooled)	
8mm nut	16-17 ft.-lb. (2.2-2.3 mkg)
10mm nut	26-29 ft.-lb. (3.6-4.0 mkg)

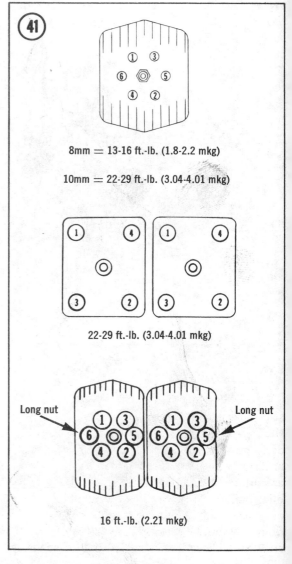

(41)

8mm = 13-16 ft.-lb. (1.8-2.2 mkg)

10mm = 22-29 ft.-lb. (3.04-4.01 mkg)

22-29 ft.-lb. (3.04-4.01 mkg)

Long nut   Long nut

16 ft.-lb. (2.21 mkg)

ft.-lb. Install the water pump. Lightly grease the O-ring that fits between the cylinder and the pump. Install the drive belt and adjust it so there is ¼ in. deflection. Tighten the mounting nuts to 15 ft.-lb.

9. Refer to *Engine Removal/Installation* in this chapter and install the engine and the support hardware. Refer to Chapter Two, *Tune-Up*, and tune the engine as described. Remember, a rebuilt upper end must be broken-in in the same manner as a new engine if it is to enjoy long service life.

10. On liquid-cooled engines, remove the bleed vent valve from the cylinder head (**Figure 42**). Pour fresh coolant into the surge tank until coolant runs out of the vent valve hole. Install the vent valve with a new gasket and fill the surge tank to the filler neck. Start the engine and run it at 4,000 rpm until the thermostat opens, as evidenced by coolant flowing into the top of the surge tank. If necessary, continue to add coolant until the level indicated by the mark on the tank is stable.

LOWER END OVERHAUL

Lower end overhaul as described here consists of removal and installation of the crankshaft assembly. A surface plate, Vee-blocks, and dial indicator stands and bases are required to accurately check the condition of the crankshaft assembly. In addition, early crankshaft assemblies cannot be serviced and must be replaced as an assembly, while the latest crankshafts require a hydraulic press and considerable experience to disassemble, assemble, and align them.

It is recommended that the crankcase halves be parted and the crankshaft assembly entrusted to a dealer for inspection and repair.

Disassembly

1. Refer to *Engine Removal/Installation* and *Upper End Disassembly* and remove the engine from the machine and disassemble upper end.

2. Remove the flywheel, rotor, and stator as described in Chapter Six. Unscrew the screws that attach the magneto base to the crankcase (**Figure 43**). An impact driver should be used to loosen the screws and prevent damage to the screw slots. Tap the magneto base off the crankcase with a soft mallet.

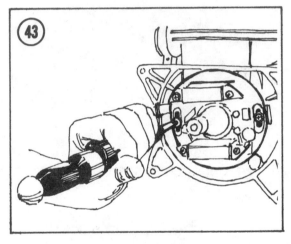

3. Unscrew the bolts from the bottom of the crankcase in the appropriate pattern shown in **Figure 44** to reduce the possibility of warping the crankcase halves.

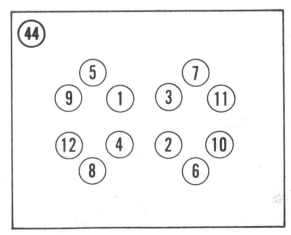

4. Part the cases by tapping on the large bosses on the upper case half with a soft mallet. See **Figure 45**.

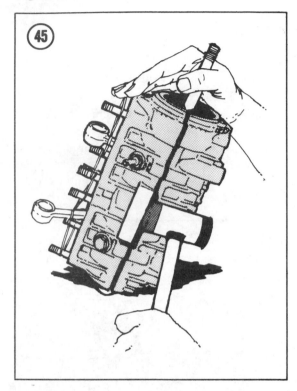

CAUTION
Do not pry the cases apart with a screwdriver or any other similar tool; damage to the sealing surfaces is likely to result.

5. Lift the crankshaft assembly out of the lower case half. Pay particular attention to shims and half rings in the bottom case, and make a detailed drawing to indicate their locations.

6. Clean the crankcase halves and the crankshaft assembly with solvent and dry them with compressed air. Have the crankshaft assembly inspected and serviced by a Polaris dealer or engine specialist.

Assembly

1. Fill the open face of each crankshaft seal with grease and install the seals on the ends of the shaft with the open faces inward. Oil the connecting rod and main bearings.

2. Lightly coat the sealing surface of both crankcase halves with a pliable crankcase sealer such as Liquid Gasket, RTV Silicone Seal or Permatex Form-A-Gasket.

3. Set the crankshaft assembly in the bottom case half, making sure the dowels in the bearings engage the alignment holes in the cases.

4. Set the top case half in place and press it down by hand until it contacts the sealing surface of the lower case half. If it does not, retrace the above steps to find the reason; no force is required to assemble the case halves if everything is lined up.

5. Install all of the crankcase bolts finger-tight. Then, tighten them in the sequence shown in **Figure 44** to the correct torque (**Table 7**).

Table 7   CRANKCASE BOLT TORQUE

| Engine | Crankcase | |
	8mm	10mm
EC25PS	18-20 ft.-lb. (2.5-2.8 mkg)	23-25 ft.-lb. (3.2-3.5 mkg)
All twin cylinder	18-20 ft.-lb. (2.5-2.8 mkg)	23-25 ft.-lb. (3.2-3.5 mkg)
EC34PL-01 (liquid cooled)	18-20 ft.-lb. (2.5-2.8 mkg)	23-25 ft.-lb. (3.2-3.5 mkg)

6. Reverse the remaining disassembly steps to assemble the engine. Refer to the instructions for assembling the upper end and installing the engine in this chapter. Refer to Chapter Two for engine tune-up.

NOTE: If you own a 1978 or later model, first check the Supplement at the back of the book for any new service information.

CHAPTER FIVE

FUEL SYSTEM

The fuel system consists of a fuel tank, fuel line of lines, in-line fuel filter and carburetor.

The Mikuni carburetor is shown in **Figures 1 and 2**. An auxiliary impulse pump (**Figure 3**) provides fuel to the carburetor. The fuel pump operates off differential pressure in the engine crankcase.

An air intake silencer is used to quiet incoming air and to catch fuel that may spit back out of the carburetor.

This chapter covers removal, installation, and replacement and/or repair of carburetors, fuel pump, in-line filter, and fuel tanks. Carburetor tuning is covered in Chapter Two.

CARBURETOR

Removal

Refer to **Figure 4** for this procedure.

1. Disconnect the fuel line from the carburetor and plug the line.

2. Unscrew the carburetor top (**Figure 5**) and withdraw the slide assembly.

3. Unscrew the choke assembly (**Figure 6**) from the carburetor and withdraw it.

4. Loosen the screws in the clamping bands on the air silencer and remove the silencer.

5. Loosen the clamping bands on the manifold

A. Spring	D. Fuel line	F. Carburetor
B. Top half	E. Clamp	G. Lower half
C. Clamp		

(**Figure 7**) and remove the carburetor. On carburetors with integral flanges, unscrew the mounting nuts, collect the washers, and remove the carburetor.

Disassembly

Refer to **Figure 8** for this procedure.

1. Remove the drain plug from bottom of the

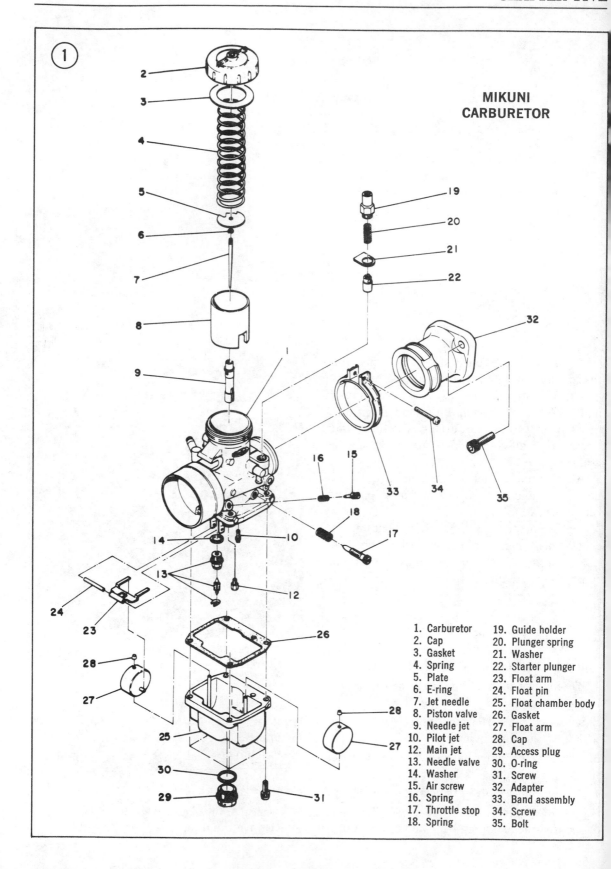

MIKUNI
CARBURETOR

1. Carburetor
2. Cap
3. Gasket
4. Spring
5. Plate
6. E-ring
7. Jet needle
8. Piston valve
9. Needle jet
10. Pilot jet
12. Main jet
13. Needle valve
14. Washer
15. Air screw
16. Spring
17. Throttle stop
18. Spring
19. Guide holder
20. Plunger spring
21. Washer
22. Starter plunger
23. Float arm
24. Float pin
25. Float chamber body
26. Gasket
27. Float arm
28. Cap
29. Access plug
30. O-ring
31. Screw
32. Adapter
33. Band assembly
34. Screw
35. Bolt

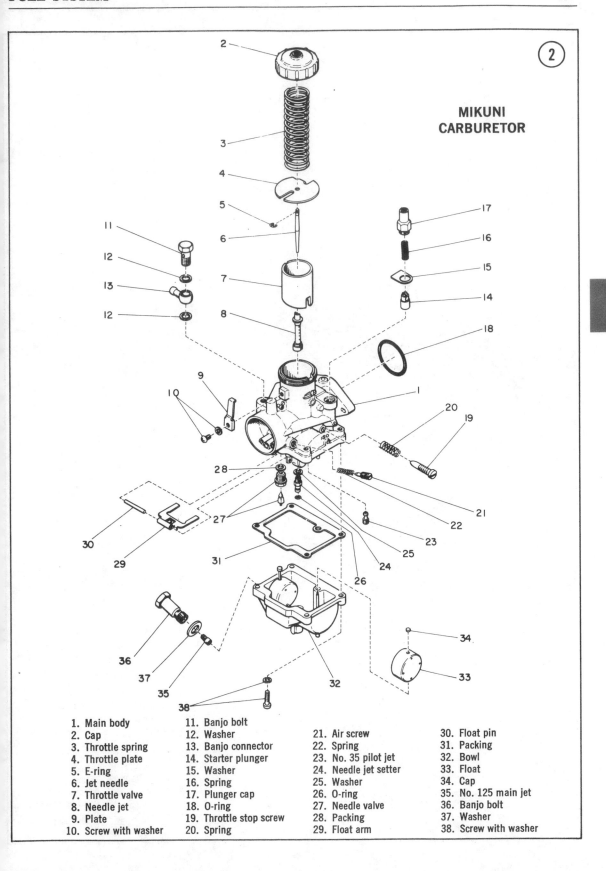

MIKUNI
CARBURETOR

5

1. Main body	11. Banjo bolt		30. Float pin
2. Cap	12. Washer	21. Air screw	31. Packing
3. Throttle spring	13. Banjo connector	22. Spring	32. Bowl
4. Throttle plate	14. Starter plunger	23. No. 35 pilot jet	33. Float
5. E-ring	15. Washer	24. Needle jet setter	34. Cap
6. Jet needle	16. Spring	25. Washer	35. No. 125 main jet
7. Throttle valve	17. Plunger cap	26. O-ring	36. Banjo bolt
8. Needle jet	18. O-ring	27. Needle valve	37. Washer
9. Plate	19. Throttle stop screw	28. Packing	38. Screw with washer
10. Screw with washer	20. Spring	29. Float arm	

③

AUXILIARY IMPULSE PUMP

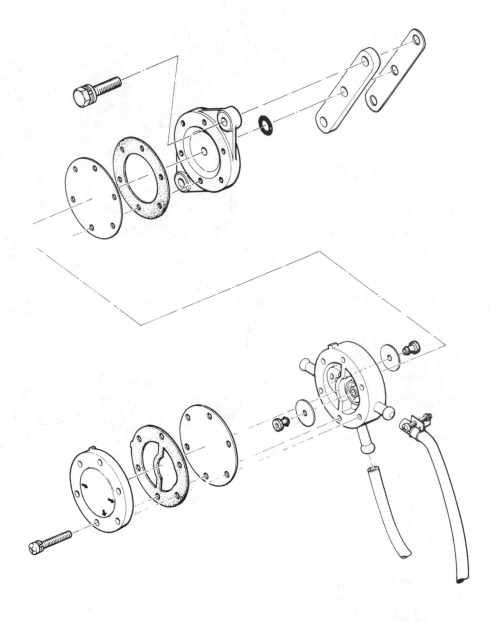

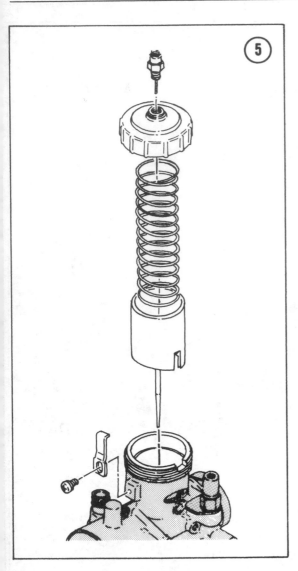

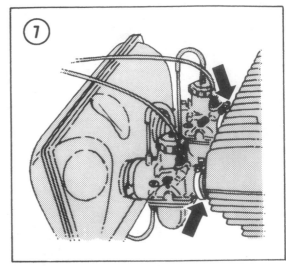

5

float chamber. Drain the fuel into a suitable container. Install the drain plug.

WARNING
Handle and dispose of drained fuel carefully or a serious or fatal fire may occur.

2. Remove the throttle stop screw and spring.

3. Remove the air screw and spring.

4. Remove the float chamber as shown in **Figure 9**. Carefully lift out the floats from the carburetor body.

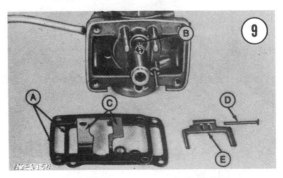

A. Gaskets	C. Baffle plate
B. Inlet needle	D. Float air pin
valve assembly	E. Float arm

5. Using a 6mm socket or box end wrench carefully remove the main jet and ring.

6. Remove the float arm pin and float arm. Lift off the baffle plate and gaskets (**Figure 9**).

7. Carefully remove the inlet needle valve assembly with washer.

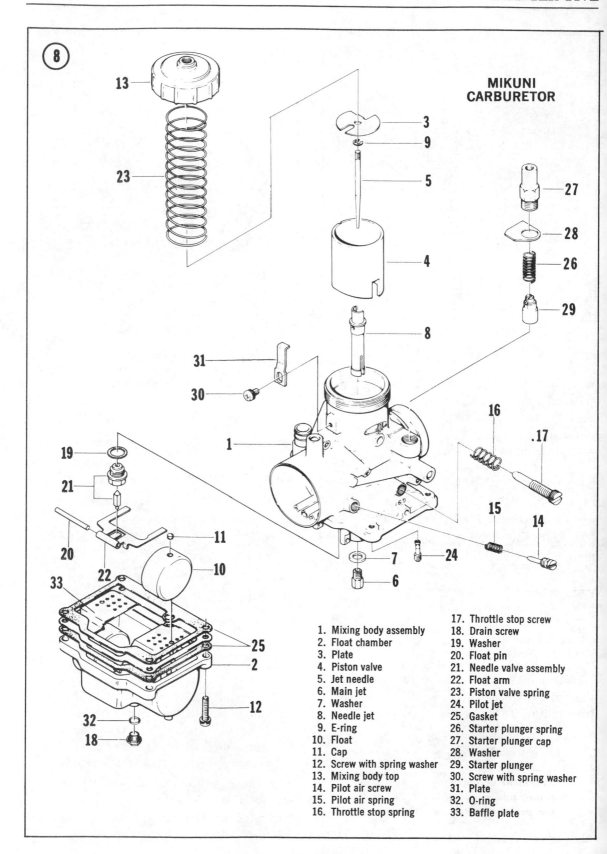

⑧

13

23

**MIKUNI
CARBURETOR**

3
9
5

27

28

26

4

29

8

31

30

16

.17

1

19

21

20

11

15

14

10

22

7

24

33

6

25

2

12

32

18

1. Mixing body assembly
2. Float chamber
3. Plate
4. Piston valve
5. Jet needle
6. Main jet
7. Washer
8. Needle jet
9. E-ring
10. Float
11. Cap
12. Screw with spring washer
13. Mixing body top
14. Pilot air screw
15. Pilot air spring
16. Throttle stop spring

17. Throttle stop screw
18. Drain screw
19. Washer
20. Float pin
21. Needle valve assembly
22. Float arm
23. Piston valve spring
24. Pilot jet
25. Gasket
26. Starter plunger spring
27. Starter plunger cap
28. Washer
29. Starter plunger
30. Screw with spring washer
31. Plate
32. O-ring
33. Baffle plate

8. Carefully push the needle jet from mixing chamber using an awl or similar sharp pointed device. See **Figure 10**.

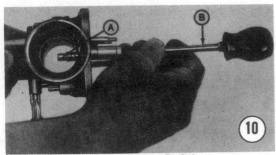

A. Needle jet   B. Awl

9. Compress the throttle slide spring and remove the cable lock plate from the top of the slide. Disconnect the end of the cable from the throttle slide. Remove the needle valve from the slide. Note the position of the E-ring on the needle valve; the E-ring locates the needle with respect to the needle valve and a change in position can affect fuel mixture and performance. If the carburetor has been performing correctly, you will want to reinstall the E-ring on the notch from which it was removed.

Cleaning and Inspection

A special carburetor cleaning solution, tank and basket (**Figure 11**) can be purchased at auto parts stores for a few dollars. When not in use the tank can be sealed to prevent the reusable solution from evaporating.

WARNING
Most carburetor cleaners are highly caustic. They must be handled with extreme care or skin burns and possible eye injury may result.

1. Clean all metallic parts in carburetor cleaning solvent. Do not place gaskets in solvent or they will be destroyed.

CAUTION
Never clean holes or passages with small drill bits or wire; a slight enlargement or burring of the hole will result, and drastically affect carburetor performance.

2. Inspect the float chamber and carburetor

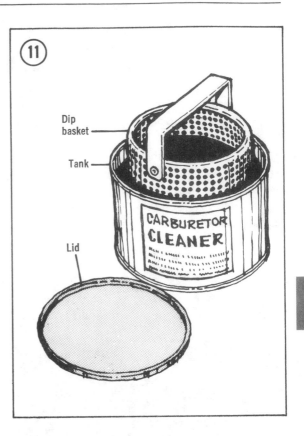

Dip basket

Tank

Lid

body for fine cracks or evidence of fuel leaks.

3. Check the throttle spring for distortion or damage.

4. Inspect the air screw and throttle stop screw for surface damage or stripped threads.

5. Inspect the pilot jet and main jet for damage or stripped threads.

CAUTION
The pilot jet and main jet must be scrupulously clean and shiny. Any burring, roughness, or abrasion will cause a lean fuel and air mixture and possible engine damage.

6. Remove the retainer and inlet valve from the valve seat. Carefully examine the seating surface on the inlet valve and seat for damage. Make sure the retainer does not bind and hinder movement of the inlet valve.

7. Inspect the jet needle and needle jet for damage. The jet needle must slide freely within the needle jet.

8. Install the float guides in the float chamber. Move the floats up and down several times to

ensure that they are not binding on the float guides.

9. Inspect the float arm and float pin to ensure that the float arm does not bind on the pin.

10. Inspect the choke plunger. The plunger must move freely in the passage of the carburetor body.

11. Install the throttle valve in the carburetor body and move it up and down several times to check for sticking motion or looseness. Ensure that the guide pin in the carburetor body is not broken.

Assembly

Refer to **Figure 8** for this procedure.

1. Using a small screwdriver install the pilot jet in the carburetor body as shown in **Figure 12**.

2. Install the gaskets and baffle plate on the carburetor body (**Figure 13**). Install the second gasket on top of baffle plate.

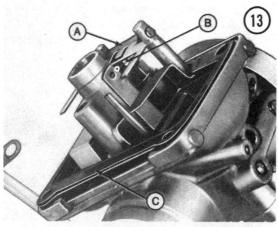

A. Float arm   B. Inlet valve   C. Baffle plate and gaskets

3. Place the washer on the inlet needle valve seat and install the seat in the carburetor body (**Figure 13**). Install the inlet valve (point down) and retainer.

4. Install the float arm and secure it with the float arm pin.

5. Invert the carburetor body and check the float level. The float bowl sealing surface of the carburetor body (**Figure 14**) must be parallel with the float arm. If necessary, adjust it by bending the float arm actuating tab.

A. Mixing chamber   B. Float arm

6. Install the needle jet. Make sure the notch on the needle jet is correctly aligned with the pin in bore of the carburetor body (**Figure 15**). Install the ring over the needle jet bore (recess in ring next to bore) and screw the main jet into the needle jet.

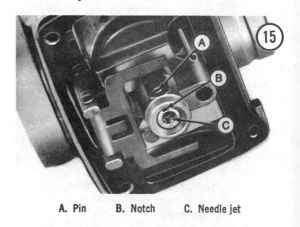

A. Pin   B. Notch   C. Needle jet

7. Slide the floats over the float pins. The pins

on the float must be down and point to the inside of float chamber as shown in **Figure 16**.

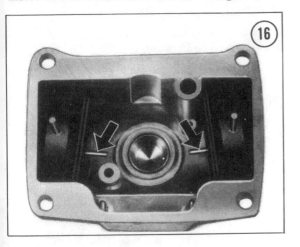

8. Install the float chamber on the carburetor body and secure it with 4 screws.

9. Slide the air screw spring over the air screw and screw in air screw gently.

CAUTION
Do not force the air screw or seat damage may occur.

10. Install the throttle stop screw and spring. Install the screw until it is just flush with the inside of the bore.

Installation

1. Position the carburetor in rubber mount and tighten the clamp screw. On flanged carburetors, install the washers and screw on and tighten the nuts.

2. Connect the fuel line from the pump to the carburetor.

3. Install the E-ring in the groove in the needle valve from which it was removed. Install the needle valve in the throttle slide (see **Figure 17**).

4. Route the throttle cable end button through cap, spring, lock plate, and slot in throttle slide as shown in **Figure 17**.

5. Slide the cable into the narrow part of the slot in the throttle valve. Install the lock plate between the spring and throttle slide with the tab on the plate in the slot of the throttle slide.

6. Install the throttle assembly in the carburetor body, making sure the needle engages the needle

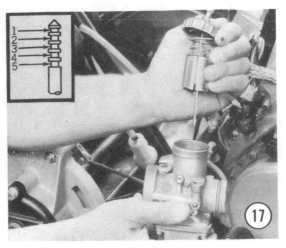

valve and the slot in the throttle engages the knob in the throttle bore (**Figure 18**).

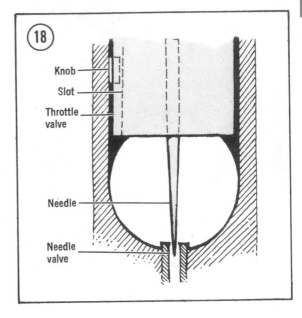

Compress the throttle valve spring and tighten the cap on the carburetor body.

7. Move the choke lever on the instrument panel to the OFF position. Route the choke cable end button in the choke plunger as shown in **Figure 19** and place the washer on the carburetor body. Install the assembly and tighten cap.

8. Perform carburetor adjustments as described in Chapter Two, *Carburetor Adjustment and Synchronization*.

9. Install the air intake silencer.

10. Install windshield and console if removed.

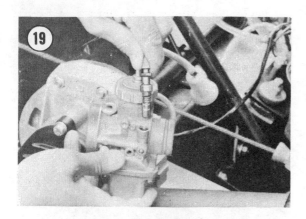

2. Remove seat and tank hold-on clip or spring.

3. Remove seat by sliding tank rearward.

4. Installation is the reverse of these steps.

Pick-up Screen Cleaning

1. Disconnect the fuel lines from the fitting and remove the fitting from the fuel tank. See **Figure 21**.

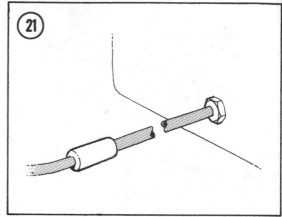

INTAKE SILENCERS

Intake silencers are installed on snowmobiles to quiet the sound of rushing air and to catch fuel that spits back out of the carburetor throat.

The silencer is not intended to filter incoming air. Operate snowmobiles only in clean, snow-covered areas.

> CAUTION
> *Never operate the snowmobile with the silencer removed. Loss of power and engine damage will result from a lean fuel mixture.*

Service of air intake silencers is limited to removal and cleaning of components.

FUEL TANK

The fuel tank (**Figure 20**) incorporates a fuel gauge in the filler cap and a spill ledge to prevent spilled fuel from spilling on to the seat. The fuel tank cap is sealed and the tank is vented by a line to the top of the tank.

A fuel shutoff valve is located between the fuel pick-up line and the in-line fuel filter.

> NOTE: *If the snowmobile has been transported on a trailer without the fuel valve shut off, the engine may be flooded.*

Removal/Installation

1. Disconnect fuel lines and vent lines.

2. Remove the pick-up screen from the end of the line.

3. Rinse the screen carefully in solvent and blow it dry with compressed air. Replace the screen if it is damaged. Replace gasket on the fuel line fitting if necessary.

IN-LINE FUEL FILTER

Service of the in-line fuel filter is limited to annual replacement or replacement when contamination builds up at the base of the cone in the filter unit.

FUEL PUMP

To check fuel pump operation, disconnect the fuel line from the pump to the carburetor at the carburetor. Make sure the ignition switch is OFF and pull the recoil starter handle and check for fuel flow at the fuel line. If fuel flow from the pump is unsatisfactory, replace it.

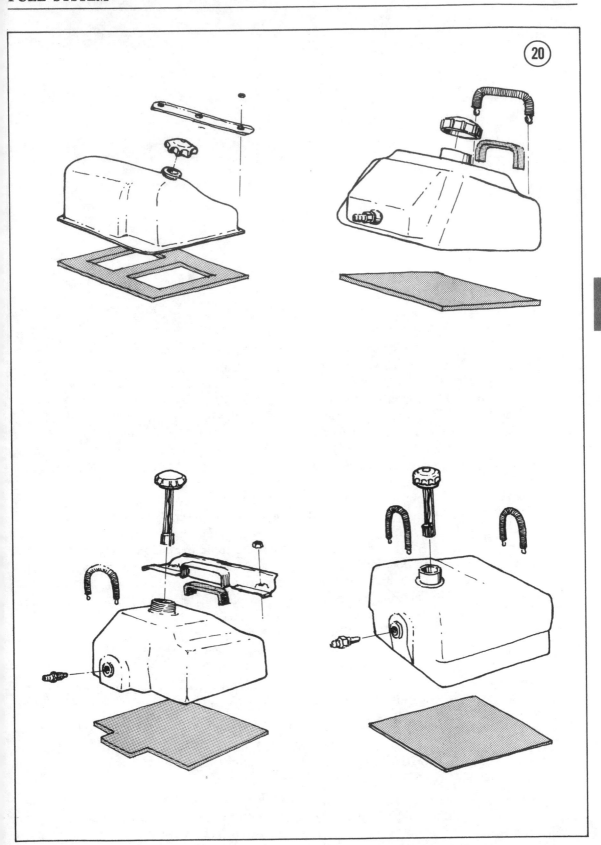

CHAPTER SIX

ELECTRICAL SYSTEM

The electrical system on Polaris snowmobiles consists of an ignition system, lighting system, and an electric starting system on some models.

Two types of ignition systems are used: a magneto (Colt and Electra racing models) and (capacitor discharge ignition) CDI (others).

The lighting system consists of a headlight, brake/taillight, and console lights.

The electric starting system on some models consists of a battery, a starter and solenoid, and charging equipment.

This chapter includes testing and repair of some components of the ignition, lighting, and charging systems. Some testing and repair tasks referenced in this chapter require special testing equipment and tools. These tasks are best accomplished by an authorized dealer or competent auto electric shop.

Wiring diagrams for all models are included at the end of the book.

Refer to Chapter Two for ignition timing and breaker point adjustment.

CAPACITOR DISCHARGE IGNITION (CDI)

The capacitor discharge ignition system (**Figure 1**) consists of a permanent magnet flywheel, alternator, and solid-state capacitor. The system supplies high voltage for ignition and generates current required for the lighting system.

The flywheel incorporates a magnet and is mounted on the engine crankshaft. The flywheel and magnet revolve around the stator assembly, which is fixed to the engine. Current is generated in the pole windings of the stator.

Nine poles supply power for the lighting system and 3 poles supply power for the ignition.

The ignition timing ring, alternator stator, and electronic pack require special test equipment to troubleshoot malfunctions and monitor performance. If trouble exists in any of these units, refer the testing and repair to an authorized dealer.

Testing Engine Emergency Shutoff Switch

Refer to the appropriate wiring diagram for this procedure.

1. Disconnect the wires leading to the terminal block.

2. Connect test leads of a continuity test light to the wires.

3. Turn the ignition switch to the ON position.

4. With the shutoff switch in the OFF position, the test light should light. The test light should

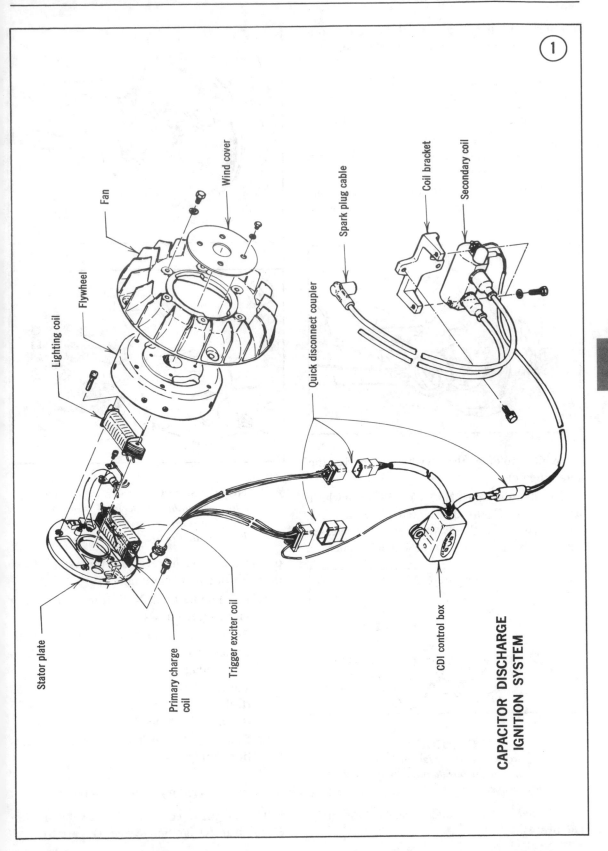

Wind cover

Fan

Coil bracket

Secondary coil

Spark plug cable

Flywheel

Lighting coil

Quick disconnect coupler

Stator plate

Primary charge coil

Trigger exciter coil

CDI control box

**CAPACITOR DISCHARGE
IGNITION SYSTEM**

not light with the shutoff switch in the ON position. Replace the switch if it is defective.

Flywheel, Alternator Stator, and Trigger Removal/Installation

It is necessary to remove the engine to perform the following procedure.

1. Remove the recoil starter, flywheel housing, and lower fan sheave.

2. Hold the flywheel with a strap wrench (part No. 2870336) or locally fabricated equivalent (**Figure 2**).

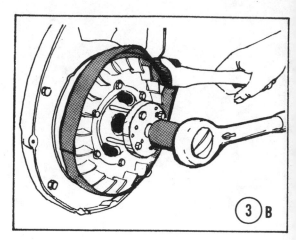

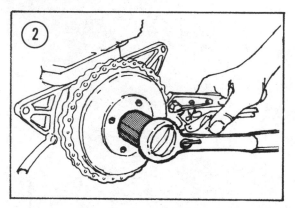

3. While holding the flywheel, remove the retaining nut.

4. Install puller (part No. 2870159) to flywheel as shown in **Figure 3**. Tighten puller and remove flywheel. If the flywheel does not release, rap sharply on the puller bolt with a hammer.

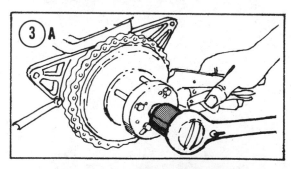

CAUTION
Do not strike flywheel with a steel hammer or serious damage to flywheel may occur.

5. Remove stator and trigger assembly (**Figure 4**).

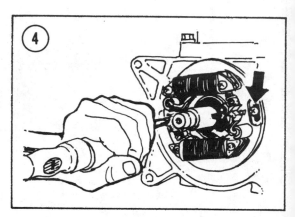

NOTE: *Screws securing stator and trigger assembly are secured with Loctite. Tap screwdriver with hammer to help break Loctite loose.*

6. Installation is the reverse of these steps. Keep the following points in mind:

a. Use Loctite Lock-N' Seal to secure stator and trigger screws.

b. Position screws on trigger assembly in the center of their slots for preliminary ignition timing.

c. Torque flywheel retaining nut to 60-65 ft.-lb. (8.3-8.9 mkg); 175 engines—30-35 ft.-lb. (4.5-4.8 mkg).

d. Refer to Chapter Two and perform ignition timing.

MAGNETO IGNITION

The magneto equipped models feature an energy transfer ignition system (**Figure 5**).

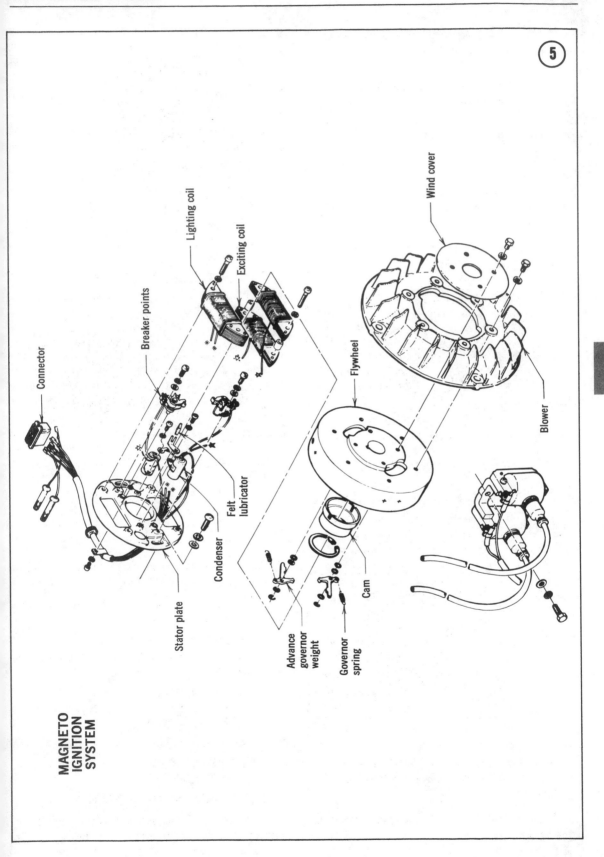

MAGNETO IGNITION SYSTEM

5

6

Connector

Breaker points

Lighting coil

Exciting coil

Wind cover

Flywheel

Blower

Stator plate

Condenser

Felt lubricator

Advance governor weight

Governor spring

Cam

The ignition system consists of an ignition generating coil, a set of breaker points, a condenser, and an ignition coil.

Refer to Chapter Two for breaker points and timing adjustments.

Emergency Stop Switch Test

1. Disconnect the coupler to emergency stop switch.

2. Connect a light-type continuity tester between the terminals in coupler.

3. The test light must light when the switch is pressed and go out when the stop switch is in the operating position.

Ignition Switch Test

Check the ignition switch with a light-type continuity tester. Refer to the schematic, and check for continuity between switch terminals.

Stator Assembly Removal

Remove recoil starter, fan cover, and flywheel to gain access to stator assembly. Remove the backing plate if the stator assembly is to be removed.

Refer to **Figure 6** for following procedures.

Condenser

1. Loosen the soldered leads on the condenser terminal with a soldering iron.

2. Remove screw that secures the condenser to the stator plate and remove condenser.

3. Install a new condenser and solder the leads to terminal.

CAUTION
Exercise care when resoldering wire to the condenser; too much heat can destroy the condenser.

Breaker Points

1. Loosen the breaker point terminal and disconnect the leads.

2. Remove the screw that attaches the breaker points to the stator plate and remove the breaker point assembly.

3. Install a new breaker point assembly and attach the leads. Perform breaker point adjustment as described in Chapter Two.

Felt Oil Pads

Replace the felt oil pads (**Figure 7**) if their lubricating capacity is questionable. Oil the

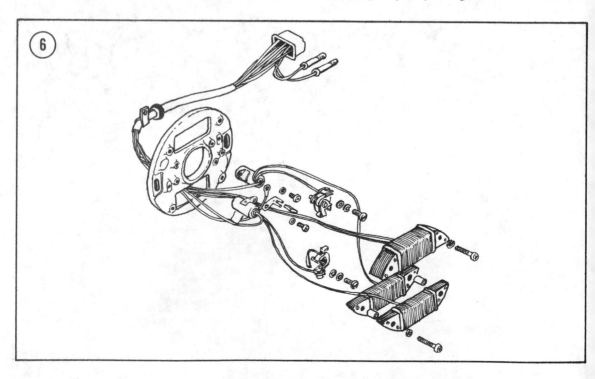

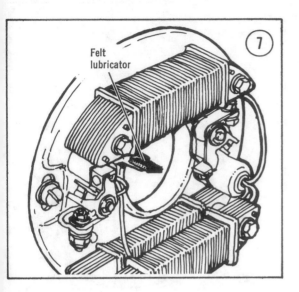

Felt lubricator

⑦

pads with a couple of drops of light oil whenever breaker points are replaced.

LIGHTING SYSTEM

The lighting system consists of a headlight and brake/taillight unit, instrument lights, and an AC (alternating current) generating device. Switches control all lighting circuits.

On models equipped with an electric starter, AC is converted to DC (direct current) by a rectifier and then used to keep the battery charged.

Testing

If the lights fail to work, do not immediately assume the worst—a major failure in the alternator, regulator, or lighting coils. Very often the problem can be found in the lamps; look for burned out filaments or bulbs that are loose in their sockets. In addition, check the harness connectors to ensure that they are clean and tight and have not become disconnected.

Four things are required for the lights to function. You must have current and an uninterrupted, non-shorted path for it to follow. The switch must work correctly. A good ground is required. The light bulbs must be in good condition and correctly installed in clean, dry sockets.

ELECTRIC START SYSTEM

The electric starting system consists of a 12-volt battery, starter motor, starter solenoid, rectifier, and fuse.

The starter motor engages a ring gear on the flywheel to turn the engine over. The battery is kept charged by the alternator. A fuse is used to protect the system from overloads or short circuits.

If difficulty is experienced with the optional electric start system installed on some models, check the most likely cause of trouble—the battery. Make certain the battery and starter connections are clean and tight. Check and service the battery as described below. If the battery is satisfactory, proceed to test the starter and solenoid as described. A schematic for the electric start models is located at the end of this book.

Battery Removal/Installation

1. Disconnect the negative (—) battery cable. Then disconnect the positive (+) cable.

2. Loosen hold-down bolts and unhook bolts from battery box. Remove hold-down clamp.

3. Disconnect vent tube from battery Carefully lift battery out of battery box.

4. Installation is the reverse of these steps. Keep the following points in mind:

    a. Be sure exterior of battery and terminals are clean and free from corrosion.

    b. Connect positive (+) cable to battery first.

CAUTION
Be sure battery connections are correct or serious damage to electrical components will occur.

Battery Cleaning and Service

Electrolyte level in the battery should be checked periodically, especially during periods of regular operation. Use only distilled water and top off battery to bottom of ring (filler neck) so the tops of the plates are covered. *Do not overfill.*

Battery corrosion is a normal reaction; however, it should be cleaned off periodically to keep battery deterioration to a minimum.

Remove battery and wire brush terminals and cable ends. Wash terminals and exterior of bat-

6

tery with about a 4:1 solution of warm water and baking soda.

> **CAUTION**
> *Do not allow any baking soda solution to enter battery cells or serious battery damage may result.*

Wash battery box and hold-down bolts with baking soda solution. Rinse all parts in clear water and wipe dry.

In freezing weather, never add water to a battery unless the machine will be operated for a period of time to mix electrolyte and water.

> **CAUTION**
> *Keep battery fully charged. A discharged battery will freeze, causing the battery case to break.*

Remove the battery from the machine during extended non-use periods and keep battery fully charged. Perform periodic specific gravity tests with a hydrometer to determine the level of charge and how long charge stays up before it starts to deteriorate.

Battery Specific Gravity Test

Determine the state of charge of the battery with a hydrometer. To use this instrument, place the suction tube (**Figure 8**) into the filler opening and draw in just enough electrolyte to lift the float. Hold the instrument in a vertical position and take the reading at eye level.

Specific gravity of electrolyte varies with temperature, so it is necessary to apply a temperature correction to the reading you obtain. For each 10° that the battery temperature exceeds 80°F, add 0.004 to the indicated specific gravity. Subtract 0.004 from the indicated value for each 10° that the battery temperature is below 80°F.

> **WARNING**
> *Do not smoke or permit an open flame in any area where batteries are being charged. Highly explosive hydrogen gas is formed during the charging process.*

The specific gravity of a fully charged battery is 1.260. If the specific gravity is below 1.220, recharge the battery (**Figure 9**).

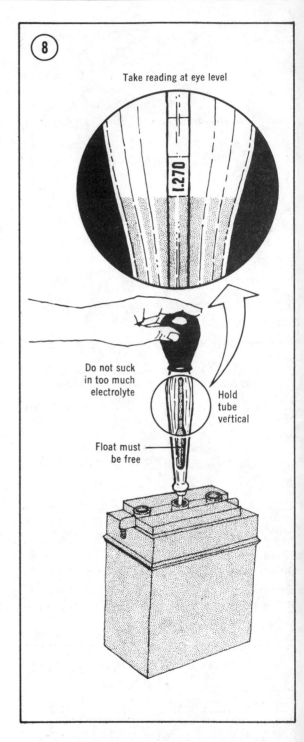

(8)

Take reading at eye level

1.270

Do not suck in too much electrolyte

Hold tube vertical

Float must be free

Starter Test

If starter fails to crank engine or cranks engine very slowly, perform the following:

1. Inspect cranking circuit wiring for loose or badly corroded connections or damaged wiring.

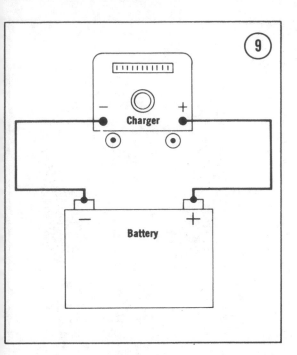

2. Perform *Battery Specific Gravity Test* to be certain battery is charged and not defective.

3. Crank engine with recoil starter to make sure engine turns freely and is not seized.

> NOTE: *Remove spark plug wires. The following bypasses the ignition switch.*

4. If starter will not crank engine, place a heavy jumper lead from positive (+) battery terminal directly to starter terminal (**Figure 10**). This bypasses the ignition switch, circuit breaker, and starter solenoid. If starter now cranks the engine, then one of these items is defective. If starter still will not crank engine, starter is defective.

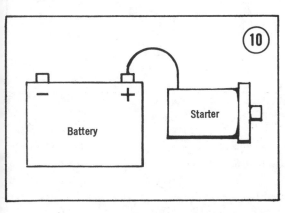

Starter Removal/Installation

Refer to **Figure 11** for this procedure. Starter repair consists of armature and/or brush replacement. It is recommended that all starter service and repair be referred to an authorized dealer or competent auto electric shop.

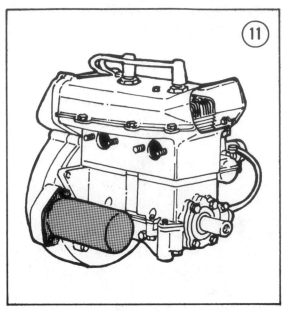

1. Disconnect ground cable from battery.

2. Disconnect solenoid-to-starter cable from starter terminal.

3. Remove mounting bolts securing starter to engine and mounting bracket to engine. Remove starter and mounting bracket.

4. Remove mounting bracket from starter.

5. Installation is the reverse of these steps.

Starter Solenoid Test

1. The starter solenoid is a sealed magnet switch and cannot be repaired. If defective, it must be replaced.

2. Remove and insulate cable from starter terminal. Connect test light across 2 large terminals (**Figure 12**) of starter solenoid.

3. With a jumper lead, connect positive (+) battery post to small terminal on solenoid. The solenoid plunger should snap in; light the test lamp, and hold until the jumper is removed. If this does not occur, the solenoid is defective and should be replaced.

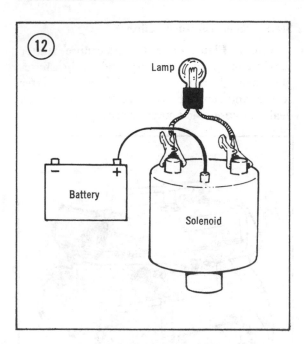

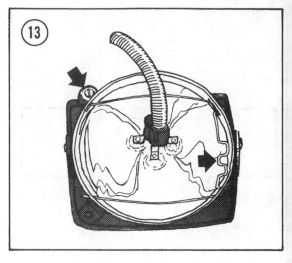

HEADLIGHT BULB REPLACEMENT

1. Raise the hood to gain access to the rear of the headlight.

2. Unplug the harness connector by pulling on the connector—not the wiring harness.

3. Remove the retaining clip from the housing (**Figure 13**).

4. Remove the old bulb and install a new one of the same rating. The rating appears on the bulb. Install the retaining clip. Reconnect the wiring harness.

HEADLIGHT AIMING

1. Refer to Chapter Two, *Suspension Adjustment*, and check (and adjust if necessary) the suspension.

2. Set the snowmobile on a level surface, 25 ft. (7.6m) from a vertical surface such as a wall (**Figure 14**).

3. Measure the distance from the floor to the center of the headlight lens. Make a mark on the vertical surface the same distance from the floor. For instance, if the center of the headlight lens is 24 in. above the floor, mark "A" (**Figure 14**) should also be 24 in. above the floor.

4. Start the engine, turn on the headlight and set the beam selector at HIGH; do not adjust the light with the selector set at LOW.

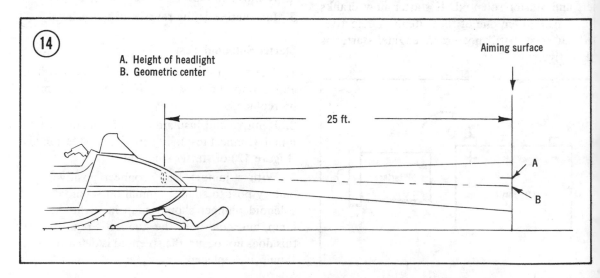

5. The most intense area of the beam on the wall must be 2 in. below the "A" mark (**Figure 15**).

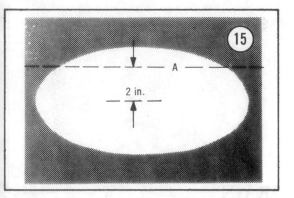

6. If the beam aim is not correct, move the headlight up or down as required by turning the spring loaded adjuster screws in or out. See **Figure 16**.

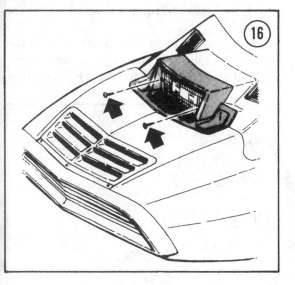

BRAKE/TAILLIGHT BULB REPLACEMENT

1. Refer to **Figure 17** (typical lens) and unscrew the screws that attach the lens to the rear housing or toolbox. Remove the lens and remove the defective bulb by pressing in on it and turning it counterclockwise.

2. Clean the socket to remove any corrosion, dirt, or moisture.

3. Line up the guide pins on the new bulb with the slots in the socket and press the bulb in and turn in clockwise to lock it in place.

> NOTE: *On dual filament bulbs (combination brake/taillight) the pins are at different distances from the base of the bulb; make sure they correspond with the different length slots in the socket.*

4. Clean the inside of the lens with a mild detergent and warm water before installing. Install all of the screws finger-tight before tightening, then tighten them securely, but not so tightly that they damage the lens.

6

CHAPTER SEVEN

POWER TRAIN

The power train consists of a drive belt, drive and driven sheaves, drive chain and sprockets, secondary shaft, drive shaft, and a brake assembly. Refer to **Figure 1** for a typical example of drive train components.

All machines are equipped with a hydraulic disc brake.

Some procedures in this chapter require the use of special tools for removal and repair work. If such tools are not available, and sub-

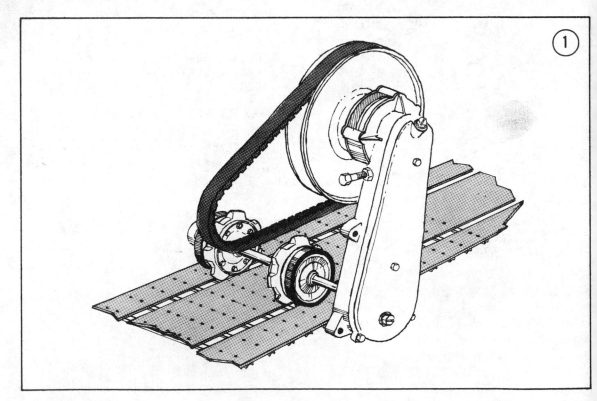

stitutes cannot be locally fabricated, refer the removal and repair work to an authorized dealer.

DRIVE BELT

Inspect the drive belt (**Figure 2**) for wear, cracking, stretching, or other damage or deterioration. If the belt is not in good condition, full power will not be transmitted from the drive clutch to the driven pulley. If the belt is not in good condition, replace it.

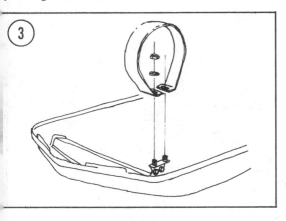

Replacement

1. Remove the clutch guard (**Figure 3**). Set the parking brake.

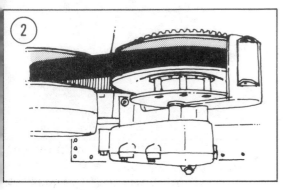

2. Push against the moveable sheave and rotate it clockwise until the sheaves are apart.

3. Hold the sheaves apart, pull the drive belt up, and roll it over the stationary sheave (**Figure 4**). When the belt is completely off the drive pulley, slowly release the moveable sheave. Then, remove the belt from the drive clutch. Reverse these steps to install the belt.

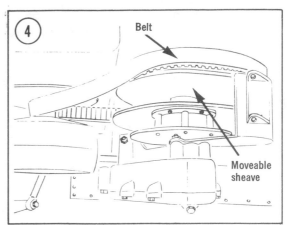

Belt Alignment

The alignment and center-to-center distances of the drive clutch and the driven pulley were set at the time the snowmobile was built; adjustment is rarely required, other than when the clutch and driven pulley are removed and reinstalled.

Special tools are required to' measure alignment and parallelism and to remove and install the clutch. If misalignment is indicated by rapid belt wear or loss of power, it is recommended that the work be entrusted to a dealer.

DRIVE CLUTCH

Removal/Installation

Service of the drive clutch should be entrusted to a dealer. The cost of service can be reduced by removing and installing it yourself.

1. Remove the clutch shield (**Figure 3**) and remove the drive belt as described above.

2. Hold the stationary sheave with a chain or strap wrench and unscrew the bolt that attaches the drive pulley to the crankshaft and collect the washer (**Figure 5**).

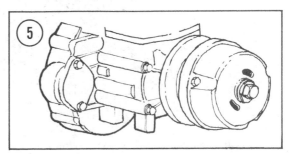

3. Screw the Polaris clutch puller bolt (part No. 2870130) into the clutch (**Figure 6**). Tighten the bolt to withdraw the clutch from the crankshaft.

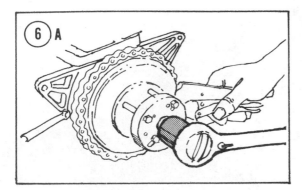

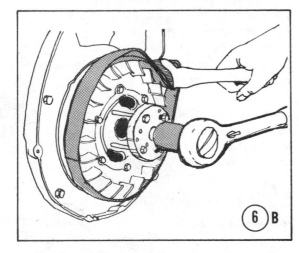

4. To install the drive clutch, install the drive belt on the driven pulley, then loop it around the drive clutch.

5. Set the drive clutch on the shaft and screw in the bolt, with a washer installed, and tighten it to 40-45 ft.-lb. (5.5-6.2 mkg); for 175cc engines, 18-20 ft.-lb. (2.5-2.8 mkg).

6. Have the alignment of the drive clutch and driven pulley checked by a dealer.

DRIVEN PULLEY

Removal/Installation

As with the drive clutch, service of the driven pulley should be entrusted to a dealer.

1. Remove the clutch shield and the drive belt as described above. Remove the air box.

NOTE: *On TX and Starfire models only the belt and shield need be removed.*

2. Unscrew the pulley bolt and remove the washer (**Figure 7**).

3. Remove the pulley from the shaft and note the number of shims and washers. Remove the key from the shaft.

4. To install the driven pulley, return all the shims that were removed from the shaft.

5. Install the pulley on the shaft and rotate it to line up its keyway with the keyway on the shaft. Tap the key into place. Screw in the pulley bolt, with a washer and any shims that were removed from the outer face of the pulley, and tighten it.

6. Have the alignment of the driven pulley and the drive clutch checked by a dealer. Install the drive belt as described in Chapter Two, *Drive Belt*. Install the clutch shield.

DRIVE CHAIN AND SPROCKETS

Removal/Installation

1. Drain the fuel tank. Turn the machine onto its right side to prevent oil from the chaincase spilling into the belly pan.

2. Unscrew the bolts that hold the chaincase cover in place and remove the washers. Tap the cover to break it loose and remove it and the gasket.

3. Loosen the locknut on the chain tensioner

(**Figure 8**) and unscrew the bolt to relieve the tension on the chain.

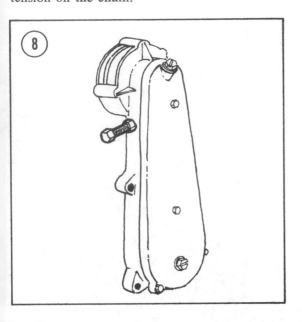

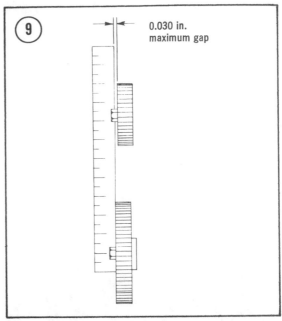

4. Unscrew the sprocket bolts and remove the washers. Slide both sprockets off their shafts with the chain in place.

5. To install the sprockets and chain, assemble them with the chain looped over both sprockets, line them up with the shafts, and slide them on.

6. Screw in the bolts, with the washers installed, and tighten them.

7. Place a straightedge across the sprockets (**Figure 9**) and check their alignment. If alignment is incorrect, add to or remove shims from behind the bottom sprocket. A gap of 0.030 in. (0.76mm) is allowable if a shim of the precise thickness to make the sprockets parallel is not available.

8. Refer to either **Figure 10A or 10B** and adjust the chain tension. When the chain wheels are turned a small distance in reverse (arrow A), the deflection of the chain at point B should be 3/8 in. If adjustment is required, loosen the locknut on the chain tension adjuster bolt (C) and screw the bolt either in or out as required. When the tension is correct, hold the bolt to keep it from turning further and tighten the locknut.

9. If the gasket is in good condition, install it. If there is any question about its condition,

replace it with a new one. Install the chaincase cover and thread in all bolts before tightening them.

JACKSHAFT

Removal/Installation

It is recommended that removal and installation of the jackshaft be entrusted to a dealer; a special alignment tool is required to accurately center the shaft in the bearing flangettes to avoid rapid premature wear.

TRACK DRIVE SHAFT AND TRACK

Removal/Installation

1. Refer to *Drive Chain and Sprockets Removal/Installation* (this chapter) and remove the drive chain and sprockets. Refer to *Suspension Removal/Installation*, Chapter Nine, and remove the skid frame.

2. Refer to **Figure 11** and unscrew the nuts from the right (left for TX and TXL) bearing flange for the drive shaft. Remove the flange, bearing, and O-ring.

3. Loosen the set screws in the bearing collar (**Figure 12**) and rotate the collar in direction of normal shaft rotation until it turns freely.

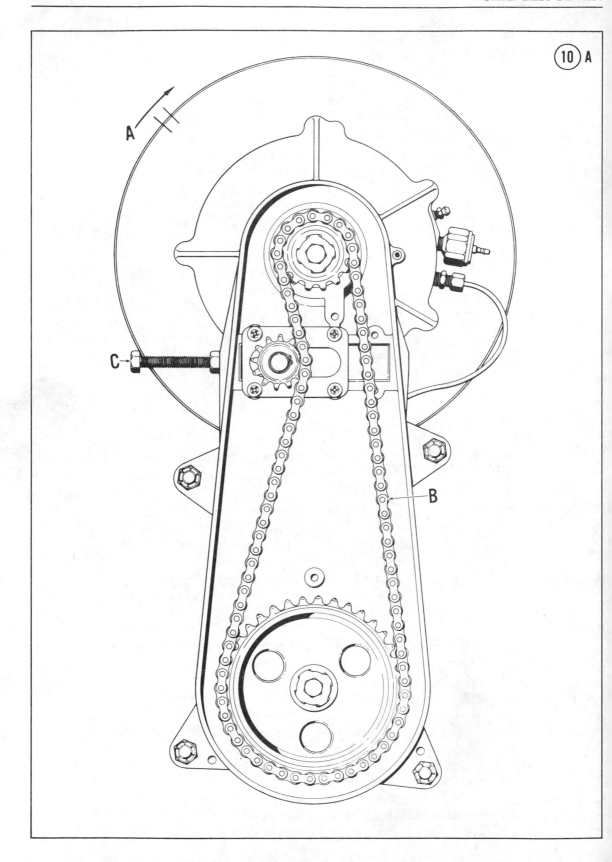

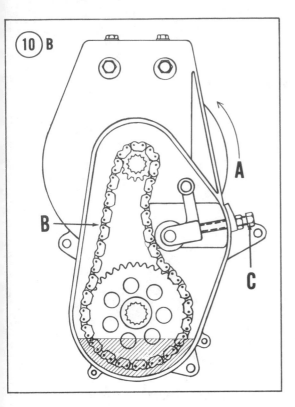

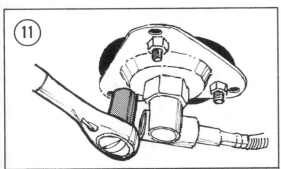

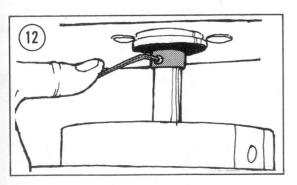

the track. Withdraw the drive shaft from the chaincase.

5. Clean all the parts thoroughly. Use solvent for metal parts, and soap and water for rubber and plastic pieces such as O-rings. Dry them thoroughly, preferably with compressed air.

6. Inspect the track and replace any missing rivets and damaged cleats. Rotate the bearings by hand to check for roughness and excessive radial play. Replace them if there is any doubt about their condition. Inspect the drive shaft for damaged threads and fretted splines and replace it if it is not in good condition.

7. To install the track and drive shaft, set the shaft assembly in the track with the splined end of the shaft on the right side.

8. On the unsplined end of the shaft, install the lock collar with the large ID end out. Install the retainer plate (with the lock flange toward the lock collar), bearing, outer retainer plate (with the flange toward the end of the shaft).

9. Set the track and drive shaft assembly in place and guide the splined end of the shaft into the chaincase.

10. Align the opposite end of the shaft with the holes in the tunnel. Install the 3 carriage bolts through the tunnel from the inside, through the retainer plates, the tunnel, front end, and the speedometer drive head.

11. Install the right side bearing on the shaft with the sealed side toward the sprockets. Then install the O-ring and the retainer plate. Screw on the nuts finger-tight.

12. Align the track drive sprockets equidistant from the inside edges of the tunnel. When the distance is equal, tighten the bearing lock collar by rotating it opposite normal shaft rotation. Tighten the set screws.

13. Tighten the nuts for each of the bearing retainers.

14. Refer to *Suspension Removal/Installation*, Chapter Nine, and install the skid frame. Refer to *Drive Chain and Sprockets Removal/Installation*, this chapter, and install the chain and sprockets.

15. Refer to *Track Tension, Track Alignment*, and *Suspension Adjustment* in Chapter Two and adjust and align the suspension and track.

4. Move the drive shaft to the right and pull the opposite end out of the front mounting hole. Tilt the shaft away from the tunnel and remove

7

CHAPTER EIGHT

FRONT SUSPENSION AND STEERING

The front suspension and steering consists of spring mounted skis on spindles connected to the steering column by tie rods (**Figure 1**).

The skis have replaceable wear rods (skags). All machines are equipped with leaf springs. Some are equipped with shock absorbers.

The handlebar steering column on some models is equipped with Zerk-type fittings that must be lubricated at 40-hour intervals. All snowmobiles use a one-piece steering column.

The tie rod and drag link ends have both right-hand and left-hand threads. The tie rods, drag link, and spindles are designed to bend rather than break if extreme shock loads are encountered.

SKI WEAR BARS

The ski wear bars, or skags, aid turning the snowmobile, and they protect the bottoms of the skis from wear caused by road crossings and bare terrain. The bars are expendable and should be checked weekly to ensure that they have not worked down to the point where they no longer afford adequate protection to the running surfaces of the skis and cease to aid turning. If the wear bars are excessively worn, turning will be imprecise and control, marginal.

Removal/Installation

1. The fuel tank should be no more than ¼ full to prevent spillage of fuel. Turn the machine on its side and protect the finish by placing cardboard on the floor.

2. Remove ice and snow from the skis.

3. Unscrew the locknut and remove the flat washer from each ski (**Figure 2**).

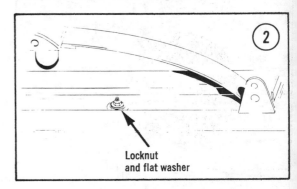

Locknut
and flat washer

4. Pry the wear bar off the bottom of each ski until the stud is out of the hole. Place a block of wood between the ski and the wear bar, *behind* the stud, and rap it with a hammer to drive the rear of the wear bar out of the hole in the rear of the ski (**Figure 3**). Then, pull the wear bar out of the hole in the front of the ski.

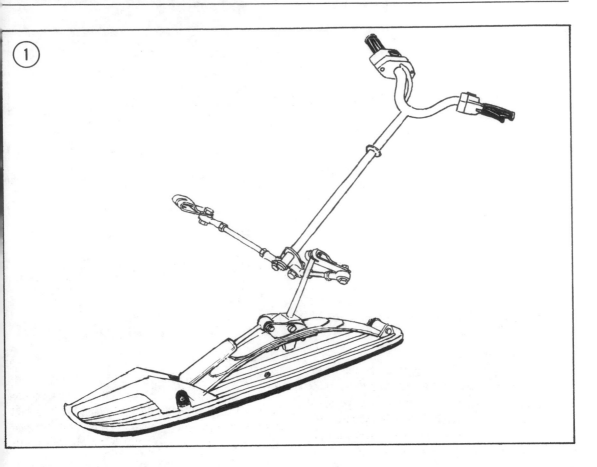

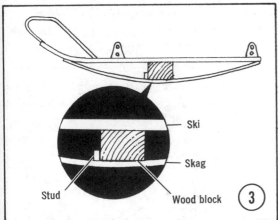

Ski

Skag

Stud

Wood block ③

5. Install a new wear bar by first inserting the forward end into the hole in the front of the ski. Insert the wooden block between the ski and the wear bar *ahead* of the stud. Tap on the block to drive the wear bar to the rear, at the same time, guide the rear end of the wear bar into the hole in the rear of the ski until the stud lines up with the hole in the top of the ski.

6. Remove the wooden block and push the stud into the hole. Install the washer, and screw on and tighten the locknut on the stud.

8

SKIS

Removal/Disassembly

1. Unscrew the locknut and bolt that attach the ski to the spindle and remove the ski (**Figure 4**). Remove the rubber damper from the spring saddle.

2. Unscrew the nuts and bolts from the shock absorber mounts and remove the shock absorber and bushings.

3. With a vise, compress the spring about an inch and remove the nut and bolt and clevis from the front spring mount. Collect the wear plate. Carefully release the pressure on the spring.

4. Unscrew the nut and bolt (or remove the cotter key and clevis) from the rear spring mount and remove the spring.

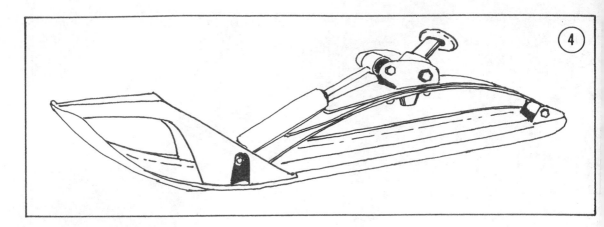

Assembly/Installation

1. Place the rear of the spring in the rear mount, and screw in and tighten the bolt and locknut. The nut must be on the inside of the ski. On some models, a clevis and cotter key are used.

2. Place the wear plate and the spring in the front mount. Compress the spring with a vise to line up the holes in the front mount with the spring and wear plate. Install the nut and bolt, with the nut on the inside of the ski, and the clevis. Install the clevis washer and a new cotter key. Release the pressure and remove the ski from the vise.

3. Set 2 plastic bushings into each eye of the shock absorber. Install the shock absorber, body down, and tighten the nuts and bolts, with the nuts on the inside.

4. Set the rubber damper and spacer in the spring saddle (**Figure 5**) and attach the ski assembly to the spindle. Make sure the threaded

hole in the saddle is to the inside. Tighten the bolt in the saddle. Then, screw on the locknut and tighten it.

TIE ROD

Removal/Installation

The tie rods are designed to bend rather than break, upon severe ski impact. If they are severely bent, they should be replaced rather than straightened. In either case, the rods must be removed.

1. Refer to Chapter Four, *Engine Removal,* and remove the engine from the machine.

2. Remove the nuts and bolts that attach the tie rods to the spindle arms and steering post (**Figure 6**).

3. Disassemble the tie rods by loosening the jam nuts on either end and unscrewing the adjuster bolts.

4. To assemble and install the tie rods, reverse

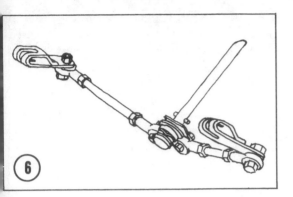

the above. Note that the adjuster bolts have both right-hand and left-hand threads. The end of the bolt with the brass colored jam nut screws into the tie rod, and the silver nut end screws into the tie rod end.

5. Install the tie rods with the adjuster end at the spindles.

6. Reinstall the engine as described in Chapter Four, *Engine Installation,* and align the skis as described below.

SKI ALIGNMENT

Ski alignment must be checked and corrected if necessary when any of the steering components (steering post, tie rods, spindles) are disconnected or replaced. It should also be checked during major service such as at the end of the season.

1. Set the handlebar in the straight ahead position and loosen the jam nuts on both tie rod ends (**Figure 7**).

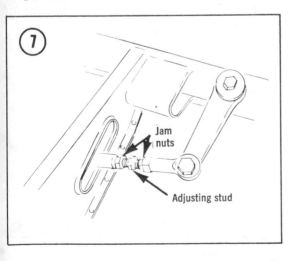

2. Raise and block the machine about 6 in. off the floor. Determine which ski is most closely aligned with the machine and measure the distance between the skis at 2 locations (**Figure 8**). The measurements should be identical.

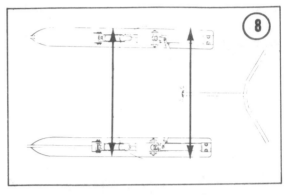

3. If adjustment is required, one or both adjusting studs in the tie rods must be turned to make the skis parallel and square with the handlebars.

4. When adjustment is correct, tighten the jam nuts against the tie rods and the tie rod ends, taking care not to turn the adjusting stud further after the adjustment is correct.

SPINDLE

Removal/Installation

1. Remove the ski assemblies from the spindles as described earlier under *Ski Removal/Disassembly.* It is first necessary to raise and support the front of the machine.

2. Mark the spindle and spindle arm for location (**Figure 9**). Loosen the pinch bolt in the arm. Remove the arm from the spindle.

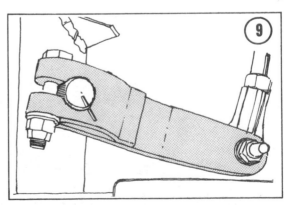

3. Pull down on the spindle to remove it. It may be necessary to tap the spindle out of its mount with a soft drift.

4. To install the spindle, slide it up into the mount and install the washers in the order they were removed.

5. Install the spindle arm with the marks aligned, and tighten the pinch bolt.

6. Refer to *Ski Assembly/Installation* and install the skis.

7. Refer to *Ski Alignment* and align the skis.

THROTTLE HANDLE

Removal/Installation

1. Remove the pad from the center of the handlebar after removing the clips. Remove the handle grip.

2. Loosen the set screw in the throttle (**Figure 10**). Slide it toward the center of the bar, and disconnect the cable from the throttle lever. Pull the throttle assembly off the bar.

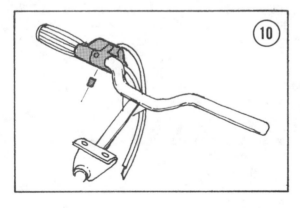

3. Reverse the above steps to install the throttle handle. Before installing the pad on the handle-

bar, check the operation of the throttle to ensure that it moves freely and returns when released. If it is not satisfactory, find the cause and correct it before operating the machine.

BRAKE HANDLE

Removal/Installation

1. Remove the pad from the center of the handlebar after removing the clips. Remove the handle grip.

2. Remove the cover from the reservoir. Loosen the set screw in the master cylinder (**Figure 11**). Rotate it on the bar and catch the fluid in a container.

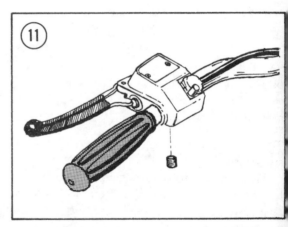

3. Disconnect the brake line and pull the master cylinder off the bar.

4. Reverse the above to assemble and install the master cylinder assembly. Fill the cylinder with fresh fluid and bleed and adjust as described in Chapter Two. Test the operation of the brake and the lights when assembly is complete, and correct any unsatisfactory conditions.

NOTE: If you own a 1978 or later model, first check the Supplement at the back of the book for any new service information.

CHAPTER NINE

REAR SUSPENSION AND TRACK

Polaris snowmobiles, with the exception of the TC model, are equipped with slide rail rear suspension which utilizes a rear idler assembly. The TC is equipped with bogey wheel suspension.

The slide rail suspension (**Figure 1**), except for the basic Colt model, is fitted with adjustable springs, shock absorbers, and replaceable wear bars. The suspension also includes weight transfer adjustment to vary the amount of pressure on the skis.

This chapter includes removal and installation procedures for suspension components and tracks. Refer to Chapter Two for suspension and track adjustments and Chapter Three for *Track Wear Analysis*.

SUSPENSION

Removal/Installation

1. Unscrew the bolts that attach the skid frame to the tunnel (**Figure 2**).

2. Loosen the track adjusting screws (**Figure 3**).

3. Raise the rear of the machine a couple of feet and support it. Pull the skid frame out of the

9

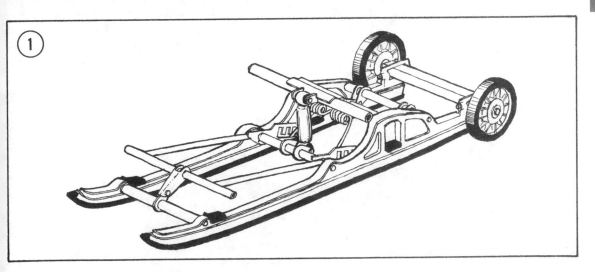

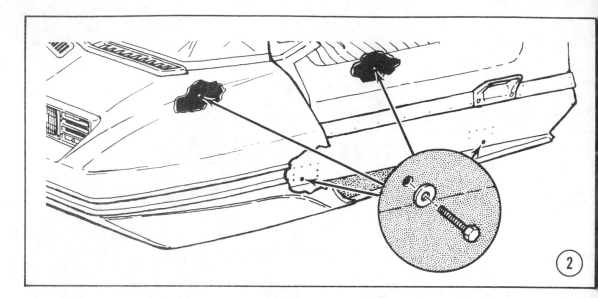

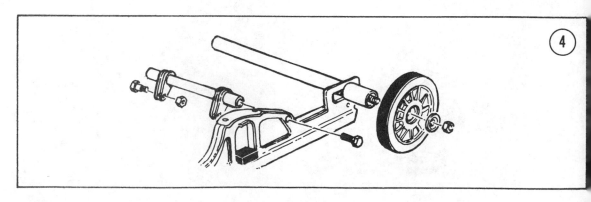

track and remove the pivot shafts, axle, and idler wheels (**Figure 4**).

4. Thoroughly wash the skid frame with detergent and water and dry it completely with clean rags and compressed air. Lightly sand the paint in chipped areas and repaint them. Inspect the Hi-Fax slides and replace them if they are severely worn. See *Hi-Fax Slide Replacement*, this chapter.

5. Lightly coat the pivot shafts and axle with low-temperature grease.

6. Turn the snowmobile on its side and pull the track out of the tunnel. Set the skid frame in the track and then install the pivot shafts and rear axle and wheels.

7. Hold the track and frame at a 45° angle to the tunnel and line up the forward holes in the skid frame with the forward holes in the tunnel. Screw in the bolts, with a flat washer installed, but do not tighten them until the rear bolts have been installed. It will be necessary to tip the snowmobile from one side to the other to install both bolts.

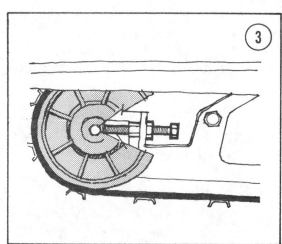

CAUTION
*The fuel tank and chaincase should be
drained before performing Step 6.*

8. Push the skid frame and track into the tunnel and line up the rear holes in the skid frame with the holes in the tunnel. Tighten the bolts after all four have been installed.

9. Refer to Chapter Two, *Track Tension, Track Alignment,* and *Suspension Adjustment* (in this chapter), and adjust and align the suspension and track.

HI-FAX SLIDE REPLACEMENT

1. Invert the skid frame on a clean surface. Unscrew the bolts from the Hi-Fax slides (**Figure 5**). With a block and hammer (**Figure 6**), tap the slide rearward to remove it.

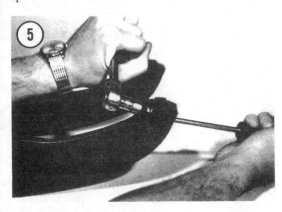

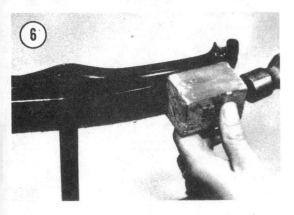

2. The new Hi-Fax strips must be at room temperature (70°F) before being installed. Tap the strip in from the rear of the skid frame.

3. Heat the Hi-Fax with a propane torch, bend it around the front of the frame, and bolt it in place. Saw off excess length with a hacksaw. Do not attempt to bend the Hi-Fax without heating it; breakage is likely to occur. Install the other strip in the manner just described.

4. Refer to *Suspension Removal/Installation* (this chapter) and install the skid frame.

SUSPENSION ADJUSTMENT

Colt

The Colt suspension is not adjustable, other than for track tension and alignment.

Electra and TX (1975 and Earlier)

The E-slot adjuster on the Electra and TX suspension provides 6 different positions that alter ski pressure to compensate for differences in rider weight (**Figure 7**). For example, position 1 would provide the greatest ski pressure and would be used for a light rider. At the other end, position 6 provides the least ski pressure and would be used for a heavy rider.

To adjust the suspension, loosen the bolt on each side and move the E-slot to the position desired. Then tighten the bolts. Both E-slots must be located at the same position.

TX, TXL (1976 on)

There are 3 adjustments possible with late TX and TXL suspension: spring tension, chassis mounting position, and front limiter pivot arm position.

To adjust the spring tension, the position of the spring leg is moved from one shoulder bolt to the other (**Figure 8**). The lower position is for normal riding conditions and average loads. The upper position is for loads in excess of 190 lb. To alter the position, unscrew the bolts and change the location of the spring legs.

The chassis mounting position adjustment (**Figure 9**) affords a wide range of riding and handling characteristic options. These are:

a. High ski pressure (normally not used)

b. Less ski pressure than A, more than C

c. Average riding conditions

d. Basic position

e. Deep snow and hill climbing

9

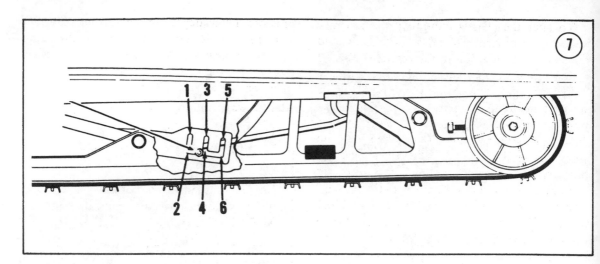

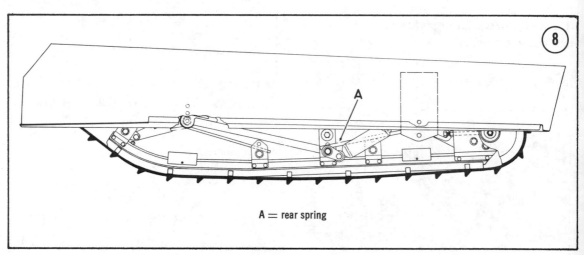

A = rear spring

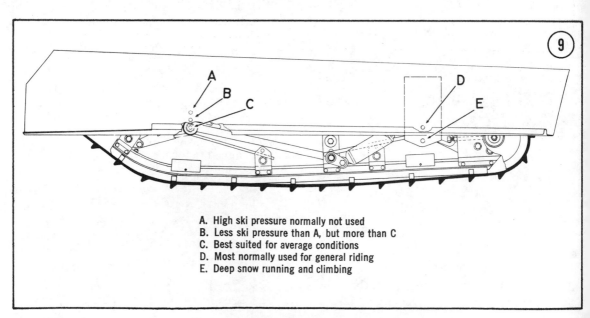

A. High ski pressure normally not used
B. Less ski pressure than A, but more than C
C. Best suited for average conditions
D. Most normally used for general riding
E. Deep snow running and climbing

To alter the chassis mounting position, unscrew the appropriate bolts, on both sides, and relocate the suspension in the tunnel. Reinstall the bolts and tighten them firmly.

The front limiter pivot arm position, like spring tension, alters ski pressure. The upper position (**Figure 10**) provides greater ski lift during acceleration and is best suited for deep snow and hill climbing. The lower position offers more ski pressure and is better suited for good maneuverability on hard-packed surfaces.

To alter the front limiter pivot arm position, unscrew the bolts, on both sides, and relocate the pivot arm. Reinstall the bolts and tighten them firmly.

TX Rear Spring Adjustment (1975 and Earlier)

The rear spring adjustment on TX models, used in conjunction with the E-slot adjustment,

provides a fine degree of suspension tailoring. Turn the bolt (**Figure 11**) counterclockwise to provide a firmer ride and to reduce weight transfer during acceleration. Turn it clockwise to soften the ride and increase weight transfer.

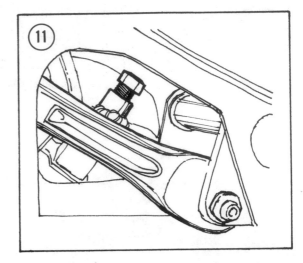

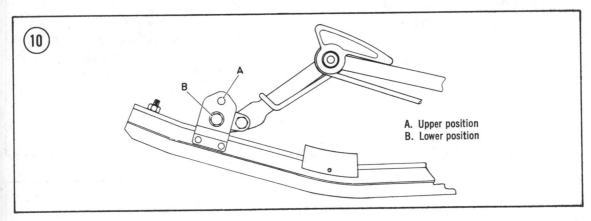

A. Upper position
B. Lower position

9

CHAPTER TEN

BRAKES

Polaris snowmobiles are equipped with a hydraulic brake system consisting of a handlebar-mounted master cylinder, slave cylinder mounted in the chaincase cover, adjustable caliper, and a disc.

ADJUSTMENT

Adjustment is described in Chapter Two.

BLEEDING

Bleeding the brake system is described in Chapter Two.

MASTER CYLINDER REBUILD

Work on the brake hydraulic system must be done on a scrupulously clean bench, with oil- and grease-free tools, clean lint-free rags, and clean hands. Grease, oil, and foreign matter can easily contaminate the system and render it inoperative.

1. Cover the machine, in the area beneath the master cylinder, with old rags to prevent spilled brake fluid from contacting the painted surfaces. Disconnect the brake line and wrap the end of it with a clean rag, taped in place; this prevents spillage of the fluid and at the same time prevents the entry of moisture and contaminants into the brake line.

2. Remove the master cylinder from the handlebar. Remove the top from the master cylinder reservoir and empty the old fluid into a disposable container.

3. Remove the pivot pin that holds the lever in place. If the master cylinder is molded Velox, drill out the head of the rivet (**Figure 1**), and then push it out with a small drift.

4. Pull the piston and spring out of the master cylinder. Discard the O-rings and the rubber cup.

5. Clean all of the parts in brake fluid or brake component cleaner. Blow them dry with compressed air.

CAUTION
Do not clean brake parts in common solvent or any fluid with a petroleum base.

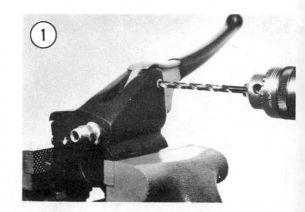

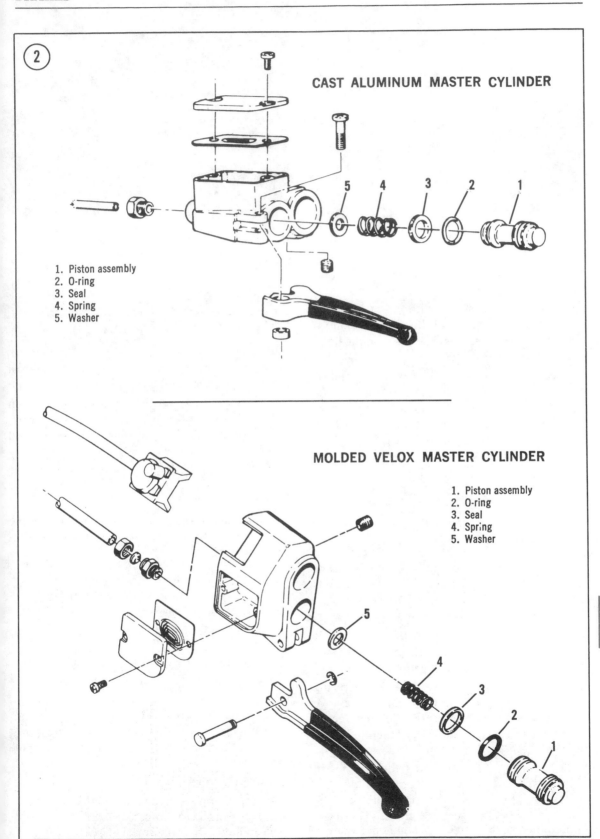

② CAST ALUMINUM MASTER CYLINDER

5   4   3   2   1

1. Piston assembly
2. O-ring
3. Seal
4. Spring
5. Washer

MOLDED VELOX MASTER CYLINDER

1. Piston assembly
2. O-ring
3. Seal
4. Spring
5. Washer

5

4

3

2

1

10

6. Install a new cup and O-rings on the piston (**Figure 2**). Coat the assembly with fresh brake fluid.

7. Coat the cylinder bore with fresh brake fluid and install the spring and the piston assembly. Be careful not to damage the seals on the lip of the cylinder.

8. Install the lever with a new pivot pin and retainer. The original rivet used in Velox master cylinders should be replaced with a pin (part No. 7661615) and retainer (part No. 7710401).

9. Install the master cylinder on the handlebar and connect the brake line.

10. Refer to Chapter Two and bleed and adjust the brake.

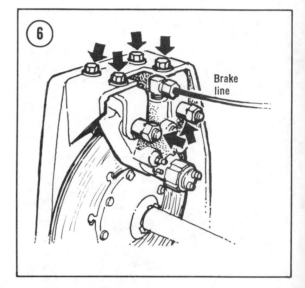

Brake line

TYPE I SLAVE CYLINDER REBUILD

1. Remove the air box, driven clutch, brake line, and brake light wires. Unscrew the bolts from the rear chaincase cover (**Figure 3**).

2. Heat the cover around the bearing boss (**Figure 4**) and pull the cover off the shaft. It may be necessary to loosen the chaincase bolts for the rear cover to clear the mounting plates.

3. Refer to **Figure 5** and remove the snap ring that retains the piston in the cylinder. Remove the washer, spring, and piston. Remove the O-rings from the piston and discard them.

4. Clean the parts, including the cylinder bore, in fresh brake fluid and blow them dry with compressed air. Inspect the bore for damage and corrosion. Minor imperfections can be removed with fine crocus cloth. The bore should then be thoroughly cleaned once again.

5. Install new O-rings on the piston and wet the assembly with fresh brake fluid. Wet the cylinder bore as well.

6. Install the piston in the cylinder bore. Then install the spring, washer, and snap ring. Make certain the snap ring is correctly seated in its groove.

7. Install the cover on the chaincase, screw in the bolts, and tighten them progressively in a crisscross pattern.

8. Connect the brake line. Refer to Chapter Two and bleed and adjust the brake system.

TYPE II BRAKE CALIPER REBUILD

1. Place a shop rag beneath the brake line connection to protect painted surfaces from brake fluid spillage. Disconnect the line (**Figure 6**) and

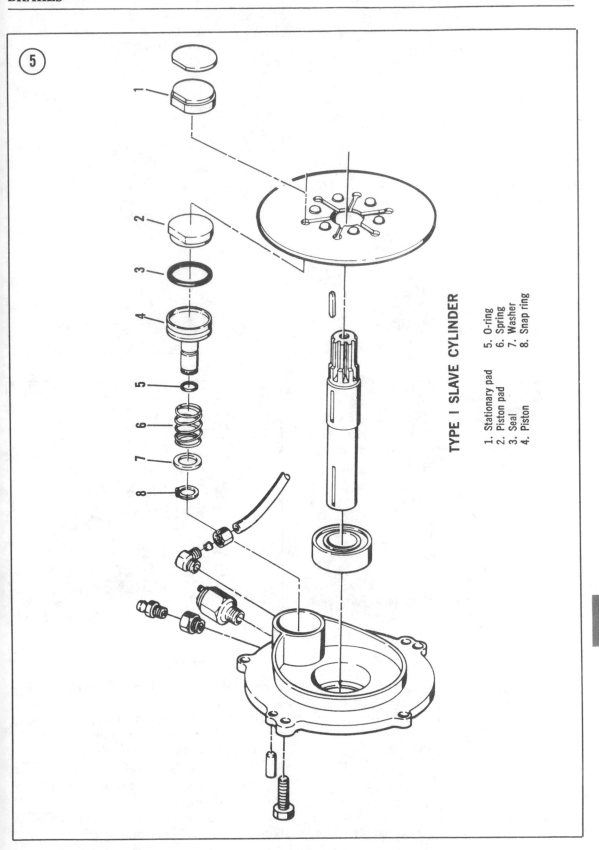

TYPE I SLAVE CYLINDER

1. Stationary pad   5. O-ring
2. Piston pad   6. Spring
3. Seal   7. Washer
4. Piston   8. Snap ring

10

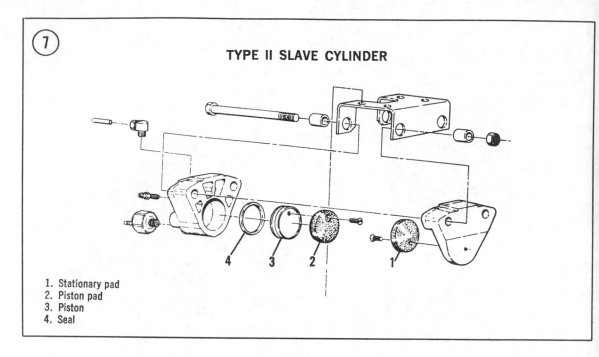

TYPE II SLAVE CYLINDER

4   3   2   1

1. Stationary pad
2. Piston pad
3. Piston
4. Seal

wrap it in a clean rag to prevent the entry of moisture and contamination.

2. Remove the 2 bolts which hold the caliper halves together. Remove the 4 mounting bolts from the top of the chaincase. See **Figure 6**.

3. Remove the screws that hold the pads in the caliper halves. Remove the pads. Note that the stationary pad is different from the piston pad (**Figure 7**).

> NOTE: *If only the pads are being replaced, and the caliper is not being rebuilt, carefully push the piston back into the cylinder to make room for the increased thickness of the new pads. Then install the pads, coat the retaining screw threads with Loctite Lock 'N' Seal, and screw them in snug.*

4. Cover the piston side of the caliper with a shop rag, apply compressed air to the brake line fitting, and drive the piston out of the cylinder (**Figure 8**).

CAUTION

Hold the piston side away from you to prevent fluid from getting into your eyes.

5. Clean all of the parts in fresh brake fluid. Discard the old O-ring. Inspect the piston and

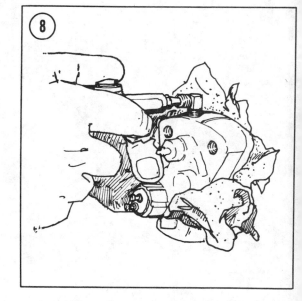

cylinder for wear, damage, and corrosion. Minor imperfections can be removed with fine crocus cloth, after which the parts must be recleaned. If wear or damage is extensive, the housing and piston must be replaced.

6. Install a new O-ring on the piston and wet the assembly with fresh brake fluid. Wet the cylinder bore also.

7. Line up the piston squarely with the cylinder bore and press it in carefully to prevent it from

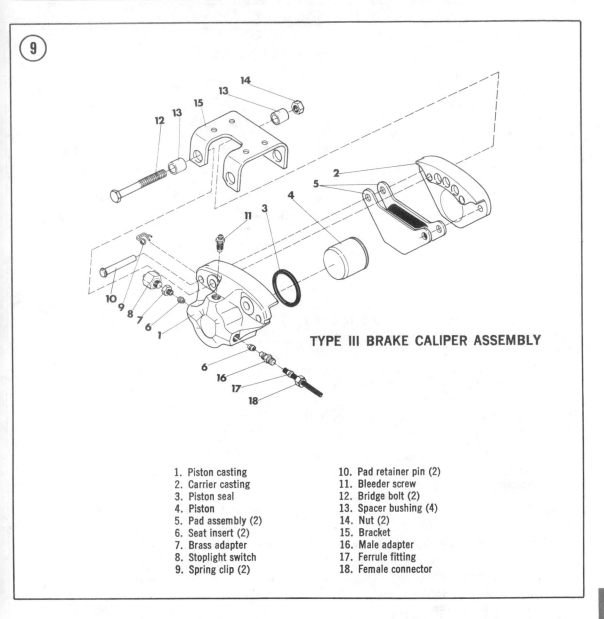

TYPE III BRAKE CALIPER ASSEMBLY

1. Piston casting	10. Pad retainer pin (2)
2. Carrier casting	11. Bleeder screw
3. Piston seal	12. Bridge bolt (2)
4. Piston	13. Spacer bushing (4)
5. Pad assembly (2)	14. Nut (2)
6. Seat insert (2)	15. Bracket
7. Brass adapter	16. Male adapter
8. Stoplight switch	17. Ferrule fitting
9. Spring clip (2)	18. Female connector

10

scoring the bore or damaging the O-ring. Push the piston all the way in.

8. Reverse the disassembly steps to assemble and install the caliper. Apply Loctite Lock 'N' Seal to the threads of the caliper carrier bolts and the four small bolts that attach the caliper to the top of the chaincase. Tighten the carrier bolts to 25-30 ft.-lb. (3.4-4.1mkg); tighten the upper mounting bolts to 8 ft.-lb. (1.1 mkg).

9. Refer to Chapter Two and bleed and adjust the brake system. Check for leaks and correct any that are found. Make sure the caliper floats freely on the carrier bolts.

TYPE III BRAKE CALIPER REBUILD

1. Place a shop rag beneath the brake line connection to protect painted surfacs from brake fluid spillage. Disconnect the line from the caliper and cover it with a clean rag to prevent the entry of moisture and contaminants.

2. Refer to **Figure 9**. Remove the spring clips from the pad retaining pins. Disconnect the brake switch lead.

3. Unscrew the bridge bolts **(Figure 10)** and the 4 bolts from the top of the chaincase. Remove the caliper assembly and separate the 2 halves.

NOTE: *If only the pads are being replaced, and the caliper is not being rebuilt, carefully push the piston back into the cylinder to make room for the increased thickness of the new pads. Replace the pads only as a set.*

4. Open the bleeder screw, invert the caliper over a disposable container, and slowly push the piston back into the cylinder to expel the fluid. Take care not to get fluid in your eyes.

5. Cover the caliper with a shop rag and apply a short burst of compressed air to eject the piston. Make sure it is directed away from you.

6. Remove the seal from the piston bore with a small wood or plastic stick. Do not use a metal object to remove it; the bore can be easily scratched.

7. Clean all the parts in fresh brake fluid and blow them dry with compressed air. Blow out the passages as well. Inspect the cylinder and piston for wear, damage, and corrosion. Minor imperfections can be removed with crocus cloth, after which the parts must be recleaned. If wear or damage is extensive, the caliper and piston must be replaced.

NOTE: *When using crocus cloth to dress the cylinder or piston, use light pressure and move around the circumference — not in and out or back and forth.*

8. Unscrew the male brake line adapter and inspect the seat insert. Replace it if it is damaged.

9. Reverse the disassembly steps to assemble the caliper. Wet the cylinder bore and a new seal with fresh brake fluid. Work the seal into the groove, making sure it is seated all around. Wet the piston in brake fluid, line it up squarely with the bore, and press it in all the way, taking care not to cock it to one side. Install the pads, assemble the caliper halves, and install the pad retaining pins and spring clips. Coat the threads of the bridge bolts and install them along with the bushings. Screw on and tighten the bridge bolt nuts to 30 ft.-lb. (4.1mkg). Apply Loctite

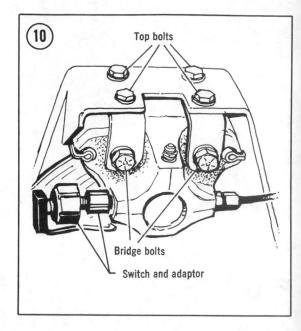

to the threads of the four upper mounting bolts; screw them in and tighten them to 8 ft.-lb (1.1 mkg). Connect the brake line and the stoplight switch lead.

10. Refer to Chapter Two and bleed and adjust the brake system. Check for leaks and correct any that are found. Make sure the caliper floats freely on the bridge bolts.

BRAKE LIGHT SWITCH REPLACEMENT

1. Disconnect the lead from the brake light switch. Place a rag beneath the switch to catch any fluid that may leak out.

2. Unscrew the switch and screw in a new one. Tighten it snugly. Reconnect the brake switch lead.

CAUTION
A switch adapter is used on all models except the Centurion; the Centurion switch does not require an adapter. When replacing the switch, make sure it is the correct size. The Centurion switch has a 3/8 x 24 NF thread; all others have a 1/8 in. NP thread.

SUPPLEMENT

1978-1979 SERVICE INFORMATION

The following supplement provides service and repair procedures unique to 1978-1979 Polaris snowmobiles. All other service procedures are identical to those described for earlier models in the main body of the book.

The chapter headings in this supplement correspond to those in the main portion of the book. If a change is not included in the supplement, there are no changes affecting the 1978-1979 models.

CHAPTER ONE

GENERAL INFORMATION

Polaris models for sale in 1978-1979 are shown in **Table 1**. With the exception of the 500cc liquid-cooled engine used in the 1979 Centurion, 1978-1979 engines are virtually the same as earlier engines with the same identification numbers; some minor improvements have been made but these do not affect service or repair unless they are specified in this supplement.

TABLE 1   1978-1979 POLARIS MODELS

1978 Models	
Model Designation	
05—TX	11—S/S 340
06—TX-L	15—RXL
10—Colt	18—Cobra
Engine Designation	
23—EC25PT-07	Twin, free-air cooled
24—EC25PC	Twin, free-air cooled
25—EC25PS	Single, fan cooled
37—EC34PT-05	Twin, free-air cooled
37—EC34PL-03	Twin, liquid cooled
38—EC34PM-03/04	Twin, fan cooled
39—EC34PL-02	Twin, liquid cooled
43—EC44PM-01	Twin, fan cooled
45—EC44PT-05	Twin, free-air cooled
1979 Models	
Model Designation	
05-TX	11—Apollo 340
06—TX-L/Centurion	18—Cobra
10—Gemini	
Engine Designation	
23—EC25PT-07	Twin, free-air cooled
25—EC25PS	Single, fan cooled
26—EC25PM-01	Twin, fan cooled
37—EC34PT-05	Twin, free-air cooled
38—EC34PM-03/04	Twin, fan cooled
39—EC34PL-02	Twin, liquid cooled
43—EC44PM-01	Twin, fan cooled
45—EC44PT-05	Twin, free-air cooled
53—EC51PL-01	Triple, liquid cooled

CHAPTER TWO

PERIODIC MAINTENANCE
AND TUNE-UP

TYPE III SUSPENSION
(EXTRUDED ALUMINUM)

Removal/Installation

1. Unscrew the front and rear suspension bolts. Make sure the gas cap is tight, then place cardboard or another protective material next to the machine and tip it up onto its side. Remove the rear suspension (**Figure 1**).

2. Loosen the Allen setscrew in the lock collar (**Figure 2**).

3. Loosen the lock collar with a punch and hammer. Turn it in the normal direction of shaft rotation to loosen it and against the direction of rotation to tighten it.

4. Unscrew the screws from the left bearing housing (**Figure 3**) and remove the housing and bearing assembly from the shaft.

5. Remove the cover from the chaincase. Remove the top and bottom sprockets. Pull the drive shaft out of the chaincase and then out of the left side of the machine to remove it (**Figure 4**).

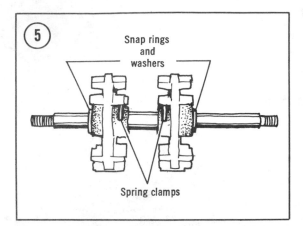

A. Eye bolt

Cam

6. If the drive sprockets are to be removed from the shaft, first remove the outer snap rings (**Figure 5**) and washers. Loosen the spring clamps and pull the sprockets off the shaft.

7. Reverse the above to install the suspension. When installing the sprockets on the shaft, make sure they are correctly indexed with the drive lugs aligned. After the front suspension bolts have been installed, use Polaris tool No. 2870354 to compress the rear torque arm and align the suspension.

Track Tension Adjustment and Alignment

Track tension and alignment of the Type III suspension are the same as described in Chapter Two, *Track Tension* and *Track Alignment*. The adjustments described below are unique to the Type III suspension. Refer to **Figure 6**.

Rear Spring Adjustment

Rear spring adjustment is a comfort adjustment.

1. Raise the rear of the machine to relax the suspension. Then, sit on it and check the movement from unladen to laden standing height; it should drop ½-1 in.

2. If adjustment is required, tighten the eye bolts (**Figure 7**) to raise the machine, or loosen them to lower it.

Front Spring and Limiter Adjustment

Low preload on the rear spring will increase ski pressure, particularly at low speeds. To decrease ski pressure, increase the spring

A. Shock absorber mount

preload by turning the spring tensioner cam clockwise (**Figure 8**). Increase ski pressure by turning the cam counterclockwise.

Additional ski pressure can be obtained for high-speed operation by shortening the limiter belt travel; conversely, lengthening the belt will reduce ski pressure.

Rear Shock Absorber Position

The mounting position of the forward end of the rear shock absorber affects ride firmness. In the lower position, the shock absorber has increased mechanical advantage and provides a firmer ride. In the lower position (**Figure 9**), the mechanical advantage is reduced, resulting in a softer ride.

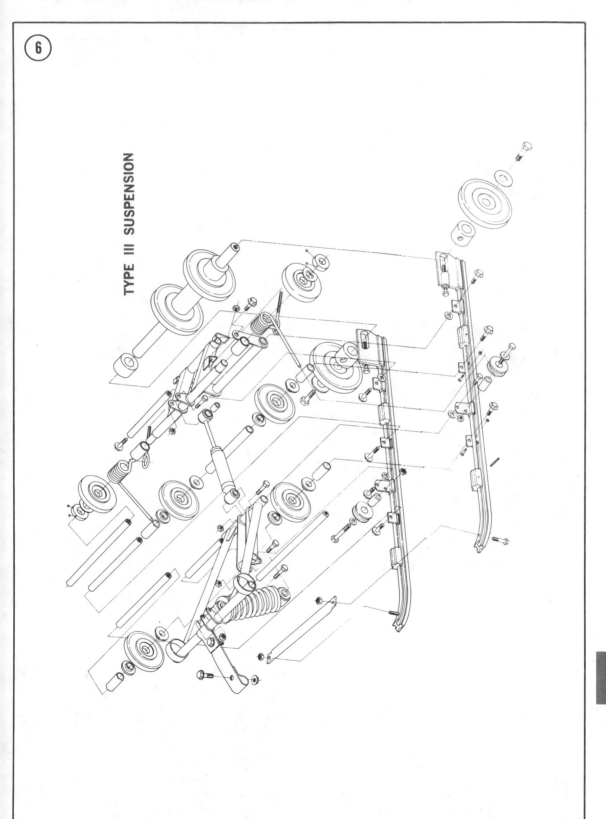

TYPE III SUSPENSION

Table 2   1978-1979 TUNE-UP SPECIFICATIONS

Engine Model	Static Timing (mm) BTDC	Inches BTDC	Deg. BTDC	Running Timing (mm) BTDC	Inches BTDC	Deg. BTDC
EC25PS*	0.360	0.014	8 ± 3	2.96	0.116	23 @ 2,000
EC25PC*	0.360	0.014	8 ± 3	2.96	0.116	23 @ 2,000
EC25PM-01*	0.048	0.002	3 ± 3	1.69	0.067	18 @ 2,000
EC34PM-03*	0.048	0.002	3 ± 3	1.69	0.067	18 @ 2,000
EC34PM-04*	0.048	0.002	3 ± 3	1.69	0.067	18 @ 2,000
EC44PM-01*	0.051	0.002	3 ± 3	1.83	0.072	18 @ 2,000
EC25PT-07	—	—	—	4.31**[1]	0.17**[1]	29 @ 3,000**[1]
EC34PT-05	—	—	—	4.31**[1]	0.17**[1]	29 @ 3,000**[1]
EC44PT-05	—	—	—	4.19**[2]	0.16**[2]	27.5 @ 3,000**[2]
EC34PL-02	—	—	—	5.05**[3]	0.198**[3]	31.5 @ 3,000**[3]
EC51PL-01	—	—	—	3.75**[4]	0.147**[4]	27 @ 3,000**[4]

*Point gap = 0.014 in. (0.35mm)
**Timing specified at 3,000 rpm
1. Acceptable variance = 4.02-4.59mm (0.158-0.180 in.); 28-30°
2. Acceptable variance = 3.76-4.65mm (0.148-0.183 in.); 26-29°
3. Acceptable variance = 4.60-5.52mm (0.181-0.217 in.); 30-33°
4. Acceptable variance = 3.48-4.02mm (0.137-0.158 in.); 26-28°

Lubrication

The long travel of the Type III suspension causes an increase in pivot shaft movement. Five lubrication fittings have been provided to reduce the possibility of accelerated wear of the shafts and bushings. The suspension should be lubricated every 300 miles with low-temperature, high-adhesion grease.

Rear Suspension Spring Replacement

1. Remove the suspension as described earlier.

2. With assistance, press in on the idler wheel (**Figure 10**) and loosen the set screws in the lock collar.

3. Relax the pressure on the idler wheel and remove the lock collar, wave washer, idler wheel, and spring.

4. Reverse the above to install the spring and idler wheel. Press in on the idler wheel (about 80 pounds) to compress the wave washer before tightening the setscrews in the lockwasher.

TUNE-UP

Tune-up specifications for 1978-1979 models are shown in **Table 2**. Recommended spark plugs are shown in **Table 3**.

Table 3   1978-1979 SPARK PLUG TYPE

Engine	NGK (Gap = 0.020 in.)	Champion
EC25PS	BR8ES	N-3
EC25PC	BR9ES	N-2
EC25PM-01	BR8ES	N-3
EC34PM-03	BR8ES	N-3
EC34PM-04	BR9ES	N-2
EC44PM-01	BR8ES	N-3
EC25PT-07	BR9ES	N-2
EC34PT-05	BR9ES	N-2
EC44PT-05	BR9ES	N-2
EC34PL-02	BR9ES	N-2
EC51PL-01	BR9ES	N-2

CHAPTER FOUR

ENGINE

With the exception of the 500cc liquid-cooled engine used in 1979 TX-L and Centurion models, service to 1978-1979 engines is essentially the same as described in Chapter Four in the main body of the book. Critical specifications for all 1978-1979 engines are provided in **Table 4**.

500cc TX-L/CENTURION ENGINE (EC51PL-01)

The 500cc TX-L/Centurion engine is a three-cylinder, piston-port two-stroke design with full coolant jacketing on the cylinders and cylinder heads. Coolant is circulated by a vane pump driven by a belt from the crankshaft. Engine heat is dissipated through radiators attached to the lower surface of the running boards.

Service and repair procedures for the 500cc engine follow. Critical specifications are presented in **Table 4**.

Removal/Installation

1. Lift the clutch guard and remove the drive belt (**Figure 11**).

2. Unscrew the exhaust manifold nuts and release the springs that attach the manifold to the expansion chamber. Remove the manifold and chamber; the resonator can be left in place.

3. Remove the recoil starter assembly and set it aside in the body (**Figure 12**).

4. Remove the radiator cap and the plugs on the radiators. Unscrew the bleeder plugs from the top of each cylinder (**Figure 13**). Place a drip pan beneath the engine, open the drain

Table 4   1978-1979 ENGINE SPECIFICATIONS

Engine Model	Cyl. Disp., cc	Bore		Stroke	
		mm	Inches	mm	Inches
EC25PS	244	72	2.835	60	2.362
EC25PC	250	53.5	2.106	55.6	2.189
EC25PM-01	244	52.9	2.082	55.6	2.189
EC34PM-03	333	61.78	2.432	55.6	2.189
EC34PM-04	333	61.78	2.432	55.6	2.189
EC44PM-01	432	67.72	2.656	60	2.362
EC25PT-07	249	53.4	2.102	55.6	2.189
EC34PT-05	336	62	2.441	55.6	2.189
EC44PT-05	432	67.75	2.667	60	2.362
EC34PL-02	333	61.78	2.432	55.6	2.189
EC51PL-01	500	61.78	2.432	55.6	2.189

Engine Model	Cylinder Head cc Uninstalled	Piston Rings	Piston/Cylinder Bore Clearance ± 0.002 in.
EC25PS	26.5	(2) 2.0mm Standard	0.009
EC25PC	11.0	L + 1.5mm Standard	0.006
EC25PM-01	11.5	(2) 1.5mm Keystone	0.005
EC34PM-03	21.0	(2) 1.5mm Keystone	0.006
EC34PM-04	21.0	(2) 1.5mm Keystone	0.006
EC44PM-01	22.9	(2) 1.5mm Keystone	0.008
EC25PT-07	11.8	(1) 1.2mm Keystone	Dress with fine stone only*
EC34PT-05	19.7	(1) 1.2mm Keystone	Dress with fine stone only*
EC44PT-05	22.8	(1) 1.2mm Keystone	Dress with fine stone only*
EC34PL-02	18.5	(1) 1.2mm Keystone	0.005
EC51PL-01	19.5	(1) 1.2mm Keystone	0.005

*Chrome cylinders may be de-glazed and refinished using fine stones.

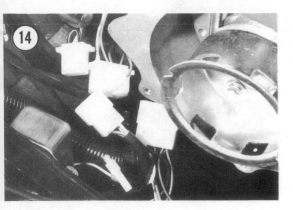

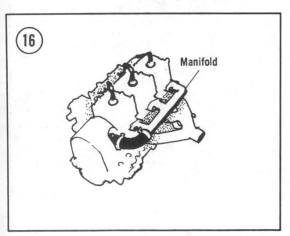

Manifold

plug and allow several minutes for the coolant to drain. Disconnect the throttle and choke cables.

5. Disconnect the coolant lines, the temperature gauge sending unit, and the spark plug high-tension leads.

6. Disconnect the electrical plugs (**Figure 14**).

7. Disconnect the fuel line from the fuel pump and plug it.

8. Disconnect the headlight harness and pull it out from between the engine and the engine plate (**Figure 15**).

9. Remove the bolts from the engine mounting plate. Carefully lift the engine out of the vehicle.

10. Reverse the above to install the engine. Refer to **Table 5** for critical torque values.

UPPER-END OVERHAUL

An orderly sequence should be followed to efficiently and correctly disassemble the engine upper end once the engine has been removed from the vehicle:

   a. Remove exterior components (carburetors, spark plugs, coil, CDI "black box," etc.).

   b. Remove the water pump.

   c. Remove the cylinder heads and gaskets.

   d. Remove the cylinders.

   e. Remove the pistons.

1. Remove the carburetors and spark plugs. Remove the coil and CDI "black box." Remove the coolant return manifold (**Figure 16**).

2. Remove the water pump cover and remove the water pump (**Figure 17**).

Table 5   **ENGINE INSTALLATION TORQUES**

Bolt Size	Description	Torque
7/16 in.	Engine mounting bolt	55-60 ft.-lb.
7/16 in.	Drive clutch bolt	40-45 ft.-lb.
3/8 in.	Engine mounting bolt	34-38 ft.-lb.
	Flywheel nut — 175cc	30-35 ft.-lb.
	Flywheel nut — all other	60-65 ft.-lb.

11

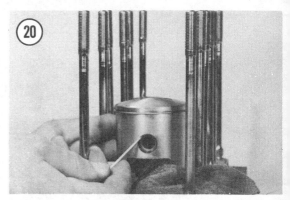

3. Unscrew the cylinder head nuts progressively in a crisscross pattern. The heads can be removed separately after the coolant manifold has been removed, or they can be removed together with manifold attached (**Figure 18**). If they are removed individually, mark them for cylinder location (left, center, and right).

4. Mark the cylinders and pistons for location (**Figure 19**). Tap around the base of each cylinder with a soft mallet to break them loose from the crankcase. Pull straight up on the cylinders to remove them; don't twist them as they are raised or it's likely that the rings will snag in the ports and break. Place clean rags in the crankcase beneath each piston.

5. Use a sharp-point tool such as an awl to remove the keepers from the wrist pin bores in the pistons (**Figure 20**).

6. Remove the pins with a piston pin puller (**Figure 21**). Remove the pistons. Carry out the inspection described in the next section.

7. Reverse the above to assemble the upper end. Install the small-end bearings in the rods,

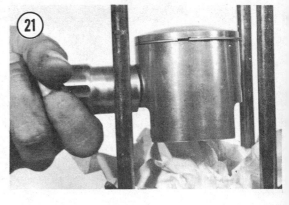

locate the side spacers on the rod with a dab of grease to hold them in place, and position the piston on the rod with the F mark facing the flywheel end of the engine (**Figure 22**). If there is no mark on the piston, locate the ring locating pin toward the intake port. Install the wrist pin keepers in the piston with one end of each keeper crossing the removal notch in the piston.

8. Install the piston rings so the beveled side faces up (**Figure 23**). Rotate the rings so the end gap engages the locating pin in the piston.

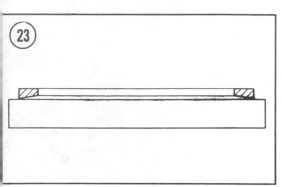

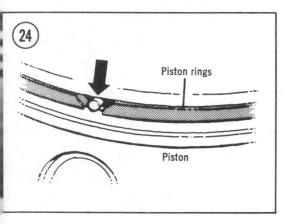

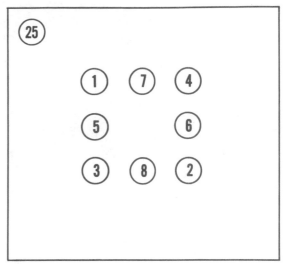

9. Install new cylinder base gaskets. Lightly coat the pistons with fresh engine oil and place a wooden block beneath one of the pistons to support it (**Figure 22**). Set the correct cylinder in place over the studs, making sure it is correctly oriented. Compress the ring, making sure it is lined up with the locating pin in the ring groove (**Figure 24**). Slide the cylinder down over the piston until it contacts the block, then remove the block. Slide the cylinder all the way down. Install the remaining cylinders in the same manner.

10. Spray new head gaskets with high-temperature aluminum paint, allow them to dry, then install them with the small discharge hole toward the intake side of the engine.

11. Install the cylinder heads on their respective cylinders. Progressively tighten the cylinder head nuts in the pattern shown in **Figure 25**. Tightening the torque for the 8mm nuts is 16-17 ft.-lb (2.2-2.3 mkg); for the 10mm nuts, the torque is 26-29 ft.-lb. (3.6-4.0 mkg).

12. If the water manifold was removed during disassembly, install it with new gaskets and tighten the nuts to 5-6 ft.-lb. (0.7-0.8 mkg). See **Figure 26**.

13. Install the water pump and the drive belt. Adjust the belt so it deflects about ¼ in. under moderate thumb pressure (**Figure 27**). Then tighten the lockbolt to 15 ft.-lb. (2 mkg). See **Figure 28**. Install the bypass hose and the elbow that connects the manifold to the water pump.

11

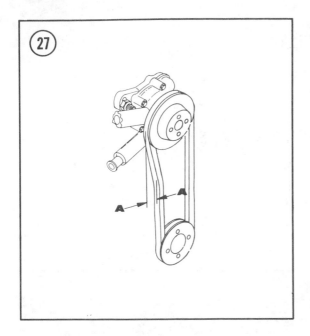

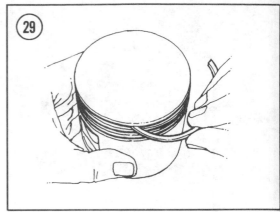

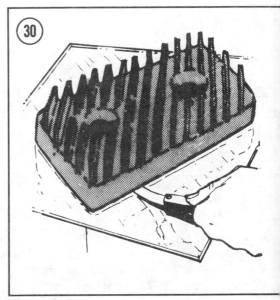

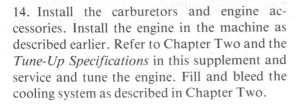

14. Install the carburetors and engine accessories. Install the engine in the machine as described earlier. Refer to Chapter Two and the *Tune-Up Specifications* in this supplement and service and tune the engine. Fill and bleed the cooling system as described in Chapter Two.

Inspection

1. Scrape carbon from the combustion chambers in the cylinder heads and the exhaust ports in the cylinders using a soft metal (aluminum) or wood scraper. Do not use a hard metal scraper; it will burr the surfaces and create hot spots.

2. Clean the heads and cylinders with solvent and dry them with compressed air if possible.

3. Remove the rings from the pistons and clean the crowns with a soft scraper. Clean the ring grooves with a piece of old piston ring (**Figure 29**). Clean the piston with solvent and dry it with compressed air.

> ### CAUTION
> *Do not clean the ring grooves with a ring groove scraper; the pistons are fitted with keystone profile rings and must be cleaned with a piece of old ring to prevent damage to the grooves.*

4. Check the flatness of the cylinder heads on a surface plate or a piece of glass (**Figure 30**). If the head does not make contact over the entire sealing surface, it must be trued; this is a job for a specialist.

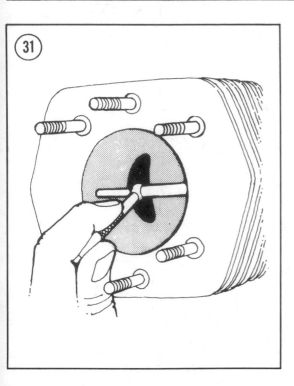

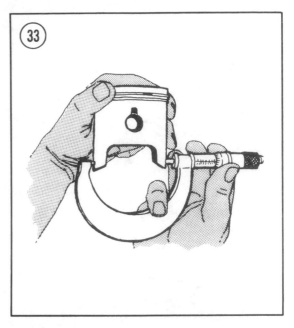

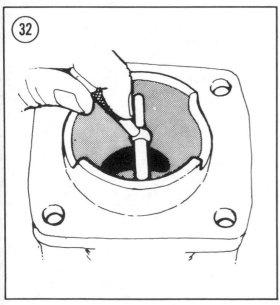

below the top of the cylinder in 2 locations, 90 degrees apart (**Figure 31**). If the measurements differ by more than 0.002 in. (0.05mm), the cylinder is out-of-round beyond specification and must be bored or replaced. Measure again in 2 locations 90 degrees apart just above the intake port. If these 2 measurements differ by more than 0.002 in. (0.05mm), the cylinder taper is beyond specification and the cylinder must be bored or replaced. If one cylinder is out of specification, all 3 cylinders must be bored and new pistons fitted.

7. Check piston skirt-to-cylinder clearance by first measuring the cylinder bore front to back (**Figure 32**) at the base. Then, measure the piston skirt, front and rear, about 1.4 in. from the bottom with an outside micrometer (**Figure 33**). Subtract the piston measurement from the cylinder measurement to determine the actual piston skirt-to-cylinder clearance. The clearance must be 0.003-0.007 in. (0.08-0.17mm). If the clearance is excessive but the cylinder dimensions are acceptable (**Table 4**), the piston should be replaced with a new unit that includes a matched pin and bearing as well as ring.

8. Measure the piston ring end gap. Place each ring into its respective cylinder, ³⁄₈ in. from the top. Use the piston to square the ring with the bore by pressing down on the ring with the

5. Check the cylinders and pistons for wear, galling, scuffing, and burning. Minor irregularities can be removed from the pistons with crocus cloth and light oil. The cylinders may be cleaned up with a light honing, provided they are within the specifications described below.

6. Measure the cylinder bore with an inside micrometer or a cylinder gauge. Measure ³⁄₈ in.

11

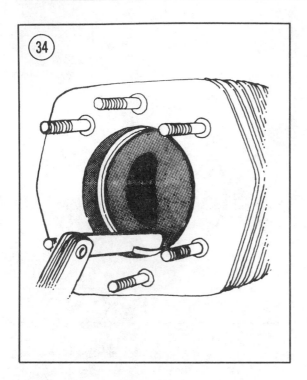

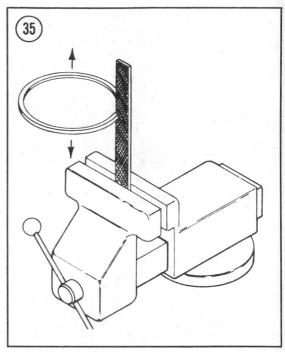

piston skirt. Measure the gap as shown in **Figure 34**. The gap should be 0.005-0.008 in (0.13-0.20mm). If the gap is too large for any one ring, replace them as a set and recheck the gap of the new rings. If the gap is too small, carefully file the rings as shown in **Figure 35** until they are correct.

9. Inspect the piston pin for galling at the ends — an indication that the pin is rotating in the piston. If this type of damage is apparent, the piston and pin must be replaced as a set. (The pin bores in the piston will no doubt be similarly damaged.)

10. Set the bearing and pin in the small end of each connecting rod and check for rocking movement, back and forth and up and down (**Figure 36**). If movement is apparent recheck with a new bearing and pin. If movement is still apparent, the rod is worn and must be replaced; this is a job for a dealer.

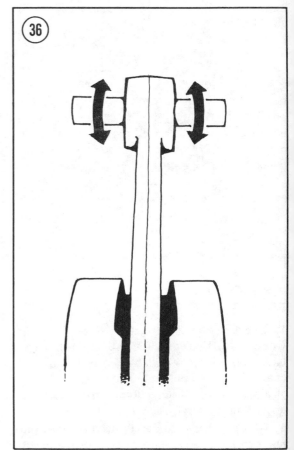

LOWER-END OVERHAUL

Lower-end overhaul as described here consists of removal and installation of the crankshaft assembly. Sophisticated tools and experience are required to accurately check the condition of the crankshaft assembly. In addi-

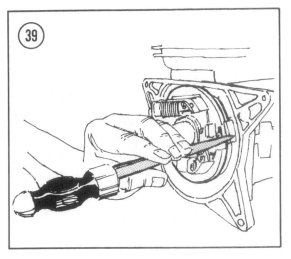

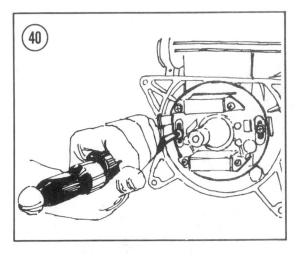

tion, a hydraulic press and considerable experience are required to disassemble, assemble, and accurately align the crankshaft assembly. It is recommended that the crankcase halves be parted and the crankshaft assembly be entrusted to a dealer for inspection and repair.

Seal replacement should also be entrusted to a dealer. A leaking crankshaft-to-crankcase seal can cause the engine to run lean, creating a situation that could result in severe damage, or if it is leaking severely, it will prevent the engine from running at all.

Disassembly

1. Refer to *Engine Removal/Installation* and *Upper-End Overhaul* and remove the engine from the machine and disassemble the upper end.

2. Remove the recoil starter cup and unscrew the flywheel nut **(Figure 37)**.

3. Install a puller on the flywheel (Polaris part No. 2870384) and secure it with a chain wrench.

Turn the puller bolt with an impact wrench or driver to remove the flywheel **(Figure 38)**.

4. Make a reference mark on the stator and crankcase with a chisel **(Figure 39)** to ensure correct engine timing when the stator is installed later. Loosen the 3 stator screws with an impact driver **(Figure 40)**, unscrew them, and remove the stator. Carefully pull the wiring harness through the rubber grommet in the crankcase.

5. Progressively loosen the 20 crankcase through bolts in a crisscross pattern beginning at the center. When all of the bolts are loose, unscrew them and separate the crankcase halves. It may be necessary to tap along the mating edge of the crankcase halves with a soft mallet to break them loose. Remove the crankshaft assembly from the upper case half.

11

6. Clean the crankcase halves and the crankshaft assembly with fresh solvent and blow them dry with compressed air. Remove the sealer from the mating surfaces of the crankcase halves, using a soft scraper and take care not to damage the sealing surfaces. Carefully inspect the bearing beds for damage. If damage is apparent, have your dealer inspect the cases to determine if they are salvageable; minor roughness can be removed with an oilstone, but if damage is extensive, the cases should be replaced.

Assembly

1. Invert the upper crankcase and stand it on the through studs. Set the crankshaft assembly in place (**Figure 41**). Make sure the seals are correctly seated in the grooves in the case.

2. Coat the sealing surface of the upper case half with an appropriate non-hardening sealer. If your dealer cannot supply a sealer, Gasgacinch, purchased from an auto supply house, or Yamaha Bond No. 4 purchased from a motorcycle dealer will work very well.

3. Line up the 7 bearing locater pins (**Figure 42**) so the are vertical and will engage the holes in the lower crankcase half. Set the lower case half in place and carefully press it down into place, making sure the pins engage the holes. Press the upper case half all the way down by hand until the mating surfaces meet.

CAUTION
The cases must meet before the crankcase bolts are installed; do not use the bolts to pull the case halves together.

4. Screw in and tighten the crankcase bolts in the pattern shown in **Figure 43**. Tighten the 8mm bolts to 18-20 ft.-lb. (2.5-2.8 mkg); tighten the 10mm bolts to 23-25 ft.-lb. (3.2-3.5 mkg).

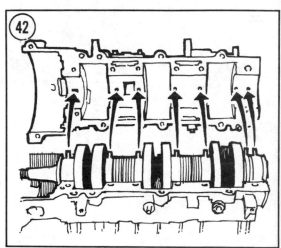

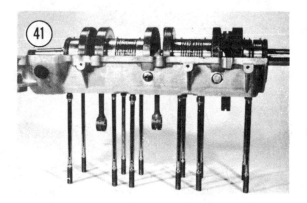

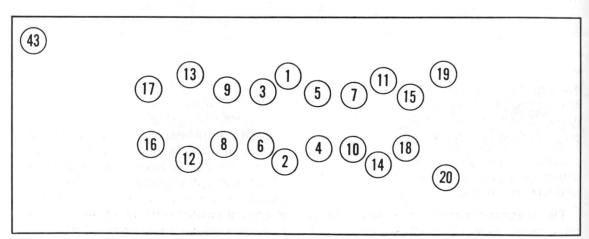

5. Rotate the crankshaft several revolutions to make sure it is not binding. Take care not to allow the connecting rods to strike the openings in the crankcase. If binding is felt, look for and correct the problem before continuing; the problem isn't going to correct itself and there is no sense in continuing until it has been taken care of.

6. Carefully feed the electrical harness from the stator plate through the rubber grommet in the crankcase. Install the stator plate with the chisel marks lined up. Hold the stator to prevent it from turning and screw in and tighten the 3 screws. Set them with an impact driver.

7. Set the key in place in the crankshaft. Install the flywheel, water pump pulley, and the starter cup **(Figure 44)**. Screw on and tighten the flywheel nut to 60 ft.-lb. (8.3 mkg). Tighten the starter cup bolts.

8. Refer to *Upper-End Overhaul* in this supplement and complete assembly of the engine. Refer to *Removal/Installation* and install the engine in the machine.

CHAPTER FIVE

FUEL SYSTEM

Altitude and air temperature have a marked effect on engine performance and must be compensated for with suitable jet sizes and appropriate needle positions.

Correct jetting and adjustment is largely a matter of experience gained through careful trial-and-error tuning.

The original-equipment jets and settings represent a compromise and will not provide best performance at all temperatures and altitudes. **Table 6** is provided as a guide for selecting optimum jetting.

Before beginning, estimate the lowest temperature at which the machine will be operated. Also, determine the lowest altitude at which it will be operated. If you are unsure about either parameter, always go for the larger of two jets; a too-lean mixture often results in a damaging piston seizure or burned piston crowns.

11

Table 6   JETTING/ALTITUDE—TEMPERATURE COMPENSATION

EC25PS
Outside Air Temperature ° F

Altitude — Feet	−40	−20	0	+20	+40	+60
1000	122.5	120	117.5	115	112.5	110
3000	120	117.5	115	112.5	110	107.5
5000	115	115	112.5	110	107.5	105
7000	112.5	110	110	107.5	105	102.5
9000	110	107.5	107.5	105	102.5	100

Main Jet Number

Production Setting
Main Jet — 117.5   Pilot Jet — 35
Cut Away — 3.0   Air Screw — 1.0 turn
Jet Needle — 5DP7—4

Outside Air Temperature, °F

Altitude — Feet	−40	−20	0	+20	+40	+60
1000	115	115	112.5	110	107.5	105
3000	112.5	110	110	107.5	105	102.5
5000	110	107.5	107.5	105	102.5	100
7000	107.5	105	105	102.5	100	95
9000	105	102.5	102.5	100	95	90

Main Jet Number

Production Setting
Main Jet — 112.5   Pilot Jet — 35
Cut Away — 3.0   Air Screw — 1.0 turn
Jet Needle — 5DP7-5
         5DP3-3

Table 6   JETTING/ALTITUDE—TEMPERATURE COMPENSATION (continued)

EC25PM—01

Outside Air Temperature ° F

Altitude — Feet	−40	−20	0	+20	+40	+60
1000	130	120	120	120	110	110
3000	120	120	110	110	110	100
5000	120	110	110	100	100	90
7000	110	100	100	100	90	90
9000	100	100	90	90	90	80

Main Jet Number

Production Setting
Main Jet — 120   Pilot Jet — 35
Cut Away — 2.5   Air Screw — 1.0 turn
Jet Needle — 5DP7—2

EC34PM—03

Outside Air Temperature ° F

Altitude — Feet	−40	−20	0	+20	+40	+60
1000	140	140	130	130	120	110
3000	130	130	120	120	110	110
5000	130	120	120	120	110	100
7000	120	120	110	110	100	100
9000	110	110	100	100	90	90

Main Jet Number

Production Setting
Main Jet — 130   Pilot Jet — 35
Cut Away — 2.5   Air Screw — 1.0 turn
Jet Needle — 5DP7—2

11

Table 6   JETTING/ALTITUDE—TEMPERATURE COMPENSATION (continued)

EC34PM—04

Outside Air Temperature ° F

Altitude — Feet	−40	−20	0	+20	+40	+60
1000	140	130	120	120	110	110
3000	130	120	120	110	110	100
5000	120	110	110	110	100	100
7000	110	110	100	100	100	90
9000	110	100	100	90	90	90

Main Jet Number

Production Setting

Main Jet — 130	Pilot Jet — 35
Cut Away — 3.0	Air Screw — 1.0 turn
Jet Needle — 5DP7—3	

EC44PM—01

Outside Air Temperature ° F

Altitude — Feet	−40	−20	0	+20	+40	+60
1000	210	200	190	180	180	170
3000	200	190	180	170	170	160
5000	190	180	170	160	160	150
7000	170	170	160	150	150	140
9000	160	160	150	140	140	130

Main Jet Number

Production Setting

Main Jet — 200	Pilot Jet — 35
Cut Away — 2.5	Air Screw — 1.0 turn
Jet Needle — 6DP1—3	

Table 6   JETTING/ALTITUDE—TEMPERATURE COMPENSATION (continued)

EC25PT—07

Outside Air Temperature ° F

Altitude — Feet	−40	−20	0	+20	+40	+60
1000	230	220	210	200	190	180
3000	220	210	200	190	180	170
5000	200	200	190	180	170	160
7000	190	180	180	170	160	150
9000	180	170	170	160	150	140

Main Jet Number

Production Setting

Main Jet — 220   Pilot Jet — 35

Cut Away — 2.5   Air Screw — 1.0 turn

Jet Needle — 5DP7—3

EC34PT—05

Outside Air Temperature ° F

Altitude — Feet	−40	−20	0	+20	+40	+60
1000	310	300	290	280	270	260
3000	300	290	280	270	260	240
5000	280	270	260	250	240	230
7000	260	250	240	240	230	220
9000	250	240	230	220	210	200

Main Jet Number

Production Setting

Main Jet — 290   Pilot Jet — 30

Cut Away — 2.0   Air Screw — 1.0 turn

Jet Needle — 6DH7—2

11

Table 6   JETTING/ALTITUDE—TEMPERATURE COMPENSATION (continued)

EC44PT—05

Outside Air Temperature ° F

Altitude — Feet	−40	−20	0	+20	+40	+60
1000	340	330	320	310	300	280
3000	330	310	300	290	280	270
5000	310	300	290	280	260	250
7000	290	280	270	260	250	240
9000	270	260	250	240	230	220

Main Jet Number

Production Setting
Main Jet — 320   Pilot Jet — 30
Cut Away — 2.5   Air Screw — 1.0 turn
Jet Needle — 6DH7—2

EC34PL—02

Outside Air Temperature ° F

Altitude — Feet	−40	−20	0	+20	+40	+60
1000	280	270	260	250	240	230
3000	270	260	250	240	230	220
5000	250	240	230	220	220	200
7000	240	230	220	210	200	190
9000	220	210	200	200	190	180

Main Jet Number

Production Setting
Main Jet — 260   Pilot Jet — 45
Cut Away — 2.5   Air Screw — 1.0 turn
Jet Needle — 6DH4—3

Table 6   JETTING/ALTITUDE—TEMPERATURE COMPENSATION (continued)

EC51PL—01

Outside Air Temperature ° F

Altitude — Feet	−40	−20	0	+20	+40	+60
1000	230	220	210	200	190	190
3000	220	210	200	190	180	180
5000	200	200	190	180	170	170
7000	190	180	180	170	160	160
9000	180	170	170	160	150	150

Main Jet Number

Production Setting

Main Jet — 210	Pilot Jet — 35
Cut Away — 3.0	Air Screw — 1.5 turn
Jet Needle — 6DH7—2	

CHAPTER SIX

ELECTRICAL SYSTEM

Wiring diagrams for 1978-1979 models are included at the end of the book.

CHAPTER NINE

REAR SUSPENSION
AND TRACK

**TYPE III SUSPENSION
(EXTRUDED ALUMINUM)**

Adjustments to the Type III suspension used on TX-L and Centurion models are described in the Chapter Two portion of this supplement.

INDEX

12

NOTES

NOTES

NOTES

WIRING DIAGRAM—1973 CONSUMER TX (140 WATT ALTERNATOR, 2 CYL.)

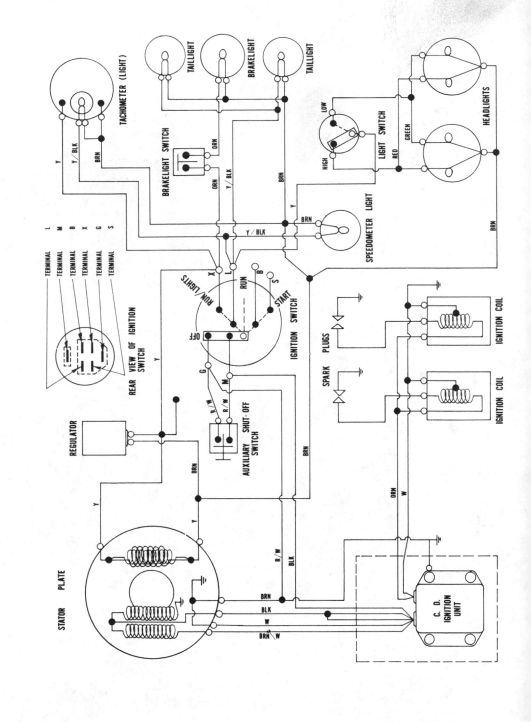

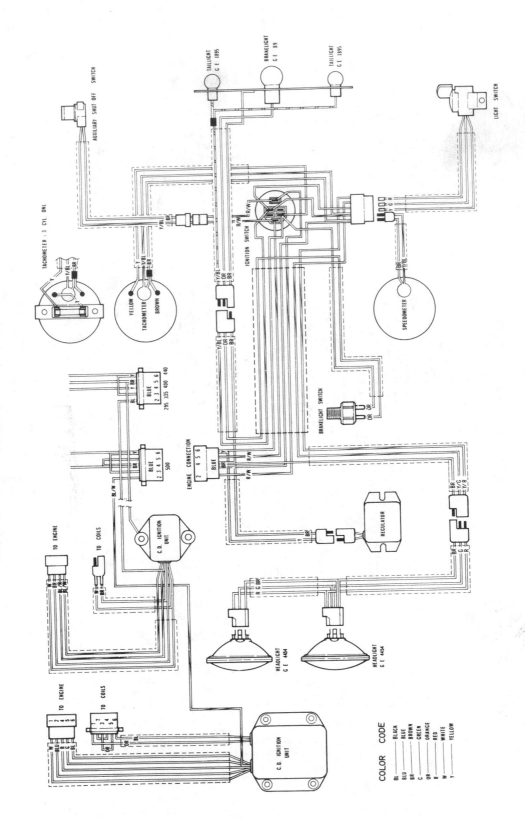

WIRING DIAGRAM — 1973 CONSUMER TX

COLOR CODE

BL —— BLACK
BLU —— BLUE
BR —— BROWN
G —— GREEN
OR —— ORANGE
R —— RED
W —— WHITE
Y —— YELLOW

13

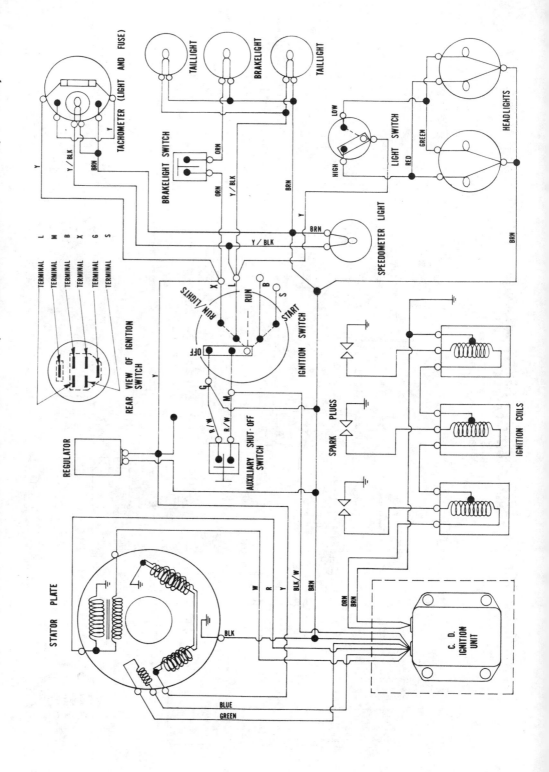

WIRING DIAGRAM — 1973 CONSUMER TX (140 WATT ALTERNATOR, 3 CYL.)

WIRING DIAGRAM — 1973 530 CHARGER, MUSTANG (140 WATT ALTERNATOR)

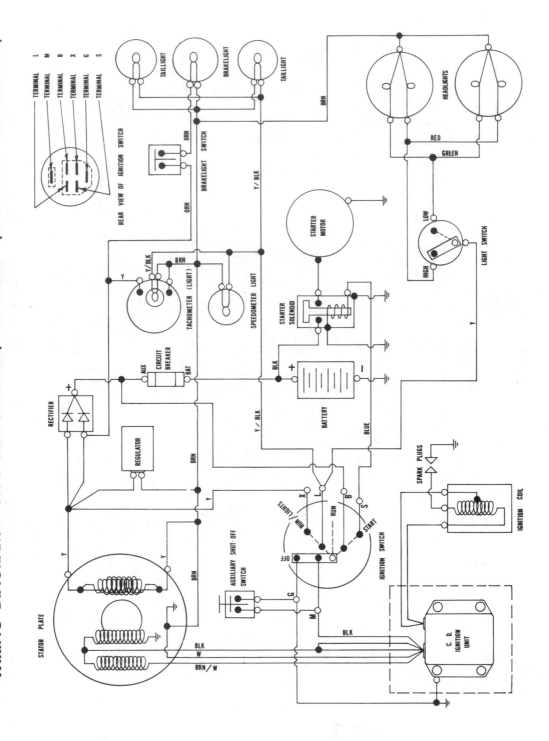

13

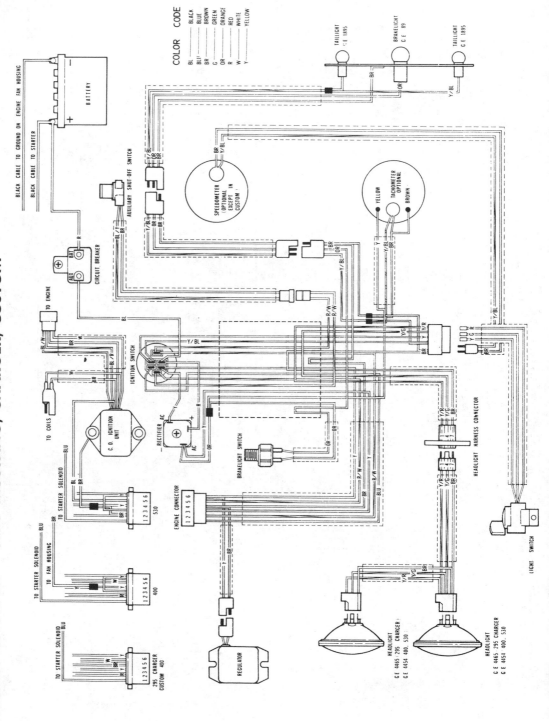

WIRING DIAGRAM — 1973 MUSTANG, CHARGER, CUSTOM

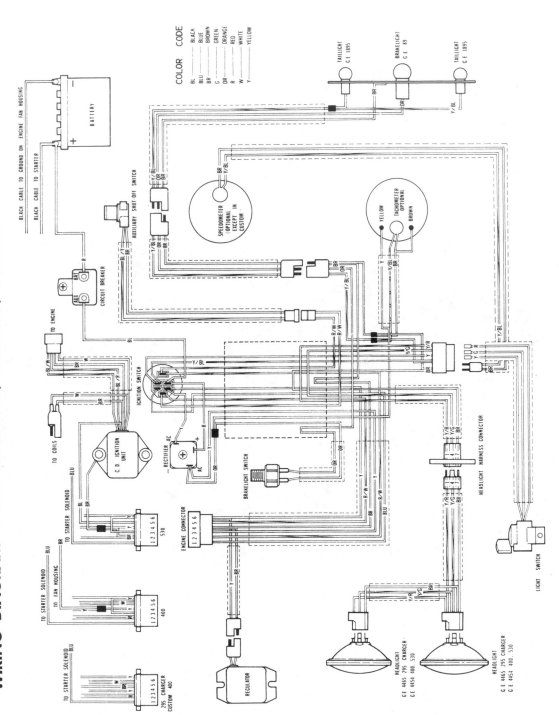

WIRING DIAGRAM — 1973 MUSTANG, CHARGER, CUSTOM

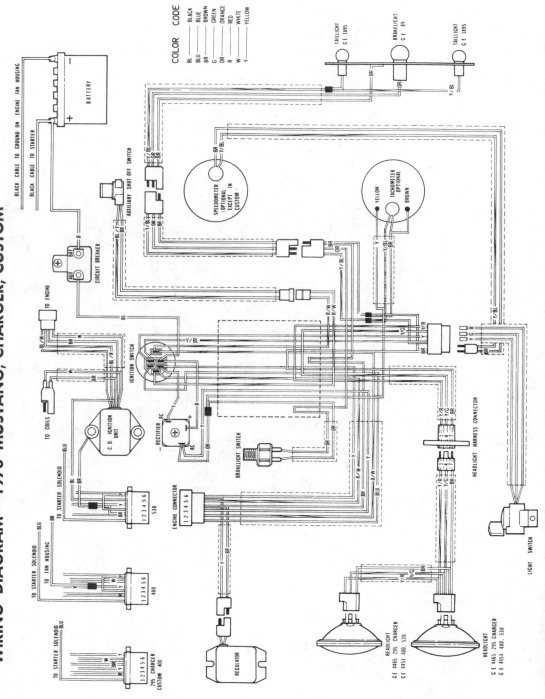

WIRING DIAGRAM — 1973 MUSTANG, CHARGER, CUSTOM

WIRING DIAGRAM – 1973 295 CHARGER, 398 CUSTOM (75 WATT ALTERNATOR)

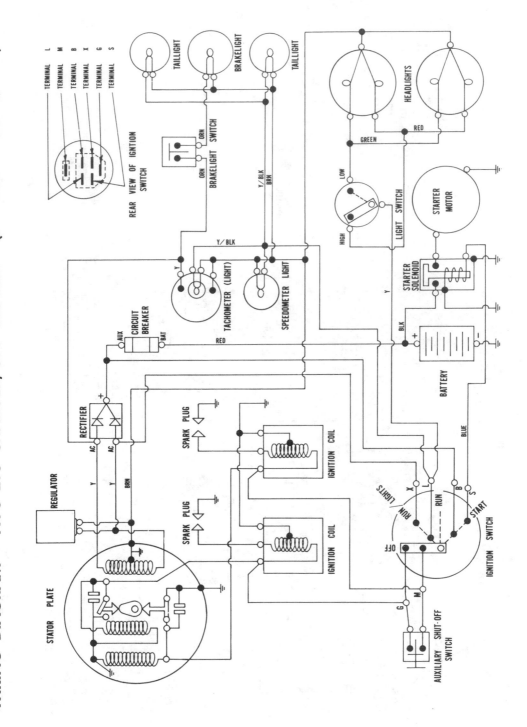

WIRING DIAGRAM — 1973 398 CHARGER, MUSTANG (140 WATT ALTERNATOR)

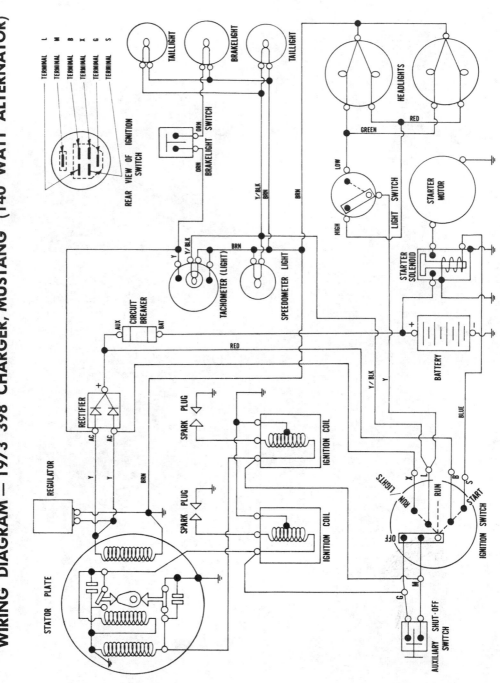

WIRING DIAGRAM – 1973 COLT (75 WATT ALTERNATOR)

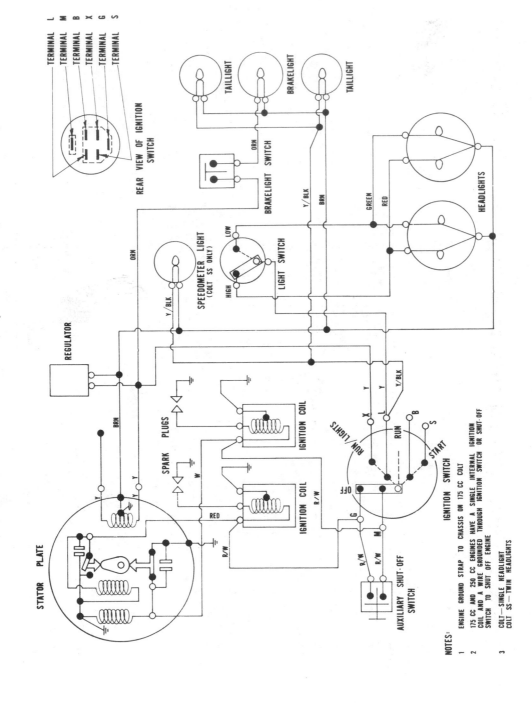

NOTES:

1 ENGINE GROUND STRAP TO CHASSIS ON 175 CC COLT

2 175 CC AND 250 CC ENGINES HAVE A SINGLE INTERNAL IGNITION
   COIL AND A WIRE GROUNDED THROUGH IGNITION SWITCH OR SHUT-OFF
   SWITCH TO SHUT OFF ENGINE

3 COLT – SINGLE HEADLIGHT
   COLT SS – TWIN HEADLIGHTS

13

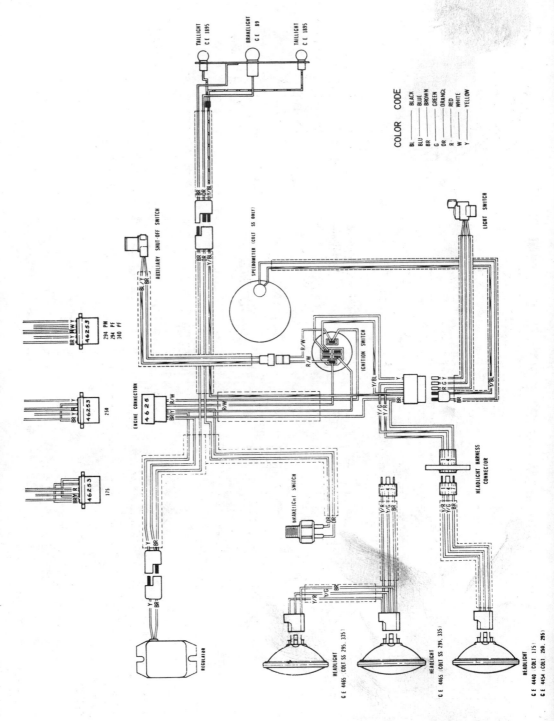

WIRING DIAGRAM – 1973 COLT

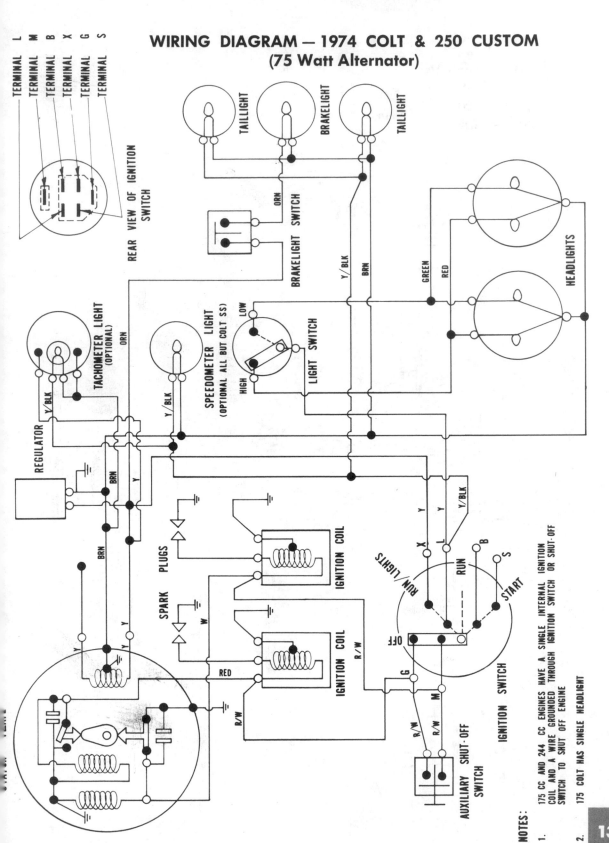

WIRING DIAGRAM — 1974 COLT & 250 CUSTOM
(75 Watt Alternator)

NOTES:

1. 175 CC AND 244 CC ENGINES HAVE A SINGLE INTERNAL IGNITION COIL AND A WIRE GROUNDED THROUGH IGNITION SWITCH OR SHUT-OFF SWITCH TO SHUT OFF ENGINE

2. 175 COLT HAS SINGLE HEADLIGHT

13

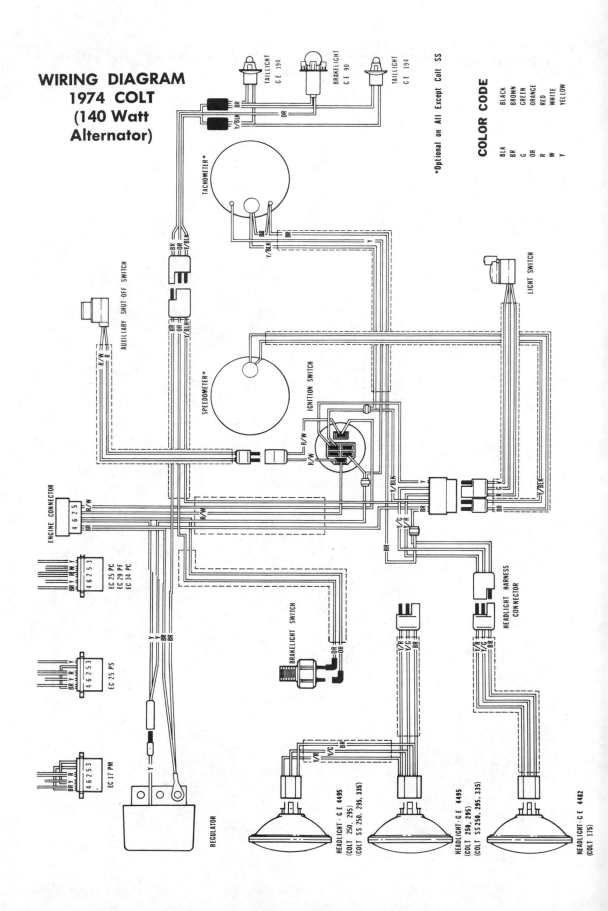

WIRING DIAGRAM
1974 COLT
(140 Watt Alternator)

COLOR CODE

BLK	BLACK
BR	BROWN
G	GREEN
OR	ORANGE
R	RED
W	WHITE
Y	YELLOW

*Optional on All Except Colt SS

TAILLIGHT GE 194
BRAKELIGHT GE 90
TAILLIGHT GE 194

TACHOMETER*

SPEEDOMETER*

IGNITION SWITCH

AUXILIARY SHUT-OFF SWITCH

LIGHT SWITCH

ENGINE CONNECTOR

EC 25 PC
EC 29 PF
EC 34 PC

EC 25 PS

EC 17 PM

REGULATOR

BRAKELIGHT SWITCH

HEADLIGHT HARNESS CONNECTOR

HEADLIGHT - GE 4495
(COLT 250, 295)
(COLT SS 250, 295, 335)

HEADLIGHT - GE 4495
(COLT 250, 295)
(COLT SS 250, 295, 335)

HEADLIGHT - GE 4002
(COLT 175)

WIRING DIAGRAM — 1974 400 CUSTOM (140 Watt Alternator)

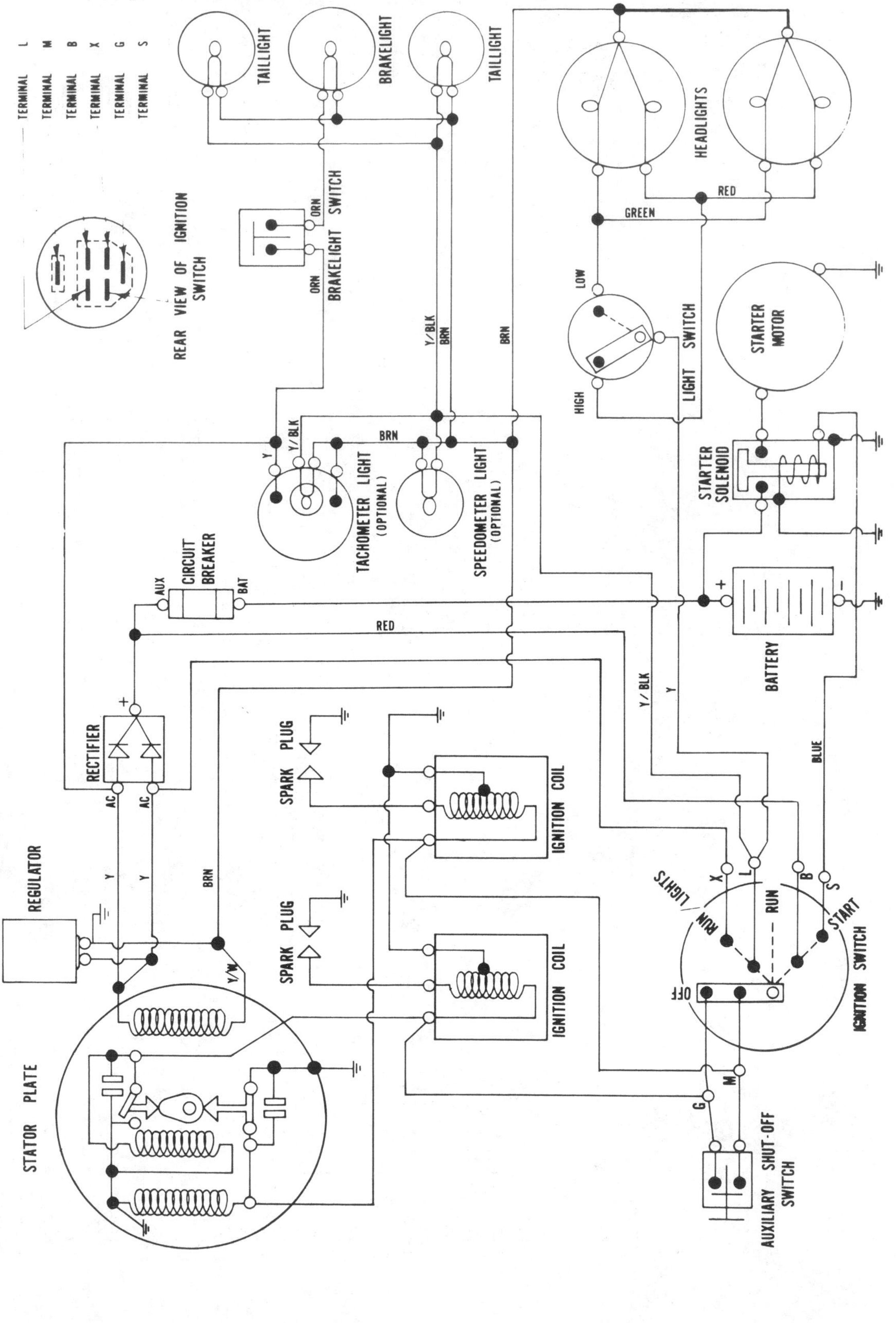

WIRING DIAGRAM — 1974 340, 440 ELECTRA & 530 CUSTOM
(140 Watt Alternator)

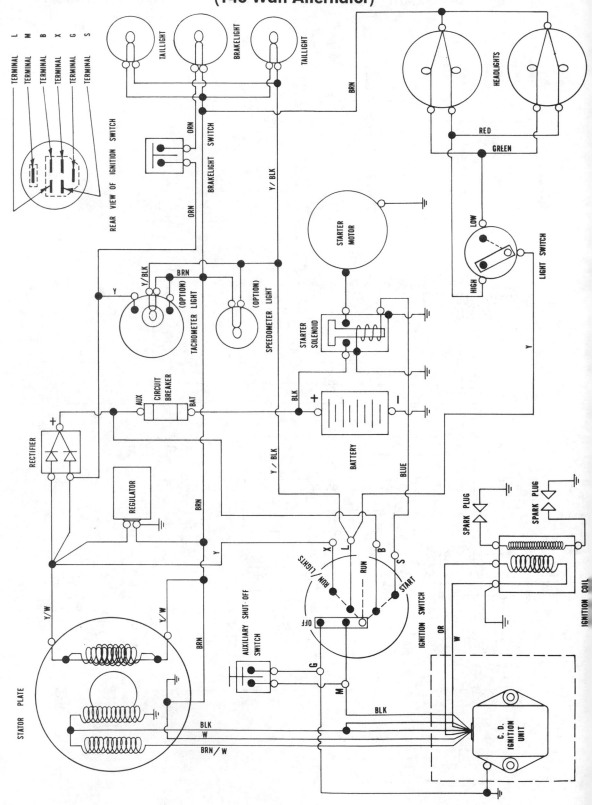

WIRING DIAGRAM — 1974 ELECTRA CUSTOM

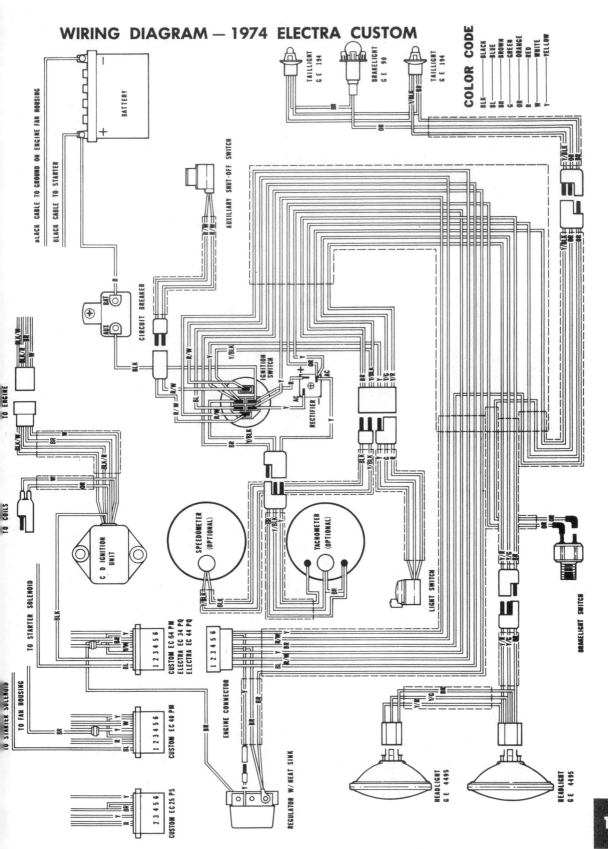

WIRING DIAGRAM – 1974 CONSUMER TX

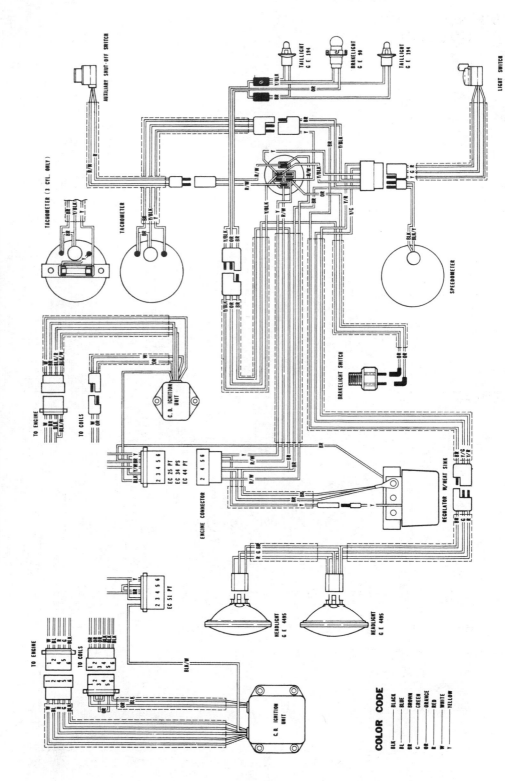

COLOR CODE

BLK —— BLACK
BL —— BLUE
BR —— BROWN
G —— GREEN
OR —— ORANGE
R —— RED
W —— WHITE
Y —— YELLOW

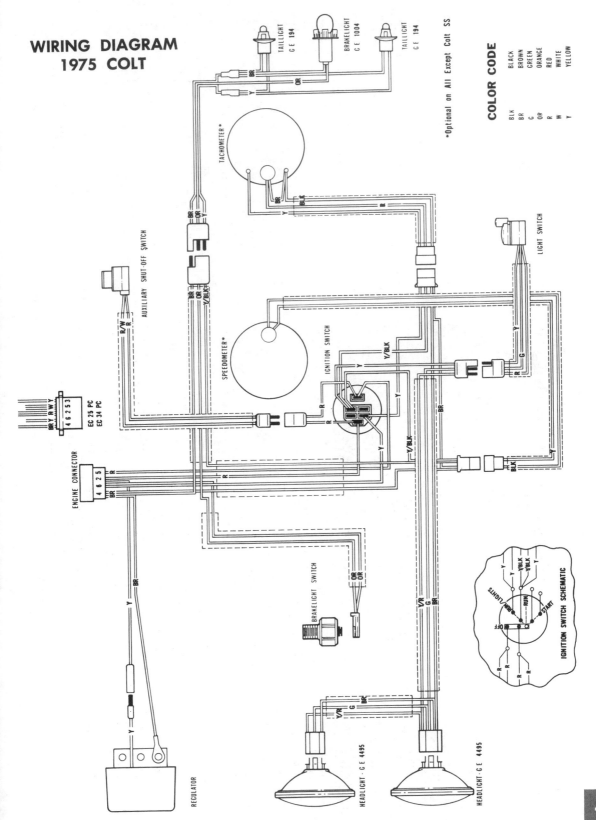

WIRING DIAGRAM 1975 COLT

COLOR CODE

BLK	BLACK
BR	BROWN
G	GREEN
OR	ORANGE
R	RED
W	WHITE
Y	YELLOW

*Optional on All Except Colt SS

TAILLIGHT G E 194

BRAKELIGHT G E 1004

TAILLIGHT G E 194

TACHOMETER*

AUXILIARY SHUT-OFF SWITCH

SPEEDOMETER*

IGNITION SWITCH

LIGHT SWITCH

ENGINE CONNECTOR

EC 25 PC
EC 34 PC

BRAKELIGHT SWITCH

IGNITION SWITCH SCHEMATIC

OFF
RUN
START
LIGHTS

REGULATOR

HEADLIGHT - G E 4495

HEADLIGHT - G E 4495

13

WIRING DIAGRAM — 1975 ELECTRA

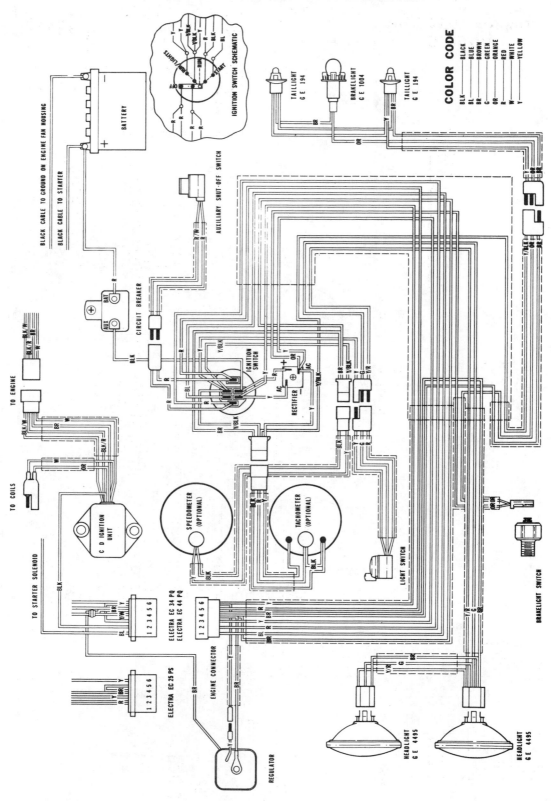

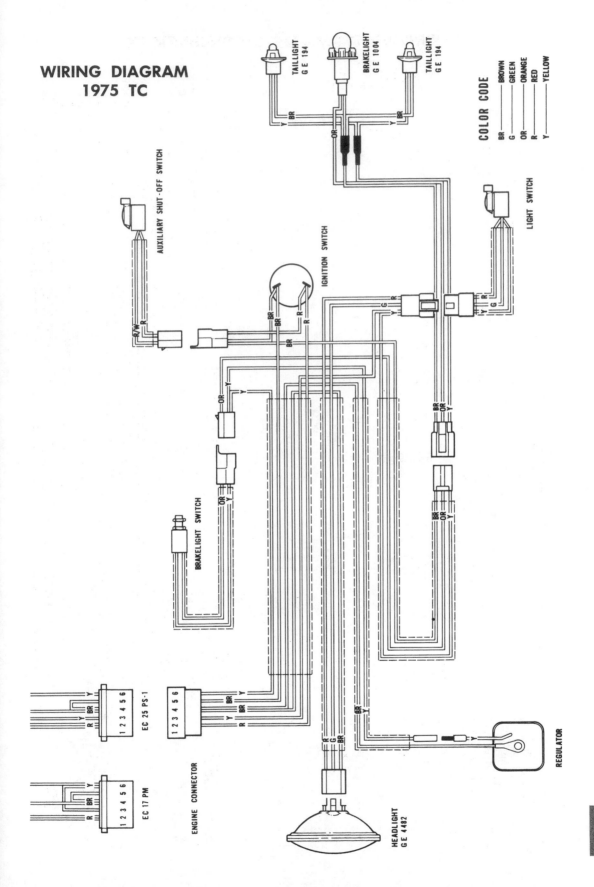

WIRING DIAGRAM 1975 TC

TAILLIGHT G E 194

BRAKELIGHT G E 1004

TAILLIGHT G E 194

COLOR CODE

BR ———— BROWN
G ———— GREEN
OR ———— ORANGE
R ———— RED
Y ———— YELLOW

AUXILIARY SHUT-OFF SWITCH

LIGHT SWITCH

IGNITION SWITCH

BRAKELIGHT SWITCH

EC 25 PS-1

EC 17 PM

ENGINE CONNECTOR

REGULATOR

HEADLIGHT G E 4482

13

WIRING DIAGRAM — 1975 CONSUMER TX

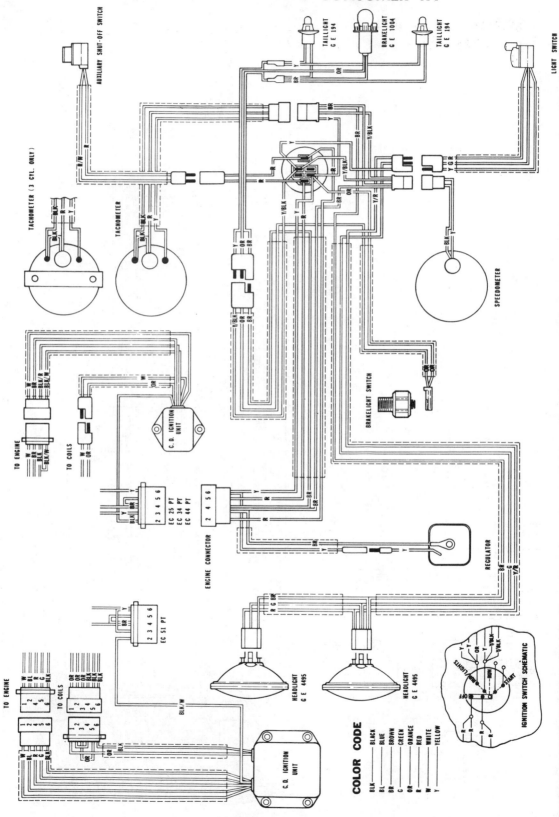

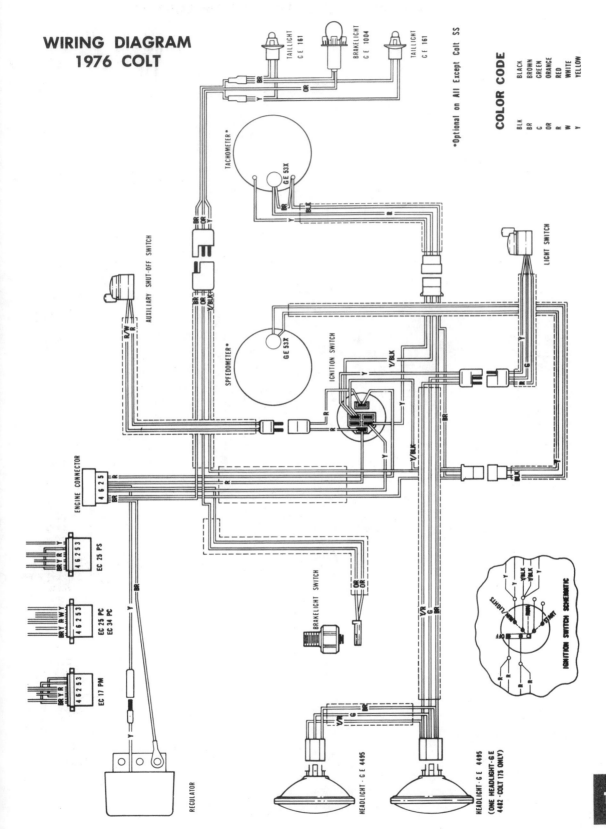

WIRING DIAGRAM
1976 COLT

*Optional on All Except Colt SS

COLOR CODE

BLK	BLACK
BR	BROWN
C	GREEN
OR	ORANGE
R	RED
W	WHITE
Y	YELLOW

TAILLIGHT G E 161

BRAKLIGHT G E 1004

TAILLIGHT G E 161

TACHOMETER*

GE 53X

LIGHT SWITCH

AUXILIARY SHUT-OFF SWITCH

SPEEDOMETER*

GE 53X

IGNITION SWITCH

IGNITION SWITCH SCHEMATIC

ENGINE CONNECTOR

EC 25 PS

EC 25 PC
EC 34 PC

EC 17 PM

BRAKELIGHT SWITCH

REGULATOR

HEADLIGHT - G E 4495

HEADLIGHT - G E 4495
(ONE HEADLIGHT - G E
4482 - COLT 175 ONLY)

13

WIRING DIAGRAM — 1976 ELECTRA

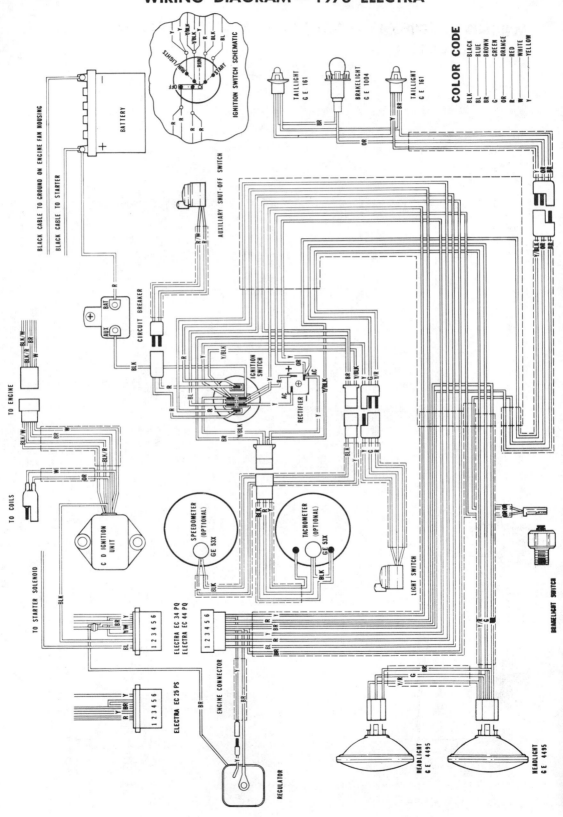

WIRING DIAGRAM — 1976 TX STARFIRE

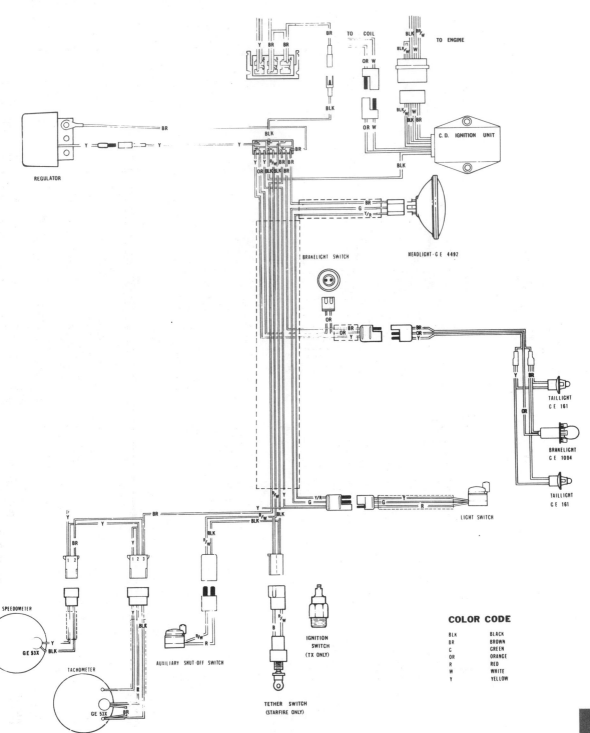

COLOR CODE

BLK	BLACK
BR	BROWN
G	GREEN
OR	ORANGE
R	RED
W	WHITE
Y	YELLOW

REGULATOR

TO COIL

TO ENGINE

C.D. IGNITION UNIT

BRAKELIGHT SWITCH

HEADLIGHT-G E 4492

TAILLIGHT G E 161

BRAKELIGHT G E 1004

TAILLIGHT G E 161

LIGHT SWITCH

SPEEDOMETER
GE 53X

TACHOMETER
GE 53X

AUXILIARY SHUT-OFF SWITCH

IGNITION SWITCH (TX ONLY)

TETHER SWITCH (STARFIRE ONLY)

13

WIRING DIAGRAM — 1977 COLT

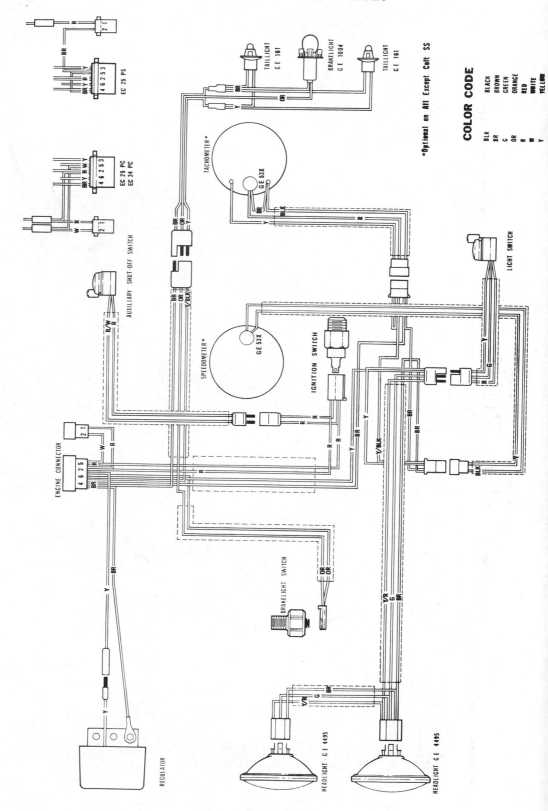

WIRING DIAGRAM — 1977 ELECTRA

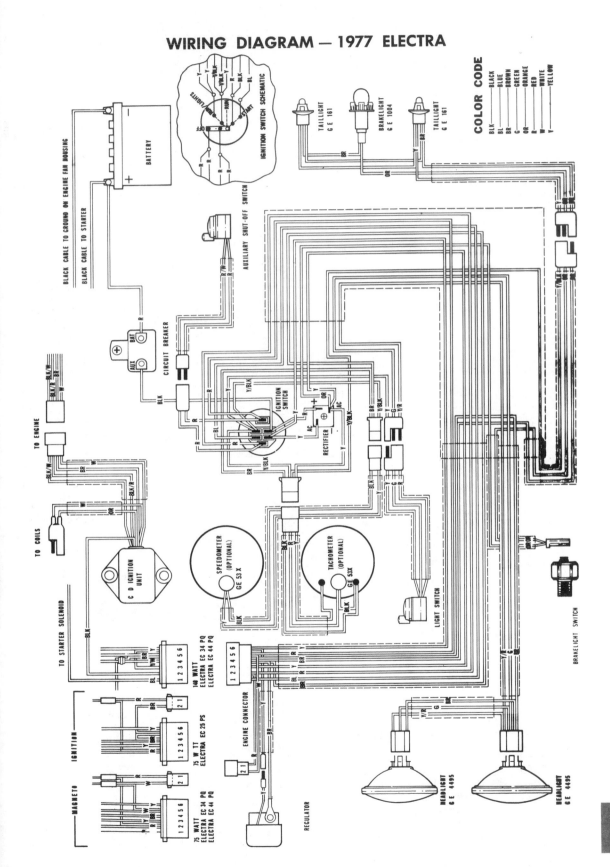

WIRING DIAGRAM – 1977 TX and TXL

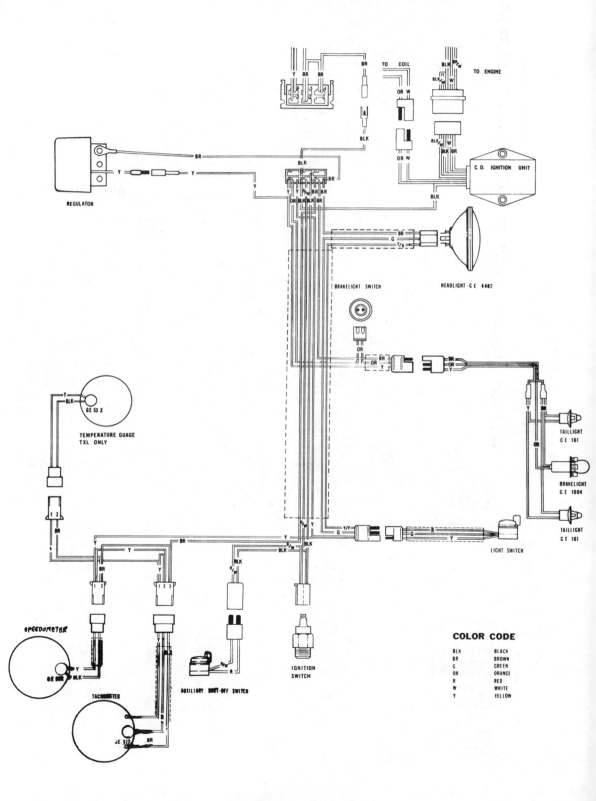

COLOR CODE

BLK	BLACK
BR	BROWN
G	GREEN
OR	ORANGE
R	RED
W	WHITE
Y	YELLOW

WIRING DIAGRAM — 1978 TX, TX-L (75 WATT ALTERNATOR)

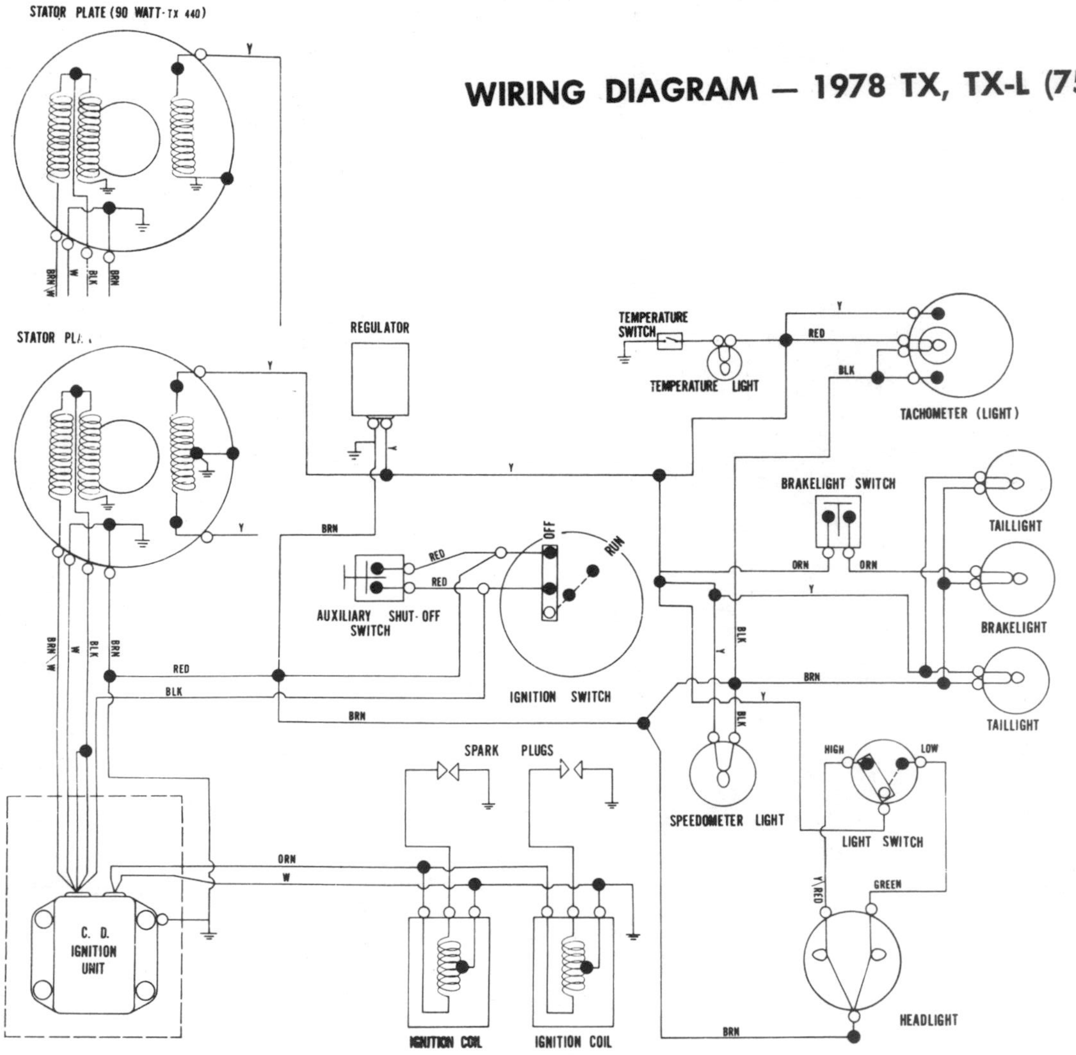

STATOR PLATE (90 WATT-TX 440)
Y
BRN\W
W
BLK
BRN
STATOR PL...
Y
Y
REGULATOR
Y
Y
BRN
TEMPERATURE SWITCH
TEMPERATURE LIGHT
Y
RED
BLK
TACHOMETER (LIGHT)
BRAKELIGHT SWITCH
ORN
ORN
TAILLIGHT
BRAKELIGHT
TAILLIGHT
Y
BLK
Y
BRN
Y
BLK
RED
RED
OFF
RUN
AUXILIARY SHUT-OFF SWITCH
IGNITION SWITCH
RED
BLK
BRN
SPARK PLUGS
SPEEDOMETER LIGHT
HIGH
LOW
LIGHT SWITCH
Y\RED
GREEN
HEADLIGHT
BRN
ORN
W
C. D. IGNITION UNIT
IGNITION COIL
IGNITION COIL

WIRING DIAGRAM — 1978 TX, TX-L

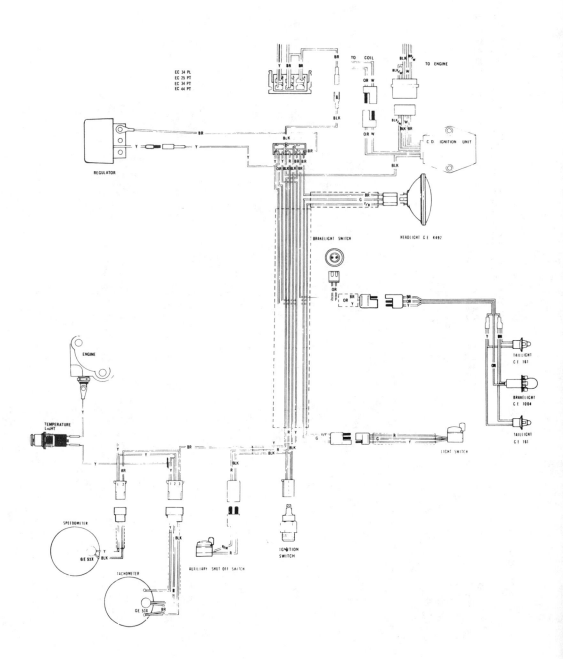

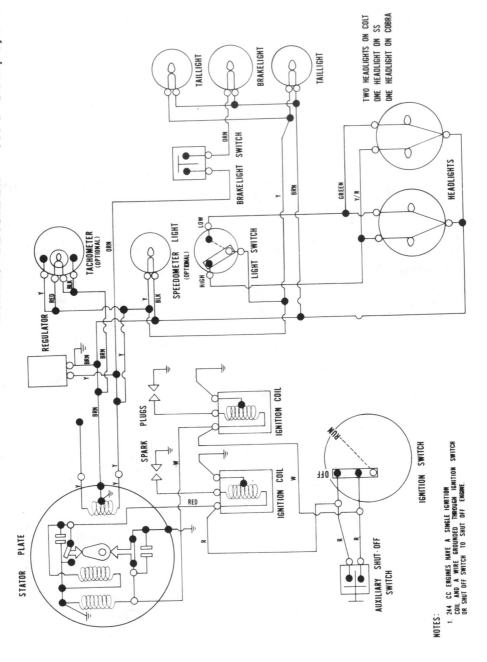

WIRING DIAGRAM — 1978 COLT, S/S 340, COBRA

NOTES:

1. 244 CC ENGINES HAVE A SINGLE IGNITION COIL AND A WIRE GROUNDED THROUGH IGNITION SWITCH OR SHUT OFF SWITCH TO SHUT OFF ENGINE.

WIRING DIAGRAM – 1978 COLT, S/S 340, COBRA

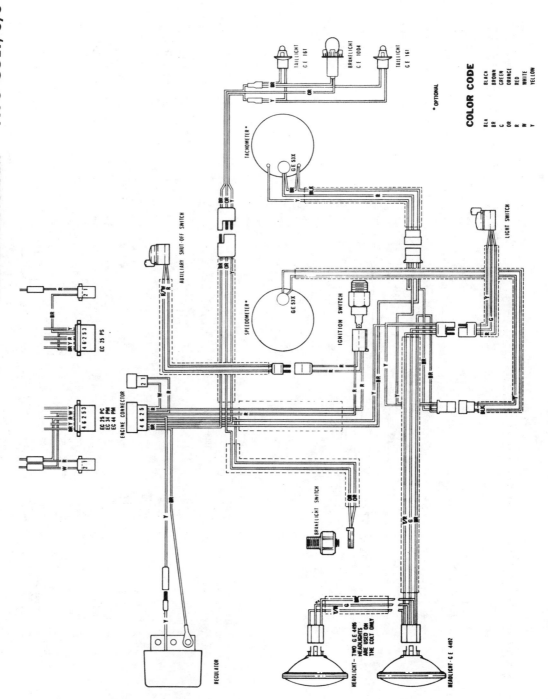

COLOR CODE

BLA — BLACK
BR — BROWN
G — GREEN
OR — ORANGE
R — RED
W — WHITE
Y — YELLOW

* OPTIONAL

WIRING DIAGRAM – 1979 TX (90 WATT ALTERNATOR)

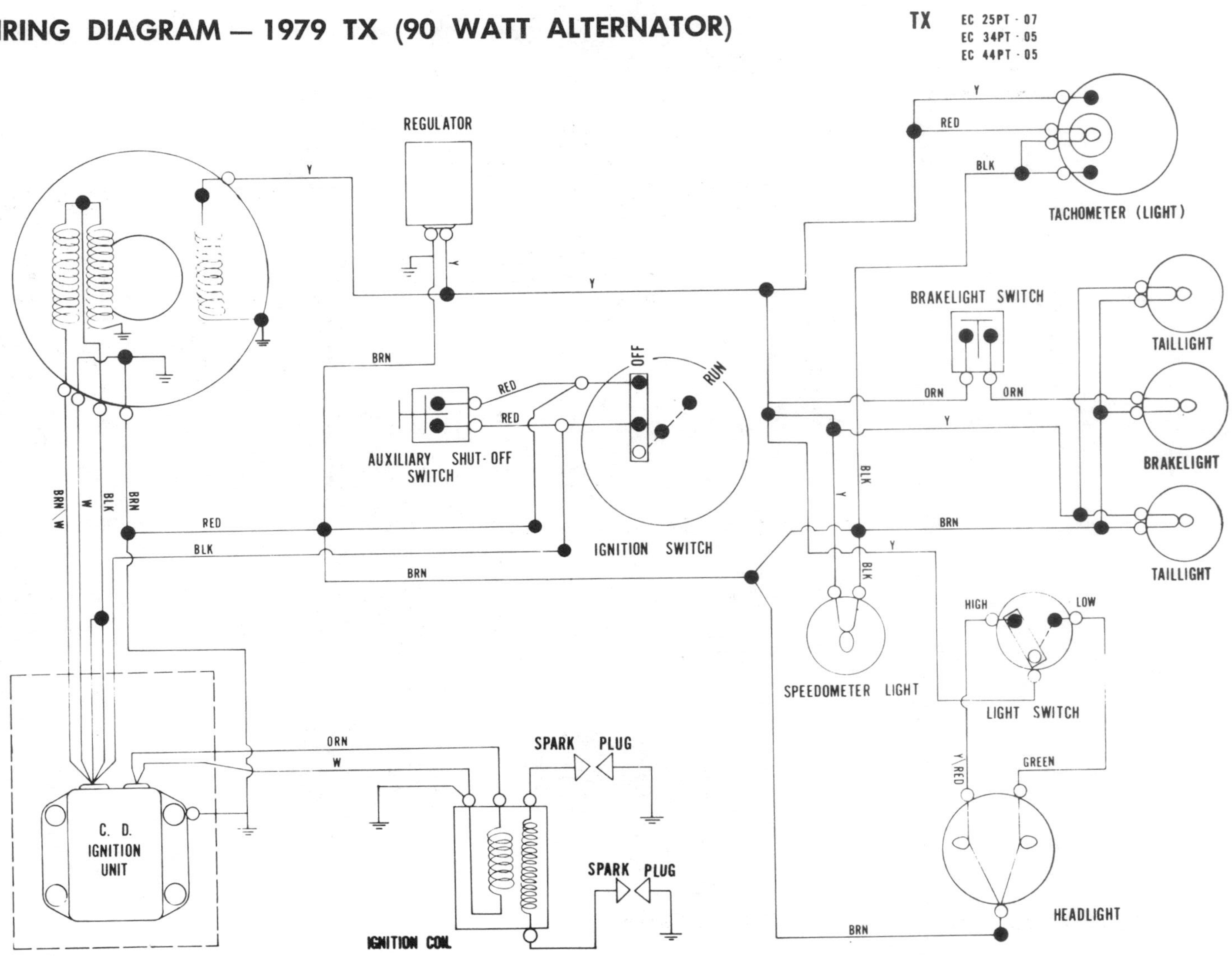

TX

EC 25PT - 07
EC 34PT - 05
EC 44PT - 05

TACHOMETER (LIGHT)

TAILLIGHT

BRAKELIGHT

TAILLIGHT

HEADLIGHT

LIGHT SWITCH

LOW

HIGH

GREEN

Y\RED

BRAKELIGHT SWITCH

ORN

ORN

Y

BRN

Y

BLK

BLK

Y

SPEEDOMETER LIGHT

BRN

RED

BLK

Y

Y

IGNITION SWITCH

RUN

OFF

RED

RED

AUXILIARY SHUT-OFF SWITCH

BRN

REGULATOR

Y

Y

BRN

RED

BLK

BRN

SPARK PLUG

SPARK PLUG

IGNITION COIL

ORN

W

BRN

BLK

W

BRN\W

C. D.
IGNITION
UNIT

13

WIRING DIAGRAM — 1979 TX

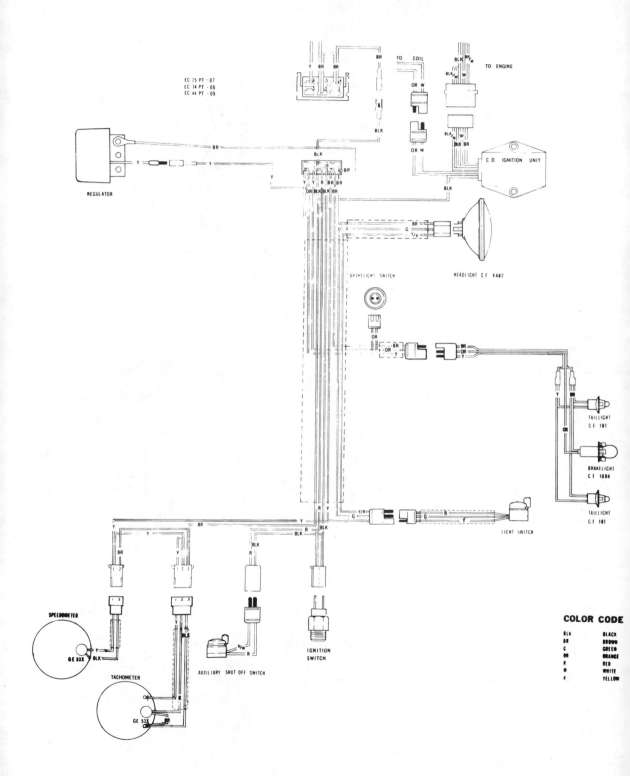

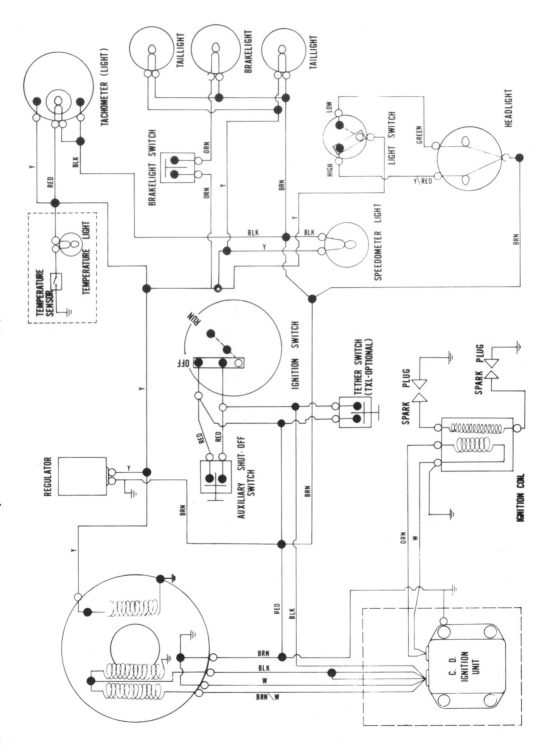

WIRING DIAGRAM—1979 TX-L 340 (90 WATT ALTERNATOR)

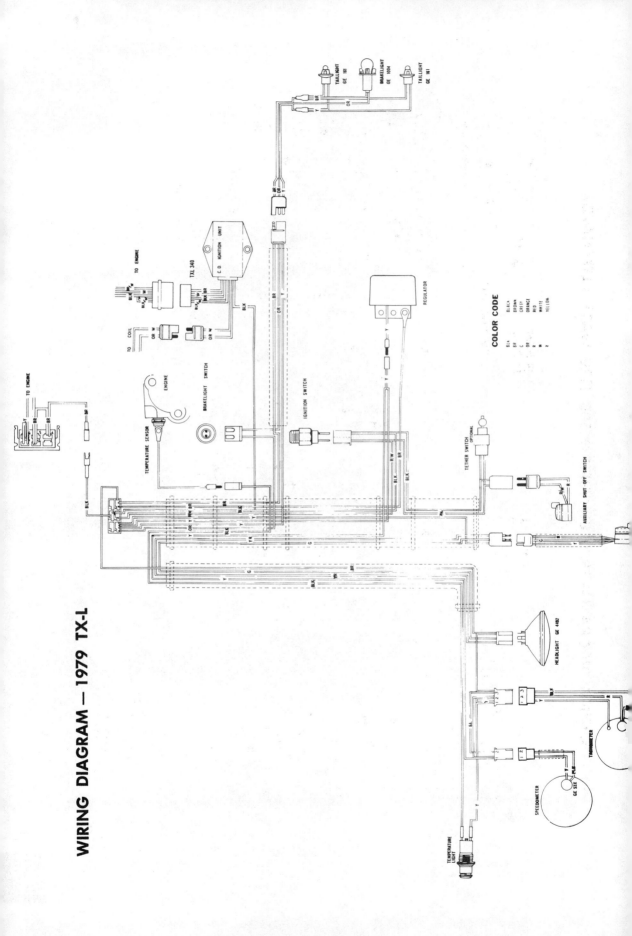

WIRING DIAGRAM — 1979 TX-L

COLOR CODE

BLK   BLACK
BR   BROWN
G   GREY
OR   ORANGE
R   RED
W   WHITE
Y   YELLOW

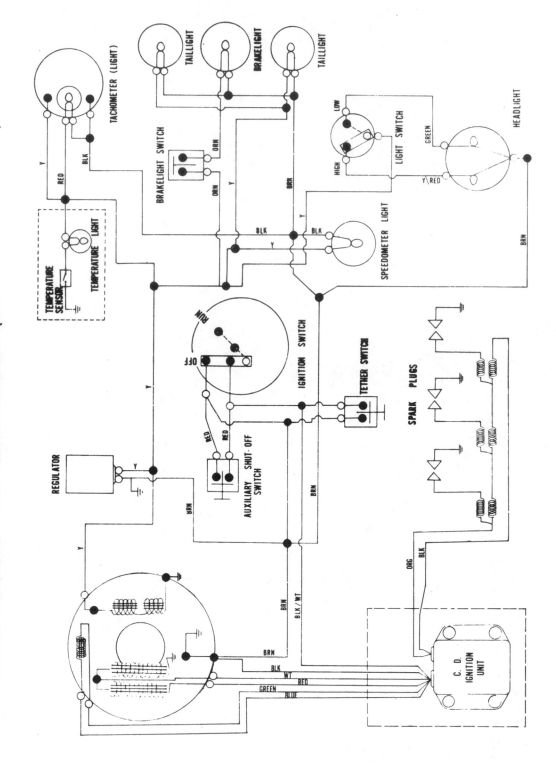

WIRING DIAGRAM — 1979 CENTURION 500 (120 WATT ALTERNATOR)

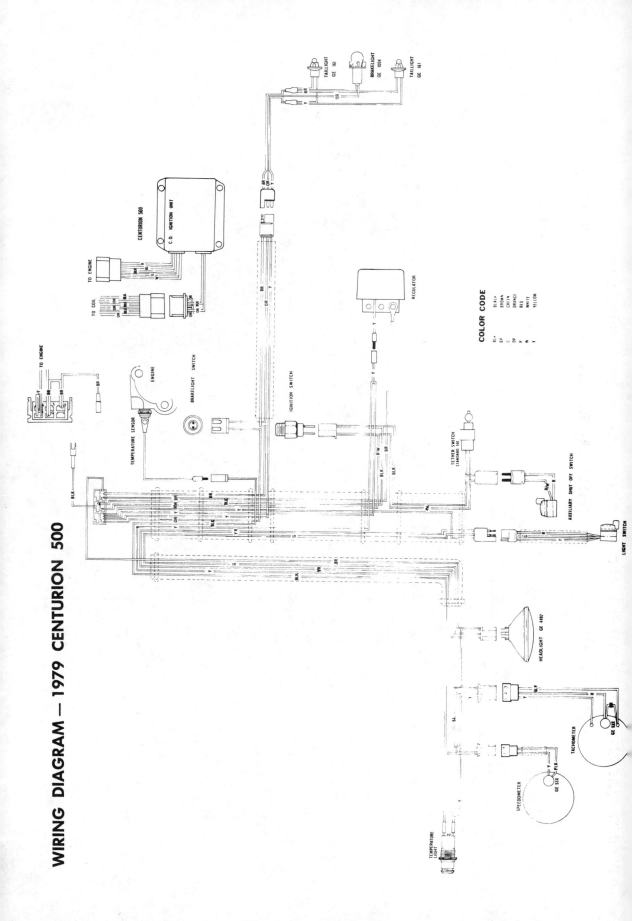

WIRING DIAGRAM – 1979 CENTURION 500

WIRING DIAGRAM — 1979 GEMINI, APOLLO, COBRA (75 WATT ALTERNATOR)

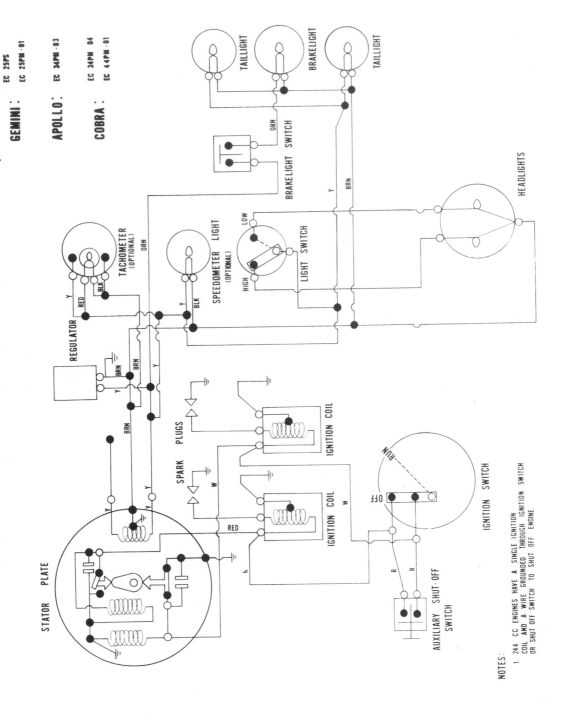

GEMINI : EC 25PS
EC 25PM-01

APOLLO : EC 34PM-03

COBRA : EC 34PM 04
EC 44PM-01

NOTES:
1. 244 CC ENGINES HAVE A SINGLE IGNITION COIL AND A WIRE GROUNDED THROUGH IGNITION SWITCH OR SHUT OFF SWITCH TO SHUT OFF ENGINE.

STATOR PLATE

REGULATOR

TACHOMETER (OPTIONAL)

SPEEDOMETER LIGHT (OPTIONAL)

LIGHT SWITCH

HIGH
LOW

HEADLIGHTS

TAILLIGHT
BRAKELIGHT
TAILLIGHT

BRAKELIGHT SWITCH

SPARK PLUGS

IGNITION COIL

IGNITION COIL

IGNITION SWITCH

RUN
OFF

AUXILIARY SHUT-OFF SWITCH

13

WIRING DIAGRAM — 1979 GEMINI, APOLLO, COBRA

GEMINI:	EC 25PS
	EC 25PM - 01
APOLLO:	EC 34PM - 03
COBRA:	EC 34PM - 04
	EC 44PM - 01

To Engine
W R
BR Y R W Y
4 6 2 5 3
2 1
To Engine
BR
BR Y R Y
4 6 2 5 3
EC 25 PS
R
2 1
ENGINE CONNECTOR
4 6 2 5
2 1
REGULATOR
Y
BR
W
R
R/W
AUXILIARY SHUT-OFF SWITCH
BR
OR
Y
SPEEDOMETER*
GE 53X
TACHOMETER*
GE 53X
BLK
TAILLIGHT
GE 161
BRAKELIGHT
GE 1004
TAILLIGHT
GE 161
BRAKELIGHT SWITCH
OR
OR
IGNITION SWITCH
Y/R
G
BR
HEADLIGHT - GE 4492
LIGHT SWITCH

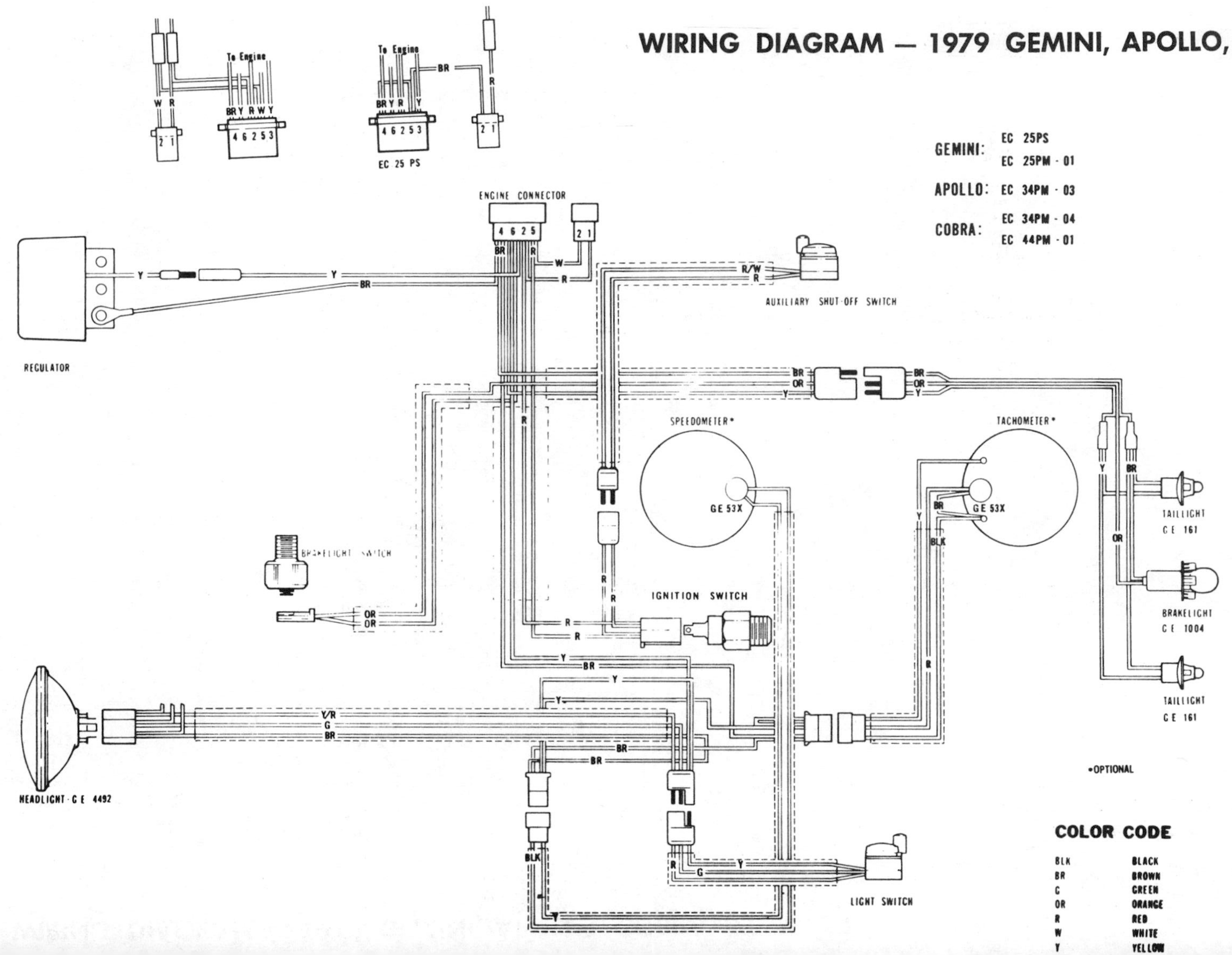

*OPTIONAL

COLOR CODE

BLK	BLACK
BR	BROWN
G	GREEN
OR	ORANGE
R	RED
W	WHITE
Y	YELLOW

Clymer Collection Series

VINTAGE

S N O W M O B I L E S

VOLUME II

POLARIS, 1973-1979

➤ YAMAHA, 1975-1980

SKI-DOO, 1970-1979

CONTENTS

YAMAHA

1975-1980
SERVICE•REPAIR•MAINTENANCE

QUICK REFERENCE DATA

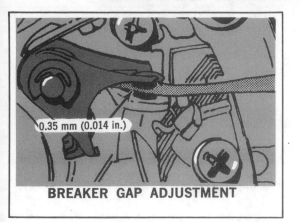

0.35 mm (0.014 in.)

BREAKER GAP ADJUSTMENT

CYLINDER HEAD FASTENER TORQUE

Model	Torque, mkg (Ft.-lb.)
ET250, ET300, ET340, GS340, GP440, EX340, EX440, PR440, EXCEL V, SRX, SSR, GP338, GP433	2.5 (18)
GPX338, GPX433	
Nuts	2.5 (18)
Bolts	2.2 (16)

CARBURETOR ADJUSTMENT SPECIFICATIONS

Model	Mainjet, Standard (Optional)	Main Adjuster, Turns Out	Slow Jet	Pilot/Intermediate Jet	Idle Air Screw, Turns Out
ET250 A/B/C	130 (125, 135)	—	50	40	1
ET300C	210 (180, 190, 200, 220)	—	90	—	$1\frac{1}{4}$
GS340	140 (130, 135, 145)	—	60	70	$1\frac{1}{4}$
GS340A	140 (130, 135, 145)	—	60	70	$1\frac{1}{4}$
GPX338F	—	$\frac{7}{8}$-$1\frac{1}{8}$	$\frac{3}{4}$ turn out	85	—
GPX433F	—	$\frac{7}{8}$-$1\frac{1}{8}$	45	65	—
GP338F	—	$1\frac{3}{8}$	$1\frac{1}{2}$ turns out	—	—
GP433F	200 (180, 190, 210)		1 turn out	—	—
ET340 B/C/EC	220 (200, 210, 230, 240)	—	—	75	1
GP440	195 (190, 200, 205)	—	48	95	1
GP440A	190 (185, 195, 200)	—	48	95	1
PR440	195 (190, 200, 205)	—	48	95	$1\frac{1}{4}$
EX340	155[1] (145, 150, 160)	—	50	90	1
EX440	155[2] (145, 150, 160)	—	50	100	$1\frac{1}{4}$
EXCEL V	145 (120, 125, 130, 135, 140)	—	95	200	$2\frac{1}{4}$
SRX440 SSR440	200[1] (180, 190, 210)	1-1-1-2	—	30/Left—170 Right—165	$\frac{1}{4}$-$\frac{3}{4}$

1. Set slide needle at 3rd notch.   2. Set slide needle at 4th notch.

IGNITION SPECIFICATIONS

Model	Timing, BTDC, mm (in.)	Spark Plug Type and Gap, mm (in.)
ET250A	1.6-1.8 (0.063-0.071)	NGK BR-8HV—0.5-0.6 (0.020-0.024)
ET250B	1.7-1.9 (0.067-0.075)	NGK BR-8HV—0.5-0.6 (0.020-0.024)
ET250C	1.1-1.3 (0.043-0.051)	NGK B-8HS—0.5-0.6 (0.020-0.024)
ET300C	1.3-1.5 (0.051-0.059)	NGK BR-9EV—0.7-0.8 (0.028-0.031)
GP338F	1.4-1.6 (0.055-0.063)	NGK B-8EV—0.4 (0.016)
GP433F	1.7-1.9 (0.067-0.075)	Champion N-3G—0.4 (0.016)
GPX338F	1.5-1.7 (0.059-0.067)	NGK B-9EV—0.5-0.6 (0.020-0.024)
GPX433F	1.5-1.7 (0.059-0.067)	Champion N-2G—0.5-0.6 (0.020-0.024)
GS340	1.4-1.6 (0.055-0.063)	NGK BR-7HS—0.5-0.6 (0.020-0.024)
GS340A	1.4-1.6 (0.055-0.063)	NGK BR-7HS—0.5-0.6 (0.020-0.024)
GS440A	1.5-1.7 (0.059-0.067)	NGK BR-8EV—0.5-0.6 (0.020-0.024)
ET340B	1.5-1.7 (0.059-0.067)	NGK BR-9EV—0.5-0.6 (0.020-0.024)
ET340C	1.5-1.7 (0.059-0.067)	NGK BR-9EV—0.5-0.6 (0.020-0.024)
ET340EC	1.5-1.7 (0.059-0.067)	NGK BR-9EV—0.7-0.8 (0.028-0.031)
EX340	1.5-1.7 (0.059-0.067)	NGK BP-9EV—0.5-0.6 (0.020-0.024)
EX340A	1.5-1.7 (0.059-0.067)	NGK BR-9EV—0.5-0.6 (0.020-0.024)
EX340B	1.5-1.7 (0.059-0.067)	NGK BR-9EV—0.5-0.6 (0.020-0.024)
EX340C	1.5-1.7 (0.059-0.067)	NGK BR-9EV—0.5-0.6 (0.020-0.024)
EX440	1.5-1.7 (0.059-0.067)	NGK BR-9EV—0.5-0.6 (0.020-0.024)
EX440A	1.5-1.7 (0.059-0.067)	NGK BR-9EV—0.5-0.6 (0.020-0.024)
EX440B	1.5-1.7 (0.059-0.067)	NGK BR-9EV—0.5-0.6 (0.020-0.024)
EX440C	1.5-1.7 (0.059-0.067)	NGK BR-9EV—0.5-0.6 (0.020-0.024)
PR440	1.5-1.7 (0.059-0.067)	NGK BR-9EV—0.5-0.6 (0.020-0.024)
GP440	1.4-1.6 (0.055-0.063)	NGK BR-9EV—0.5-0.6 (0.020-0.024)
EXCEL V	1.4-1.6 (0.055-0.063)	NGK BR-9ES—0.7-0.8 (0.028-0.031)
SRX440	1.5-1.7 (0.059-0.067) −40 to −20°C (−40 to −4°F) 1.7-1.9 (0.067-0.075) −20 to 0°C (−4 to 32°F) 1.9-2.1 (0.075-0.083) above 0°C (32°F)	NGK B-9EV—0.5-0.6 (0.020-0.024)
SSR440	0.74-0.76 (0.029-0.030) −40 to −20°C (−40 to −4°F) 0.89-0.91 (0.035-0.036) −20 to 0°C (−4 to 32°F) 0.93-1.13 (0.037-0.044) above 0°C (32°F)	Champion N-82G—0.5-0.6 (0.020-0.024)

SHEAVE DISTANCE/OFFSET

Model	Distance, Center-to-Center	Offset
SSR, SRX, EXCEL V, EX340, EX440	269-271 mm (10.56-10.64 in.)	5.0-6.0 mm (0.197-0.236 in.)
GP338, GP433, GP340, GP440	269-271 mm (10.56-10.64 in.)	4.5-6.5 mm (0.18-0.26 in.)
GPX338, GPX433, ET250, ET340	269-271 mm (10.56-10.64 in.)	10-12 mm (0.39-0.47 in.)
ET300	264-268 mm (10.39-10.55 in.)	10-12 mm (0.39-0.47 in.)

CHAPTER ONE

GENERAL INFORMATION

Snowmobiling has, in recent years, become one of the most popular outdoor winter recreational pastimes. It provides an opportunity for an entire family to experience the splendor of winter and enjoy a season previously regarded by many as miserable.

Snowmobiles also provide an invaluable service in the form of rescue and utility vehicles in areas that would otherwise be inaccessible.

As with all sophisticated machines, snowmobiles require specific periodic maintenance and repair to ensure their reliability and usefulness.

MANUAL ORGANIZATION

This manual provides information for periodic maintenance, tune-up, and general repair procedures for Yamaha snowmobiles manufactured in 1976 and later.

This chapter provides general information and hints to make all snowmobile work easier and more rewarding. Additional sections cover snowmobile operation, safety, and survival techniques.

Chapter Two provides all tune-up and periodic maintenance required to keep your snowmobile in top running condition.

Chapter Three provides numerous methods and suggestions for finding and fixing troubles fast. The chapter also describes how a 2-cycle engine works, to help you analyze troubles logically. Troubleshooting procedures discuss typical symptoms and logical methods to pinpoint the trouble.

Subsequent chapters describe specific systems such as the engine, fuel system, electrical system, and power train. Each provides disassembly, inspection, repair, and reassembly procedures in easy-to-follow, step-by-step form. If a repair is impractical for the owner/mechanic, it is so indicated. Usually, such repairs are quicker and more economically done by a Yamaha dealer or other competent snowmobile repair shop.

Tables are found at the end of the chapter.

Some of the procedures in this manual call for special tools. In all cases, the tool is illustrated, often in actual use.

The terms NOTE, CAUTION, and WARNING have specific meanings in this book. A NOTE provides additional information to make a step or procedure easier or clearer. Disregarding a NOTE could cause inconvenience, but would not cause damage or personal injury.

A CAUTION emphasizes areas where equipment damage could result. Disregarding a CAUTION could cause permanent mechanical damage; however, personal injury is unlikely.

A WARNING emphasizes areas where personal injury or death could result from negligence. Mechanical damage may also occur. WARNINGS are to be taken seriously. In some cases, severe injury or death has been caused by mechanics disregarding similar warnings.

IDENTIFICATION AND
PARTS REPLACEMENT

Each snowmobile has a serial number applicable to the machine and a model and serial number for the engine.

Figure 1 shows the location of the machine serial number on the right side of the tunnel. **Figure 2** shows the location of engine model and serial numbers on the fan case for air-cooled models. On liquid-cooled models the number is on the right side of the crankcase. Unless specifically noted, all serial numbers called out in procedures in this manual are machine serial numbers and not engine numbers.

Write down all serial and model numbers applicable to your machine and carry the numbers with you when you order parts from a dealer. Always order by year and engine and machine numbers. If possible, compare the old parts with the new ones before purchasing them. If the parts are not alike, have the parts man explain the reason for the difference and insist on assurance that the new parts will fit and are correct.

OPERATION

With the exception of SRX and SSR models, Yamaha snowmobiles are equipped with Autolube and require no pre-mixing of fuel and oil.

WARNING
Serious fire hazards always exist around gasoline. Do not allow any smoking in areas where fuel is mixed or when re-fueling your snowmobile.

Always use fresh fuel. Gasoline loses its potency after sitting for a period of time. Old fuel can cause engine failure and leave you stranded in severe weather.

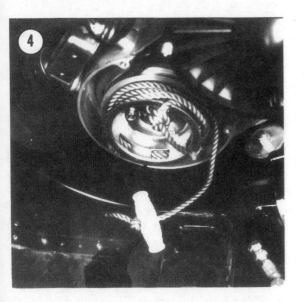

Correct fuel/oil mixing is essential for the life and efficiency of the engine. Engine lubrication for SRX models is provided by oil mixed with the gasoline. Always mix fuel in exact proportions. A "too lean" mixture can cause serious and expensive damage, and a "too rich" mixture can cause poor performance and fouled spark plugs which make the engine difficult or impossible to start.

Use a premium grade gasoline with an octane rating of 90 or higher. Mix gasoline and oil in a separate tank — not the snowmobile fuel tank. The mixing tank should be larger than the amount of fuel being mixed to permit room for the fuel to agitate and mix thoroughly.

Use Yamalube oil or an equivalent. Use a fuel/oil ratio of 20:1 (SRX models — **Table 1**) or 15:1 (SSR models — **Table 2**).

1. Pour the required amount of oil into a clean and empty mixing can.

2. Add ½ the gasoline required and mix thoroughly.

3. Add the remainder of required gasoline and mix thoroughly once again.

4. Fill the snowmobile tank with "mix" using a funnel equipped with a fine-mesh filter screen.

Pre-start Inspection

1. Familiarize yourself with your machine, the owner's manual, and all the decals on the snowmobile.

2. Clean the windshield with a clean, damp cloth. *Do not* use gasoline, solvents, or abrasive cleaners.

3. Check all ski and steering components for wear and loose parts. Correct any unsatisfactory conditions.

4. Check track tension and adjust it if necessary.

5. Check the operation of the throttle and brake controls and ensure that they are free and correctly adjusted.

6. Check the fuel level and top it up if necessary.

7. Check the coolant on liquid-cooled models.

> **WARNING**
> *Before starting the engine, be sure no bystanders are in front of or behind the snowmobile; a sudden lurch of the machine could cause serious injury.*

8. Start the engine and test the operation of the emergency kill switch and the tether switch. Check to make sure all the lights are working.

Emergency Starting

Always carry a small tool kit with you, and carry an extra starting rope for emergency starting.

1. Open the hood.

2. Remove recoil starter assembly (**Figure 3**).

3. Wind the starting rope around the starter pulley and pull to crank the engine (**Figure 4**).

Emergency Stopping

To stop the engine in case of an emergency, pull the tether string or switch the emergency kill switch to STOP or OFF.

Towing

When preparing for a long trip, pack extra equipment in a sled; do not try to haul it on the snowmobile. A sled is also ideal for transporting small children.

> **WARNING**
> *Never tow a sled with ropes or pull straps. Always use a rigid tow bar. The use of ropes or flexible straps could result in a tailgate accident if the tow vehicle stops suddenly.*

If it is necessary to tow a disabled snowmobile, securely fasten the disabled machine's skis to the hitch of the tow machine. Remove the drive belt from the disabled machine and tow it at low to moderate speeds.

Clearing the Track

If the snowmobile has been operated in deep or slushy snow, it is necessary to clear the track after stopping to prevent the track from freezing and making starting and running difficult the next time.

WARNING
Make sure no one is behind the machine when clearing the track. Ice and rocks thrown from the track can cause injury.

Tip the snowmobile on its side until the track clears the ground *completely*. Run the track at a moderate speed until all the ice and snow is thrown clear.

CAUTION
If the track does freeze, it must be broken loose manually. Attempting to force a frozen track with the engine will burn and damage the drive belt.

Proper Clothing

Warm and comfortable clothing is essential to provide protection from frostbite. Even mild temperatures can be very uncomfortable and dangerous when combined with a strong wind or when traveling at high speed. See **Table 3** for wind chill factors. Always dress according to what the wind chill factor is, not the temperature. Check with your dealer for suggested types of snowmobile clothing.

WARNING
To provide additional warmth as well as protection against head injury, always wear an approved safety helmet when snowmobiling.

SERVICE HINTS

All procedures described in this book can be performed by anyone reasonably handy with tools. Special tools are required for some procedures; their operation is described and illustrated. These may be purchased at Yamaha dealers. If you are on good terms with the dealer's service department, you may be able to borrow from them; however, it should be kept in mind that many of the tools will pay for themselves after the first or second use, particularly such tools as sheave alignment and distance gauges. If special tools are required, make arrangements to have them on hand before starting. It is frustrating and sometimes more expensive to begin a job and then find out you are unable to finish it.

Service will be far easier if the machine is clean before you begin work on it. There are special cleaners for washing the engine and related parts. Just brush or spray on the cleaning solution, let it stand, then rinse it away with a garden hose. Clean all oily or greasy parts with cleaning solvent as they are removed.

WARNING
Never use gasoline as a cleaning agent. It represents an extreme fire hazard. Be sure to work in a well-ventilated area when using cleaning solvent. Keep a fire extinguisher handy, just in case.

Observe the following practices and you will save time, effort, and frustration as well as prevent possible expensive damage.

1. Tag all internal parts for location and mark all mating parts for position. Small parts such as bolts can be identified by placing them in plastic bags and sealing and labeling the bags with masking tape.

2. Frozen or very tight bolts and screws can often be loosened by by soaking them with penetrating oil such as WD-40® , then sharply striking the bolt head a few times with a hammer and punch (or screwdriver for screws). A hammer driven impact tool can also be very effective. However, ensure tool is seated squarely on the bolt or nut before striking. Avoid heat unless absolutely necessary, since it may melt, warp, or remove the temper from many parts.

3. Avoid flames or sparks when working near flammable liquids such as gasoline.

4. No parts, except those assembled with a press fit, require unusual force during assembly. If a part is hard to remove or install, find out why before proceeding.

5. Cover all openings after removing parts to keep dirt, small tools, etc., from falling in.

6. Clean all parts as you go along and keep them separated into subassemblies. The use of trays, jars, or cans will make reassembly that much easier.

7. Make diagrams whenever similar-appearing parts are found. You may *think* you can remember where everything came from — but mistakes are costly. There is also the possibility you may be sidetracked and not return to work for days or even weeks — in which interval carefully laid out parts may become disturbed.

8. Wiring should be tagged with masking tape and marked as each wire is removed. Again, do not rely on memory alone.

9. When reassembling parts, be sure all shims and washers are replaced exactly as they came out. Whenever a rotating part butts against a stationary part, look for a shim or washer. Use new gaskets if there is any doubt about the condition of old ones. Generally, you should apply gasket cement to only one mating surface so the parts may be easily disassembled in the future. A thin coat of oil on gaskets helps them seal effectively.

10. Heavy grease can be used to hold small parts in place if they tend to fall out during assembly. However, keep grease and oil away from electrical and brake components.

11. High spots may be sanded off a piston with sandpaper, but emery cloth and oil do a much more professional job.

12. Carburetors are best cleaned by disassembling them and soaking the parts in a commercial carburetor cleaner. Never soak gaskets and rubber parts in these cleaners. Never use wire to clean out jets and air passages; they are easily damaged. Use compressed air to blow out the carburetor only if the float has been removed first.

13. Take your time and do the job right. Do not forget that a newly rebuilt snowmobile engine must be broken in the same as a new one. Keep rpm's within the limits given in your owner's manual when you get back on the snow.

14. Work safely in a good work area with adequate lighting and allow sufficient time for a repair task.

15. When assembling 2 parts, start all fasteners, then tighten evenly.

16. Before undertaking a job, read the entire section in this manual which pertains to it. Study the illustrations and text until you have a good idea of what is involved. Many procedures are complicated and errors can be disastrous. When you thoroughly understand what is to be done, follow the prescribed procedure step-by-step.

TOOLS

Every snowmobiler should carry a small tool kit to help make minor adjustments as well as perform emergency repairs.

A normal assortment of ordinary hand tools is required to perform the repair tasks outlined in this manual. The following list represents the minimum requirement:

   a. American and metric combination wrenches
   b. American and metric socket wrenches
   c. Assorted screwdrivers
   d. Pliers
   e. Feeler gauges
   f. Spark plug wrench
   g. Small hammer
   h. Plastic or rubber mallet
   i. Parts cleaning brush

When purchasing tools, always get quality tools. They cost more initially but in most cases will last a lifetime. Remember, the initial expense of new tools is easily offset by the money saved on a few repair jobs.

Tune-up and troubleshooting require a few special tools. All of the following special tools are used in this manual, however all tools are not necessary for all machines. Read the procedures applicable to your machine to determine what your special tool requirements are.

1. *Ignition gauge* (**Figure 5**). This tool combines round wire spark plug gap gauges with narrow breaker point feeler gauges. The device costs about $3 at auto accessory stores.

2. *Impact driver* (**Figure 6**). This tool might have been designed with the snowmobiler in mind. It makes removal of screws easy, and eliminates damaged screw slots. Good ones run about $12 at larger hardware stores.

3. *Hydrometer* (**Figure 7**). This instrument measures state of charge of the battery, and tells much about battery condition. Such an instrument is available at any auto parts store and through most larger mail order outlets. Satisfactory ones cost as little as $3.

4. *Multimeter or* VOM (**Figure 8**). This instrument is invaluable for electrical system troubleshooting and service. A few of its functions may be duplicated by locally fabricated substitutes, but for the serious hobbyist, it is a must. Its uses are described in the applicable sections of this book. Prices start at around $10 at electronics hobbyists stores and mail order outlets.

5. *Timing gauge* (**Figure 9**). This device is used to precisely locate position of piston before top dead center to achieve the most accurate ignition timing. The instrument is screwed into the spark plug hole and indicates inches and/or milimeters. The tool shown costs about $20 and

is available from most dealers and mail order houses. Less expensive tools, which use a vernier scale instead of a dial indicator, are also available.

6. *Air flow meter or carburetor synchronizer* (**Figure 10**). This device is used on engines with multiple carburetors to fine tune the synchronization and idle speed. The tool shown costs about $10-15 at most dealers, auto parts stores, and mail order houses.

7. *Compression gauge* (**Figure 11**). The compression gauge measures the compression pressure built up in each cylinder. The results, when properly interpreted, indicate general piston, cylinder, ring, and head gasket condition. Gauges are available with, or without, the flexible hose. Prices start around $5 at most auto parts stores and mail order outlets.

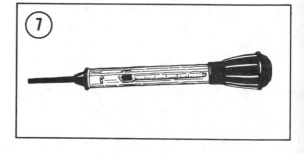

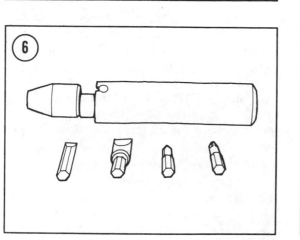

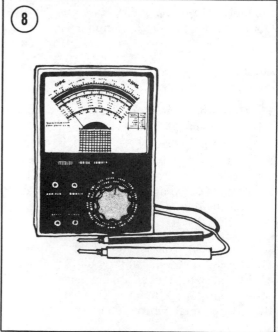

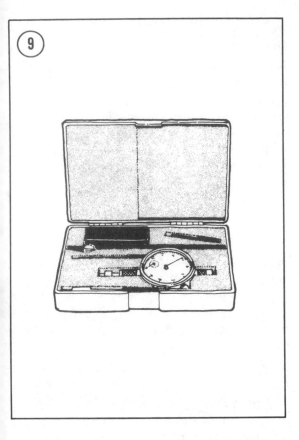

EXPENDABLE SUPPLIES

Certain expendable supplies are also required. These include grease, oil, gasket cement, wiping rags, cleaning solvent, and distilled water. Solvent is available at many service stations. Distilled water, required for the battery, is available at every supermarket. An increasing number of mechanics clean oily parts with a solution of common household detergent or laundry powder.

WORKING SAFELY

Professional mechanics can work for years without sustaining serious injury. If you observe a few rules of common sense and safety, you can enjoy many safe hours servicing your own machine. You can also hurt yourself or damage the machine if you ignore these rules.

1. Never use gasoline as a cleaning solvent.

2. Never smoke or use a torch in the area of flammable liquids, such as cleaning solvent in open containers.

3. Never smoke or use a torch in an area where batteries are charging. Highly explosive hydrogen gas is formed during the charging process.

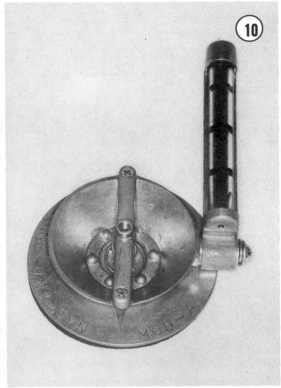

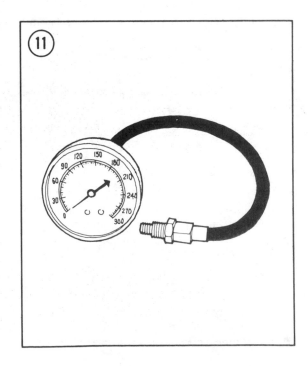

4. If welding or brazing is required on the machine, remove the fuel tank to a safe distance, at least 50 feet away.

5. Be sure to use properly sized wrenches for nut turning.

6. If a nut is tight, think for a moment what would happen to your hand should the wrench slip. Be guided accordingly.

7. Keep your work area clean and uncluttered.

8. Wear safety goggles in all operations involving drilling, grinding, or use of a chisel.

9. Never use worn tools.

10. Keep a fire extinguisher handy. Be sure it is rated for gasoline and electrical fires.

SNOWMOBILE CODE OF ETHICS

When snowmobiling, always observe the following code of ethics as provided by the International Snowmobile Industry Association.

1. I will be a good sportsman. I recognize that people judge all snowmobile owners by my actions. I will use my influence with other snowmobile owners to promote sportsmanlike conduct.

2. I will not litter trails or camping areas. I will not pollute streams or lakes.

3. I will not damage living trees, shrubs, or other natural features.

4. I will respect other people's property and rights.

5. I will lend a helping hand when I see someone in distress.

6. I will make myself and my vehicle available to assist search and rescue parties.

7. I will not interfere with or harass hikers, skiers, snowshoers, ice fishermen, or other winter sportsmen. I will respect their rights to enjoy our recreation facilities.

8. I will know and obey all federal, state, and local rules regulating the operation of snowmobiles in areas where I use my vehicle. I will inform public officials when using public lands.

9. I will not harass wildlife. I will avoid areas posted for the protection or feeding of wildlife.

10. I will stay on marked trails or marked roads open to snowmobiles. I will avoid country travel unless specifically authorized.

SNOWMOBILE SAFETY

General Tips

1. Read your owner's manual and know your machine.

2. Check throttle and brake controls before starting the engine. Frozen controls can cause serious injury.

3. Know how to make an emergency stop.

4. Know all state, provincial, federal, and local laws concerning snowmobiling. Respect private property.

5. Never add fuel while smoking or when engine is running. Always use fresh, properly mixed fuel. Improper fuel mixtures can cause engine failure, and can leave you stranded in severe weather.

6. Wear adequate clothing to avoid frostbite. Never wear any loose scarves or belts that could catch in moving parts or on tree limbs.

7. Wear eye and head protection. Wear tinted goggles or face shields to guard against snow-blindness. Never wear yellow eye protection.

8. Never allow anyone to operate the snowmobile without proper instruction.

9. Use the "buddy system" for long trips. A snowmobile travels farther in 30 minutes than you can walk in a day.

10. Take along sufficient tools and spare parts for emergency field repairs.

11. Use a sled with a stiff tow bar for carrying extra supplies. Do not overload your snowmobile.

12. Carry emergency survival supplies when going on long trips. Notify friends and relatives of your destination and expected arrival time.

13. Never attempt to repair your machine while the engine is running.

14. Check all machine components and hardware frequently, especially skis and steering.

15. Never lift rear of machine to clear the track. Tip machine on its side and be sure no one is behind machine.

16. Winch snowmobile onto a tilt-bed trailer, never drive it on. Secure machine firmly to trailer and ensure trailer lights operate.

Operating Tips

1. Never operate the vehicle in crowded areas, or steer toward persons.

2. Avoid avalanche areas and other unsafe terrain.

3. Cross highways (where permitted) at a 90 degree angle after looking in both directions. Post traffic guards if crossing in groups.

4. Do not ride snowmobile on or near railroad tracks. The snowmobile engine can drown out the sound of an approaching train. It is difficult to maneuver the snowmobile from between the tracks.

5. Do not ride snowmobile on ski slope areas with skiers.

6. Always check the thickness of the ice before riding on frozen lakes or rivers. Do not panic if you go through ice; conserve energy.

7. Keep headlight and taillight areas free of snow and never ride at night without lights.

8. Do not ride snowmobile without shields, guards, and protective hoods.

9. Do not attempt to open new trails at night. Follow established trails or unseen barbed wire or guy wires may cause serious injury or death.

10. Always steer with both hands.

11. Be aware of terrain and avoid operating snowmobile at excessive speed.

12. Do not panic if throttle sticks. Pull "tether" string or push emergency stop switch.

13. Drive more slowly when carrying a passenger, especially a child.

14. Always allow adequate stopping distance based on ground cover conditions. Ice requires a greater stopping distance to avoid skidding. Apply brakes gradually on ice.

15. Do not speed through wooded areas. Hidden obstructions, hanging limbs, unseen ditches, and even wild animals can cause accidents.

16. Do not tailgate. Rear end collisions can cause injury and machine damage.

17. Do not mix alcoholic beverages with snowmobiling.

18. Keep feet on footrests at all times. Do not permit feet to hang over sides or attempt to stabilize machine with feet when making turns or in near-spill situations; broken limbs could result.

19. Do not stand on seat, stunt, or show-off.

20. Do not jump snowmobile. Injury or machine damage could result.

21. Always keep hands and feet out of the track area when engine is running. Use extra care when freeing snowmobile from deep snow.

22. Check fuel supply regularly. Do not travel further than your fuel will permit you to return.

23. Whenever you leave your machine unattended, remove the "tether" switch.

Preparing for a Trip

1. Check all bolts and fasteners for tightness. Do not operate your snowmobile unless it is in top operating condition.

2. Check weather forecasts before starting out on a trip. Cancel your plans if a storm is possible.

3. Study maps of the area before the trip and know where help is located. Note locations of phones, resorts, shelters, towns, farms, and ranches. Know where fuel is available. If possible, use the buddy system.

4. Do not overload your snowmobile. Use a sled with a stiff tow bar to haul extra supplies.

5. Do not risk a heart attack if your snowmobile gets stuck in deep snow. Carry a small block and tackle for such situations. Never allow anyone to manually pull on the skis while you attempt to drive machine out.

6. Do not ride beyond one-half the round trip cruising range of your fuel supply. Keep in mind how far it is home.

7. Always carry emergency survival supplies when going on long trips or traveling in unknown territory. Notify friends and relatives of your destination and expected arrival time.

8. Carry adequate eating and cooking utensils (small pans, kettle, plates, cups, etc.) on longer trips. Carry matches in a waterproof container, candles for building a fire, and easy-to-pack food that will not be damaged by freezing. Carry dry food or space energy sticks for emergency rations.

9. Pack extra clothing, a tent, sleeping bag, hand axe, and compass. A first aid kit and snow shoes may also come in handy. Space age blankets (one side silverfoil) furnish warmth and can be used as heat reflectors or signaling devices for aerial search parties.

Emergency Survival Techniques

1. Do not panic in the event of an emergency. Relax, think the situation over, then decide on a course of action. You may be within a short distance of help. If possible, repair your snowmobile so you can drive to safety. Conserve your energy and stay warm.

2. Keep hands and feet active to promote circulation and avoid frostbite while servicing your machine.

3. Mentally retrace your route. Where was the last point where help could be located? Do not attempt to walk long distances in deep snow. Make yourself comfortable until help arrives.

4. If you are properly equipped for your trip you can turn any undesirable area into a suitable campsite.

5. If necessary, build a small shelter with tree branches or evergreen boughs. Look for a cave or sheltered area against a hill or cliff. Even burrowing in the snow offers protection from the cold and wind.

6. Prepare a signal fire using evergreen boughs and snowmobile oil. If you cannot build a fire, make an S-O-S in the snow.

7. Use a policeman's whistle or beat cooking utensils to attract attention or frighten off wild animals.

8. When your camp is established, climb the nearest hill and determine your whereabouts. Observe landmarks on the way, so you can find your way back to your campsite. Do not rely on your footprints. They may be covered by blowing snow.

Table 1   20:1 FUEL/OIL MIXING RATIO —
SRX MODELS

Fuel	Oil	
U.S. Gallons	oz.	cc
0.5	3.2	95
1.0	6.4	189
1.5	9.6	283
2.0	12.8	378
2.5	16.0	473
5.0	32.0	946
Liters		cc
1.0		50
2.0		100
3.0		150
4.0		200
5.0		250
6.0		300

Table 2   15:1 FUEL/OIL MIXING
RATIO — SSR MODELS

Fuel	Oil	
U.S. Gallons	oz.	cc
0.5	4.25	126
1.0	8.5	252
1.5	12.75	377
2.0	17.0	502
2.5	21.25	628
5.0	42.5	1256
Liters		cc
1.0		67
2.0		134
3.0		200
4.0		266
5.0		333
6.0		400

Table 3   WIND CHILL FACTORS

Estimated Wind Speed in MPH	Actual Thermometer Reading (° F)											
	50	40	30	20	10	0	—10	—20	—30	—40	—50	—60
	Equivalent Temperature (° F)											
Calm	50	40	30	20	10	0	—10	—20	—30	—40	—50	—60
5	48	37	27	16	6	—5	—15	—26	—36	—47	—57	—68
10	40	28	16	4	—9	—21	—33	—46	—58	—70	—83	—95
15	36	22	9	—5	—18	—36	—45	—58	—72	—85	—99	—112
20	32	18	4	—10	—25	—39	—53	—67	—82	—96	—110	—124
25	30	16	0	—15	—29	—44	—59	—74	—88	—104	—118	—133
30	28	13	—2	—18	—33	—48	—63	—79	—94	—109	—125	—140
35	27	11	—4	—20	—35	—49	—67	—82	—98	—113	—129	—145
40	26	10	—6	—21	—37	—53	—69	—85	—100	—116	—132	—148

*									
	Little Danger (for properly clothed person)				**Increasing Danger**		**Great Danger**		
					• Danger from freezing of exposed flesh •				

*Wind speeds greater than 40 mph have little additional effect.

CHAPTER TWO

PERIODIC MAINTENANCE

A program of regular routine maintenance will ensure that your snowmobile will provide many hours of efficient, trouble-free service. An afternoon or evening spent now, cleaning, inspecting, and adjusting, can prevent costly mechanical problems in the future and unexpected and often dangerous breakdowns on the trail.

The procedures described in this chapter are simple and straightforward. They are arranged by service interval so that tasks that should be carried out at one time are grouped together to make servicing easy and more enjoyable. Tables are at the end of the chapter.

SERVICE INTERVALS

Factory-recommended service intervals are shown in **Tables 1 and 2**. Service interval requirements may vary depending on type of use; for example, for extremely hard use, over rough and uncertain terrain, track adjustment and condition should be checked more frequently than recommended in the table.

Although many of the items to be checked won't require any actual service, even after many hours of use, it's a good idea to follow the recommendations to help you to develop the habit of carrying out a systematic inspection. It can serve to warn of impending trouble and it will allow you to become familiar with your machine and gain some confidence about its condition and your ability to take care of it. A day of riding is much more pleasant if you're not worrying about the condition of your snowmobile.

PRE-RIDE CHECKS

The checks and inspection that follow should be carried out before each ride.

Fuel Level

Check the fuel gauge (**Figure 1**) and top up the tank if it is not full. Even if you are planning on riding a short distance, it's a good idea to begin with a full tank of gas; an unexpected change in weather or trail conditions could require you to be out longer than you had anticipated.

Drive Belt

Raise the hood and check the condition of the drive belt. If it is severely worn, cracked, damaged, or deteriorated, it should be replaced.

Oil Level

Check the level in the oil tank and fill it if it is less than half full. Use Yamalube 2-Cycle Oil or an equivalent.

Engine Stop Switch

Start the engine and allow it to warm up to the point that it will idle the throttle unattended. Then, operate the engine STOP switch, and if the engine does not shut off, refer to Chapter Six and locate and correct the trouble before riding the machine.

Tether Switch

Start the engine and allow it to idle. Disconnect the tether switch, and if the engine does not shut off, refer to Chapter Six and locate and correct the trouble before riding the machine.

Lights

Check the operation of the headlight, taillight, and stoplight. If any are not operating, refer to Chapter Six and locate and correct the trouble before riding the machine.

Track

Before riding, check the track to make sure it's not frozen. If it is, lean the machine over and free the track by hand; *do not free the track with the engine, otherwise the drive belt may wear and burn.*

20 HOURS OR 250 MILES (400 KM)

The following checks and corrections should be made every 20 hours or 250 miles (400 km) of operation.

Engine Mounts and Fasteners

Check the engine mounting bolts (2 front and 2 rear — **Figure 2**) to make sure they are tight. Check the bolts on the air shroud (**Figure 3**), manifolds (**Figures 4 and 5**), and starter assembly (**Figure 6**).

Oil and Fuel Lines

Inspect the oil and fuel lines for loose connections and damage. Tighten all connections and replace any lines that are damaged or cracked.

Spark Plugs

Remove the spark plugs, clean them, and check and reset the gap if necessary. Refer to Table 2 in Chapter Six for gap and spark plug specifications.

Drive System Fasteners

Check the mounting bolts on the chaincase for tightness (**Figure 7**).

Check the track assembly mounting bolts (**Figure 8**) for tightness.

Ski Runners

Inspect the ski runners (skags) for wear (**Figure 9**) and replace them if they are more than half worn down or are cracked at the mounting studs. Refer to Chapter Eight.

Drive Belt

Check the condition of the drive belt and replace it if it is severely worn.

Check the adjustment of the belt as described in Chapter Seven.

Body Fasteners

Tighten any loose body bolts. Replace loose rivets by first drilling out the old rivet and then installing a new one with a pop-riveter. This tool, along with an assortment of rivets, is available through many hardware and auto parts stores. Follow the manufacturer's instructions for installing rivets.

Electrical Leads

Inspect the high-tension electrical leads to the spark plugs for cracks and breaks in the insulation and replace the leads if they are less than perfect; breaks in the insulation allow the spark to arc to ground and will impair engine performance.

Check primary ignition wiring and lighting wiring for damaged insulation. Usually minor damage can be repaired by wrapping the damaged area with electrical insulating tape. If insulation damage is extensive, the affected section of wire should be replaced.

40 HOURS OR
500 MILES (800 KM)

The following checks and corrections should be carried out every 40 hours or 500 miles (800 km) of operation.

Recoil Starter

Pull out the starter rop and inspect it for fraying. If its condition is questionable, refer to Chapter Four, *Starter,* and replace the rope.

Check the action of the starter. It should be smooth, and when the rope is released, it should return all the way. If the action of the starter is rough, or if the rope does not return, refer to Chapter Four, *Starter,* and service the starter as described.

Starter Valve

Routinely check the operation and adjustment of the starter valve at this interval or at any time starting is difficult. Pull up on the starter cable sheath **(Figure 10)** and check the free play of the sheath and the adjuster. The free play should be 0.5-1.0 mm (0.02-0.04 in.).

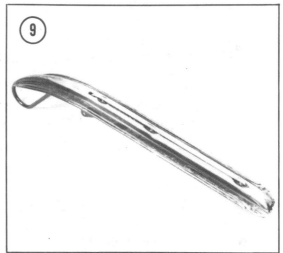

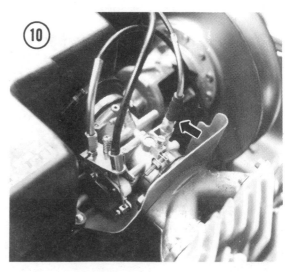

See **Figure 11**. If adjustment is required, loosen
the locknut and turn the adjuster in or out until
the free play is correct. Then, without further
turning the adjuster, tighten the locknut.

Oil Pump

Check and adjust the oil pump stroke as
described in Chapter Four, *Oil Pump*.

Primary Drive

Check the clutch bolt for tightness. It should
be 43 ft.-lb. (6 mkg).

Check the contact surfaces of the sheaves. If
they are scored or severely worn, the clutch
should be replaced.

Secondary Drive

Check the spring tension of the secondary
drive sheaves by pressing in on the moveable
sheave while turning it clockwise. There should
be a great deal of spring resistance.

Check the contact surfaces of the secondary
sheaves. If they are scored or severely worn, the
sheave assembly should be replaced.

Sheave Distance

Measure the distance between the sheave
centers (**Figure 12**). If the distance is not as
specified in **Table 3**, loosen the mounting bolts
on the primary chaincase (**Figure 13**) and move
the case forward or back as required. Then
tighten the bolts and recheck the distance.

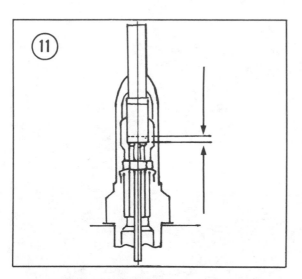

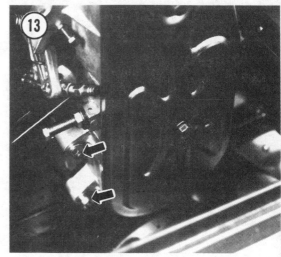

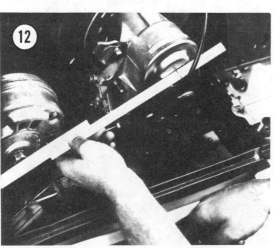

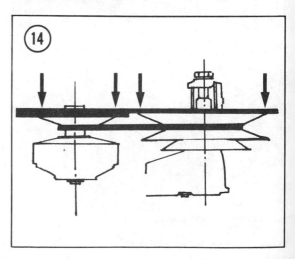

Sheeve Offset

Measure the sheave offset with a sheave gauge (**Figure 14**). If the offset is not as specified in **Table 3**, loosen the engine mounting bolts (**Figure 15** — 2 front and 2 rear) and move the engine right or left as required. Then tighten the bolts and recheck the offset.

> NOTE: *Sheave gauges are available through dealers for just a few dollars, or one can be made using the offset dimension shown in* **Table 3**.

Brake

There are 3 distinct brake designs used on Yamaha models covered in this handbook, designated Type I, Type II, and Type III (**Figure 16**).

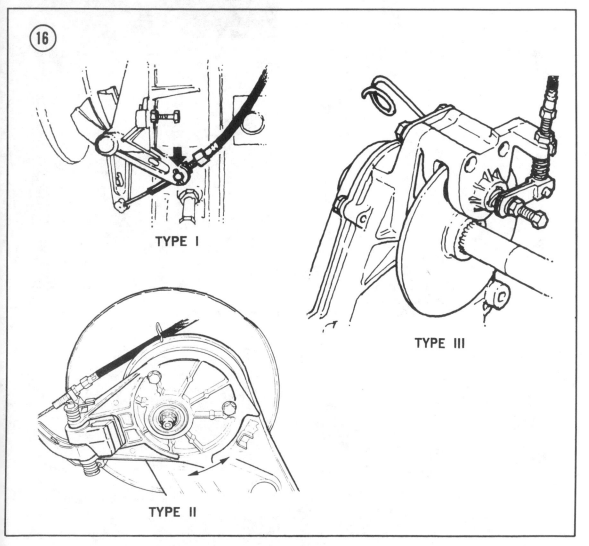

TYPE I

TYPE III

TYPE II

NOTE: *These designations are not Yamaha's. They are used in this handbook for convenience and understanding when describing the different brake types.*

Type I

Inspect the brake pads for wear. If the material thickness is less than 1 mm (0.04 in.), replace the pads as described in Chapter Seven, *Brake, Pad Replacement — Type I.*

Check brake adjustment. The clearance between the pads and the disc should be 0.1-1.0 mm (0.008-0.04 in.). If the clearance is not correct, adjust the outer pad by loosening the locknut on the adjuster bolt (**Figure 17**) and screwing the bolt in or out as required. Then, without further turning the bolt, tighten the locknut.

Adjust the inner pad by loosening the locknut on the cable adjuster (**Figure 18**) and turning the adjuster sleeve in or out as required. Then, without further turning the adjuster, tighten the locknut.

Check the operation of the brake to make sure the pads clamp the disc firmly when the brake is applied, and that they retract when the brake is released.

NOTE: *Do not lubricate the brake cable; extremely cold temperatures would cause the lubricant to thicken and make operation of the brake difficult. A small amount of low-temperature grease should be applied to the end of the cable where it engages the hand lever.*

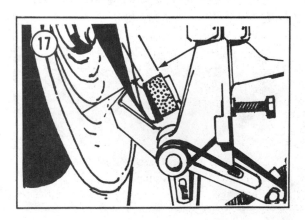

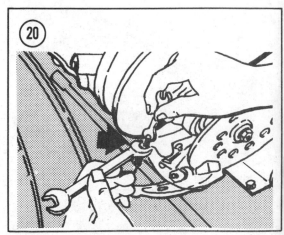

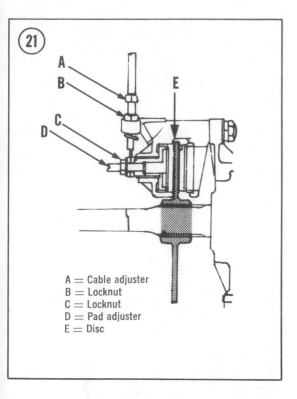

A = Cable adjuster
B = Locknut
C = Locknut
D = Pad adjuster
E = Disc

Type II

Inspect the brake pads for wear. If the material is less than 5 mm (0.2 in.) thick, replace the pads as described in Chapter Seven, *Brake, Pad Replacement — Type II.*

Check brake adjustment. The clearance between the pads and the disc should be 1 mm (0.04 in.). Adjust the inner pad by loosening the locknut (**Figure 19**) and turning the adjuster in (to decrease clearance) or out (to increase clearance) until the clearance is correct. Then, tighten the locknut.

Adjust the outer pad by loosening the locknut on the cable adjuster (**Figure 20**) and turning the adjuster out (to decrease clearance) or in (to increase clearance) until the clearance is correct. Then, tighten the locknut.

Type III

Inspect the brake pads for wear. If the material is less than 4 mm (0.16 in.) thick, replace the pads as described in Chapter Seven, *Brake, Pad Replacement — Type III.*

Check brake adjustment. Insert a flat feeler gauge (0.15 mm-0.006 in.) between the disc and the inner pad (**Figure 21**). Loosen the locknut on the adjuster and turn the adjuster in just until the pad makes contact with the gauge. Then, hold the adjuster to prevent it from turning further and tighten the locknut.

Loosen the locknut on the cable adjuster and turn the adjuster in or out to obtain a free play of 5 mm (0.21 in.) for the cable sheath when it is pulled away from the adjuster. Then tighten the locknut on the cable adjuster.

Guide Wheels

Inspect the rubber on the guide (idler) wheels for wear and damage (**Figure 22**). Replace the wheels if they are in poor condition. Refer to Chapter Nine, *Suspension Removal/Installation* for the correct procedure.

Drive Sprocket

Inspect the teeth on the drive sprockets for wear and damage (**Figure 23**). If the sprockets are damaged, replace them. Refer to Chapter Seven.

Track

Check the adjustment and alignment of the track as described in Chapter Nine.

Inspect the track for damage and wear. Refer to Chapter Three and determine the reasons for wear and damage before installing a new track so that the cause can be corrected beforehand to prevent damage to the new track.

Suspension

Inspect the suspension for damage, such as bent axles, and for loose or missing fasteners.

Drive Chain

Check the adjustment of the drive chain. Remove the inspection plug from the chaincase cover (**Figure 24**) and check the movement of the chain. It should be 8-15 mm (0.32-0.6 in.).

If adjustment is required, loosen the locknut and turn the adjuster bolt (**Figure 25**) in or out as required. Then, without further turning the adjuster, tighten the locknut.

Check the chaincase oil level by removing the level plug from the rear of the chaincase. The plug can be reached through a vent hole in the body (**Figure 26**). Oil should just seep out the hole. If not, slowly add oil (API GL-3, SAE 75 or 80) through the inspection hole until it begins to seep out the level hole. Then, install and tighten the level plug and install the inspection plug.

Ski Alignment

Check the alignment of the skis (**Figure 27**). Toe-out (the difference that dimension A is greater than dimension B) should be no greater than 0.6 mm (¼ in.).

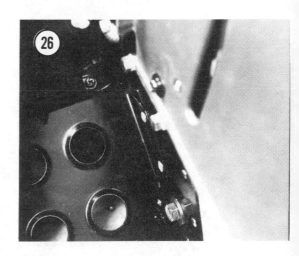

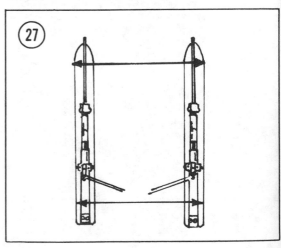

2

If adjustment is required, loosen the locknut on the steering cross-rod (**Figure 28**) and turn the rod in or out until toe-out is correct. Then, without further turning the rod, tighten the locknut.

Fuel Tank and Lines

Remove the seat and fuel tank cover and inspect the tank for cracks and abrasion (see Chapter Five, *Fuel Tank*). If the tank is damaged and leaking or is likely to leak in the near future, replace it.

Check the lines for loose connections and damage and replace any that are damaged.

Oil Tank

Inspect the oil tank for cracks and abrasions that are leaking or may soon be and replace the tank if its condition is in doubt.

80 HOURS OR 1,000 MILES (1,600 KM)

Following 80 hours or 1,000 miles (1,600 km) of operation, measure cylinder compression to determine if the bore and piston rings are still sealing correctly.

Start the engine and allow it to warm up, then shut it off. Remove the spark plug and insert a compression gauge into the plug bore. With assistance, crank the engine several times, until the gauge ceases to rise. The gauge should indicate 110-130 lb. If the pressure is substantially lower, i.e., less than 100 lb., the engine upper end should be serviced. Refer to Chapter Four, *Upper-end Service.*

ANNUALLY

The following checks, inspections, and adjustments should be carried out at the end of the winter season, when the machine is taken out of service prior to being stored for summer.

Upper-end Decarbonization

Decarbonization of the upper end involves cleaning the piston crown, combustion chamber, and exhaust port in the cylinder. Refer to Chapter Four, *Upper-end Service*, for the correct procedures.

Ignition Timing

Check and adjust the ignition timing as described in Chapter Six, *Ignition Timing*.

Carburetor Service

Clean, inspect, and adjust the carburetor as described in Chapter Five.

Fuel Tank

Refer to Chapter Five, *Fuel Tank,* and remove, clean, and reinstall the fuel tank.

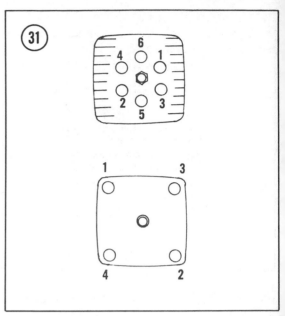

Fuel Filter

Refer to Chapter Five, *Fuel Filter,* and replace the fuel filter.

Oil Filter

Replace the oil filter (**Figure 29**).

LUBRICATION

The lubrication services that follow should be carried out at the intervals shown in **Table 4**. The table also lists recommended lubricants.

Lubrication of the primary or drive sheave should be entrusted to a dealer; special tools are required to disassemble and assemble the unit.

40 HOURS OR
400 MILES (600 KM)

Primary Sheave

Lubricate the weights and roller pins in the primary sheave.

Secondary Sheave

Refer to Chapter Seven, *Driven Sheave,* and remove the sheave assembly and lubricate the shaft and the movable sheave.

Front Axle Housing

Refer to Chapter Seven, *Front Axle,* and

remove the front axle and grease the right axle housing.

Drive Chain Oil

Refer to Chapter Seven, *Drive Chain,* and drain and refill the chaincase.

Steering

Refer to Chapter Eight, *Steering,* lubricate the steering post and linkage.

Skis

Refer to Chapter Eight, *Skis,* and lubricate the ski pivot shafts, wear plates, and retaining pins.

TUNE-UP

The factory-recommended intervals for checking the factors relating to engine tuning (spark plug condition and gap, ignition timing, carburetion) would seem to be at odds with experience. This occurs because experience has shown that required service intervals differ from one system to the next. For example, while spark plug condition and gap should be checked for all models at 20-hour intervals, along with contact breaker gap and ignition timing for flywheel magneto models, ignition timing on CDI-equipped models need be checked

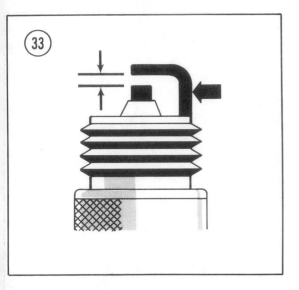

only if the ignition assembly has been removed and reinstalled.

However, a complete tune-up procedure is presented here for convenience, and only a little extra time is required to ensure that all engine tuning variables are correct.

Because the different systems in the engine interact, the tune-up procedure should be done in the following order:

 a. Check and tighten cylinder head fasteners

 b. Work on ignition system

 c. Adjust carburetion

CYLINDER HEAD FASTENERS

1. On air-cooled models, disconnect the spark plug high-tension leads and remove the cooling shroud (**Figure 30**).
2. On all models, tighten the cylinder head fasteners in the pattern shown (**Figure 31**) to the value shown in **Table 5**.
3. Install the cooling shroud on air-cooled models.

IGNITION SYSTEM

Spark plug service is described below. Ignition timing and adjustment is described in Chapter Six. For models equipped with CDI (capacitor discharge ignition) this work can be sidestepped; once the ignition has been installed and adjusted, timing will remain constant for as

long as the ignition remains installed and undisturbed.

For flywheel magneto (contact breaker) equipped models, the point gap and timing should be checked and corrected each time the spark plugs are checked (20 hours or 250 miles — 400 km).

Spark Plugs

For all models, spark plugs should be routinely checked and their gap adjusted at 20-hour or 250-mile (400-km) intervals. In addition, they should be checked any time hard starting or poor performance indicates that they may be faulty or that carburetion may be out of adjustment.

1. Carefully disconnect the high-tension leads from the plugs by grasping the caps and turning them slightly as you pull them loose. Don't pull on the wires.
2. Clean the area around the base of the plug with compressed air.
3. Unscrew the plugs from the cylinder heads and compare their condition with **Figure 32**.
4. Check the heat range of the plugs and compare them with the specifications in Table 2, Chapter Six. If the heat range is not correct, replace them with correct plugs.
5. If the plugs are in good condition and are the correct heat range, clean them with a fine wire brush and solvent and dry them with compressed air.
6. Check the electrode gap (see Table 2, Chapter Six) with a round wire gauge, and if adjustment is required, carefully bend the side electrode (**Figure 33**).
7. Install the plugs in the cylinder heads until they are firmly seated. Then, tighten them an additional ¼ turn.

> NOTE: *On models equipped with contact breaker ignition, don't install the spark plugs until the timing and contact breaker gap have been checked and adjusted.*

Capacitor Discharge Ignition (CDI)

For models equipped with CDI (capacitor discharge ignition), ignition timing and adjust-

SPARK PLUG CONDITIONS   32

NORMAL USE

OIL FOULED

CARBON FOULED

OVERHEATED

GAP BRIDGED

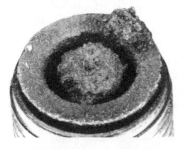

SUSTAINED PREIGNITION

WORN OUT

Photos courtesy of Champion Spark Plug Company.

ment are unnecessary during a routine tune-up. However, if poor performance or spark plug condition indicates a potential problem, refer to Chapter Six, *Capacitor Discharge Ignition (CDI),* and check static and strobe timing as described.

Flywheel Magneto Ignition

For models equipped with flywheel magneto ignition, refer to Chapter Six, *Flywheel Magneto,* and adjust the contact breaker gap and timing as described.

CARBURETION

Check control cable adjustments described in Chapter Five; cables stretch with use and require adjustment of free play.

Check idle speed and mixture adjustment as described in Chapter Five.

2

Tables are on the following pages.

Table 1   SERVICE INTERVALS — STANDARD MODELS

Interval	Item
Before each ride	• Check fuel level • Check fan belt condition • Check oil level • Check operation of engine stop switch • Check operation of tether switch • Check operation of lights • Check track for icing
Every 20 hours or 250 miles (400 km)	• Check engine mounts and fasteners • Check oil and fuel lines • Clean and regap spark plugs • Check point gap and timing (flywheel magneto ignition only) • Check drive system fasteners • Check ski runners (skags) • Check drive belt adjustment • Check body fasteners • Check electrical leads
Every 40 hours or 500 miles (800 km)	• Check recoil starter and rope • Check starter valve (choke) • Check oil pump • Check secondary (driven) sheaves • Check sheave distance • Check sheave offset • Check brake adjustment and condition • Inspect guide and idler wheels • Inspect drive sprockets • Check track adjustment • Inspect suspension • Check drive chain tension • Check ski alignment • Inspect fuel tank and lines • Inspect oil tank
Every 80 hours or 1,000 miles (1,600 km)	• Check compression in cylinders
Annually	• Remove carbon from engine upper end • Check and adjust ignition timing • Clean, inspect, and adjust carburetor • Clean and inspect fuel tank • Replace fuel filter • Replace oil filter

Table 2   SERVICE INTERVALS — SRX AND SSR MODELS

Interval	Item
Before each race	• Check engine mounts and fasteners • Check oil and fuel lines • Check carburetor mounts • Check carburetor adjustments • Check ignition timing • Check compression in cylinders • Check muffler mounts • Check spark plug condition and gap • Check coolant system for leaks • Check coolant level • Inspect drive belt • Check sheave offset • Check sheave distance • Check brake pad wear • Check brake adjustment • Check track adjustment • Inspect track for damage • Check tightness of body fasteners • Adjust suspension • Inspect skags for wear • Inspect electrical leads and connections • Check operation of engine stop switch • Check operation of tether switch
Every 4 hours or 200 miles (300 km)	• Inspect recoil starter rope • Check carburetor float level • Check cylinder head fastener torque • Check operation of drive and driven sheaves • Inspect drive sprockets • Inspect guide and idler wheels • Check axles for damage • Check drive chain adjustment • Inspect fuel tank
When poor performance indicates trouble	• Adjust carburetion • Check ignition timing • Check spark plug condition and gap • Check piston-to-cylinder clearance • Check piston ring end gap • Check piston ring side clearance • Check cylinder wear • Check operation of drive and driven sheaves • Check sheave distance • Check sheave offset • Check track adjustment • Check ski alignment • Check suspension adjustment
Annually	• Clean, inspect, and adjust carburetion • Disassemble and inspect engine • Replace brake pads • Clean fuel tank

2

Table 3   SHEAVE DISTANCE/OFFSET

Model	Distance, Center-to-Center	Offset
SSR, SRX, EXCEL V, EX340, EX440	269-271 mm (10.56-10.64 in.)	5.0-6.0 mm (0.197-0.236 in.)
GP338, GP433, GS340, GP440	269-271 mm (10.56-10.64 in.)	4.5-6.5 mm (0.18-0.26 in.)
GPX338, GPX433, ET250, ET340	269-271 mm (10.56-10.64 in.)	10-12 mm 0.39-0.47 in.)
ET300	264-268 mm (10.39-10.55 in.)	10-12 mm (0.39-0.47 in.)

Table 4   LUBRICATION INTERVALS

Interval	Item	Lubricant
Every 40 hours or 500 miles (800 km)	Drive sheave weights and roller pins	Low-temperature moly-disulfide grease
	Driven sheave shaft and sliding sheave	Low-temperature moly-disulfied grease
	Front axle housing	Low-temperature all-purpose grease
	Replace drive chain oil	API GL-3, SAE 75 or 80
	Steering column bottom bushing	Low-temperature all-purpose grease
	Steering column top bushing	Engine oil
	Tie rod/drag link ends	Low-temperature all-purpose grease
	Ski spindles	Low-temperature all-purpose grease
	Ski wear plates	Low-temperature all-purpose grease
	Ski mounting bolts	Low-temperature all-purpose grease
	Brake cable end at control	Aeroshell No. 7A or Esso Beacon 325 or an equivalent
Every 80 hours or 1,000 miles (1,600 km)	Oil pump drive	Aeroshell No. 7A or Esso Beacon 325 or an equivalent
	Oil pump drive cover	Aeroshell No. 7A or Esso Beacon 325 or an equivalent
	Suspension axles	Low-temperature all-purpose grease
Annually	Recoil starter mechanism	Aeroshell No. 7A or Esso Beacon 325 or an equivalent
As required	Engine oil tank	YAMALUBE 2-Cycle Oil

Table 5   CYLINDER HEAD FASTENER TORQUE

Model	Torque, mkg (ft.-lb.)
ET250, ET300, ET340, GS340, GP440, EX340, EX440, PR440, EXCEL V, SRX, SSR, GP338, GP433	2.5 (18)
GPX338, GPX433	
Nuts	2.5 (18)
Bolts	2.2 (16)

2

CHAPTER THREE

TROUBLESHOOTING

Diagnosing snowmobile ills is relatively simple if you use orderly procedures and keep a few basic principles in mind.

Never assume anything. Do not overlook the obvious. If you are riding along and the snowmobile suddenly quits, check the easiest most accessible problem spots first. Is there gasoline in the tank? Has a spark plug wire fallen off? Check the ignition switch. Maybe that last mogul caused you to accidentally switch the emergency switch to OFF or pull the emergency stop "tether" string.

If nothing obvious turns up in a cursory check, look a little further. Learning to recognize and describe symptoms will make repairs easier for you or a mechanic at the shop. Describe problems accurately and fully. Saying that "it won't run" isn't the same as saying "it quit at high speed and wouldn't start," or that "it sat in my garage for three months and then wouldn't start."

Gather as many symptoms together as possible to aid in diagnosis. Note whether the engine lost power gradually or all at once, what color smoke (if any) came from the exhaust, and so on. Remember that the more complicated a machine is, the easier it is to troubleshoot because symptoms point to specific problems.

You do not need fancy equipment or complicated test gear to determine whether repairs can be attempted at home. A few simple checks could save a large repair bill and time lost while the snowmobile sits in a dealer's service department. On the other hand, be realistic and do not attempt repairs beyond your abilities. Service departments tend to charge heavily for putting together disassembled components that may have been abused. Some won't even take on such a job — so use common sense; don't get in over your head.

OPERATING REQUIREMENTS

An engine needs 3 basics to run properly correct gas/air mixture, compression, and spark at the right time. If one or more are missing, the engine will not run. The electric system is the weakest link of the three. Most problems result from electrical breakdown than from any other source. Keep that in mind before you begin tampering with carburetor adjustments.

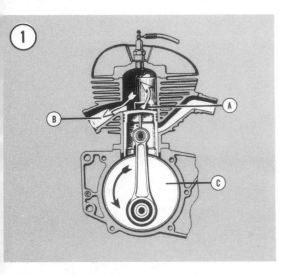

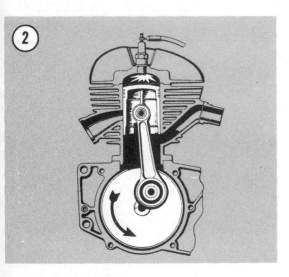

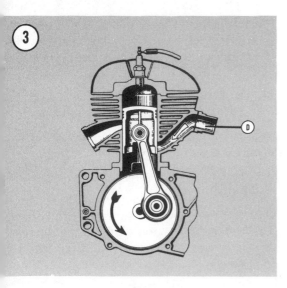

If the snowmobile has been sitting for any length of time and refuses to start, check the battery (if the machine is so equipped) for a charged condition first, and then look to the gasoline delivery system. This includes the tank, fuel petcock, lines, and the carburetor. Sediment may have formed in the tank, obstructing fuel flow. Gasoline deposits may have gummed up carburetor jets and air passages. Gasoline tends to lose its potency after standing for long periods. Condensation may contaminate it with water. Drain old gas and try starting with a fresh tankful.

Compression, or the lack of it, usually enters the picture only in the case of older machines. Worn or broken pistons, rings, and cylinder bores could prevent starting. Generally a gradual power loss and harder and harder starting will be readily apparent in this case.

PRINCIPLES OF 2-CYCLE ENGINES

The following is a general discussion of a typical 2-cycle piston-port engine.

Figures 1 through 4 illustrate operating principles of piston-port engines. During this discussion, assume that the crankshaft is rotating counterclockwise. In **Figure 1**, as the piston travels downward, a transfer port (A) between the crankcase and the cylinder is uncovered. Exhaust gases leave the cylinder through the exhaust port (B), which is also opened by downward movement of the piston. A fresh fuel/air charge, which has previously been compressed slightly by the descending piston, travels from the crankcase (C) to the cylinder through transfer ports (A) as the ports open. Since the incoming charge is under pressure, it rushes into the cylinder quickly and helps to expel exhaust gases from the previous cycle.

Figure 2 illustrates the next phase of the cycle. As the crankshaft continues to rotate, the piston moves upward, closing the exhaust and transfer ports. As the piston continues upward, the air/fuel mixture in the cylinder is compressed. Notice also that a low pressure area is created in the crankcase by the ascending piston at the same time. Further upward movement of the piston uncovers the intake port (D). A fresh fuel/air charge is then drawn into the crankcase through the intake port because of the low pressure created by the upward piston movement.

The third phase is shown in **Figure 3**. As the piston approaches top dead center, the spark plug fires, igniting the compressed mixture. The piston is then driven downward by the expanding gases.

When the top of the piston uncovers the exhaust port, the fourth phase begins, as shown in **Figure 4**. The exhaust gases leave the cylinder through the exhaust port. As the piston continues downward, the intake port is closed and the mixture in the crankcase is compressed in preparation for the next cycle. Every downward stroke of the piston is a power stroke.

ENGINE STARTING

An engine that refuses to start or is difficult to start can try the patience of anyone. More often than not, the problem is very minor and can be found with a simple and logical troubleshooting approach.

The following items provide a beginning point from which to isolate engine starting problems.

Engine Fails to Start

Perform the following spark test to determine if the ignition system is operating properly.

1. Remove a spark plug.

2. Connect the spark plug connector to the spark plug and clamp the base of spark plug to a good grounding point on the engine. A large alligator clip makes an ideal clamp. Position the spark plug so you can observe the electrode.

3. Turn on the ignition and crank the engine over. A fat blue spark should be evident across the spark plug electrode.

> WARNING
> *On machines equipped with* CDI *(capacitor discharge ignition), do not hold spark plug, wire, or connector or a serious electrical shock may result.*

4. If the spark is good, check for one or more of the following possible malfunctions:

   a. Fouled or defective spark plugs

   b. Obstructed fuel filter or fuel line

   c. Defective fuel pump

   d. Leaking head gasket — perform the compression test

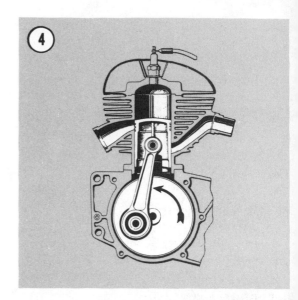

5. If spark is not good, check for one or more of the following:

   a. Burned, pitted, or improperly gapped breaker points

   b. Weak ignition coil or condenser

   c. Loose electrical connections

   d. Defective CDI components — have CDI system checked by an authorized dealer

Engine Difficult to Start

Check for one or more of the following possible malfunctions:

   a. Fouled spark plugs

   b. Improperly adjusted choke

   c. Defective or improperly adjusted breaker points

d. Contaminated fuel system

e. Improperly adjusted carburetor

f. Weak ignition coil

g. Incorrect fuel mixture

h. Crankcase drain plugs loose or missing

i. Poor compression — perform the compression test

Engine Will Not Crank

Check for one or more of the following possible malfunctions:

a. Defective recoil starter

b. Seized piston

c. Seized crankshaft bearings

d. Broken connecting rod

Compression Test

Perform a compression test to determine condition of piston ring sealing qualities, piston wear, and condition of head gasket seal.

1. Remove the spark plugs. Insert a compression gauge in one spark plug hole (**Figure 5**). Refer to Chapter One for a suitable type of compression tester.

2. Crank the engine vigorously and record compression reading. Repeat for other cylinder. Compression readings should be from 120 to 175 psi (8.44-12.30 kg/cm²). Maximum allowable variation between cylinders is 10 psi (0.70 kg/cm²).

3. If compression is low or variance between cylinders is excessive, check for defective head gaskets, damaged cylinders and pistons, or stuck piston rings.

ENGINE PERFORMANCE

The following items are a starting point from which to isolate a performance malfunction. It is assumed the engine runs but is not operating at peak efficiency.

The possible causes for each malfunction are listed in a logical sequence and in order of probability.

Engine Will Not Idle

a. Carburetor incorrectly adjusted

b. Fouled or improperly gapped spark plugs

c. Head gasket leaking — perform the compression test

d. Fuel mixture incorrect

e. Spark advance mechanism not retarding

f. Obstructed fuel pump impulse tube

g. Crankcase drain plugs loose or missing

Engine Misses at High Speed

a. Fouled or improperly gapped spark plugs

b. Defective or improperly gapped breaker points

c. Improper ignition timing

d. Defective fuel pump

e. Improper carburetor high-speed adjustment or improper main jet selection

f. Weak ignition coil

g. Obstructed fuel pump impulse tube

h. Obstructed fuel filter

Engine Overheating

a. Too lean fuel mixture — incorrect carburetor adjustment or jet selection

b. Improper ignition timing

c. Incorrect spark plug heat range

d. Intake system or crankcase air leak

e. Cooling fan belt broken or slipping

f. Cooling fan defective

g. Damaged or blocked cooling fins

Engine Smokes and Runs Rough

a. Carburetor adjusted incorrectly — mixture too rich

b. Incorrect fuel/oil mixture

c. Choke not operating properly

d. Obstructed muffler

e. Water or other contaminates in fuel

Engine Loses Power

a. Carburetor incorrectly adjusted

b. Engine overheating

c. Defective or improperly gapped breaker points

3

d. Improper ignition timing

e. Incorrectly gapped spark plugs

f. Weak ignition coil

g. Obstructed muffler

h. Dragging brakes

Engine Lacks Acceleration

a. Carburetor mixture too lean

b. Defective fuel pump

c. Incorrect fuel/oil mixture

d. Defective or improperly gapped breaker points

e. Improper ignition timing

f. Dragging brakes

ENGINE FAILURE ANALYSIS

Overheating is the major cause of serious and expensive engine failures. It is important that each snowmobile owner understand all the causes of engine overheating and take the necessary precautions to avoid expensive overheating damage. Proper preventive maintenance and careful attention to all potential problem areas can often prevent serious malfunction before it happens.

Fuel

All snowmobile engines rely on a proper fuel/oil mixture for engine lubrication. Always use an approved oil and mix the fuel carefully as described in Chapter One.

Gasoline must be of sufficiently high octane (88 or higher) to avoid "knocking" and "detonation."

Fuel/Air Mixture

Fuel/air mixture is determined by carburetor adjustment or main jet selection. Always adjust carburetors carefully and pay particular attention to avoid a "too-lean" mixture.

Heat

Excessive external heat on the engine can be caused by the following:

a. Hood louvers plugged with snow

b. Damaged or plugged cylinder and head cooling fins

c. Slipping or broken fan belt

d. Damaged cooling fan

e. Operating snowmobile in hot weather

f. Plugged or restricted exhaust system

See **Figures 6 and 7** for examples of cylinder and piston scuffing caused by excessive heat.

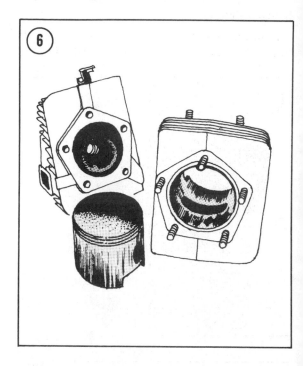

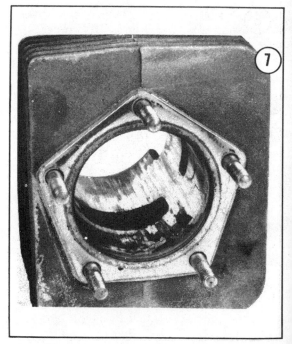

Dirt

Dirt is a potential problem for all snowmobiles. The air intake silencers on all models are not designed to filter incoming air. Avoid running snowmobiles in areas that are not completely snow covered.

Ignition Timing

Ignition timing that is too far advanced can cause "knocking" or "detonation." Timing that is too retarded causes excessive heat buildup in the cylinder exhaust port area.

Spark Plugs

Spark plugs must be of a correct heat range. Too hot a heat range can cause pre-ignition and detonation which can ultimately result in piston burn-through as shown in **Figure 8**.

Refer to Chapter Two for recommended spark plugs.

Pre-ignition

Pre-ignition is caused by excessive heat in the combustion chamber due to a spark plug of improper heat range and/or too lean a fuel mixture. See **Figure 9** for an example of a melted and scuffed piston caused by pre-ignition.

Detonation (Knocking)

Knocking is caused by a too lean fuel mixture and/or too low octane fuel.

ELECTRICAL SYSTEM

The following items provide a starting point from which to troubleshoot electrical system malfunctions. The possible causes for each malfunction are listed in a logical sequence and in order of probability.

Ignition system malfunctions are outlined under *Engine Starting* and *Engine Performance*.

Lights Will Not Light

    a. Bulbs are burned out
    b. Loose electrical connections
    c. Defective switch
    d. Defective lighting coil or alternator
    e. Defective voltage regulator
    f. Defective battery (electric-start models)

Bulbs Burn Out Rapidly

    a. Incorrect bulb type
    b. Defective voltage regulator

Lights Too Bright or Too Dim

    a. Defective voltage regulator
    b. Defective alternator

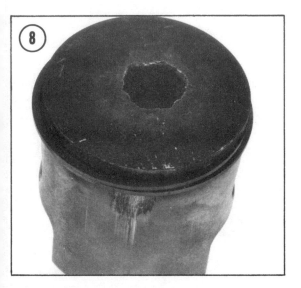

Discharged Battery
(Electric-start Models)

   a. Defective battery

   b. Low electrolyte level

   c. Dirty or loose electrical connections

   d. Defective voltage regulator

   e. Defective lighting coil

   f. Defective rectifier

   g. Defective circuit breaker

Cracked Battery Case

   a. Discharged battery allowed to freeze

   b. Improperly installed hold-down clamp

   c. Improperly attached battery cables

Starter Motor Does Not Operate

   a. Loose electrical connections

   b. Discharged battery

   c. Defective starter solenoid

   d. Defective starter motor

   e. Defective circuit breaker

   f. Defective ignition switch

Poor Starter Performance

   a. Commutator or brushes worn, dirty, or oil soaked

   b. Binding armature

   c. Weak brush springs

   d. Armature open, shorted, or grounded

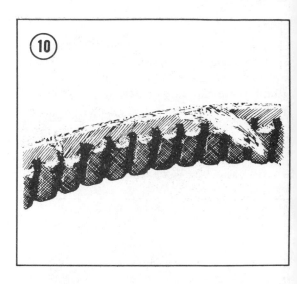

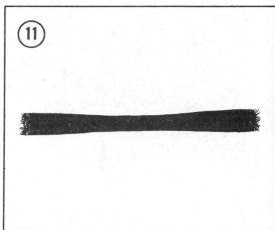

POWER TRAIN

The following items provide a starting point from which to troubleshoot power train malfunctions. The possible causes for each malfunction are listed in a logical sequence and in order of probability. Also refer to *Drive Belt Wear Analysis*.

Drive Belt Not Operating
Smoothly in Drive Sheave

   a. Face of drive sheave is rough, grooved, pitted, or scored

   b. Defective drive belt

Uneven Drive Belt Wear

   a. Misaligned drive and driven sheaves

   b. Loose engine mounts

Glazed Drive Belt

   a. Excessive slippage

   b. Oil or grease on sheave surfaces

Drive Belt Worn Narrow in One Place

   a. Excessive slippage caused by stuck track

   b. Too high engine idle speed

Drive Belt Too Tight at Idle

   a. Engine idle speed too fast

   b. Distance between sheaves incorrect

   c. Belt length incorrect

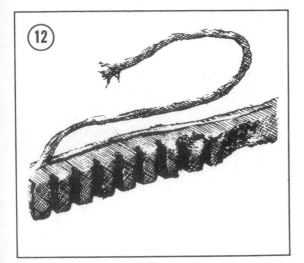

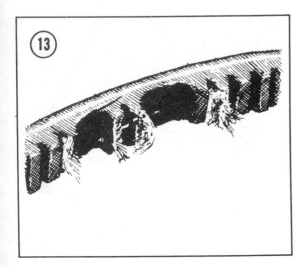

Drive Belt Edge Cord Failure

a. Misaligned sheaves

b. Loose engine mounting bolts

Brake Not Holding Properly

a. Incorrect brake cable adjustment

b. Brake lining or pucks worn

c. Oil saturated brake lining or pucks

d. Sheared key on brake pulley or disc

e. Incorrect brake adjustment

Brake Not Releasing Properly

a. Weak or broken return spring

b. Bent or damaged brake lever

c. Incorrect brake adjustment

Leaking Chaincase

a. Gaskets on drive shaft bearing flanges or secondary shaft bearing flanges damaged

b. Damaged O-ring on drive shaft or secondary shaft

c. Cracked or broken chaincase

Rapid Chain and Sprocket Wear

a. Insufficient chaincase oil

b. Misaligned sprockets

c. Broken chain tension blocks

DRIVE BELT WEAR ANALYSIS

Frayed Edge

A rapidly wearing drive belt with a frayed edge cord indicates the drive belt is misaligned (see **Figure 10**). Also check for loose engine mounting bolts.

Worn Narrow in One Section

Excessive slippage due to a stuck track or too high an engine idle speed will cause the drive belt to be worn narrow in one section (see **Figure 11**).

Belt Disintegration

Drive belt disintegration is usually caused by misalignment. Disintegration can also be caused by using an incorrect belt or oil or grease on sheave surfaces (see **Figure 12**).

Sheared Cogs

Sheared cogs as shown in **Figure 13** are usually caused by violent drive sheave engagement. This is an indication of a defective or improperly installed drive sheave.

SKIS AND STEERING

The following items provide a starting point from which to troubleshoot ski and steering malfunctions. The possible causes for each malfunction are listed in a logical sequence and in order or probability.

Loose Steering

a. Loose steering post bushing

b. Loose steering post or steering column cap screw

c. Loose tie rod ends

d. Worn spindle bushings

e. Stripped spindle splines

Unequal Steering

a. Improperly adjusted tie rods

b. Improperly installed steering arms

Rapid Ski Wear

a. Skis misaligned

b. Worn out ski wear rods (Skags)

c. Worn out spring wear plate

TRACK ASSEMBLY

The following items provide a starting point from which to troubleshoot track assembly malfunctions. The possible causes for each are listed in a logical sequence and in order of probability. Also refer to *Track Wear Analysis*.

Frayed Track Edge

Track misaligned

Track Grooved on Inner Surface

a. Track too tight

b. Frozen rear idler shaft bearing

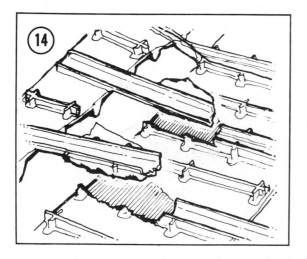

Track Drive Ratcheting

Track too loose

Rear Idlers Turning on Shaft

Frozen rear idler shaft bearings

TRACK WEAR ANALYSIS

The majority of track failures and abnormal wear patterns are caused by negligence, abuse, and poor maintenance. The following items il-

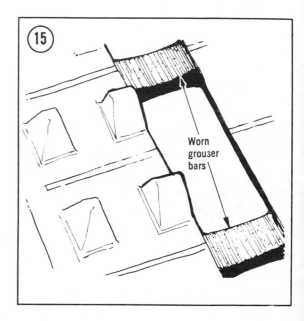

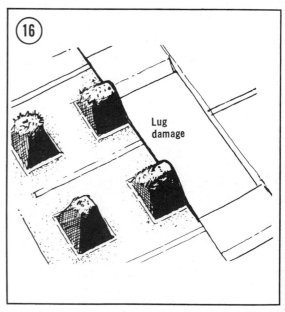

lustrate typical examples. In all cases the damage could have been avoided by proper maintenance and good operator technique.

Obstruction Damage

Cuts, slashes, and gouges in the track surface are caused by hitting obstructions such as broken glass, sharp rocks or buried steel (see **Figure 14**).

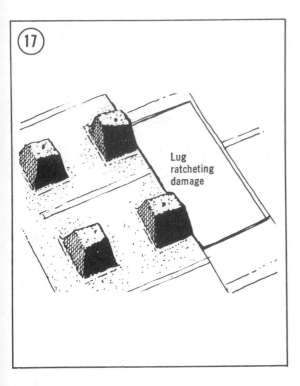

Lug ratcheting damage

Worn Grouser Bars

Excessively worn grouser bars are caused by snowmobile operation over rough and non-snow covered terrain such as gravel roads and highway roadsides (**Figure 15**).

Lug Damage

Lug damage as shown in **Figure 16** is caused by lack of snow lubrication.

Ratcheting Damage

Insufficient track tension is a major cause of ratcheting damage to the top of the lugs (**Figure 17**). Ratcheting can also be caused by too great a load and constant ''jack-rabbit'' starts.

Over-tension Damage

Excessive track tension can cause too much friction on the wear bars. This friction causes the wear bars to melt and adhere to the track grouser bars. See **Figure 18**. An indication of this condition is a ''sticky'' track that has a tendency to ''lock up.''

Loose Track Damage

A track adjusted too loosely can cause the outer edge to flex excessively. This results in the type of damage shown in **Figure 19**. Excessive weight can also contribute to the damage.

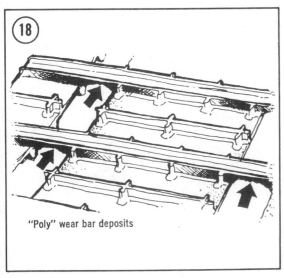

''Poly'' wear bar deposits

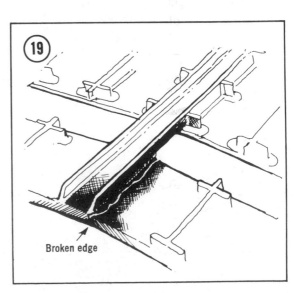

Broken edge

Impact Damage

Impact damage as shown in **Figure 20** causes the track rubber to open and expose the cord. This frequently happens in more than one place. Impact damage is usually caused by riding on rough or frozen ground or ice. Also, insufficient track tension can allow the track to pound against the track stabilizers inside the tunnel.

Edge Damage

Edge damage as shown in **Figure 21** is usually caused by tipping the snowmobile on its side to clear the track and allowing the track edge to contact an abrasive surface.

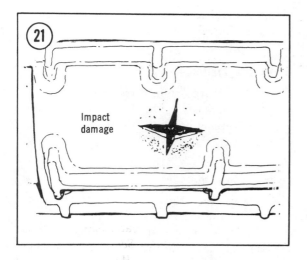

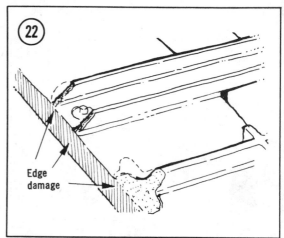

CHAPTER FOUR

ENGINE

All Yamaha snowmobiles are powered with either single- or twin-cylinder 2-stroke engines. Refer to Chapter Three for *Principles of Operation* of 2-cycle engines. Work on all engines is essentially similar, although some differences do exist between models (air cooling vs liquid cooling; piston-port intake control vs reed valve; etc.) and where the differences are important to the work being described they will be pointed out. Tables are at the end of the chapter.

All engines are equipped with ball-type main crankshaft bearings and needle bearings on both ends of the connecting rods. Crankshaft components are available as individual parts; however, other than replacement of outer seals, it is recommended that crankshaft work be entrusted to a dealer or other competent engine specialist. Experience and special measuring equipment, along with a hydraulic press, are required to service the crankshaft. Engine removal and disassembly are covered in detail so that the cost of lower-end service can be minimized.

An upper end overhaul is within the abilities of the average hobbyist mechanic equipped with a reasonable range of hand tools, and inside and outside micrometers. Before beginning any work on the engine, read Chapter One, and particularly the headings *Service Hints, Tools, Expendable Supplies,* and *Working Safely.* The information they contain will contribute to the efficiency, effectiveness, and safety of your work.

Also, carefully read and understand the appropriate procedures in this chapter before picking up a wrench. It is also a good idea to physically compare the instructions with the actual machine, as far as possible, beforehand, to familiarize yourself with the procedure and the equipment.

A complete upper-end overhaul can be performed without removing the engine from the machine. However, if you have the time, you may find it more convenient to have the engine on a workbench. Should a small part or tool or bit of dirt fall into the crankcase, it is easier to remove if the engine can be inverted. For these reasons, engine removal is described first.

The removal/installation procedures, as well as most service procedures, are virtually identical for all Yamaha engines. Exceptions are noted where they apply.

When measuring wear surfaces for critical dimensions, be sure to consult the table for your particular engine. This holds true for critical tightening torque values as well.

Finally, if you are disassembling the upper end even for a routine inspection and carbon removal (anticipating no parts replacement) purchase a gasket set beforehand. You can't reassemble the upper end without it, and if the pistons, rings, and bores are in good condition you will save time by being able to complete the job right away.

ENGINE REMOVAL (AIR COOLED)

Engine removal is virtually the same for all Yamaha snowmobiles, with a few exceptions that are noted as they occur. The machine illustrated is an ET300C and is the most typical example.

1. Open the hood all the way. Unplug the harness from the headlamp and free the harness from the clip inside the hood (**Figure 1**). Disconnect the hood restraining cable and with assistance, support the hood and remove the bolts that attach the hood hinge to the chassis (**Figure 2**). Remove the hood and set it well out of the way to prevent it from being damaged.

2. Disconnect the springs that secure the head-pipe to the manifold (**Figure 3**). Remove the long spring that holds the muffler in its cradle. Unscrew the bolt that attaches the tailpipe to the chassis (**Figure 4**). Remove the exhaust system and collect the rubber shock mount at the tailpipe.

3. Disconnect the fuel line from the carburetor (**Figure 5**) and plug the line to prevent fuel from leaking. A golf tee makes an excellent fuel line plug.

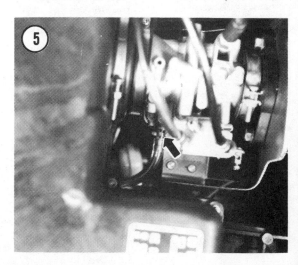

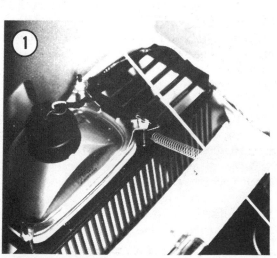

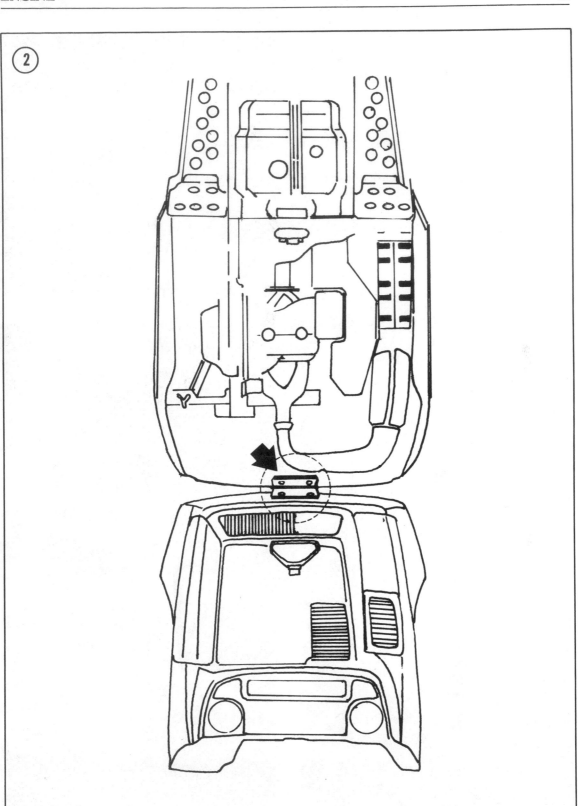

4. Disconnect the fuel pump pulse line from the engine and plug it with a golf tee (**Figure 6**).

5. Disconnect the oil feed line (**Figure 7**) and plug it with a golf tee.

6. Disconnect the throttle cable (**Figure 8**) and the starter cable.

7. Unplug the wiring harness connectors (**Figure 9**).

8. Remove the drive belt guard (**Figure 10**). Lock the brake to prevent the driven sheaves from turning. Push against the moveable driven sheave and rotate it clockwise to separate it from the fixed driven sheave. Roll the belt over the moveable sheave (**Figure 11**). Remove the belt from the drive sheave (clutch).

9. Remove the bolts that attach the starter rope guide to the body (**Figure 12**). Remove the bolts that attach the starter to the engine (**Figure 13**) and remove the starter assembly.

10. Remove the clutch bolt (**Figure 14**). Install a puller in the end of the crankshaft (**Figure 15**) and turn the puller bolt clockwise to break the clutch loose from the crankshaft. The clutch must be held to prevent it from turning with a pin spanner or a tool such as the one shown. This tool, called a Grab-It, can be used for the clutch, the starter pulley, and the alternator rotor. It's available through some motorcycle shops or directly from the manufacturer.

> NOTE: *It may be necessary to rap sharply on the head of the puller bolt during clutch removal to break the clutch loose.*

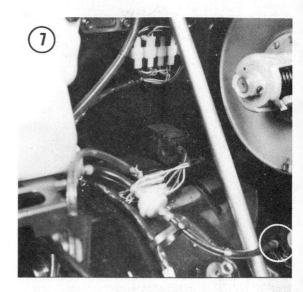

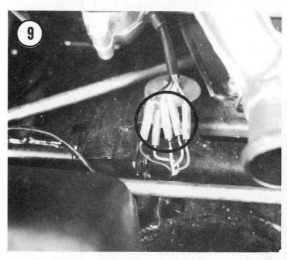

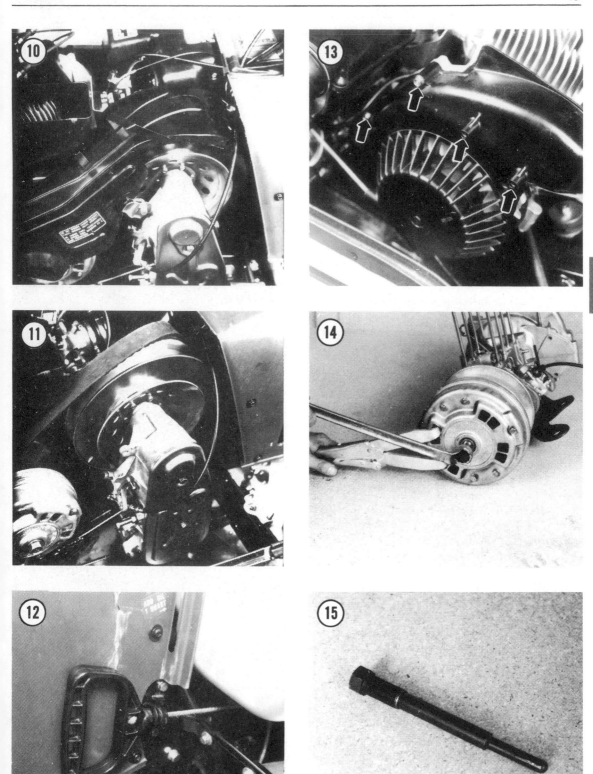

4

11. Unscrew the engine mounting bolts (**Figure 16**). There are 2 bolts in front of the engine and 2 behind it.

12. Carefully check to make sure that all cables, lines, and electrical leads between the engine and the machine have been disconnected. Then, with assistance, lift the engine out of the machine and set it on a workbench.

ENGINE REMOVAL (LIQUID-COOLED)

Removal of the liquid-cooled engine is virtually the same as for the air-cooled engines. However, the cooling system must first be drained and the coolant hoses disconnected.

> WARNING
> *Do not drain the system or disconnect the coolant hoses when the engine and coolant are hot; serious burns are likely to result.*

1. Carefully loosen the radiator cap to relieve system pressure.

2. Remove the drain bolt from the front of each cylinder and allow the coolant to drain into a clean container.

> NOTE: *The bolts are located immediately below the exhaust outlets.*

3. Disconnect the bypass line from the thermostat housing, direct the end of the line down and into a container (**Figure 17**), and allow several minutes for the heat exchanger and water pump to drain. Then, disconnect the top and bottom coolant hoses from the engine.

ENGINE INSTALLATION
(AIR-COOLED)

1. Make sure the rubber engine mount shock absorbers are in place and set the engine into the machine. Tighten the engine mounting bolts and nuts finger-tight (**Figure 18**).

2. Clean the taper on the clutch-end of the crankshaft and then clean the internal taper in the clutch. Install the clutch on the crankshaft. Hold the clutch to prevent it from turning, screw in the clutch bolt, and tighten it to the value shown in **Table 1** at the end of the chapter (**Figure 19**).

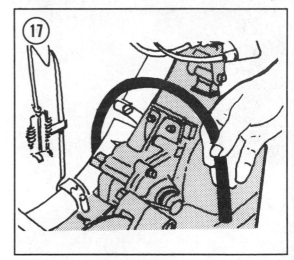

3. Install the starter assembly (**Figure 20**). Attach the starter rope guide to the body (**Figure 21**).

4. Install the drive belt on the clutch. Roll the belt over the movable driven sheave (**Figure 22**).

> NOTE: *Refer to Chapter Seven, **Drive Belt Adjustment**, and adjust the center-to-center distance of the sheaves and the sheave offset as described.*

5. Connect the wiring harness (**Figure 23**).

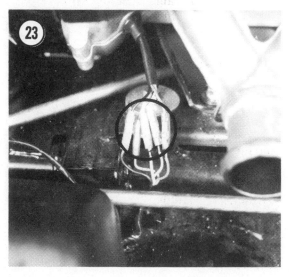

6. Connect the starter cable (**Figure 24**) and the throttle cable.

7. Remove the golf tee from the oil feed line and reconnect the line (**Figure 25**).

8. Remove the golf tee from the fuel pump pulse line and reconnect the line (**Figure 26**).

9. Remove the golf tee from the fuel line and reconnect it to the carburetor (**Figure 27**).

10. Set the exhaust system in place. Don't forget the rubber shock mount at the tailpipe. Screw in the tailpipe bolt (**Figure 28**). Install the spring that holds the muffler in its cradle and install the springs that connect the headpipe to the exhaust manifold (**Figure 29**).

11. With assistance, line up the hood hinge with the body and screw in and tighten the bolts (**Figure 30**). Connect the restraining cable.

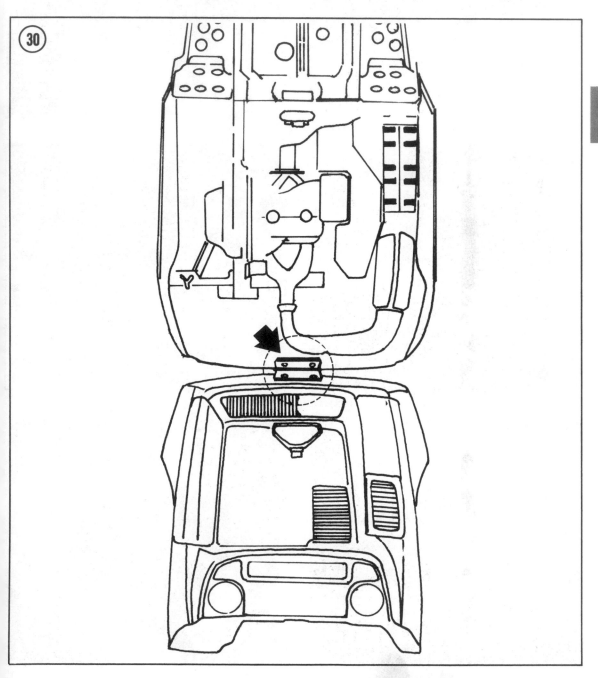

4

12. Route the headlamp wiring harness through the clip in the hood and plug the wiring connector into the headlamp (**Figure 31**).

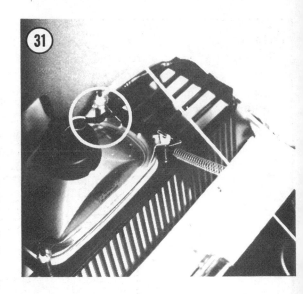

ENGINE INSTALLATION
(LIQUID-COOLED)

Installation of the liquid-cooled engine is essentially the same as that described for air-cooled engines above. When the installation steps described have been carried out, proceed as follows.

1. Connect the top and bottom coolant hoses to the engine and tighten the hose clamps securely.

2. Connect the bypass hose to the thermostat housing.

3. Loosen the air bleeder bolt on the top of the thermostat housing (**Figure 32**) 4 or 5 turns.

4. Pour coolant into the radiator filler opening until coolant begins to flow out of the bleeder bolt hole and is free of air bubbles. Then, tighten the bleeder bolt. Refer to *Filling and Bleeding the Cooling System* in Chapter Three and fill and bleed the system as described.

UPPER-END SERVICE
(AIR-COOLED)

The engine upper-end can be serviced and repaired with the engine installed in the machine. Many mechanics find that upper-end engine work is easier with the engine on a bench, but a great deal of time can be saved with the procedure that follows. This procedure also applies when the engine has been removed from the vehicle.

Disassembly

1. Open the hood all the way. Unplug the harness from the headlamp and free the harness from the clip inside the hood (**Figure 33**). Disconnect the hood restraining cable. With assistance, support the hood and remove the bolts that attach the hood hinge to the chassis (**Figure 34**). Remove the hood and set it well out of the way to prevent it from being damaged.

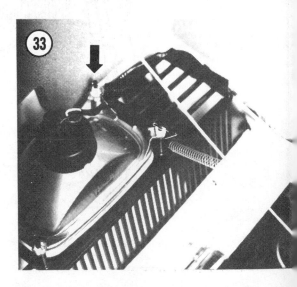

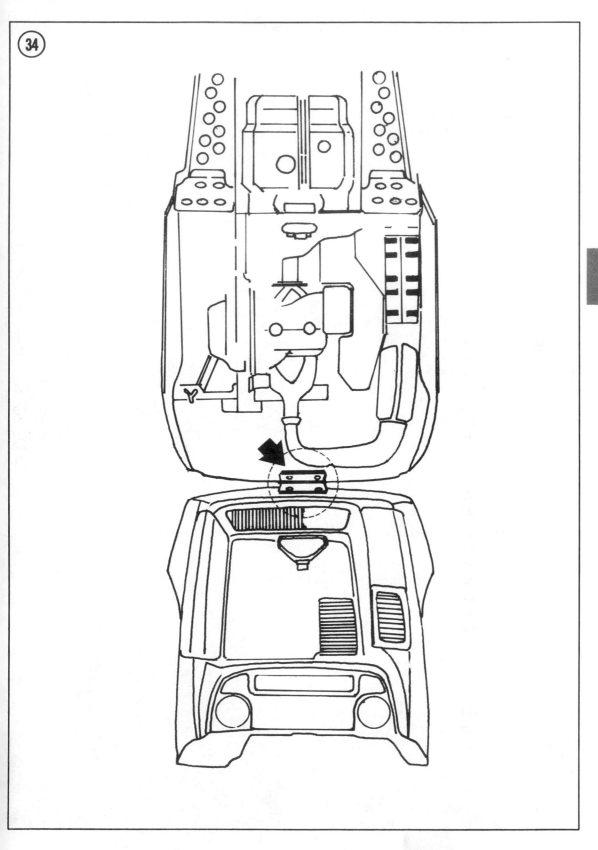

2. Disconnect the springs that secure the head-pipe to the manifold (**Figure 35**). Remove the long spring that holds the muffler in its cradle. Unscrew the bolt that attaches the tailpipe to the chassis (**Figure 36**). Remove the exhaust system and collect the rubber shock mount at the tailpipe.

3. Disconnect the fuel line from the carburetor (**Figure 37**) and plug the line to prevent fuel from leaking. A golf tee makes an excellent fuel line plug.

4. Disconnect the oil feed line (**Figure 38**) and plug it with a golf tee.

5. Disconnect the throttle cable (**Figure 39**) and the starter cable.

6. Disconnect the high-tension leads from the spark plugs. Remove the screws that attach the coil to the cooling shroud (**Figure 40**), disconnect the coil leads from the clip, and set the coil out of the way, in the tool box.

7. Remove the air intake silencer (**Figure 41**).

8. Remove the starter assembly (**Figure 42**), and remove the bolts that connect the rope guide to the machine (**Figure 43**).

9. Remove the cooling shroud (**Figure 44**). On

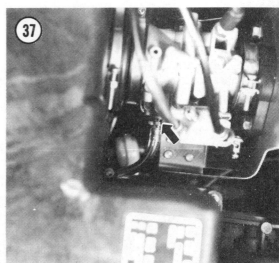

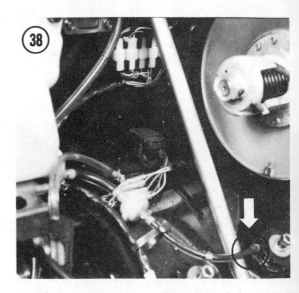

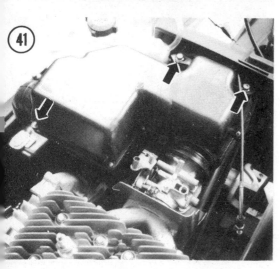

4

EXCEL V models, first remove the outer fan case (**Figure 45**). Remove the 3 screws from the starter pulley (**Figure 46**) and remove the pulley along with the fan drive pulley and fan belt (**Figure 47**). Remove the fan case assembly (**Figure 48**).

10. Loosen the carburetor clamping band and remove the carburetor (**Figure 49**). *Be careful of the sharp edge on the carburetor heat shield*.

11. Remove the exhaust manifold (**Figure 50**).

12. Remove the intake manifold (**Figure 51**) and the carburetor shield (**Figure 52**). Remove the reed valve (if so equipped).

13. Loosen the cylinder head nuts 2 full turns,

½ turn at a time, in a crisscross pattern, to prevent warping the heads. Then, unscrew the nuts completely. Mark the heads for location and position — "L" for left and "R" for right (**Figure 53**). Remove the heads and the head gaskets.

14. Remove the cylinders by lifting straight up — do not twist them as you remove them, otherwise the piston rings may be damaged. Mark the cylinders for location.

15. Place a clean shop rag in the crankcase to prevent dirt and small parts and tools from falling into the engine. Remove the piston pin clip from the outside of each piston (**Figure 54**), press the pin out, and remove the pistons.

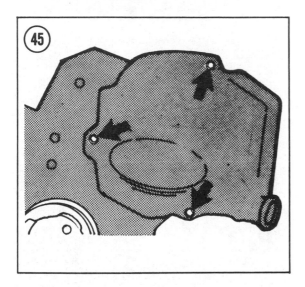

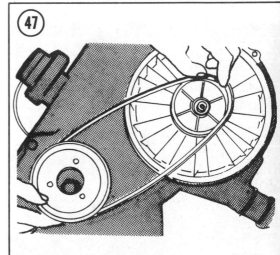

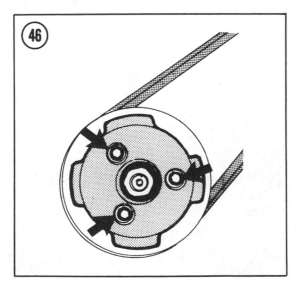

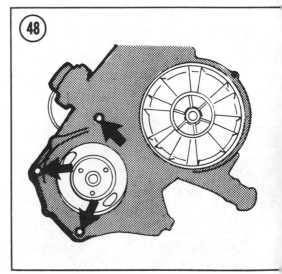

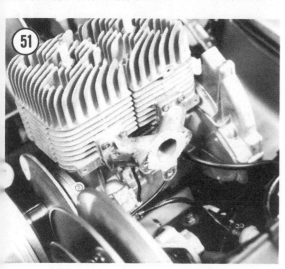

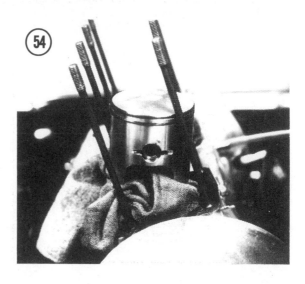

4

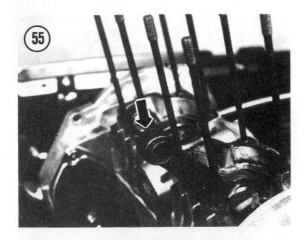

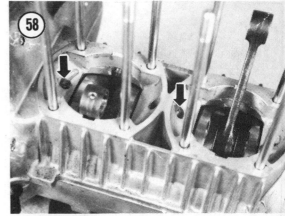

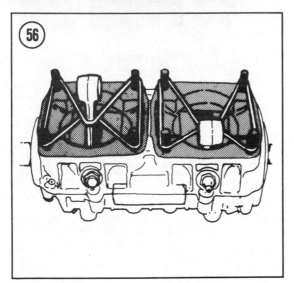

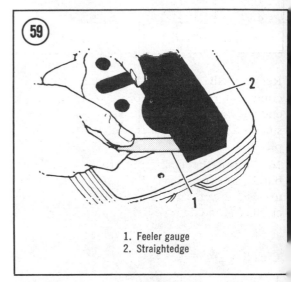

1. Feeler gauge
2. Straightedge

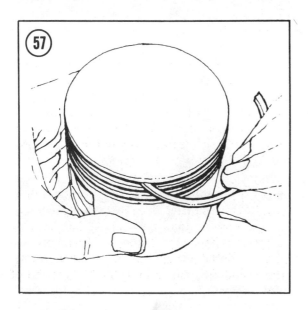

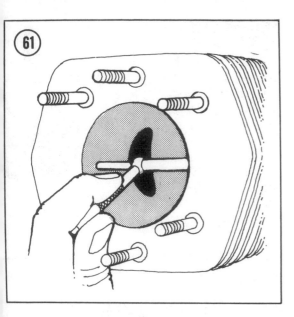

Remove the small-end bearing from the connecting rod (**Figure 55**). For twin cylinder engines, keep the piston sets (piston, pin, clips, small-end bearing) separated; do not mix the pieces.

16. Secure the connecting rods with rubber bands stretched over the cylinder studs (**Figure 56**) to prevent the rods from striking the crankcase and damaging it.

Cleaning

1. Scrape carbon from the combustion chamber in the head and the exhaust port in the cylinder, using a soft metal (aluminum) or wood scraper. Do not use a hard metal scraper; it will burr the surfaces and create hot spots.

2. Clean the head and cylinder with solvent and dry them with compressed air if possible.

3. Remove the rings from the piston and clean the piston crown with a soft scraper. Clean the ring grooves with a ring groove scraper or a piece of old piston ring (**Figure 57**). Clean the piston with solvent and dry it with compressed air.

CAUTION
Pistons fitted with Keystone cross-section rings must not be cleaned with a ring groove scraper; instead, use a piece of old ring.

4. Clean the small-end bearing in fresh solvent and blow it dry with compressed air.

5. Clean the oil passages in the transfer ports in the crankcase (**Figure 58**). If these ports are clogged, oil is prevented from reaching the upper end and damage is sure to result.

6. Remove old cylinder base gasket from the top of the crankcase and the bottom of the cylinder, using a soft scraper. Be careful not to allow any pieces to fall into the crankcase.

Inspection

1. Inspect the reed valve petals (if so equipped) for fatigue cracks. The petals should fit flush or nearly so with the neoprene seats. If the petals must be replaced, refer to Chapter Five, *Reed Valve*.

2. Check the flatness of the cylinder head on a surface plate or piece of glass (**Figure 59**). If the head does not make contact over the entire sealing surface it must be trued. This is a job for a specialist.

3. Check the piston and cylinder for wear, galling, scuffing, or burning. Minor irregularities can be removed from the piston with crocus cloth and light oil. The cylinder may be cleaned up with a light honing, provided it is within specifications as described below.

4. Inspect the inside of the piston for cracks in the corners of the transfer notches (**Figure 60**). Fatigue in this area can cause the piston skirt to collapse. If cracks are visible, the piston must be replaced.

5. Measure the bore with an inside micrometer or cylinder gauge. Measure $\frac{3}{8}$ in. below the top of the cylinder, in 2 locations 90° apart (**Figure 61**). If the 2 measurements differ by more than 0.05 mm (0.002 in.), the cylinder is out-of-round beyond specification and must be bored or replaced.

6. Measure the cylinder again in 2 locations 90° apart just above the intake port. If these measurements differ from those made in Step 5 above by more than 0.05 mm (0.002 in.), the cylinder is tapered beyond specifications and must be bored or replaced. Acceptable cylinder dimensions are shown in **Table 2** at the end of this chapter.

7. Check piston skirt-to-cylinder clearance by first measuring the base of the cylinder bore, front to back (**Figure 62**). With an outside micrometer, measure the piston skirt, front to back, about 6 mm (¼ in.) from the bottom (**Figure 63**). Subtract the piston measurement from the cylinder measurement to determine actual piston skirt-to-cylinder clearance. Refer to **Table 2** for acceptable clearance. If the bore is OK, but the clearance is excessive, the piston must be replaced with a new unit that includes a matched pin and bearing, as well as rings. Also, for twin cylinder engines, the pistons must be replaced as a set.

8. Measure the piston ring end gap. Place a ring into the cylinder, 6 mm (¼ in.) from the top. Use the piston to square the ring with the cylinder by pressing down on the ring with the piston skirt. Measure the gap as shown in **Figure 64**. Refer to **Table 2** for acceptable ring end gap. If the gap is too large for either ring, replace them as a set. Check new rings in the manner just described, and if the gap is too small, file material off the ends of the rings (**Figure 65**).

9. Inspect the piston pin for wear and discoloration and replace it along with the bearing if it is less than perfect.

10. Inspect the bearing cage for cracks at the corners of the roller beds (**Figure 66**). Inspect the rollers for flat spots and replace the bearing if either condition is apparent.

11. Inspect the bearing bore in the small end of the connecting rod. It should have a uniform

surface. If the bore is worn or scored, the rod should be replaced. This is a job for a specialist.

12. Lightly oil the bearing and pin and install them in the connecting rod. Check for play and rotation (**Figure 67**). There should be no vertical play and the pin should rotate smoothly. If play or binding are apparent, the pin and bearing should be replaced. If play is still apparent with new parts, the connecting rod should be replaced. This is a job for your dealer or an engine specialist.

Assembly

1. Oil the connecting rod big end bearing (**Figure 68**). Oil the main bearings (**Figure 69**). Oil the upper-end bearing and install it in the connecting rod (**Figure 70**).

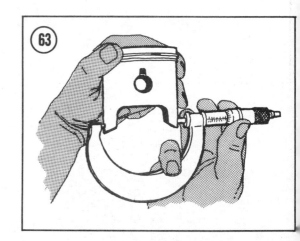

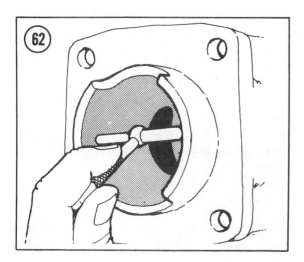

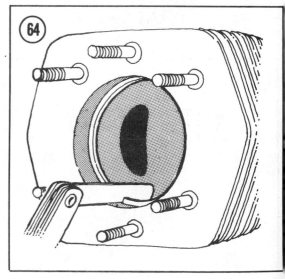

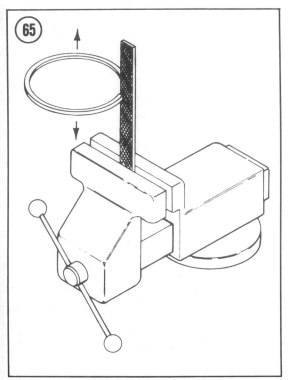

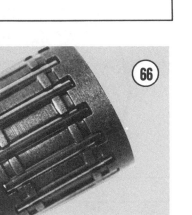

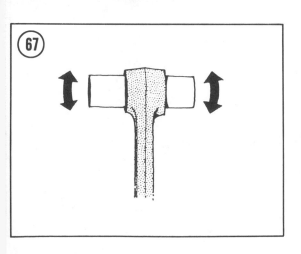

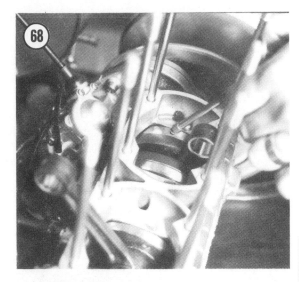

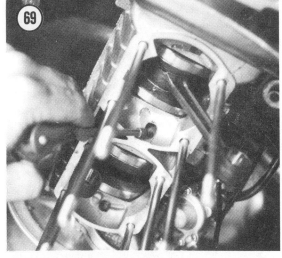

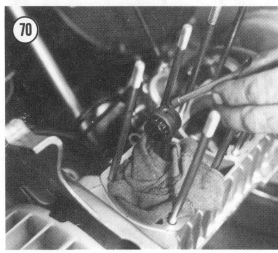

4

2. Oil the piston pin. Install the piston with the arrow on the piston crown facing forward — toward the exhaust port. This is essential so the piston ring ends will be correctly positioned and will not snag in the ports (**Figure 71**). Install the piston pin clips, making sure they are completely seated in their grooves with the open ends of the clips facing down (**Figure 72**).

3. Coat both sides of the cylinder base gasket with gasket cement and install the gasket on the crankcase or on the cylinder base (**Figure 73**).

4. Lightly oil the piston and the cylinder bore. Line up the ends of the piston rings with the locating pins in the ring grooves (**Figure 74**). A ring compressor or large hose clamp can be used to compress the rings; however, the tapered lead on the bottom of the cylinder is generous and the cylinder can be installed without the aid of a compressor.

5. Line up the cylinder with the piston, hold the piston to prevent it from rocking, and push the cylinder down over the piston. Some resistance is normal, but if binding is felt, remove the cylinder and locate and correct the problem before proceeding; *don't force the cylinder down over the piston.* If the cylinder does bind, it is likely that a ring is not correctly seated in its groove, or its ends may not be aligned with the locating pin in the ring groove.

6. Install the head gasket (**Figure 75**).

7. Install the head, washers, and nuts. Run the nuts down finger-tight.

NOTE: *On twin cylinder engines, install the intake and exhaust manifolds (Figures 76 and 77) and install reed valves if the engine is so equipped. Tighten the manifold nuts and bolts before tightening the cylinder head nuts. Coat the sealing surface of the intake manifold and the gaskets with Yamaha Bond No. 3 and connect the oil lines (Figure 78). If the cylinder head nuts are tightened before the manifolds are installed, the bolt holes in the manifolds will very likely not line up with the bolt holes in the cylinders.*

8. When the manifolds have been installed, tighten the cylinder head nuts in a crisscross pattern to the torque specified in **Table 1** at the end of this chapter.

NOTE: *Before installing the carburetor heat shield (Figure 79), deburr the top edge of the plate to preclude injuries later on.*

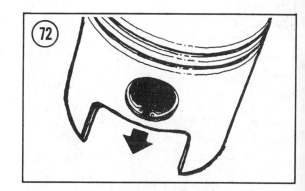

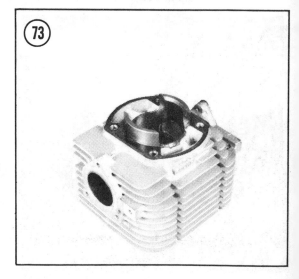

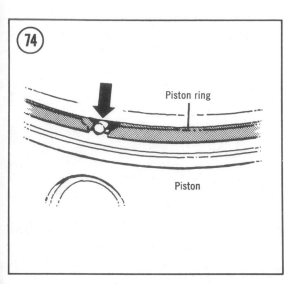

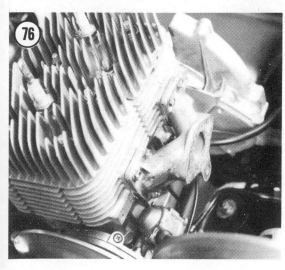

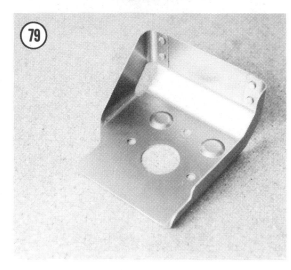

4

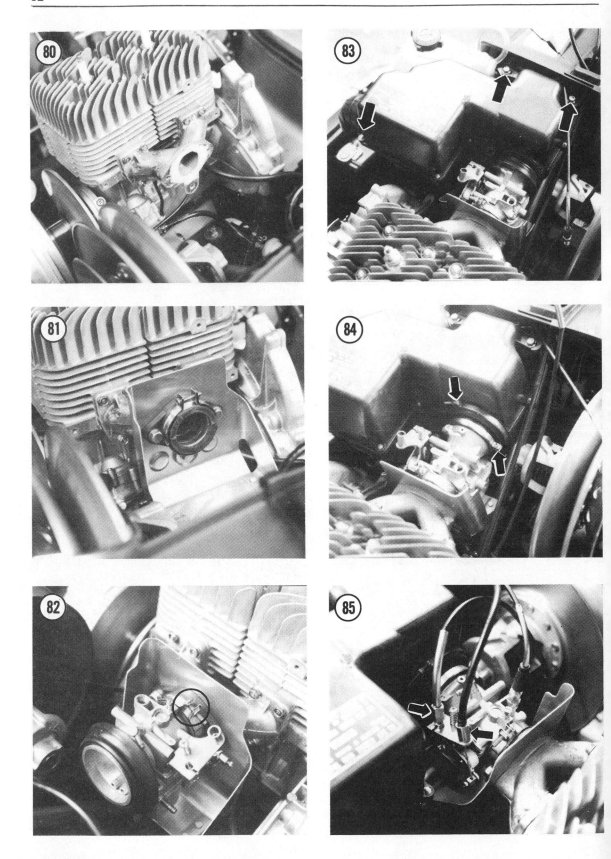

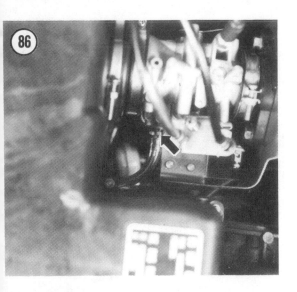

9. Apply Yamaha Bond No. 3 to both sides of the manifold gasket and set it on the manifold (**Figure 80**). Install the heat shield and the carburetor connector (**Figure 81**).

10. Install the carburetor in the connector and tighten the clamping band (**Figure 82**). Remove the large band from the carburetor-to-silencer boot and roll the boot back (**Figure 82**). Install the silencer (**Figure 83**). Roll the boot over the flange on the silencer and install and tighten the clamping bands (**Figure 84**).

11. Connect the oil pump, starter, and throttle cables (**Figure 85**). Connect the starter cable. Remove the plug from the fuel line and connect the line to the carburetor (**Figure 86**).

12. Bolt the starter rope guide to the body (**Figure 87**). Bolt the starter assembly to the engine (**Figure 88**).

13. Install the cooling shroud on the engine (**Figure 89**). On EXCEL V models, install the fan case assembly (**Figure 90**), the fan belt and

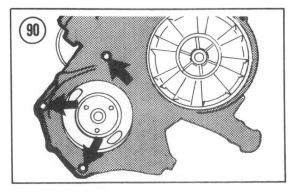

fan drive pulley (**Figure 91**), the starter pulley and bolts (**Figure 92**), and the outer fan case (**Figure 93**).

14. Check to make sure the electrical leads at the front of the engine are connected (**Figure 94**).

15. Install the coil (**Figure 95**) and connect the high-tension leads to the spark plugs.

16. Set the exhaust system in place and connect the springs that attach the head pipe to the manifold and the long spring that holds the muffler in its cradle (**Figure 96**). Position the rubber shock mount between the body and the bracket on the exhaust system tailpipe and screw in and tighten the bolt (**Figure 97**).

17. Double check to make sure all lines, cables, hoses, and wires have been reconnected and are correctly routed.

18. Refer to Chapter Two and tune the engine and service the machine as described.

> NOTE: *Following upper-end service, if any parts were replaced or if the cylinders were bored or honed, the engine should be broken in just as though it were new. In addition, it's a good idea to retorque the cylinder head nuts after several hours of operation.*

UPPER-END SERVICE (LIQUID-COOLED)

Upper-end service for liquid-cooled engines is essentially the same as that described for air-cooled engines with the exception of those points noted below.

Disassembly

Before disassembling the upper end, the coolant must first be drained.

> **WARNING**
> *Do not drain the system or disconnect the coolant hoses when the engine and coolant are hot; serious burns are likely to result.*

1. Carefully loosen the radiator cap to relieve system pressure.

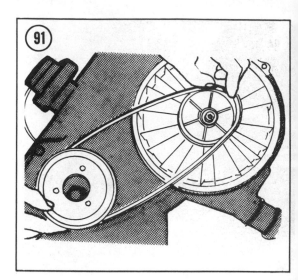

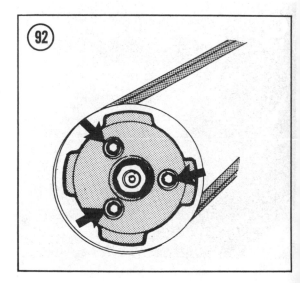

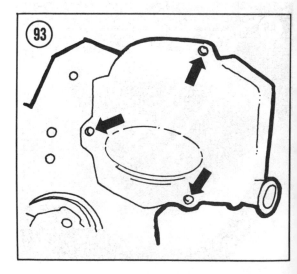

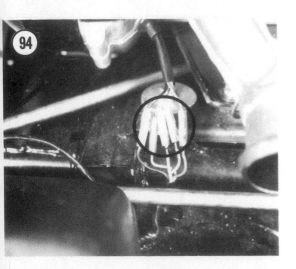

2. Remove the drain bolt from the front of each cylinder and allow the coolant to drain into a clean container.

> NOTE: *The bolts are located immediately below the exhaust outlets.*

3. Disconnect the bypass line from the thermostat housing, direct the end of the line down and into a container (**Figure 98**), and allow several minutes for the heat exchanger and the water pump to drain. Then, disconnect the top coolant hoses from the engine.

4. Refer to **Figure 99**. Remove the thermostat housing from the rear water manifold, then remove the thermostat.

4

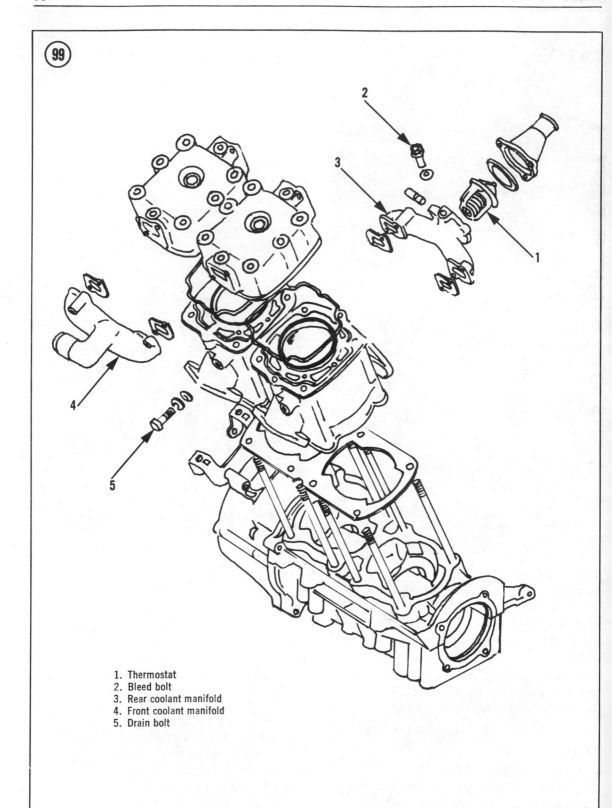

99

1. Thermostat
2. Bleed bolt
3. Rear coolant manifold
4. Front coolant manifold
5. Drain bolt

5. Unscrew the cylinder head nuts progressively in a crisscross pattern to prevent warping the heads, then unscrew the nuts. Tap around the base of the heads with a soft mallet to break them loose from the gaskets. Then, lift up on the heads and remove them.

> CAUTION
> *Be careful to keep residual coolant that may remain in the heads from leaking into the cylinders.*

6. Disconnect the exhaust system from the cylinders.

7. Loosen the clamping bands at the carburetor mounts and remove the carburetors. The carburetors need not be disconnected from their cables but can be set out of the way.

8. Tap around the bases of the cylinders to break them loose from the gaskets and then slide them up the studs to remove them.

9. Remove the outer piston pin clip from each piston (**Figure 100**), push the pins out, remove the pistons, and collect the bearings.

Cleaning

1. Scrape carbon from the combustion chamber in the heads and the exhaust ports in the cylinder, using a soft metal (aluminum) or wood scraper. Do not use a hard metal scraper; it will burr the surfaces and create hot spots.

2. Scrape old gasket material from the sealing surfaces of the heads and cylinders with a soft metal or wood scraper, taking care not to damage the surfaces. Clean the openings in the water passages and then clean the heads and cylinder with solvent and blow them dry with compressed air.

3. Remove the rings from the pistons and clean the piston crowns with a soft scraper. Clean the ring grooves with a piece of old ring. Clean the pistons with solvent and blow them dry with compressed air.

4. Clean the small-end bearings with solvent and dry them with compressed air.

5. Clean the thermostat and the passages in the water manifolds with solvent and dry them with compressed air.

Inspection

The inspection of the cylinder heads, cylinders, pistons, and bearings is the same as for air-cooled engines described earlier. However, the cylinder bores in the liquid-cooled engine are chrome plated and must be checked for damage. Check for peeling chrome toward the top of the cylinder and around the edges of the ports. If only slight peeling is apparent, the cylinders are satisfactory. But, if peeling is extensive, replace the cylinders.

Critical dimensions and tolerances are shown in **Table 2** at the end of this chapter.

Assembly

Assembly of the liquid-cooled engine is essentially the same as for air-cooled engines described earlier.

Use new cylinder base gaskets and coat both surfaces lightly with Yamaha Bond No. 3.

After installing the cylinders and heads, and before tightening the head nuts, install both front and rear coolant manifolds. Coat both sides of new gaskets with Yamaha Bond No. 4. Tighten the manifold bolts securely to align the cylinders and heads, then tighten the head nuts in a crisscross pattern to the torque specified in **Table 1** at the end of this chapter.

When assembly is complete, refer to Chapter Two and fill and bleed the cooling system, perform routine service, and tune the engine.

4

NOTE: *Following upper-end service, if any of the parts were replaced, the engine should be broken in just as though it were new. In addition, it's a good idea to retorque the cylinder head nuts after several hours of operation.*

LOWER-END SERVICE

Lower-end service as described here consists of removal, inspection, and installation of the crankshaft assembly. Inspection requires V-blocks or another suitable centering device such as a lathe or a dial indicator with base and stand. It also requires a working knowledge of precision measurement. If you lack the skills or the equipment, your dealer can make the measurements and determine what service is required.

The detailed inspection procedures are included for those equipped for the job. Critical dimensions and tolerances are shown in **Table 3** at the end of this chapter.

Crankshaft service — replacement of unsatisfactory parts or alignment of the crankshaft components — should be entrusted to your dealer or an engine specialist. A hydraulic press and considerable experience are necessary to disassemble, assemble, and accurately align the crankshaft assembly, which, in the case of the average twin cylinder engine, is made up of 7 pressed-together pieces, not counting the bearings, seals, and connecting rods.

Disassembly

1. Refer to *Engine Removal* and *Upper-end Service, Disassembly* and remove the engine from the machine and disassemble the upper end.

2. Loosen the flywheel bolt and remove the starter pulley (**Figure 101**).

3. Unscrew the fan bolts and remove the fan (**Figure 102**).

4. Unscrew the flywheel bolt, install a puller (**Figure 103**) (see **Table 3** for puller identification), and tighten the puller to break the flywheel loose from the crankshaft. It may be necessary to rap sharply on the head of the

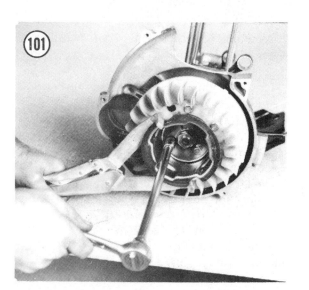

puller to break the flywheel loose. *Do not heat the flywheel.*

5. Mark the stator and the crankcase for reference during assembly (**Figure 104**). Unscrew the stator screws and remove the stator.

6. Remove the oil pump housing (**Figure 105**).

7. Remove the engine mount plate (**Figure 106**).

8. Unscrew the crankcase bolts in the order in which they are numbered (**Figure 107**).

9. Tap on the large bolt bosses with a soft mallet to break the crankcase halves apart and then remove the bottom half.

CAUTION
Do not pry the cases apart with a screwdriver or any other sharp tool, otherwise the sealing surfaces will be damaged.

10. Lift the crankshaft assembly out of the upper case half. Pay particular attention to the locating ring and alignment pins for reference during assembly.

Cleaning

1. Clean the case halves and the crankshaft assembly in *fresh solvent* and dry them with compressed air.

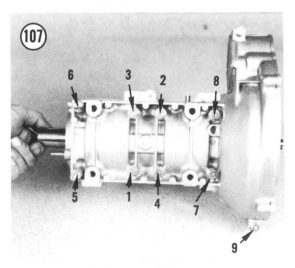

2. Clean the oil passages in the transfer ports in the upper crankcase half (**Figure 108**) and apply compressed air to them to ensure they are clean.

Inspection

1. Rotate the bearings by hand and feel for play and roughness. The bearings should turn freely and smoothly and should have no apparent play. If you are uncertain about their condition, have them checked by your dealer or an engine specialist and replaced if they are less than perfect.

2. Check the lips of the oil seals (**Figure 109**) for damage and replace them if their condition is doubtful.

3. Check the axial play of the connecting rod by measuring its side-to-side movement at the small end with a dial indicator (**Figure 110**). If the play exceeds 2 mm (0.08 in.), the big-end bearings or the connecting rod or both must be replaced. Refer this work to your dealer or an engine specialist.

4. Support the crankshaft assembly in V-blocks or a lathe and measure the runout of the shaft with a dial indicator (**Figure 111**). Maximum allowable runout for the ends is 0.03 mm (0.0012 in.) and 0.04 mm (0.0016 in.) for the center bearings. If runout exceeds these tolerances, have the assembly trued by your dealer or an engine specialist.

Assembly

1. Install the clip in the groove in the bearing (**Figure 112**).

2. Install the oil seal with the lip facing out (**Figure 113**).

3. Set the crankshaft into the upper case half, and at the same time line up the punch marks on the bearings with the edge of the case (**Figure 114**).

> NOTE: *Before the crankshaft seats in the case, the marks will actually be slightly above the edge of the case (Figure 115). It's helpful to envision the marks as being 90° from the alignment pins on the bearing.*

4. Make certain the oil seal lips line up with the grooves in the case (**Figure 116**). Then press the crankshaft down into place. Double check to make sure all the bearings and seals are seated.

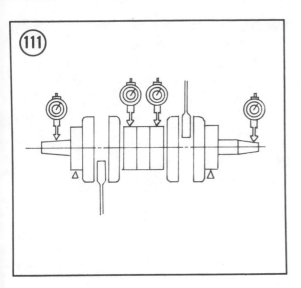

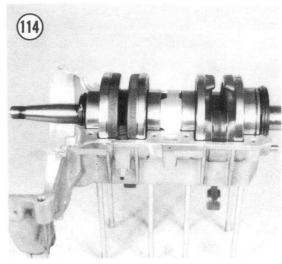

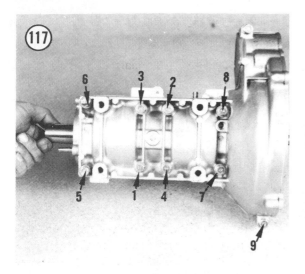

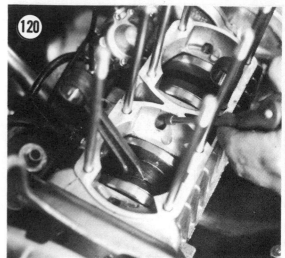

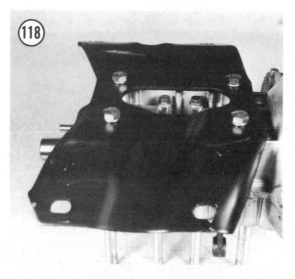

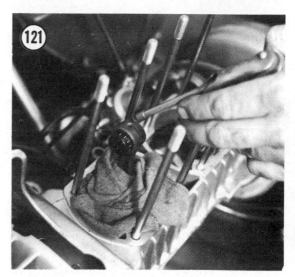

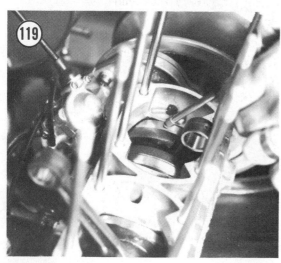

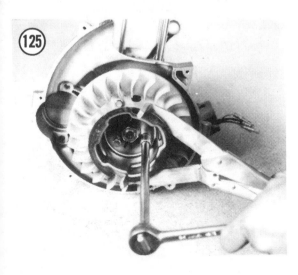

5. Coat the sealing surfaces of both case halves with Yamaha Bond No. 4.

6. Set the lower case half in place, making sure it contacts the upper case half along the entire sealing surface.

7. Screw in the crankcase bolts and run them down finger-tight. Rotate the crankshaft several complete revolutions to make sure it is correctly seated and not binding. Then, tighten the bolts progressively in numerical order (**Figure 117**) and occasionally rotate the crankshaft and check for binding and resistance. If the shaft binds, stop and locate and correct the trouble before continuing. Finally, tighten the bolts in numerical order to the torque specified in **Table 1** at the end of this chapter.

8. Install the engine mounting plate (**Figure 118**).

9. Invert the crankcase assembly and oil the big-end bearings (**Figure 119**), the main bearings (**Figure 120**), and the small-end bearings (**Figure 121**).

10. Grease the oil pump drive gears and install the oil pump housing (**Figure 122**). Refer to *Oil Pump* below.

11. Line up the mark on the stator with the mark on the crankcase (**Figure 123**) and screw in and tighten the stator screws.

12. Set the key in the crankshaft, line it up with the keyway in the rotor, and install the rotor on the crankshaft. Screw the bolt into the end of the crankshaft and tighten it to the torque specified in **Table 1** at the end of this chapter.

13. Install the fan. Line up the mark on the fan with the keyway (**Figure 124**). Install the starter pulley (**Figure 125**) and screw in and tighten the 3 bolts.

14. Refer to *Upper-End Service, Assembly* and *Engine Installation* and assemble the upper end and install the engine in the machine.

15. When installation is complete, refer to Chapter Two and service the machine and tune the engine.

> NOTE: *If any parts were replaced, break in the engine as though it were new. After several hours of operation, check the engine mounting bolts and retorque the cylinder head nuts.*

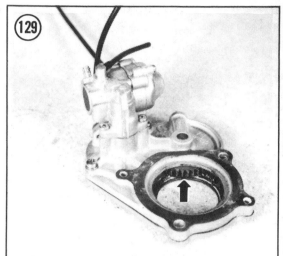

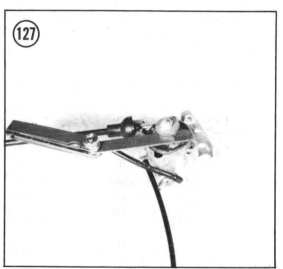

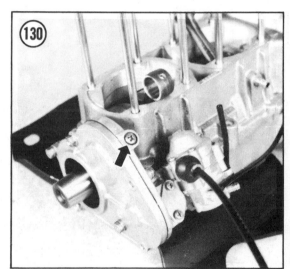

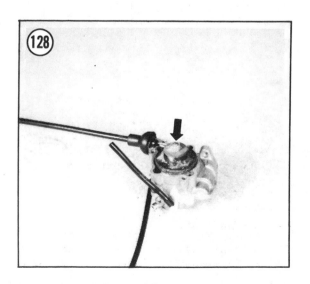

OIL PUMP

It's unlikely that the oil pump will require service at any time throughout the life of the engine. However, if oil delivery problems are suspected, the pump delivery rate can be adjusted. Work on the pump is easier when the engine is out of the machine and on a bench.

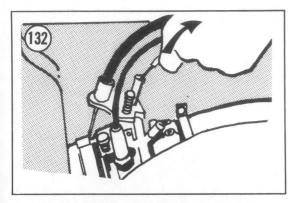

1. Remove the pump housing and the pump (**Figure 126**).

2. Extend the pump plunger and measure the gap between the boss on the adjuster pulley and the plate (**Figure 127**). The gap should be 0.020-0.025 mm (0.008-0.0098 in.).

3. If adjustment is required, remove the locknut and plate (**Figure 128**) and add or remove shims behind the plate.

4. When adjustment is correct, install the pump (**Figure 126**). Grease the drive gears and install the pump housing (**Figure 129**).

5. Connect the pump cable. Remove the Phillips screw from the pump housing (**Figure 130**) and inject grease into the housing. Then, install and tighten the screw.

6. Remove the bleed screw from the pump (**Figure 131**) and allow oil to run out until it is free of air bubbles. Then, screw in and tighten the bleed screw.

NOTE: *The oil supply tank must be connected to the pump for this initial bleeding.*

7. After the engine has been installed in the machine and is capable of running, start the engine and pull the pump cable all the way out so the pump stroke is at maximum (**Figure 132**). Run the engine at about 2,000 rpm for a couple of minutes to bleed the oil distributor and delivery line. Then, adjust the throttle cable free play as described in Chapter Two. Pull up the oil pump cable sheath (**Figure 133**) and adjust the pump cable free play to 25 mm (0.98 in.). When the adjustment is correct, tighten the cable adjuster locknut.

STARTER

Starter service and repair usually involves replacement of the starter rope. However, after long usage the starter may require complete servicing including cleaning and lubrication and replacement of worn or broken parts.

Removal/Installation

1. Unscrew the bolts that attach the rope guide to the body (**Figure 134**).

2. Unscrew the bolts that attach the starter assembly to the engine (**Figure 135**) and remove the starter.

3. Reverse the above to install the starter.

Disassembly

1. Unscrew the nut from the center of the starter drum (**Figure 136**). Remove the washers and the plate.

2. Remove the pawl and return spring (**Figure 137**).

3. Carefully remove the spring cap (**Figure 138**) and try not to release the drive spring.

> **WARNING**
> *The drive spring is under considerable tension and if it is released suddenly, it could cause injury.*

Cleaning and Inspection

1. Clean the parts in solvent and dry them with compressed air.

2. Inspect the pawl for wear and replace it if wear or damage are excessive.

3. Inspect the drive spring for breaks and cracks.

Assembly

1. The drive spring can be installed one of 2 ways — either by winding it to a small size and then installing it in the starter case, or, with assistance, it can be wound into the case beginning with the outside end of the spring. If assistance is available, the second method is recommended. Note the direction and location of the spring and the spring ends (**Figure 139**). After the spring has been installed, grease it liberally.

2. Hook the knot in the rope in the notch in the drum (**Figure 140**).

3. Wind the rope on the drum counterclockwise, leaving about an 8 in. tail (**Figure 141**).

4. Remove the knot from the notch and wind the drum 4 turns counterclockwise to preload the spring (**Figure 142**). Pull the rope and test for resistance.

5. Install the drive plate spring (**Figure 143**), the spring cap, and the pawl and return spring

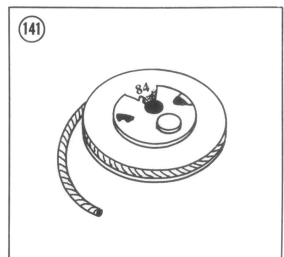

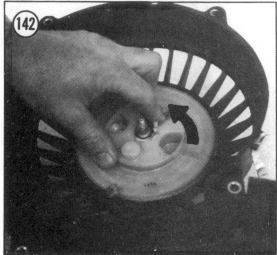

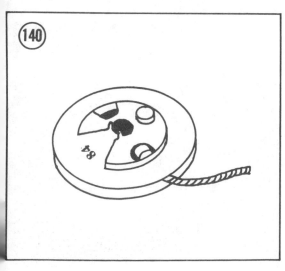

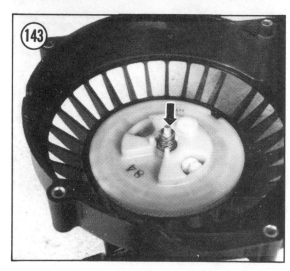

4

(Figure 144). Grease the pawl pivot and install the plate, washers, and nut **(Figure 145)**.

6. Thread the rope through the rope guide and the handle. Tie a knot in the end of the rope and fuse the knot with heat before testing the starter **(Figure 146)**. Then, pull the rope about 5 in. and check to make sure the pawl extends **(Figure 147)**.

7. Install the starter as described earlier.

EMERGENCY STARTING

If the starter rope breaks or the starter will not function, remove it **(Figure 148)** and wrap a rope around the drum on the flywheel **(Figure 149)** and pull the engine through just as you would with the starter.

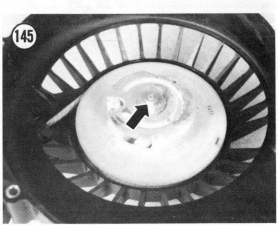

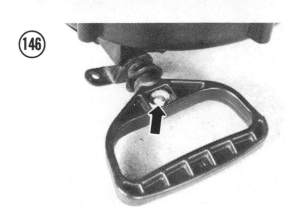

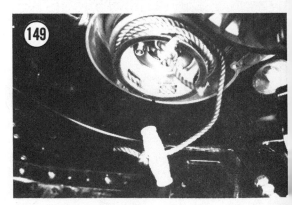

Table 1   ENGINE FASTENER TIGHTENING TORQUE

Model	Cylinder Head	Ignition Rotor	Crankcase	Engine Mounts	Drive Sheave*
		Torque, mkg (ft.-lb.)			
ET250	2.0 (15) step 1	7.3 (53)	1 & 2 (7 & 15)	3 (22)	10/6 (72/43)
ET300	2.0 (15) step 1	7.3 (53)	1 & 2 (7 & 15)	3 (22)	10/6 (72/43)
ET340	2.0 (15) step 1	7.3 (53)	1 & 2 (7 & 15)	3 (22)	12/6 (88/43)
GS340	2.0 (15) step 1	7.3 (53)	2 (15)	3.8 (27)	6/5 (43/36)
GP440	2.0 (15) step 1	7.3 (53)	2 (15)	3.8 (27)	6/5 (43/36)
EX340	2.0 (15) step 1	7.3 (53)	1 & 2 (7 & 15)	3.8 (27)	6/5 (43/36)
EX440	2.5 (18) step 2	7.3 (53)	1 & 2 (7 & 15)	3.8 (27)	6/5 (43/36)
PR440	2.5 (18) step 2	7.3 (53)	2 (15)	3 (22)	11-13 (80-90)
EXCEL V	2.5 (18) step 2	7.3 (53)	1 & 2 (7 & 15)	3.8 (27)	12/6 (88/43)
SRX	2.5 (18) step 2	7.3 (53)	2 (15)	3 (22)	6/5 (43/36)
SSR	2.5 (18) step 2	7.3 (53)	1 & 2.5 (7 & 18)	3.8 (27)	12/6 (88/43)
GP338	2.5 (18) step 2	7.3 (53)	1 & 2.5 (7 & 18)	3.8 (27)	12/6 (88/43)
GP433	2.5 (18) step 2	7.3 (53)	1 & 2.5 (7 & 18)	3.8 (27)	12/6 (88/43)
GPX338	2.5 (18) step 2	7.3 (53)	1 & 2 (7 & 15)	3 (22)	6/4 (43/28)
Nuts	2.0 (15) step 1	7.3 (53)			
	2.5 (18) step 2				
Bolts	1.8 (13) step 1	7.3 (53)			
	2.2 (16) step 2	7.3 (53)			
GPX433			1 & 2 (7 & 15)	3 (22)	6/4 (43/28)
Nuts	2.0 (15) step 1	7.3 (53)			
	2.5 (18) step 2	7.3 (53)			
Bolts	1.8 (13) step 1	7.3 (53)			
	2.2 (16) step 2	7.3 (53)			

*Tighten to first value to set sheave on crankshaft taper. Then loosen and tighten to second value.

Table 2   UPPER END SPECIFICATIONS

Model	Piston-to-Cylinder Clearance, mm (in.)	Cylinder Service Limit, mm (in.)	Ring End Gap, mm (in.)
ET250	0.045-0.050 (0.0018-0.0020)	73.05 (2.872)	0.4 (0.016)
ET300	0.040-0.045 (0.0016-0.0018)	55.95 (2.208)	0.3-0.5 (0.012-0.020)
ET300C	0.040-0.045 (0.0016-0.0018)	56.10 (2.214)	0.3-0.5 (0.012-0.020)
ET340	0.040-0.045 (0.0016-0.0018)	60.10 (2.366)	0.35-0.55 (0.014-0.022)
GS340	0.045-0.050 (0.0018-0.0020)	60.10 (2.366)	0.3-0.4 (0.012-0.016)
GP440	0.045-0.050 (0.0018-0.0020)	68.10 (2.681)	0.3-0.4 (0.012-0.016)
PR440	0.045-0.050 (0.0018-0.0020)	68.10 (2.681)	0.35-0.55 (0.014-0.022)
EX340	0.045-0.050 (0.0018-0.0020)	60.10 (2.366)	0.35-0.55 (0.014-0.022)
EX440	0.045-0.050 (0.0018-0.0020)	68.10 (2.680)	0.35-0.55 (0.014-0.022)
GP338	0.045-0.050 (0.0018-0.0020)	60.10 (2.366)	0.35-0.55 (0.014-0.022)
GP433	0.045-0.050 (0.0018-0.0020)	68.10 (2.680)	0.35-0.55 (0.014-0.022)
GPX338	0.045-0.050 (0.0018-0.0020)	60.10 (2.366)	0.35-0.55 (0.014-0.022)
GPX433	0.045-0.050 (0.0018-0.0020)	68.10 (2.680)	0.35-0.55 (0.014-0.022)
SRX440	0.065-0.070 (0.0026-0.0028)	68.60 (2.700)	0.35-0.55 (0.014-0.022)
SSR440	0.060-0.075 (0.0024-0.0030)	68.10 (2.683)	0.35-0.55 (0.014-0.022)
EXCEL V	0.055-0.060 (0.0022-0.0024)	73.10 (2.878)	0.30-0.50 (0.012-0.020)

CHAPTER FIVE

FUEL AND EXHAUST SYSTEMS

The fuel system consists of a carburetor, fuel pump, fuel tank, lines, and an in-tank fuel filter. On some models, the fuel pump is integrated with the carburetor. All fuel pumps used are operated by differential pressure in the crankcase.

Table 1 identifies the carburetors used for each model. All tables are at the end of the chapter.

An air intake silencer is used to quiet incoming air and catch fuel that may spit back through the carburetor.

This chapter covers removal, installation, repair or replacement of carburetors, fuel pumps, filters, tanks and exhaust system. Adjustment is also described along with recommended jetting procedures.

CARBURETORS

Removal/Installation

With only a few minor differences, removal and installation of carburetors on all models covered in this book are the same.

1. Raise the hood.

2. Disconnect the choke or starter cable, the throttle cable, and the oil pump cable (**Figure 1**). On slide type carburetors, unscrew the carburetor top and withdraw the slide and nee-

dle assembly (**Figure 2**). It's not necessary to disconnect the slide from the cable.

3. Disconnect the fuel line and plug it (**Figure 3**).

4. Remove the band from the intake boot at the air intake silencer (**Figure 4**) and peel the boot back (**Figure 5**).

5. Unscrew the carburetor mounting nuts or loosen the clamping band (**Figure 6**) and remove the carburetor.

6. Reverse the above to install the carburetor. When installation is complete, adjust the carburetor as described later in this chapter. Adjustment procedures follow each of the carburetor service procedures.

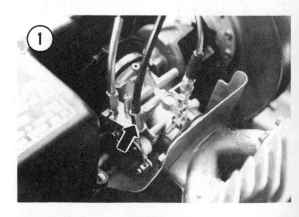

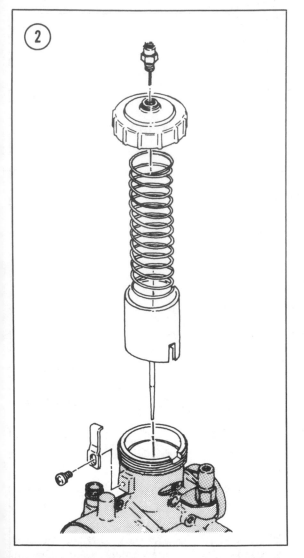

5

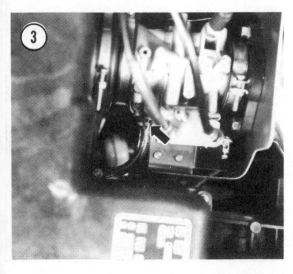

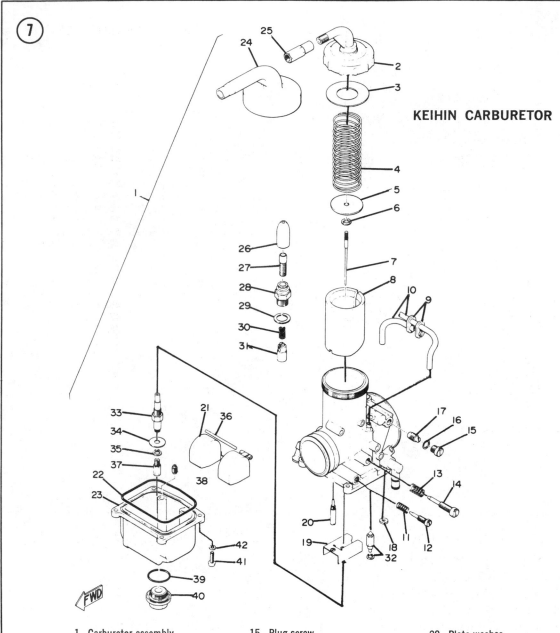

KEIHIN CARBURETOR

1. Carburetor assembly
2. Mixing chamber top
3. Gasket
4. Throttle valve spring
5. Spring seat
6. Clip
7. Needle jet
8. Throttle valve
9. Clip
10. Hose
11. Adjust screw spring
12. Adjust screw
13. Stop screw spring
14. Stop screw
15. Plug screw
16. Washer
17. Power jet
18. Ring
19. Buffer plate
20. Slow jet
21. Float
22. O-ring
23. Float chamber body
24. Cap
25. Wire adjuster
26. Starter plunger cap cover
27. Cable adjuster
28. Starter plunger cap
29. Plate washer
30. Starter plunger spring
31. Starter plunger
32. Valve seat assembly
33. Needle jet
34. Plate washer
35. Clip
36. Float pin
37. Main jet
38. Starter jet
39. O-ring
40. Drain bolt
41. Pan head screw
42. Spring washer

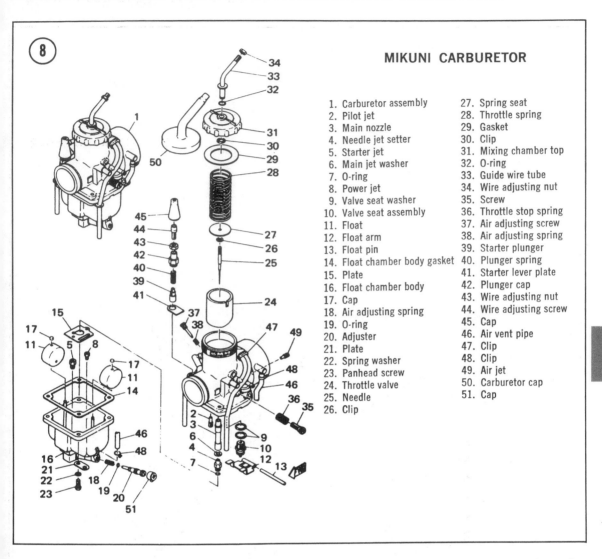

MIKUNI CARBURETOR

1. Carburetor assembly
2. Pilot jet
3. Main nozzle
4. Needle jet setter
5. Starter jet
6. Main jet washer
7. O-ring
8. Power jet
9. Valve seat washer
10. Valve seat assembly
11. Float
12. Float arm
13. Float pin
14. Float chamber body gasket
15. Plate
16. Float chamber body
17. Cap
18. Air adjusting spring
19. O-ring
20. Adjuster
21. Plate
22. Spring washer
23. Panhead screw
24. Throttle valve
25. Needle
26. Clip
27. Spring seat
28. Throttle spring
29. Gasket
30. Clip
31. Mixing chamber top
32. O-ring
33. Guide wire tube
34. Wire adjusting nut
35. Screw
36. Throttle stop spring
37. Air adjusting screw
38. Air adjusting spring
39. Starter plunger
40. Plunger spring
41. Starter lever plate
42. Plunger cap
43. Wire adjusting nut
44. Wire adjusting screw
45. Cap
46. Air vent pipe
47. Clip
48. Clip
49. Air jet
50. Carburetor cap
51. Cap

SLIDE CARBURETORS

EX340/440 and EX340A/440A machines are equipped with Keihin PW slide carburetors. SRX and SSR models are equipped with Mikuni VM slide carburetors. Both carburetors are nearly identical in construction and service requirements; however, parts, including jets, are not interchangeable.

Disassembly

Refer to **Figure 7** for Keihin carburetors, or **Figure 8** for Mikuni.

1. Unscrew the 4 screws that attach the float bowl to the carburetor and remove the bowl. Empty the gasoline into a sealable container.

2. Remove the float hinge pin and float. Tap out the valve needle and unscrew the valve body.

3. Unscrew the main jet.

4. Unscew the slow jet (2, **Figure 7** or 2, **Figure 8**).

5. For Keihin carburetors, unscrew the needle jet (33, **Figure 7**). For Mikuni carburetors, press the jet out of the body.

6. Unscrew the power jet (17, **Figure 7** — Keihin only).

7. Remove the throttle stop screw (14, **Figure 7** or 35, **Figure 8**).

8. Unscrew the idle mixture screw (12, **Figure 7** or 37, **Figure 8**.)

9. Remove the starter (28, **Figure 7** or 42, **Figure 8**).

Cleaning and Inspection

A special carburetor cleaning solvent, tank, and basket can be purchased at auto parts stores for just a few dollars. When not in use, the tank can be sealed to prevent the reuseable solvent from evaporating.

> **WARNING**
> *Most carburetor cleaning solvents are highly caustic. Handle them with extreme care to prevent skin burns and eye injury.*

1. Clean all metal parts in the carburetor cleaning solvent.

> **CAUTION**
> *Do not place gaskets, O-rings, floats, or other non-metal parts in the solvent or they will be damaged.*

2. Dry the parts with compressed air. Blow out all jets and passages to ensure that no solvent or residue remains.

> **CAUTION**
> *Never clean passages or jets with small drill bits or wire; the soft metal is very easily burred resulting in changes in the effective size of the hole and altered fuel flow rate.*

3. Inspect the carburetor body and float bowl for fine cracks or evidence of fuel leaks. Minor damage can be repaired with epoxy or a "liquid aluminum" type filler.

4. Inspect the taper of the idle mixture air scew for scoring and replace it if it is less than perfect. Inspect the threads of the throttle stop screw for damage which could cause binding.

5. Inspect the jets for internal damage and damaged threads. Replace any jet that is less than perfect. Make certain replacement jets are the same size as the original.

> **CAUTION**
> *The jets must be scrupulously clean and shiny. Any burring, roughness, or abrasion could cause a lean mixture that will result in major engine damage.*

6. Inspect the float valve seat and needle taper for scoring, wear, or any other signs of damage and replace them as a set if they are less than

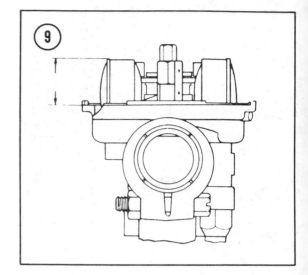

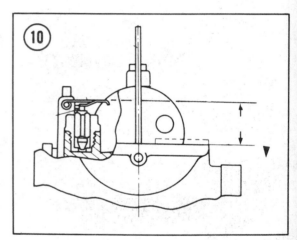

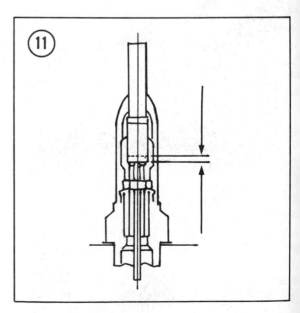

perfect. A damaged float valve will result in flooding of the float chamber and impair performance. In addition, accumulation of raw gasoline in the engine compartment presents a severe fire hazard.

7. Inspect the jet needle and needle jet for scoring, wear, or damage and replace them as a set if they are less than perfect. Check the movement of the needle in the needle jet. It must move freely in and out without binding.

8. Check the movement of the float on the pivot pin. It must move freely without binding.

9. Check the movement of the starting plunger (choke) in the passage in the carburetor. It should move freely in and out.

10. Check the movement of the throttle slide in the carburetor. It should move freely up and down without binding and it should not be loose. If either the slide or the slide bore in the carburetor body appear to be worn, one or both pieces should be replaced.

Assembly

Refer to **Figure 7** or **Figure 8**.

1. Install the starter assembly (28, **Figure 7**, or 42, **Figure 8**).

2. Install the idle mixture screw (12, **Figure 7** or 37, **Figure 8**). Screw it in carefully, just until it seats. *Don't tighten it; the screw and seat are easily damaged.* For Keihin carburetors, back the screw out one full turn. For Mikuni carburetors, back the screw out ½ turn. This provides a basic setting that will permit the engine to start and idle well enough to allow the correct adjustment to be made.

3. Install the throttle stop screw (14, **Figure 7** or 36, **Figure 8**).

4. Install the power jet (17, **Figure 7** — Keihin only).

5. Install the needle jet (33, **Figure 7** or 3, **Figure 8**).

6. Install the slow jet (20, **Figure 7** or 2, **Figure 8**).

7. Install the main jet (37, **Figure 7** or 5, **Figure 8**). Don't overtighten the jet and damage the threads.

8. Screw the float valve into the carburetor. Set the float needle in the valve. Install the float

and the float hinge pin. Make sure the pin is seated.

9. Measure the float height, and correct it if necessary, as described below.

10. Install the float bowl gasket and the float bowl. Start all the screws in before tightening them.

Float Level Adjustment

The float level should be routinely checked and adjusted whenever the carburetor is disassembled and cleaned, or when flooding indicates that the level may be incorrect.

1. Invert the carburetor. Allow the float arm to contact the needle valve, but don't compress the spring-loaded plunger on the needle.

2A. For Keihin carburetors, measure the distance from the top of the float to the float bowl flange on the carburetor (**Figure 9**). The distance should be 19-21 mm (0.75-0.83 in.). If necessary, carefully bend the float arm until the distance is correct.

2B. For Mikuni carburetors, measure the distance from the float arm to the float bowl flange on the carburetor (**Figure 10**). The distance should be 18 mm (0.71 in.). If necessary, carefully bend the tang that depresses the needle valve until the distance is correct.

Adjustment

There are 5 adjustments possible with slide type carburetors, because they are interdependent, they should be carried out in the following order for best results.

a. Starter cable free play

b. Throttle cable free play

c. Idle mixture screw/throttle stop screw

d. Slide needle position (mid-range)

e. Main jet/jetting adjustment

1. Pull up on the starter cable and measure the distance between the end of the sheath and the adjuster (**Figure 11**). It should be 1.5-2.5 mm (0.06-0.1 in.) for Mikuni carburetors, and 0.5-1.0 mm (0.2-0.4 in.) for Keihin carburetors.

5

If adjustment is required, loosen the locknut on the adjuster (**Figure 12**) and turn the adjuster in or out until the free play is correct. Then, hold the adjuster to prevent it from turning further and tighten the locknut.

2. Pull up on the throttle cable sheath and measure the distance between the end of the sheath and the adjuster (**Figure 13**). It should be 0.5-1.0 mm (0.2-0.4 in.). If the free play is incorrect, loosen the locknut on the adjuster (**Figure 14**) and turn the adjuster in or out until the free play is correct. Then, without further turning the adjuster, tighten the locknut.

3. Start the engine and allow it to warm up to operating temperature. Set the idle speed at about 2,000 rpm with the throttle stop screw (**Figure 15**). Set the idle mixture screws on both carburetors as specified in **Table 2**. Then, turn the screws in or out, equally, until the idle speed is at its highest pioint.

CAUTION
If the idle speed rises to the point where it is approaching clutch engagement speed, reduce the speed by backing off the throttle stop screw. Idle speed should be 1,500-2,000 rpm.

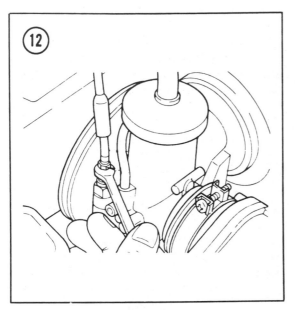

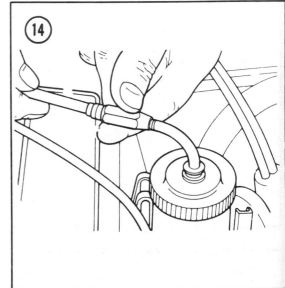

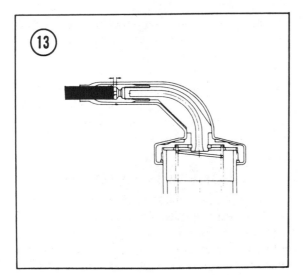

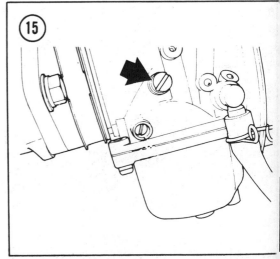

4. To check the mid-range setting (slide needle position), first warm up the engine, then accelerate the machine hard, with full throttle, and "feel" the engine response. If the engine seems starved or if it knocks, the mid-range mixture is too lean. In this case, remove the carburetor top and slide assembly and raise the needle in the slide by moving the needle clip to the next lower notch (**Figure 16**). Then recheck the performance and if the mixture is still too lean, raise the needle one more position; move the needle one position at a time.

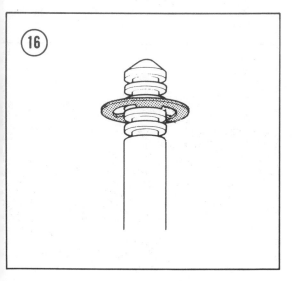

If the engine "blubbers" or if there is excessive exhaust smoke during hard acceleration, the mixture is too rich in mid-range. In this case, lower the needle in the slide by moving the clip to a higher notch. Then recheck the performance and if it is still too rich, lower the needle another position.

CAUTION
After adjusting the slide needle position, check the operation of the throttle to make sure the slide moves freely in its bore and closes when throttle is closed.

5. Check the condition of the high-speed mixture ratio by conducting a "plug chop" as described under *Jetting* later in this chapter. For carburetors equipped with a main jet adjuster screw (**Figure 17**), the mixture can be made leaner by turning the screw clockwise and made richer by turning it counterclockwise.

CAUTION
During testing and adjustment, turn the screw no more than $\frac{1}{8}$ turn at a time. Massive changes, such as $\frac{1}{2}$ turn at a time, may take the mixture beyond the optimum point and yield inaccurate information, or, at the worst, the mixture could be made so lean that engine damage may result.

If the carburetors are not eqipped with main jet adjusting screws, high-speed mixture corrections must be made by changing main jet sizes. In this case, also refer to *Jetting* and make any required adjustments and changes as described.

When all the adjustments discussed have been made, test the machine in all modes of carburetor performance — starting, idle, acceleration, and sustained high-speed operation. If performance is deficient in any mode, readjust the carburetors as just described until total performance is satisfactory.

BD44-38 KEIHIN CARBURETOR

The Keihin BD44-38 carburetor is equipped with a butterfly throttle valve and a mixture enrichment valve for cold starting. Fuel is supplied to the carburetor by a remote pulse-type pump.

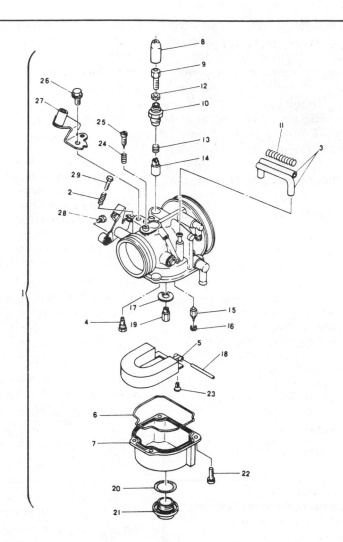

BD44-38 KEIHIN
CARBURETOR

1. Carburetor assembly
2. Spring
3. Hose
4. Slow jet
5. Float
6. O-ring
7. Float chamber body
8. Starter plunger cap cover
9. Cable adjuster
10. Starter plunger cap
11. Spring
12. Nut
13. Starter plunger spring
14. Starter plunger
15. Valve seat assembly

16. Clip
17. Clip
18. Float pin
19. Main jet
20. O-ring
21. Drain bolt
22. Panhead screw with washer
23. Flathead screw
24. Spring
25. Adjust screw
26. Bolt with washer
27. Stay
28. Bolt
29. Panhead screw
30. Spring

Disassembly

Refer to **Figure 18** for the procedure that follows.

1. Unscrew the 4 screws that attach the float bowl to the carburetor. Remove the bowl, the float pivot pin (18), and the float (5).

2. Remove the slow jet (4), the main jet (19) and clip (17), and the float needle valve (15) and clip (16).

3. Remove the idle mixture (pilot) screw (25) and spring (24).

4. Remove the throttle stop screw (29) and spring (2).

> **CAUTION**
> *Do not remove the throttle butterfly valve or the throttle shaft. The screws that locate the butterfly in the shaft are staked during assembly at the factory to prevent them from coming loose and being drawn into the engine. Also, the air bypass hole is precisely machined into the butterfly, and if the butterfly is disturbed, it's unlikely that the hole will be correctly aligned during reassembly.*

Cleaning and Inspection

1. Clean all metal parts in carburetor cleaning solvent.

> **CAUTION**
> *Do not place gaskets, O-rings, floats, or other non-metal parts in the solvent or they will be damaged.*

> **WARNING**
> *Most carburetor cleaning solvents are highly caustic. Handle them with care to prevent skin burns and eye injury.*

2. Dry the parts with compressed air. Blow out all jets and passages to ensure that no solvent or residue remains.

> **CAUTION**
> *Never clean jets and passages with small drill bits or wire; the soft metal is easily burred and as a result the jet size will be changed and affect mixture ratio.*

3. Inspect the carburetor body and float bowl for fine cracks or evidence of fuel leaks. Minor damage can be repaired with epoxy or "liquid aluminum" type filler.

4. Inspect the taper of the idle mixture air screw for scoring and replace it if it is less than perfect. Inspect the threads of the throttle stop screw for damage which could cause binding.

5. Inspect the jets for internal damage and damaged threads. Replace any jet that is less than perfect. Make certain replacement jets are the same size as the originals.

> **CAUTION**
> *The jets must be scrupulously clean and shiny. Any burring or roughness could cause a lean mixture that could result in major engine damage.*

6. Inspect the float valve seat and needle taper for scoring, wear, or other signs of damage and replace them as a set if they are less than perfect. A damaged float valve will result in flooding of the float chamber and impair performance. In addition, accumulation of raw gasoline in the engine compartment presents a servere fire hazard.

7. Check the movement of the float arm on the pivot pin. It must move freely without binding.

8. Check the movement of the starter plunger (choke) in the passage in the carburetor. It should move freely in and out. Check also to make sure the plunger assembly is clean.

9. Check the movement of the throttle shaft and butterfly. They should move freely. If they do not, look for burring in the venturi where the butterfly contacts it in the closed position. Minor imperfections can be removed with crocus cloth and oil, but if damage is extensive, replace the carburetor body.

Assembly

Refer to **Figure 18** for the procedure that follows.

1. Install throttle stop screw (29) and spring (2).

2. Install the idle air mixture screw (25) and spring (24). Carefully run the screw in just until it contacts its seat. Then, screw it out the number of turns specified in **Table 2**. This provides a basic setting that will permit the engine to run while final adjustment is being made.

3. Install the float needle valve (15) and clip (16).

5

4. Install the slow jet (4) and the main jet (19) and clip (17).

5. Install the float (5) and float pivot pin (18). Check the float level (see *Float Level* below) and correct it if necessary.

6. Install the float bowl. Make sure the O-ring gasket is correctly seated in the groove in the bowl. Start all 4 screws in before tightening them.

Float Level

1. Hold the carburetor so the weight of the float valve does not pull it down from the float arm (**Figure 19**).

2. Measure the distance from the float chamber flange on the carburetor to the float arm. It should be 15-17 mm (0.59-0.67 in.).

> NOTE: *The float arm should contact the spring-loaded plunger in the needle valve but should not depress it.*

3. If the distance is not correct, remove the float and carefully bend the contact tang as required.

Adjustment

There are 5 adjustments for the B44-38 Keihin carburetor. Because they are interdependent, they must be carried out in the order described below for best results.

    a. Throttle cable adjustment

    b. Starter cable adjustment

    c. Oil pump cable adjustment

    d. Idle mixture adjustment

    e. Jetting (main jet)

1. Check the free play of the throttle lever (**Figure 20**). It should be 0.5-1.0 mm (0.02-0.04 in.). If it's not correct, loosen the screw that attaches the throttle cable to the throttle arm (**Figure 21**) and move the cable in or out as required; then tighten the screw.

2. Pull up on the starter cable sheath and measure the distance between the end of the sheath and the adjuster (**Figure 22**). It should be 0.5-1.0 mm (0.02-0.04 in.). If adjustment is required, loosen the locknut on the adjuster and run the adjuster in or out as required. When ad-

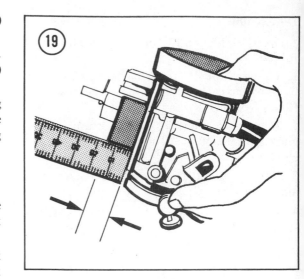

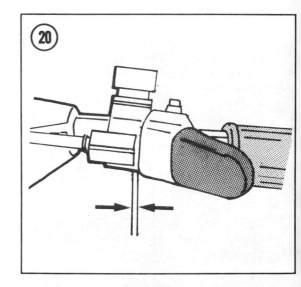

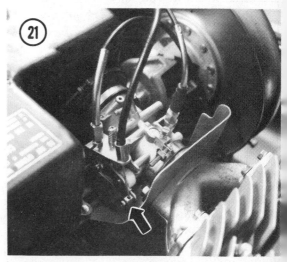

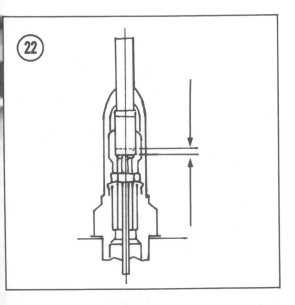

justment is correct, hold the adjuster to prevent it from turning further and tighten the locknut.

3. Pull up on the oil pump cable sheath and measure the distance from the end of the sheath to the adjuster (**Figure 23**). The free play should be 25 mm (1 in.). If adjustment is required, loosen the locknut on the adjuster and run the adjuster in or out as required. When free play is correct, hold the adjuster to prevent it from turning further and tighten the locknut.

4. Set the idle mixture screw as specified in **Table 2**. Start the engine, warm it up, and adjust the idle to 1,500-2,000 rpm with the throttle stop screw (**Figure 24**). Turn the idle mixture screw (**Figure 25**) in or out, $\frac{1}{8}$ turn at a time, until the engine idles at the fastest speed. Then, adjust the idle speed to 1,500-2,000 rpm with the throttle stop screw.

CAUTION

If the idle speed rises to the point where it is approaching clutch engagement speed, reduce the speed by backing off the throttle stop screw.

5. Refer to *Jetting* later in this chapter and adjust the main jet circuit as described through changes in main jet size.

B38-34 MIKUNI CARBURETOR

The B38-34 Mikuni carburetor is fitted with a butterfly throttle valve and mixture enrichment valve for cold starting. Fuel is supplied by a remote pulse-type pump.

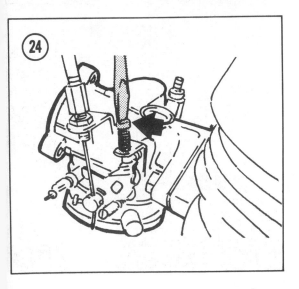

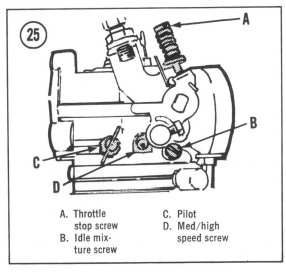

A. Throttle stop screw
B. Idle mixture screw
C. Pilot
D. Med/high speed screw

5

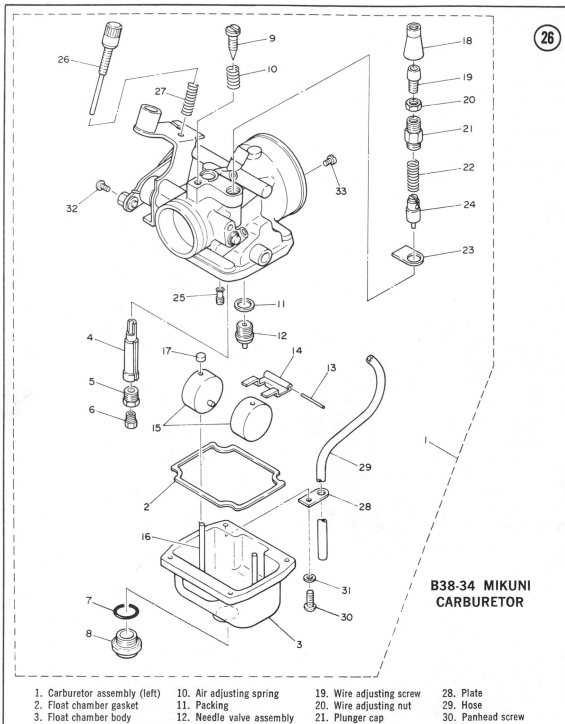

B38-34 MIKUNI CARBURETOR

26

1. Carburetor assembly (left)
2. Float chamber gasket
3. Float chamber body
4. Main nozzle
5. Holder guide
6. Main jet
7. O-ring
8. Screw guide
9. Pilot adjusting screw
10. Air adjusting spring
11. Packing
12. Needle valve assembly
13. Pin
14. Arm
15. Float
16. Pin
17. Cap
18. Cap
19. Wire adjusting screw
20. Wire adjusting nut
21. Plunger cap
22. Plunger spring
23. Plate
24. Plunger assembly
25. Pilot jet
26. Screw assembly
27. Spring
28. Plate
29. Hose
30. Panhead screw
31. Spring washer
32. Panhead screw
33. Air pilot jet

Disassembly

Refer to **Figure 26** for the procedure that follows.

1. Unscrew the 4 screws that attach the float bowl to the carburetor. Remove the bowl and float assembly.

2. Push the float arm pivot pin (13) out of the posts in the carburetor body and remove the float arm (14).

3. Unscrew the main jet (6) and pilot jet (25).

4. Unscrew the main jet block (5) and press the needle jet (4) out of the carburetor.

5. Remove the float needle valve (12).

6. Remove the idle air mixture control screw (9) and spring (10).

7. Remove the throttle stop screw (26) and spring (27).

CAUTION
Do not remove the throttle butterfly valve or the throttle shaft. The screws that locate the butterfly in the shaft are staked to prevent them from coming loose and being drawn into the engine. Also, an air bypass hole is precisely machined into the butterfly during assembly at the factory, and if the butterfly is disturbed, it's unlikely that the hole will be correctly aligned during reassembly.

Cleaning and Inspection

1. Clean all metal parts in carburetor cleaning solvent.

CAUTION
Do not place gaskets, O-rings, floats, or other non-metal parts in the solvent or they will be damaged.

WARNING
Most carburetor cleaning solvents are highly caustic. Handle them with care to prevent skin burns and eye injuries.

2. Blow the parts dry with compressed air. Blow out all the jets and passages to ensure that no solvent or residue remains.

CAUTION
Never clean jets and passages with small drill bits or wire; the soft metal is easily burred and as a result the jet size will be changed and affect mixture ratio.

3. Inspect the carburetor body and float bowl for fine cracks or evidence of fuel leaks. Minor damage can be repaired with epoxy or liquid aluminum type filler.

4. Inspect the taper of the idle mixture air screw for scoring and replace it if it is less than perfect. Inspect the threads of the throttle stop screw for damage which could cause binding.

5. Inspect the jets for internal damage and damaged threads. Replace any jet that is less than perfect. Make certain replacement jets are the same size as the originals.

CAUTION
The jets must be scrupulously clean and shiny. Any burring, roughness, or abrasion could cause a lean mixture that could result in major engine damage.

6. Inspect the float valve seat and needle taper for scoring, wear, or other signs of damage and replace them as a set if they are less than perfect. A damaged float valve will result in flooding of the float chamber and impair performance. In addition, accumulation of raw gasoline in the engine compartment presents a severe fire hazard.

7. Check the movement of the float arm on the pivot pin. It must move freely without binding.

8. Check the movement of the starter plunger (choke) in the passage in the carburetor. It should move freely in and out. Check also to make sure the plunger assembly is clean.

9. Check the movement of the throttle shaft and butterfly. They should move freely. If they do not, look for burring in the venturi where the butterfly contacts it in the closed position. Minor imperfections can be removed with crocus cloth and oil, but if damage is extensive, replace the carburetor body.

Assembly

Refer to **Figure 26** for the procedure that follows.

1. Install the throttle stop screw (26) and spring (27).

2. Install the idle air mixture control screw (9) and spring (10). Carefully run the screw in just

5

until it contacts its seat. Then, screw it out the number of turns specified in **Table 2**. This provides a basic setting that will permit the engine to run while final adjustment is being made.

3. Install the float needle valve (12).

4. Install the spray nozzle (4) and the main jet holder (5).

5. Install the main jet (6) and the pilot jet (25). Take care not to overtighten them and strip the threads.

6. Install the float arm (14) and the float arm pivot pin (13). Check the float level (see *Float Level* below) and correct it if necessary.

7. Install the float bowl. Start all of the 4 screws in before tightening them.

Float Level

1. Hold the carburetor so the weight of the float valve does not pull it down from the float arm (**Figure 27**).

2. Measure the distance from the float chamber flange on the carburetor to float arm. It should be 15-17 mm (0.59-0.67 in.).

> NOTE: *The float arm should rest on the spring-loaded plunger but should not depress it.*

3. If the distance is not correct, remove the float arm and carefully bend the contact tang as required.

Adjustment

There are 5 adjustments for the B38-34 Mikuni carburetor. Because they are interdependent, they must be carried out in the order described below for best results.

   a. Throttle cable adjustment

   b. Starter cable adjustment

   c. Oil pump cable adjustment

   d. Idle mixture adjustment

   e. Jetting (main jet)

1. Check the free play of the throttle lever (**Figure 28**). It should be 0.5-1.0 mm (0.02-0.04 in.). If it's not correct, loosen the screw that attaches the throttle cable to the throttle arm (**Figure 29**) and move the cable in or out as required and then tighten the screw.

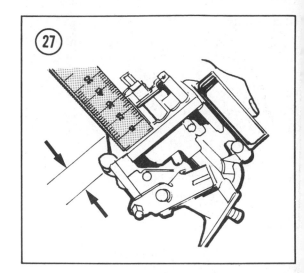

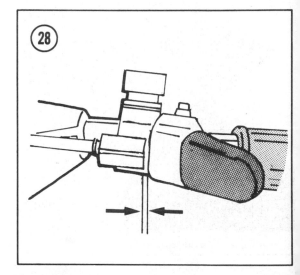

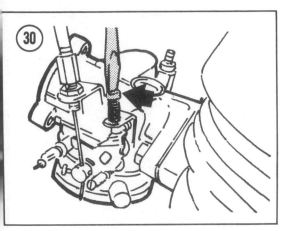

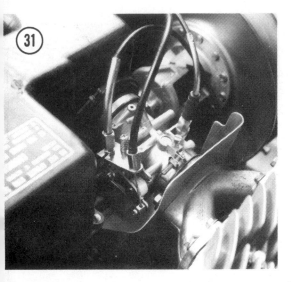

2. Pull up on the starter cable sheath and measure the distance between the end of the sheath and the adjuster (**Figure 30**). It should be 0.5-1.0 mm (0.02-0.04 in.). If adjustment is required, loosen the locknut on the adjuster and run the adjuster in or out as required. When adjustment is correct, hold the adjuster to prevent it from turning further and tighten the locknut.

3. Pull up on the oil pump cable sheath and measure the distance from the end of the sheath to the adjuster (**Figure 31**). The free play should be 25 mm (1 in.). If adjustment is required, loosen the locknut on the adjuster and run the adjuster in or out as required. When free play is correct, hold the adjuster to prevent it from turning further and tighten the locknut.

4. Set the idle mixture screw as specified in **Table 2**. Start the engine, warm it up, and adjust the idle to 1,500-2,000 rpm with the throttle stop screw (**Figure 32**). Turn the idle mixture screw (**Figure 33**) in or out, $\frac{1}{8}$ turn at a time, until the engine idles at the fastest speed. Then, adjust the idle speed to 1,500-2,000 rpm with the throttle stop screw.

5

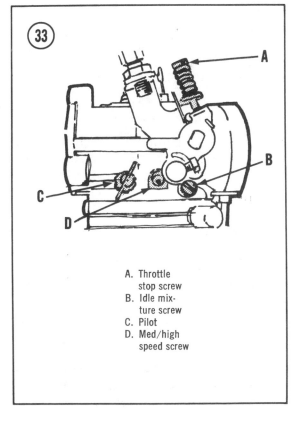

A. Throttle
   stop screw
B. Idle mix-
   ture screw
C. Pilot
D. Med/high
   speed screw

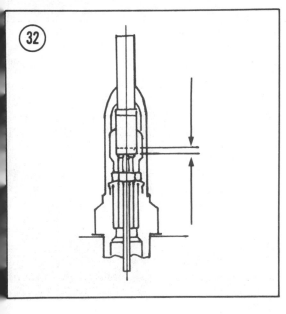

CAUTION
If the idle speed rises to the point where it is approaching clutch engagement speed, reduce the engine speed by backing off the throttle stop screw.

5. Refer to *Jetting* later in this chapter and adjust the main jet circuit as described through changes in main jet size.

BN38-34SH MIKUNI CARBURETOR

The Mikuni BN38-34SH carburetor is equipped with a butterfly throttle and a mixture enrichment valve for cold starting. The carburetor incorporates an integral pulse-type fuel pump.

Disassembly

Refer to **Figure 34** for the procedure that follows.

1. Remove the bottom cover (22) and gasket (21). Remove the No. 3 body (20), check valve (19), gasket (18), No. 2 body (17), gaskets (14), pump diaphragm (16), No. 1 body (15), and main diaphragm (13).

2. Remove lever pin (11), diaphragm arm (9), spring (10), and valve (5).

3. Remove the valve plate (6) and needle valve body (5). Remove the check valve plate (3), check valve seat (2), and gasket (1).

CAUTION
Take care not to damage the check valve seat.

4. Remove the idle air mixture screw (36) and spring (35). Remove the main adjusting screw (34).

CAUTION
Remove the O-rings from the main mixture screw seat, carefully, only if the carburetor body is to be submerged in carburetor solvent.

5. Remove the pilot jet (38).

CAUTION
Do not remove the throttle butterfly and shaft. The screws that locate the butterfly in the shaft are staked to prevent them from backing out and being drawn into the engine. Also, an air bypass hole

is precisely machined in the throttle butterfly during assembly at the factory and if the butterfly is disturbed, it's unlikely that the hole will be correctly aligned during assembly.

Cleaning and Inspection

1. Clean all metal parts in carburetor cleaning solvent.

CAUTION
Do not place gaskets, O-rings, diaphragms, or other non-metal parts in the solvent or they will be damaged.

WARNING
Most carburetor cleaning solvents are highly caustic. Handle them with care to prevent skin burns and eye injury.

2. Dry the parts with compressed air. Blow out all the jets and air passages to ensure that no solvent or residue remains.

CAUTION
Never clean jets and passages with small drill bits or wire; the soft metal is easily burred and as a result the jet size will be changed and affect the mixture ratio.

3. Inspect the carburetor and pump bodies for fine cracks and evidence of fuel leaks. Minor damage can be repaired with epoxy or "liquid aluminum" type filler.

4. Inspect the taper of the idle mixture air screw and the main adjusting screw for scoring and replace them if they are less than perfect. Inspect the threads of the throttle stop screw which could cause binding.

5. Inspect the jets for internal damage and damaged threads. Replace any jet that is less than perfect. Make certain replacement jets are the same size as the originals.

CAUTION
The jets must be scrupulously clean and shiny. Any burring or roughness could cause a lean mixture ratio that could result in major engine damage.

6. Check the movement of the diaphragm arm on its pivot pin. It must move freely without binding.

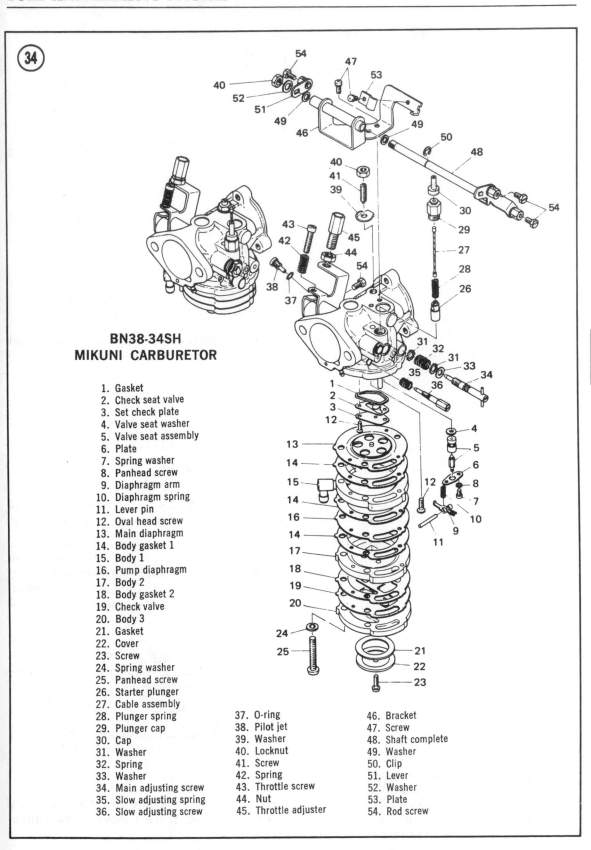

**BN38-34SH
MIKUNI CARBURETOR**

1. Gasket
2. Check seat valve
3. Set check plate
4. Valve seat washer
5. Valve seat assembly
6. Plate
7. Spring washer
8. Panhead screw
9. Diaphragm arm
10. Diaphragm spring
11. Lever pin
12. Oval head screw
13. Main diaphragm
14. Body gasket 1
15. Body 1
16. Pump diaphragm
17. Body 2
18. Body gasket 2
19. Check valve
20. Body 3
21. Gasket
22. Cover
23. Screw
24. Spring washer
25. Panhead screw
26. Starter plunger
27. Cable assembly
28. Plunger spring
29. Plunger cap
30. Cap
31. Washer
32. Spring
33. Washer
34. Main adjusting screw
35. Slow adjusting spring
36. Slow adjusting screw

37. O-ring
38. Pilot jet
39. Washer
40. Locknut
41. Screw
42. Spring
43. Throttle screw
44. Nut
45. Throttle adjuster

46. Bracket
47. Screw
48. Shaft complete
49. Washer
50. Clip
51. Lever
52. Washer
53. Plate
54. Rod screw

5

7. Check the diaphragm springs for resiliency.

8. Check movement of the throttle butterfly and shaft. They should move freely. If they do not, look for burring in the venturi where the butterfly contacts it when it is closed. Minor imperfections can be removed with crocus cloth and oil, but if damage is extensive, replace the carburetor body.

9. Inspect the diaphragms and gaskets and replace any that are damaged.

10. Inspect the check valve for damage and replace it if it is less than perfect.

Assembly

Refer to **Figure 34** for the procedure that follows.

1. Install the pilot jet (38).

2. Install the idle mixture screw (36) and spring (35). Install the main adjusting screw (34). Carefully run the screws in just until they contact their seats. Then, back them out the number of turns specified in **Table 2**. This provides a basic setting that will permit the engine to run while final adjustment is being made.

3. Install the check valve gasket (1), check valve seat (2), and check valve plate (3). Install the needle valve body (5) and the valve plate (6).

4. Install the valve needle (5), spring (10), diaphragm arm (9), and lever pin (11).

5. Refer to **Figure 35** and assemble the pump bodies, diaphragms, and springs. Make sure the rim of the main diaphragm fits into the flange on the pump body.

Adjustment

There are 4 adjustments for the BN38-34SH carburetor. They are interdependent and must be carried out in the order shown below for best results.

   a. Idle mixture adjustment

   b. Throttle stop adjustment

   c. Pilot jet adjustment

   d. Main mixture screw adjustment

1. Set the idle mixture screw as specified in **Table 2**. Then, start the engine and allow it to idle. Turn the idle mixture screw either in or

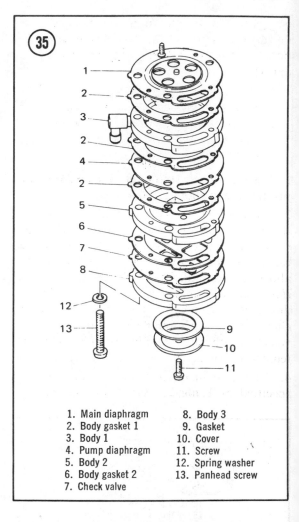

1. Main diaphragm	8. Body 3
2. Body gasket 1	9. Gasket
3. Body 1	10. Cover
4. Pump diaphragm	11. Screw
5. Body 2	12. Spring washer
6. Body gasket 2	13. Panhead screw
7. Check valve	

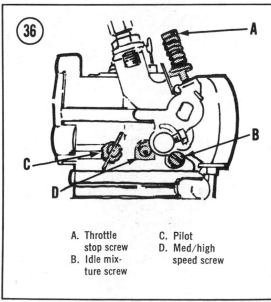

A. Throttle	C. Pilot
stop screw	D. Med/high
B. Idle mix-	speed screw
ture screw	

out, ⅛ turn at a time, until the engine idles at the fastest speed. Then, back it out an additional ¼ turn to ensure sufficient fuel supply during acceleration.

CAUTION
If the idle speed rises to the point where it approaches clutch engagement speed, reduce the speed by backing off the throttle stop screw.

2. Use the throttle stop screw (**Figure 36**) to adjust the idle to about 2,100 rpm.

3. The pilot jet is a fixed jet and adjustment of the pilot jet circuit is made by replacing the jet with one of another size. If operation in the range controlled by the pilot jet (from just above idle to mid-range) is rough, refer to *Jetting* later in this chapter and use the guidelines discussed to change the pilot jet. Generally, a change to a larger pilot jet is required if the vehicle is operated at low altitudes and the temperature is significantly below freezing.

4. Set the main mixture adjustment screw as specified in **Table 2**. Then, start the engine, allow it to warm up, and accelerate the machine hard, with full throttle, and check the "feel" of the carburetion. The machine should accelerate smoothly without "blubbering" (too rich) and without feeling starved (too lean). If adjustment is required, turn the main mixture screw ⅛ turn at a time until the mixture is correct. Turn the screw in to richen the mixture and out to lean it.

When the adjustments are complete and correct, refer to *Jetting* later in this chapter and conduct a "plug chop" to check the correctness of the mixture control adjustments.

CDX38-34/42-38
KEIHIN CARBURETOR

Keihin CDX38-34 and CDX42-38 carburetors are equipped with butterfly throttle and choke valves and incorporate an integral pulse-type fuel pump.

Disassembly

Refer to **Figure 37** or **Figure 38** for the procedure that follows.

5

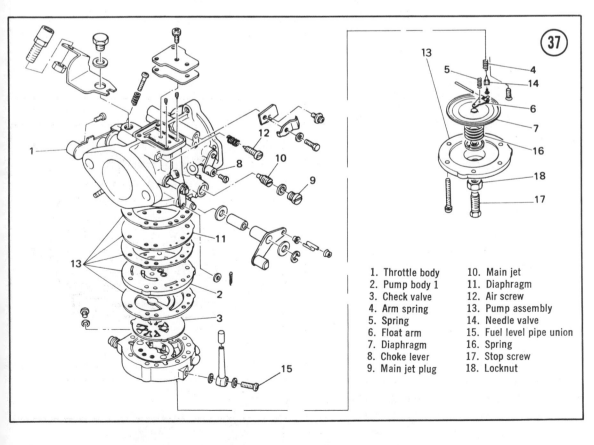

37

1. Throttle body	10. Main jet
2. Pump body 1	11. Diaphragm
3. Check valve	12. Air screw
4. Arm spring	13. Pump assembly
5. Spring	14. Needle valve
6. Float arm	15. Fuel level pipe union
7. Diaphragm	16. Spring
8. Choke lever	17. Stop screw
9. Main jet plug	18. Locknut

1. For CDX42-38 carburetors, remove the accelerator pump linkage (41-47). Remove the No. 4 pump body and disassemble it. Pay close attention to the actual parts and compare them with the illustration for reference during assembly later on.

2. Remove the No. 2 pump body (6) and the check valve (5) and gasket (4). Remove the pin (11), float arm (10), and valve (7) and pin (8) from the pump body. Remove the fuel level pipe (17).

3. Remove the No. 1 pump body (3), gaskets (1), and diaphragm (2).

4. Remove the throttle stop screw (65) and the idle air mixture screw (58).

5. Remove the cover (62) from the top of the carburetor and unscrew the slow (59) and intermediate (60) jets.

> CAUTION
> *Do not remove the throttle and choke butterflies and shafts. The screws that locate the butterflies in the shafts are staked to prevent them from becoming loose and being drawn into the engine. Also, an air bypass hole is precisely machined into the throttle butterfly during assembly at the factory and if the butterfly is disturbed it's unlikely that the hole will be correctly aligned during reassembly.*

Cleaning and Inspection

1. Clean all metal parts in carburetor cleaning solvent.

> CAUTION
> *Do not place gaskets, O-rings, diaphragms, or other non-metal parts in the solvent or they will be damaged.*

> WARNING
> *Most carburetor cleaning solvents are highly caustic. Handle them with care to prevent skin burns and eye injury.*

2. Dry the parts with compressed air. Blow out all the jets and passages to ensure that no solvent or residue remains.

> CAUTION
> *Never clean jets and passages with small drill bits or wire; the soft metal is easily burred and as a result the jet size will be altered and will affect mixture ratio.*

3. Inspect the carburetor and pump bodies for fine cracks and evidence of fuel leaks. Minor damage can be repaired with epoxy or "liquid aluminum" type filler.

4. Inspect the tapers of the idle mixture and main mixture screws for scoring and replace them if they are less than perfect. Inspect the threads of the throttle stop screw for damage which could cause binding.

5. Inspect the jets for internal damage and damaged threads. Replace any jet that is less than perfect. Make certain replacement jets are the same size as the originals.

> CAUTION
> *The jets must be scrupulously clean and shiny. Any burring or roughness could cause a lean mixture that could result in major engine damage.*

6. Inspect the fuel level valve seat and needle taper for scoring, wear, or other damage and replace them as a set if they are less than perfect. A damaged fuel level valve will allow the carburetor to flood and impair performance. In addition, accumulation of raw gasoline in the engine compartment presents a severe fire hazard.

7. Check the movement of the float arm on the pivot pin. It must move freely without binding.

8. Check the diaphragm and float arm springs for resiliency. The springs should feel lively. Take care not to stretch the springs; otherwise, fuel level and flow rate could be adversely affected.

9. Check the movement of the throttle and choke butterflies and shafts. They should move freely. If they do not, look for burring in the venturi where the butterflies contact it when they are closed. Minor imperfections can be removed with crocus cloth and oil, but if damage is extensive replace the carburetor body.

10. Inspect the diaphragms and gaskets and replace any that are damaged.

Assembly

Refer to **Figure 37** or **Figure 38** for the procedure that follows.

1. Install the slow (59) and intermediate (60) jets in the carburetor body and install the gasket (62) and cover (61).

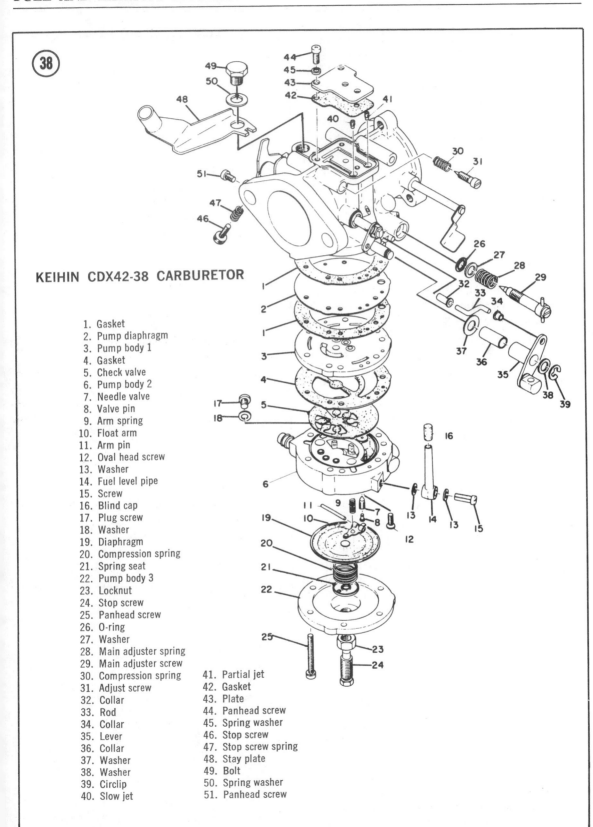

KEIHIN CDX42-38 CARBURETOR

1. Gasket
2. Pump diaphragm
3. Pump body 1
4. Gasket
5. Check valve
6. Pump body 2
7. Needle valve
8. Valve pin
9. Arm spring
10. Float arm
11. Arm pin
12. Oval head screw
13. Washer
14. Fuel level pipe
15. Screw
16. Blind cap
17. Plug screw
18. Washer
19. Diaphragm
20. Compression spring
21. Spring seat
22. Pump body 3
23. Locknut
24. Stop screw
25. Panhead screw
26. O-ring
27. Washer
28. Main adjuster spring
29. Main adjuster screw
30. Compression spring
31. Adjust screw
32. Collar
33. Rod
34. Collar
35. Lever
36. Collar
37. Washer
38. Washer
39. Circlip
40. Slow jet
41. Partial jet
42. Gasket
43. Plate
44. Panhead screw
45. Spring washer
46. Stop screw
47. Stop screw spring
48. Stay plate
49. Bolt
50. Spring washer
51. Panhead screw

5

2. Install the throttle stop screw (65) and the idle mixture screw (58) and main mixture screw (48). Carefully run the mixture screws in just until they contact their seats. Then, screw them out the number of turns specified in **Table 2**. This provides a basic setting that will permit the engine to run while final adjustment is being made.

3. Install the No. 1 pump body (3), gaskets (1), and diaphragm (2).

4. Install the float arm (10), valve (7), valve pin (8), arm spring (9), and arm pin (11) in the No. 2 pump body. Install the pump body (6), check valve (5), and gasket (4). Install the fuel level pipe (17).

5. Assemble and install the No. 3 pump body as illustrated in **Figure 39**. Then, assemble the No. 4 pump body (if fitted), and connect the accelerator linkage (41-47).

Adjustment

There are 4 adjustments for the CDX carburetor. They are interdependent and must be carried out in the order shown below for best results.

   a. Fuel level adjustment

   b. Idle mixture adjustment

   c. Throttle stop adjustment

   d. Medium/high-speed mixture adjustment

1. Back off the locknut on the fuel regulator screw all the way and run the screw into the pump body 6 full turns (**Figure 40**). Remove the cap from the fuel level pipe. Start the engine and allow it to idle. Turn the fuel level regulator screw either in or out to align the fuel level with the joint of the pump body and the carburetor body (**Figure 41**). Turn the screw in to raise the level, out to lower it. When the level is correct, tighten the locknut without further turning the regulator screw.

2. Set the idle mixture and medium/high-speed mixture screws as specified in **Table 2**. Then, start the engine and allow it to idle. Turn the idle mixture screw either in or out, ⅛ turn at a time, until the engine idles at the fastest speed. Then, turn the screw out an additional ¼ turn to ensure sufficient fuel supply during acceleration.

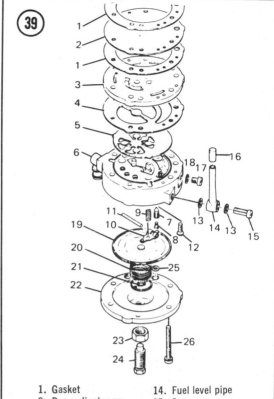

1. Gasket	14. Fuel level pipe
2. Pump diaphragm	15. Screw
3. Pump body 1	16. Blind cap
4. Gasket	17. Plug screw
5. Check valve	18. Washer
6. Pump body 2	19. Diaphragm
7. Needle valve	20. Compression spring
8. Valve pin	21. Spring seat
9. Arm spring	22. Pump body 3
10. Float arm	23. Locknut
11. Arm pin	24. Stop screw
12. Oval head screw	25. U-ring
13. Washer	26. Panhead screw

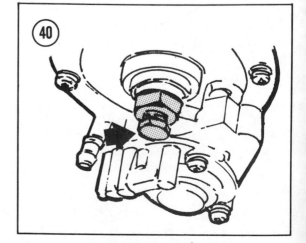

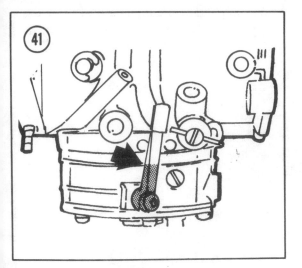

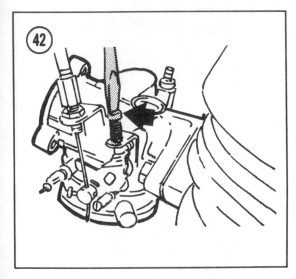

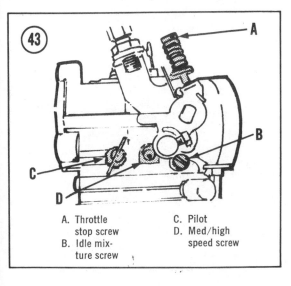

A. Throttle
   stop screw
B. Idle mix-
   ture screw

C. Pilot
D. Med/high
   speed screw

CAUTION
If the idle speed rises to the point where it is approaching clutch engagement speed, reduce the engine speed by backing off the throttle stop screw.

3. Use the throttle stop screw (**Figure 42**) to adjust the idle to 2,000 rpm.

4. Adjust the medium/high-speed mixture screw (**Figure 43**) as specified in **Table 2**. Then, start the engine, allow it to warm up, and accelerate the machine hard, with full throttle, and check the "feel" of the carburetion. The engine should accelerate smoothly, without "blubbering" (too rich) and without feeling starved (too lean). If adjustment is required, turn the main screw $\frac{1}{8}$ turn at a time until the mixture is correct. Turn the screw out to lean the mixture, in to richen it.

When the adjustments are complete and correct, refer to *Jetting* later in this chapter and conduct a "plug chop" to check the correctness of the mixture control adjustments.

JETTING

The air/fuel mixture ratio has a significant effect on engine performance and service life. For purposes of discussion, a ratio of 15 parts air to one part fuel is generally accepted. If there are proportionately more parts of fuel — say 12 to 1 — the mixture is fuel-rich and there is not enough air to properly oxidize the fuel, allowing some of it to go unburned and provide less work than it's capable of. Not only is fuel efficiency reduced, but, in more immediate terms, engine performance is poor. The engine tends to be sluggish and respond poorly.

On the other hand, if the ratio is perhaps 20 parts air to one part fuel, the mixture is fuel-lean, and while the engine may not seem sluggish and in fact will often seem to be performing better than normal, a lean condition raises temperature in the combustion chamber, often to the point of melting the piston crown, combustion chamber, and the insulation and electrodes on the spark plug.

Mixture ratio is affected by changes in air density which varies with changes in temperature and altitude. Air density increases as temperature decreases, and decreases as altitude increases.

5

SPARK PLUG CONDITIONS

(44)

NORMAL USE

OIL FOULED

CARBON FOULED

OVERHEATED

GAP BRIDGED

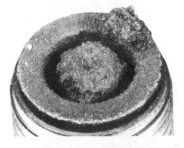

SUSTAINED PREIGNITION

WORN OUT

Photos courtesy of Champion Spark Plug Company.

The standard jets and settings shown in **Table 2** are the basic factory settings. They are selected for operation in outside air temperatures of −4° to 32°F (−20° to 0°C) at sea level.

As a rule of thumb, main jet size should be decreased one size (for example, from a No. 210 to a No. 200 jet) for each 4,000 foot increase in altitude if the outside temperature remains in the basic range (−4° to 32°F).

However, if the outside temperature is significantly lower than the basic range — say −36° to −4°F — an increase in jet size is required. Thus, it can be seen that if the machine is to be operated at higher altitude (4,000 feet) and colder temperature than the basic range, the standard jet may very well be correct.

It is important to understand that changes in altitude and temperature from the basic ranges can offset one another.

NOTE: *The values used above to explain the relationship of temperature and altitude as they affect air density are selected only for illustration; correct jetting can be achieved only by patient experimenting under actual conditions.*

Before making any changes in jetting, make the basic adjustments described under *Adjustment* for your particular carburetor and carry out ignition adjustments described in Chapter Six. Then, test ride the machine and check for the symptoms described in **Table 2**.

Next, conduct a "plug chop." Accelerate the machine at full throttle for about 100 yards on hard-packed snow. Then, kill the engine with the ignition switch and stop the machine with the brake — not with engine compression.

WARNING
Make certain you have clear snow ahead of you before accelerating to make a plug chop. Check the area you will be accelerating over beforehand to make sure there are no hidden obstacles.

Unscrew the spark plugs from the cylinder heads and compare their condition to **Figure 44**. If the spark plugs indicae a lean mixture, the main jet size should be increased, and if a rich condition is indicated, the main jet size should be decreased.

NOTE: *If the carburetor is equipped with a high-speed adjuster screw, turn the screw in to richen the mixture or out to lean it.*

Make jet changes one size at a time and recheck with a plug chop as described above. (If the high-speed circuit has an adjuster screw, turn the screw ⅛ turn at a time.) Be patient and don't be satisfied until the jetting is correct; the little bit of additional time required to do a thorough job can mean the difference between fair and excellent performance — and it may very well prevent expensive engine damage.

REED VALVE

The reed valve should be inspected routinely when the engine upper-end is serviced, or when a decline in engine performance that can't be corrected with ignition and carburetion tuning indicates that the reed valve may have broken reed petals.

Removal

1. Loosen the carburetor clamping bands (**Figure 45**) and remove the carburetor. It is not necessary to disconnect the cables and clamps from the carburetor — just hang it out of the way.

2. Unscrew the intake manifold nuts, tap the manifold with a soft mallet to break it loose, and remove it.

3. Remove the reed valve assembly from the cylinder.

Inspection

1. Check the reed petals for fatigue cracks. Check to see if the petals fit flush against the seats. Check the fit by applying suction to the carburetor side of the valve. Replace the petals as described below (*Reed Petal Replacement*) if they are less than perfect.

2. Check the clearance of the valve stoppers (**Figure 46**). It should be 10.2-10.6 mm (0.402-0.418 in.). If the clearance is greater than specified, the reed petals will break, and if it is less the petals won't open completely and performance will be poor.

If the clearance is incorrect, carefully bend the stoppers as required.

Reed Petal Replacement

1. Remove the screws that attach the stopper plates and reeds to the valve block (**Figure 47**). Mark the stoppers and valve so the stoppers can be installed on the sides from which they were removed.

2. Clean the reed block and stopper plates in solvent and dry them.

3. Coat the threads of the screws with Loctite or a similar compound.

4. Position the new reeds and the stoppers with notched corner positioned as shown (**Figure 48**). Screw in and tighten the screws.

5. Check the stopper clearance as described above.

Installation

1. Install the reed valve assembly and gasket in the cylinder.

2. Install the intake manifold and gaskets. Start all the nuts on and run them down finger-tight before tightening them with a wrench.

3. Install the carburetor and tighten the clamping bands.

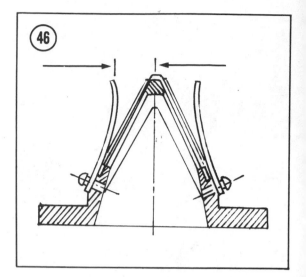

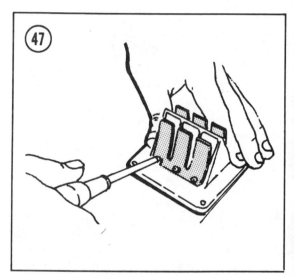

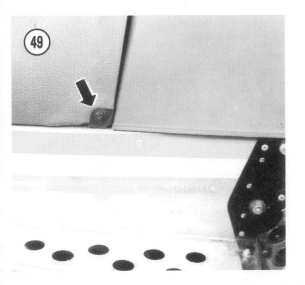

FUEL TANK

Removal/Installation

1. Remove the seat by first unscrewing the bolts beneath the rear of the body and then the bolts on either side of the front of the seat (**Figure 49**). Slide the seat back several inches, disconnect the wiring harness for the taillight (**Figure 50**), and remove the seat.

2. Remove the fuel tank cover (**Figure 51**).

3. Remove the filler/filter assembly from the tank (**Figure 52**).

4. Disconnect the fuel tank hold-down strap at the rear of the fuel tank (**Figure 53**). Raise the strap and remove the tank by pulling it to the rear.

5. Reverse the above to install the tank. Make certain the tank is correctly seated before connecting the hold-down strap.

5

Cleaning/Inspection

1. Pour old gasoline from the tank into a sealable container manufactured specifically for gasoline storage.

2. Pour about 1 quart of fresh gasoline into the tank and slosh it around for several minutes to loosen sediment. Then pour the contents into a sealable container.

3. Examine the tank for cracks and abrasions, particularly at points where the tank contacts the body. Abraded areas can be protected and cushioned by coating them with a non-hardening silicone sealer and allowing it to dry before installing the tank. However, if abrading is extensive, or if the tank is leaking, replace it.

FUEL FILTER

Replace the fuel filter at the end of the winter season, before storing the machine for the summer, and after the fuel tank has been cleaned as described above.

Remove the filler/filter assembly from the tank and remove the filter from the pickup line (**Figure 54**). Install a new filter, making sure the hose is pushed all the way down onto the filter nipple and the hose clamp is seated between the shoulder on the nipple and the filter body.

FUEL PUMP

On models not equipped with a carburetor that incorporates an integral fuel pump, a remote pump is installed just ahead of the fuel tank (**Figure 55**).

If the pump is not serviceable, and if it's faulty it must be replaced.

Disconnect the fuel and pulse lines at the pump, plug the fuel line from the tank with a golf tee, and remove the pump. Install a new pump and connect the fuel and pulse lines.

EXHAUST SYSTEM

The exhaust system requires no service other than an annual cleaning of carbon that builds up in the headpipe.

Removal/Installation

1. Raise the hood.

2. Disconnect the springs that attach the head-pipe to the manifold (**Figure 56**) and remove the hold-down spring over the muffler.

3. Unscrew the bolt that attaches the tailpipe to the body (**Figure 57**) and collect the rubber shock mount.

4. Remove the exhaust system from the machine.

5. Reverse the above to install the system. Make sure rubber shock mount is reinstalled at the tailpipe.

Cleaning

1. Fray the end of a 2-foot section of old control cable. Attach the opposite end to a drill motor (**Figure 58**).

2. Use a glove or shop rag to protect your hand, spin the cable with the drill motor, and feed it into the headpipe. Work the cable in and out as you spin it to break the carbon deposits loose. Take your time and do a thorough job.

3. Shake the large pieces out into a trash container. Then, apply compressed air through the tailpipe to blow out the remaining soot.

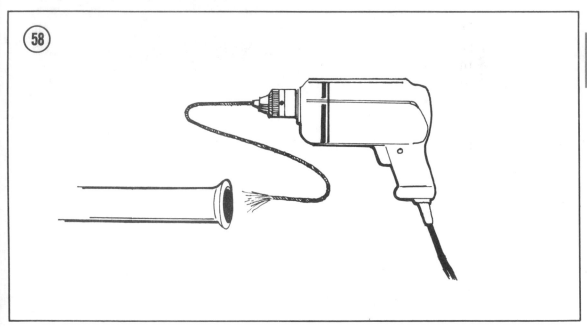

5

Table 1   CARBURETOR APPLICATIONS

Model	Carburetor
ET250A/B/C; GS340/A; GP338F; GP433F; GP440/A; GPX433F; PR440	Keihin CDX38-32/38-34/42-38
EX340/A; EX440/A	Keihin PW42-38
SRX440; SSR440	Mikuni VM40
GPX338F	Mikuni BN38-34SH
EX340B; EX440B/C; EXCEL V	Keihin BD44-38
ET300C; ET340B/C; ET340EC	Mikuni B38-32/38-34

Table 2   CARBURETOR ADJUSTMENT SPECIFICATIONS

Model	Main Jet, Standard (Optional)	Main Adjuster, Turns Out	Slow Jet	Pilot/Intermediate Jet	Idle Air Screw, Turns Out
ET250 A/B/C	130 (125, 135)	—	50	40	1
ET300C	210 (180, 190, 200, 220)	—	90	—	1¼
GS340	140 (130, 135, 145)	—	60	70	1¼
GS340A	140 (130, 135, 145)	—	60	70	1¼
GPX338F	—	⅞-1⅛	¾ turn out	85	—
GPX433F	—	⅞-1⅛	45	65	—
GP338F	—	1⅜	1½ turns out	—	—
GP433F	200 (180, 190, 210)	—	1 turn out	—	—
ET340 B/C/EC	220 (200, 210, 230, 240)	—	—	75	1
GP440	195 (190, 200, 205)	—	48	95	1
GP440A	190 (185, 195, 200)	—	48	95	1
PR440	195 (190, 200, 205)	—	48	95	1¼
EX340	155[1] (145, 150, 160)	—	50	90	1
EX440	155[2] (145, 150, 160)	—	50	100	1¼
EXCEL V	145 (120, 125, 130, 135, 140)	—	95	200	2¼
SRX440 SSR440	200[1] (180, 190, 210)	1-1-1-2	—	30/Left—170 Right—165	¼-¾

1. Set slide needle at 3rd notch.
2. Set slide needle at 4th notch.

CHAPTER SIX

ELECTRICAL SYSTEM

The electrical system consists of an ignition system, lighting system, and, on some models, an electric starting system.

Two types of ignition systems are used — a contact breaker flywheel magneto and a CDI (capacitive discharge ignition) electronic system.

The lighting system consists of a headlight, brake/taillight, and console lights.

The electric starting system on some models consists of a battery, starter and solenoid, and a generator.

Ignition and starter applications are shown in **Table 1**. All tables are at the end of the chapter.

This chapter includes testing and repair of some components of the ignition, lighting, and charging systems. Some testing and repair tasks require special test equipment and tools, and are best left to a dealer or competent auto electric shop.

Wiring diagrams for all models covered are included at the end of the book.

CAPACITIVE DISCHARGE IGNITION (CDI)

The capacitive discharge ignition (CDI) system consists of a flywheel-mounted alternator and a control "black box" that houses the solid-state capacitor and trigger and amplifier devices.

In addition to powering the ignition, the alternator also powers the lights.

In operation, a permanent-magnet rotor attached to the end of the crankshaft, revolves around a fixed stator which holds the generating coils and the ignition timing coils.

As the magnets in the flywheel/rotor pass the coils they induce a voltage in them which flows to the electronic control module (as well as to the lights). The voltage is stepped up, or increased, in the module and is stored in the capacitor.

The rotor also induces voltage in the timing coil and this voltage flows to an electronic "switch" that releases the stored energy in the capacitor. This energy discharges to the primary winding in the ignition coil which induces high voltage in the secondary coil winding. This high voltage then jumps the spark plug electrodes and ignites the air/fuel mixture in the combustion chamber.

The primary feature of electronic ignition is that it requires virtually no maintenance other than timing adjustment following installation and a periodic check (annually) to ensure that the timing has not changed.

The system has a drawback and that is that the electronic control module is not repairable; failure of just one component in the module requires replacement of the entire unit. However, the likelihood of an ignition failure is remote and the unit will probably last for the life of the machine.

Removal

It is not necessary to remove the engine from the machine to remove the alternator/ignition assembly; the procedure that follows is illustrated with the engine on a workbench for clarity.

1. Remove the starter assembly (**Figure 1**).

2. Loosen the flywheel/rotor nut and remove the starter pulley (**Figure 2**).

3. Unscrew the fan bolts and remove the fan (**Figure 3**).

4. Unscrew the flywheel nut and install a puller (**Figure 4** — Yamaha tool/part No. 90890-01850) and tighten the puller bolt to break the flywheel/rotor loose from the crankshaft. It may be necessary to rap sharply on the head of the puller to shock the flywheel/rotor loose.

CAUTION
Do not strike the flywheel/rotor with a hammer and do not heat it with a torch, or it's likely to be damaged.

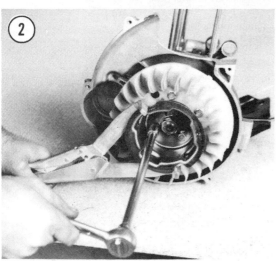

5. Mark the stator and crankcase for reference during installation (**Figure 5**). Disconnect the ignition wiring harness, unscrew the stator screws (**Figure 6**), and remove the stator.

Testing

Have the stator tested by your dealer. Circuit resistances are critical and require the use of a bench tester to accurately assess the condition of the ignition and timing coils.

Installation

1. Set the stator in place and install the bolts finger-tight. Line up the reference mark on the stator with the reference mark on the crankcase (**Figure 5**) and tighten the stator mounting screws.

2. Line up the keyway in the flywheel/rotor with the key in the crankshaft and press the flywheel onto the crankshaft. Screw the flywheel/rotor nut onto the crankshaft and tighten it to 7.0-7.5 mkg (50-54 ft.-lb.).

3. Install the fan. Line up the mark on the fan with the keyway (**Figure 7**) and screw in and tighten the fan bolts.

4. Install the starter pulley and screw in and tighten the 3 bolts (**Figure 8**).

6

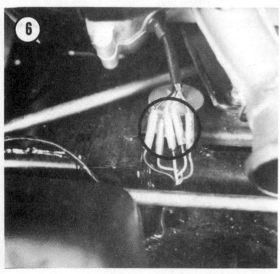

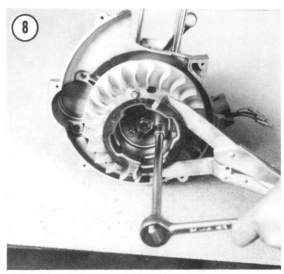

5. Check and adjust the timing as described below.

6. Install the starter assembly (**Figure 9**).

Static Timing

Ignition timing must be checked and adjusted following installation of the ignition stator and rotor.

1. Remove the starter assembly (**Figure 9**).

2. Unscrew the spark plug from the right cylinder and install a timing gauge adapter (Yamaha part No. 90890-01195) and insert a dial gauge into the adapter (**Figure 10**).

3. Rotate the crankshaft to bring the piston to TDC as indicated by the gauge. Then zero the gauge.

4. Rotate the crankshaft counterclockwise (viewed from the right) until the gauge needle has made approximately 3 ½ revolutions. Then, carefully turn the crankshaft clockwise until the gauge indicates the timing shown in **Table 2**.

5. Check the static timing marks on the stator and rotor (**Figure 11**). They should line up. If they do not, loosen the stator bolts and rotate the stator to align the marks. Then tighten the stator bolts.

> NOTE: *The stator bolts can be reached through the cutouts in the rotor.*

6. Remove the gauge and adapter, install the spark plug and connect the high-tension lead, and install the starter.

Strobe Timing

Strobe timing can be used instead of static timing. However, static timing may be necessary first if the timing is so far off that the engine won't run.

1. Connect a timing light to the left spark plug lead in accordance with the manufacturer's instructions.

2. Start the engine and run it at 1,000-3,000 rpm. Direct the timing light at the starter case at about the 2 o'clock position (**Figure 12**).

3. The projection on the fan should line up with the mark on the crankcase (**Figure 13**). If it does not, shut off the engine, remove the starter

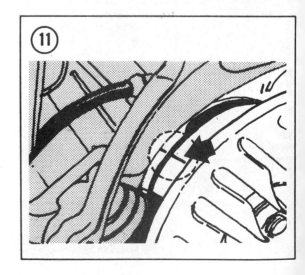

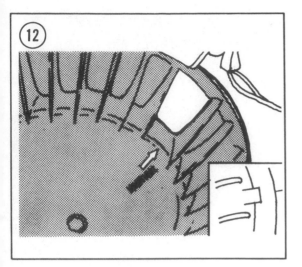

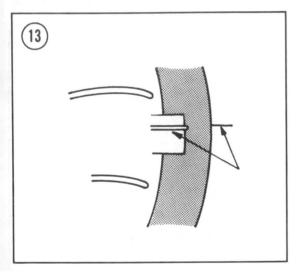

assembly, loosen the stator bolts, and rotate the stator as required.

Then, tighten the stator bolts, install the starter assembly, and recheck the timing as just described.

If the timing is still not correct, be patient and continue checking and adjusting until the marks line up correctly.

FLYWHEEL MAGNETO

More than one-third of the snowmobiles covered in this handbook are equipped with flywheel magneto ignition (see **Table 1**).

The system consists of a magnetic rotor, stationary ignition source coil, lighting coils, contact breaker assembly (points), ignition coil and ignition switch, safety switch, and kill switch.

The contact breaker gap should be checked and adjusted if necessary every 20 hours or 250 miles (400 km) of operation, and the breaker should be replaced annually. Contact breaker adjustment should be done in conjunction with a timing check and adjustment (see *Timing/Adjustment* later in this chapter).

Removal

It is not necessary to remove the engine from the machine to remove the alternator/ignition assembly.

1. Remove the starter assembly (**Figure 14**).

2. Loosen the flywheel nut and remove the starter pulley (**Figure 15**).

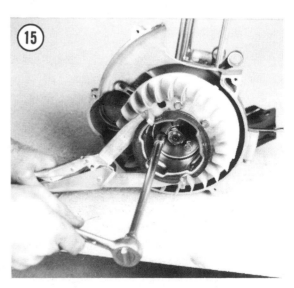

3. Unscrew the flywheel nut and install a puller (**Figure 16** — Yamaha tool/part No. 90890-01850) and tighten the puller to break the flywheel loose from the crankshaft. It may be necessary to rap sharply on the head of the puller bolt to shock the flywheel/rotor loose.

> CAUTION
> *Do not strike the flywheel/rotor with a hammer and do not heat it with a torch, or it's likely to be damaged.*

4. Mark the stator and crankcase for reference during assembly (**Figure 17**). Disconnect the ignition wiring harness, unscrew the stator screws and remove the stator (**Figure 18**).

Testing

Have the stator tested by your dealer. Circuit resistances are critical and require the use of a bench tester to accurately assess the condition of the source coils.

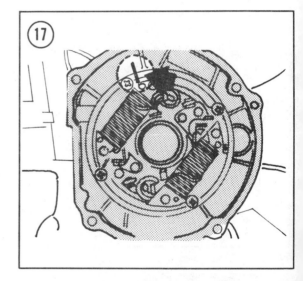

Installation

1. Set the stator in place and install the bolts finger-tight. Line up the reference mark on the stator with the reference mark on the crankcase (**Figure 19**) and tighten the stator mounting screws.

2. Line up the keyway in the flywheel/rotor with the key in the crankshaft and press the flywheel onto the crankshaft. Screw the flywheel/rotor nut onto the end of the crankshaft and tighten it to 7.0-7.5 mkg (50-54 ft.-lb.).

3. Install the starter pulley (**Figure 20**) and screw in and tighten the 3 bolts.

4. Check and adjust the static timing and the contact breaker gap as described below.

5. Install the starter assembly (**Figure 21**).

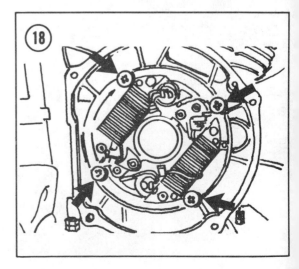

Timing/Adjustment

Ignition timing must be checked and adjusted following installation of the ignition stator and rotor. Contact breaker gap must be adjusted at 20-hour or 250-mile (400 km) intervals and when the contact breaker assembly is replaced.

For assured good performance, the timing and contact breaker gap adjustment should be done at the same time.

1. Remove the starter assembly (**Figure 21**) and the starter pulley (**Figure 20**).

2. Dip a stiff business card in lacquer thinner or a similar non-petroleum base solvent such as ethyl alcohol, place the card between the contact breaker points, and draw it through the points several times, until the points are clean and no discoloration remains on the card. Inspect the contact surfaces of the points and if they are smooth and parallel, dress them with a couple of strokes of a point file. Then clean them with lacquer thinner.

3. Rotate the crankshaft until the contact breaker lobe opens the breaker to its widest point. Then measure the gap with a flat feeler gauge (**Figure 22**). The gap should be 0.35 mm (0.014 in.). If it's not, loosen the breaker mounting screw and move the stationary plate as required. Then, tighten the screw and recheck the gap to make sure it has not changed.

4. Remove the spark plug from the right cylinder, install a dial gauge adapter (Yamaha part No. 90890-01039) and a dial gauge

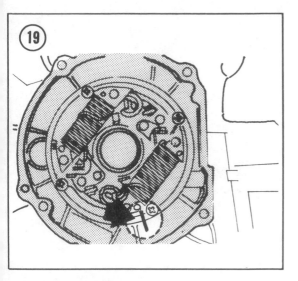

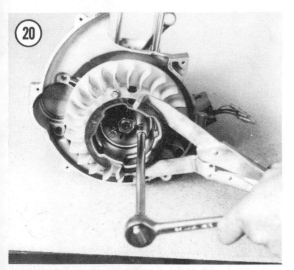

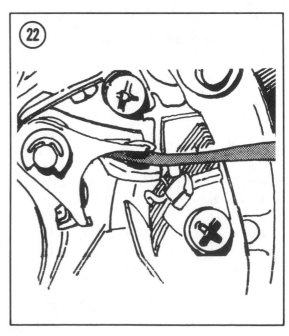

(Yamaha part No. 90890-03002 or an equivalent). See **Figure 23**.

5. Disconnect the magneto primary lead and connect a buzz-box or continuity light to the gray lead and ground (**Figure 24**).

> NOTE: *At the precise instant the light goes out or the buzz-box ceases to make noise, the points are just beginning to open.*

6. Rotate the crankshaft to bring the piston to TDC, as indicated by the dial gauge. Zero the gauge. Then, turn the crankshaft counterclockwise until the gauge indicates the timing shown in **Table 2**. This is the firing point.

7. Slightly loosen the stator mounting screws (**Figure 25**) and slowly turn the stator until the points just begin to open (indicated by the light or buzz-box) with the crankshaft at the firing point. Check the dial gauge to make sure the crankshaft has not moved. Then, tighten the stator screws.

8. Recheck the contact breaker gap at its widest point. It may not be possible to achieve both correct timing and contact breaker gap if the breaker assembly has been in use for awhile. In such case, it will be necessary to compromise by turning the stator plate slightly to alter the firing point within the limits shown in **Table 2**.

9. On twin cylinder engines, adjust the timing and contact breaker gap for the left cylinder in the manner just described for the right cylinder.

Contact Breaker Replacement

The contact breaker assembly should be replaced annually or when accurate contact breaker gap adjustment is no longer possible because of point wear.

1. Remove the contact breaker mounting screw (**Figure 26**) and remove the breaker assembly.

2. Loosen the terminal nut and disconnect the primary lead.

3. Connect the primary lead to a new breaker assembly and tighten the nut.

4. Install the contact breaker assembly on the stator.

5. Refer to *Timing/Adjustment* and adjust the contact breaker gap.

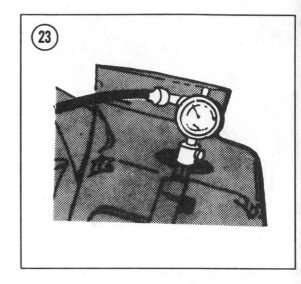

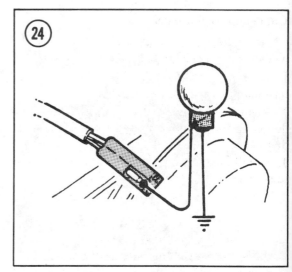

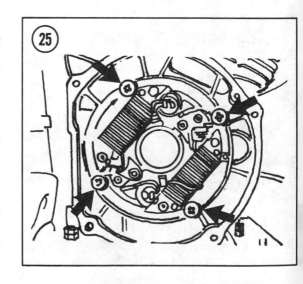

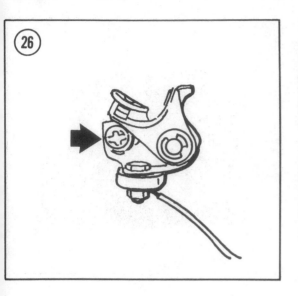

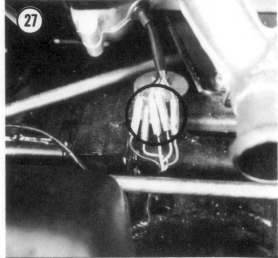

Condenser Replacement

The condenser should be replaced routinely when the contact breaker assembly is replaced.

1. Loosen the soldered leads on the condenser terminal with a soldering iron.

2. Remove the screw that attaches the condenser to the stator plate and remove the condenser.

3. Install a new condenser and solder the leads to the terminal.

> CAUTION
> *Be careful when soldering the leads to the condenser; too much heat can destroy the condenser.*

LIGHTING SYSTEM

The lighting system consists of a headlight and brake/taillight unit, instrument lights, and an AC (alternating current) generating device. Switches control all lighting circuits.

Testing

If the lights fail to work, do not immediately assume the worst — a major failure in the alternator, regulator, or lighting coils. Very often the problem can be found in the lamps; look for burned out filaments or bulbs that are loose in their sockets. Also check the harness connec-

tors to ensure they are clean, dry, and tight and have not come disconnected.

Four things are required for the lights to function. You must have current and an uninterrupted, non-shorted path for it to follow. The switch must work correctly. A good ground is required. And the bulbs must be in good condition and correctly installed in clean, dry sockets.

A lighting coil resistance test and a regulator test can confirm both good and bad conditions.

Lighting Coil Resistance Test

1. Unplug the main wiring harness connector at the engine (**Figure 27**).

2. Connect an ohmmeter to the leads on the engine side of the connector and measure the resistance (see **Table 3**).

If the resistance is not correct, replace the lighting coil on the stator. If it is correct, remove the regulator and have it tested by your dealer. The test requires only a few minutes of your dealer's time and is very inexpensive. The equipment required for the test (two 12-volt batteries and a regulator checker) is costly and would probably not be used more than once.

HEADLIGHT BULB REPLACEMENT

1. Raise the hood to gain access to the rear of the headlight.

6

2. Unplug harness connector by pulling on the connector — not the wiring harness (**Figure 28**).

3. Turn the retaining ring counterclockwise to release it from the housing (**Figure 29**).

4. Remove the old bulb and install a new one of the same rating. The rating appears on the bulb. Set the retaining ring in place and turn it clockwise to lock it. Reconnect the wiring harness.

HEADLIGHT AIMING

1. Set the snowmobile on a level surface, 25 feet (7.6 m) from a vertical surface such as a wall (**Figure 30**).

2. Measure the distance from the floor to the center of the headlight lens. Make a mark on the wall the same distance from the floor. For instance, if the center of the headlight lens is 2 feet above the floor, mark ''A'' in **Figure 30** should also be 2 feet above the floor.

3. Start the engine, turn on the headlight, and set the beam selector at HIGH; do not adjust the headlight beam with the selector set at LOW.

4. The most intense area of the beam on the wall should be 2 in. (50 mm) below the ''A'' mark (**Figure 31**) and in line with imaginary vertical centerlines from the headlight to the wall.

5. To raise the beam, tighten the top adjuster screws and loosen the bottom screws (**Figure**

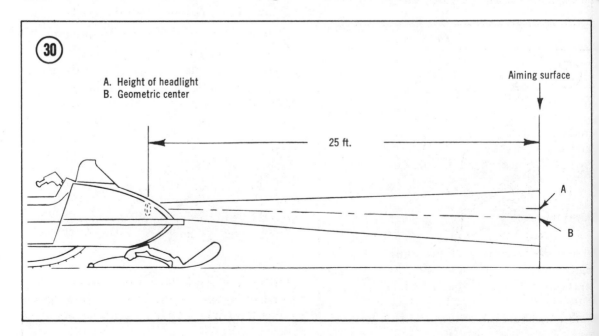

A. Height of headlight
B. Geometric center

Aiming surface

25 ft.

A

B

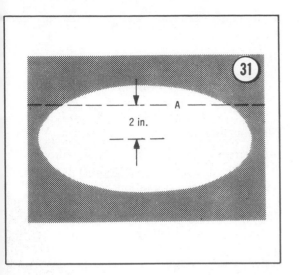

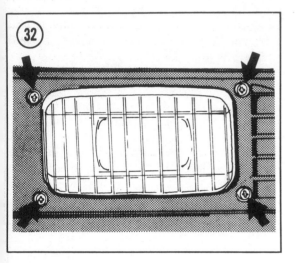

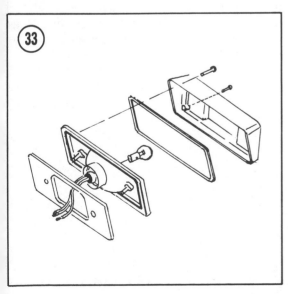

32). To lower the beam, tighten the bottom screws and loosen the top screws. To move the beam to the right, tighten the right screws and loosen the left. To move the beam to the left, tighten the left screws and loosen the right.

BRAKE/TAILLIGHT
BULB REPLACEMENT

1. Refer to **Figure 33** (a typical brake/taillight assembly) and remove the screws that attach the lens to the seat or toolbox door. Remove the lens and remove the defective bulb by pressing in on it, turning it counterclockwise, and pulling it out of the socket.

2. Clean the socket to remove any corrosion, dirt, and moisture.

3. Line up the guide pins of the new bulb with the solts in the socket, press the bulb in, and turn it clockwise to lock it in place.

> NOTE: *On dual filament bulbs (combination brake/taillight) the pins are at different distances from the base of the bulb. Make sure they correspond with the different length slots in the socket.*

4. Clean the inside of the lens with a mild detergent and warm water before installing it. Also make sure that the lens is completely dry. Install all of the screws fingertight before tightening them, and then tighten them securely but not so tight that they damage the lens.

ELECTRIC START SYSTEM

The electric start system on EXCEL V and EC models consists of a 12-volt battery, starter motor, starter solenoid, AC to DC rectifier, and fuse.

The starter motor pinion gear engages a ring gear on the flywheel to turn the engine over. The battery is charged by the alternator. The rectifier changes the alternating current (AC) produced by the alternator to direct current (DC) which is stored in the battery. The fuse protects the system from overloads and short circuits.

If difficulty is experienced with the electric start system, check the obvious and most likely cause of trouble — the battery. Make certain the battery and starter connections are clean and tight. Check and service the battery as described below. If the battery has sufficient charge and the connections are good, test the starter and solenoid as described. Refer to the wiring diagrams for EXCEL V and EC models at the end of the book for reference when troubleshooting the starter system.

BATTERY

With proper care, the battery should last for 2 to 3 years. Incorrect care or neglect (described below) can cut battery service life short and lead to chronic starting problems.

a. *Electrolyte Level:* Correct electrolyte level must be maintained at all times for the battery to be able to accept and maintain a full charge (see *Cleaning and Service*).

b. *Charge Level:* The battery must be maintained at full charge all the time to prevent premature sulfation which will result in internal shorts that destroy the battery. This is a point that is often overlooked during summer storage. The battery should be removed from the machine and cleaned and serviced and fully charged. It should be stored in a dry, warm place, and should be periodically tested and recharged to prevent it from sulfating.

c. *Overcharging:* Overcharging or charging the battery at too high a rate creates excessive heat that will destroy the battery.

d. *Freezing:* If the machine is left outdoors for long periods in freezing temperatures, freezing of the electrolyte is likely to occur, resulting in deterioration of the battery's service life. Guard against this by removing the battery and storing it in a warm place until the machine will be used.

Removal/Installation

1. Disconnect the cables from the battery — first the negative (−) then the positive (+).

2. Disconnect the battery hold-down strap.

3. Slide the battery part way out and note the routing of the vent tube for reference during installation, then remove the battery.

4. Reverse the above the install the battery. Make sure the vent tube is correctly routed and

is not kinked. Connect the positive cable first, then the negative.

> CAUTION
> *Be sure the battery connections are correct or serious damage to electrical components will occur.*

Cleaning and Service

Electrolyte level in the battery should be checked frequently, especially during periods of regular, sustained operation. Use only distilled water and top off the level to the ring in the bottom of the filler neck. The tops of the plates should be covered but take care not to overfill the battery.

Corrosion of the terminals is normal but it must be removed before it creates excessive electrical resistance. Wash the terminals and cable ends with a solution of 4 parts water and one part baking soda.

> CAUTION
> *Keep the baking soda solution out of the battery cells or it will dilute the electrolyte and damage the battery.*

Clean the battery carrier with baking soda solution and rinse the battery and the case with fresh water. Dry them with an old towel or shop rag.

Specific Gravity Test

Use a hydrometer to check the state of charge of the battery. Place the suction tube of the hydrometer in one of the filler openings (**Figure 34**) and draw off just enough electrolyte to lift the float. Hold the hydrometer vertical and read the specific gravity level. Then, return the electrolyte to the cell from which it was removed and check the next cell. Continue until all cells have been tested.

Specific gravity for a battery that is fully charged is 1.260. If the specific gravity is below 1.220, recharge the battery as described below.

> NOTE: *Specific gravity varies with temperature. For each 10° F that the battery temperature is less than 80° F, subtract 0.004 from the value shown on the hydrometer. For every 10° F that the battery temperature exceeds 80° F, add 0.004 to the indicated reading.*

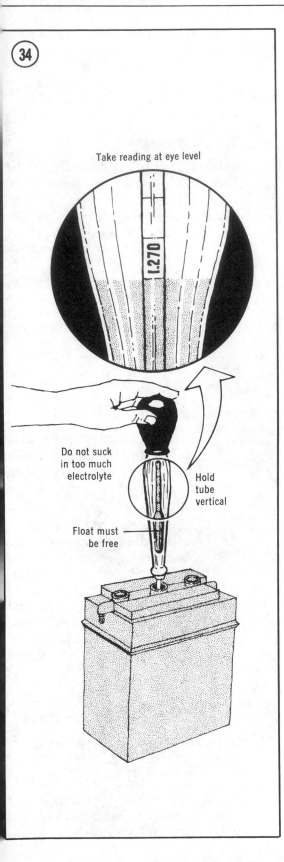

Take reading at eye level

1.270

Do not suck
in too much
electrolyte

Hold
tube
vertical

Float must
be free

Battery Charging

Connect the battery to a charger — positive
to positive, negative to negative (**Figure 35**). If
the charger is equipped with a variable-rate
selector, select a low setting (1-1½ amps). Turn
the charger on or plug it in and allow the battery to charge for at least 8 hours.

NOTE: *Remove the caps from the cells
during charging and periodically check
and correct the electrolyte level if
necessary.*

After the battery has had a sufficient time to
charge, turn off the charger, disconnect the
cables, and check the specific gravity as described above. Then, allow the battery to sit for
about an hour and check the specific gravity
again. If the level has not dropped, the battery
can be considered to be fully charged and in
good condition.

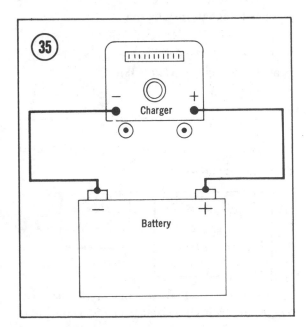

Charger

Battery

STARTER

If the starter fails to crank the engine, or if it cranks it very slowly, test the starter as described below.

Testing

1. Inspect the starter wiring for loose and corroded terminals and connections and for damaged insulation. Clean and tighten any corroded connections and replace any damaged wires. Inspect the fuse.

2. Perform *Specific Gravity Test* to make sure the battery is fully charged and not defective.

3. Crank the engine with the recoil starter to make sure the engine turns freely and is not seized.

4. Disconnect the high-tension leads from the spark plugs. Connect a heavy jumper wire from the positive (+) terminal of the battery directly to the starter (**Figure 36**) to bypass the starter switch and solenoid. If the starter turns, it can be assumed to be all right. In such case, check the continuity of the switch (see the wiring diagram at the end of the book) with an ohmmeter. Also test the solenoid as described below.

If the starter does not turn, it's defective and should be replaced (see *Starter Removal/ Installation*).

Starter Removal/Installation

1. Disconnect ground cable from the battery.

2. Remove the intake silencer, carburetor, and heat shield (**Figures 37 and 38**).

3. Remove recoil starter assembly (**Figure 39**).

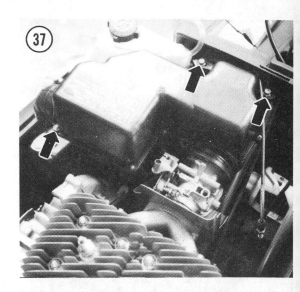

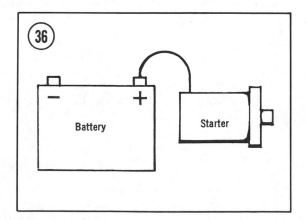

4. Disconnect cable from starter **(Figure 40)**.

5. Unscrew starter mounting bolts **(Figure 41)** and remove the starter.

6. Reverse the above steps to install the starter. Clean the threads of the starter mounting bolts and coat them with Loctite or a similar thread locking compound before installing and tightening them.

Starter Solenoid Test

The starter is a sealed magnetic switch that cannot be repaired. If it's defective, replace it.

1. Disconnect the leads from the solenoid and connect a test light between the 2 large terminals **(Figure 42)**.

2. Connect a jumper wire between the small post on the solenoid and the positive terminal of the battery. The solenoid plunger should snap in, light the test light, and hold until the jumper wire is disconnected. If this does not occur, the solenoid is defective and must be replaced.

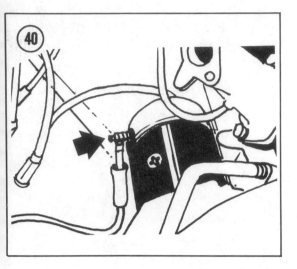

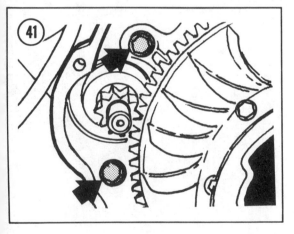

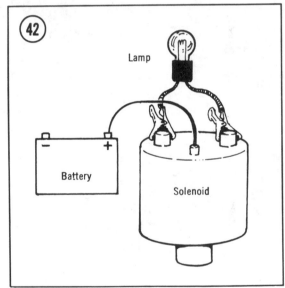

Table 2   IGNITION SPECIFICATIONS

Model	Timing, BTDC, mm (in.)	Spark Plug Type and Gap, mm (in.)
ET250A	1.6-1.8 (0.063-0.071)	NGK BR-8HV—0.5-0.6 (0.020-0.024)
ET250B	1.7-1.9 (0.067-0.075)	NGK BR-8HV—0.5-0.6 (0.020-0.024)
ET250C	1.1-1.3 (0.043-0.051)	NGK B-8HS—0.5-0.6 (0.020-0.024)
ET300C	1.3-1.5 (0.051-0.059)	NGK BR-9EV—0.7-0.8 (0.028-0.031)
GP338F	1.4-1.6 (0.055-0.063)	NGK B-8EV—0.4 (0.016)
GP433F	1.7-1.9 (0.067-0.075)	Champion N-3G—0.4 (0.016)
GPX338F	1.5-1.7 (0.059-0.067)	NGK B-9EV—0.5-0.6 (0.020-0.024)
GPX433F	1.5-1.7 (0.059-0.067)	Champion N-2G—0.5-0.6 (0.020-0.024)
GS340	1.4-1.6 (0.055-0.063)	NGK BR-7HS—0.5-0.6 (0.020-0.024)
GS340A	1.4-1.6 (0.055-0.063)	NGK BR-7HS—0.5-0.6 (0.020-0.024)
GS440A	1.5-1.7 (0.059-0.067)	NGK BR-8EV—0.5-0.6 (0.020-0.024)
ET340B	1.5-1.7 (0.059-0.067)	NGK BR-9EV—0.5-0.6 (0.020-0.024)
ET340C	1.5-1.7 (0.059-0.067)	NGK BR-9EV—0.5-0.6 (0.020-0.024)
ET340EC	1.5-1.7 (0.059-0.067)	NGK BR-9EV—0.7-0.8 (0.028-0.031)
EX340	1.5-1.7 (0.059-0.067)	NGK BR-9EV—0.5-0.6 (0.020-0.024)
EX340A	1.5-1.7 (0.059-0.067)	NGK BR-9EV—0.5-0.6 (0.020-0.024)
EX340B	1.5-1.7 (0.059-0.067)	NGK BR-9EV—0.5-0.6 (0.020-0.024)
EX340C	1.5-1.7 (0.059-0.067)	NGK BR-9EV—0.5-0.6 (0.020-0.024)
EX440	1.5-1.7 (0.059-0.067)	NGK BR-9EV—0.5-0.6 (0.020-0.024)
EX440A	1.5-1.7 (0.059-0.067)	NGK BR-9EV—0.5-0.6 (0.020-0.024)
EX440B	1.5-1.7 (0.059-0.067)	NGK BR-9EV—0.5-0.6 (0.020-0.024)
EX440C	1.5-1.7 (0.059-0.067)	NGK BR-9EV—0.5-0.6 (0.020-0.024)
PR440	1.5-1.7 (0.059-0.067)	NGK BR-9EV—0.5-0.6 (0.020-0.024)
GP440	1.4-1.6 (0.055-0.063)	NGK BR-9EV—0.5-0.6 (0.020-0.024)
EXCEL V	1.4-1.6 (0.055-0.063)	NGK BR-9ES—0.7-0.8 (0.028-0.031)
SRX440	1.5-1.7 (0.059-0.067) −40 to −20°C (−40 to −4°F) 1.7-1.9 (0.067-0.075) −20 to 0°C (−4 to 32°F) 1.9-2.1 (0.075-0.083) above 0°C (32°F)	NGK B-9EV—0.5-0.6 (0.020-0.024)
SSR440	0.74-0.76 (0.029-0.030) −40 to −20°C (−40 to −4°F) 0.89-0.91 (0.035-0.036) −20 to 0°C (−4 to 32°F) 0.93-1.13 (0.037-0.044) above 0°C (32°F)	Champion N-82G—0.5-0.6 (0.020-0.024)

Table 1 IGNITION AND STARTER APPLICATIONS

Model	Ignition	Starter
ET250A/B; GS340A; GP338F; GP440/A; GP433F; PR440	Contact breaker/ flywheel magneto	Manual recoil
ET250C; ET300C; GPX338F; ET340B/C; EX340A/B; EX440A/B/C; GPX433F; SRX440; SSR440	CDI	Manual recoil
ET340EC; EXCEL V	CDI	Electric/ manual recoil

Table 3 LIGHTING COIL RESISTANCE

Model	Resistance
SRX440	0.24 ± 10 percent at $20\,°C$ ($68\,°F$)
All others	0.18 ± 10 percent at $20\,°C$ ($68\,°F$)

6

CHAPTER SEVEN

DRIVE TRAIN

The drive train consists of a drive sheave on the end of the crankshaft, connected to a driven sheave on the chaincase by a belt; a drive chain and sprockets inside the chaincase; a drive shaft with 2 drive sprockets; and a brake. A typical drive train is shown in **Figure 1**.

Some of the procedures in this chapter require the use of special tools, a press, and considerable experience.

For instance, work on the drive and driven sheaves should be entrusted to your dealer. Not only are several special tools required, but experience is required to determine if changes need be made to the clutch weights when the drive sheave is being serviced.

DRIVE BELT

The drive belt should be inspected every 20 hours or 250 miles (400 km) of operation for wear, cracking, damage, or deterioration. If the belt is in poor condition, full power won't be transmitted from the drive sheave to the driven sheave.

Measure the width of the belt (**Figure 2**). A new belt is 31.8 mm (1.24 in.) wide. If it is less than 26 mm (1.02 in.), replace it.

Removal/Installation

1. Remove the belt guard (**Figure 3**).
2. Lock the brake to prevent the driven sheave from turning.
3. Push against the movable driver and rotate it clockwise to separate the sheaves.
4. Roll the belt over the movable sheave (**Figure 4**) to remove it.

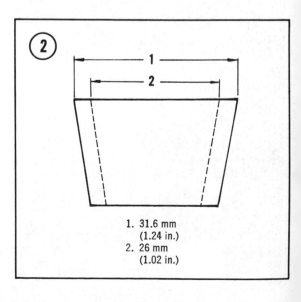

1. 31.6 mm
   (1.24 in.)
2. 26 mm
   (1.02 in.)

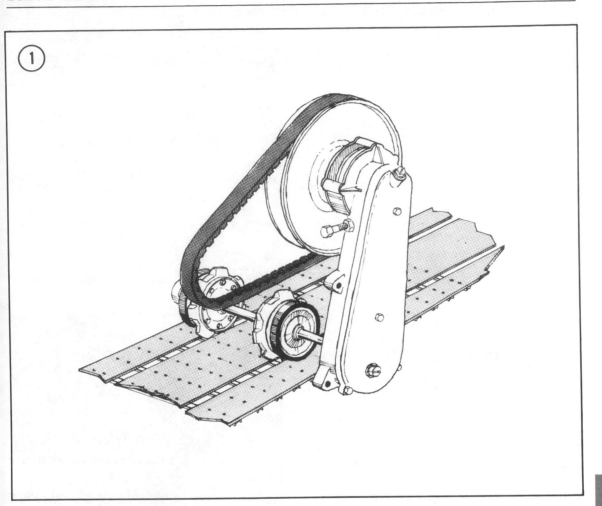

7

5. Remove the belt from the drive sheave.

6. Reverse the above to install the belt.

Drive Belt Adjustment

The center-to-center distance from the drive sheave to the driven sheave, and the offset of the sheaves must be correctly maintained for good performance and long belt life.

1. Measure the distance between the sheave centers (**Figure 5**). It should be 264-268 mm (10.39-10.55 in.).

2. If adjustment is required, loosen the chaincase mounting bolts (**Figure 6**) and move the chaincase back or forward as required. When the distance is correct, tighten the chaincase mounting bolts without further moving the chaincase.

3. Measure the offset of the sheaves. This is easily done with a sheave gauge available through your dealer. It should be part of your tool inventory (**Figure 7**). Set the gauge against the sheaves (**Figure 7**). The gauge should contact each sheave at 2 places at the same time. If it does not, loosen the engine mounting bolts (**Figure 8** — 2 in front of the engine and 2 behind it), and move the engine right or left until the offset is correct. Then, tighten the bolts and recheck the offset.

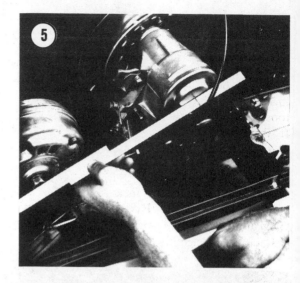

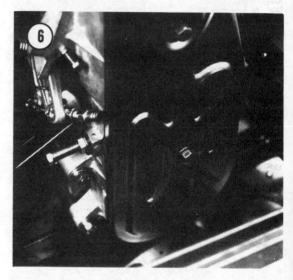

DRIVE SHEAVE REMOVAL/INSTALLATION

Work on the drive sheave should be entrusted to your dealer. The drive sheave can be removed without removing the engine from the machine; the work is illustrated with the engine on a bench for clarity.

1. Remove the drive belt as described above.

2. Unscrew the bolt from the end of the crankshaft (**Figure 9**) and install a puller (see **Table 1** at the end of the chapter for puller identification).

3. Hold the sheave to prevent it from turning and tighten the puller bolt (**Figure 10**).

NOTE: *It may be necessary to rap sharply on the head of the puller bolt to shock the drive sheave loose from the crankshaft.*

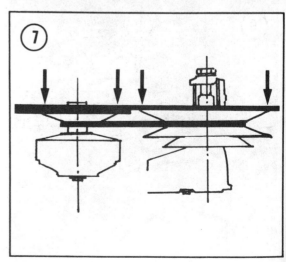

4. To install the drive sheave, reverse the above. Make sure the taper on the crankshaft and inside the sheave are clean, oil-free, and dry before installing the sheave on the shaft. Screw in and tighten the bolt to 10 mkg (72 ft.-lb.) to seat the sheave on the shaft. Then, loosen the bolt and retighten it to 6 mkg (44 ft.-lb.).

DRIVEN SHEAVE

Service of the driven sheave should be entrusted to your dealer. However, you can save time and money by inspecting, removing, and installing the assembly yourself.

Inspection

1. Press in on the movable driven sheave and rotate it clockwise. Check the feel of the spring. It should be extremely stiff. If it is not, if it pushes in without much resistance, the spring should be replaced.

2. Check the ramp shoes for wear (**Figure 11**) and have them replaced if they are worn thin or are damaged.

3. Inspect the contact surfaces of the sheaves for wear and scoring. If the surfaces are in poor condition, they will rapidly wear the drive belt.

4. Check the sheaves and brake disc for warping and replace them if they are not true.

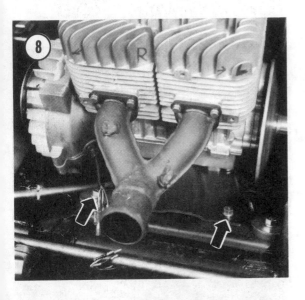

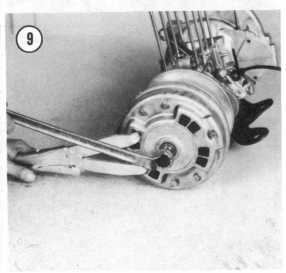

7

Removal/Installation

1. Remove the drive belt as described earlier.

2. Turn the machine onto its right side and rest it on cardboard to prevent damage to the finish.

3. Remove the chaincase cover (**Figure 12**) and the gasket.

4. Lock the brake. Remove the cotter key from the driven sheave shaft and unscrew the nut (**Figure 13**). Release the brake and slacken the cable adjuster.

5. Loosen the locknut on the chain tensioner (**Figure 14**) and unscrew the tensioner bolt several turns to relax the chain tension.

6. Pull the sprocket off the driven sheave shaft and remove the spacer (**Figure 15**).

7. Tap the sheave assembly out of the chain-case with a soft mallet, and at the same time disengage it from the brake.

8. Reverse the above to install the driven sheave. Make sure the brake disc engages the brake and the shaft is lined up with the bearing before tapping it into the chaincase. Adjust the brake (see Chapter Two, *Brake*) and lock the brake to prevent the sheave from turning.

Install the spacer and the sprocket and chain. Screw on and tighten the nut to 4 mkg (29 ft.-lb.) and install a new cotter key in the shaft. Adjust the chain tension as described under *Chaincase, Installation*.

CHAINCASE

The chaincase houses sprockets and a drive chain that connects the driven sheave to the

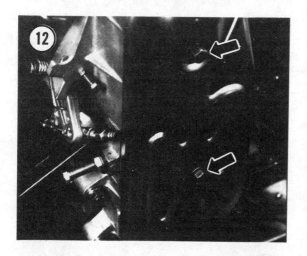

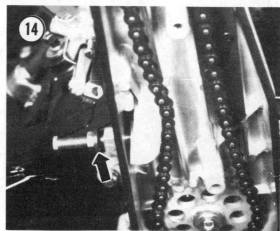

drive axle. The case is sealed to contain the oil bath in which the chain and sprockets run.

The only service required by the chaincase assembly is a periodic check of the chain tension and oil level. Annually, the chaincase should be drained and refilled. Chain tension and oil level are discussed in Chapter Two, *Drive Chain*.

To change the oil in the chaincase, carry out the first 3 steps of the procedure that follows and fill the case with 450 cc (15 oz.) of GL-3 SAE 75 or 80 gear oil. Then, install the gasket and cover.

Removal

1. Remove the drive belt as described at the beginning of this chapter.

2. Tilt the machine onto its right side and rest it on cardboard to prevent damage to the finish.

3. Remove the chaincase cover (**Figure 16**) and gasket.

4. Drain the oil from the chaincase. A turkey baster, available in markets and variety stores for about a dollar, is handy for siphoning the oil from the case.

5. Loosen the locknut on the chain tensioner (**Figure 17**) and unscrew the tensioner bolt several turns to relax the chain.

6. Lock the brake, remove the cotter key from the driven sheave shaft, and unscrew the sprocket bolts (**Figure 18**). Release the brake and disconnect the cable.

7. Remove the sprockets and chain together. Remove the spacers located behind the sprockets (**Figure 19**).

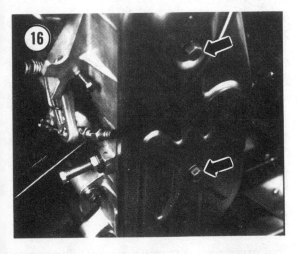

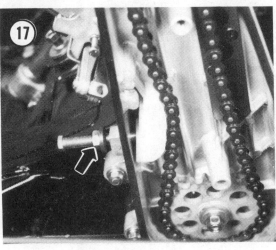

8. Tap the driven sheave assembly out of the case and disengage it from the brake.

9. Loosen the locknuts on the track tension bolts (**Figure 20**) and slack the bolts off several turns to relax the track tension on the drive axle.

> NOTE: *Loosen the track tension bolts an equal number of turns and write down the number of turns for reference during assembly; it will save time when the tension is adjusted later on.*

10. Unscrew the chaincase mounting bolts (**Figure 21**) and remove the chaincase. Pull out on the case to disengage it from the drive axle.

Inspection

1. Clean the case, cover, chain, and sprockets with solvent and dry them with compressed air.

2. Inspect the case for cracks and damage. Minor cracks or porous areas where seeping could occur can be repaired with epoxy or a liquid aluminum type filler.

3. Inspect the seals for wear and damage and replace them if they are unsatisfactory (see **Figure 22**).

4. Inspect the sprockets for wear and undercutting of the teeth and replace them if they are not satisfactory.

> NOTE: *Unless the chaincase has been run dry, chain wear will be negligible.*

5. Check the wear of the tensioner (**Figure 23**) and replace it if it's worn beyond the limit shown.

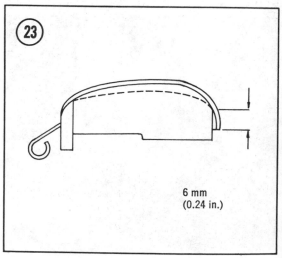

6 mm
(0.24 in.)

Installation

1. Install the chaincase on the drive axle. Install the mounting bolts and tighten them finger-tight.

2. Press the driven sheave into the case, taking care to engage the brake disc with the brake and line up the shaft squarely with the bearing. Install the spacers on the shafts (**Figure 24**).

3. Install the sprockets and chain. Make sure the shoulder on the bottom sprocket faces out (**Figure 25**).

4. Connect the brake cable and run the adjuster out far enough so the brake will lock the driven sheave. Screw on and tighten the top sprocket nut to 4 mkg (29 ft.-lb.) and install a new cotter key in the shaft. Screw on and tighten the bottom sprocket nut to 3.5 mkg (25 ft.-lb.).

5. Adjust the chain tension so there is 8-15 mm (0.32-0.6 in.) of back-and-forth movement of the chain on the rear run. Then, tighten the tension adjuster locknut (**Figure 26**).

6. Install the cover gasket on the chaincase with the break in the gasket located at the top (**Figure 27**).

7. Pour 450 cc (15 oz.) of GL-3 SAE 75 or 80 gear oil into the chaincase.

7

8. Install the cover and tighten the bolts (**Figure 28**).

9. Set the machine upright and install the drive belt as described earlier (see *Drive Belt, Removal/Installation*).

10. Screw in the track tensioner bolts the number of turns they were loosened earlier. Refer to Chapter Nine, *Track Adjustment,* and adjust the track tension and alignment. Refer to Chapter Two, *Brake,* and adjust the brake.

DRIVE AXLE

Service to the drive axle includes drive wheel and bearing replacement. Replacement of the drive wheels should be entrusted to your dealer; the wheels must be pressed off and on the axle and they must be precisely spaced to avoid unnecessary track and drive wheel wear.

Removal

1. Unscrew the nut from the right end of the drive axle (**Figure 29**).

2. Remove the chaincase assembly as described earlier (see *Chaincase, Removal*). Refer to Chapter Nine and remove the rear suspension assembly (see *Suspension Removal/Installation*).

3. Pull the track forward to disengage the track lugs from the lugs on the drive wheels.

4. Pull up on the drive axle to disengage it from the right bearing (**Figure 30**) and remove the axle from the machine.

Inspection

1. Inspect the lugs on the drive wheels for damage and wear. If they are in poor condition, have them replaced by your dealer.

2. Turn the right bearing (**Figure 31**) by hand and check it for roughness and play. If the bearing is in poor condition, unscrew the bear-

ing carrier bolts **(Figure 32)**, remove the old bearing, and install a new one.

Installation

1. Guide the left end of the axle through the hole in the body and then set the right end into the bearing **(Figure 33)**.

2. Engage the track lugs with the lugs on the drive wheels.

3. Install the chaincase assembly as described earlier (see *Chaincase, Installation*).

4. Refer to Chapter Nine, *Suspension Removal/Installation*, and install the suspension.

5. Set the machine upright and install the Bellville washer and nut on the right end of the axle **(Figure 34)**. Tighten the nut to 8 mkg (58 ft.-lb.).

6. Adjust the track tension and alignment as described in Chapter Nine, *Track Adjustment*.

BRAKE

All models covered in this handbook are equipped with a mechanical disc brake. Three distinct types are used, designated in this handbook as Type I, Type II, and Type III **(Figure 35)**.

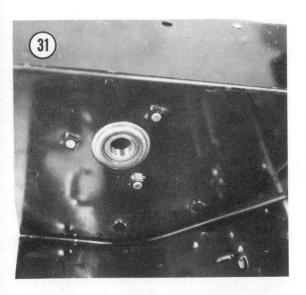

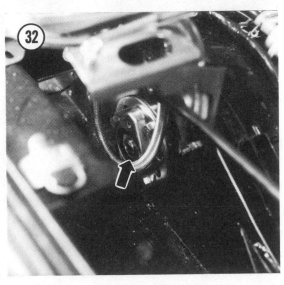

7

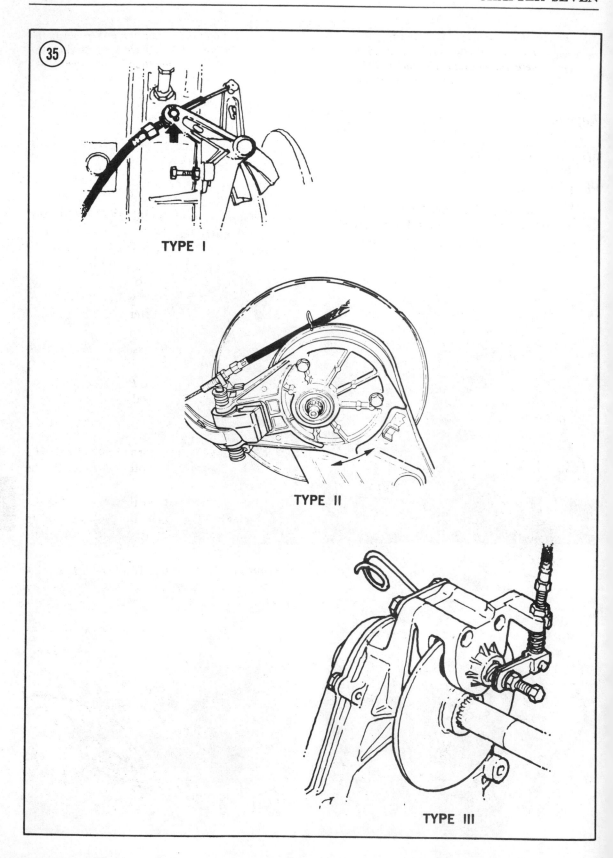

TYPE I

TYPE II

TYPE III

NOTE: *These designations (Types I, II, and III) are not Yamaha's. They are used here for convenience and understanding when describing and discussing the 3 brake types.*

Adjustment

Adjustment of all 3 brake types is described in Chapter Two, *Brake*.

Pad Replacement (Type I)

If either brake pad is worn to a thickness of 1 mm (0.04 in.), both pads should be replaced.

1. Remove the chaincase assembly as described earlier (see *Chaincase, Removal*).

NOTE: *While this may seem to be a lot of extra work for a job seemingly as simple as replacing brake pads, the task of disassembling the brake and then assembling it again with the chaincase installed in the machine is almost impossible. At best, the job would be frustrating and probably consume at least as much time as if the case were removed and worked on on a bench —*

and without the assurance that the return springs and pivot shaft cotter key are correctly installed. It's for these reasons that brake pad replacement should be considered when the chaincase is removed from the machine for drive train service.

2. Remove the cotter key from the end of the brake pivot shaft (**Figure 36**) and remove the shaft.

3. Remove the calipers and install new pads.

4. Grease the brake pivot shaft with low-temperature grease.

5. Assemble the caliper halves, springs, and shaft. Make sure the springs are located on the bosses on the chaincase so they will pull the pads away from the disc when the brake is released. Install a new cotter key in the end of the brake pivot shaft.

6. Install the chaincase assembly (see *Chaincase, Installation*).

7. Refer to Chapter Two, *Brake, Type I,* and adjust the brake as described.

Pad Replacement (Type II)

If either brake pad is worn to a thickness of 5 mm (0.2 in.) or less, both pads should be replaced.

1. Loosen the locknut on the brake cable adjuster (**Figure 37**), turn the adjuster in to slacken the cable, and disconnect the cable from the caliper.

2. Remove the cotter key from the brake pivot pin (**Figure 38**) and remove the pin, the caliper halves, and the spring.

7

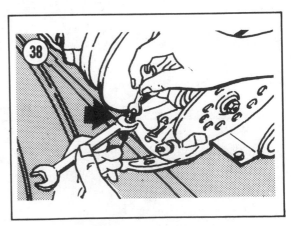

3. Install new pads in the caliper halves.

4. Assemble the caliper halves, spring, washers, and the pin with the brake carriers. Install a new cotter key in the end of the brake pivot pin to lock the pin in place.

5. Connect the cable to the caliper and adjust the brake as described in Chapter Two, *Brake, Type II.*

Pad Replacement (Type III)

If either brake pad is worn to a thickness of 4 mm (0.16 in.) or less, both pads should be replaced.

Refer to **Figure 39** for the procedure that follows.

1. Loosen the locknut on the cable adjuster and screw the adjuster in to slacken the cable. Loosen the locknut on the adjuster cam bolt and back the cam bolt out several turns. Disconnect the cable from the brake caliper.

2. Unscrew the bolts that attach the caliper to the chaincase and remove the caliper from the case and the brake disc.

3. Rotate the brake lever *clockwise* to remove the adjuster cam from the caliper.

4. Clean the caliper and the adjuster cam with a non-petroleum solvent such as ethyl alcohol and dry them with compressed air. Grease the adjuster cam threads with low-temperature grease and install the cam in the caliper.

5. Install the backup plate and new pads in the caliper.

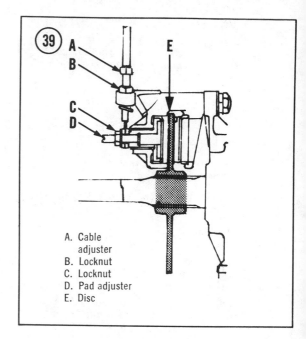

A. Cable adjuster
B. Locknut
C. Locknut
D. Pad adjuster
E. Disc

6. Set the caliper in place over the disc and in line with the bolt holes in the chaincase.

NOTE: *It may be necessary to back off the cam adjuster bolt several additional turns to provide enough clearance for the pads to slide down over the disc.*

7. Screw in and tighten the caliper mounting bolts.

8. Connect the brake cable to the brake arm.

9. Refer to Chapter Two, *Brake, Type III,* and adjust the brake as described.

Table 1   SHEAVE PULLER IDENTIFICATION

Model	Puller No.
EX340, EX440, GPX338, GPX433	90890-01836
GS340, GP440, ET250, GP338, GP433	90890-01850
ET340, EXCEL V, SSR, SRX	90890-01859
ET300	90890-01878

CHAPTER EIGHT

FRONT SUSPENSION AND STEERING

The front suspension and steering consists of spring-mounted skis carried on spindles that are connected to the steering column by a tie rod and drag link.

All models except the SSR are equipped with single leaf springs attached to the skis, front and rear. SSR models are equipped with coil springs and integral shock absorbers that attach to the ski spindles and the body. The springs have 5 pre-load settings.

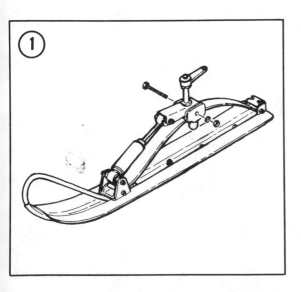

All models are equipped with a single-piece steering column that is mounted in nylon bushings.

Tie rods and drag links are fitted with adjustable ends to accommodate ski alignment.

SKIS

The skis are equipped with wear bars, or skags, that aid turning the machine and protect the bottoms of the skis from wear and damage caused by road crossings and bare terrain. The bars are expendable and should be checked for wear and damage at 20-hour or 250-mile (400 km) intervals and replaced when they are worn to the point they no longer protect the skis or aid turning.

Removal/Installation
(All Except SSR Models)

1. Support the front of the machine so both skis are off the ground.

2. Unscrew the top shock absorber bolt and the ski-to-spindle bolt (**Figure 1**) and remove the ski assembly.

3. Unscrew the spring-to-ski mounting bolts and remove the spring from the ski.

4. Reverse the above to install the skis. Clean and grease the spring-to-ski mounting bolts and eyes and the wear plates (**Figure 2**) with low-temperature grease.

Wear Bar (Skag)
Replacement (All Models)

1. Remove the skis as described above.

2. Unscrew the locknuts that attach the skag to the ski (**Figure 3**) and remove the skag.

3. Install a new skag (**Figure 4**) and screw on and tighten the locknuts.

> NOTE: *If the locking inserts in the nuts are worn or extruded, replace the nuts.*

Removal/Installation (SSR Models)

1. Support the front of the machine so the skis are off the ground.

2. Unscrew the ski-to-spindle bolts (**Figure 5**) and remove the skis.

3. Reverse the above to install the skis. Replace locknuts if their inserts are worn or extruded.

Ski Spindle Lubrication

1. Support the front of the machine so the skis are off the ground.

2. Straighten the lock tab on the ski spindle nut (**Figure 6**) and unscrew the nut. Scribe a mark on the spindle and steering arm for reference during installation.

3. Tap the ski spindle out of the arm with a soft mallet and remove the ski.

4. Clean the spindle and bore with solvent and dry them with compressed air.

5. Grease the spindle with low-temperature grease.

6. Install the spindle in the bore, align the reference marks on the spindle and the steering arm, and install the arm.

7. Screw on and tighten the nut and lock it in place with the tab lock.

8. Refer to *Ski Alignment* in this chapter and align the skis as described.

STEERING

Steering service includes lubrication and replacement of the steering column bushings,

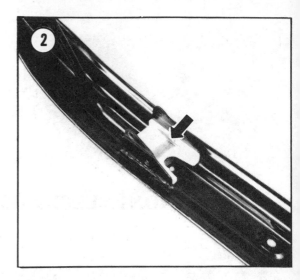

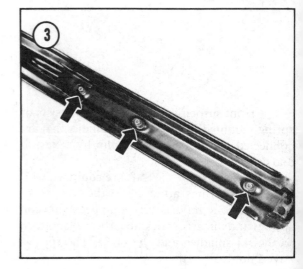

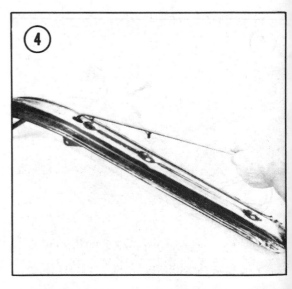

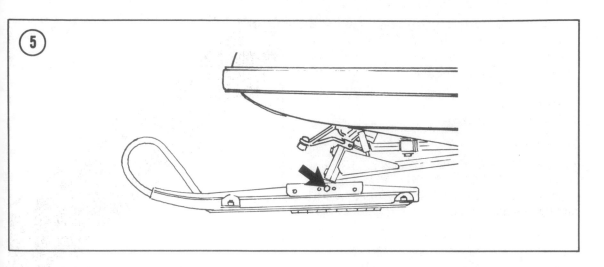

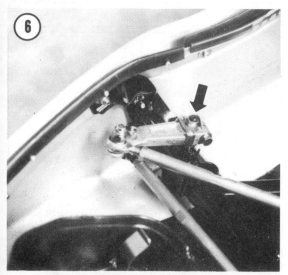

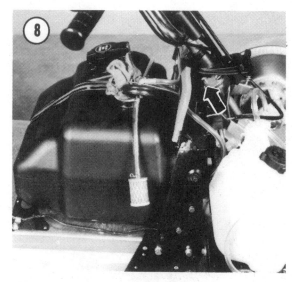

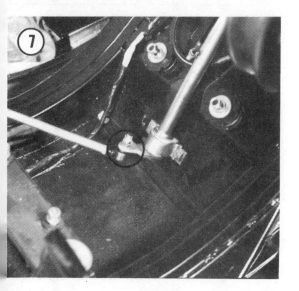

lubrication and replacement of the tie rod and drag link ends, and ski alignment.

STEERING COLUMN

Removal/Installation

1. Disconnect the drag link from the end of the steering column **(Figure 7)**. Unscrew the bottom column mounting bolts.

2. Unscrew the top column mounting bolts **(Figure 8)**.

> NOTE: *It's not necessary to disturb the controls or remove the handlebar.*

3. Clean, inspect, and lubricate the bushings as described below and then install the column by reversing the above. Refer to *Ski Alignment* and align the skis as described.

8

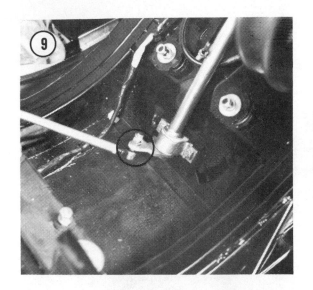

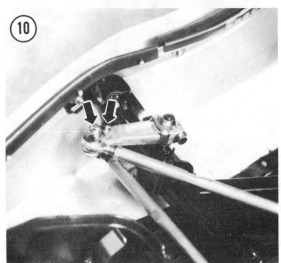

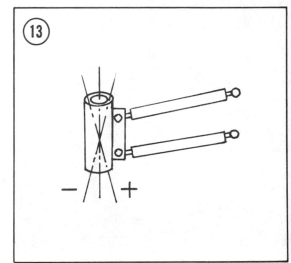

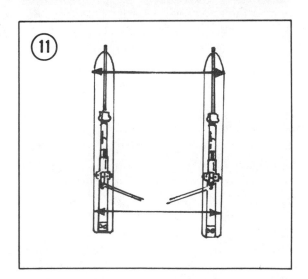

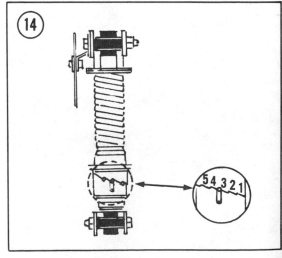

**Steering Bushing Cleaning,
Inspection, and Lubrication**

1. Clean the column and bushings with solvent and dry them with compressed air.

2. Inspect the bushings for wear and damage and replace them if they are scored or if they are sloppy on the column.

3. Lubricate the bushings with low-temperature grease.

TIE ROD AND DRAG LINK

Removal/Installation

1. Disconnect the drag link from the bottom of the steering column (**Figure 9**).

2. Unscrew the locknuts from the drag link and tie rod spindles (**Figure 10**) and tap the spindles out of the steering arm with a soft mallet.

3. Clean, inspect, and lubricate the spindles as described below and install them by reversing the above. Replace any locknuts with worn or extruded inserts. Refer to *Ski Alignment* and align the skis as described.

**Cleaning, Inspection,
and Lubrication**

1. Clean the spindles and spindle bores with solvent and dry them with compressed air.

2. Inspect the spindles and bores for wear and damage and replace any parts that are scored or severely worn.

3. Lubricate the spindles with low-temperature grease.

SKI ALIGNMENT

Check the alignment of the skis (**Figure 11**). Toe-out (the amount by which dimension A is greater than dimension B) should be no greater than 0.6 mm (¼ in.).

If adjustment is required, loosen the locknut on the steering tie rod (**Figure 12**) and turn the rod in or out until the toe-out is correct. Then, without further turning the rod, tighten the locknut.

SSR SUSPENSION ADJUSTMENT

The front suspension on SSR models must be adjusted in conjunction with rear suspension adjustments (see Chapter Nine, *SSR Racing Adjustments*).

Refer to **Table 1** for the procedure that follows.

1. Set the camber as recommended (**Figure 13**). To achieve 0° camber, L1 must equal L2. For negative camber, L1 must be 2.5 mm (0.098 in.) longer than L2. For positive camber, L1 must be 2.5 mm (0.098 in.) shorter than L2.

2. Set the spring pre-load as recommended (**Figure 14**). For smooth surfaces, increase the pre-load, and decrease it for rough surfaces.

3. Set the stabilizer as recommended (**Figure 15**). For cross-country racing or oval track racing on courses with large radius turns, both stabilizers should be adjusted equally. On courses with sharp radius turns, the outside stabilizer should be adjusted one position shorter than the inside stabilizer (e.g., outside — No. 2; inside — No. 1).

8

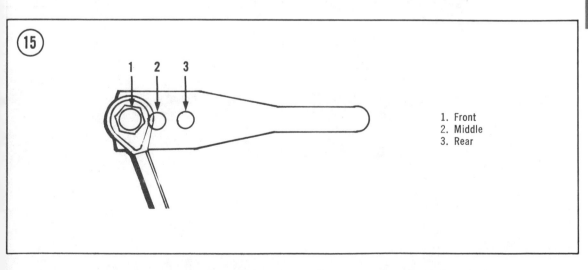

15

1   2   3

1. Front
2. Middle
3. Rear

CONTROL CABLE REPLACEMENT

Throttle Cable

1. Loosen the throttle cable adjuster locknut at the carburetor (**Figure 16**) and run the adjuster all the way in and disconnect the cable.

2. Disconnect the cable at the hand control (**Figure 17**).

3. Connect a new cable to the hand control and route the cable alongside the old one. Then, remove the old cable from the machine. Connect the new cable to the carburetor.

4. Adjust the new cable as described in Chapter Five, under *Adjustment* for the carburetor with which your machine is equipped.

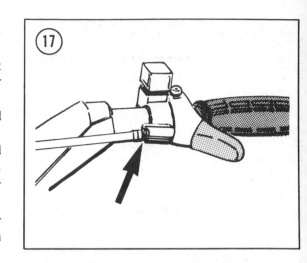

Brake Cable

1. Loosen the locknut on the brake cable adjuster at the brake (**Figure 18**) and run the adjuster all the way in and disconnect the cable from the brake.

2. Disconnect the cable from the hand control (**Figure 19**).

3. Connect a new cable to the hand control and route it alongside the old cable. Then, remove the old cable from the machine and connect the new cable to the brake.

4. Refer to Chapter Two, *Brake — Type I, Type II,* or *Type III* and adjust the brake as described.

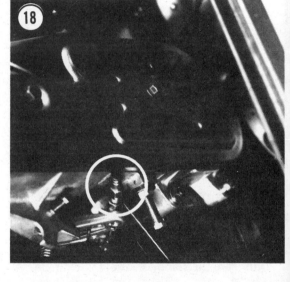

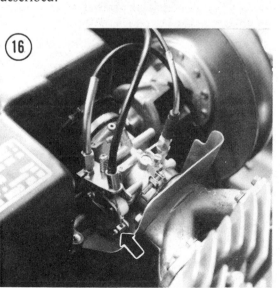

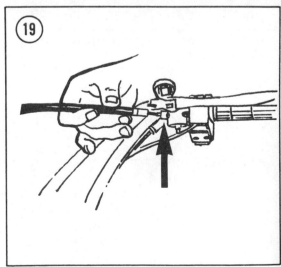

Table 1   SUSPENSION ADJUSTMENT GUIDE — SSR MODELS

Surface	Course Turns	Camber	Spring Pre-Load Position	Stabilizer (Inside/Outside)
Hard ice	Large radius (more than 50 meters)	0° or positive	Middle (3)	1/1
	Small radius (less than 45 meters)	0° or negative	Increase (see text)	½ or ⅔ (see text)
Soft ice or hard-packed snow	Large radius	0° or positive	Increase (see text)	2/2 (see text)
	Small radius	0° or negative	Increase (see text)	½ or ⅔ (see text)
Soft or wet snow	Large radius	0° or positive	Increase (see text)	2/2 (see text)
	Small radius	0° or negative	Increase (see text)	½ or ⅔ (see text)

8

CHAPTER NINE

REAR SUSPENSION AND TRACK

Yamaha snowmobiles are equipped with slide-rail suspension which utilizes a rear idler wheel assembly to control track tension and alignment.

Several variations of the slide-rail design are used and include fixed-axle idlers and spring-controlled top and bottom idlers.

All the systems are equipped with adjustable springs, shock absorbers, and replaceable wear bars.

Tables are found at the end of the chapter.

SUSPENSION

Removal/Installation

1. Loosen the locknuts on the track adjusting bolts (**Figure 1**) and back the bolts out to relieve the tension on the track.

2. Disconnect the rear springs from their hangers (**Figure 2**).

3. Unscrew the 2 bolts that connect the rear of the suspension to the body (**Figure 3**). Then, unscrew the 2 forward bolts (**Figure 4** — one on each side).

4. Turn the machine on its side and rest it on a sheet of cardboard to protect the finish.

5. Swing the rear of the suspension and track frame out of the body and lift the suspension assembly out of the track.

6. Reverse the above steps to install the suspension. Set the suspension into the track, making sure the lugs in the track are inboard of the idler wheels (**Figure 5**).

Screw in all 4 suspension bolts before tightening them. Then, connect the rear springs. Refer to *Track Adjustment* described later in this chapter and adjust the track tension and alignment.

Cleaning/Inspection

1. Thoroughly wash the suspension with detergent and warm water and dry it thoroughly with clean rags and compressed air.

2. Inspect the slide runners (**Figures 6, 7,** and **8**) for wear and damage. If the runners are severely abraded or worn to less than 10 mm (0.40 in.) (**Figure 9**), replace them as described under *Slide Runner Replacement* after the suspension has been cleaned and painted.

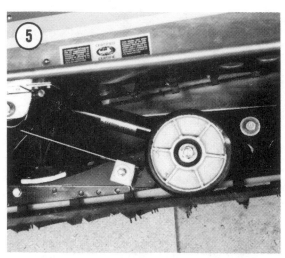

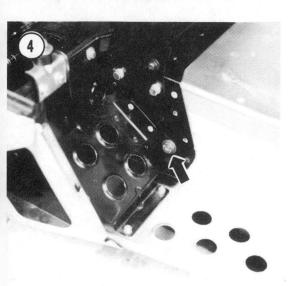

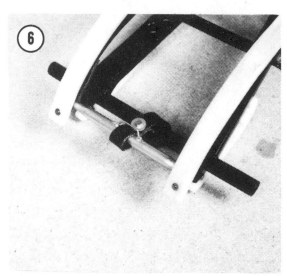

9

3. Remove the axles (**Figure 10**) and clean them and the axle sleeves with solvent. Dry them with compressed air.

4. Inspect the idler wheels for wear and damage and replace them if the rubber is severely worn or abraded.

5. Lightly sand and feather all chipped painted areas, using a 320 grit wet-or-dry paper. Wash away the sanding residue with water and dry the suspension thoroughly. Paint the sanded areas with a rust-inhibiting paint, such as Rustoleum Gloss Black. Spray on several light coats, allowing the paint to dry between coats to prevent it from running.

6. After the suspension frame has been painted (and slide runners replaced, if required), lightly coat the axles with low-temperature grease and install them in the axle sleeves.

7. Install the suspension as described earlier and adjust the track tension and alignment as described under *Track Adjustment*.

Slide Runner Replacement

1. Remove the screws that attach the slide runners to the suspension (**Figure 11**). It may be necessary to break the screws loose with an impact driver.

2. Slide the runners off the suspension frame.

3. Thoroughly clean the suspension where the runners contact it to remove grit, corrosion, and old paint. Sand and paint the affected area as described above (*Cleaning/Inspection*).

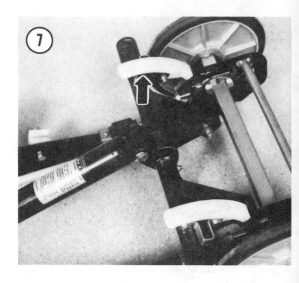

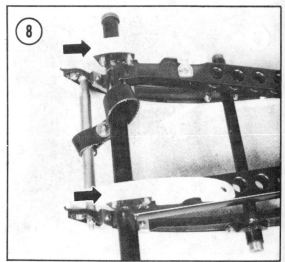

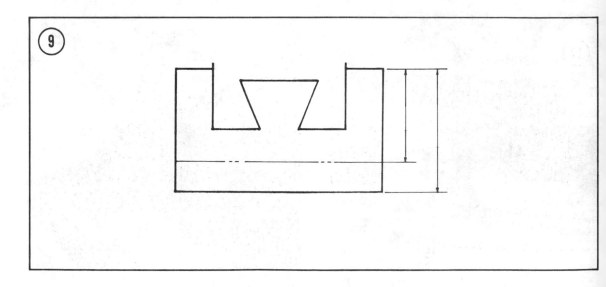

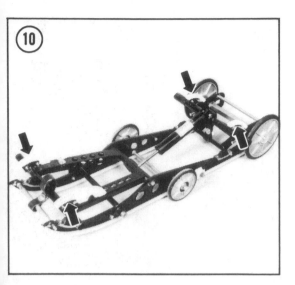

4. Install new runner material. Coat the screw threads with Loctite or a similar fastener locking compound.

TRACK

There are 2 track adjustments — tension and alignment — that should be carried out every 40 hours or 500 miles (800 km) of operation.

Tension Adjustment

Correct track tension is important because if the track is too loose, it will slap on the bottom of the tunnel and wear both the track and the tunnel. Also, a loose track can ratchet on the drive sprockets and damage both the track and the sprockets.

If the track is too tight, it will rapidly wear the slide runner material and the rubber on the idler wheels, and degrade performance because of increased friction and drag on the drive system.

1. Turn the machine onto its side and rest it on a piece of cardboard to protect the finish.

2. Clean ice, snow, and dirt from the track and suspension.

3. Pull the track away from the suspension frame at midpoint with moderate force (**Figure 12**) and measure the distance. It should be ¾-1 in. (19-25 mm).

4. If adjustment is required, loosen the locknuts on the track adjuster bolt (**Figure 13**). If the track-to-runner distance is more than 1

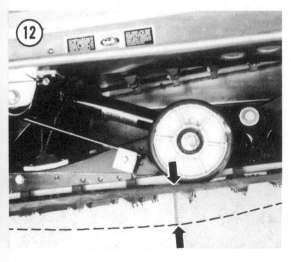

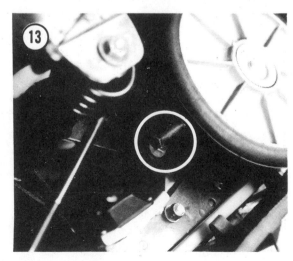

9

in. (25 mm), tighten the adjuster bolts equally until the distance is correct. Then, tighten the locknuts.

If the track-to-runner distance is less than ¾ in. (19 mm), loosen the adjuster bolts equally until the distance is correct. Then, tighten the locknuts.

Alignment

Track alignment is related to track tension and should be checked and adjusted when the tension is checked and adjusted. If the track is misaligned, the rear idler wheels, drive sprocket lugs, and track lugs will wear rapidly. Also, performance will be poor because of resistance of the track against the sides of the wheels.

1. Adjust the track tension as described above.

2. Position the machine, on its skis, so the tips of the skis are against a wall or other immovable barrier. Elevate and support the machine so the track is completely clear of the ground and free to rotate.

3. Start the engine and apply just enough throttle to turn the track several complete revolutions. Then, shut off the engine and allow the track to coast to a stop; don't stop it with the brake.

> WARNING
> *Don't stand behind or in front of the machine when the engine is running, and take care to keep hands, feet, and clothing away from the track when it is turning.*

4. Check the alignment of the rear idler wheels and the track lugs (**Figure 14**). If the idlers are equal distances from the lugs and the openings in the track are centered with the slide runners (**Figure 15**), the alignment is correct. However, if the track is offset to one side or the other, alignment adjustment is required.

5. Loosen the locknuts on the track adjuster bolts (**Figure 16**). If the track is offset to the left, tighten the left adjuster bolt and loosen the right one equal amounts until the track is centered. Then, tighten the locknuts.

If the track is offset to the right, tighten the right adjuster bolt and loosen the left one equal amounts. Then, tighten the locknuts.

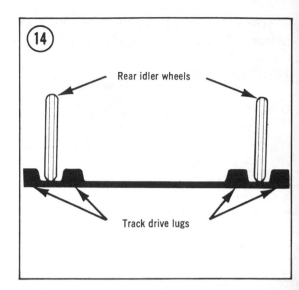

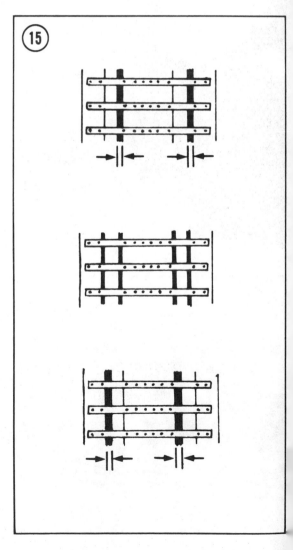

6. Repeat Steps 3 and 4 and if alignment is still not correct, repeat Step 5 and then Steps 3 and 4 again until the track is correctly aligned. Then recheck track tension.

Removal/Installation

If track damage or wear is experienced (see Chapter Three, *Track Wear Analysis*) the track should be replaced.

1. Refer to *Suspension Removal/Installation* in this chapter and remove the rear suspension assembly from the machine.

2. Refer to *Drive Axle, Removal,* in Chapter Seven and remove the drive axle.

3. Remove the track from the machine.

4. Install a new track by reversing the above steps.

> NOTE: *Orient the lugs on the new track as shown in Figure 17.*

5. After installation is complete, adjust the track as described under *Tension Adjustment and Alignment* in this chapter. Recheck and correct adjustment after 5 hours and then 10 hours of operation, and then at the intervals recommended in Chapter Two.

SUSPENSION ADJUSTMENT

The suspension can be adjusted to accommodate rider weight (rear springs) and driving conditions (front springs and snubber strap).

Correct suspension adjustment is arrived at largely through a matter of trial-and-error "tuning." There are several fundamental points that must be understood and applied before the suspension can be successfully adjusted to your needs.

Ski pressure — the load on the skis relative to the load on the track — is the primary factor controlling handling performance. If the ski pressure is too light, the front of the machine tends to float and steering control becomes vague, with the machine tending to drive straight ahead rather than turn, and wander when running straight at steady throttle.

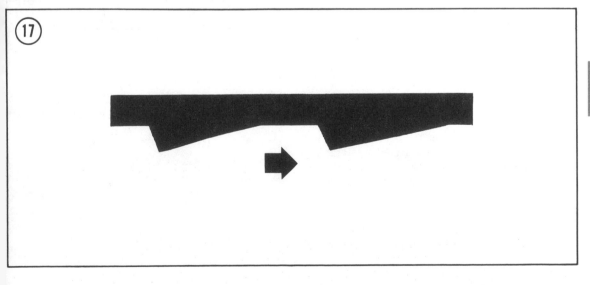

9

On the other hand, if ski pressure is too heavy, the machine tends to plow during cornering and the skis dig in during straight line running rather than stay on top of the snow.

Ski pressure for one snow condition is not necessarily good for another condition. For instance, if the surface is very hard and offers little steering traction, added ski pressure — to permit the skis to "bite" into the snow — is desirable; also, the hard surface will support the skis and not allow them to penetrate when the machine is running in a straight line under power.

On the other hand, if the surface is soft and tacky, lighter ski pressure is desirable to prevent the skis from sinking into the snow. Also, the increased traction afforded by the snow will allow the skis to turn with light pressure.

It's apparent, then, that good suspension adjustment involves some thought and analysis relating to ski pressure versus conditions. Ski pressure is increased by softening front springs or pulling the front end down with the snubber strap, and it's decreased by stiffening the front springs or extending the snubber.

Trail Riding Adjustments

If the machine is heavily loaded, either with the addition of a passenger or with equipment, the rear tends to squat, taking weight off the skis and making steering uncertain.

To compensate for an increased load, disconnect the rear springs from their hangers (**Figure 18**), move the hangers up one position, and reconnect the springs.

On ice and hard-packed snow, increased ski pressure is desirable. This could be achieved by stiffening the rear suspension as just described, but if the machine is not heavily laden, the ride would be hard and uncomfortable. Instead, the front suspension can be pulled down by shortening the snubber strap (**Figure 19**).

If the machine is equipped with front springs, ski pressure can also be increased by relaxing the springs.

SRX Racing Adjustments

Correct suspension adjustment is essential for good racing performance.

Refer to **Table 1** for the procedure that follows.

1. Set the front (**Figure 20**) and rear (**Figure 21**) stopper bands as recommended.

2. Set the rear spring position (**Figure 22**) as recommended.

3. Set the front arm position (**Figure 23**) as recommended.

4. Set the rear arm position (**Figure 24**) as recommended.

5. Refer to **Figure 25** for the basic spike arrangement and number of spikes. KK-8 spikes should be added only if forward traction is poor, and KK-19 spikes should be added if side slip is excessive.

> NOTE: *Do not use more spikes than are actually required for good traction; an excessive number of spikes will hamper performance.*

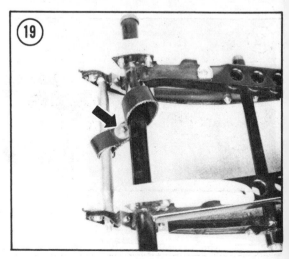

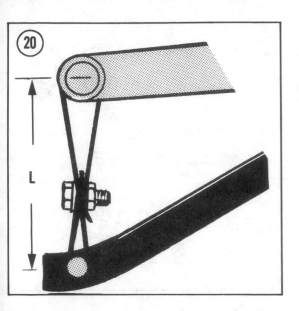

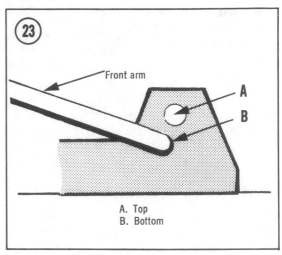

A. Top
B. Bottom

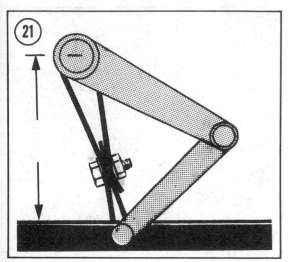

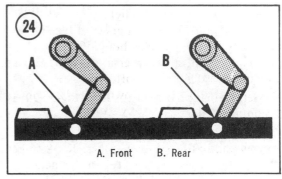

A. Front   B. Rear

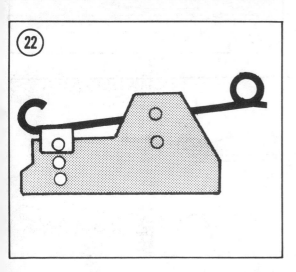

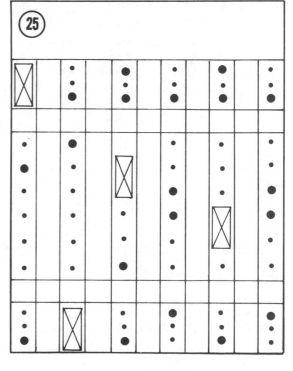

9

SSR Racing Adjustments

There are 4 adjustments possible with the rear suspension on SSR models to accommodate varied surface conditions and track layouts. In addition, there are several adjustments to the front suspension (see Chapter Eight, *SSR Racing Adjustments*) that must be made in conjunction with the rear suspension adjustments described here.

Refer to **Table 2** for the procedure that follows.

1. Set the length of the front stopper bolt (**Figure 26**) as recommended. Shorten the stopper to increase oversteer and lengthen it to increase understeer.

2. Set the tension of the front spring adjuster (**Figure 27**) as recommended. This adjustment greatly affects ski pressure; if the adjuster is too loose, ski pressure will be very high.

3. Set the rear spring position (**Figure 28**) as recommended.

4. Set the rear pivot arm position (**Figure 29**) as recommended.

5. Refer to **Figure 30** for the basic spike arrangement and number of spikes. KK-8 spikes should be added only if forward traction is poor, and KK-19 (or Woody's Gold Diggers, No. 1316) should be added if side slip is excessive.

> NOTE: *Do not use more spikes than are actually required for good traction; an excessive number of spikes will hamper performance.*

6. Refer to Chapter Eight, *SSR Racing Adjustments,* and adjust the front suspension as recommended.

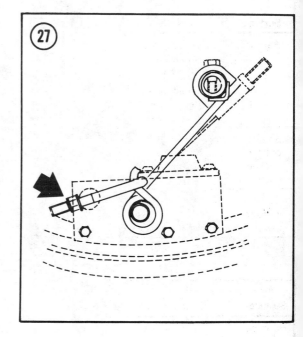

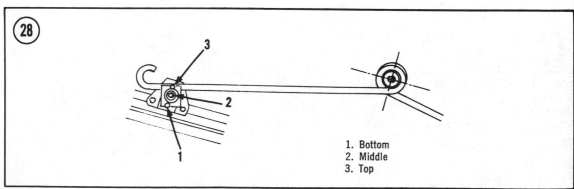

1. Bottom
2. Middle
3. Top

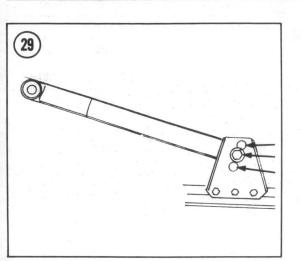

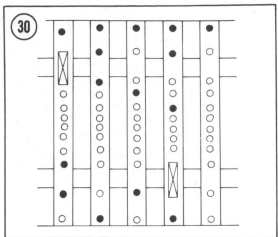

Table 1   SUSPENSION ADJUSTMENT GUIDE — SRX MODELS

Surface	Course Turns	Stoppers Front/Rear	Rear Spring Position	Front Arm Position	Rear Arm Position
Hard ice	Large radius (more than 50 meters)	3/2	Bottom	Lower	Front
	Small radius (less than 45 meters)	3/2	Middle	Lower	Rear
Soft ice or hard-packed snow	Large radius	3/2	Middle	Lower	Front
	Small radius	4/2	Middle	Upper	Rear
Soft or wet snow	Large radius	4/2	Middle	Lower	Rear
	Small radius	4/2	Top	Lower	Rear

Table 2   SUSPENSION ADJUSTMENT GUIDE — SSR MODELS

Surface	Course Turns	Front Stopper	Front Spring	Rear Spring Position	Pivot Arm Position
Hard ice	Large radius (more than 50 meters)	Normal	Normal	Middle	Bottom
	Small radius (less than 45 meters)	Shorten	Tighten	Middle	Top
Soft ice or hard-packed snow	Large radius	Shorten	Tighten	Middle	Top
	Small radius	Shorten	Tighten	Middle	Top
Soft or wet snow	Large radius	Shorten	Tighten	Bottom	Top
	Small radius	Shorten	Tighten	Bottom	Top

9

INDEX

10

10

WIRING DIAGRAMS

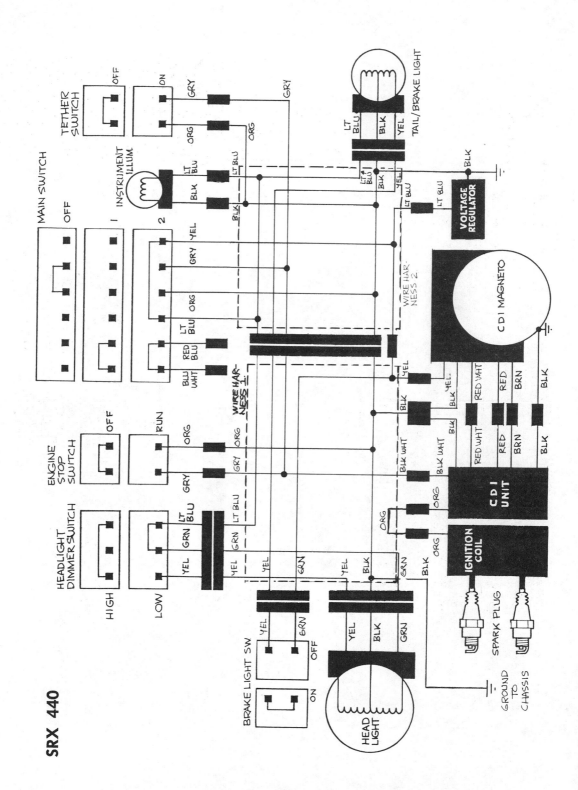

SRX 440

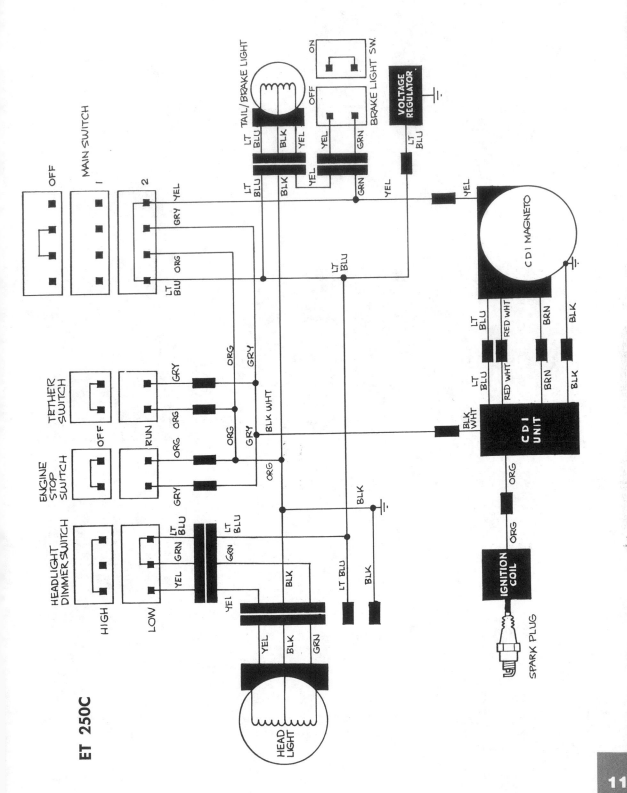

ET 250C

SSR 440

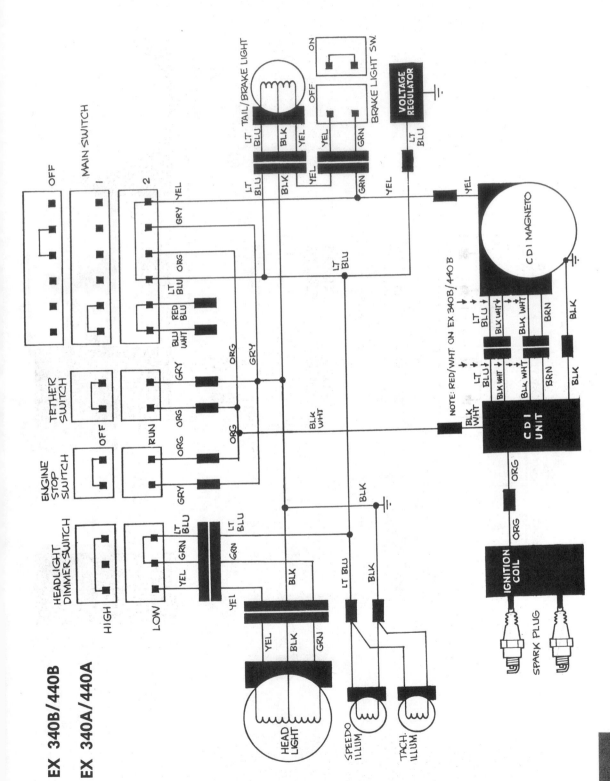

EX 340B/440B

EX 340A/440A

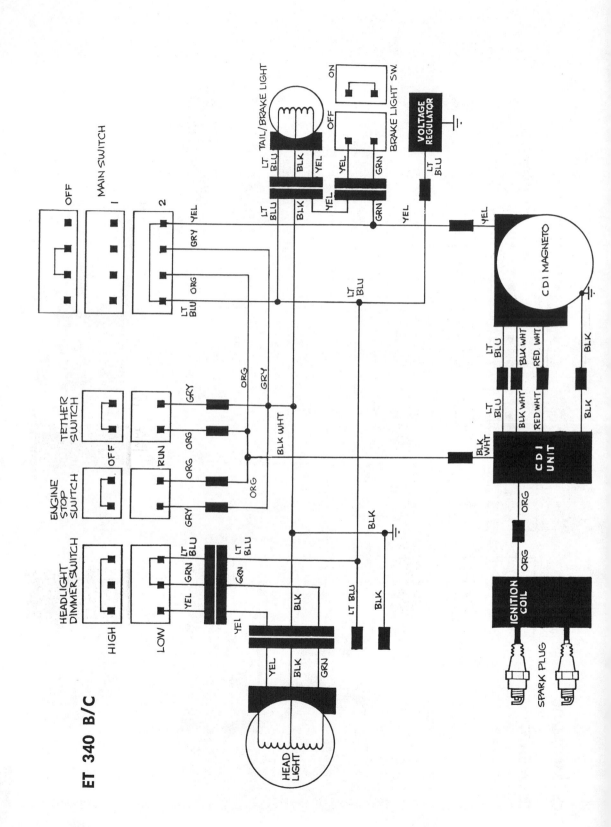

ET 340 B/C

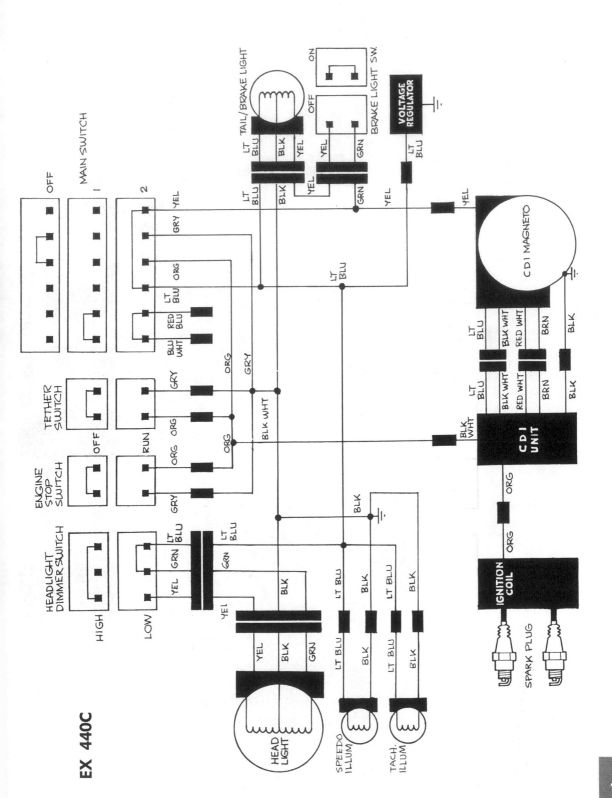

EX 440C

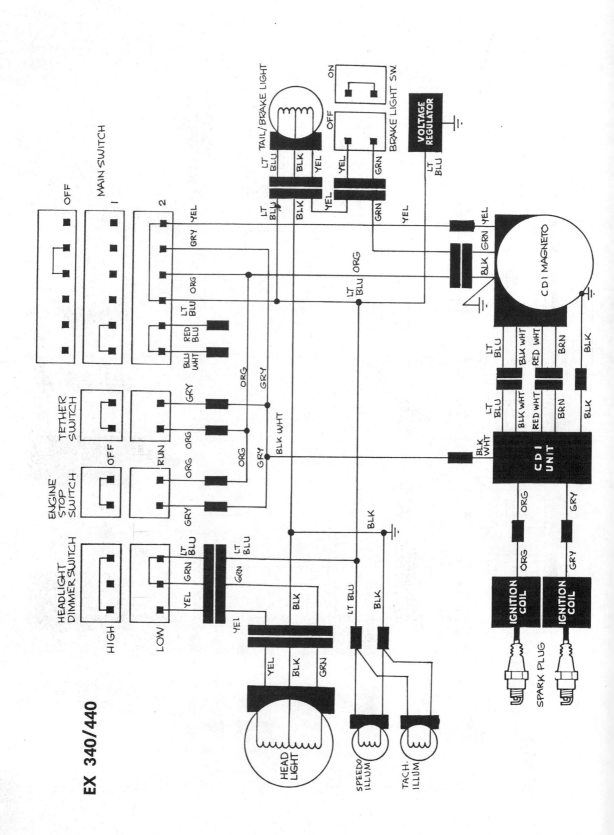

EX 340/440

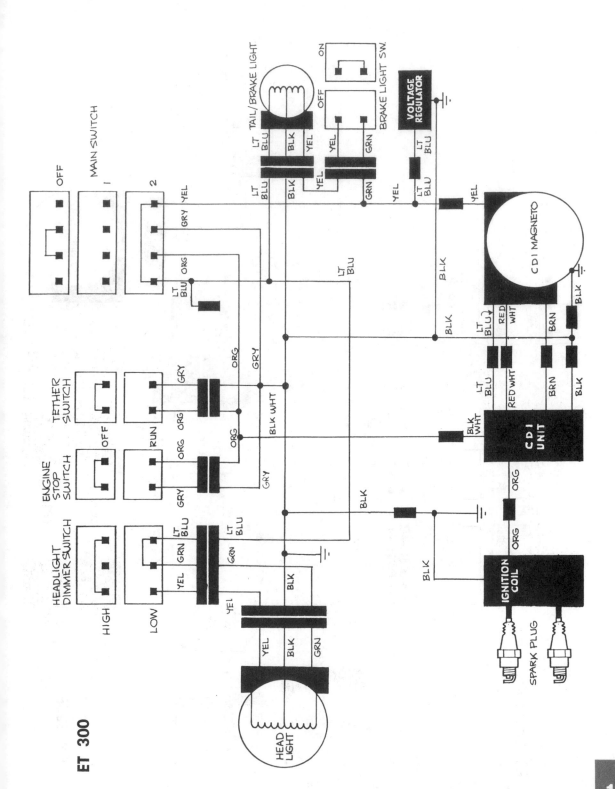

ET 300

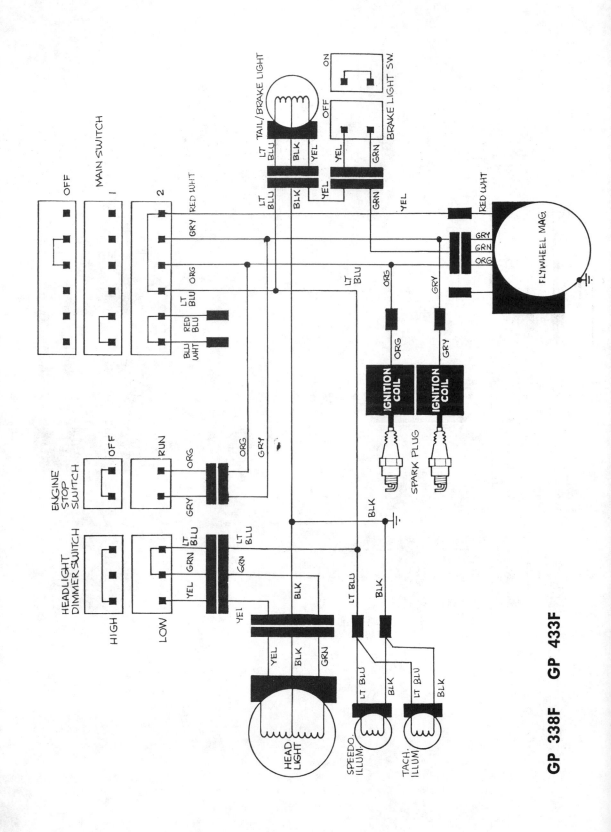

GP 338F   GP 433F

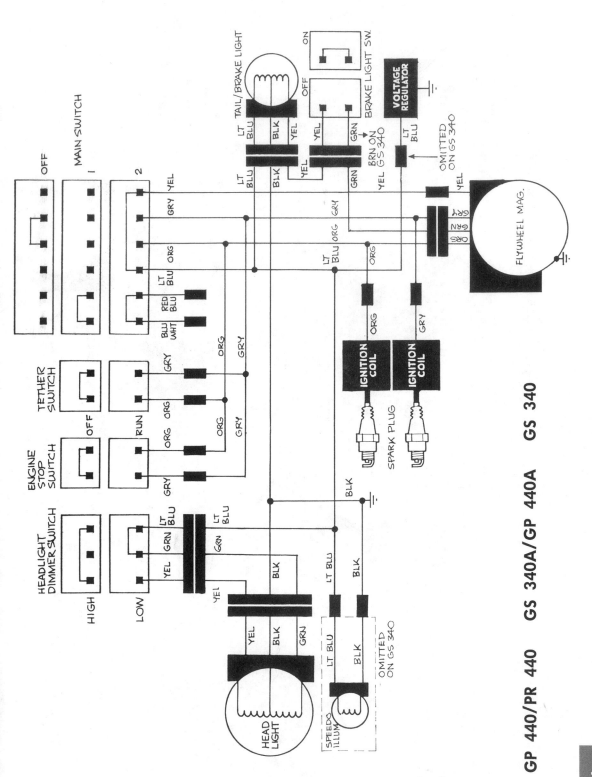

GP 440/PR 440   GS 340A/GP 440A   GS 340

11

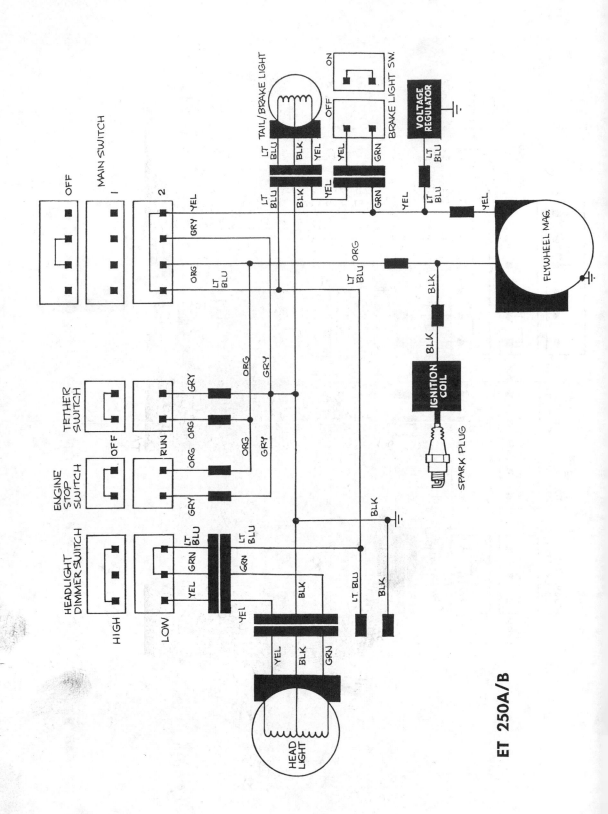

ET 250A/B

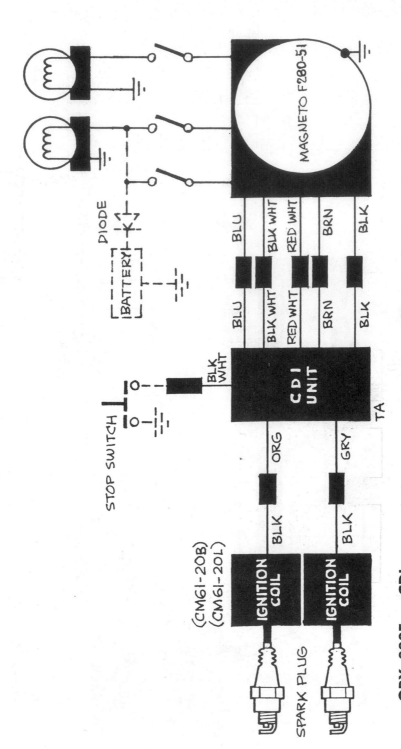

GPX 338F   CDI

(SEE G-338F/433F FOR BODY WIRING)

GPX 433F

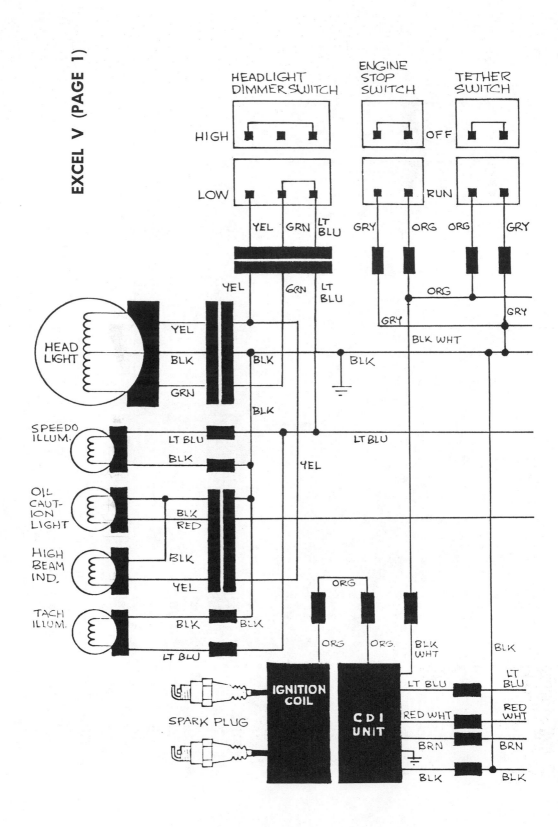

EXCEL V (PAGE 1)

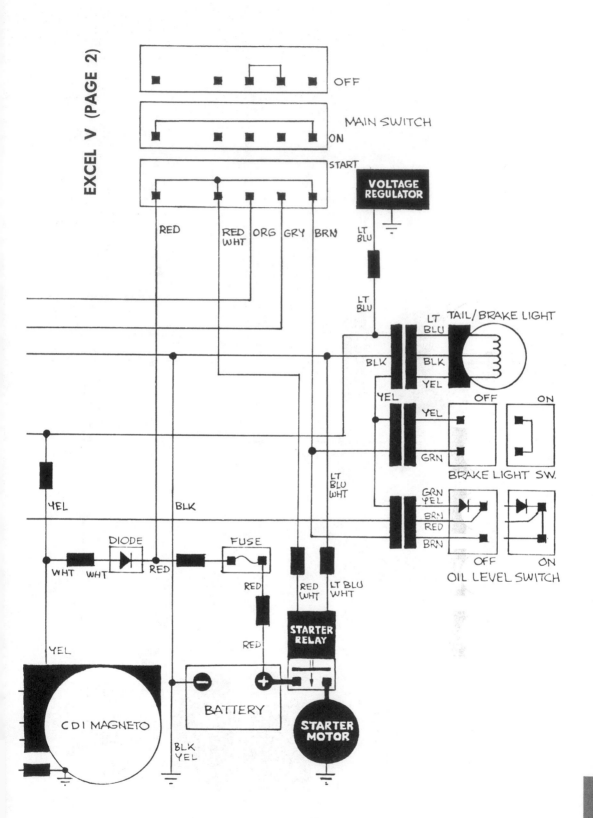

EXCEL V (PAGE 2)

OFF

MAIN SWITCH

ON

START

VOLTAGE REGULATOR

RED — RED WHT — ORG — GRY — BRN

LT BLU

LT BLU

LT BLU

TAIL/BRAKE LIGHT

BLK — BLK

YEL

YEL — YEL

GRN

OFF   ON

BRAKE LIGHT SW.

LT BLU WHT

GRN YEL
BRN RED
BRN

OFF   ON

OIL LEVEL SWITCH

YEL

BLK

DIODE

FUSE

RED

WHT — WHT — RED

RED

YEL

RED WHT — LT BLU WHT

STARTER RELAY

CDI MAGNETO

BATTERY

BLK YEL

STARTER MOTOR

11

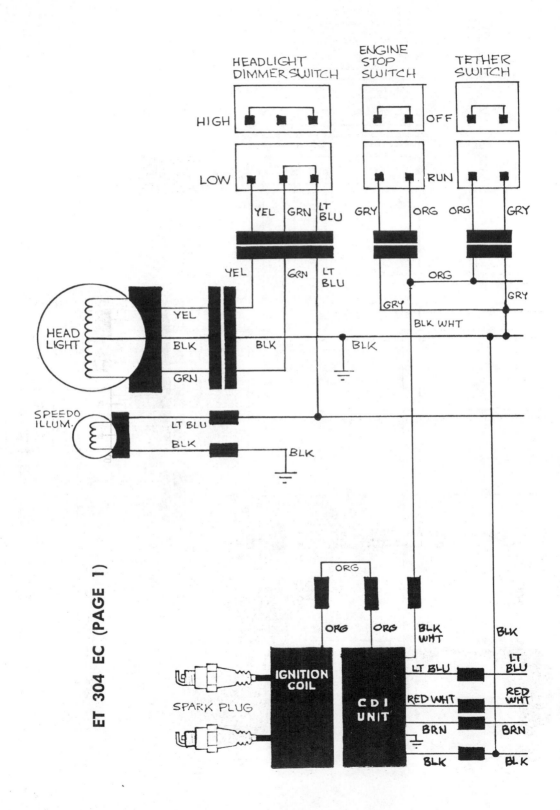

ET 304 EC (PAGE 1)

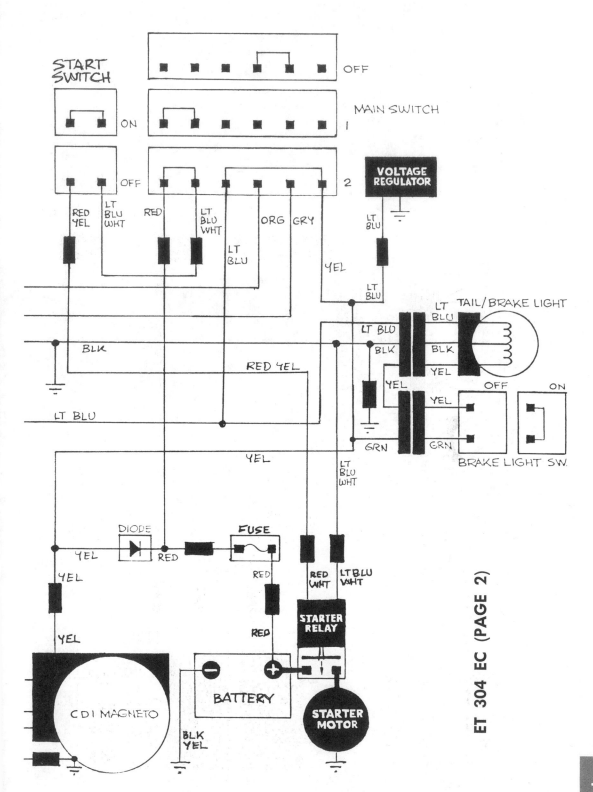

START SWITCH

OFF

ON

MAIN SWITCH

1

OFF

2

VOLTAGE REGULATOR

RED YEL

LT BLU WHT

RED

LT BLU WHT

LT BLU

ORG

GRY

LT BLU

YEL

LT BLU

TAIL/BRAKE LIGHT

LT BLU

BLK

YEL

LT BLU

BLK

BLK

RED YEL

YEL

YEL

OFF

ON

LT BLU

GRN

GRN

BRAKE LIGHT SW.

YEL

LT BLU WHT

DIODE

YEL

RED

FUSE

RED

RED WHT

LT BLU WHT

YEL

YEL

RED

STARTER RELAY

YEL

CDI MAGNETO

BATTERY

STARTER MOTOR

BLK YEL

ET 304 EC (PAGE 2)

NOTES

Clymer Collection Series

VINTAGE

S N O W M O B I L E S

VOLUME II

Polaris, 1973-1979

Yamaha, 1975-1980

➤ Ski-Doo, 1970-1979

CONTENTS

CHAPTER TEN

LIQUID COOLING SYSTEM

QUICK REFERENCE DATA

TUNE-UP SPECIFICATIONS

Spark plug gap	0.020 in. (0.51mm)
Spark plug torque	14mm plugs — 20 ft.-lb. (2.8 mkg) 18mm plugs — 30 ft.-lb. (4.1 mkg)
Breaker point gap	0.014-0.018 in. (0.35-0.45mm)

SPARK PLUG APPLICATION

Model	Champion Standard	Bosch Standard
Elan 250; Olympique 300 (299 engine)	K-9	M175T1
Olympique 335, 440 (1973) Olympique 300 (1976)	K-9	M225T1
T'NT F/A, T'NT R/V, T'NT 440 (1973) (14mm heads) and R/V 340	RM-2	W280MZ2
Elan 250 Twin and Deluxe to 1977 Olympique 300T, 340, 399, T'NT 399	L-81	W240T1
Olympique 300 Twin (1978 and later) Olympique 340, 340E (1978 and later) Citation 300 (1978 and later) Everest 340, 340E (1978 and later)	L-78	W280MZ1
T'NT 340 (1978)	L-78	W260MZ1
Blizzard 6500, 7500, 9500	—	W340S2S
Blizzard 5500		W275T2
Everest 440, 440E; T'NT 440 L/C	K-7	M260T1
Everest 444 L/C	N-3	W260MZ2 or W280MZ2 with 2 gaskets
Elan 250SS, 300SS; T'NT 294, 300, 340 Everest 340 (to 1977); Olympique 340 (to 1977); T'NT 292 single; T'NT 440; Everest 440 (to 1977)	L-78	M260T1

FUEL AND LUBRICATION REQUIREMENTS

FUEL	Regular grade for all except high performance models Premium grade for high performance models
ENGINE OIL TYPE MIXTURE RATIO	Ski-Doo 2-cycle oil 1970-1972 models—20:1 1973 models—40:1 1974 and later—50:1
ROTARY VALVE OIL RESERVOIR	Castrol injector oil
CHAINCASE OIL	Ski-Doo chaincase oil or equivalent (SAE 30)

TRACK TENSION ADJUSTMENT SPECIFICATIONS

Bogie wheel suspension

1970-1971 models (measured from bottom edge of center bogie wheel to inside edge of track)	$2\frac{1}{2}$-3 in. (6.4-7.6 cm)
All other models (measured from top inside edge of track to bottom of footboard)	
Elan	$1\frac{1}{4}$-$1\frac{1}{2}$ in. (3.2-3.8 cm)
Olympique	$2\frac{1}{8}$-$2\frac{3}{8}$ in. (5.4-6.0 cm)

Slide suspension

All models 1970-1973 (measure from footboard to inside track)	$5\frac{3}{4}$-6 in. (14.6-15.2 cm)
1974 and later (measure between bottom of slider shoe and inside of track)	
Ground leveller suspension	$\frac{1}{2}$-$\frac{5}{8}$ in. (1.3-1.6 cm)
High performance suspension	$\frac{5}{8}$ in. (1.6 cm)

Torque reaction suspension

Olympique; all 1978-1979 models	$\frac{1}{2}$ in. (1.3 cm)
All other models	$\frac{3}{4}$ in. (1.9 cm)

IGNITION TIMING SPECIFICATIONS

Engine	Direct Timing BTDC[1]	Indirect Timing BTDC[1]
245 (1976)*	0.035-0.055 in. (0.90-1.40mm)	N/A
245 (1975)*	0.037-0.057 in. (0.95-1.45mm)	N/A
247	0.147-0.167 in. (3.73-4.23mm)	N/A[2]
248, 249	0.077-0.097 in. (1.97-2.47mm)	0.080-0.100 in. (2.04-2.54mm)
250	0.150-0.170 in. (3.81-4.31mm)	0.150-0.160 in. (3.81-4.06mm)
292 (1970-1971)	0.140-0.160 in. (3.55-4.06mm)	0.195-0.221 in. (4.95-5.61mm)
292, 302 (1972)	0.147-0.167 in. (3.73-4.23mm)	0.195-0.215 in. (4.95-5.46mm)
294	0.084-0.104 in. (2.14-2.64mm)	0.087-0.110 in. (2.19-2.79mm)
300	0.150-0.170 in. (3.81-4.31mm)	0.205-0.241 in. (5.20-6.12mm)
302	0.147-0.167 in. (3.73-4.23mm)	0.212-0.244 in. (5.38-6.20mm)
305	0.111-0.131 in. (2.82-3.32mm)	0.135-0.159 in. (3.43-4.03mm)
305, 343[3] (1978)	0.073-0.093 in. (1.86-2.36mm)	0.087-0.107 in. (2.21-2.71mm)
335	0.160-0.180 in. (4.06-4.57mm)	0.220-0.250 in. (5.59-6.35mm)
337	0.157-0.177 in. (3.99-4.49mm)	0.229-0.249 in. (5.81-6.32mm)
338	0.111-0.131 in. (2.82-3.32mm)	0.132-0.154 in. (3.35-3.89mm)
340 (1970)	0.160-0.180 in. (4.06-4.57mm)	0.198-0.228 in. (5.02-5.79mm)
340 (1971)	0.160-0.180 in. (4.06-4.57mm)	0.193-0.220 in. (4.90-5.59mm)
343 (1972)	0.137-0.157 in. (3.48-3.98mm)	0.159-0.179 in. (4.03-4.55mm)
343 (1973)	0.111-0.131 in. (2.82-3.32mm)	0.131-0.154 in. (3.33-3.91mm)
343	0.111-0.131 in. (2.82-3.32mm)	0.135-0.159 in. (3.43-4.03mm)
345*	0.035-0.055 in. (0.90-1.40mm)	N/A
345 (1978)*	0.034-0.054 in. (0.87-1.37mm)	N/A
346 (1973)*	0.109-0.129 in. (2.77-3.28mm)	N/A
396 (1973)*	0.060-0.080 in. (1.52-2.03mm)	N/A
346, 396 (1974)*	0.071-0.091 in. (1.82-2.32mm)	N/A
354*, 454*	0.045-0.065 in. (1.14-1.64mm)	N/A
399, 440 (1970, 1971)	0.160-0.180 in. (4.06-4.57mm)	0.148-0.171 in. (3.76-4.34mm)
401, 434, 435 (1972)	0.137-0.157 in. (3.48-3.98mm)	0.146-0.166 in. (3.71-4.22mm)
401	0.111-0.131 in. (2.82-3.32mm)	0.135-0.159 in. (3.43-4.03mm)
434, 440[4]	0.111-0.131 in. (2.82-3.32mm)	0.118-0.144 in. (2.99-3.66mm)
435	0.111-0.131 in. (2.82-3.32mm)	0.119-0.141 in. (3.02-3.58mm)
436*	0.071-0.091 in. (1.82-2.32mm)	N/A
440 (1975)*	0.071-0.091 in. (1.82-2.32mm)	0.077-0.097 in. (1.96-2.46mm)
440 (1978-1979)	0.111-0.131 in. (2.82-3.32mm)	0.120-0.140 in. (3.05-3.55mm)
444	0.082-0.102 in. (2.10-2.60mm)	N/A
503	0.068-0.088 in. (1.82-2.32mm)	N/A

*Engines equipped with CDI.

1. Use direct timing for engines with vertical spark plug holes and indirect timing for engines with spark plug on an angle.
2. On 1972 models, indirect specification is the same as direct.
3. On 343 engines serial number 3,019,645 to 3,020,644 direct timing is 0.147-0.167 in. (3.73-4.23mm).
4. Except 1975 440 with CDI.

SKI-DOO

1970-1979
SERVICE•REPAIR•MAINTENANCE

CHAPTER ONE

GENERAL INFORMATION

Snowmobiling has in recent years become one of the most popular outdoor winter recreational pastimes. It provides an opportunity for an entire family to experience the splendor of winter and enjoy a season previously regarded by many as miserable.

Snowmobiles also provide an invaluable service in the form of rescue and utility vehicles in areas that would otherwise be inaccessible.

As with all sophisticated pieces of machinery, snowmobiles require specific periodic maintenance and repair to ensure their reliability and usefulness.

MANUAL ORGANIZATION

This manual provides periodic maintenance, tune-up, and general repair procedures for Ski-Doo snowmobiles manufactured since 1970.

This chapter provides general information and hints to make all snowmobile work easier and more rewarding. Additional sections cover snowmobile operation, safety, and survival techniques.

Chapter Two provides all tune-up and periodic maintenance required to keep your snowmobile in top running condition.

Chapter Three provides numerous methods and suggestions for finding and fixing troubles

fast. The chapter also describes how a 2-cycle engine works, to help you analyze troubles logically. Troubleshooting procedures discuss typical symptoms and logical methods to pinpoint the trouble.

Subsequent chapters describe specific systems such as engine, fuel system, and electrical system. Each provides disassembly, repair, and reassembly procedures in easy to follow, step-by-step form. If a repair is impractical for the owner/mechanic, it is so indicated. Usually, such repairs are quicker and more economically done by a Ski-Doo dealer or other competent snowmobile repair shop.

Some of the procedures in this manual specify special tools. In all cases, the tool is illustrated in actual use or alone.

The terms NOTE, CAUTION, and WARNING have specific meaning in this book. A NOTE provides additional information to make a step or procedure easier or clearer. Disregarding a NOTE could cause inconvenience, but would not cause damage or personal injury.

A CAUTION emphasizes areas where equipment damage could result. Disregarding a CAUTION could cause permanent mechanical damage; however, personal injury is unlikely.

A WARNING emphasizes areas where personal injury or death could result from negligence.

Mechanical damage may also occur. WARNINGS are to be taken seriously. In some cases, serious injury or death has been caused by mechanics disregarding similar warnings.

MACHINE IDENTIFICATION AND PARTS REPLACEMENT

Each snowmobile has a serial number applicable to the machine and a model and serial number for the engine.

Figure 1 shows the location of the machine serial number on the right side of the tunnel. **Figure 2** shows the location of engine model and serial numbers.

Write down all serial and model numbers applicable to your machine and carry the numbers with you. When you order parts from a dealer, always order by year and engine and machine numbers. If possible, compare old parts to the new ones before purchasing them. If parts are not alike, have the parts manager explain the difference.

OPERATION

Fuel Mixing

WARNING
Serious fire hazards always exist around gasoline. Do not *allow any smoking in areas where fuel is mixed or when refueling your snowmobile.*
Always use fresh fuel. Gasoline loses its potency after sitting for a period of time. Old fuel can cause engine failure and leave you stranded in severe weather.

Proper fuel mixing is very important for the life and efficiency of the engine. All engine lubrication is provided by the oil mixed with the gasoline. Always mix fuel in exact proportions. A "too lean" mixture can cause serious and expensive damage. A "too rich" mixture can cause poor performance and fouled spark plugs which can make an engine difficult or impossible to start.

Use a gasoline with an octane rating of 90 or higher. Use premium grade gasoline in all high performance racing machines. Mix gasoline in a separate tank, not the snowmobile fuel tank. Use a tank with a larger volume than necessary to allow room for the fuel to agitate and mix completely.

Use Ski-Doo Snowmobile oil and mix with fresh gasoline in a 20:1 ratio for 1970-1973 models, 40:1 for 1974 models and 50:1 for all later models.

1. Pour required amount of oil into a *clean* container.

2. Add ½ the necessary gasoline and mix thoroughly.

3. Add remainder of gasoline and mix entire contents thoroughly.

4. Always use a funnel equipped with a fine screen while adding fuel to the snowmobile.

Pre-start Inspection

1. Familiarize yourself with your machine, the owner's manual, and all decals on the snowmobile.

2. Clean the windshield with a clean, damp cloth. *Do not* use gasoline, solvents, or abrasive cleaners.

3. Check all ski and steering components for wear and loose parts. Correct as necessary.

4. Check track tension.

5. Check operation of throttle and brake controls and ensure that they are free and properly adjusted.

6. Check fuel level.

WARNING
Before starting engine, be sure no bystanders are in front of, or behind, the snowmobile or a sudden lurch may cause serious injuries.

7. Start engine and test operation of emergency kill switch. Check that all lights are working.

Emergency Starting

Always carry a small tool kit with you. Carry an extra starting rope for emergency starting or use the recoil starter rope.

1. Remove hood.

2. Remove recoil starter.

3. Wind rope around starter pulley and pull to crank engine.

Emergency Stopping

To stop the engine in case of an emergency, switch emergency kill switch to STOP or OFF position.

Towing

When preparing for a long trip, pack extra equipment in a sled, do not try to haul it on the snowmobile. A sled is also ideal for transporting small children.

WARNING
Never tow a sled with ropes or pull straps, always use a solid tow bar. Use of ropes or flexible straps could result in a tailgate accident, when the snowmobile is stopped, with subsequent serious injury.

If it is necessary to tow a disabled snowmobile, securely fasten the disabled machine's skis to the hitch of the tow machine. Remove the drive belt from the disabled machine before towing.

Clearing the Track

If the snowmobile has been operated in deep or slushy snow, it is necessary to clear the track after stopping or the track may freeze, making starting the next time difficult.

WARNING
Always be sure no one is behind the machine when clearing the track. Ice and rocks thrown from the track can cause serious injury.

Tip the snowmobile on its side until the track clears the ground *completely*. Run the track at a moderate speed until all the ice and snow is thrown clear.

CAUTION
If track does freeze, it must be broken loose manually. Attempting to force a frozen track with the engine running will burn and damage the drive belt.

Proper Clothing

Warm and comfortable clothing are a must to provide protection from frostbite. Even mild temperatures can be very uncomfortable and dangerous when combined with a strong wind or when traveling at high speed. See **Table 1** for wind chill factors. Always dress according to what the wind chill factor is, not the temperature. Check with an authorized dealer for suggested types of snowmobile clothing.

WARNING
To provide additional warmth as well as protection against head injury, always wear an approved helmet when snowmobiling.

SERVICE HINTS

All procedures described in this book can be performed by anyone reasonably handy with tools. Special tools are required for some procedures; their operation is described and illustrated. These may be purchased at Ski-Doo dealers. If you are on good terms with the dealer's service department, you may be able to borrow from them, however, it should be borne in mind that many of these tools will pay for

Table 1   WIND CHILL FACTORS

Estimated Wind Speed in MPH	Actual Thermometer Reading (° F)											
	50	40	30	20	10	0	—10	—20	—30	—40	—50	—60
	Equivalent Temperature (° F)											
Calm	50	40	30	20	10	0	—10	—20	—30	—40	—50	—60
5	48	37	27	16	6	—5	—15	—26	—36	—47	—57	—68
10	40	28	16	4	—9	—21	—33	—46	—58	—70	—83	—95
15	36	22	9	—5	—18	—36	—45	—58	—72	—85	—99	—112
20	32	18	4	—10	—25	—39	—53	—67	—82	—96	—110	—124
25	30	16	0	—15	—29	—44	—59	—74	—88	—104	—118	—133
30	28	13	—2	—18	—33	—48	—63	—79	—94	—109	—125	—140
35	27	11	—4	—20	—35	—49	—67	—82	—98	—113	—129	—145
40	26	10	—6	—21	—37	—53	—69	—85	—100	—116	—132	—148

*

Little Danger (for properly clothed person)	Increasing Danger	Great Danger
		• Danger from freezing of exposed flesh •

*Wind speeds greater than 40 mph have little additional effect.

---

themselves after the first or second use. If special tools are required, make arrangements to get them before starting. It is frustrating and sometimes expensive to get under way and then find that you are unable to finish up.

Service will be far easier if the machine is clean before beginning work. There are special cleaners for washing the engine and related parts. Just brush or spray on the cleaning solution, let it stand, then rinse it away with a garden hose. Clean all oily or greasy parts with cleaning solvent as they are removed.

WARNING
Never use gasoline as a cleaning agent, as it presents an extreme fire hazard. Be sure to work in a well-ventilated area when using cleaning solvent. Keep a fire extinguisher handy, just in case.

Observing the following practices will save time, effort, and frustration as well as prevent possible expensive damage:

1. Tag all similar internal parts for location and mark all mating parts for position. Small parts such as bolts can be identified by placing them in plastic sandwich bags and sealing and labeling the bags with masking tape.

2. Frozen or very tight bolts and screws can often be loosened by soaking them with penetrating oil such as WD-40®, then sharply striking the bolt head a few times with a hammer and punch (or screwdriver for screws). A hammer driven impact tool can also be very effective. However, ensure tool is seated squarely on the bolt or nut before striking. Avoid heat unless absolutely necessary, since it may melt, warp, or remove the temper from many parts.

3. Avoid flames or sparks when working near flammable liquids such as gasoline.

4. No parts, except those assembled with a press fit, require unusual force during assembly. If a part is hard to remove or install, find out why before proceeding.

5. Cover all openings after removing parts to keep dirt, small tools, etc., from falling in.

6. Clean all parts as you go along and keep them separated into subassemblies. The use of trays, jars, or cans will make reassembly that much easier.

7. Make diagrams whenever similar-appearing parts are found. You may *think* you can remember where everything came from — but mistakes are costly. There is also the possibility you

may be sidetracked and not return to work for days or even weeks — in which interval carefully laid out parts may have become disturbed.

8. Wiring should be tagged with masking tape and marked as each wire is removed. Again, do not rely on memory alone.

9. When reassembling parts, be sure all shims and washers are replaced exactly as they came out. Whenever a rotating part butts against a stationary part, look for a shim or washer. Use new gaskets if there is any doubt about the condition of old ones. Generally, you should apply gasket cement to only one mating surface so the parts may be easily disassembled in the future. A thin coat of oil on gaskets helps them seal effectively.

10. Heavy grease can be used to hold small parts in place if they tend to fall out during assembly. However, keep grease and oil away from electrical and brake components.

11. High spots may be sanded off a piston with sandpaper, but emery cloth and oil do a much more professional job.

12. Carburetors are best cleaned by disassembling them and soaking the parts in a commercial carburetor cleaner. Never soak gaskets and rubber parts in these cleaners. Never use wire to clean out jets and air passages; they are easily damaged. Use compressed air to blow out the carburetor only if the float has been removed first.

13. Take your time and do the job right. Do not forget that a newly rebuilt snowmobile engine must be broken in the same as a new one. Keep rpm's within the limits given in your owner's manual when you get back on the snow.

14. Work safely in a good work area with adequate lighting and allow sufficient time for a repair task.

15. When assembling 2 parts, start all fasteners, then tighten evenly.

16. Before undertaking a job, read the entire section in this manual which pertains to it. Study the illustrations and text until you have a good idea of what is involved. Many procedures are complicated and errors can be disastrous. When you thoroughly understand what is to be done, follow the prescribed procedure step-by-step.

TOOLS

Every snowmobiler should carry a small tool kit to help make minor adjustments as well as perform emergency repairs.

A normal assortment of ordinary hand tools is required to perform the repair tasks outlined in this manual. The following list represents the minimum requirement:

a. American and metric combination wrenches

b. American and metric socket wrenches

c. Assorted screwdrivers

d. Pliers

e. Feeler gauges

f. Spark plug wrench

g. Small hammer

h. Plastic or rubber mallet

i. Parts cleaning brush

When purchasing tools, always get quality tools. They cost more initially but in most cases will last a lifetime. Remember, the initial expense of new tools is easily offset by the money saved on a few repair jobs.

Tune-up and troubleshooting require a few special tools. All of the following special tools are used in this manual, however all tools are not necessary for all machines. Read the procedures applicable to your machine to determine what your special tool requirements are.

1. *Ignition gauge* (**Figure 3**). This tool combines round wire spark plug gap gauges with narrow breaker point feeler gauges. The device costs about $3 at auto accessory stores.

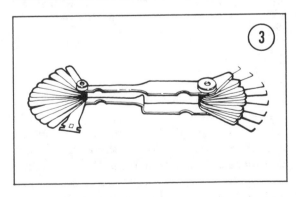

2. *Impact driver* (**Figure 4**). This tool might have been designed with the snowmobiler in mind. It makes removal of screws easy, and

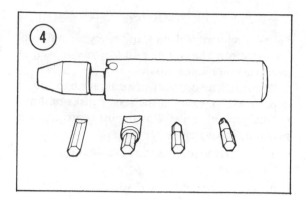

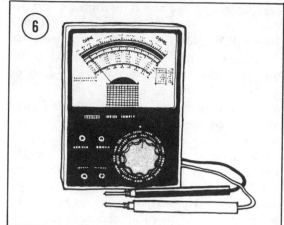

eliminates damaged screw slots. Good ones run about $12 at larger hardware stores.

3. *Hydrometer* (**Figure 5**). This instrument measures state of charge of the battery, and tells much about battery condition. Such an instrument is available at any auto parts store and through most larger mail order outlets. Satisfactory ones cost as little as $3.

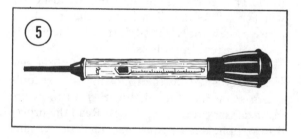

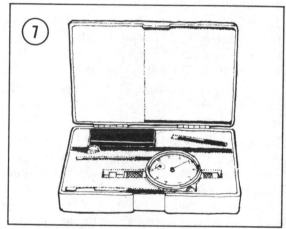

4. *Multimeter or* VOM (**Figure 6**). This instrument is invaluable for electrical system troubleshooting and service. A few of its functions may be duplicated by locally fabricated substitutes, but for the serious hobbyist, it is a must. Its uses are described in the applicable sections of this book. Prices start at around $10 at electronics hobbyists stores and mail order outlets.

5. *Timing gauge* (**Figure 7**). This device is used to precisely locate the position of the piston before top dead center to achieve the most accurate ignition timing. The instrument is screwed into the spark plug hole and indicates inches and/or millimeters. The tool shown costs about $20 and is available from most dealers and mail order houses. Less expensive tools, which use a vernier scale instead of a dial indicator, are also available.

6. *Air flow meter or carburetor synchronizer* (**Figure 8**). This device is used on engines with multiple carburetors to fine tune the synchronization and idle speed. The tool shown costs about $10-15 at most dealers, auto parts stores, and mail order houses.

7. *Compression gauge* (**Figure 9**). The compression gauge measures the compression pressure built up in each cylinder. The results, when properly interpreted, indicate general piston, cylinder, ring, and head gasket condition. Gauges are available with, or without, the flexible hose. Prices start around $5 at most auto parts stores and mail order outlets.

EXPENDABLE SUPPLIES

Certain expendable supplies are also required. These include grease, oil, gasket cement, wiping rags, cleaning solvent, and distilled water. Solvent is available at many service stations. Distilled water, required for the battery,

1

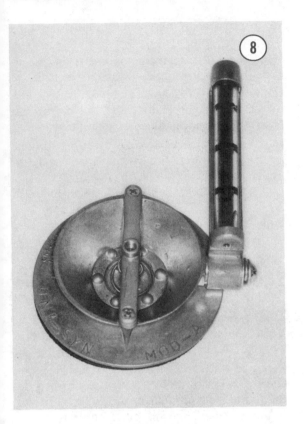

own machine. You can also hurt yourself or damage the machine if you ignore these rules.

1. Never use gasoline as a cleaning solvent.

2. Never smoke or use a torch in the area of flammable liquids, such as cleaning solvent in open containers.

3. Never smoke or use a torch in an area where batteries are charging. Highly explosive hydrogen gas is formed during the charging process.

4. If welding or brazing is required on the machine, remove the fuel tank to a safe distance, at least 50 feet away.

5. Be sure to use properly sized wrenches for nut turning.

6. If a nut is tight, think for a moment what would happen to your hand should the wrench slip. Be guided accordingly.

7. Keep your work area clean and uncluttered.

8. Wear safety goggles in all operations involving drilling, grinding, or use of a chisel.

9. Never use worn tools.

10. Keep a fire extinguisher handy. Be sure it is rated for gasoline and electrical fires.

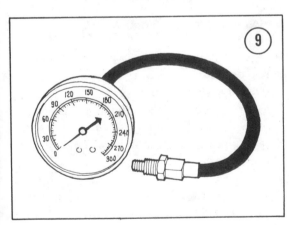

is available at every supermarket. An increasing number of mechanics clean oily parts with a solution of common household detergent or laundry powder.

WORKING SAFELY

Professional mechanics can work for years without sustaining serious injury. If you observe a few rules of common sense and safety, you can enjoy many safe hours servicing your

SNOWMOBILE CODE OF ETHICS

When snowmobiling, always observe the following code of ethics as provided by the International Snowmobile Industry Association.

1. I will be a good sportsman. I recognize that people judge all snowmobile owners by my actions. I will use my influence with other snowmobile owners to promote sportsmanlike conduct.

2. I will not litter trails or camping areas. I will not pollute streams or lakes.

3. I will not damage living trees, shrubs, or other natural features.

4. I will respect other people's property and rights.

5. I will lend a helping hand when I see someone in distress.

6. I will make myself and my vehicle available to assist search and rescue parties.

7. I will not interfere with or harass hikers, skiers, snowshoers, ice fishermen, or other winter sportsmen. I will respect their rights to enjoy our recreation facilities.

8. I will know and obey all federal, state, and local rules regulating the operation of snowmobiles in areas where I use my vehicle. I will inform public officials when using public lands.

9. I will not harass wildlife. I will avoid areas posted for the protection or feeding of wildlife.

10. I will stay on marked trails or marked roads open to snowmobiles. I will avoid country travel unless specifically authorized.

SNOWMOBILE SAFETY

General Tips

1. Read your owner's manual and know your machine.

2. Check throttle and brake controls before starting the engine. Frozen controls can cause serious injury.

3. Know how to make an emergency stop.

4. Know all state, provincial, federal, and local laws concerning snowmobiling. Respect private property.

5. Never add fuel while smoking or when engine is running. Always use fresh, properly mixed fuel. Improper fuel mixtures can cause engine failure, and can leave you stranded in severe weather.

6. Wear adequate clothing to avoid frostbite. Never wear any loose scarves or belts that could catch in moving parts or on tree limbs.

7. Wear eye and head protection. Wear tinted goggles or face shields to guard against snow-blindness. Never wear yellow eye protection.

8. Never allow anyone to operate the snowmobile without proper instruction.

9. Use the "buddy system" for long trips. A snowmobile travels farther in 30 minutes than you can walk in a day.

10. Take along sufficient tools and spare parts for emergency field repairs.

11. Use a sled with a stiff tow bar for carrying extra supplies. Do not overload your snowmobile.

12. Carry emergency survival supplies when going on long trips. Notify friends and relatives of your destination and expected arrival time.

13. Never attempt to repair your machine while the engine is running.

14. Check all machine components and hardware frequently, especially skis and steering.

15. Never lift rear of machine to clear the track. Tip machine on its side and be sure no one is behind machine.

16. Winch snowmobile onto a tilt-bed trailer, never drive it on. Secure machine firmly to trailer and ensure trailer lights operate.

Operating Tips

1. Never operate the vehicle in crowded areas, or steer toward persons.

2. Avoid avalanche areas and other unsafe terrain.

3. Cross highways (where permitted) at a 90 degree angle after looking in both directions. Post traffic guards if crossing in groups.

4. Do not ride snowmobile on or near railroad tracks. The snowmobile engine can drown out the sound of an approaching train. It is difficult to maneuver the snowmobile from between the tracks.

5. Do not ride snowmobile on ski slope areas with skiers.

6. Always check the thickness of the ice before riding on frozen lakes or rivers. Do not panic if you go through ice; conserve energy.

7. Keep headlight and taillight areas free of snow and never ride at night without lights.

8. Do not ride snowmobile without shields, guards, and protective hoods.

9. Do not attempt to open new trails at night. Follow established trails or unseen barbed wire or guy wires may cause serious injury or death.

10. Always steer with both hands.

11. Be aware of terrain and avoid operating snowmobile at excessive speed.

12. Do not panic if throttle sticks. Pull "tether" string or push emergency stop switch.

13. Drive more slowly when carrying a passenger, especially a child.

14. Always allow adequate stopping distance based on ground cover conditions. Ice requires a greater stopping distance to avoid skidding. Apply brakes gradually on ice.

15. Do not speed through wooded areas. Hidden obstructions, hanging limbs, unseen ditches, and even wild animals can cause accidents.

16. Do not tailgate. Rear end collisions can cause injury and machine damage.

17. Do not mix alcoholic beverages with snowmobiling.

18. Keep feet on footrests at all times. Do not permit feet to hang over sides or attempt to stabilize machine with feet when making turns or in near-spill situations; broken limbs could result.

19. Do not stand on seat, stunt, or show-off.

20. Do not jump snowmobile. Injury or machine damage could result.

21. Always keep hands and feet out of the track area when engine is running. Use extra care when freeing snowmobile from deep snow.

22. Check fuel supply regularly. Do not travel further than your fuel will permit you to return.

23. Whenever you leave your machine unattended, remove the "tether" switch.

Preparing for a Trip

1. Check all bolts and fasteners for tightness. Do not operate your snowmobile unless it is in top operating condition.

2. Check weather forecasts before starting out on a trip. Cancel your plans if a storm is possible.

3. Study maps of the area before the trip and know where help is located. Note locations of phones, resorts, shelters, towns, farms, and ranches. Know where fuel is available. If possible, use the buddy system.

4. Do not overload your snowmobile. Use a sled with a stiff tow bar to haul extra supplies.

5. Do not risk a heart attack if your snowmobile gets stuck in deep snow. Carry a small block and tackle for such situations. Never allow anyone to manually pull on the skis while you attempt to drive machine out.

6. Do not ride beyond one-half the round trip cruising range of your fuel supply. Keep in mind how far it is home.

7. Always carry emergency survival supplies when going on long trips or traveling in unknown territory. Notify friends and relatives of your destination and expected arrival time.

8. Carry adequate eating and cooking utensils (small pans, kettle, plates, cups, etc.) on longer trips. Carry matches in a waterproof container, candles for building a fire, and easy-to-pack food that will not be damaged by freezing. Carry dry food or space energy sticks for emergency rations.

9. Pack extra clothing, a tent, sleeping bag, hand axe, and compass. A first aid kit and snow shoes may also come in handy. Space age blankets (one side silverfoil) furnish warmth and can be used as heat reflectors or signaling devices for aerial search parties.

Emergency Survival Techniques

1. Do not panic in the event of an emergency. Relax, think the situation over, then decide on a course of action. You may be within a short distance of help. If possible, repair your snowmobile so you can drive to safety. Conserve your energy and stay warm.

2. Keep hands and feet active to promote circulation and avoid frostbite while servicing your machine.

3. Mentally retrace your route. Where was the last point where help could be located? Do not attempt to walk long distances in deep snow. Make yourself comfortable until help arrives.

4. If you are properly equipped for your trip you can turn any undesirable area into a suitable campsite.

5. If necessary, build a small shelter with tree branches or evergreen boughs. Look for a cave or sheltered area against a hill or cliff. Even burrowing in the snow offers protection from the cold and wind.

6. Prepare a signal fire using evergreen boughs and snowmobile oil. If you cannot build a fire, make an S-O-S in the snow.

7. Use a policeman's whistle or beat cooking utensils to attract attention or frighten off wild animals.

8. When your camp is established, climb the nearest hill and determine your whereabouts. Observe landmarks on the way, so you can find your way back to your campsite. Do not rely on your footprints. They may be covered by blowing snow.

CHAPTER TWO

PERIODIC MAINTENANCE AND TUNE-UP

To gain the utmost in safety, performance, and useful life from your machine, it is necessary to make periodic inspections and adjustments. It frequently happens that minor problems are found during such inspections that are simple and inexpensive to correct at the time, but which could lead to major problems later.

This chapter includes routine maintenance and inspections as well as complete tune-up procedures for all models. **Table 1** summarizes this important information. Keep detailed records of inspections, adjustments, and tune-ups. Such records can help identify recurring trouble areas as well as ensure that required maintenance and tune-up items are accomplished as recommended by the manufacturer.

INLINE FUEL FILTER

Replace the inline fuel filter at the beginning of each season's operation. Examine the filter periodically as specified in **Table 1** and replace it if there is evidence of fuel line contamination.

FAN BELT TENSION

Check fan belt tension at specified intervals **(Table 1)**.

1. Remove the fan cover and recoil starter mechanism.

2. Deflect belt with your fingers as shown in **Figure 1**. Examine belt for signs of fraying or deterioration. Adjust belt if deflection is more than ¼ in. (6mm) as outlined under *Fan Belt Adjustment,* Chapter Four. Replace belt if necessary.

DRIVE AND DRIVEN PULLEYS

All drive and driven pulleys should be removed, disassembled, cleaned, and inspected for worn parts annually. The majority of work on

Table 1   SCHEDULED MAINTENANCE

Check the following items at indicated intervals:	Annually	Monthly (or 40 hrs. operation)	Weekly (or 10 hrs. operation)	Daily
Windshield	X	X	X	X
Condition of skis and steering components	X	X	X	X
Track condition and tension	X	X	X	X
Throttle control	X	X	X	X
Brake	X	X	X	X
Emergency stop switch	X	X	X	X
Lighting system	X	X	X	X
Chaincase oil level	X	X	X	
In-line filter for contamination	X	X	X	
Drive belt	X	X	X	
Carburetor adjustments	X	X		
Ski alignment	X	X		
Fan belt tension	X	X		
Headlight adjustment	X	X		
Ski runner shoes	X	X		
Slide suspension wear bars	X	X		
All components for condition and tightness	X			
Drive and driven pulleys	X			

these components requires special tools and expertise. Refer to Chapter Seven for work you can perform. Refer all other work to an authorized dealer.

DRIVE BELT

Examine drive belt periodically as specified in **Table 1**. If belt shows unusual signs of wear, refer to Chapter Three for drive belt analysis and troubleshooting. Replace drive belt if its width is reduced by ⅛ in. (3mm). Refer to Chapter Seven for standard width and drive belt replacement for your model. Drive belts are not interchangeable between different models even though belt width may be the same.

Removal/Installation

Refer to **Figure 2** for this procedure.

1. Tilt cab and remove pulley guard.

2. Twist and push sliding half of driven pulley to open pulley.

3. Hold pulley in open position and slip drive belt off of driven pulley and then off the drive pulley.

CAUTION
Do not pry belt off over pulleys or belt and/or pulleys may be damaged.

4. Installation is the reverse of these steps. Check drive belt tension as outlined in Chapter Seven.

BRAKES

Check brake operation as scheduled in **Table 1**. Brakes are operating properly if the track is locked when the brake control lever is the specified distance from handlebar grip. If brake control lever movement is excessive, perform brake adjustment.

Brake Adjustment
(Bombardier Self-Adjusting Disc)

1. Rotate cable, adjusting nuts until no free play exists between brake lever and brake housing on handlebar.

2. Measure gap between brake lever and brake caliper. Gap should be $2 \pm \frac{1}{8}$ in. (50 ± 3mm) on floating caliper type and $1\frac{1}{2} \pm \frac{1}{8}$ in. (38 ± 3mm) on floating disc type (**Figure 3**). On Blizzard 5500 models, gap should be $2\frac{1}{4} \pm \frac{1}{8}$ in. (57 ± 3mm). Rotate adjuster nut until specified dimension is achieved.

> NOTE: *On floating caliper type it may be necessary to move brake light switch support to achieve specified gap.*

3. Check operation of brake light and loosen and adjust light switch locknuts if necessary (**Figure 4**).

Brake Adjustment (Except
Bombardier Self-Adjusting Disc)

1. Firmly apply brake and measure distance between brake control lever and handlebar grip. Distance should be as follows:

    a. Pivot brake and 1970-1971 drum brakes, $\frac{1}{4}$ in. (6.4mm).

    b. All drum and disc except self-adjusting disc, 1 in. (25mm).

    c. Self-adjusting disc, $\frac{1}{2}$ in. (13mm).

2. If distance between brake lever and handlebar grip is excessive, loosen locknuts on brake cable and adjust cable for specified dimension (**Figure 5**).

3. Tighten brake cable locknuts and recheck. Readjust if necessary.

4. Check operation of brake light and loosen and adjust light switch locknuts if necessary (**Figure 6**).

Hydraulic Disc Brake Bleeding

Check that fluid level is within $\frac{1}{8}$ in. (3.2mm) from the top of master cylinder reservoir. Use only brake fluid specified SAE 70R3, DOT 3, or DOT 4 for automotive disc brake application.

If brake work has been performed or if brake operation is ''spongy,'' bleeding may be necessary to expel any air from the system.

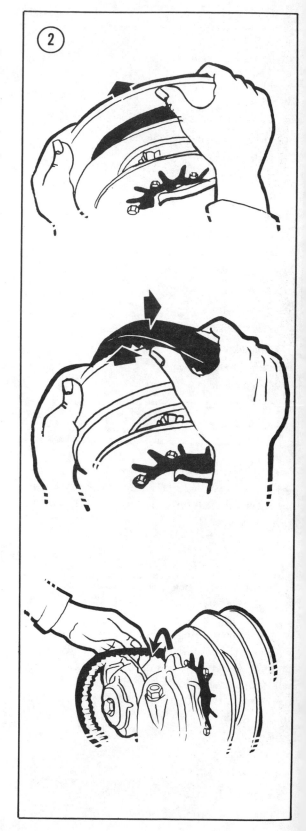

2

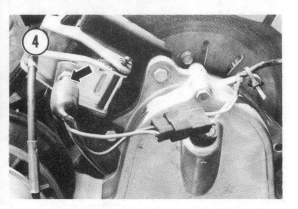

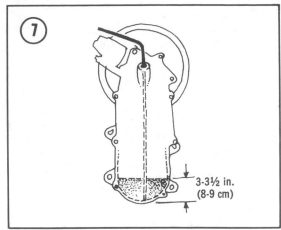

3-3½ in.
(8-9 cm)

NOTE: *During bleeding operation, be sure master cylinder reservoir is kept topped up to the specified level. If level is allowed to drop too low, air may be ingested, requiring complete rebleeding.*

1. Connect a plastic or rubber hose to brake bleeder nipple. Place other end of hose in a container with a few inches of clean brake fluid. Keep hose end below the level of the brake fluid.

2. Open brake bleed valve slightly.

3. Operate brake lever and note air bubbles released in jar. Continue operating brakes until all air is expelled. Be sure to keep master cylinder level topped off.

4. After all air has been expelled, close bleeder valve while slowly squeezing brake lever. Check all connections for leaks and remove bleeder hose.

CAUTION
Do not use brake fluid from bleed jar to top off reservoir as the fluid is already aerated.

CHAINCASE OIL LEVEL

Check level of chaincase oil at intervals specified in **Table 1** earlier in this chapter.

NOTE: *On models where oil level is difficult to see, because of tool box, use a long piece of stiff wire as a dipstick and measure oil level through filler hole (Figure 7). Ensure that dipstick touches bottom of chaincase. Oil level should be 3-3½ in. (8-9 cm).*

On machines with pressed steel chaincase and aluminum chaincase (without external tension adjuster) oil level should be flush with indicator level or plug (**Figure 8**).

On models with aluminum chaincase with external tension adjuster, total quantity of oil is 6 oz. (180cc).

On later model Blizzards oil level should be to bottom of the oil level opening as shown in **Figure 9**.

Top off oil level if necessary with Ski-Doo chaincase oil or equivalent (SAE 30).

Use a syringe or oil suction device to remove old oil when changing oil for machine storage preparation.

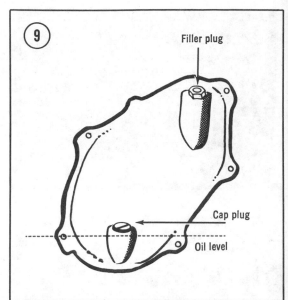

Rotary Valve Oil Reservoir

Check level of oil in reservoir frequently on rotary valve models. Do not allow oil level to fall below line on reservoir as shown in **Figure 10**. Top off reservoir with Castrol Injector Oil.

Liquid Coolant Level

Coolant level should be 1 in. (25mm) below filler neck of coolant tank. Start engine and run at least one minute after thermostat opens; 110°F (43°C). Stop engine and check coolant level. Top up if necessary with a 60% antifreeze and 40% water mixture.

> WARNING
> *Always remove pressure cap from a hot engine very carefully with a rag over the cap. Unscrew the cap to the first step only, until all pressure is released or serious burns from hot coolant may result.*

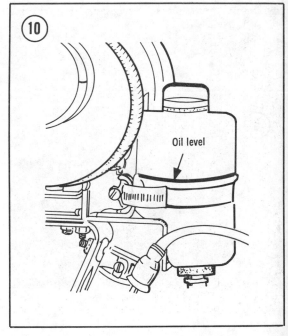

TRACK TENSION ADJUSTMENT

Proper track tension is very important to obtain maximum life and service from the track. Check for track "ratcheting" and proper tension at intervals specified in **Table 1** earlier in this chapter.

Track "ratcheting" occurs if track is too loose and drive lugs on the track slip over the cogs on the drive wheel.

Table 2   TRACK TENSION ADJUSTMENT SPECIFICATIONS

Suspension	Adjustment
Bogie wheel suspension	
1970-1971 models (measured from bottom edge of center bogie wheel to inside edge of track)	2½-3 in. (6.4-7.6 cm)
All other models (measured from top inside edge of track to bottom of foot board)	
Elan	1¼-1½ in. (3.2-3.8 cm)
Olympique	2⅛-2⅜ in. (5.4-6.0 cm)
Slide suspension	
All models 1970-1973 (measure from foot board to inside of track)	5¾-6 in. (14.6-15.2 cm)
1974 and later (measure between bottom of slider shoe and inside of track)	
Ground leveller suspension	½-⅝ in. (1.3-1.6 cm)
High performance suspension	⅝ in. (1.6 cm)
Torque reaction suspension	
All Olympique; all 1978-1979 models	½ in. (1.3 cm)
All other models	¾ in. (1.9 cm)

2

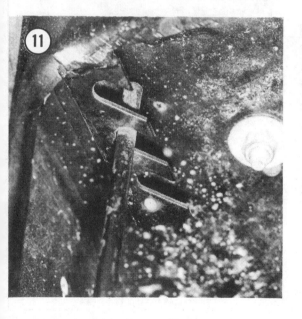

(Figure 11). Do not *attempt to correct track tension by changing position of link plate springs.*

Bogie Suspension

1. Raise rear of snowmobile; block securely.

2. Measure track tension as specified in **Table 2**.

3. If track tension is incorrect perform the following:

   NOTE: *On models with 3-position link plate spring anchors, ensure that link plate springs are in middle position*

a. Loosen link plate spring locknuts on inner side of link plate springs (**Figure 12**).

b. Turn adjuster bolts clockwise to increase tension and counterclockwise to release tension (**Figure 13**).

c. Adjust track tension to specified value and tighten locknuts.

4. Check track alignment as follows:

WARNING
Before rotating track, ensure that track is clear. Any tools or other objects on track could be thrown back causing serious injury.

a. Start engine and rotate track *slowly*.

b. Check that track is well-centered and distance between edge of track and link plate is the same on each side (**Figure 14**).

c. If track is not aligned, loosen link plate spring locknut and turn adjuster (on side where track is closer to link plate) clockwise until track is realigned.

d. Tighten locknut and recheck track tension. Readjust if necessary.

NOTE: *Track tension and alignment are interrelated.* Do not *adjust one without checking the adjustment of the other.*

5. Remove block from rear of snowmobile.

Slide Suspension

1. Raise rear of snowmobile; block securely.

2. Measure track tension as in **Table 2**.

3. If track tension is incorrect perform the following:

a. Loosen locknuts on adjuster bolts located inside of rear idler wheels (**Figure 15**).

b. Turn adjuster bolts clockwise to increase tension and counterclockwise to release tension.

c. Adjust track tension to specified valuve and tighten locknuts.

4. Check track alignment as follows:

WARNING
Before rotating track ensure that track is clear. Any tools or other objects on track could be thrown back causing serious injury.

NOTE: *Track tension and alignment are interrelated. Do not adjust one without checking the adjustment of the other.*

a. Start engine and rotate track *slowly*.

b. Check that track is well-centered and distance between edge of track and frame is the same on each side.

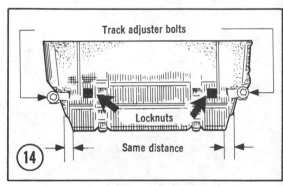

c. If track is not aligned, loosen locknuts securing adjuster bolts and tighten adjuster on side where track is closer to frame.

d. Tighten locknuts and recheck track tension. Readjust if necessary.

5. Remove block from rear of snowmobile.

SLIDE SUSPENSION RIDE ADJUSTMENT

See **Table 3** for model application.

Ground Leveller and High Performance Suspension

1. Raise rear of snowmobile and block up securely.

2. Tighten nuts on front spring adjuster bolts until outside of nut is ⅝-⅞ in. (15.9-22.2mm) from end of bolt (**Figure 16**). Ensure that both nuts are adjusted equally.

Table 3   SLIDE SUSPENSION MODEL

Model	Suspension
Olympique 1970-1974 T'NT F/C 1970-1973 Elan 294 SS 1974 Elan 300 SS 1975	Ground leveller
T'NT F/A 1973-1974	High performance
All other models	Torque reaction

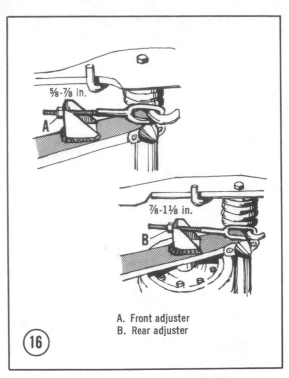

A. Front adjuster
B. Rear adjuster

3. Tighten nuts on rear spring adjuster bolts until outside of nut is ⅞-1⅛ in. (22.2-28.6mm) from end of bolt (**Figure 16**). Ensure that both nuts are adjusted equally.

4. Adjuster nuts can be tightened further if firmer ride is desired. Best all-around traction and ride are obtained if 5 in. (13 cm) clearance exists between rear of foot rest and the ground when driver is seated on snowmobile.

Torque Reaction Suspension

1. Measure distance between rear of foot rest and ground with driver in snowmobile. Distance should be 4½-5½ in. (11-14 cm).

> NOTE: *Front cam adjusters are for various snow conditions. Cams should be in lower position for deep snow and higher position for icy snow. Rear cams are adjusted for differing driver weights.*
>
> *A spark plug wrench makes an ideal adjusting tool.*

2. Adjust front cams as desired for snow conditions (**Figure 17**). Adjust rear cams for specified distance between foot rest and ground (**Figure 18**).

CAUTION
Always turn left side adjustment cams clockwise and right side cams counterclockwise. *Ensure that left front cam is set at the same elevation as right front and left rear is set the same as right rear.*

HARDWARE AND COMPONENT TIGHTNESS CHECK

Hardware and components on all machines should be checked at least once a year. An ideal time is when the machine is placed in or removed from storage. Check the tightness of all bolts, nuts, and fasteners. Check for any damaged or worn parts, and areas that require special attention or repair. Refer to **Figure 19** for forward engine models and **Figure 20** for mid-engine models.

ENGINE TUNE-UP

In order to maintain your snowmobile in proper running condition, the engine must receive periodic tune-ups. Since different systems in an engine interact to affect overall performance, the tune-up procedures should be performed in a sequence with time spent to double check all adjustments.

Normal tune-up procedures should begin with ignition adjustment, then be followed by carburetor adjustment. Since all adjustments interact, recheck items like idle adjustments after completing the entire tune-up procedure.

Always check the condition of spark plug wires, ignition wires, and fuel lines for splitting, loose connections, hardness, and other signs of deterioration. Check that all manifold nuts and carburetor nuts are tight and no crankcase leaks are present. A small air leak can make a good

1. Ski runner nuts	7. Engine mounting bolts
2. Ski bolts	8. Carburetor attaching nuts on band
3. Shock absorber attaching bolt	9. Air silencer and fuel lines
4. Steering arm cap screws	10. Driven pulley support
5. Tie rod end locknuts	11. Suspension components
6. Drive pulley retaining bolt	

tune-up impossible as well as affect performance. A small air leak can also cause serious damage by allowing the engine to run on a "too-lean" fuel mixture.

Tune-up Hints

The following list of general hints will help make a tune-up easier and more successful:

1. Always use good tools and tune-up equipment. The money saved from one or two home tune-ups will more than pay for good tools; from that point you're money ahead. Refer to Chapter One for suitable types of tune-up/test equipment.

2. The purchase of a small set of ignition wrenches and one or two "screwholding" or magnetic screwdrivers will ease the work in replacing breaker points and help eliminate losing small screws.

3. Always purchase quality ignition components.

4. When using a feeler gauge to set breaker points, ensure that the blade is wiped clean before inserting between the points.

5. Ensure that points are fully open when setting gap with a feeler gauge.

6. Be sure that feeler gauge is not tilted or twisted when it is inserted between the contacts. Closely observe the points and withdraw the feeler gauge slowly and carefully. A slight resistance should be felt, however, the movable contact point must *not* "spring back" even slightly when the feeler gauge blade is removed.

7. If breaker points are only slightly pitted, they can be "dressed down" lightly with a small ignition point file. *Do not* use sandpaper as it leaves a residue on the points.

8. After points have been installed, always ensure that they are properly aligned, or premature pitting and burning will result (**Figure 21**). Bend only the *fixed* half of the points; not the movable arm.

1. Ski runner nuts
2. Ski bolts
3. Steering arm cap screws
4. Tie rod end locknuts
5. Drive pulley retaining bolt
6. Engine mounting bolts
7. Carburetor attaching nuts
8. Air silencer and fuel lines
9. Driven pulley support on hinge rod
10. Suspension components

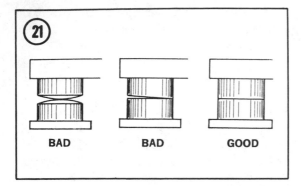

BAD   BAD   GOOD

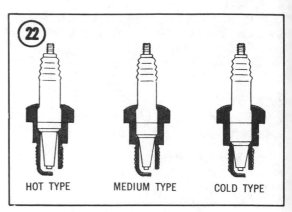

HOT TYPE   MEDIUM TYPE   COLD TYPE

9. When point gap has been set, spring points open and insert a piece of clean paper or cardboard between the contacts. Wipe the contact a few times to remove any trace of oil or grease. A small amount of oil or grease on the contact surfaces will cause the points to prematurely burn or arc.

10. When connecting a timing light or timing tester, always follow the manufacturer's instructions.

Spark Plugs

Among the first steps to be done during any tune-up is to remove and examine the spark plug. Condition of a used spark plug can tell much about engine condition and carburetion to a trained observer.

To remove the spark plug, first clean the area around its base to prevent dirt or other foreign material from entering the cylinder. Next, unscrew the spark plug, using a $^{13}/_{16}$ in. deep socket. If difficulty is encountered removing a spark plug, apply penetrating oil to its base and allow some 20 minutes for the oil to work in. It may also be helpful to rap the cylinder head lightly with a rubber or plastic mallet; this procedure sets up vibrations which helps the penetrating oil to work in.

The proper heat range for spark plugs is determined by the requirement that the plugs operate hot enough to burn off unwanted deposits, but not so hot that they burn themselves or cause preignition. A spark plug of the correct heat range will show a light tan color on the portion of the insulator within the cylinder after the plug has been in service. **Figure 22** illustrates the different construction of the various heat ranges.

Table 4   CAUSES OF FOULED PLUGS

• Improper fuel/oil mixture	• Weak ignition
• Wrong type of oil	• Excessive idling
• Idle speed too low	• Wrong spark plugs
• Clogged air silencer	(too cold)

Figure 23 illustrates various conditions which might be encountered upon plug removal.

1. *Normal condition* — If plugs have a light tan or gray colored deposit and no abnormal gap wear or erosion, good engine, carburetion, and ignition condition are indicated. The plug in use is of the proper heat range, and may be serviced and returned to use.

2. *Oil fouled* — This plug exhibits a black insulator tip, damp oily film over the firing end, and a carbon layer over the entire nose. Electrodes will not be worn. Common causes for this condition are listed in **Table 4**.

Oil fouled spark plugs may be cleaned in a pinch, but it is better to replace them. It is important to correct the cause of fouling before the engine is returned to service.

3. *Overheated* — Overheated spark plugs exhibit burned electrodes. The insulator tip will be light gray or even chalk white. The most common cause of this condition is using a spark plug of the wrong heat range (too hot). If it is known that the correct plug is used, other causes are lean fuel mixture, engine overloading or lugging, loose carburetor mounting, or timing advanced too far. Always correct the fault before putting the snowmobile back into service. Such plugs cannot be salvaged; replace with new ones.

SPARK PLUG CONDITIONS   ㉓

NORMAL USE

OIL FOULED

CARBON FOULED

OVERHEATED

GAP BRIDGED

SUSTAINED PREIGNITION

WORN OUT

Photos courtesy of Champion Spark Plug Company.

4. *Preignition* — If electrodes are melted, preignition is almost certainly the cause. Check for carburetor mounting or intake manifold leaks, also overadvanced ignition timing. It is also possible that a plug of the wrong heat range (too hot) is being used. Find the cause of preignition before placing the engine back into service.

5. *Carbon fouled* — Soft, dry sooty deposits are evidence of incomplete combustion and can usually be attributed to rich carburetion. This condition is also sometimes caused by weak ignition, retarded timing, or low compression. Such a plug may usually be cleaned and returned to service, but the condition which causes fouling should be corrected.

6. *Gap bridging* — Plugs with this condition exhibit gaps shorted out by combustion chamber deposits used between electrodes. On 2-stroke engines either of the following may be the cause:

    a. Improper fuel/oil mixture

    b. Clogged exhaust

Be sure to locate and correct the cause of this spark plug condition. Such plugs must be replaced with new ones.

7. *Worn out* — Corrosive gases formed by combustion and high voltage sparks have eroded the electrodes. Spark plugs in this condition require more voltage to fire under hard acceleration; often more than the ignition system can supply. Replace them with new spark plugs of the same heat range.

The spark plugs recommended by the factory are usually the most suitable for your machine. If riding conditions are mild, it may be advisable to go to spark plugs one step hotter than normal. Unusually severe riding conditions may require slightly colder plugs. See **Table 5**.

CAUTION

> *Ensure that spark plugs used have the correct thread reach. A thread reach too short will cause the exposed threads in the cylinder head to accumulate carbon, resulting in stripped cylinder head threads when the proper plug is installed. A thread reach too long will cause the exposed spark plug threads to accumulate carbon resulting in stripped cylinder head threads when the plug is removed.*

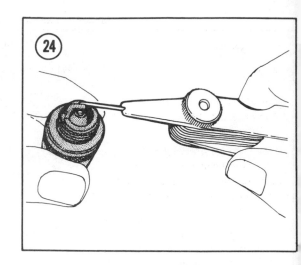

It may take some experimentation to arrive at the proper plug heat range for your type of riding. As a general rule, use as cold a spark plug as possible without fouling. This will give the best performance.

Remove and clean spark plugs at least once a season. After cleaning, inspect them for worn or eroded electrodes. Replace them if in doubt about their condition. If the plugs are serviceable, file the center electrodes square, then adjust the gaps by bending the outer electrodes only. Measure the gap with a round wire spark plug gauge only; a flat gauge will yield an incorrect reading. **Figure 24** illustrates proper spark plug gap measurement. Gap should be 0.020 in. (0.51mm).

Be sure to clean the seating area on the cylinder head and use a new gasket whenever you replace a spark plug. Install the plug finger-tight, then tighten it an additional ½ turn. If using a torque wrench, torque spark plugs to 20 ft.-lb. (2.8 mkg), for 14mm plugs and 30 ft.-lb. (4.1 mkg) for 18mm plugs.

Single Cylinder Engine Breaker Point and Timing Adjustment

Refer to list of general tune-up hints as outlined under *Engine Tune-Up*.

1. Remove spark plug.

2. Remove recoil starter and starting pulley from magneto ring (**Figure 25**).

3. Rotate crankshaft until breaker points are fully open (viewed through magneto ring). See **Figure 26**.

Table 5   SPARK PLUG APPLICATION

| Model | Champion | | Bosch | |
	Standard	Gold Palladium	Standard	Silver Sport
Elan 250; Olympique 300 (299 engine)	K-9	K-8G	M175T1	—
Olympique 335, 440 (1973) Olympique 300 (1976)	K-9	K-8G	M225T1	—
T'NT F/A, T'NT R/V, T'NT 440 (1973) (14mm heads) and R/V 340	RM-2	N-2G	W280MZ2	W280S1S
Elan 250 Twin and Deluxe to 1977 Olympique 300T, 340, 399, T'NT 399	L-81	L-6G	W240T1	W260S1S
Olympique 300 Twin (1978 and later) Olympique 340, 340E (1978 and later) Citation 300 (1978 and later) Everest 340, 340E (1978 and later)	L-78	L-4G	W280MZ1	—
T'NT 340 (1978)	L-78	L-4G	W260MZ1	—
Blizzard 6500, 7500, 9500	—		W340S2S	—
Blizzard 5500			W275T2	—
Everest 440, 440E; T'NT 440 L/C	K-7	K-5G	M260T1	W260S1S
Everest 444 L/C	N-3	N-3G	W260MZ2 or W280MZ2 with 2 gaskets	
Elan 250SS, 300SS; T'NT 294, 300, 340 Everest 340 (to 1977); Olympique 340 (to 1977); T'NT 292 single; T'NT 440; Everest 440 (to 1977)	L-78	L-4G	M260T1	—

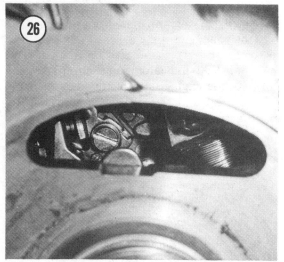

4. Carefully examine points and dress with file or replace as necessary.

5. Loosen screw securing breaker points. Using a feeler gauge set breaker point gap to 0.014-0.018 in. (0.35-0.45mm). Tighten screw securing breaker points. Recheck gap as gap can change when screw is tightened, readjust if necessary.

6. Disconnect electrical junction block at engine and connect a flashlight-type or tone-type timing tester. Connect one lead to black wire leading from engine and the other lead to a good ground such as fan cowl.

> NOTE: *More precise timing can be achieved by using a dial indicator-type gauge as described in Chapter One. If dial indicator gauge is used proceed to Step 9. If gauge is not used perform next step.*

7. Turn on flashlight or tone tester and rotate magneto until timing marks align (**Figure 27**).

8. Loosen 3 screws retaining armature plate (**Figure 28**, magneto/fan assembly removed for clarity) and rotate plate until timing light fluctuates or tone signal changes. This indicates points are just starting to open. Tighten armature plate retaining screws. Recheck point gap and timing and readjust if necessary. Proceed to Step 14.

> NOTE: *In order to get breaker points to just begin to open when timing marks are aligned, it may be necessary to slightly change breaker point gap, however never vary gap beyond specified tolerance of 0.014-0.018 in. (0.35-0.45mm).*

9. Install dial indicator gauge in spark plug hole. Rotate engine until piston is at TDC (top dead center) and "zero" gauge according to manufacturer's instructions (**Figure 29**).

10. Rotate engine until dial indicator gauge indicates piston is BTDC (before top dead center) the amount specified in **Table 6**.

> NOTE: *On engines with vertical spark plug hole use direct timing specification, Table 6. Engines with spark plug hole on an angle use indirect timing specifications.*

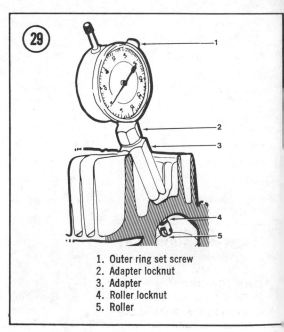

1. Outer ring set screw
2. Adapter locknut
3. Adapter
4. Roller locknut
5. Roller

Table 6   IGNITION TIMING SPECIFICATIONS

Engine	Direct Timing BTDC[1]	Indirect Timing BTDC[1]
245 (1976)*	0.035-0.055 in. (0.90-1.40mm)	N/A
245 (1975)*	0.037-0.057 in. (0.95-1.45mm)	N/A
247	0.147-0.167 in. (3.73-4.23mm)	N/A[2]
248, 249	0.077-0.097 in. (1.97-2.47mm)	0.080-0.100 in. (2.04-2.54mm)
250	0.150-0.170 in. (3.81-4.31mm)	0.150-0.160 in. (3.81-4.06mm)
292 (1970-1971)	0.140-0.160 in. (3.55-4.06mm)	0.195-0.221 in. (4.95-5.61mm)
292, 302 (1972)	0.147-0.167 in. (3.73-4.23mm)	0.195-0.215 in. (4.95-5.46mm)
294	0.084-0.104 in. (2.14-2.64mm)	0.087-0.110 in. (2.19-2.79mm)
300	0.150-0.170 in. (3.81-4.31mm)	0.205-0.241 in. (5.20-6.12mm)
302	0.147-0.167 in. (3.73-4.23mm)	0.212-0.244 in. (5.38-6.20mm)
305	0.111-0.131 in. (2.82-3.32mm)	0.135-0.159 in. (3.43-4.03mm)
304, 343[3] (1978)	0.073-0.093 in. (1.86-2.36mm)	0.087-0.107 in. (2.21-2.71mm)
335	0.160-0.180 in. (4.06-4.57mm)	0.220-0.250 in. (5.59-6.35mm)
337	0.157-0.177 in. (3.99-4.49mm)	0.229-0.249 in. (5.81-6.32mm)
338	0.111-0.131 in. (2.82-3.32mm)	0.132-0.154 in. (3.35-3.89mm)
340 (1970)	0.160-0.180 in. (4.06-4.57mm)	0.198-0.228 in. (5.02-5.79mm)
340 (1971)	0.160-0.180 in. (4.06-4.57mm)	0.193-0.220 in. (4.90-5.59mm)
343 (1972)	0.137-0.157 in. (3.48-3.98mm)	0.159-0.179 in. (4.03-4.55mm)
343 (1973)	0.111-0.131 in. (2.82-3.32mm)	0.131-0.154 in. (3.33-3.91mm)
343	0.111-0.131 in. (2.82-3.32mm)	0.135-0.159 in. (3.43-4.03mm)
345*	0.035-0.055 in. (0.90-1.40mm)	N/A
345 (1978)*	0.034-0.054 in. (0.87-1.37mm)	N/A
346 (1973)*	0.109-0.129 in. (2.77-3.28mm)	N/A
396 (1973)*	0.060-0.080 in. (1.52-2.03mm)	N/A
346, 396 (1974)*	0.071-0.091 in. (1.82-2.32mm)	N/A
354*, 454*	0.045-0.065 in. (1.14-1.64mm)	N/A
399, 440 (1970, 1971)	0.160-0.180 in. (4.06-4.57mm)	0.148-0.171 in. (3.76-4.34mm)
401, 434, 435 (1972)	0.137-0.157 in. (3.48-3.98mm)	0.146-0.166 in. (3.71-4.22mm)
401	0.111-0.131 in. (2.82-3.32mm)	0.135-0.159 in. (3.43-4.03mm)
434, 440[4]	0.111-0.131 in. (2.82-3.32mm)	0.118-0.144 in. (2.99-3.66mm)
435	0.111-0.131 in. (2.82-3.32mm)	0.119-0.141 in. (3.02-3.58mm)
436*	0.071-0.091 in. (1.82-2.32mm)	N/A
440 (1975)*	0.71-0.091 in. (1.82-2.32mm)	0.077-0.097 in. (1.96-2.46mm)
440 (1978-1979)	0.111-0.131 in. (2.82-3.32mm)	0.120-0.140 in. (3.05-3.55mm)
444	0.082-0.102 in. (2.10-2.60mm)	N/A
503	0.068-0.088 in. (1.82-2.32mm)	N/A

*Engines equipped with CDI.
1. Use direct timing for engines with vertical spark plug holes and indirect timing for engines with spark plug on an angle.
2. On 1972 models, indirect specification is the same as direct.
3. On 343 engines serial number 3,019,645 to 3,020,644 direct timing is 0.147-0.167 in. (3.73-4.23mm).
4. Except 1975 440 with CDI.

11. Turn on flashlight or tone tester and loosen 3 screws securing armature plate (**Figure 28**).

12. Hold advance mechanism weight in full advance position (toward magneto ring). See **Figure 30**.

13. Slowly rotate armature plate until timing light fluctuates or tone signal changes. This indicates points are just starting to open. Tighten armature plate retaining screws. Recheck point gap and timing, readjust if necessary.

14. Remove timing tester. Remove dial indicator gauge if used. Connect electrical junction block.

15. Install starting pulley and recoil starter. Install spark plug.

Twin Cylinder Engine Breaker Point and Timing Adjustment

Refer to list of general tune-up hints as outlined under *Engine Tune-Up*.

1. Remove spark plugs.

2. Remove recoil starter and fan cover.

3. Remove starting pulley and fan drive belt (**Figure 31**).

4. Rotate crankshaft until breaker points are fully open (viewed through magneto ring opening). See **Figure 32**.

> NOTE: *Upper breaker points apply to magneto side piston; lower points apply to* PTO *(power take off) side.*

5. Carefully examine points and dress with file or replace as necessary.

6. Loosen screw securing breaker points. Using a feeler gauge set breaker point gap to 0.014-0.0l8 in. (0.35-0.45mm). See **Figure 32**. Tighten screw securing breaker points. Recheck gap as gap can change when screw is tightened; readjust if necessary. Repeat for other set of breaker points.

7. Disconnect electrical junction block at engine and connect a flashlight-type or tone-type timing tester. Connect one lead to blue wire (magneto side points) leading from engine. Connect other lead to a good ground such as fan cowl.

> NOTE: *More precise timing can be achieved by using a dial indicator-type*

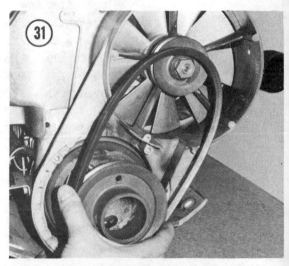

2

gauge as described in Chapter One. If dial indicator gauge is used proceed to Step 13. If gauge is not used perform next step.

8. Loosen 2 screws or nuts securing armature plate (**Figure 33**, magneto removed for clarity).

9. Turn on flashlight or tone tester and rotate crankshaft until magneto side piston approaches TDC (top dead center) and timing marks align (**Figure 34**).

10. Rotate armature plate until timing light fluctuates or tone signal changes. This indicates points are just starting to open. Tighten armature plate retaining screws. Rotate crankshaft counterclockwise approximately ¼ turn and then slowly rotate crankshaft back clockwise until timing marks are aligned. Check that points just start to open. Tightening armature plate retaining screws can cause timing to shift slightly. Readjust timing if necessary.

> NOTE: *It is necessary to hold centrifugal advance mechanism in the fully advanced position (toward magneto rim) while rotating armature plate to set timing (Figure 35) on the following engines:*
> *305 engines*
> *343 engines, serial No. 2,670,920*
>   *and subsequent*
> *346 engines*
> *402 engines*
> *440 engines, serial No. 2,748,146*
>   *and subsequent*
> *444 engines*

11. Disconnect timing tester lead from blue wire and connect to blue/red (PTO side points) leading from engine.

12. Turn on timing tester and rotate crankshaft until timing marks align. Timing light should fluctuate or tone signal should change. If timing is incorrect adjust lower set of points as follows:

  a. If timing is too early, decrease point gap toward lower limit, 0.014 in. (0.35mm), until correct timing is achieved.

  b. If timing is too late, increase point gap toward upper limit, 0.018 in. (0.45mm), until correct timing is achieved.

c. After tightening breaker point retaining screw, recheck timing and readjust if necessary. Proceed to Step 19.

13. Install dial indicator gauge in magneto side spark plug hole. Rotate crankshaft until piston is at TDC (top dead center) and "zero" gauge according to manufacturer's instructions (**Figure 29**).

14. Loosen 2 screws or nuts securing armature plate (**Figure 33**, magneto removed for clarity). Turn on timing tester and rotate crankshaft until piston is specified distance BTDC (before top dead center), **Table 6**.

> NOTE: *On engines with vertical spark plug hole use* direct *timing specifications,* **Table 6**. *Engines with spark plug hole on an angle use* indirect *timing specifications.*

15. Hold advance mechanism in fully advanced position (toward magneto ring) and slowly rotate armature plate until light fluctuates or tone signal changes (**Figure 35**). Tighten plate retaining screws and recheck timing. Readjust if necessary.

16. Disconnect timing tester lead from blue wire and connect to blue/red wire (PTO side points) leading from engine.

17. Remove dial indicator gauge from magneto side and install in PTO side spark plug hole and "zero" gauge when piston is at TDC.

18. Hold advance mechanism in fully advanced position and rotate crankshaft until piston is specified distance BTDC, **Table 6**. Timing light should fluctuate or tone signal should change. If timing is incorrect, adjust lower set of points as follows:

> NOTE: *Do not loosen screws on armature ring or magneto side timing will be changed, requiring complete timing procedure to be repeated.*

a. If timing is too early, decrease point gap toward lower limit, 0.014 in. (0.35mm), until correct timing is achieved.

b. If timing is too late, increase point gap toward upper limit, 0.018 in. (0.45mm), until correct timing is achieved.

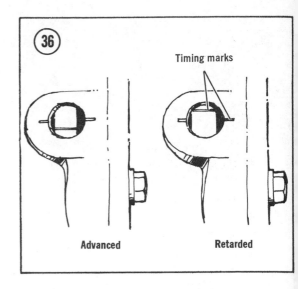

Timing marks

Advanced   Retarded

c. After tightening breaker point retaining screw, recheck timing and readjust if necessary.

19. Remove timing tester. Remove dial indicator gauge if used. Connect electrical junction block.

20. Install starting pulley and fan belt.

21. Install recoil starter, fan cover, and spark plugs.

CDI Ignition Timing (Except 354 Engines)

1. Raise rear of snowmobile off ground and block up securely.

> WARNING
> *Ignition timing requires engine be run at 5,000 rpm. Ensure that track area is clear, pulley guard is in place, and no one walks behind track or serious injuries may result.*

2. Remove rubber plug from upper crankcase.

3. Connect an external powered timing light to magneto side spark plug wire.

> NOTE: *If DC powered timing light is used, connect light to an external battery.*

4. Start engine and run up to 5,000 rpm. Timing marks on crankcase and magneto ring should align (**Figure 36**). If marks do not align perform the following:

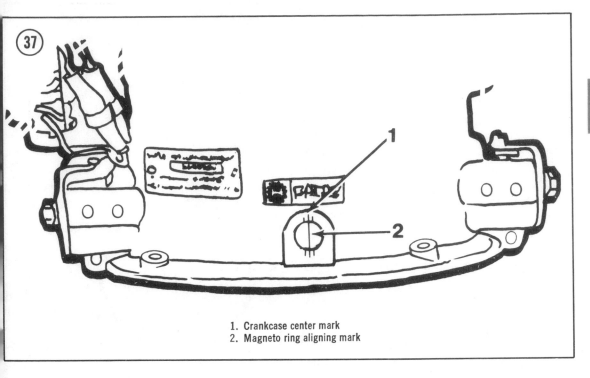

1. Crankcase center mark
2. Magneto ring aligning mark

CAUTION
*Do not run engine more than necessary
or excessive slider shoe wear may result.*

a. Remove recoil starter and starting pulley.

b. Loosen Allen screws securing armature plate. Rotate plate clockwise to retard timing and counterclockwise to advance timing.

c. Recheck timing and readjust if necessary.

5. With engine off, connect timing light to PTO (power take off) side spark plug wire.

6. Start engine and run up to 5,000 rpm. Timing should coincide with magneto side timing. If PTO timing is incorrect perform the following:

a. Remove PTO spark plug and install a dial indicator timing gauge (described in Chapter One) in spark plug hole.

b. Rotate engine until piston is at TDC (top dead center) and "zero" gauge according to manufacturer's instructions.

c. Rotate crankshaft until piston is specified distance BTDC (before top dead center). See **Table 6**.

d. Scribe marks on magneto rings for lower and upper limits of specified dimension. Repeat for magneto side piston.

e. Position armature plate so both cylinders fire within upper and lower limits of specified timing tolerance.

7. Remove timing light and install rubber plug in crankcase.

8. Install starting pulley and recoil starter if removed.

9. Remove block from rear of snowmobile.

CDI Ignition Timing (354 Engines)

1. Raise rear of snowmobile off ground and block up securely.

WARNING
Ignition timing requires engine be run at 6,000 rpm. Ensure that track area is clear, pulley guard is in place, and no one walks behind track or serious injuries may result.

2. Remove rubber plug from upper crankcase.

3. Install dial indicator gauge in spark plug hole. Rotate crankshaft until piston is at TDC (top dead center) and "zero" gauge according to manufacturer's instructions (**Figure 29**).

4. With piston at TDC, rotate crankshaft until piston is positioned 0.055 in. (1.40mm) BTDC.

Check that timing mark on the magneto ring aligns with the center mark on the crankcase as shown in **Figure 37**. If timing marks are incorrect, remark magneto ring. Repeat for the other piston.

5. Check air gap between the magneto ring and each trigger coil as shown in **Figure 38**. If air gap is incorrect, magneto ring will have to be removed and the armature plate repositioned (refer to *Flywheel and Magneto Removal* in Chapter Four). Air gap for each trigger coil should be 0.040-0.063 in. (1-1.6mm).

6. Connect an external powered timing light to magneto side spark plug wire. Use an external battery if using a DC powered timing light.

7. Start engine and run up to 6,000 rpm. Timing mark on magneto ring should align as shown in **Figure 37**. If marks do not align, perform the following:

   a. Loosen screw securing trigger coil bracket and adjust bracket up or down slightly until timing is correct (**Figure 39**). Repeat for the other cylinder.

NOTE: *Magneto trigger coil is on carburetor side and* PTO *trigger coil is on exhaust side.*

   b. If insufficient travel of trigger coil bracket prevents correct timing, remove bracket and slightly move trigger coil on the bracket (**Figure 40**).

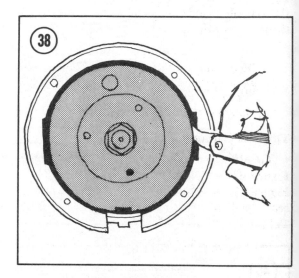

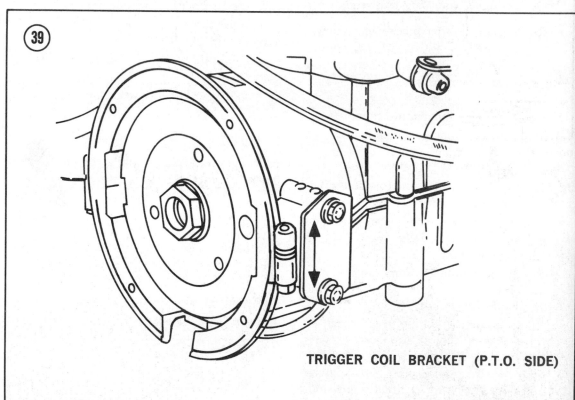

TRIGGER COIL BRACKET (P.T.O. SIDE)

2

8. Remove timing light and install rubber plug in crankcase.

9. Remove block from rear of snowmobile.

Throttle Cable Adjustment
(Tillotson Carburetors)

Adjust throttle cable (A, **Figure 41**) so throttle lever on carburetor is fully open when throttle control on the handlebar is in the wide-open throttle position.

> **CAUTION**
> *Do not adjust cable too tightly (throttle on carburetor is wide-open before throttle control is fully against handlebar) or cable may break due to excessive strain.*

Tillotson Carburetor Adjustment

1. Gently close low-speed mixture needle (B, **Figure 41**) and high-speed mixture needle (A, **Figure 42**), if adjustable, until needle contacts seat. Back off mixture needles as specified in **Table 7**.

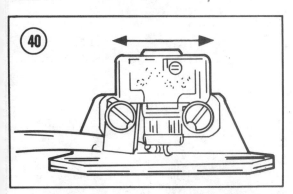

> **CAUTION**
> *Close mixture needles carefully or damage to needle and/or seat may result.*

2. Start and warm up engine. Turn idle speed adjustment screw (C, **Figure 41**) to achieve specified idle speed, **Table 7**.

3. Ensure that the high-speed needle (if adjustable) is set at specified preliminary setting, **Table 7**. Check and adjust mixture as follows:

> **CAUTION**
> *If snowmobile is equipped with an air silencer, adjustments must be made with silencer installed or a "too lean" mixture and subsequent engine damage may result.*

a. Drive snowmobile approximately 1 mile at 6,000 rpm. Shut off engine with ignition switch or kill button; do not allow engine to idle.

b. Remove spark plug(s) and examine insulator. A brownish tip indicates correct mixture. Black insulator indicates a "too rich" mixture and light grey insulator indicates a "too lean" mixture.

c. If mixture is incorrect, adjust high-speed mixture needle. Turn needle clockwise to obtain a leaner mixture or counterclockwise to obtain a richer mixture. Adjust needle ⅛ turn at a time and repeat high-speed run and spark plug examination after each run.

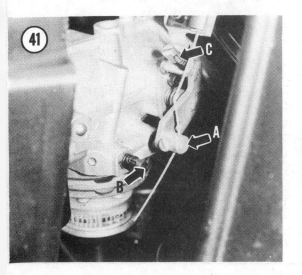

Table 7   TILLOTSON CARBURETOR SPECIFICATIONS

Model	Carburetor	Low Speed Adjustment (Turns)**	High Speed Adjustment (Turns)**	Idle Speed (rpm)
Elan				
250, 250 E (1971,1972, early 1973)	HR-73A	¾	1¼ ①	*
250 (late 1973-1975)	HR-133A	¾	Fixed	*
292 SS (1972)	HD-22B	¾	1¼	*
250 T (1973)	HR-136A	¾	Fixed	*
250 T, 250 Deluxe (1974)	HR-155A	1	Fixed	*
250 Deluxe (1975)	HR-165A	1	Fixed	*
250 (1976)	HR-173A	1	Fixed	*
250 SS (1973)	HR-143A (2)	¾	Fixed	*
294 SS (1974)	HR-161A	¾	Fixed	*
300 SS (1975)	HR-166A	¾	Fixed	*
250 SS (1976)	HR-172A	1	Fixed	1,500-1,800
250 (1978-1979)	HR-173A	1	Fixed	1,800-2,000
250 Deluxe (1978-1979)	HR-172A	1	Fixed	1,800-2,200
Olympique				
300 (1971-early 1973)	HR-74A	¾	1¼	*
300 (late 1973-1974)	HR-132A	¾	1	*
300 (1975 and 1976 twin)	HR-169A	1	Fixed	1,500-1,800
300 (1976 single)	HR-174A	1	Fixed	1,200-1,500
335 (1970)	HR-176	¾	1¼	*
335 (1971-1973)	HR-75A	¾ ②	1¼ ②	*
340 (1973-1974)	HR-131A	¾	Fixed	*
340 (1975-1976)	HR-170A, B	1	Fixed	1,500-1,800
399 (1970)	HR-16B	¾	1¼	*
399 (1971-1972)	HR-76A	¾	1¼	*
400 (early 1973)	HR-76A	1	1¹⁄₁₆	*
400 (late 1973-1974)	HR-134A	¾	Fixed	*
440 (1973-1974)	HR-135A	⅞	Fixed	*
440 plus (1976)	HR-176A	1	Fixed	1,500-1,800
T'NT				
292, 340 (1970, 1971, and 1972 292)	HD-22A, B	¾	1¼	*
340 (1972)	HD-98A	1⅛	1	*
294 (1973)	HR-137A (2)	¾	Fixed	*
340 (1973)	HD-107A	⅞	Fixed	*
300 (1974)	HR-164A	1	1	*
340 (1974-1975)	HD-134A	1	1	*
340 (1976)	HD-148A	1	1	1,500-1,800
399 (1970)	HD-21A	¾	1¼	*
440 (1971)	HD-73A	¾	1¼	*

(continued)

Table 7 TILLOTSON CARBURETOR SPECIFICATIONS (continued)

Model	Carburetor	Low Speed Adjustment (Turns)**	High Speed Adjustment (Turns)**	Idle Speed (rpm)
T'NT (con't.)				
440 (1972)	HD-83A	1¼	1¼	*
440 (1973)	HD-109A	1	1	*
440 and Everest (1974-1975)	HD-138A	1	1	*
440 and Everest (1976)	HD-147A	1	1	1,500-1,800
400 F/A (1972)	HD-104A (2)	¾	1¼	*
340 F/A (1973-1974)	HR-149A (2)	1	1⅛	*
400 F/A (1973-1974)	HD-123A (2)	1	⅝	*
340 F/A (1975)	HR-168A (2)	1	1⅛	*
440 F/A (1974)	HRM-3A (2)	1	1¼	*
440 F/A (1975)	HRM-5A (2)	1	1	*

* Unless otherwise specified, idle speed is 1,800-2,200 rpm.

** Tolerance for all adjustments is +⅛-0 turn.

① Fixed jet on later 1973 models.

② On 1973 models turn low-speed needle ⅞ and high-speed needle 1 1/16.

43

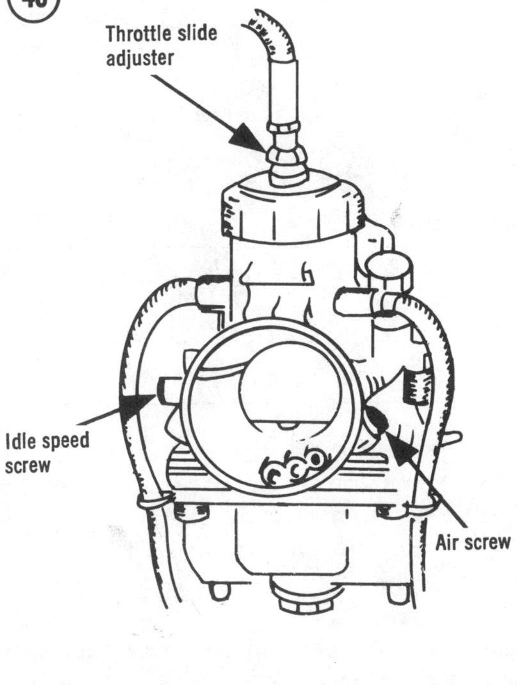
Throttle slide adjuster
Idle speed screw
Air screw

CAUTION

Continued operation with a "too lean" mixture can cause engine overheating and serious engine damage.

d. If final adjustment is a considerable change from preliminary mixture needle setting, check for engine and/or carburetor air leaks, defective crankcase seals, or incorrect spark plug heat range.

Mikuni Carburetor Adjustment and Synchronization

This procedure includes throttle cable adjustments and idle speed adjustments for all models equipped with Mikuni carburetors.

On models equipped with 2 carburetors, more precise synchronization can be achieved with an air flow meter as described in Chapter One. If such a device is available, perform the following procedure as a preliminary adjustment and proceed to *Mikuni Carburetor Air Flow Meter Synchronization* for the final fine tuning.

Refer to **Figure 43** for this procedure.

Table 8   MIKUNI CARBURETOR SPECIFICATIONS

Model	Carburetor	E-ring Position (From Top)	Air Screw Turns (± ¼ Turn)
T'NT R/V 245 (1975)	VM 34-72	2	1
T'NT 340-340E kit (1976)	VM 34-109	3	1
T'NT 440-440E kit (1976)	VM 34-105	2	1
Olympique 340-340E kit (1976)	VM 34-104	3	1
Olympique 300-300E kit (1976)	VM 34-103	3	1
T'NT R/V 250 (1976)	VM 34-93	2	1
T'NT R/V 340 (1976)	VM 34-94	2	1
Olympique 440 plus kit (1976)	VM 32-117	3	1½
Olympique 300 (twin—1977-1978)	VM 30-90	3	1½
Olympique 340-340E (1977-1979)	VM 30-91	3	1½
Everest 340-340E kit (1977-1979)	VM30-98	3	1½
Olympique 440 (1977)	VM 32-113	4	1½
T'NT 340 F/A (1977-1978)	VM 34-118	3	1
T'NT 440 F/A (1977)	VM 36-53	2	1
T'NT 440 (1977)	VM 34-110	3	1½
R/V 340 (1977-1978)	VM 34-135	4	1
Everest 440-440E (1977)	VM 34-110	3	1½
Everest 440 L/C (1977)	VM 34-150	4	1
Citation 300 (1978)	VM30-94	3	1½
Citation 300 (1979)	VM 30-104	3	1½
Everest 440, 440E (1978)	VM 34-165	3	2
T'NT 440 F/C (1978)	VM 34-165	3	2
Everest 444 L/C	VM 34-150	4	1½
Blizzard 6500	VM 34-184	4	1½
Blizzard 9500	VM 36-78	4	1
Blizzard 5500	VM 34-203	3	1½
Blizzard 7500 and Cross Country	VM 34-199	2	1½

1. Remove air intake silencer.

2. Use a strong rubber band and clamp throttle lever to handlebar grip in the wide-open-throttle position.

3. Loosen locknut securing throttle slide adjuster. Feel inside carburetor bore and turn adjuster until cut-out portion of throttle valve is flush with inside of carburetor bore (**Figure 44**).

4. Turn adjuster sleeve counterclockwise the required number of additional turns to position the backside of the throttle valve flush with the carburetor bore.

5. Rotate idle speed screw counterclockwise until the tip is flush with inside of carburetor bore.

6. Remove rubber band clamp from handlebar and allow throttle to return to idle position.

7. Turn in idle speed screw until tip just contacts throttle slide valve. Turn in stop screw 2 additional turns for a preliminary idle setting.

8. Slowly operate throttle lever on handlebar

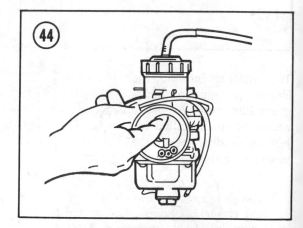

and observe that throttle valve begins to rise. On models with 2 carburetors, ensure that throttle valves move an equal amount together. Readjust throttle cables if necessary.

9. Slowly turn in pilot air screw until light seating is felt. *Do not* force or air screw may be damaged. Back out pilot air screw number of turns specified in **Table 8**.

2

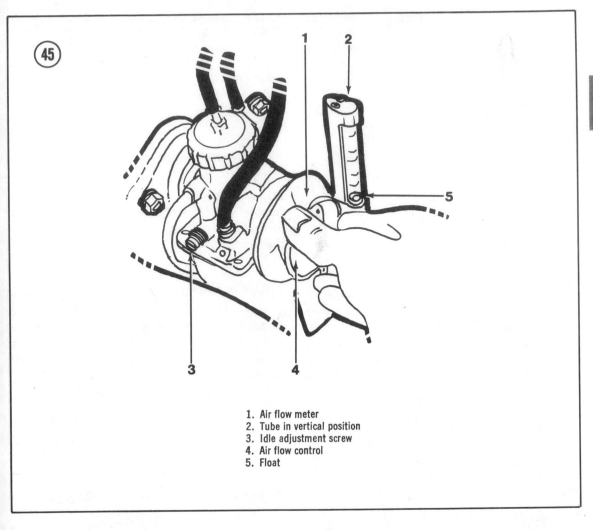

1. Air flow meter
2. Tube in vertical position
3. Idle adjustment screw
4. Air flow control
5. Float

10. Install air intake silencer and start engine. Warm up engine to operating temperature and check idle speed. Adjust throttle stop screw as necessary for specified idle speed. On 2 carburetor models, ensure that both throttle stop screws are adjusted an equal amount.

CAUTION
Do not use pilot air screws to attempt to set engine idle speed. Pilot air screws must be set as specified in Table 8, or a "too lean" mixture and subsequent engine damage may result.

Mikuni Carburetor Air Flow Meter Synchronization

To obtain a precise synchronization of twin carburetor models, use an air flow meter device as described in Chapter One. Perform *Mikuni*

Carburetor Adjustment and Synchronization to obtain proper preliminary adjustments.

Refer to **Figure 45** for this procedure.

WARNING
The following procedure is performed with the engine running. Ensure that arms and clothing are clear of drive belt or serious injury may result.

1. Raise and support rear of snowmobile so track is clear of the ground.

2. Start engine. Wedge in throttle lever to maintain engine speed at 4,000 rpm.

3. Open air flow control of air flow meter and place meter over right carburetor throat. Tube on meter must be vertical.

4. Slowly close air flow control until float in tubes aligns with a graduated mark on tube.

5. Without changing adjustment of air flow control, place air flow meter on left carburetor. If carburetors are equal, no adjustment is necessary.

6. If adjustment is necessary, loosen cable adjuster locknut on carburetor with lowest float level and turn adjustor until air flow matches other carburetor. Tighten locknut.

7. Return engine to idle and repeat Steps 3, 4, and 5. Adjust throttle stop screws as necessary for a balanced idle.

Mikuni Carburetor Main Jet Selection

The main jet controls the fuel metering when the carburetor is operating in the ½ to full throttle range. Since temperature and altitude affect the air density, each snowmobile owner will have to perform the following trial and error method of jet selection to obtain peak engine efficiency and performance for his own particular area of operation.

CAUTION
Air intake silencer must be installed during the following procedure or a "too lean" mixture may result. A "too lean" fuel mixture can cause engine overheating and subsequent serious damage.

NOTE: *Snowmobile must be operated on a flat, well-packed area for best results.*

1. Operate machine at wide-open throttle for several minutes. If peak rpm cannot be achieved or engine appears to be laboring, main jet needs to be changed.

2. Make another trial run and shut off ignition while throttle is still wide open. Examine the exhaust and spark plugs to determine if mixture is too rich or too lean. Mixture is too rich if exhaust manifold or spark plug insulator is dark brown or black. Refer to *Spark Plugs* in this chapter. Decrease jet size if mixture is too rich.

NOTE: *Change jet sizes one increment at a time and test after each change to obtain best results.*

If manifold or spark plug insulator is a very light color, mixture is too lean. Correct by increasing jet size.

3. If state of fuel/air mixture cannot be determined by color of exhaust manifold or spark plug insulator, assume mixture is too lean and increase jet size. If operation improves, continue increasing jet size until maximum performance is achieved. If operation gets worse, decrease jet size until best results are obtained.

OFF-SEASON STORAGE

Proper storage techniques are essential to help maintain your snowmobile's life and usefulness. The off-season is also an excellent time to perform any maintenance and repair tasks that are necessary.

Placing in Storage

1. Use soap and water to thoroughly clean the exterior of your snowmobile. Use a hose to remove rocks, dirt, and debris from the track area. Clean all dirt and debris from the hood and console areas.

CAUTION
Do not spray water around the carburetor or engine. Be sure you allow sufficient time for all components to dry.

2. Use a good automotive type cleaner wax and polish the hood, pan, and tunnel. Use a suitable type of upholstery cleaner on the seat. Touch up any scratched or bare metal parts with paint. Paint or oil the skis to prevent rust.

3. Drain the fuel tank. Start the engine and run it at idle to burn off all fuel left in the carburetor. Check the fuel filter and replace if contaminated.

4. Wrap up carburetor(s) and intake manifold in plastic and tie securely.

5. Remove spark plugs and add a teaspoon of snowmobile oil to each cylinder. Pull the engine over several times with the starter rope to spread the oil over the cylinder walls. Replace the spark plugs.

6. Remove the drive belt. Apply a film of light grease to drive and driven pulleys to prevent rust and corrosion.

7. Change chaincase oil.

8. Raise rear of snowmobile off the ground. Loosen the track adjusting screws to remove any tension on the track.

9. Carefully examine all components and assemblies. Make a note of immediate and future maintenance and repair items and order the necessary parts. Perform *Hardware and Component Tightness Check*.

10. Cover snowmobile and store inside if possible.

Removing From Storage

1. Perform *Hardware and Component Tightness Check*.

2. Remove grease from the drive and driven pulleys and install the drive belt.

3. Fill the fuel tank with new gasoline/oil mixture. Refer to Chapter One.

4. Check throttle and brake controls for proper operation and adjust if necessary.

5. Adjust the track to proper tension.

6. Familiarize yourself with all safety and operating instructions.

7. Start the engine and check the operation of the emergency stop switch. Check that all lights and switches operate properly. Replace any burned out bulbs.

8. Start out slowly on short rides until you are sure your machine is operating properly and is dependable.

2

CHAPTER THREE

TROUBLESHOOTING

Diagnosing snowmobile ills is relatively simple if you use orderly procedures and keep a few basic principles in mind.

Never assume anything. Do not overlook the obvious. If you are riding along and the snowmobile suddenly quits, check the easiest, most accessible problem spots first. Is there gasoline in the tank? Has a spark plug wire fallen off? Check the ignition switch. Maybe that last mogul caused you to accidentally switch the emergency switch to OFF or pull the emergency stop "tether" string.

If nothing obvious turns up in a cursory check, look a little further. Learning to recognize and describe symptoms will make repairs easier for you or a mechanic at the shop. Describe problems accurately and fully. Saying that "it won't run" isn't the same as saying "it quit at high speed and wouldn't start," or that "it sat in my garage for 3 months and then wouldn't start."

Gather as many symptoms together as possible to aid in diagnosis. Note whether the engine lost power gradually or all at once, what color smoke (if any) came from the exhaust, and so on. Remember that the more complicated a machine is, the easier it is to troubleshoot because symptoms point to specific problems.

You do not need fancy equipment or complicated test gear to determine whether repairs can

be attempted at home. A few simple checks could save a large repair bill and time lost while the snowmobile sits in a dealer's service department. On the other hand, be realistic and do not attempt repairs beyond your abilities. Service departments tend to charge heavily for putting together disassembled components that may have been abused. Some will not even take on such a job — so use common sense; do not get in over your head.

OPERATING REQUIREMENTS

An engine needs three basics to run properly: correct gas/air mixture, compression, and a spark at the right time. If one or more are missing, the engine will not run. The electrical system is the weakest link of the three. More problems result from electrical breakdowns than from any other source; keep this in mind before you begin tampering with carburetor adjustments.

If the snowmobile has been sitting for any length of time and refuses to start, check the battery (if the machine is so equipped) for a charged condition first, and then look to the gasoline delivery system. This includes the tank, fuel petcocks, lines, and the carburetor. Rust may have formed in the tank, obstructing fuel flow. Gasoline deposits may have gummed up carburetor jets and air passages. Gasoline tends to lose its potency after standing for long periods. Condensation may contaminate it with water. Drain old gas and try starting with a fresh tankful.

Compression, or the lack of it, usually enters the picture only in the case of older machines. Worn or broken pistons, rings, and cylinder bores could prevent starting. Commonly, a gradual power loss and harder and harder starting will be readily apparent in this case.

PRINCIPLES OF 2-CYCLE ENGINES

The following is a general discussion of a typical 2-cycle piston-ported engine. The same principles apply to rotary valve engines except that during the intake cycle, the fuel/air mixture passes through a rotary valve assembly into the crankcase. During this discussion, assume that the crankshaft is rotating counterclockwise.

In **Figure 1**, as the piston travels downward, a scavenging port (A) between the crankcase and the cylinder is uncovered. Exhaust gases leave the cylinder through the exhaust port (B), which is also opened by downward movement of the piston. A fresh fuel/air charge, which has previously been compressed slightly, travels from the crankcase (C) to the cylinder through scavenging port (A) as the port opens. Since the incoming charge is under pressure, it rushes into the cylinder quickly and helps to expel exhaust gases from the previous cycle.

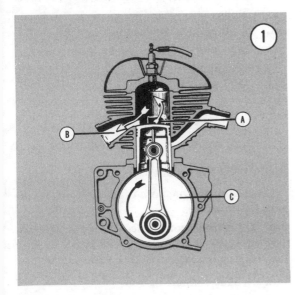

Figure 2 illustrates the next phase of the cycle. As the crankshaft continues to rotate, the piston moves upward, closing the exhaust and scavenging ports. As the piston continues upward, the air/fuel mixture in the cylinder is compressed. Notice also that a low pressure area is created in the crankcase at the same time. Further upward movement of the piston uncovers intake port (D). A fresh fuel/air charge is then drawn into the crankcase through the intake port because of the low pressure created by the upward piston movement.

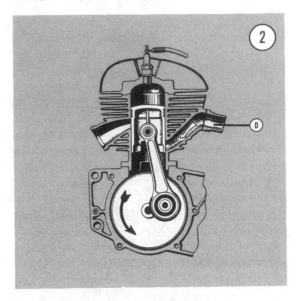

The third phase is shown in **Figure 3**. As the piston approaches top dead center, the spark plug fires, igniting the compressed mixture. The piston is then driven downward by the expanding gases.

When the top of the piston uncovers the exhaust port, the fourth phase begins, as shown in **Figure 4**. The exhaust gases leave the cylinder through the exhaust port. As the piston continues downward, the intake port is closed and the mixture in the crankcase is compressed in preparation for the next cycle. Every downward stroke of the piston is a power stroke.

ENGINE STARTING

An engine that refuses to start or is difficult to start can try anyone's patience. More often than not, the problem is very minor and can be

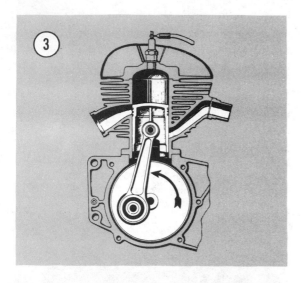

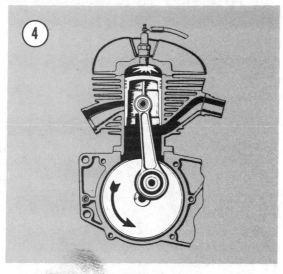

3. Turn on ignition and crank engine over. A fat blue spark should be evident across spark plug electrode.

> **WARNING**
> *On machines equipped with* CDI *(capacitor discharge ignition), do not hold spark plug, wire, or connector or a serious electrical shock may result.*

4. If spark is good, check for one or more of the following possible malfunctions:
   a. Fouled or defective spark plugs
   b. Obstructed fuel filter or fuel line
   c. Defective fuel pump
   d. Leaking head gasket (see *Compression Test)*

5. If spark is not good, check for one or more of the following:
   a. Burned, pitted, or improperly gapped breaker points
   b. Weak ignition coil or condenser
   c. Loose electrical connections
   d. Defective CDI components — have CDI system checked by an authorized dealer.

Engine Difficult to Start

Check for one or more of the following possible malfunctions:
   a. Fouled spark plugs
   b. Improperly adjusted choke
   c. Defective or improperly adjusted breaker points
   d. Contaminated fuel system
   e. Improperly adjusted carburetor
   f. Weak ignition coil
   g. Incorrect fuel mixture
   h. Defective reed valve
   i. Crankcase drain plugs loose or missing
   j. Poor compression (see *Compression Test)*

Engine Will Not Crank

Check for one or more of the following possible malfunctions:
   a. Defective recoil starter
   b. Seized piston
   c. Seized crankshaft bearings
   d. Broken connecting rod

found with a simple and logical troubleshooting approach.

The following items provide a beginning point from which to isolate an engine starting problem.

Engine Fails to Start

Perform the following spark test to determine if the ignition system is operating properly.

1. Remove a spark plug.

2. Connect spark plug connector to spark plug and clamp base of spark plug to a good grounding point on the engine. A large alligator clip makes an ideal clamp. Position spark plug so you can observe the electrode.

Compression Test

Perform compression test to determine condition of piston ring sealing qualities, piston wear, and condition of head gasket seal.

1. Remove spark plugs. Insert a compression gauge in one spark plug hole (**Figure 5**). Refer to Chapter One for a suitable type of compression tester.

2. Crank engine vigorously and record compression reading. Repeat for other cylinder. Compression readings should be from 120-175 psi (8.4-12.30 kg/cm²). Maximum allowable variation between cylinders is 10 psi (0.70 kg/cm²).

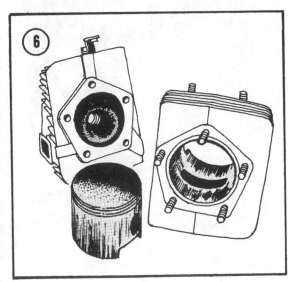

3. If compression is low or variance between cylinders is excessive, check for defective head gaskets, damaged cylinders and pistons, or stuck piston rings.

ENGINE PERFORMANCE

In the following discussion, it is assumed that the engine runs, but is not operating at peak efficiency. This will serve as a starting point from which to isolate a performance malfunction.

The possible causes for each malfunction are listed in a logical sequence and in order of probability.

Engine Will Not Idle

   a. Carburetor incorrectly adjusted
   b. Fouled or improperly gapped spark plugs
   c. Head gasket leaking — perform compression test
   d. Fuel mixture incorrect
   e. Spark advance mechanism not retarding
   f. Obstructed fuel pump impulse tube
   g. Crankcase drain plugs loose or missing

Engine Misses at High Speed

   a. Fouled or improperly gapped spark plugs
   b. Defective or improperly gapped breaker points
   c. Improper ignition timing
   d. Defective fuel pump
   e. Improper carburetor high-speed adjustment (Walbro and Bendix carburetors) or improper main jet selection (Mikuni carburetor)
   f. Weak ignition coil
   g. Obstructed fuel pump impulse tube

Engine Overheating

   a. Too lean fuel mixture — incorrect carburetor adjustment or jet selection
   b. Improper ignition timing
   c. Incorrect spark plug heat range
   d. Intake system or crankcase air leak
   e. Cooling fan belt or coolant pump drive belt broken or slipping
   f. Cooling fan or coolant pump defective
   g. Leak in liquid cooling system
   h. Damaged or blocked cooling fins

3

Smoky Exhaust and Engine Runs Rough

   a. Carburetor adjusted incorrectly — mixture too rich

   b. Incorrect fuel/oil mixture

   c. Choke not operating properly

   d. Obstructed muffler

   e. Water or other contaminants in fuel

Engine Loses Power

   a. Carburetor incorrectly adjusted

   b. Engine overheating

   c. Defective or improperly gapped breaker points

   d. Improper ignition timing

   e. Incorrectly gapped spark plugs

   f. Weak ignition coil

   g. Obstructed muffler

   h. Defective reed valve

Engine Lacks Acceleration

   a. Carburetor mixture too lean

   b. Defective fuel pump

   c. Incorrect fuel/oil mixture

   d. Defective or improperly gapped breaker points

   e. Improper ignition timing

   f. Defective rotary valve

ENGINE FAILURE ANALYSIS

Overheating is the major cause of serious and expensive engine failures. It is important that each snowmobile owner understand all the causes of engine overheating and take the necessary precautions to avoid expensive overheating damage. Proper preventive maintenance and careful attention to all potential problem areas can often eliminate a serious malfunction before it happens.

Fuel

All Ski-Doo snowmobile engines rely on a proper fuel/oil mixture for engine lubrication. Always use an approved oil and mix the fuel carefully as described in Chapter One.

Gasoline must be of sufficiently high octane (90 or higher) to avoid "knocking" and "detonation."

Fuel/Air Mixture

Fuel/air mixture is determined by carburetor adjustment (Tillotson) or main jet selection (Mikuni). Always adjust carburetors carefully and pay particular attention to avoiding a "too lean" mixture.

Heat

Excessive external heat on the engine can be caused by the following:

   a. Hood louvers plugged with snow

   b. Damaged or plugged cylinder and head cooling fins

   c. Slipping or broken fan belt

   d. Damaged cooling fan or coolant pump

   e. Operating snowmobile in hot weather

   f. Plugged or restricted exhaust system

See **Figures 6 and 7** for examples of cylinder and piston scuffing caused by excessive heat.

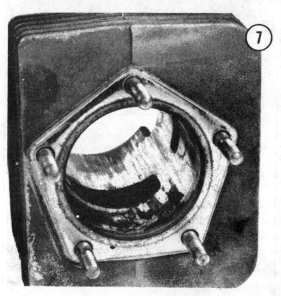

Dirt

Dirt is a potential problem for all snowmobiles. The air intake silencers on all models are not designed to filter incoming air. Avoid running snowmobiles in areas that are not completely snow covered.

Ignition Timing

Ignition timing that is too far advanced can cause "knocking" or "detonation." Timing that is too retarded causes excessive heat buildup in the cylinder exhaust port areas.

Spark Plugs

Spark plugs must be of a correct heat range. Too hot a heat range can cause preignition and detonation which can ultimately result in piston burn-through as shown in **Figure 8**.

Refer to Chapter Two for recommended spark plugs.

Preignition

Preignition is caused by excessive heat in the combustion chamber due to a spark plug of improper heat range and/or too lean a fuel mixture. See **Figure 9** for an example of a melted and scuffed piston caused by preignition.

Detonation (Knocking)

Knocking is caused by a "too lean" fuel mixture and/or "too low" octane fuel.

ELECTRICAL SYSTEM

The following items provide a starting point from which to troubleshoot electrical system malfunctions. The possible causes for each malfunction are listed in a logical sequence and in order of probability.

Ignition system malfunctions are outlined under *Engine Starting* and *Engine Performance,* covered earlier.

Lights Will Not Light

    a. Bulbs are burned out
    b. Loose electrical connections
    c. Defective switch
    d. Defective lighting coil

Bulbs Burn Out Rapidly

Incorrect bulb type

Lights Too Bright or Too Dim

Defective lighting coil

Discharged Battery

    a. Defective battery
    b. Low electrolyte level
    c. Dirty or loose electrical connections
    d. Defective lighting coil
    e. Defective rectifier

Cracked Battery Case

    a. Discharged battery allowed to freeze
    b. Improperly installed hold-down clamp
    c. Improperly attached battery cables

Starter Motor Does Not Operate

a. Loose electrical connections
b. Discharged battery
c. Defective starter solenoid
d. Defective starter motor
e. Defective ignition switch

Poor Starter Performance

a. Commutator or brushes worn, dirty, or oil soaked
b. Binding armature
c. Weak brush springs
d. Armature open, shorted, or grounded

POWER TRAIN

The following items provide a starting point from which to troubleshoot power train malfunctions. The possible causes for each malfunction are listed in order of probability. Also refer to *Drive Belt Wear Analysis,* later in this chapter.

Drive Belt Not Operating Smoothly in Drive Pulley

a. Face of drive pulley is rough, grooved, pitted, or scored
b. Defective drive belt

Uneven Drive Belt Wear

a. Misaligned drive and driven pulleys
b. Loose engine mounts

Glazed Drive Belt

a. Excessive slippage
b. Oil on pulley surfaces

Drive Belt Worn Narrow in One place

a. Excessive slippage caused by stuck track
b. Too high engine idle speed

Drive Belt Too Tight at Idle

a. Engine idle speed too fast
b. Distance between pulley incorrect
c. Belt length incorrect

Drive Belt Edge Cord Failure

a. Misaligned pulleys
b. Loose engine mounting bolts

Brake Not Holding Properly

a. Incorrect brake cable adjustment or air in hydraulic brake system
b. Brake lining or pucks worn
c. Oil saturated brake lining or pucks
d. Sheared key on brake pulley or disc

Brake Not Releasing Properly

a. Weak or broken return spring
b. Bent or damaged brake lever

Leaking Chaincase

a. Gaskets on drive shaft bearing flange
b. Cracked or broken chaincase

Rapid Chain and Sprocket Wear

a. Insufficient chaincase oil
b. Misaligned sprockets
c. Broken chain tension blocks

DRIVE BELT WEAR ANALYSIS

Uneven Belt Wear

Uneven belt wear on only one side as shown in **Figure 10** is usually caused by a loose engine mount or pulley misalignment. Also check for rough or scratched pulley surfaces.

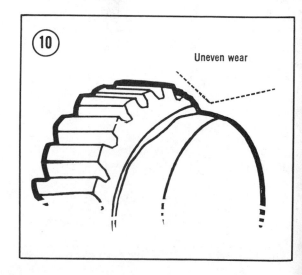

Uneven wear

Glazed Belt

A glazed or baked appearance on the edge of the belt as shown in **Figure 11** is usually the result of some mechanical difficulty. Pulley shafts may be rusted or the drive pulley may have worn or missing flyweights/rollers. Refer this type of belt wear to a dealer. He has the expertise to pinpoint the malfunction.

Worn Top Width

Excessive wear in the top width of the belt (**Figure 12**) can be caused by erratic drive pulley actuation or rough or scratched pulley surfaces. If all mechanical systems are functioning properly, the belt may just be worn out. Replace drive belt if its width is ⅛ in. (3mm) less than new. Refer to Chapter Seven.

Belt Worn In One Section

Spot wear such as shown in **Figure 13** is often caused by a frozen or too tight track. Check also for a too high idle speed, incorrect belt length, incorrect pulley distance, or a malfunction in the drive pulley.

Belt Edges Worn Concave

Concave edge wear as shown in **Figure 14** is caused by using an improper drive belt or roughness on pulley surfaces.

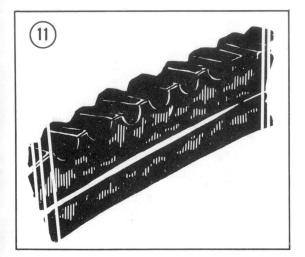

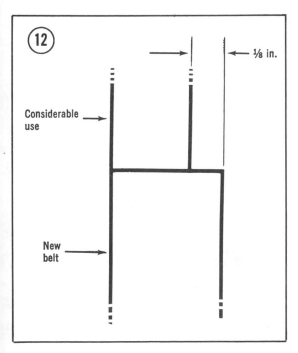

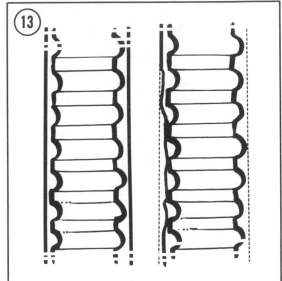

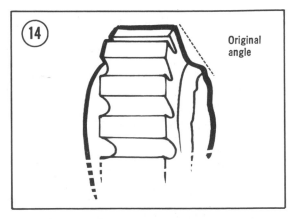

Belt Disintegration

Belt disintegration as illustrated in **Figure 15** is the result of excessive belt speed caused by using an improper drive belt or oil on pulley surfaces. Incorrect gear ratio may also cause belt disintegration. Refer malfunction to a dealer for his analysis.

Edge Cord Breakage

The type of edge cord breakage shown in **Figure 16** is usually caused by pulley misalignment. Refer to Chapter Seven for applicable pulley alignment procedure.

Flex Crack Between Cogs

Cracks appearing between belt cogs (**Figure 17**) generally indicate that the belt has lost its flexibility and must be replaced.

Sheared Drive Cogs

Sheared cogs as shown in **Figure 18** can be a result of improper belt installation as well as violent erratic drive pulley engagement. Enlist the help of a dealer to determine the full nature of the malfunction.

Belt "Flip-Over"

Drive belt "flip-over" at high speed (**Figure 19**) is usually caused by improper pulley alignment. Also check that the belt is the exact type specified for your machine.

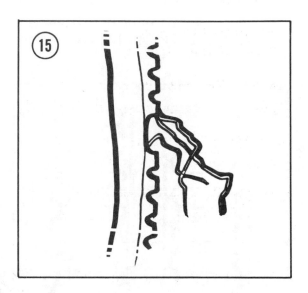

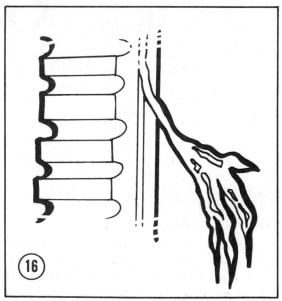

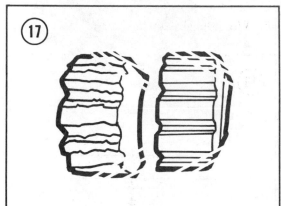

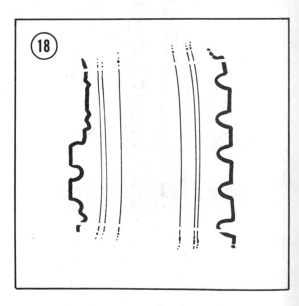

SKIS AND STEERING

The following items provide a starting point from which to troubleshoot ski and steering malfunctions. The possible causes for each malfunction are listed in order of probability.

Loose Steering

  a. Loose steering post bushing

  b. Loose tie rod ends

  c. Worn spindle bushings

  d. Stripped spindle splines

Unequal Steering

  a. Improperly adjusted tie rods

  b. Improperly installed steering arms

Rapid Ski Wear

  a. Skis misaligned

  b. Worn out ski runner shoes

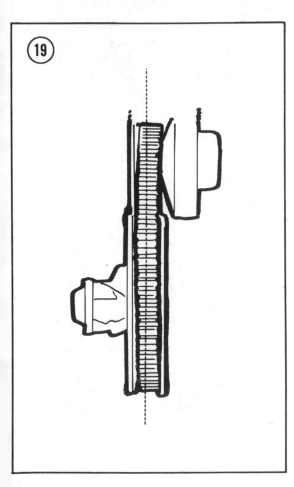

TRACK ASSEMBLY

The following items provide a starting point from which to troubleshoot track assembly malfunctions. The possible causes for each malfunction are listed in order of probability.

Frayed Track Edge

Track is misaligned.

Track Grooved on Inner Surface

  a. Track too tight

  b. Frozen bogie wheel(s)

  c. Frozen rear idle-shaft bearing

Track Driving Ratcheting

Track is too loose.

Rear Idlers Turning on Shaft

Rear idler shaft bearings are frozen.

Bogie Wheels Not Turning Freely

Bogie wheel bearing is defective.

Bogie Assemblies Not Pivoting Freely

Bogie tube and axle are bent.

TRACK WEAR ANALYSIS

The majority of track failures and abnormal wear patterns are caused by negligence, abuse, and poor maintenance. The following items illustrate typical examples. In all cases the damage could have been avoided by proper maintenance and good operator technique.

Obstruction Damage

Cuts, slashes, and gouges in the track surface are caused by hitting obstructions such as broken glass, sharp rocks, or buried steel. See **Figure 20**.

Worn Grouser Bars

Excessively worn grouser bars are caused by snowmobile operation over rough and non-snow covered terrain such as gravel roads and highway roadsides (**Figure 21**).

Lug Damage

Lug damage as shown in **Figure 22** is caused by lack of snow lubrication.

Ratcheting Damage

Insufficient track tension is a major cause of ratcheting damage to the top of the lugs. See **Figure 23**. Ratcheting damage can also be caused by too great a load and constant "jack-rabbit" starts.

Overtension Damage

Excessive track tension can cause too much friction on the wear bars. This friction causes the wear bars to melt and adhere to the track grouser bars. See **Figure 24**. An indication of this condition is a "sticky" track that has a tendency to "lock up."

Loose Track Damage

A track adjusted too loosely can cause the outer edge to flex excessively. This results in the

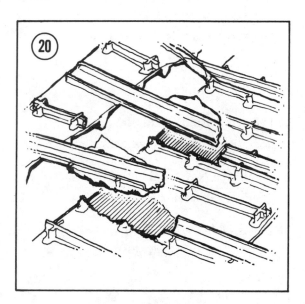

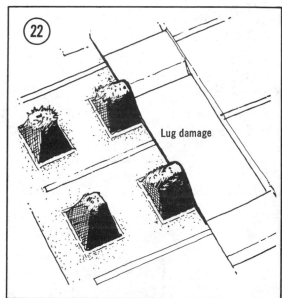

Lug damage

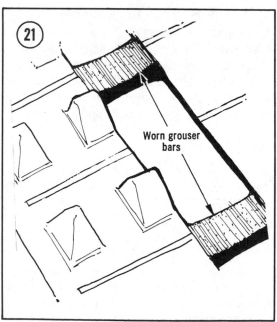

Worn grouser bars

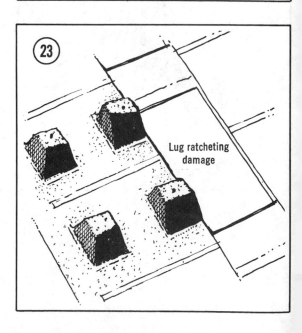

Lug ratcheting damage

type of damage shown in **Figure 25**. Excessive weight can also contribute to the damage.

Impact Damage

Impact damage as shown in **Figure 26** causes the track rubber to open and expose the cord. This frequently happens in more than one place. Impact damage is usually caused by riding on rough or frozen ground or ice. Insuf-

ficient track tension can allow the track to pound against the track stabilizers inside the tunnel.

Edge Damage

Edge damage as shown in **Figure 27** is usually caused by tipping the snowmobile on its side to clear the track and allowing the track edge to contact an abrasive surface.

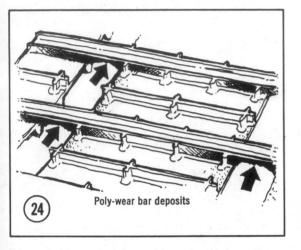

Poly-wear bar deposits

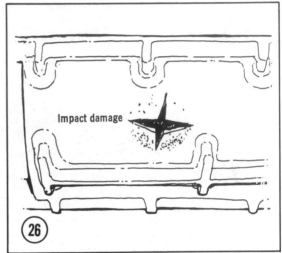

Impact damage

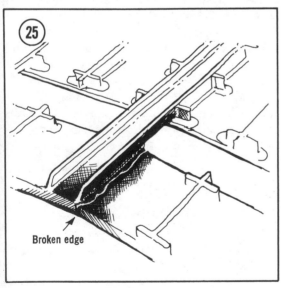

Broken edge

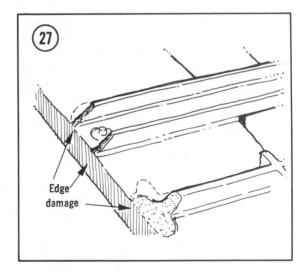

Edge damage

CHAPTER FOUR

ENGINE

Ski-Doo snowmobiles are equipped with single and twin cylinder 2-cycle engines. The high performance twin cylinder engines are equipped with rotary valves, all other engines use piston-porting.

All engines have ball or roller main crankshaft bearings and needle bearings on the lower and upper bearings of the connecting rods.

This chapter includes removal and repair procedures for most engine components. However, due to the special tools and expertise required, all crankshaft assembly inspection and alignment should be performed by an authorized dealer or competent machine shop. Some procedures in this chapter require the use of special tools. In all cases the special tools are illustrated and in many cases can be easily fabricated or substituted by a well-equipped home mechanic. However, each snowmobile owner must be honest with himself about his own supply of tools and expertise and avoid repair procedures that are not within his capabilities. It is often cheaper and easier in the long run to remove the engine and take it to an authorized dealer for required service and repair than to risk expensive damage if you do not have the proper tools and facilities for the necessary work.

TOP END
AND COMPLETE OVERHAUL

The following is an orderly sequence for removing and disassembling the engine to perform a top end overhaul or complete overhaul. Proceed to the applicable engine section and perform the procedures necessary in the order indicated to achieve desired level of disassembly for the necessary repairs. Tightening torques (**Table 1**), single cylinder engine specifications (**Table 2**), and twin cylinder engine specifications (**Table 3**) are found at the end of the chapter.

Top End Overhaul

a. Remove engine.
b. Remove fan housing and shrouds.
c. Remove flywheel and magneto assembly.
d. Remove cylinder head.
e. Remove cylinder, piston, and rings.
f. Perform component inspection.

Complete Overhaul

a. Perform top end overhaul.
b. Remove crankshaft assembly.
c. Perform component inspection.

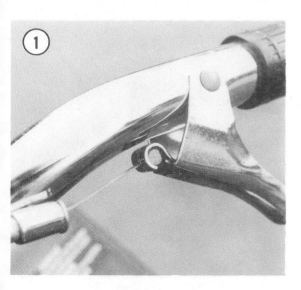

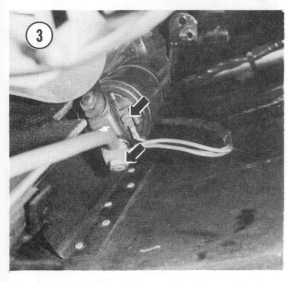

SINGLE CYLINDER ENGINES

Engine Removal/Installation

1. Disconnect brake and throttle cables and cable housings from handlebar and brake lever (**Figure 1**). On Elan models disconnect cable from handle plate and remove cable from engine bracket. Disconnect throttle cable from carburetor. Remove choke knob of necessary.

2. On all models except T'NT, remove console.

3. Remove pulley guard and drive belt as outlined in Chapter Seven.

4. Disconnect fuel lines from carburetor (**Figure 2**). Position lines up higher than level of tank to prevent tank from draining.

5. Disconnect all electrical connectors from engine. Tag wire locations to aid installation.

6. On electric start models, disconnect negative battery cable and disconnect solenoid and starter wires (**Figure 3**).

7. On applicable models, disconnect decompressor (compression release) knob from decompressor, and remove decompressor switch from holder.

8. Disconnect steering column from upper column as shown in **Figure 4**.

9. Remove engine mounting nuts and washers (**Figure 5**).

10. On Elan and T'NT models perform the following:

    a. Tilt upper column towards seat.

    b. Raise steering column and lift engine out from right side of machine.

11. On Olympique models, proceed as follows:

   a. Remove upper column.

   b. Remove engine from right side of machine.

12. Installation is the reverse of these steps. Keep the following points in mind:

   a. Torque nuts securing engine assembly as specified in **Table 1**.

   b. Adjust decompressor cable for ¹⁄₁₆ in. (1.6mm) free play between cable housing ferrule and valve lever (**Figure 6**).

   c. Adjust brakes as outlined in Chapter Two.

   d. Perform *Pulley Alignment* as outlined in Chapter Seven.

Exterior Component Removal/Installation

1. Remove air silencer, carburetor, and muffler.

2. Remove recoil starter and drive pulley.

3. Remove throttle cable bracket secured to engine. On models with 247cc engine, remove brake cable bracket from engine.

4. Remove electric starter on models so equipped.

5. Remove decompressor valve (compression release) from cylinder on models so equipped.

6. Remove engine mount from crankcase.

7. Installation is the reverse of these steps. Keep the following points in mind:

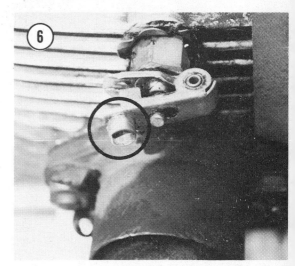

   a. Lower left screw in recoil starter on Olympique 335 E models also secures battery cable clamp.

   b. Torque decompressor valve to 10 ft.-lb. (1.4 mkg) and secure valve to cylinder by bending a section of locking and sealing sleeve over cylinder fin.

   c. Torque nuts securing engine mount to crankcase as specified in **Table 1**.

   d. When installing carburetor, assemble components in the following order: flange gasket, isolating flange, flange gasket, isolating sleeves, carburetor, isolating washers and nuts.

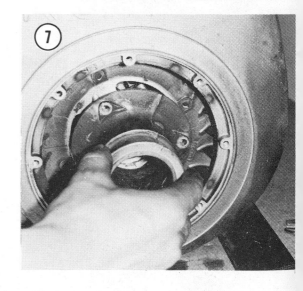

NOTE: *Be sure that the hole in plastic flange aligns with vacuum port on engine flange.*

Fan Cowl, Fan, and Magneto Assembly Removal/Installation

The following procedure requires the use of special tools to remove magneto plate/fan assembly. If special tools or locally fabricated equivalents are not available, refer task to an authorized dealer.

1. Remove engine and recoil starter.

2. Remove electric starter on models so equipped.

3. Remove nuts securing starting pulley to magneto plate (**Figure 7**) and remove pulley.

4. Remove fan cowl assembly from engine (**Figure 8**).

5. Using a hammer and small punch, bend back locking tab securing magneto nut.

6. Using special tool to hold fan, remove nut and washer securing magneto plate/fan housing assembly as shown in **Figure 9**.

7. Install special puller and tighten until magneto plate/fan assembly is removed from crankshaft (**Figure 10**).

> CAUTION
> *Always place magneto ring on a clean cloth or magneto may attract dirt and/or metal particles that can affect magneto efficiency.*

NOTE: *At this time electric starter gear or magneto plate can be removed from fan assembly if desired.*

8. Remove screws securing labyrinth ring to magneto assembly and remove ring (**Figure 11**).

9. Using a hammer and small punch, gently remove Woodruff key from crankshaft.

> CAUTION
> *Exercise care when key is removed or key and/or crankshaft may be damaged.*

10. Remove cam spring and washer from end of crankshaft (**Figure 12**).

11. Remove Allen screws securing magneto armature plate to engine (**Figure 13**). Disconnect wiring and remove armature plate. Tag wires to aid connection during installation.

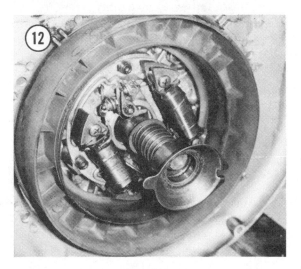

12. On electric start and T'NT 292 models, remove screws securing ignition coil and bracket and remove coil and bracket from engine.

13. Installation is the reverse of these steps. Keep the following points in mind:

CAUTION

Ensure that magneto wires are correctly positioned to avoid their being squeezed behind armature plate.

a. Lightly grease inner channel of cam with low temperature grease.

b. Be sure bevelled side of labyrinth ring is on top **(Figure 14)**.

c. Lightly grease spring seating of magneto ring plate with low temperature grease.

d. Turn crankshaft until Woodruff key is up and rotate cam until it is approximately 240° from key.

e. Torque magneto nut. See **Table 1**.

f. Perform engine timing as outlined in Chapter Two.

Cylinder Head, Cylinder, Piston, and Ring Removal

1. Remove engine and external components.

2. Remove fan and magneto assembly.

3. Remove nuts securing cylinder head (see **Figure 15**). To aid head removal, gently tap head with a rubber mallet. Remove head and discard old gasket.

4. Gently slide cylinder up over piston **(Figure 16)**.

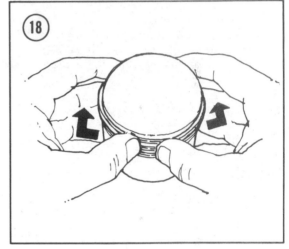

5. Note mark on piston indicating exhaust side of engine **(Figure 17)**. If no marks are visible, inscribe piston accordingly.

> NOTE: *If rings are going to be changed, but not piston, rings may now be removed. However if piston is going to be removed, leave old rings on piston to protect ring grooves until new rings are to be installed.*

6. Using a ring expander tool or your thumbs on each end of piston ring, gently expand ring and slide up and off piston. **(Figure 18)**.

7. Be sure piston is appropriately marked. Remove circlips from each end of piston pin **(Figure 19)**.

> NOTE: *Stuff clean rags around connecting rod in crankcase to help prevent circlips from dropping into crankcase.*

Using a piston pin removal tool or an appropriately sized wooden dowel, gently remove pin from piston and connecting rod.

CAUTION
Exercise care when removing pin to avoid damaging connecting rod needle bearings. If a wooden dowel is used to drive out piston pin, ensure that piston is properly supported so that lateral shock is not transmitted to lower connecting rod bearing, otherwise rod and/or bearing damage may occur.

Remove needle bearing from connecting rod.

8. Refer to *Component Inspection* and inspect cylinder, piston, pin, and rings.

Cylinder Head, Cylinder, Piston, and Ring Installation

1. Lubricate piston pin needle bearings with oil and insert bearings into connecting rod.

2. Slide piston over connecting rod. Be sure that mark or letters AUS face exhaust side of engine (**Figure 17**).

3. Using piston pin installation tool or appropriately sized wooden dowel, install piston pin through piston and rod end.

> CAUTION
> *Exercise care when installing pin to avoid damage to connecting rod needle bearing. If a wooden dowel is used to drive in piston pin, ensure that piston is properly supported so that lateral shock is not transmitted to lower connecting rod bearing, otherwise rod and/or bearing damage may occur.*

4. Secure piston pin to piston with circlips. When circlip is properly installed in groove, rotate circlip so gap in clip is not directly on notch break of piston (**Figure 19**).

> NOTE: *Stuff clean rags around connecting rod in crankcase to help prevent circlip from dropping into crankcase.*

> CAUTION
> *If possible use new circlips to secure piston pin. If old circlips are used they must snap securely into grooves in piston. A weak circlip could become disengaged during engine operation and cause severe engine damage.*

5. Using a ring expander tool or your thumbs on each end of piston ring, gently expand ring and slide over piston in ring groove (**Figure 18**). Install ring in bottom groove first. Be sure that ring groove clearance is within tolerance as outlined in *Component Inspection*.

> NOTE: *Be sure that ring end "V" is properly positioned in ring groove.*

6. Install new cylinder base gasket.

7. Thoroughly lubricate piston, rings, and cylinder bore with engine oil.

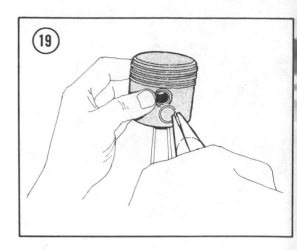

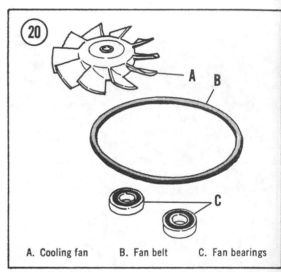

A. Cooling fan   B. Fan belt   C. Fan bearings

8. Position 2 thin, wooden supports such as tongue depressors under piston for piston support, and rotate crankshaft so that piston sits on wooden supports.

9. Compress rings with a suitable ring compressor or your fingers and carefully slide cylinder down over piston.

> CAUTION
> *Crankshaft, connecting rod, and piston must rotate freely. Any "roughness," "tight spots," or "metallic noises" must be corrected before engine is run or serious damage may result.*

10. Install cylinder head with a new head gasket. Torque head nuts in a crisscross pattern to 10 ft.-lb. (1.4 mkg) then torque as specified in **Table 1**.

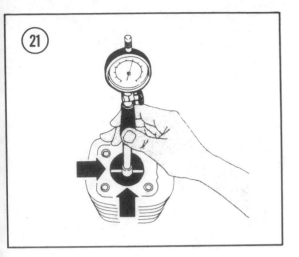

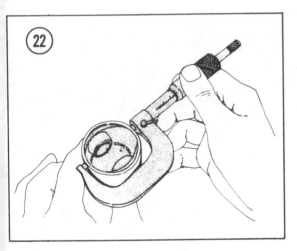

11. Install fan and magneto assembly.

12. Install external components on engine and install engine.

Crankshaft Assembly
Removal/Installation

Crankshaft assembly, removal, inspection, service and repair, including crankcase bearing and seal replacement, should be referred to an authorized dealer or competent machine shop. They are equipped with the necessary special tools and expertise to perform the work.

COMPONENT INSPECTION

Some of the following inspection procedures require the use of micrometers and dial indicators for precise wear analysis. If such precision tools are not available, refer inspection procedures to an authorized dealer or competent machine shop. Refer to **Table 2 or 3** (end of chapter) for engine component dimensions and wear tolerances.

Cooling Fan and Belt

1. Inspect fan (**Figure 20**) for cracked, broken, or damaged fins. Dress nicks or dents with a file. If fins are cracked or broken, fan must be replaced.

2. Inspect fan bearings for wear or looseness. Replace if necessary.

3. Inspect fan belt and replace if frayed, stretched, or deteriorated.

Cylinder Taper and Out-of-Round

1. To check for cylinder taper perform the following:

   a. Refer to **Figure 21** and measure cylinder diameter ⅝ in. (16mm) from top of cylinder down to just below intake port.

   b. On rotary valve models, measure just below auxiliary transfer port, facing exhaust port.

   c. If cylinder taper exceeds 0.003 in. (0.08mm) rebore and hone or replace the cylinder.

2. To check cylinder for out-of-round measure cylinder ½-⅝ in. (13-16mm) from top of cylinder. If cylinder out-of-round exceeds 0.002 in. (0.05mm) rebore and hone or replace the cylinder.

Piston-to-Cylinder Clearance

1. With a micrometer measure piston skirt at right angles to piston pin 5/16 in. (8mm) from bottom of piston (**Figure 22**).

2. Measure cylinder bore ½-⅝ in. (13-16mm) below top of cylinder (**Figure 21**).

3. Subtract the piston measurement from the cylinder measurement to obtain piston-to-cylinder clearance. If clearance exceeds wear limit specified in **Table 2 or 3** piston must be replaced. It may be necessary to bore cylinder to the next oversize.

Piston-to-Cylinder Clearance (Quick Method)

With the cylinder upside down on a workbench install the piston (without rings) into the cylinder bore. Refer to **Figure 23** and insert the thickest possible feeler gauge between the piston and cylinder wall on the intake side. If a feeler gauge larger than wear limit specified in **Table 3** can be inserted between piston and cylinder bore, a new piston or rebore is necessary.

Honing Cylinder Bore

If cylinder is within wear tolerance, but lightly scored, hone by running a fine stone cylinder hone lightly in cylinder (**Figure 24**).

Clean cylinder thoroughly with detergent and water to remove all particles.

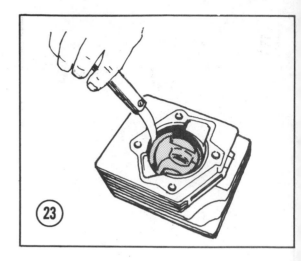

Cylinder Head

1. Carefully scrape carbon from cylinder head and exhaust ports of cylinders. Use a soft metal (nonferrous) scraper to avoid damage. A wooden spatula works well for cleaning exhaust ports.

2. Use a spark plug tap (14mm or 18mm) to clean carbon from spark plug threads in cylinder head, if required.

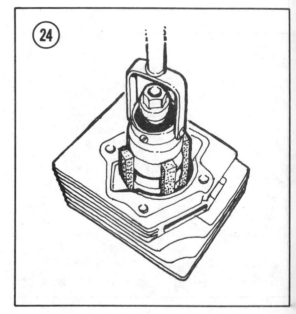

Crankcase

1. Inspect crankcase sealing surfaces (**Figure 25**) for deep scratches, scoring, or pitting.

2. Inspect bearing and oil seal retaining inserts for wear, scoring, or conditions that could cause leaks.

3. Replace crankcase halves if damaged. Crankcase halves are available only in a matched set — not individually.

Piston Ring End Gap

Slide piston ring into cylinder between transfer port and intake port. On rotary valve engines, position ring just below the transfer ports. Use piston ring to slide ring into position to ensure that ring is perfectly square inside bore. Measure ring end gap with feeler gauge as shown in **Figure 26**. Refer to **Table 2 or 3** and replace ring if end gap is excessive.

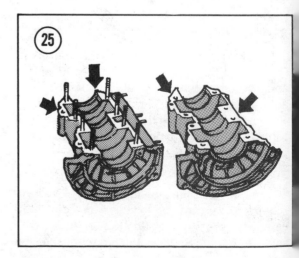

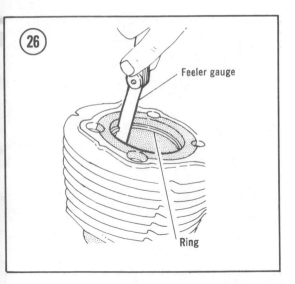

Feeler gauge

Ring

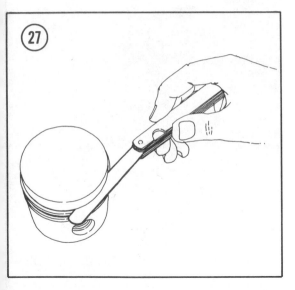

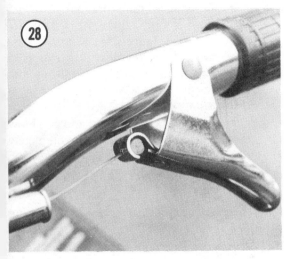

Piston Ring Groove Clearance

With a feeler gauge check side clearance of rings in grooves (**Figure 27**). If clearance is greater than 0.008 in. (0.20mm), replace the piston and rings.

Crankshaft and Connecting Rod

Refer all clearance inspection, service, and repair work on crankshaft assembly to an authorized dealer or competent machine shop.

1. Inspect threads on each end of crankshaft. Inspect keyway on flywheel end and taper on each end of crankshaft for scoring or wear.

2. Inspect ball bearings for wear, free movement, and security.

3. Inspect seals for wear or damage.

TWIN CYLINDER ENGINES

The basic procedures for removal, disassembly, and repair of twin cylinder engines are the same. Specific differences will be noted in the procedures where necessary.

Engine Removal/Installation
(Mid-Engine Models)

1. Remove pulley guard and drive belt. Remove console on Olympique models.

2. Disconnect brake and throttle cables and housings from handlebar and brake lever (**Figure 28**).

3. Disconnect kill button from handlebar on models so equipped.

4. Disconnect all electrical connections from engine. Tag all wire locations to aid installation.

5. Remove air silencer on models so equipped (**Figure 29**) and disconnect fuel lines from carburetor. On T'NT models, disconnect springs securing muffler to engine.

6. Disconnect steering column retaining bracket from upper column (**Figure 30**).

7. Remove nuts securing engine mount to frame (**Figure 31**).

8. Lift engine from machine.

> NOTE: *On T'NT models, tilt upper column toward seat and lean engine to the*

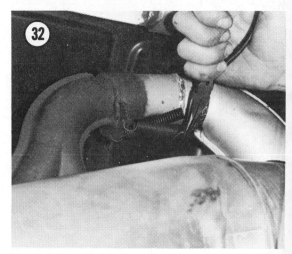

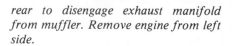

rear to disengage exhaust manifold from muffler. Remove engine from left side.

9. Installation is the reverse of these steps. Keep the following points in mind:

a. Torque engine mounting nuts to 22-25 ft.-lb. (3.0-3.5 mkg).

b. Adjust brake as outlined in Chapter Two.

c. Perform *Pulley Alignment* as outlined in Chapter Seven.

Engine Removal/Installation (Front Engine Models)

1. Remove pulley guard and drive belt.

2. Remove muffler and air silencer (**Figures 32 and 33**).

3. On liquid cooled models perform the following:

a. Remove coolant tank pressure cap and disconnect bypass hose from cylinder head fitting (**Figure 34**). Route bypass hose into a clean container if coolant is to be retained. Block off bypass fitting and keep bypass hose as low as possible to drain the system.

b. Cover filler neck with your hand and blow through tank vent tube to completely drain the system (**Figure 35**).

c. Disconnect coolant hoses from the engine.

4. If necessary disconnect the cab retaining cable.

5. Disconnect primer and impulse lines.

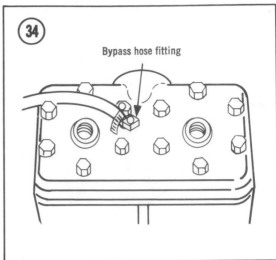

Bypass hose fitting

4

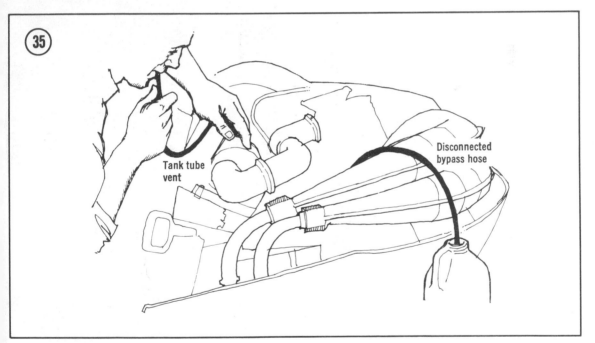

Tank tube vent

Disconnected bypass hose

6. If carburetor is to be removed with the engine, disconnect the throttle cable and fuel lines.

7. If carburetor is to be removed, perform the following:

   a. Remove nuts securing carburetor and slide carburetor off mounting studs **(Figure 36)**.

   b. With fuel lines and cables still attached, swing carburetor out of the way **(Figure 37)**.

8. On rotary valve models, disconnect oil line from bottom of oil reservoir and drain oil from reservoir and crankcase. Disconnect upper oil vent line.

> NOTE: *On models equipped with 444 liquid cooled engines, it is not necessary to disconnect oil tank lines prior to engine removal. Tank can be drained and removed after engine removal.*

9. Remove recoil starter.

10. Disconnect all electrical connections (see **Figure 38**). Tag wire locations to aid installation. On models equipped with electric starter, disconnect ground cable (−) from battery before disconnecting other wires (**Figure 39**).

11. If necessary, remove drive pulley as outlined in Chapter Seven.

12. Remove nuts securing engine mount to machine (**Figure 40**) and lift out engine.

13. Installation is the reverse of these steps. Keep the following points in mind:

    a. Torque engine mounting nuts to 22-25 ft.-lb. (3.0-3.5 mkg).

    b. Perform *Pulley Alignment* as outlined in Chapter Seven.

    c. On rotary valve models top off oil reservoir as outlined in Chapter Two.

Flywheel and Magneto Removal/Installation

The following procedure requires the use of special tools to remove the flywheel and magneto assembly. If special tools or locally fabricated equivalents are not available, refer task to an authorized dealer.

1. Remove engine.

2. Remove muffler and recoil starter if not previously removed.

3. Remove nuts securing fan belt pulley/starter pulley to magneto ring plate. Remove belt and pulley (**Figure 41**).

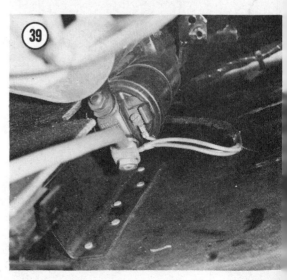

4. Using a hammer and a small punch, straighten locking tab behind magneto unit (**Figure 42**).

5. Install special crankshaft holding tool to magneto ring plate using nuts and washers from fan belt/starter pulley (**Figure 43**).

If special crankshaft holding tool is not available, perform the following:

a. Insert a length of rope such as recoil starter rope into the spark plug hole.

b. Slowly rotate crankshaft counterclockwise until the piston bears against the rope.

On 354 and 503 engines the crankshaft can be held by using the crankshaft locking bolt (**Figure 44**). Locate magneto side piston at TDC and install bolt into hole in crankshaft. On 503 models remove the aluminum spacer from under the bolt. *Do not* overtighten the bolt as it does not hold by pressure against the crankshaft.

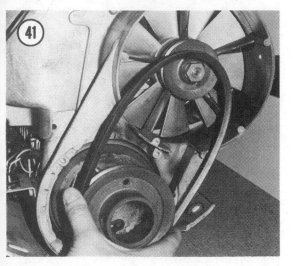

> NOTE: *On electric start engines that are being disassembled for major engine work, use special puller and remove starter gear complete with shims and spacers.*
>
> *Remove nuts securing starter motor and bracket to engine and remove starter and bracket.*

6. Remove magneto nut.

7. Install flywheel puller (**Figure 45**) and

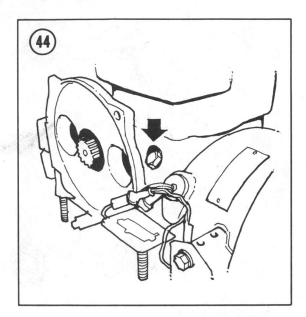

remove magneto housing (**Figure 46**). Remove puller and holding tool from magneto ring plate.

.8. If desired, on models so equipped, remove flat end screw and remove centrifugal advance weight and spring from magneto ring plate (**Figure 47**).

> NOTE: *If further disassembly is desired, remove 4 Allen screws and remove ring plate from magneto ring.*

CAUTION
Always place magneto ring on a clean cloth or magneto may attract dirt and/or metal particles that can affect magneto efficiency.

9. On models equipped with one-piece cooling shroud, perform the following:

  a. Remove bolts and washers securing shroud to cylinder head spacer nut.

  b. Remove 3 screws securing fan housing to shroud and remove shroud.

10. On models equipped with 2-piece cooling shroud, perform the following:

  a. Remove bolts securing exhaust side shroud.

  b. Remove 2 screws securing fan housing to exhaust side shroud (**Figure 48**).

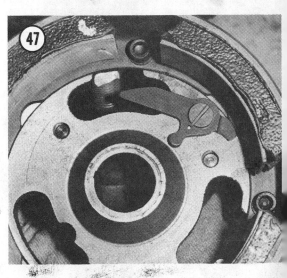

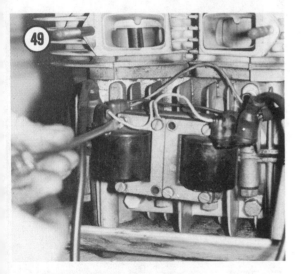

4

   c. Remove nut securing shroud stud and remove stud and shroud.

11. On models equipped with engine console, remove Allen screws securing console to cooling shroud and remove console.

12. Remove throttle cable bracket from shroud on models so equipped.

13. Disconnect wiring from ignition coils and remove coils (**Figure 49**). Tag wires to aid installation.

14. Remove coil bracket from crankcase on models equipped with one-piece cooling shroud (**Figure 50**).

15. On models equipped with 2-piece shroud, remove screws securing fan housing to intake side shroud and complete shroud removal.

16. Remove 4 nuts and washers securing fan housing (**Figure 51**) to engine and remove housing. If repair of fan housing is necessary, refer to *Cooling Fan Disassembly*.

17. Press in and hold magneto cam toward armature plate and tap out crankshaft Woodruff key with a hammer and small punch. Remove cam with spring and washer from crankshaft (**Figure 52**).

18. Remove 2 nuts or Allen screws securing armature plate and remove plate (**Figure 53**).

19. Installation is the reverse of these steps. Keep the following points in mind:

   a. Be sure armature plate wiring is routed through notch in fan housing and shroud

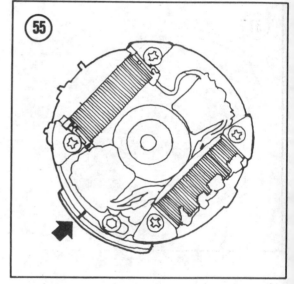

and rubber grommet is in proper position (**Figure 54**).

b. Lightly grease inner channel of cam with low temperature grease.

c. Lightly grease spring seating of magneto ring plate with low temperature grease.

d. Rotate crankshaft until Woodruff key is up and rotate cam clockwise until notch is 45° from key.

e. When installing magneto plate, align crankcase and armature plate marks (**Figure 55**) for preliminary timing adjustment. For 354 engines, position armature plate on crankcase with retaining screws in the middle of plate slots as shown in **Figure 56**.

f. Check magneto coil air gap (distance between end of coil and magnet) with a feeler gauge as shown in **Figure 57**. For 354 engines, check gap as shown in **Figure 58**. Refer to **Table 4** for air gap specifications.

g. Torque the magneto nut as specified in **Table 1**.

h. On models equipped with one-piece cooling shroud, install ignition coil bracket before mounting coils.

i. On 1978 and later models equipped with 440 engines, install fan shroud bolts as shown in **Figure 59**.

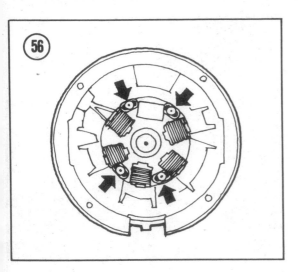

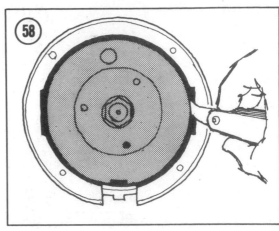

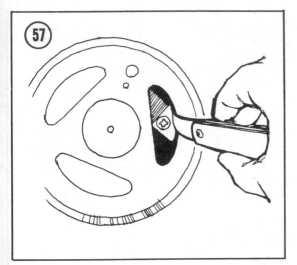

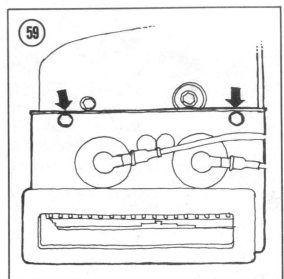

4

Table 4   MAGNETO AIR GAP SPECIFICATIONS

Engine	Air Gap
247; 302 singles	0.010-0.015 in. (0.25-0.38mm)
354 twin	0.040-0.063 in. (1.0-1.6mm)
All other twins	0.012-0.018 in. (0.30-0.45mm)

j. Perform *Fan Belt Adjustment*.

k. Perform ignition timing as outlined in Chapter Two.

Cylinder Head, Cylinder, Piston, and Ring Removal

Refer to **Figures 60 and 61** for typical examples of air and liquid cooled top end components.

1. Remove engine.

2. Remove flywheel, magneto assembly, and fan housing with cooling shrouds.

3. Remove intake manifold, gaskets, and flanges (**Figure 62**). Remove air deflector if so equipped (**Figure 63**).

4. Remove exhaust manifolds (**Figure 64**). Unscrew exhaust sockets from cylinders on engines so equipped (**Figure 65**).

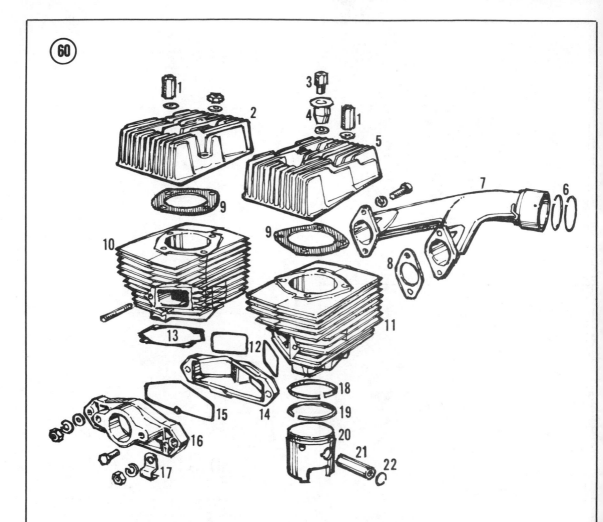

60

TYPICAL AIR COOLED TOP END

1. Distance nut
2. Cylinder head (P.T.O.)
3. Distance nut (short)
4. Support sleeve
5. Cylinder head (mag.)
6. Sealing ring
7. Exhaust manifold
8. Exhaust gasket
9. Cylinder head gasket
10. Cylinder (P.T.O.)
11. Cylinder (mag.)

12. Gasket
13. Gasket (cylinder/crankcase)
14. Intake manifold
15. Gasket
16. Intake cover
17. H.T. cable bracket
18. L-trapez ring
19. Rectangular ring
20. Piston
21. Gudgeon pin
22. Circlip

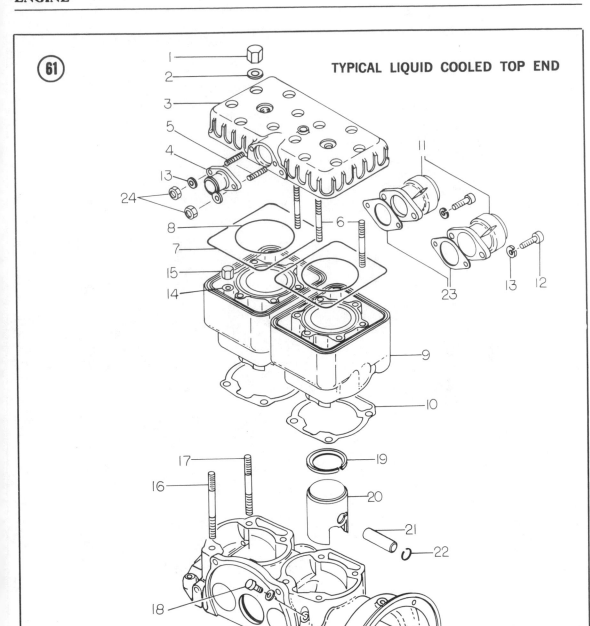

TYPICAL LIQUID COOLED TOP END

61

4

1. Capnut	7. Gasket	13. Lockwasher	19. L-ring
2. Flat washer	8. Gasket (O-ring)	14. Flat washer	20. Piston
3. Cylinder head	9. Cylinder	15. Capnut	21. Gudgeon pin
4. Coolant outlet collar	10. Cylinder/crankcase gasket	16. Cylinder stud (79mm)	22. Circlip
5. Stud	11. Exhaust socket	17. Cylinder stud (104mm)	23. Exhaust gasket
6. Stud (head)	12. Capscrew	18. Bolt	24. Nut

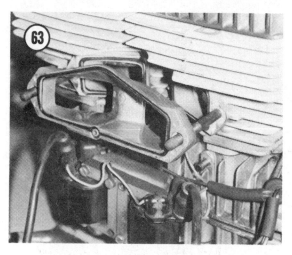

NOTE: *Cylinder installation requires that cylinders be properly aligned before head bolts are tightened. This is accomplished by first installing the intake and/or exhaust manifolds. On models with exhaust sockets and/or twin carburetors, proper alignment cannot be achieved without the use of an alignment tool. Such a tool can easily be locally fabricated from strap or angle iron and drilled to exactly match the manifold studs (Figure 66). If it is necessary to locally fabricate such a tool, do so before head bolts are loosened in order for the tool to exactly represent correct cylinder alignment.*

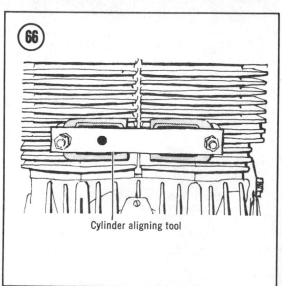

Cylinder aligning tool

5. Gradually loosen, in a crisscross pattern, then remove nuts securing cylinder heads

to be removed, leave old rings on pistons to protect ring grooves until new rings are to be installed.

(Figure 67). Note location of long nuts to aid installation. To aid head removal, gently tap head with a rubber mallet. Remove heads and discard old gaskets **(Figure 68).**

6. Gently slide cylinders up over pistons **(Figure 69).**

7. Note mark on each piston indicating exhaust side of engine **(Figure 70).** If no marks are visible, inscribe them accordingly. Also ensure that pistons are marked "1" and "2" since they are not interchangeable, if they are not to be replaced with new ones.

   NOTE: *If rings are going to be changed, but not pistons, rings may now be removed. However, if pistons are going*

8. Using a ring expander tool or your thumbs on each end of piston ring, gently expand ring and slide up and off piston **(Figure 71).**

9. Be sure pistons are appropriately marked. Remove circlips from each end of piston pins **(Figure 72).**

   NOTE: *Stuff clean rags around connecting rods in crankcase to help prevent circlips from dropping into crankcase.*

Using a piston pin removal tool or an appropriately sized wooden dowel, gently remove pins from piston and connecting rod **(Figure 73).**

CAUTION
Exercise care when removing pins to avoid damaging connecting rod needle bearings. If a wooden dowel is used to drive out piston pins, ensure that piston is properly supported so lateral shock is not transmitted to lower connecting rod bearing, otherwise rod and/or bearing damage may occur.

Remove needle bearings from connecting rods (**Figure 74**).

10. Refer to *Component Inspection* and inspect cylinders, pistons, pins, and rings.

Cylinder Head, Cylinder, Piston and Ring Installation

1. Lubricate piston pin needle bearings with oil and insert bearings into connecting rods.

2. Slide piston over connecting rod. Be sure that the mark or letters AUS face exhaust side of engine (**Figure 70**).

3. Using piston pin installation tool or appropriately sized wooden dowel, install piston pins through piston and rod ends (**Figure 73**).

CAUTION
Exercise care when installing pins to avoid damage to connecting rod needle bearings. If a wooden dowel is used to drive in piston pins, ensure that piston is properly supported so lateral shock is not transmitted to lower connecting rod bearing; otherwise rod and/or bearing damage may occur.

4. Secure piston pins to pistons with circlips. When circlip is properly installed in groove,

rotate circlip so gap in clip is not directly on notch break of piston (**Figure 75**).

> NOTE: *Stuff clean rags around connecting rods in crankcase to help prevent circlip from dropping into crankcase.*

CAUTION
If possible, use new circlips to secure piston pins. If old circlips are used, they must snap securely into grooves in pistons. A weak circlip could become disengaged during engine operation and cause severe engine damage.

5. Using a ring expander tool, or your thumbs on each end of piston ring, gently expand ring

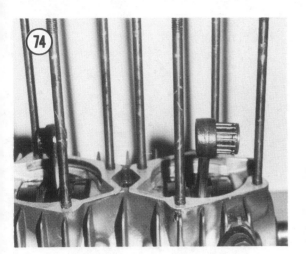

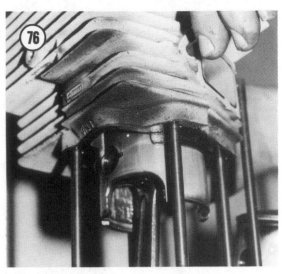

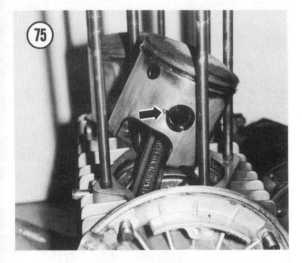

and slide over piston into ring groove (**Figure 71**). Install ring in bottom groove first. Be sure that ring groove clearance is within tolerance as outlined in *Component Inspection*.

> NOTE: *Be sure ring end "V" is properly positioned in ring groove.*

6. Install new cylinder base gaskets.

7. Thoroughly lubricate pistons, rings, and cylinder bores with engine oil.

8. Install cylinder over studs. Ensure that exhaust ports face exhaust side of engine. Compress rings with your fingers and slide cylinders down over piston (**Figure 76**).

> CAUTION
> *Cylinders must be properly aligned before head nuts are tightened or serious engine damage may result.*

9. On liquid-cooled models, keep the following points in mind:

   a. Cylinder stud length must be correct or the cap nuts will not tighten completely. Refer to **Figure 77** for 354 engines and **Figure 78** for 444 engines. If stud length is excessive, washers must be added under cap nuts to prevent nuts from bottoming on studs.

   b. Longer threaded portion of studs should be screwed into crankcase.

   c. On 354 engines, temporarily install cylinder head to align both cylinders. Torque cylinder nuts in a crisscross pattern to 12 ft.-lb. (1.6 mkg).

10. Install intake and exhaust manifolds with new gaskets on cylinders. On models with twin carburetors or exhaust sockets, install alignment tool as described in removal procedure (**Figure 66**). Tighten nuts securing manifolds and/or alignment tool.

11. Install cylinder heads with new head gaskets. On liquid-cooled models, apply silicone sealant around studs and washer seats before installing head cap nuts. Install head nuts making sure long and short nuts are properly positioned (**Figure 79**).

12. On air-cooled models, tighten head nuts in a crisscross pattern, each head separately. Refer to **Figure 80** for liquid-cooled models. Torque all nuts to 10 ft.-lb. (1.4 mkg) then to value specified in **Table 1**.

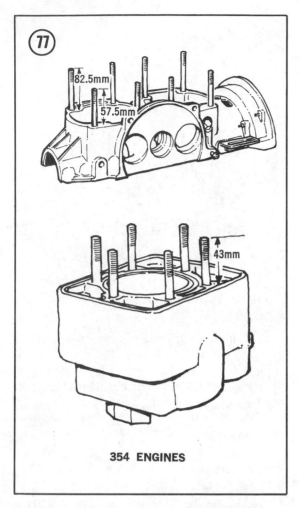

354 ENGINES

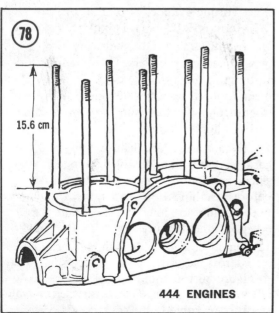

444 ENGINES

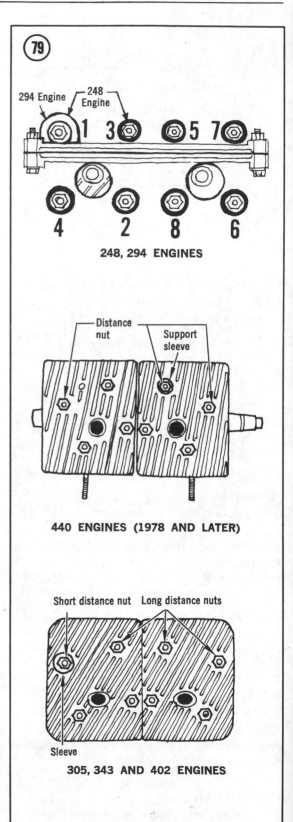

248, 294 ENGINES

440 ENGINES (1978 AND LATER)

305, 343 AND 402 ENGINES

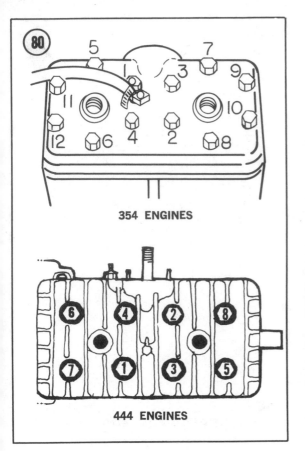

354 ENGINES

444 ENGINES

13. Install exhaust sockets or exhaust manifold. Shorter socket is installed on the PTO (power take off) side of the engine.

14. Install intake manifold, flywheel, magneto assembly, and fan housing with cooling shrouds.

15. Install engine.

Crankshaft Assembly Removal

Refer to **Figure 81** for a typical crankshaft assembly.

1. Remove cylinder heads, cylinders and pistons.

2. On rotary valve models perform *Rotary Valve Removal*.

3. Remove engine mount from crankcase if not previously performed (**Figure 82**).

4. Remove electric starter on models so equipped (**Figure 83**).

5. Remove nuts securing crankcase halves together.

6. Tap upper crankcase half lightly with a soft mallet and separate crankcase halves (**Figure 84**).

CAUTION
Never attempt to pry crankcase halves apart with screwdriver or similar object or crankcase sealing surface will be damaged.

7. Gently lift up and remove crankcase assembly (**Figure 85**).

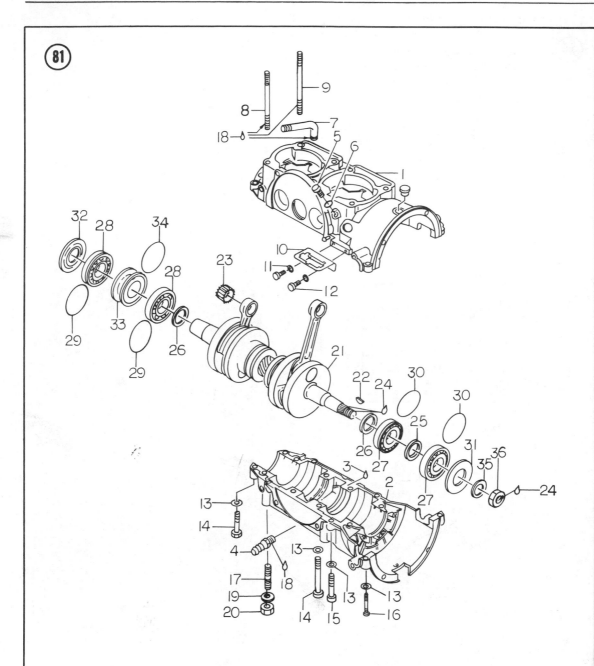

TYPICAL CRANKSHAFT ASSEMBLY

1. Crankcase (upper half)
2. Crankcase (lower half)
3. Crankcase sealant
4. Oil fitting
5. Bolt (M8 x 16)
6. Sealing ring
7. Angular tube (oil)
8. Cylinder stud (79mm)
9. Cylinder stud (104mm)
10. Junction block support
11. Lockwasher
12. Screw
13. Lockwasher
14. Bolt
15. Capscrew
16. Bolt
17. Stud
18. Loctite 242
19. Lockwasher
20. Nut
21. Crankshaft
22. Woodruff key
23. Needle cage bearing
24. Loctite 242
25. Distance ring (2mm)
26. Distance ring
27. Bearing
28. Bearing
29. O-ring
30. O-ring
31. Oil seal (mag.)
32. Oil seal (P.T.O.)
33. Labyrinth sleeve
34. O-ring
35. Lockwasher
36. Nut

8. Perform crankshaft assembly and crankcase inspection as outlined in *Component Inspection*. Refer all crankcase assembly repair and service work to an authorized dealer or competent machine shop. They are equipped with the necessary special tools and expertise for the task.

Crankshaft Assembly Installation

1. Check the condition of O-rings on outer bearing races. The O-rings are necessary to keep the outer bearing races from turning in the crankcase. Replace O-rings if necessary.

> NOTE: *On 503 engines the O-rings are replaced by rubber buttons.*

2. Install crankshaft assembly into lower crankcase half. Thoroughly lubricate crankshaft and bearings with engine oil.

> CAUTION
> *If crankshaft and/or crankcase has been repaired or replaced, ensure that end play is properly set by an authorized dealer or machine shop. See Table 3.*

3. Check that crankcase sealing surfaces are clean and not damaged. Apply an even coat of silicone rubber adhesive to sealing surfaces on both crankcase halves. Make sure no rubber adhesive runs into crankcase.

4. Install upper crankcase half. Check that the seals are correctly positioned and are not cocked down.

5. Install nuts, flat washers, and lockwashers and tighten evenly in sequence (**Figure 86**).

Torque nuts as specified in **Table 1**. Keep the following points in mind:

  a. On 245, 345, 346, 396, and 436 engines, spring washers are *not* installed on last 2 magneto side studs.

  b. On 248cc and 294cc engines, torque 2 smaller nuts on magneto side to 9 ft.-lb. (1.2 mkg).

  c. On 354 engines, torque 2 smaller bolts on magneto side to 10 ft.-lb. (1.3 mkg).

Rotary Valve Removal/Installation

Refer to **Figure 87** for a typical rotary valve assembly.

4

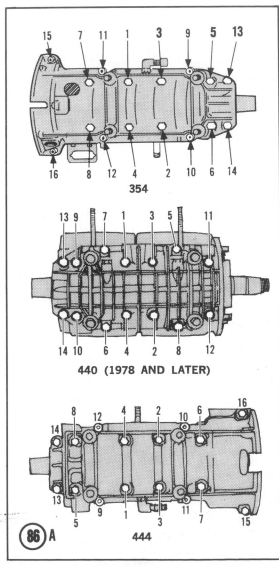

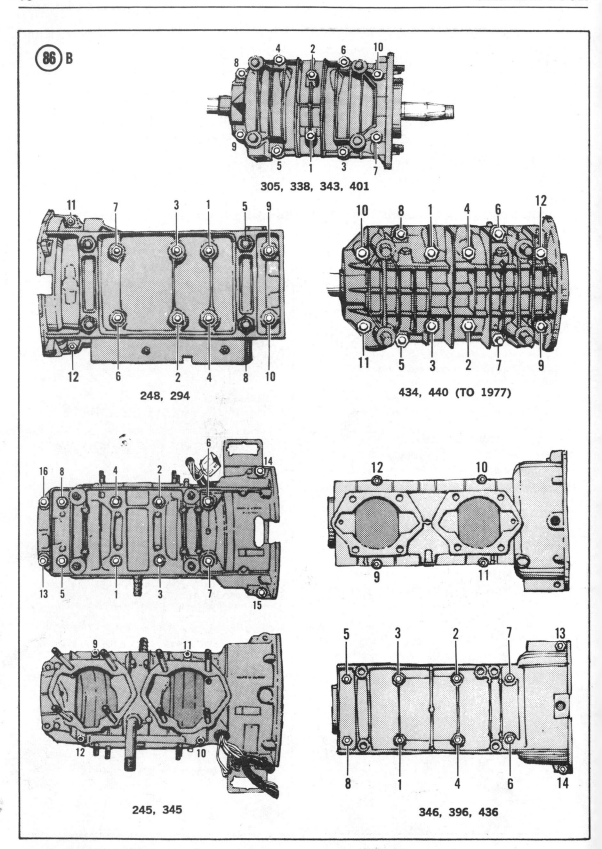

86 B

305, 338, 343, 401

248, 294

434, 440 (TO 1977)

245, 345

346, 396, 436

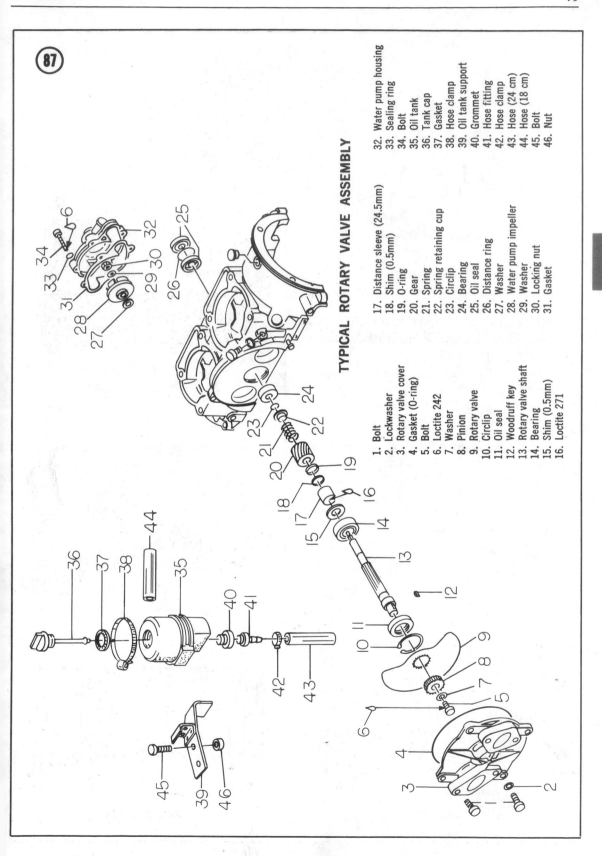

TYPICAL ROTARY VALVE ASSEMBLY

1. Bolt
2. Lockwasher
3. Rotary valve cover
4. Gasket (O-ring)
5. Bolt
6. Loctite 242
7. Washer
8. Pinion
9. Rotary valve
10. Circlip
11. Oil seal
12. Woodruff key
13. Rotary valve shaft
14. Bearing
15. Shim (0.5mm)
16. Loctite 271

17. Distance sleeve (24.5mm)
18. Shim (0.5mm)
19. O-ring
20. Gear
21. Spring
22. Spring retaining cup
23. Circlip
24. Bearing
25. Oil seal
26. Distance ring
27. Washer
28. Water pump impeller
29. Washer
30. Locking nut
31. Gasket

32. Water pump housing
33. Sealing ring
34. Bolt
35. Oil tank
36. Tank cap
37. Gasket
38. Hose clamp
39. Oil tank support
40. Grommet
41. Hose fitting
42. Hose clamp
43. Hose (24 cm)
44. Hose (18 cm)
45. Bolt
46. Nut

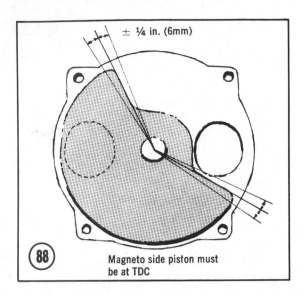

± ¼ in. (6mm)

88 Magneto side piston must be at TDC

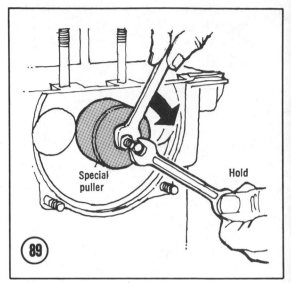

Special puller Hold

89

1. Remove carburetors and rotary valve cover. Note location of large O-ring gasket behind rotary valve cover.

2. Mark outside of valve disc with a felt tip pen to assist valve installation. Remove screw and washer retaining valve disc and remove disc.

3. To install valve disc, perform the following:

a. Rotate magneto side piston to TDC (top dead center). Use dial indicator-type timing gauge as described in Chapter One.

b. Position rotary valve on gear so edges align within ¼ in. (6mm) of timing marks on each side (**Figure 88**).

   NOTE: *If timing marks are not visible, perform Rotary Valve Timing.*

c. Rotary valve disc is asymmetrical. Position each side of valve disc on gear to determine position in which greater alignment accuracy can be achieved.

4. If rotary valve shaft assembly removal is desired, perform the following:

a. Remove circlip securing shaft assembly (10, **Figure 87**).

b. On liquid-cooled models remove water pump housing and water pump impeller.

c. Install special puller (**Figure 89**) and remove shaft assembly. If puller is not available, refer task to an authorized dealer. Refer shaft component inspection and repair to a dealer.

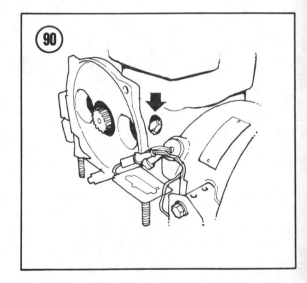

90

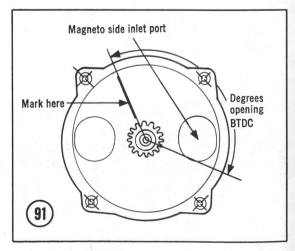

Magneto side inlet port

Mark here

Degrees opening BTDC

91

5. Secure valve disc with washer and screw. Install rotary valve cover. Ensure that O-ring is properly positioned. Install carburetors.

Rotary Valve Timing

Refer to **Table 5** for timing specifications.

1. Perform *Rotary Valve Removal*.

2. Rotate magneto side piston to TDC (top dead center). Use a dial indicator-type timing gauge as described in Chapter One. On 354 engines, install special locking bolt to hold magneto side piston at TDC (**Figure 90**).

3. Use a protractor or degree wheel and mark BTDC opening point from *bottom* edge of magneto side inlet port as shown in **Figure 91**.

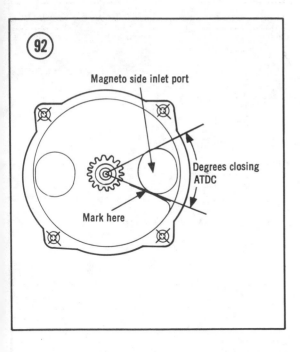

Magneto side inlet port

Degrees closing ATDC

Mark here

4. With protractor or degree wheel mark ATDC closing point from *top* edge of inlet port as shown in **Figure 92**.

5. Proceed to Step 3b of *Rotary Valve Installation*.

Cooling Fan Disassembly/Assembly

This procedure requires a special tool to remove fan from fan housing. If special tool or locally fabricated equivalent is not available, refer task to an authorized dealer.

Refer to **Figure 93** for a typical cooling fan assembly.

1. Remove fan housing.

2. Install fan holder tool to hold fan and remove fan nut (**Figure 94**).

3. Remove lockwasher with outer half of pulley, shims, inner pulley, shim, Woodruff key and fan (**Figure 95**).

> NOTE: *Newer type pulley half is constructed without a shoulder on the inner face (Figure 96). A 0.230 in. (6mm) spacer must be installed with a new style pulley half.*

4. Remove bearings from fan housing.

> NOTE: *It may be necessary to heat fan housing in an oven to 140°-160°F (60°-71°C) to aid bearing removal. Use a hammer and a block of wood to gently tap bearings from housing.*

5. Remove 2 shims from between bearings when bearings are removed. Remove circlip from fan housing if desired.

Table 5   ROTARY VALVE TIMING SPECIFICATIONS

Engine	Degrees Opening B.T.D.C.	Degrees Closing A.T.D.C.
245, 345	127	48
354 (1978)	131	52
(1979)	132	50
444 (1978)	140	51
(1979)	139	49
454	137	65

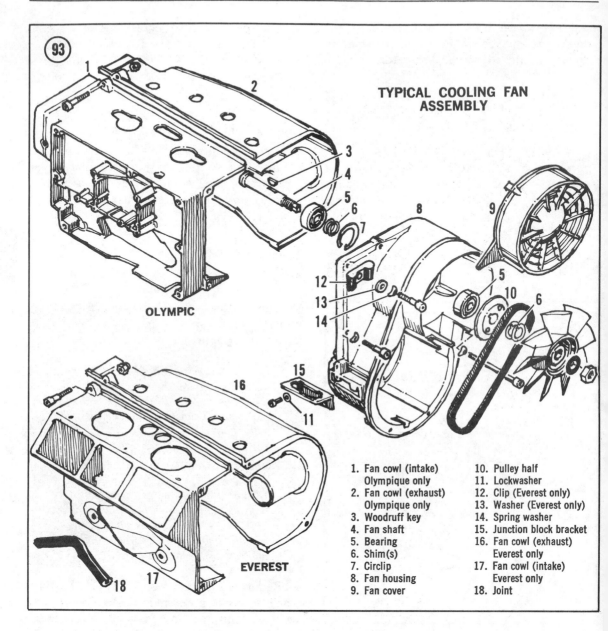

TYPICAL COOLING FAN ASSEMBLY

OLYMPIC

EVEREST

1. Fan cowl (intake) Olympique only	10. Pulley half
2. Fan cowl (exhaust) Olympique only	11. Lockwasher
3. Woodruff key	12. Clip (Everest only)
4. Fan shaft	13. Washer (Everest only)
5. Bearing	14. Spring washer
6. Shim(s)	15. Junction block bracket
7. Circlip	16. Fan cowl (exhaust) Everest only
8. Fan housing	17. Fan cowl (intake) Everest only
9. Fan cover	18. Joint

6. Carefully inspect bearings for evidences of roughness or excessive wear and replace if necessary. Refer to *Component Inspection*.

7. Assembly is the reverse of these steps. Keep the following points in mind:

a. Lubricate bearings with light oil and insert one bearing into housing. Heat fan housing if necessary to aid bearing installation.

b. Install 2 washers against face of installed bearing and install second bearing. Bearing shields must face outward.

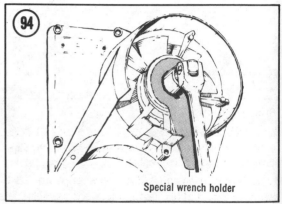

Special wrench holder

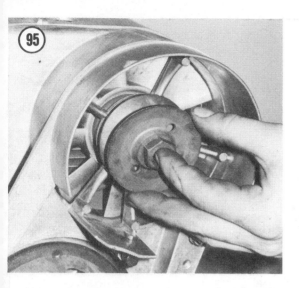

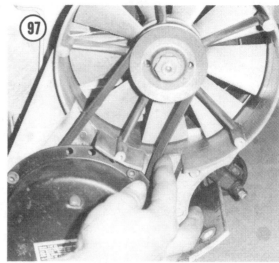

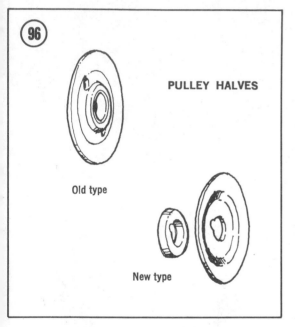

PULLEY HALVES

Old type

New type

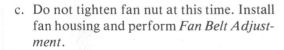

c. Do not tighten fan nut at this time. Install fan housing and perform *Fan Belt Adjustment*.

Fan Belt Adjustment

1. Check fan belt for approximately ¼ in. (6mm) deflection as shown in **Figure 97**.

2. If belt tension is incorrect, remove fan protector. Use special holding tool to hold fan and remove fan nut (**Figure 94**).

3. Remove or install shims between inner and outer pulley halves until specified tension is achieved. Extra shims can be stored under the fan nut (**Figure 98**).

4. Torque fan nut as specified in **Table 1**. Recheck fan belt tension and readjust if necessary.

5. Install fan protector onto fan housing.

RECOIL STARTER

Removal/Installation

Remove 4 bolts securing recoil starter assembly to engine and lift off starter (**Figure 99**). Installation is the reverse of removal.

Disassembly

Refer to **Figure 100** for this procedure.

1. Pull out rope and hold. Use an ice pick or similar sharp tool and disengage key clamp from rope (**Figure 101**). Remove rope from sheave and hand grip.

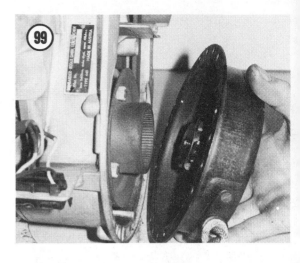

> NOTE: *On some early models, starter rope was secured by a jam pin through the center of the sheave hub. On these models, remove circlip, cover washer, and pivoting arm assembly to expose rope end loop and jam pin on back of sheave. Remove rope from sheave, taking care not to lose jam pin.*

2. Remove circlip, cover washer, and pivot arm assembly complete with friction washers. Do not disassemble pivot arm assembly unless worn and replacement parts are necessary.

3. Remove "D" washer and rope sheave.

4. Gently tap on outside starter housing to remove spring cartridge.

5. Pry spring cartridge open with a small screwdriver and remove spring.

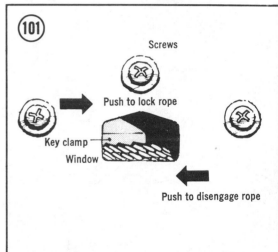

> **WARNING**
> *Exercise great care when opening spring cartridge. Spring is tightly wound and may fly out causing injury.*

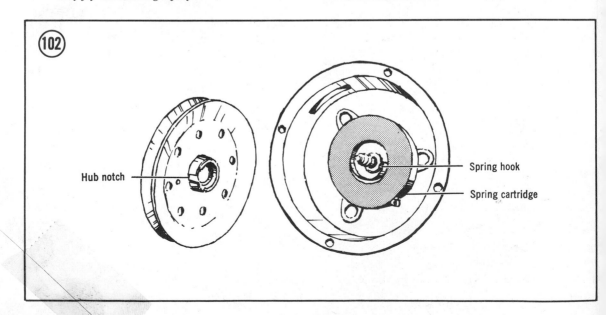

Assembly

1. Wind spring into smaller half of cartridge case. Lightly grease spring as it is wound into case. Install case cover.

2. Install spring cartridge in starter housing with large opening of cartridge facing up. Gently tap cartridge into place.

3. Install rope sheave in housing and align notch in sheave with spring hook (**Figure 102**).

> NOTE: *On early model jam pin starters, secure rope end in sheave with jam pin and tap rope end until it is flush with back of sheave.*

4. Install "D" washer and complete pivot arm assembly with friction washers.

5. Secure pivot arm assembly with circlip. Ensure that pivot arm is positioned so that arm can turn clockwise.

6. Fuse rope ends with a match.

7. Install rope end in hand grip and secure with knot.

8. Rotate sheave counterclockwise 6 turns to wind up rewind spring and hold.

9. Look through rope hole in starter housing and turn sheave until hole in sheave aligns with hole in housing.

10. Route rope through housing and into sheave hole until approximately ¾ in. (19mm) of rope is visible in housing.

11. Install key in housing and push key to lock rope (**Figure 101**).

4

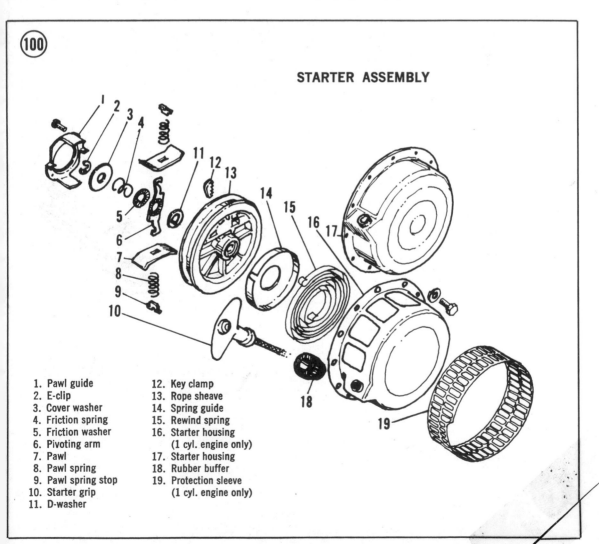

⑩⓪

STARTER ASSEMBLY

1. Pawl guide	12. Key clamp
2. E-clip	13. Rope sheave
3. Cover washer	14. Spring guide
4. Friction spring	15. Rewind spring
5. Friction washer	16. Starter housing
6. Pivoting arm	(1 cyl. engine only)
7. Pawl	17. Starter housing
8. Pawl spring	18. Rubber buffer
9. Pawl spring stop	19. Protection sleeve
10. Starter grip	(1 cyl. engine only)
11. D-washer	

Table 1   TORQUE SPECIFICATIONS

Engine	Engine Assembly to Frame	Engine Mount to Crankcase	Crankcase Bolts/Nuts	Cylinder Head Nut	Magneto Nut	Fan Nut	Intake/Exhaust Manifold Bolt/Nut
247* and 302	22-25 ft.-lb. (3.0-3.5 mkg)	to 1973 50 ft.-lb. (6.9 mkg) 1974 and later 23-29 ft.-lb. (3.2-4.0 mkg)	16 ft.-lb. (2.2 mkg)	to 1973 16-18 ft.-lb. (0.8-2.5 mkg) 14-16 1974 and later 14-16 (1.9-2.2)	50-56 ft.-lb. (6.9-7.7 mkg)	N/A	16 ft.-lb. (2.2 mkg)
245 and 345	22-25 ft.-lb. (3.0-3.5 mkg)	to 1977 23-29 ft.-lb. (3.2-4.0 mkg) 1978 and later 26 ft.-lb. (3.6 mkg)	16 ft.-lb. (2.2 mkg) Allen cap screws to 7 ft.-lb. (1.0 mkg)	to 1977 16-18 ft.-lb. (2.2-2.5 mkg) 1978 and later 12 ft.-lb. (1.5 mkg)	58-62 ft.-lb. (8.0-8.6 mkg)	N/A	16 ft.-lb. (2.2 mkg)
248 and 294	22-25 ft.-lb. (3.0-3.5 mkg)	23-29 ft.-lb. (3.2-4.0 mkg)	16 ft.-lb. (2.2 mkg) Bolts 11, 12 9 ft.-lb. (1.2 mkg)	14-16 ft.-lb. (1.9-2.2 mkg)	to 1977 42-50 ft.-lb. (5.8-6.9 mkg) 1978 and later 46 ft.-lb. (6.4 mkg)	to 1973 12-17 ft.-lb. (1.7-2.3 mkg) 1974 and later 42-50 ft.-lb. (5.8-6.9 mkg)	15 ft.-lb. (2.1 mkg)
305, 338, 343, 401, and 402	22-25 ft.-lb. (3.0-3.5 mkg)	23-29 ft.-lb. (3.2-4.0 mkg)	14-16 ft.-lb. (1.9-2.2 mkg)	14-16 ft.-lb. (1.9-2.2 mkg)	to 1977 42-50 ft.-lb. (5.8-6.9 mkg) 1978 and later 60 ft.-lb. (8.3 mkg)	to 1973 12-17 ft.-lb. (1.7-2.3 mkg) 1974 and later 42-50 ft.-lb. (5.8-6.9 mkg)	14-16 ft.-lb. (1.9-2.2 mkg)
346, 396, and 436	22-25 ft.-lb. (3.0-3.5 mkg)	30-35 ft.-lb. (4.1-4.8 mkg)	14-16 ft.-lb. (1.9-2.2 mkg)	14-16 ft.-lb. (1.9-2.2 mkg)	58-62 ft.-lb. (8.0-8.6 mkg)	N/A	14-16 ft.-lb. (1.9-2.2 mkg)
354	22-25 ft.-lb. (3.0-3.5 mkg)	26 ft.-lb. (3.6 mkg)	16 ft.-lb. (2.2 mkg) Bolts 15, 16 10 ft.-lb. (1.4 mkg)	1978 12 ft.-lb. (1.7 mkg) 1979 16 ft.-lb. (2.2 mkg)	70-72 ft.-lb. (9.7-10.0 mkg)	N/A	15 ft.-lb. (2.1 mkg)
434 and 440	22-25 ft.-lb. (3.0-3.5 mkg)	29-35 ft.-lb. (4.0-4.8 mkg)	14-16 ft.-lb. (1.9-2.2 mkg)	14-16 ft.-lb. (1.9-2.2 mkg)	434— 50-58 ft.-lb. (6.9-8.0 mkg) 440— 58-63 ft.-lb. (8.0-8.7 mkg)	to 1973 12-17 ft.-lb. (1.7-2.3 mkg) 1974 and later 42-50 ft.-lb. (5.8-6.9 mkg)	14-16 ft.-lb. (1.9-2.2 mkg)
444 and 454	22-25 ft.-lb. (3.0-3.5 mkg)	26 ft.-lb. (3.6 mkg)	16 ft.-lb. (2.2 mkg)	1978—12 ft.-lb. (1.7 mkg) 1979—28 ft.-lb. (3.9 mkg)	60 ft.-lb. (8.3 mkg)	N/A	15 ft.-lb. (2.1 mkg)
503	22-25 ft.-lb. (3.0-3.5 mkg)	26 ft.-lb. (3.6 mkg)	16 ft.-lb. (2.2 mkg)	16 ft.-lb. (2.2 mkg)	60 ft.-lb. (8.3 mkg)	46 ft.-lb. (6.4 mkg)	15 ft.-lb. (2.1 mkg)

Table 2   SINGLE CYLINDER ENGINE SPECIFICATIONS

Engine	Cylinder Bore (Standard)	Wear Limit	Ring End Gap	Crankshaft End Play
247	2.7165 in. (69.0mm)	0.0065 in. (0.165mm)	0.010-0.063 in. (0.25-1.60mm)	0.004-0.016 in. (0.10-0.40mm)
292	2.9528 in. (75.0mm)	0.0076 in. (0.195mm)	0.012-0.063 in. (0.30-1.60mm)	0.004-0.016 in. (0.10-0.40mm)
300, 302	2.9921 in. (76.0mm)	0.0076 in. (0.195mm)	0.012-0.063 in. (0.30-1.60mm)	0.004-0.016 in. (0.10-0.40mm)
335, 337	3.0708 in. (78.0mm)	0.0076 in. (0.195mm)	0.012-0.063 in. (0.30-1.60mm)	0.004-0.016 in. (0.10-0.40mm)

Table 3   TWIN CYLINDER ENGINE SPECIFICATIONS

Engine Type	Cylinder Bore (Standard)	Wear Limit	Ring End Gap	Crankshaft End Play
245	2.1260 in. (54.0mm)	0.0069 in. (0.175mm)	0.008-0.020 in. (0.020-0.50mm)	0.04-0.016 in.* (0.10-0.40mm)
248	2.1260 in. (54.0mm)	0.0053 in. (0.135mm)	0.008-0.063 in. (0.20-1.60mm)	0.004-0.016 in. (0.10-0.40mm)
248 (1978-1979)	2.1260 in. (54.0mm)	0.0053 in. (0.135mm)	0.006-0.014 in. (0.15-0.35mm)	0.004 in. (0.10mm)
294	2.2441 in. (57.0mm)	0.0053 in. (0.135mm)	0.008-0.063 in. (0.20-1.60mm)	0.004-0.016 in. (0.10-0.40mm)
305	2.1850 in. (55.5mm)	0.0053 in. (0.135mm)	0.008-0.063 in. (0.20-1.60mm)	0.004-0.106 in. (0.10-0.40mm)
305 (1978)	2.1850 in. (55.5mm)	0.0068 in. (0.172mm)	0.006-0.014 in. (0.15-0.35mm)	0.009 in. (0.10mm)
338	2.3425 in. (59.5mm)	0.0076 in. (0.195mm)	0.008-0.063 in. (0.20-1.60mm)	0.004-0.016 in. (0.10-0.40mm)
343	2.3425 in. (59.5mm)	0.0076 in. (0.195mm)	0.008-0.063 in. (0.20-1.60mm)	0.004-0.016 in. (0.10-0.40mm)
343 (1978)	2.3425 in. (59.5mm)	0.0076 in. (0.195mm)	0.006-0.014 in. (0.15-0.35mm)	0.004 in. (0.10mm)
343 (1979)	2.3425 in. (59.5mm)	0.008 in. (0.20mm)	0.006-0.014 in. (0.15-0.35mm)	0.004 in. (0.10mm)
345	2.4803 in. (63.0mm)	0.0053 in. (0.135mm)	0.008-0.020 in. (0.20-0.50mm)	N/A
345 (1978)	2.4803 in. (63.0mm)	0.0053 in. (0.135mm)	0.008-0.015 in. (0.20-0.40mm)	N/A
346	2.3425 in. (59.5mm)	0.0092 in. (0.235mm)	0.008-0.063 in. (0.20-1.60mm)	N/A

(continued)

4

Table 3   TWIN CYLINDER ENGINE SPECIFICATIONS (continued)

Engine Type	Cylinder Bore (Standard)	Wear Limit	Ring End Gap	Crankshaft End Play
346 (1978)	2.3425 in. (59.5mm)	0.0092 in. (0.235mm)	0.006-0.014 in. (0.15-0.35mm)	N/A
354 (1978)	2.3425 in. (59.5mm)	0.0076 in. (0.195mm)	0.006-0.014 in. (0.15-0.35mm)	N/A
354 (1979)	2.3425 in. (59.5mm)	0.008 in. (0.20mm)	0.006-0.014 in. (0.15-0.35mm)	0.004 in. (0.10mm)
396	2.5394 in. (64.5mm)	0.0084 in. (0.215mm)	0.010-0.063 in. (0.25-1.60mm)	N/A
401	2.5394 in. (64.5mm)	0.0076 in. (0.195mm)	0.010-0.063 in. (0.25-1.60mm)	0.004-0.016 in. (0.10-0.40mm)
434	2.6575 in. (67.5mm)	0.0076 in. (0.195mm)	0.010-0.063 in. (0.25-1.60mm)	N/A
436	2.6575 in. (67.5mm)	0.010 in. (0.255mm)	0.010-0.063 in. (0.25-1.60mm)	N/A
440	2.6575 in. (67.5mm)	0.0086 in. (0.216mm)	0.010-0.063 in. (0.25-1.60mm)	N/A
440 (1978)	2.6575 in. (67.5mm)	0.0069 in. (0.175mm)	0.008-0.016 in. (0.20-0.40mm)	N/A
440 (1979)	2.6575 in. (67.5mm)	0.007 in. (0.18mm)	0.008-0.016 in. (0.20-0.40mm)	0.004 in. (0.10mm)
444 (1978-1979)	2.7362 in. (69.5mm)	0.007 in. (0.18mm)	0.008-0.016 in. (0.20-0.40mm)	0.004 in. (0.10mm)
454	2.6575 in. (67.5mm)	0.009 in. (0.22mm)	0.008-0.016 in. (0.20-0.40mm)	0.004 in. (0.10mm)
503	2.8346 in. (72mm)	0.006 in. (0.16mm)	0.008-0.016 in. (0.20-0.40mm)	0.004 in. (0.10mm)

*Not applicable on 1976 models.

CHAPTER FIVE

FUEL SYSTEM

The fuel system consists of a fuel tank, fuel lines, inline fuel filter, and carburetor(s).

All models are equipped with one of 2 types of carburetor, a Tillotson or Mikuni. Tillotson carburetors have an integral fuel pump. Mikuni carburetors are provided fuel through an auxiliary impulse fuel pump operating off differential pressure in the engine crankcase. An air silencer is fitted on some models to quiet incoming air and catch fuel that may spit back out of the carburetor.

This chapter covers removal, installation, and replacement and/or repair of carburetors, fuel pumps, inline filters, and fuel tanks. Carburetor tuning is covered in Chapter Two.

See **Table 1 or 2** at the end of the chapter for carburetor application and specifications.

TILLOTSON CARBURETOR

Three basic types of Tillotson carburetors are used: the HR, HD, and HRM. Refer to **Table 1** for model application. Refer to **Figures 1 and 2** for typical examples of HR and HD type carburetors. Refer to **Figure 3** for a typical example of HRM types.

Removal/Installation

1. Remove air intake silencer **(Figure 4)** on models so equipped.

2. Disconnect throttle and choke cables from carburetor.

3. Disconnect fuel lines. Tag fuel line to aid installation.

4. Open tab locks **(Figure 5)** and remove nuts and washers securing carburetor to engine.

5. Remove carburetor with isolating sleeves and gaskets **(Figure 6)**. If applicable, also remove isolating flange and gasket **(Figure 7)**.

6. Installation is the reverse of these steps. Keep the following points in mind:

    a. Longer fuel line is return line and is connected to outlet nipple on carburetor.

    b. Perform carburetor adjustments as outlined in Chapter Two.

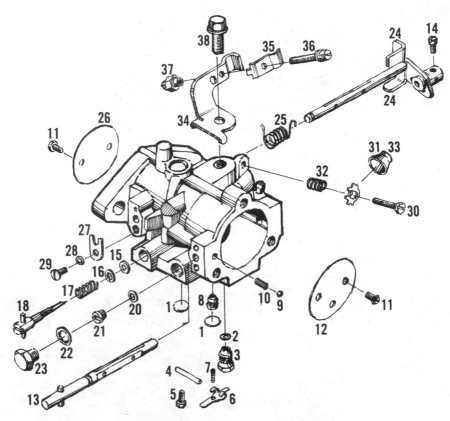

TYPICAL HR TYPE CARBURETOR

1. Welch plug
2. Inlet seat gasket
3. Inlet needle and seat
4. Fulcrum pin
5. Retaining screw
6. Fulcrum lever
7. Fulcrum lever spring
8. Main nozzle check valve
9. Friction ball
10. Friction spring
11. Shutter screw
12. Choke shutter
13. Choke shaft
14. Wire retaining screw
15. Packing
16. Washer
17. Adjusting screw spring
18. Idle mixture adjusting screw
19. High speed mixture adjusting screw
20. Main fuel jet gasket
21. Main fuel jet
22. Plug screw gasket
23. Main jet plug screw
24. Throttle shaft

25. Throttle shaft spring
26. Throttle shutter
27. Throttle shaft clip
28. Lockwasher
29. Retaining screw
30. Idle speed adusting screw
31. Washer
32. Adjusting screw spring
33. Cup
34. Throttle cable bracket
35. Throttle cable clamp
36. Cable clamp retaining screw
37. Cable clamp retaining nut
38. Retaining screw and lockwasher
39. Diaphragm gasket
40. Metering diaphragm
41. Diaphragm cover
42. Fuel pump gasket
43. Fuel pump diaphragm
44. Fuel pump body
45. Inet valve gasket
46. Inlet valve diaphragm
47. Inlet valve body
48. Fuel strainer screen
49. Fuel strainer gasket
50. Body screw and lockwasher

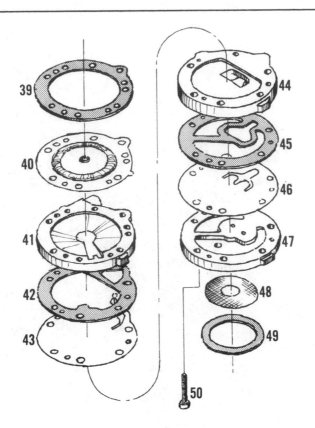

WITH INTEGRATED FUEL PUMP

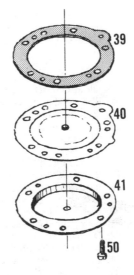

WITHOUT INTEGRATED FUEL PUMP

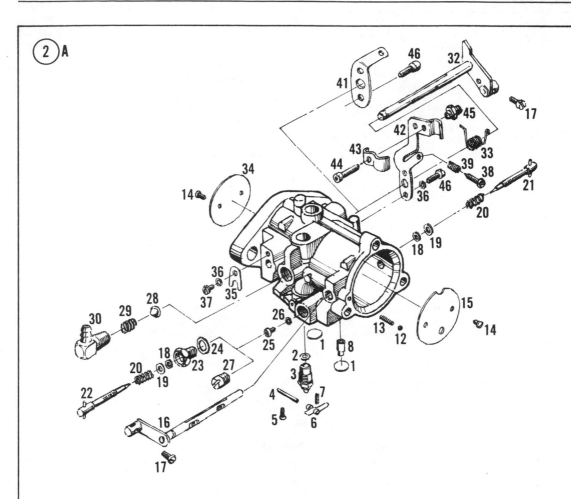

TYPICAL HD TYPE CARBURETOR

1. Welch plug
2. Inlet seat gasket
3. Inlet needle and seat
4. Fulcrum pin
5. Retaining screw
6. Fulcrum lever
7. Fulcrum lever spring
8. Main nozzle check valve
9. Main nozzle check valve/discharge tube
10. Lead shot
11. Intermediate nozzle check valve
12. Friction ball
13. Friction spring
14. Shutter screw
15. Choke shutter
16. Choke shaft
17. Wire retaining screw
18. Packing
19. Washer

20. Adjusting screw spring
21. Idle mixture adjusting screw
22. High speed mixture adjusting screw
23. Mixture screw gland
24. Fiber gasket
25. Main fuel jet
26. Main fuel jet gasket
27. Main fuel jet plug screw
28. Inlet screen
29. Inlet screen retaining spring
30. Fuel connector
31. Body channel plug screw
32. Throttle shaft
33. Throttle shaft spring
34. Throttle shutter
35. Throttle shaft clip
36. Lockwasher
37. Retaining screw
38. Idle speed screw

39. Idle speed screw spring
40. Idle speed screw cup
41. Idle speed screw gasket
42. Throttle cable bracket
43. Throttle cable clamp
44. Cable clamp retaining screw
45. Cable clamp retaining nut
46. Bracket retaining screw
47. Diaphragm gasket
48. Metering diaphragm
49. Diaphragm cover
50. Fuel pump gasket
51. Fuel pump diaphragm
52. Fuel pump body
53. Inlet valve gasket
54. Inlet valve diaphragm
55. Inlet valve body
56. Fuel strainer screen
57. Fuel strainer gasket
58. Body screw and lockwasher

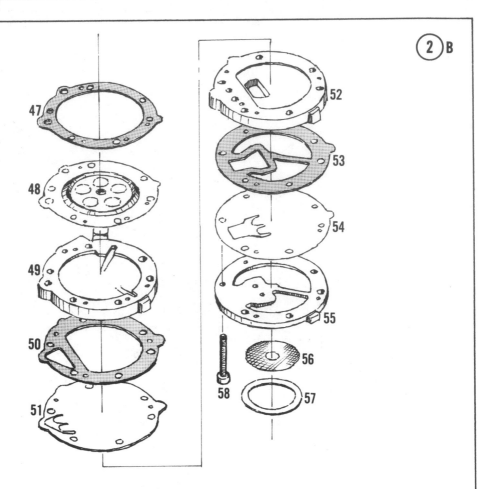

2 B

5

WITH INTEGRATED FUEL PUMP

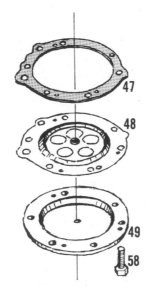

WITHOUT INTEGRATED FUEL PUMP

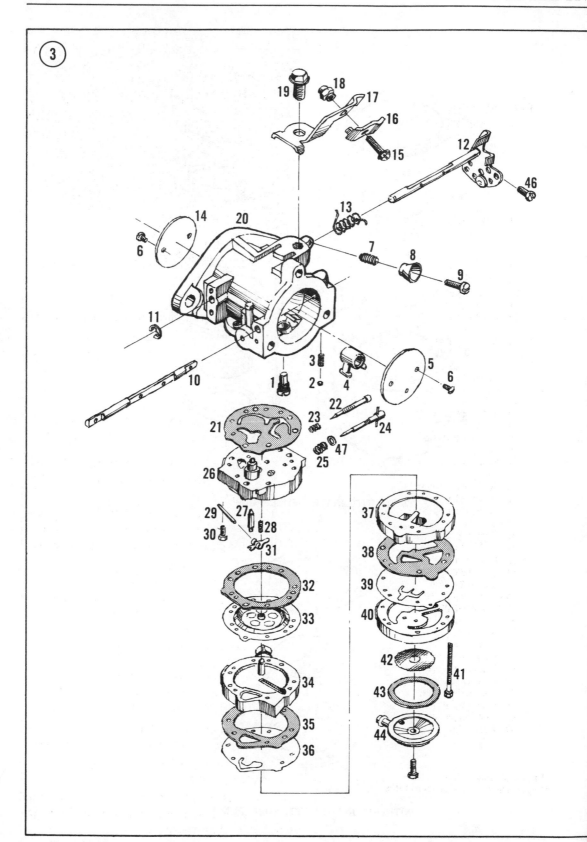

TYPICAL HRM TYPE CARBURETOR

1. Nozzle check valve
*2. Friction ball
*3. Spring
4. Primary venturi
*5. Choke shutter
*6. Screw
7. Spring
8. Cup
9. Idle speed screw
*10. Choke shaft
11. Circlip
12. Throttle shaft
13. Spring
14. Throttle shutter
*15. Screw
*16. Throttle cable clamp
*17. Throttle cable bracket
*18. Nut
*19. Bolt
20. Carburetor body
21. Adjuster
22. Idle mixture screw
23. Spring
24. High speed mixture screw
25. Spring
26. Adjustment module
27. Inlet needle
28. Inlet tension spring
29. Fulcrum pin
30. Retaining screw
31. Inlet control lever
32. Diaphragm gasket
33. Metering diaphragm
34. Diaphragm cover
35. Fuel pump gasket
36. Fuel pump diaphragm
37. Fuel pump body
38. Inlet valve gasket
39. Inlet valve diaphragm
40. Body screw and lockwasher
42. Fuel strainer screen
43. Cover gasket
44. Fuel strainer cover
45. Cover retaining screw
46. Cable retaining screw
**47. Washer

* Not applicable on HRM 5A
** Applicable only on HRM 5A and HRM 7A

Disassembly

Refer to **Figure 1 and 2** for HD and HR types and **Figure 3** for HRM type carburetors.

1. Clean exterior of carburetor with a non-flammable solvent.

CAUTION
Never use compressed air to clean an assembled carburetor or diaphragm may be damaged.

2. Carefully disassemble carburetor. Pay particular attention to location of different sized screws and springs.

3. If necessary to remove welch plugs from carburetor body, carefully pierce plug with a sharp tool such as an awl and pry plug out of carburetor.

CAUTION
Exercise care when removing choke shaft or choke friction ball and spring may fly out and be lost.
Carefully remove inlet control lever as it is spring loaded and can fly out when retainer screw is removed.
Main fuel jet has left-hand threads. To remove, turn jet clockwise.

4. If removing main nozzle check ball assembly (beneath welch plug), perform the following:

a. On HR type carburetors, unscrew main nozzle check ball assembly.

b. On HD type carburetors, use a small punch and gently tap out main nozzle check ball assembly.

5

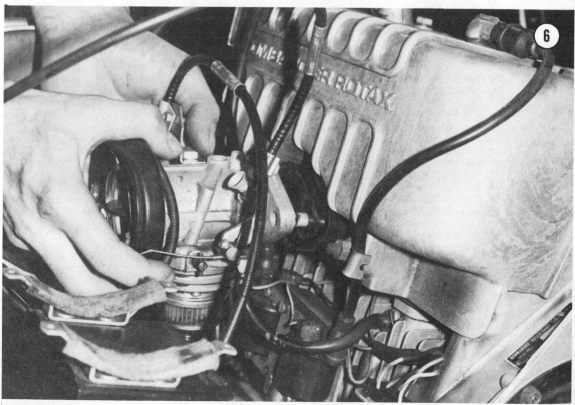

5. When carburetor is fully disassembled, perform *Cleaning and Inspection*.

Cleaning and Inspection

> **WARNING**
> *Most carburetor cleaners are highly caustic. They must be handled with extreme care or skin burns and possible eye injury may result.*

1. Clean all metallic parts in carburetor cleaning solvent. Do not place gaskets or diaphragms in solvent or they will be destroyed.

> **CAUTION**
> *Never clean holes or passages with small drill bits or wire or a slight enlargement or burring of holes will result, drastically affecting carburetor performance.*

2. After cleaning carburetor parts, dry with compressed air. Make sure all holes are open and free of carbon and dirt.

> NOTE: *Do not use rags or wastepaper to dry parts. Lint may plug jets or channels and affect carburetor operation.*

3. Inspect shaft bearing surfaces in carburetor body (**Figure 8**) for excessive wear.

> **CAUTION**
> *If excessive clearance is found between shafts and carburetor body, worn parts must be replaced. Excessive clearance will allow air to enter, causing a damaging lean mixture.*

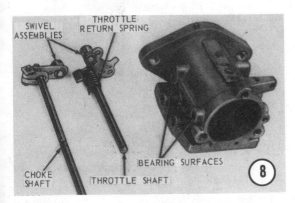

4. Inspect choke and throttle plates for damage. Inspect swivel assemblies on choke and throttle levers for wear. Inspect condition

of throttle return spring. Replace all worn parts.

5. Inspect mixture needles and needle valve seating surfaces for pitting or wear (**Figure 9**) and replace if worn or damaged.

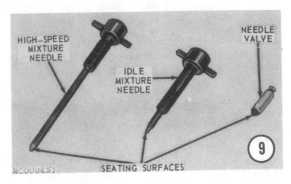

6. Inspect diaphragms for distortion, cracks, or punctures (**Figure 10**).

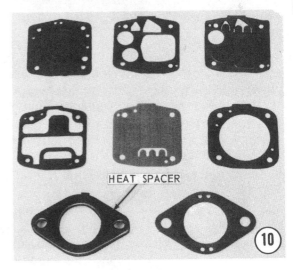

7. Inspect carburetor mounting gasket and heat spacer gasket.

Assembly

Refer to **Figures 1 and 2** for HD and HR types and **Figure 3** for HRM type carburetors.

1. Install main nozzle check ball assembly (if removed) as follows:

    a. On HR type carburetor screw assembly in carburetor body.

    b. On HD type carburetor insert nozzle assembly in carburetor body until nozzle shoulder is flush with bottom of nozzle well.

2. If welch plugs were removed, install new plugs (convex side up) and tap plug with hammer and punch until plug is flat. Ensure that plug completely seals opening.

3. Place spring, washer, and packing on idle speed mixture screw and install in carburetor. Lubricate packing with petroleum jelly.

4. Install high-speed needle with spring, washer, and packing. Lubricate packing with petroleum jelly.

5. On HR and HD types with fixed main jet install jet with gasket and turn *counterclockwise* to tighten.

6. Insert choke friction spring and ball into carburetor and hold in position while installing choke shaft.

> NOTE: *On HRM carburetors install primary venturi with largest section toward front of carburetor.*

7. Insert choke shutter on shaft and turn shaft to center shutter in carburetor body. Secure choke shutter with screws. Ensure that hole on shutter is down and mark on shutter faces out.

8. Install throttle shaft part way. Connect throttle shaft spring and turn shaft one turn clockwise and finish installing shaft.

9. Install idle speed screw bracket on HD carburetor.

10. Install throttle shaft retainer clip and secure with screw.

11. Insert throttle shutter into throttle shaft with location mark facing out. Close throttle shaft to center shutter in carburetor body and secure shutter with 2 screws.

12. Install inlet needle seat with thin wall socket. Torque seat to 25-30 in.-lb. (29-35 cmkg) on HR types and 40-45 in.-lb. (46-52 cmkg) on HD type carburetors.

13. Install needle seat and inlet control lever. Secure control lever with retaining screw. Adjust inlet control lever so that center of lever that contacts metering diaphragm is flush with metering chamber wall.

14. Assembly pump diaphragm assembly. Install assembly to carburetor and tighten 6 screws evenly in a crisscross pattern **(Figure 11)**.

15. Install fuel inlet strainer cover with strainer screen to diaphragm pump body and secure with screw.

MIKUNI CARBURETOR

Refer to **Table 2** for model application.

Removal/Installation

1. Remove air filter.

2. Disconnect fuel and primer lines.

3. Unscrew throttle chamber cover and carefully slide throttle slide assembly from carburetor **(Figure 12)**.

> NOTE: *If carburetor is being removed for cleaning or repair, disconnect throttle cable from throttle slide and remove throttle slide assembly. Note and record what notch E-ring is located in on jet needles to aid installation.*

4. Remove drain plug from bottom of float chamber and drain fuel into a suitable container. Install drain plug.

5. Loosen clamp securing carburetor and remove carburetor from rubber mount.

6. Installation is the reverse of these steps. Keep the following points in mind:

    a. Install E-ring on jet needle in same position noted during removal.

    b. Ensure that float level is correct. Refer to *Assembly*.

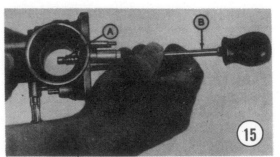

A. Needle jet   B. Awl

c. Perform carburetor adjustments as outlined in Chapter Two.

Disassembly

Refer to **Figure 13** for this procedure.

1. Remove throttle stop screw and spring.

2. Remove air screw and spring.

3. Remove float chamber as shown in **Figure 14**. Gently lift out floats from mixing chamber body.

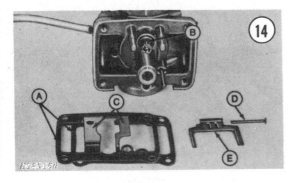

A. Gaskets
B. Inlet needle valve assembly
C. Baffle plate
D. Float air pin
E. Float arm

4. Using a 6mm socket or box end wrench, gently remove main jet and ring.

5. Remove float arm pin and float arm. Lift off baffle plate and gaskets (**Figure 14**).

6. Gently remove inlet needle valve assembly with washer.

7. Gently push needle jet from mixing chamber using an awl or similar sharp pointed device. See **Figure 15**.

Cleaning and Inspection

> **WARNING**
> *Most carburetor cleaners are highly caustic. They must be handled with extreme care or skin burns and possible eye injury may result.*

1. Clean all metallic parts in carburetor cleaning solvent. Do not place gaskets in solvent or they will be destroyed.

> **CAUTION**
> *Never clean holes or passages with small drill bits or wire or a slight enlargement or burring of hole will result, drastically affecting carburetor performance.*

2. Inspect float chamber and mixing chamber body for fine cracks or evidence of fuel leaks.

3. Check spring for distortion or damage.

4. Inspect air screw and throttle stop screw for surface damage or stripped threads.

5. Inspect pilot jet and main jet for damage or stripped threads.

> **CAUTION**
> *Pilot jet and main jet must be scrupulously clean and shiny. Any burring, roughness, or abrasion will cause a lean fuel and air mixture and possible engine damage.*

6. Remove retainer and inlet valve from valve seat. Carefully examine seating surface on inlet valve and seat for damage. Ensure that retainer does not bind and hinder movement of inlet valve.

7. Inspect jet needle and needle jet for damage. Jet needle must slide freely within needle jet.

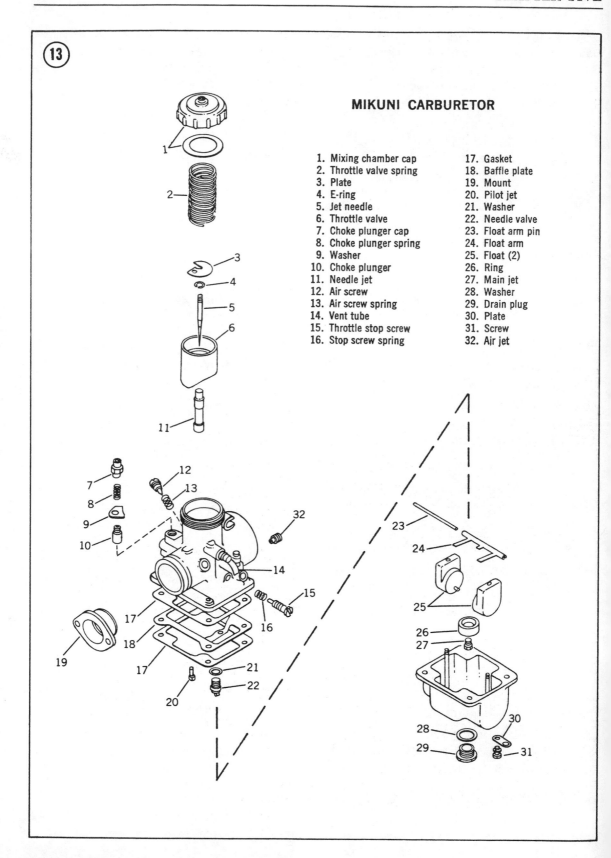

⑬

MIKUNI CARBURETOR

1. Mixing chamber cap
2. Throttle valve spring
3. Plate
4. E-ring
5. Jet needle
6. Throttle valve
7. Choke plunger cap
8. Choke plunger spring
9. Washer
10. Choke plunger
11. Needle jet
12. Air screw
13. Air screw spring
14. Vent tube
15. Throttle stop screw
16. Stop screw spring
17. Gasket
18. Baffle plate
19. Mount
20. Pilot jet
21. Washer
22. Needle valve
23. Float arm pin
24. Float arm
25. Float (2)
26. Ring
27. Main jet
28. Washer
29. Drain plug
30. Plate
31. Screw
32. Air jet

8. Install float guides in float chamber. Move floats up and down several times to ensure that they are not binding on float guides.

9. Inspect float arm and float pin to ensure that float arm does not bind on pin.

10. Inspect choke plunger. Plunger must move freely in passage of mixing chamber.

11. Install throttle valve in mixing chamber body and move several times up and down to check for sticking motion or wear. Ensure that guide pin in mixing chamber body is not broken.

Assembly

Refer to **Figure 13** for this procedure.

1. Using a small screwdriver, install pilot jet in carburetor body as shown in **Figure 16**.

2. Install gaskets and baffle plate on mixing chamber surface (**Figure 17**). Install second gasket on top of baffle plate.

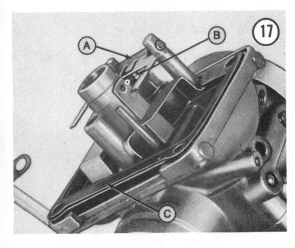

A. Float arm   B. Inlet valve   C. Baffle plate and gaskets

3. Place washer on inlet needle valve seat and install seat in mixing chamber body (**Figure 17**). Install inlet valve (point down) and retainer.

4. Install float arm and secure float arm with float arm pin.

5. Invert carburetor body. Edge of mixing chamber (**Figure 18**) must be 23-24mm (0.90-0.94 in.) from float arm. Adjust if necessary by bending float arm actuating tab.

A. Mixing chamber   B. Float arm

6. Install needle jet. Make sure notch on needle jet is correctly aligned with pin on bore of mixing chamber (**Figure 19**). Install ring over needle jet bore (recess in ring next to bore) and screw main jet into needle jet.

A. Pin   B. Notch   C. Needle jet

7. Slide floats over float pin. Pins on float must be down and point to inside of float chamber as shown in **Figure 20**.

8. Install float chamber to mixing chamber body and secure with 4 screws.

9. Slide air screw spring over air screw and install air screw gently.

> CAUTION
> *Do not force air screw or seat damage may occur.*

10. Install throttle stop screw with spring. Install screw until it is just flush with inside of bore.

AIR INTAKE SILENCERS

Air intake silencers are installed on snowmobiles to quiet the sound of rushing air and to catch fuel that spits back out of the carburetor throat. Refer to **Figures 21, 22, 23, and 24** for typical examples.

The silencer is not intended to filter incoming air. Operate snowmobiles only in clean, snow covered areas.

> CAUTION
> *Do not operate snowmobile with silencer removed. Loss of power and engine damage may result due to a leaner mixture.*

Service of air intake silencers is limited to removal and cleaning of components.

FUEL TANK

Refer to **Figures 21, 22, 23, and 24** for typical fuel tank installations.

> NOTE: *On 1970 Olympiques and some T'NT models, the fuel tank is built in. Service is limited to draining tank and removing fuel lines and fuel line adaptor.*

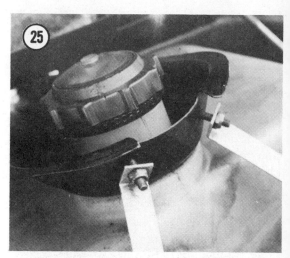

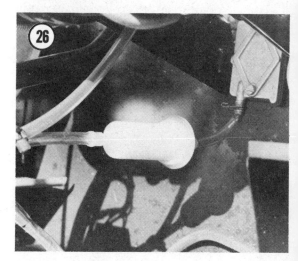

Removal/Installation

1. Siphon fuel from tank into a suitable container.

2. Disconnect fuel lines from fuel line adaptor. Tag lines to aid reconnection.

3. Loosen clamp and unscrew fuel line adaptor from tank.

4. Remove bolts and nuts securing tank mounting straps (**Figure 25**) and remove tank.

5. Installation is the reverse of these steps. Install fuel line adaptor so fuel nipples point toward rear of machine and tighten clamp.

FUEL FILTER

Service of fuel filter (**Figure 26**) is limited to cleaning of screen type filter or replacement of paper element filters.

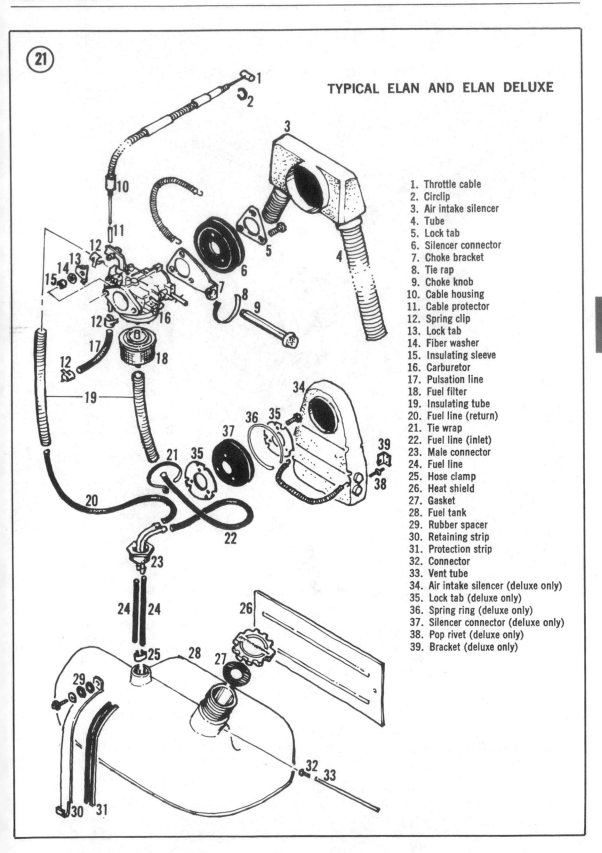

㉑

TYPICAL ELAN AND ELAN DELUXE

1. Throttle cable
2. Circlip
3. Air intake silencer
4. Tube
5. Lock tab
6. Silencer connector
7. Choke bracket
8. Tie rap
9. Choke knob
10. Cable housing
11. Cable protector
12. Spring clip
13. Lock tab
14. Fiber washer
15. Insulating sleeve
16. Carburetor
17. Pulsation line
18. Fuel filter
19. Insulating tube
20. Fuel line (return)
21. Tie wrap
22. Fuel line (inlet)
23. Male connector
24. Fuel line
25. Hose clamp
26. Heat shield
27. Gasket
28. Fuel tank
29. Rubber spacer
30. Retaining strip
31. Protection strip
32. Connector
33. Vent tube
34. Air intake silencer (deluxe only)
35. Lock tab (deluxe only)
36. Spring ring (deluxe only)
37. Silencer connector (deluxe only)
38. Pop rivet (deluxe only)
39. Bracket (deluxe only)

5

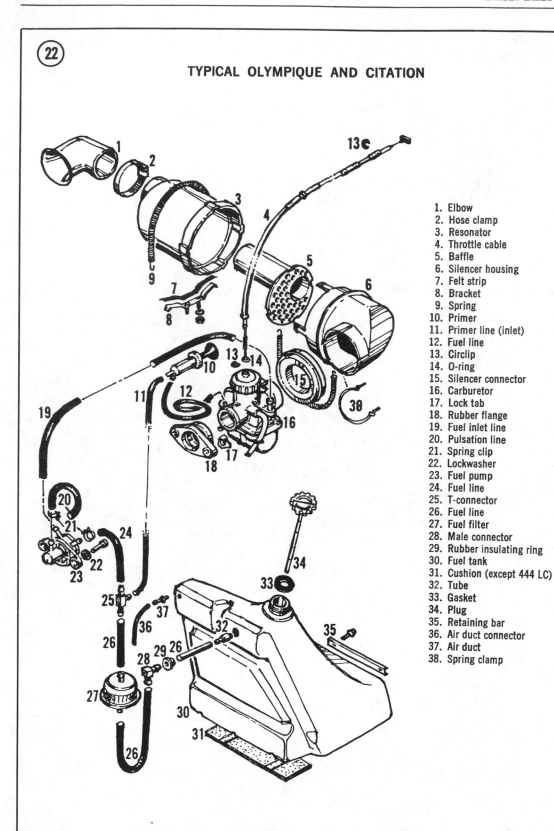

(22)

TYPICAL OLYMPIQUE AND CITATION

1. Elbow
2. Hose clamp
3. Resonator
4. Throttle cable
5. Baffle
6. Silencer housing
7. Felt strip
8. Bracket
9. Spring
10. Primer
11. Primer line (inlet)
12. Fuel line
13. Circlip
14. O-ring
15. Silencer connector
16. Carburetor
17. Lock tab
18. Rubber flange
19. Fuel inlet line
20. Pulsation line
21. Spring clip
22. Lockwasher
23. Fuel pump
24. Fuel line
25. T-connector
26. Fuel line
27. Fuel filter
28. Male connector
29. Rubber insulating ring
30. Fuel tank
31. Cushion (except 444 LC)
32. Tube
33. Gasket
34. Plug
35. Retaining bar
36. Air duct connector
37. Air duct
38. Spring clamp

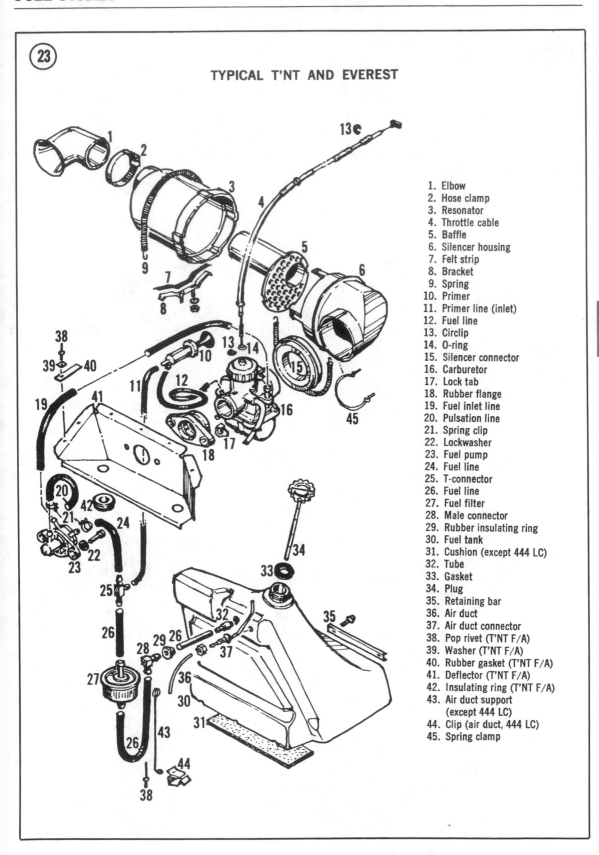

23

TYPICAL T'NT AND EVEREST

1. Elbow
2. Hose clamp
3. Resonator
4. Throttle cable
5. Baffle
6. Silencer housing
7. Felt strip
8. Bracket
9. Spring
10. Primer
11. Primer line (inlet)
12. Fuel line
13. Circlip
14. O-ring
15. Silencer connector
16. Carburetor
17. Lock tab
18. Rubber flange
19. Fuel inlet line
20. Pulsation line
21. Spring clip
22. Lockwasher
23. Fuel pump
24. Fuel line
25. T-connector
26. Fuel line
27. Fuel filter
28. Male connector
29. Rubber insulating ring
30. Fuel tank
31. Cushion (except 444 LC)
32. Tube
33. Gasket
34. Plug
35. Retaining bar
36. Air duct
37. Air duct connector
38. Pop rivet (T'NT F/A)
39. Washer (T'NT F/A)
40. Rubber gasket (T'NT F/A)
41. Deflector (T'NT F/A)
42. Insulating ring (T'NT F/A)
43. Air duct support
    (except 444 LC)
44. Clip (air duct, 444 LC)
45. Spring clamp

5

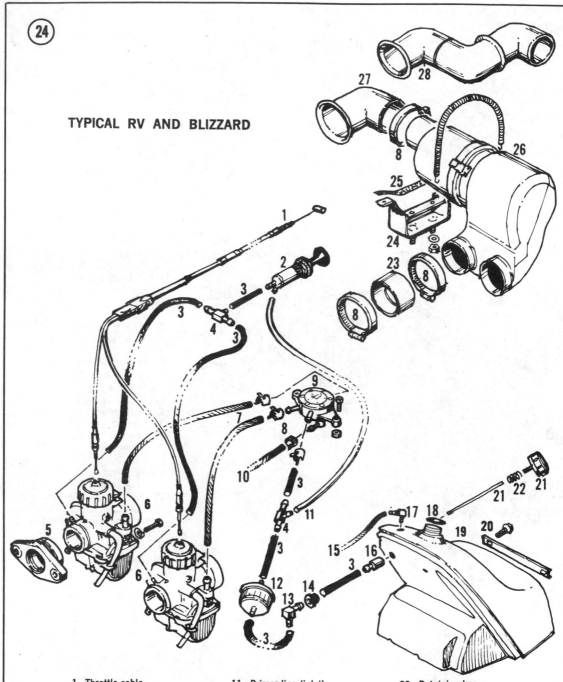

TYPICAL RV AND BLIZZARD

1. Throttle cable
2. Primer
3. Fuel line
4. T-connector
5. Rubber flanges
6. Carburetors
7. Fuel inlet lines
8. Hose clamp
9. Fuel pump
10. Pulsation line

11. Primer line (inlet)
12. Fuel filter
13. Male connector
14. Rubber insulating ring
15. Air duct
16. Tube
17. Connector (air duct)
18. Gasket
19. Fuel tank

20. Retaining bar
21. Plug
22. Spring (connector)
23. Adaptor
24. Bracket
25. Felt strip
26. Air intake silencer
27. Elbow (RV)
28. Elbow (Blizzard 6500)

To clean screen type filter, disassemble and flush with gasoline or solvent and blow dry with compressed air.

Paper element filters should be replaced annually or when contamination builds up at the base of the element.

FUEL PUMP

To check fuel pump (**Figure 27**) operation, disconnect fuel line from pump to carburetor at the carburetor. Make sure ignition is off and pull recoil starter and check for fuel flow at fuel line. If fuel flow from pump is unsatisfactory, replace pump. Refer to **Figure 28** for an exploded view of a typical fuel pump.

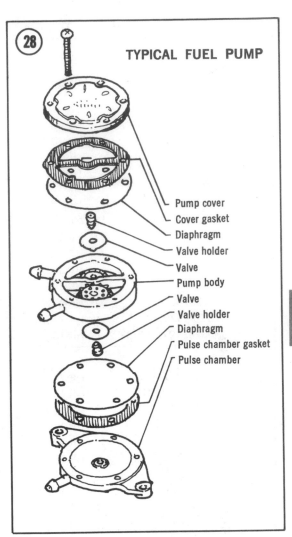

TYPICAL FUEL PUMP

- Pump cover
- Cover gasket
- Diaphragm
- Valve holder
- Valve
- Pump body
- Valve
- Valve holder
- Diaphragm
- Pulse chamber gasket
- Pulse chamber

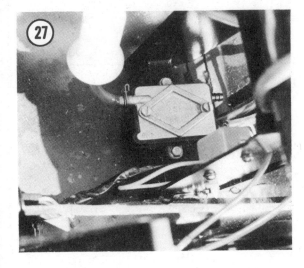

5

Table 1   TILLOTSON CARBURETOR SPECIFICATIONS

Model	Carburetor	Low Speed Adjustment (Turns)**	High Speed Adjustment (Turns)**	Idle Speed (rpm)
Elan				
250, 250 E (1971,1972, early 1973)	HR-73A	¾	1¼ ①	*
250 (late 1973-1975)	HR-133A	¾	Fixed	*
292 SS (1972)	HD-22B	¾	1¼	*
250 T (1973)	HR-136A	¾	Fixed	*
250 T, 250 Deluxe (1974)	HR-155A	1	Fixed	*
250 Deluxe (1975)	HR-165A	1	Fixed	*
250 (1976)	HR-173A	1	Fixed	*
250 SS (1973)	HR-143A (2)	¾	Fixed	*
294 SS (1974)	HR-161A	¾	Fixed	*
300 SS (1975)	HR-166A	¾	Fixed	*
250 SS (1976)	HR-172A	1	Fixed	1,500-1,800
250 (1978-1979)	HR-173A	1	Fixed	1,800-2,000
250 Deluxe (1978-1979)	HR-172A	1	Fixed	1,800-2,200
Olympique				
300 (1971-early 1973)	HR-74A	¾	1¼	*
300 (late 1973-1974)	HR-132A	¾	1	*
300 (1975 and 1976 twin)	HR-169A	1	Fixed	1,500-1,800
300 (1976 single)	HR-174A	1	Fixed	1,200-1,500
335 (1970)	HR-176	¾	1¼	*
335 (1971-1973)	HR-75A	¾ ②	1¼ ②	*
340 (1973-1974)	HR-131A	¾	Fixed	*
340 (1975-1976)	HR-170A, B	1	Fixed	1,500-1,800
399 (1970)	HR-16B	¾	1¼	*
399 (1971-1972)	HR-76A	¾	1¼	*
400 (early 1973)	HR-76A	1	1¹⁄₁₆	*
400 (late 1973-1974)	HR-134A	¾	Fixed	*
440 (1973-1974)	HR-135A	⅞	Fixed	*
440 plus (1976)	HR-176A	1	Fixed	1,500-1,800
T'NT				
292, 340 (1970, 1971, and 1972 292)	HD-22A, B	¾	1¼	*
340 (1972)	HD-98A	1⅛	1	*
294 (1973)	HR-137A (2)	¾	Fixed	*
340 (1973)	HD-107A	⅞	Fixed	*
300 (1974)	HR-164A	1	1	*
340 (1974-1975)	HD-134A	1	1	*
340 (1976)	HD-148A	1	1	1,500-1,800
399 (1970)	HD-21A	¾	1¼	*
440 (1971)	HD-73A	¾	1¼	*

(continued)

Table 1   TILLOTSON CARBURETOR SPECIFICATIONS (continued)

Model	Carburetor	Low Speed Adjustment (Turns)**	High Speed Adjustment (Turns)**	Idle Speed (rpm)
T'NT (con't.)				
440 (1972)	HD-83A	1¼	1¼	*
440 (1973)	HD-109A	1	1	*
440 and Everest (1974-1975)	HD-138A	1	1	*
440 and Everest (1976)	HD-147A	1	1	1,500-1,800
400 F/A (1972)	HD-104A (2)	¾	1¼	*
340 F/A (1973-1974)	HR-149A (2)	1	1⅛	*
400 F/A (1973-1974)	HD-123A (2)	1	⅝	*
340 F/A (1975)	HR-168A (2)	1	1⅛	*
440 F/A (1974)	HRM-3A (2)	1	1¼	*
440 F/A (1975)	HRM-5A (2)	1	1	*

* Unless otherwise specified, idle speed is 1,800-2,200 rpm.
** Tolerance for all adjustments is +⅛-0 turn.
① Fixed jet on later 1973 models.
② On 1973 models turn low-speed needle ⅞ and high-speed needle 1¹¹⁄₁₆.

Table 2   MIKUNI CARBURETOR SPECIFICATIONS

Model	Carburetor	E-ring Position (From Top)	Air Screw Turns (±¼ Turn)
T'NT R/V 245 (1975)	VM 34-72	2	1
T'NT 340-340E kit (1976)	VM 34-109	3	1
T'NT 440-440E kit (1976)	VM 34-105	2	1
Olympique 340-340E kit (1976)	VM 34-104	3	1
Olympique 300-300E kit (1976)	VM 34-103	3	1
T'NT R/V 250 (1976)	VM 34-93	2	1
T'NT R/V 340 (1976)	VM 34-94	2	1
Olympique 440 plus kit (1976)	VM 32-117	3	1½
Olympique 300 (twin—1977-1978)	VM 30-90	3	1½
Olympique 340-340E (1977-1979)	VM 30-91	3	1½
Everest 340-340E kit (1977-1979)	VM30-98	3	1½
Olympique 440 (1977)	VM 32-113	4	1½
T'NT 340 F/A (1977-1978)	VM 34-118	3	1
T'NT 440 F/A (1977)	VM 36-53	2	1
T'NT 440 (1977)	VM 34-110	3	1½
R/V 340 (1977-1978)	VM 34-135	4	1
Everest 440-440E (1977)	VM 34-110	3	1½
Everest 440 L/C (1977)	VM 34-150	4	1
Citation 300 (1978)	VM30-94	3	1½
Citation 300 (1979)	VM 30-104	3	1½
Everest 440, 440E (1978)	VM 34-165	3	2
T'NT 440 F/C (1978)	VM 34-165	3	2
Everest 444 L/C	VM 34-150	4	1½
Blizzard 6500	VM 34-184	4	1½
Blizzard 9500	VM 36-78	4	1
Blizzard 5500	VM 34-203	3	1½
Blizzard 7500 and Cross Country	VM 34-199	2	1½

5

CHAPTER SIX

ELECTRICAL SYSTEM

The electrical system on Ski-Doo snowmobiles consists of an ignition system, lighting system, and an optional electric starting system.

Two types of ignition systems are used: a breaker point magneto and capacitive discharge ignition (CDI). Refer to **Figures 1 and 2** for a typical example of each system.

The lighting system consists of a headlight, brake/taillight, and instrument lights.

The electric starting system is an optional package consisting of a battery, a starter with solenoid, and charging components.

This chapter includes testing and repair of some components of the ignition, lighting, and charging systems. Many of the testing and repair tasks referenced in this chapter require special testing equipment and tools. These tasks are best accomplished by an authorized dealer or competent auto electric shop.

Refer to Chapter Two for magneto breaker point and timing adjustments.

CDI SYSTEM

The capacitor discharge ignition system supplies high voltage to spark plugs without the use of breaker points as in a conventional magneto ignition system.

The CDI system electronic components are not repairable and must be replaced if found defective.

If ignition system malfunctions are experienced, perform the following troubleshooting procedure. Refer any additional testing and repairs to an authorized dealer.

CDI Troubleshooting

1. Check spark plugs (Chapter Two) and spark plug wires and replace if defective.

2. Disconnect junction block connected to engine kill button.

3. Start engine. If engine does not miss, replace kill button. If engine continues to miss or will not start, continue procedure.

4. On models equipped with trigger box, perform the following:

   a. Disconnect violet and black/violet wires from timing box.

   b. Connect ohmmeter between wires. Ohmmeter should indicate 55-60 ohms. If resistance is not as specified, magneto side cylinder pick-up coil is defective. Replace armature plate.

   c. Disconnect black/yellow and violet/yellow wires from timing box.

   d. Connect ohmmeter between wires. Ohmmeter should indicate 55-60 ohms. If resistance is not as specified, PTO side cylinder pick-up coil is defective. Replace armature plate.

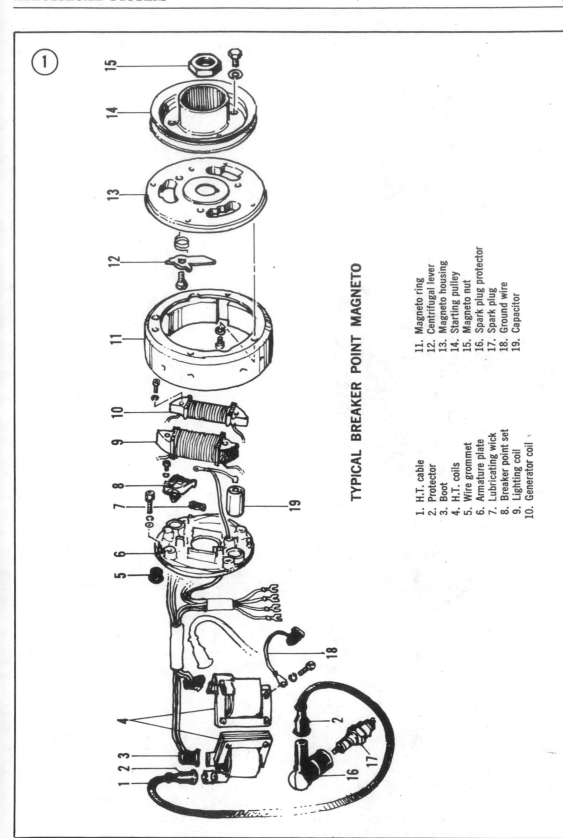

TYPICAL BREAKER POINT MAGNETO

1. H.T. cable
2. Protector
3. Boot
4. H.T. coils
5. Wire grommet
6. Armature plate
7. Lubricating wick
8. Breaker point set
9. Lighting coil
10. Generator coil

11. Magneto ring
12. Centrifugal lever
13. Magneto housing
14. Starting pulley
15. Magneto nut
16. Spark plug protector
17. Spark plug
18. Ground wire
19. Capacitor

6

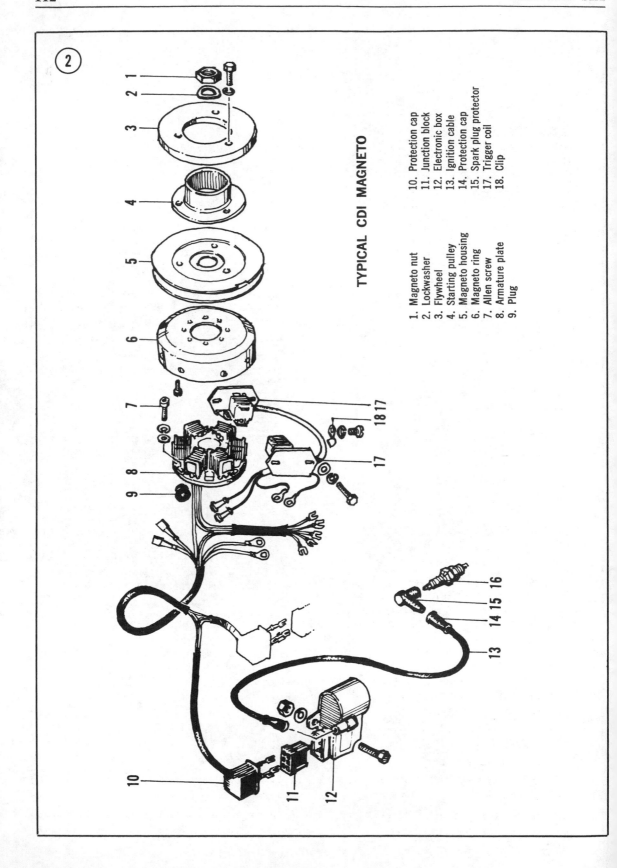

TYPICAL CDI MAGNETO

1. Magneto nut
2. Lockwasher
3. Flywheel
4. Starting pulley
5. Magneto housing
6. Magneto ring
7. Allen screw
8. Armature plate
9. Plug
10. Protection cap
11. Junction block
12. Electronic box
13. Ignition cable
14. Protection cap
15. Spark plug protector
17. Trigger coil
18. Clip

e. If either pick-up coil is defective, remove armature plate assembly from engine as described in Chapter Four.

f. If both pick-up coils check out good, proceed to Step 6.

5. On models without trigger box, perform the following:

a. Disconnect junction block from electronic box.

b. Connect ohmmeter between violet/yellow wire in junction block (not electronic box) and ground. Ohmmeter should indicate 55-60 ohms. If resistance is not as specified, PTO side cylinder pick-up coil is defective. Replace armature plate.

c. Connect ohmmeter between violet wire in junction block and ground. Ohmmeter should indicate 55-60 ohms. If resistance is not as specified, magneto side cylinder pick-up coil is defective. Replace armature plate.

d. If pick-up coils check out as specified and engine misfires on one cylinder, replace electronic box. If either pick-up coil is defective, remove armature plate assembly as outlined in Chapter Four.

e. If engine will not fire on either side, perform the next step.

6. If pick-up coils check out as specified, perform the following:

a. Disconnect junction block from electronic box if not already disconnected.

b. Connect ohmmeter between ground and red wire in junction block (not on electronic box). Ohmmeter should indicate 325-365 ohms.

c. If resistance is not as specified, remove armature plate as outlined in Chapter Four and have an authorized dealer replace ignition generator coil.

d. If resistance is within tolerance, replace electronic box.

e. Reconnect all junction blocks.

MAGNETO IGNITION

The testing of ignition generating coil, condenser, brake light coil, and ignition coils requires expensive sensitive test equipment. If a malfunction is suspected in any of these components, have it tested by an authorized dealer or competent auto electric shop. They have the equipment and expertise for the task.

If malfunctions exist in ignition generating coil or condenser, remove armature plate as outlined in Chapter Four.

Refer to Chapter Two for breaker point and timing adjustments.

LIGHTING SYSTEM

The lighting system consists of a headlight and brake/taillight unit, instrument lights and an AC (alternating current) generating device. Switches control all lighting circuits. The lighting coil on the magneto armature plate generates AC current.

On models equipped with an electric starter, AC is converted (rectified) to DC (direct current) by a rectifier and then used to keep the battery charged.

Lighting Coil

Testing of lighting coil (**Figure 3**) requires expensive sensitive test equipment. If a lighting coil malfunction is suspected, remove magneto armature plate as outlined in Chapter Four and refer testing or repair to an authorized dealer.

6

Light Switch Test

1. Remove wire connectors from light switch.

2. Use an ohmmeter or flashlight continuity tester and test operation of switch in OFF and ON positions.

3. Replace switch if defective. Connect wires to switch.

Headlight Replacement

Lift retaining clips securing bulb socket (**Figure 4**). Twist and pull out bulb. Ensure that new bulb is of the same wattage rating as the old one.

Brake/Taillight Bulb Replacement

1. Remove screws (**Figure 5**) securing light lens and remove lens. On models without lens retaining screws, unsnap lens.

2. Push in and rotate bulb counterclockwise to remove (**Figure 6**).

3. Install new bulb making sure alignment pins on bulb are properly aligned.

4. Install lens and secure with retaining screws.

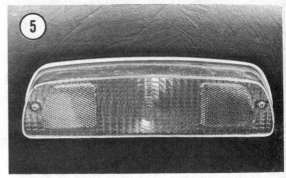

Headlight Adjustment

1. Position snowmobile on a flat surface with headlight 25 ft. (7.6m) from a vertical surface (**Figure 7**).

2. Turn on high beam. Light adjustment is correct if beam center is equal with horizontal beam line. Maximum horizontal deviation from center is 2 in. (5 cm). Maximum vertical deviation is 1 in. (2.5 cm).

3. If light alignment is incorrect, remove headlight ring and adjust upper and lower screws until beam is within specified tolerance.

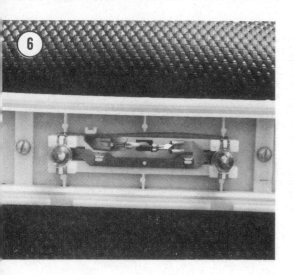

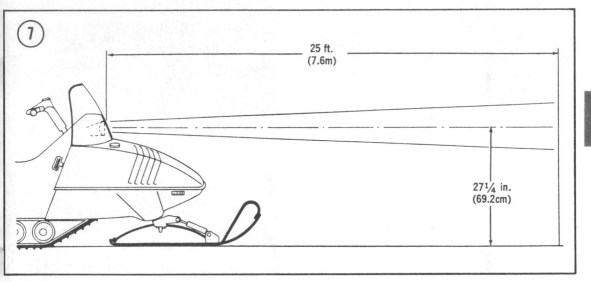

NOTE: *On older models it may be necessary to use small wedges behind headlight ring to obtain desired deflection.*

ELECTRIC STARTING SYSTEM

The electric starting system consists of a 12-volt battery, starter motor with solenoid and a rectifier.

The starter solenoid acts as a relay to route battery current to the starter as well as mechanically engage the starter drive. The starter drive engages with a ring gear on the engine to turn the engine over.

The battery is kept charged by current supplied by the lighting coil which is rectified to DC (direct current) by the rectifier.

Starter and Solenoid
Removal/Installation

Starter testing and repair requires special tools. It is recommended that all starter service and repair be referred to an authorized dealer or competent auto electric shop.

1. Disconnect battery ground cable (**Figure 8**).

2. Disconnect battery cable and switch wires from solenoid (**Figure 9**).

3. Remove capscrews and washers securing starter bracket to crankcase (**Figure 10**).

4. Remove nuts and washers securing starter bracket to starter.

5. Remove nuts and washers securing starter to engine. Remove starter and solenoid with starter bracket.

6. Installation is the reverse of these steps.

Battery Removal/Installation

1. Disconnect negative (−) cable **(Figure 8)**. Remove rubber boot and disconnect positive (+) cable.

2. Loosen hold-down bolts **(Figure 11)** and unhook bolts from battery box. Remove hold-down clamp.

3. Disconnect vent tube from battery. Carefully lift battery out of battery box.

4. Installation is the reverse of these steps. Keep the following points in mind:

> CAUTION
> *Be sure battery connections are correct or serious damage to electrical components will occur.*

   a. Be sure exterior of battery and terminals are clean and free from corrosion.

   b. Connect positive (+) cable to battery first.

Battery Cleaning and Service

Electrolyte level in the battery should be checked periodically, especially during periods of regular operation. Use only distilled water and top off battery to bottom of ring (filler neck) so the tops of the plates are covered. *Do not* overfill.

Battery corrosion is a normal reaction; however, it should be cleaned off periodically to keep battery deterioration to a minimum.

Remove battery and wire brush terminals and cable ends. Wash terminals and exterior of battery with about a 4:1 solution of warm water and baking soda.

> CAUTION
> *Do not allow any baking soda solution to enter battery cells or serious battery damage may result.*

Wash battery box and hold-down bolts with baking soda solution. Rinse all parts in clear water and wipe dry.

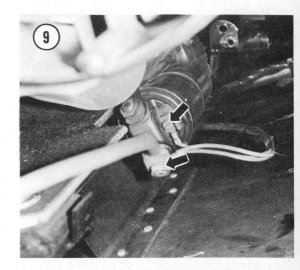

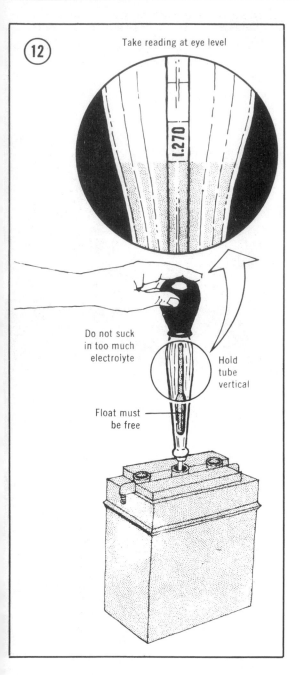

(12) Take reading at eye level

1.270

Do not suck in too much electrolyte

Hold tube vertical

Float must be free

charged. Perform periodic specific gravity tests with a hydrometer to determine the level of charge and how long charge stays up before it starts to deteriorate.

Battery Specific Gravity Test

Determine the state of charge of the battery with a hydrometer. To use this instrument, place the suction tube (**Figure 12**) into the filler opening and draw in just enough electrolyte to lift the float. Hold the instrument in a vertical position and take the reading at eye level.

Specific gravity of electrolyte varies with temperature, so it is necessary to apply a temperature correction to the reading you obtain. For each 10° that the battery temperature exceeds 80°F, add 0.004 to the indicated specific gravity. Subtract 0.004 from the indicated value for each 10° that the battery temperature is below 80°F.

WARNING
Do not smoke or permit any open flame in any area where batteries are being charged. Highly explosive hydrogen gas is formed during the charging process.

The specific gravity of a fully charged battery is 1.260. If the specific gravity is below 1.220, recharge the battery (**Figure 13**).

Starter Test

If starter fails to crank engine or cranks engine very slowly, perform the following:

1. Inspect cranking circuit wiring for loose or badly corroded connections or damaged wiring.

2. Perform *Battery Specific Gravity Test* to be certain battery is charged and not defective.

3. Crank engine with recoil starter to make sure engine turns freely and is not seized.

NOTE: *Remove spark plug wires. The following bypasses the ignition switch.*

4. If starter still will not crank engine, place a heavy jumper lead from positive (+) battery terminal directly to starter terminal (**Figure 14**). This bypasses ignition switch and starter solenoid. If starter motor operates, then one of these items is defective. If starter motor will not operate, starter is defective.

In freezing weather, never add water to a battery unless the machine will be operated for a period of time to mix electrolyte and water.

CAUTION
Keep battery fully charged. A discharged battery will freeze causing the battery case to break.

Remove the battery from the machine during extended non-use periods and keep battery fully

6

Starter Solenoid Test

1. The starter solenoid is a sealed magnetic switch and cannot be repaired. If defective, it must be replaced.

2. Remove and insulate cable from starter terminal. Connect test light across 2 large terminals of starter solenoid.

3. With a jumper lead, connect positive (+) battery post to small terminal on solenoid. Solenoid plunger should snap in, light the test lamp, and hold until the jumper is removed. If not, solenoid is defective.

Rectifier Test

1. Disconnect 4 connectors from rectifier. A diode exists between each of the 4 terminals in the rectifier. Test the 4 diodes one at a time by connecting a test light to 2 adjacent terminals.

2. Test with leads on 2 top terminals, 2 bottom terminals, 2 left terminals, and 2 right terminals. Reverse terminal contacts in each test set-up. Do not test terminals in a diagonal pattern.

3. With leads connected one way, test light should light. With leads reversed, a high resistance or open condition should be indicated. Repeat test for the other 3 diodes. Replace if defective.

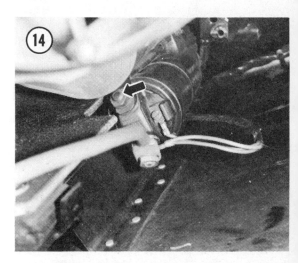

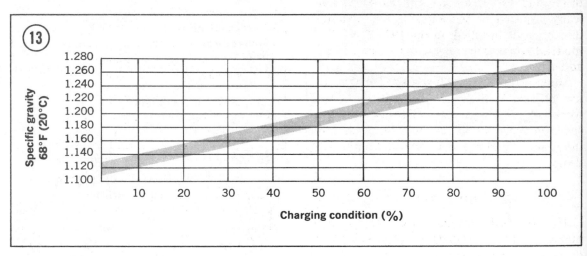

CHAPTER SEVEN

POWER TRAIN

The power train consists of a drive belt, drive and driven pulleys, drive chain and sprockets with chaincase, and a brake assembly.

Three types of brake systems are used: pivot, drum, and disc. Disc brakes are either mechanically adjusted or self-adjusting. A hydraulic disc brake is installed on the 1973 T'NT F/A model. Pivot and drum brakes are mechanically adjusted.

Some procedures in this chapter require the use of special tools for removal and repair work. If such tools are not available and substitutes cannot be locally fabricated, refer the removal and repair work to an authorized dealer.

DRIVE BELT

The drive belt transmits power from the drive pulley to the driven pulley. Refer to **Table 1** for drive belt model application. Drive belt should be replaced when its width is reduced by approximately ⅛ in. (3.0mm). Always install the drive belt specified for your type of machine. Drive belts are not interchangeable between different models even though belt width may be the same.

Removal/Installation

1. Tilt cab and remove pulley guard (**Figure 1**).
2. Twist and push sliding half of driven pulley to open pulley.

Table 1   DRIVE BELT APPLICATION

Model	Belt Width
Elan (all models)	$1\frac{3}{16}$ in.
Olympique Plus (1976)	$1\frac{3}{16}$ in.
All 1975 and earlier models except 1975 T'NT R/V 250	$1\frac{3}{16}$ in.
All other models	$1\frac{5}{16}$ in.

Note: Replace belt when width is reduced by ⅛ in. (3mm)

3. Hold pulley in open position and slip drive belt off of driven pulley then drive pulley (**Figure 2**).

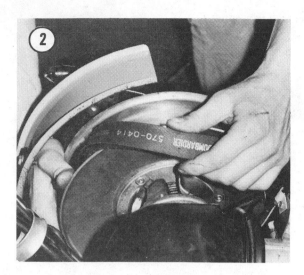

CAUTION
Do not pry belt off over pulleys or belt and/or pulleys may be damaged.

4. Installation is the reverse of these steps. Check drive belt tension.

Drive Belt Tension Adjustment

Drive belt tension must be correct or improper drive and abnormal belt wear may result.

Check tension on all machines with a drive pulley *without* bearings on the shaft.

1. Position a ruler on drive belt for a reference.

2. Using a stick and fish scale apply 15 lb. (6.8 kg) of pressure at center of belt. Belt should deflect 1 3/16 - 1 1/2 in. (30-38mm).

3. If belt tension is incorrect, decrease or increase distance between pulleys. Recheck belt deflection.

DRIVE PULLEY

The following procedures require the use of special tools for removal, installation, and repair. If special tools or locally fabricated equivalents are not available, refer work to an authorized dealer. Refer to **Table 2** for drive pulley model application.

CAUTION
Drive pulleys are matched to driven pulleys and engine. Do not use pulleys not designed for your particular machine or improper operation may result.

Pressure Lever and Roller Round Shaft Type Drive Pulley Removal/Installation

1. Remove drive belt.

2. To hold engine while removing retaining bolt, perform the following:
   a. Remove spark plug(s).
   b. Rotate crankshaft until piston (PTO piston for twin cylinder engines) is approximately 1 in. (25mm) BTDC.
   c. Insert a length of rope such as recoil starter rope into spark plug hole (**Figure 3**).
   d. Slowly rotate crankshaft counterclockwise until piston bears against rope.

3. Make sure alignment marks on pulley halves are visible. If not, make new marks.

4. Apply pressure to governor cup of pulley and remove retaining bolt (**Figure 4**).

NOTE: *Pulley is spring loaded and may spring apart if pressure is not applied during bolt removal.*

5. Gently remove sliding half of pulley with spring and spring seat (**Figure 5**).

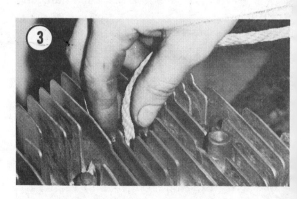

Table 2   DRIVE PULLEY SPECIFICATIONS

Model	Pulley Type	Torque Method	Bolt Torque Ft.-lb.	Mkg
Elan	1	A	37-54*	(5.1-7.5)
Olympique (1970-1974 and 1976 300 single)	2	A	37-54	(5.1-7.5)
Olympique (all 1975 and 1976 plus 440)	3	A	83-92	(11.5-12.7)
Olympique (1976 300 twin and 340)**	3	B	58-68	(8.0-9.4)
Olympique (1978-1979 300T and 340)	3	B	58-68	(8.0-9.4)
Citation (1978-1979 300)	3	A	58-68	(8.0-9.4)
T'NT F/A 340, 400, 440	4	B	58-68	(8.0-9.4)
T'NT and Everest**	3	A	83-92	(11.5-12.7)
T'NT 245, 250, 340 R/V**	3	B	58-68	(8.0-9.4)
Everest 340, 440, 444LC (1978-1979)	3	B	58-68	(8.0-9.4)
T'NT 340 F/A and 440 F/C (1978)	3	B	58-68	(8.0-9.4)
R/V 340 (1978), Blizzard 5500 and 6500	3	B	58-68	(8.0-9.4)
Blizzard 7500 plus and 9500 plus	5	B	58-68	(8.0-9.4)

Pulley Type
1 — Roller round shaft
2 — Pressure lever
3 — Roller square shaft
4 — High performance
5 — Roller square shaft with 3 ramps

Torque Method
A. Torque to specifications. loosen and retorque to specification.
B. Torque to specification. Start engine and alternately accelerate and brake. Stop engine and retorque to specification.

*On 1975 250 Deluxe models, torque to 83-92 ft.-lb. (11.5-12.7 mkg)
**Models equipped with "Duralon" bushings.

6. To remove fixed half of pulley from crankshaft, it is necessary to locally fabricate a removal tool. Perform the following:

a. Cut a piece of pipe the approximate length of exposed pulley shaft. Pipe must be large enough to slide over pulley shaft.

b. Drill a 5/16 in. hole near end of pipe.

c. Slide pipe over pulley shaft and install a 5/16 in. bolt through pipe and hole in shaft end. Secure bolt with nut.

d. Use a pipe wrench on pipe and remove fixed half of drive pulley.

7. Refer all necessary inspection and repair to an authorized dealer.

8. Installation is the reverse of these steps. Keep the following points in mind:

a. Pack inside pulley shaft with clutch lubricant available from an authorized dealer.

b. Lightly oil retaining bolt threads.

c. Ensure that pulley marks are aligned.

d. Torque retaining bolt to 37-54 ft.-lb. (5.1-7.5 mkg). Loosen bolt and retorque to specified value.

e. Perform *Pulley Alignment*.

Roller Square Shaft and High Performance Type Drive Pulley Removal/Installation

1. Remove drive belt.

2. On some models equipped with high per-

formance type pulley, it is necessary to raise engine from frame. Support engine with a wooden block between engine mount and frame cross support.

> NOTE: *Roller shaft pulleys are spring loaded. To avoid pulley springing apart during removal of retaining bolt, pressure must be applied and held against sliding half of pulley. On roller square shaft type pulleys, 1 or 2 clamps secured to outside rims of pulley halves can be used to hold spring tension (Figure 6). Exercise care when installing clamp(s) to avoid damaging or distorting pulley rims.*

3. To hold engine while removing retaining bolt, perform the following:

  a. Remove spark plug(s).

  b. Rotate crankshaft until piston (PTO piston for twin cylinder engines) is approximately 1 in. (25mm) BTDC.

  c. Insert a length of rope such as recoil starter rope into spark plug hole (**Figure 3**).

  d. Slowly rotate crankshaft counterclockwise until piston bears against rope.

4. Make sure alignment marks on pulley halves are visible. If not make new marks (**Figure 7**).

5. Loosen retaining bolt. If clamps are not used on pulley, remember to hold pressure against pulley to keep it from springing apart. Remove retaining bolt and governor cup (**Figure 8**).

6. On models equipped with high performance pulley, it is necessary to use a special puller to remove pulley assembly. Perform the following:

  a. Insert puller through pulley hub.

  b. Gradually tighten puller.

  c. Tap puller head to release pulley from crankshaft.

7. On models equipped with roller shaft pulleys, gently remove clamp(s) holding pulley halves together, and remove sliding half of pulley (**Figure 9**).

8. Loosen fixed half of pulley with a 1⅛ in. open end wrench or large adjustable (Crescent) wrench, and remove pulley half (**Figure 10**).

CAUTION
Keep wrench as close to hub as possible and ensure that wrench does not slip, or damage to pulley shaft may result.

9. Refer all necessary inspection and repair to an authorized dealer.

10. Installation is the reverse of these steps. Keep the following points in mind:

   a. Lightly oil retaining bolt threads.

   b. On models equipped with high performance pulley, clean crankshaft with fine steel wool and acetone. Dry shaft with clean, dry cloth.

   c. Always use a *new* locking tab washer.

   CAUTION
   On pulleys equipped with "Duralon" bushings (Table 2), install sliding half of pulley very carefully or "Duralon" bushing may be scratched by square edge of shaft.
   When installing governor cup ensure that shaft end is positioned in governor cup seat or a bent crankshaft may result.

   d. Torque retaining bolt as specified in **Table 2**.

   e. Perform *Pulley Alignment*.

DRIVEN PULLEY

CAUTION
Driven pulleys are matched to drive pulleys and engine. Do not use pulleys not designed for your particular machine or improper operation may result.

Removal/Installation

1. Remove drive belt.

   NOTE: *On T'NT F/A models with self-adjusting pulley (Table 3), remove bolt and washer securing driven pulley and remove pulley.*

2. On mid-engine models, remove muffler **(Figure 11)**. On models with tuned muffler, remove muffler grommet.

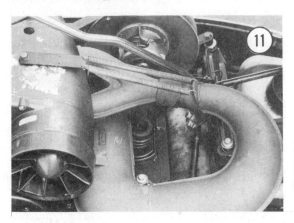

3. Loosen steering column upper bracket **(Figure 12)**.

Table 3   PULLEY ALIGNMENT SPECIFICATIONS

Model	Pulley Offset	Distance Between Pulleys
All 1970 models except T'NT 340	½ in. (12.7mm)[1]	1⅞ in. (47.6mm)[2]
All 1971 models	½ in. (12.7mm)[1]	1⅞ in. (47.6mm)[2]
All 1972-1973 except T'NT 340, 440, and T'NT F/A	½ in. (12.7mm)[1]	1⅞ in. (47.6mm)[2]
1970 T'NT 340	⅜ in. (9.5mm)	1⅞ in. (47.6mm)[2]
1972-1973 T'NT 294, 340, 440	7/16 in. (11.1mm)[3]	1⅝ in. (41.3mm)[2]
1973 T'NT F/A 340, 400	½ in. (12.7mm)[4]	10½ in. (26.7cm)[5]
1974 Elan and Olympique except Elan 294SS[7]	9/16 in. (14.3mm)[3]	1⅞ in. (47.6mm)[4]
1974-1975 Elan 294SS and 300SS[7]	9/16 in. (14.3mm)[3]	1⅞ in. (47.6mm)[4]
1974-1975 Elan 294SS and 300SS[7]	½ in. (12.7mm)[3]	1½ in. (38.1mm)[4]
1974-1975 T'NT, Everest, T'NT F/A, 245 R/V, and 1975 Olympique[7]	½ in. (12.7mm)[3]	1⅜ in. (34.9mm)[4]
1974-1975 T'NT F/A except 245 R/V	Self-adjusting	1¼ in. (31.7mm)[6]
1976 Elan	1½ in. (38.1mm)[3]	1¾ in. (44.4mm)[2]
1978-1979 Elan	1 11/32 in. (34mm)[3]	1¾ in. (44mm)[2]
1976 Olympique 300 single	1½ in. (38.1mm)[3]	1⅞ in. (47.6mm)[2]
1976 Olympique 440	1½ in. (38.1mm)[3]	1⅜ in. (34.9mm)[2]
1976 Olympique 300, 340, T'NT, Everest, and T'NT R/V	1 5/16-1⅜ in. (33.3-34.9mm)	1⅜ in. (34.9mm)[2]
1978 Blizzard 6500 Plus	1 11/32 in. (34mm)[3]	1 5/16 in. (33mm)[2]
1979 Blizzard 5500	1 11/32 in. (34mm)[3]	1⅜ in. (35mm)[2]
All other 1978-1979 models	1 11/32 in. (34mm)[3]	1 7/16 in. (36mm)[2]

1. 1971 models tolerance ± 1/32 in. (±0.8mm)
2. 1971 models tolerance ± 1/32 in. (±0.8mm), all other models tolerance +0 − 1/16 in. (+0 − 1.6mm)
3. Tolerance ± 1/32 in. (±0.8mm)
4. Tolerance ± 1/16 in. (±1.6mm)
5. Measure between pulley centers. Tolerance +0 − ⅛ in. (3.2mm). Pulley not adjustable, if out of tolerance check for mechanical wear or damage.
6. Not adjustable.
7. 1974-1975 models pulley offset achieved by using a simulator rod of specified diameter between halves of driven pulley.

4. On models so equipped, disconnect driven pulley support from upper column bracket **(Figure 13)**.

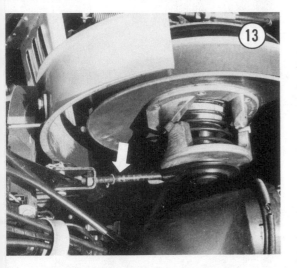

5. On models equipped with disc brakes, remove 2 bolts securing brake assembly and remove brake assembly **(Figure 14)**.

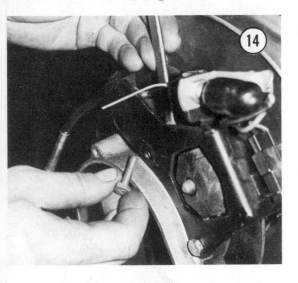

6. Remove air silencer **(Figure 15)**.

> NOTE: *On some models it may be necessary to remove carburetor to gain access to driven pulley.*

7. On models equipped with aluminum chaincase, drain oil and remove chaincase cover **(Figure 16)**.

8. On models with pressed steel chaincase, pry out inspection cover **(Figure 17)**.

9. Loosen chain tension as follows:

   a. On 1970 model chaincases, loosen locknut and adjuster bolt and rotate adjuster **(Figure 18)**.

7

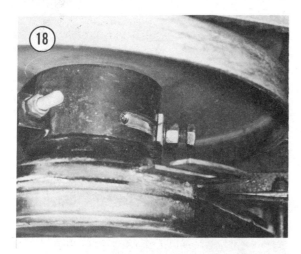

b. On aluminum chaincase models without external adjuster, release springs securing tensioner blocks **(Figure 19)**.

c. On models with aluminum chaincase and external adjuster, loosen adjuster bolt.

10. Remove cotter pin and remove nut and washer from upper sprocket shaft **(Figure 20)**.

11. Hold upper sprocket and chain and remove driven pulley **(Figure 21)**.

> NOTE: *On models equipped with pressed steel chaincase, wire sprocket to top of chaincase to prevent chain and sprocket from falling to the bottom of the chaincase.*

12. Refer all necessary inspection and repair to an authorized dealer.

13. Installation is the reverse of these steps. Keep the following points in mind:

a. On models *not* equipped with self-adjusting drive pulley **(Table 3)**, tighten nut securing driven pulley and upper sprocket then back off nut ⅙ turn. Install cotter pin **(Figure 20)**.

> CAUTION
> *Failure to back off castellated nut ⅙ turn may result in damaged bearing on drive pulley shaft.*

b. On T'NT F/A models with self-adjusting pulley **(Table 3)**, torque pulley retaining bolt to 25 ft.-lb. (3.5 mkg).

c. On 1970 models, adjust external tensioner bolt for ¼ in. (6.4mm) chain deflection. Measure deflection on chain through upper inspection hole in chaincase **(Figure 22)**.

d. On later models, chaincases with external tensioner bolt, tighten adjuster bolt for ¼ in. (6.4mm) slack measured at driven pulley (**Figure 23**).

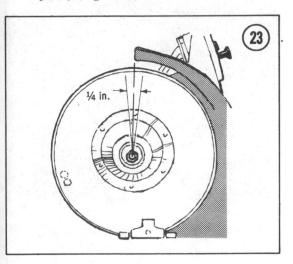

e. Use new O-ring on aluminum chaincase cover. Tighten cover bolts gradually and evenly. Torque to 5 ft.-lb. (0.7 mkg).

f. Add approved oil until level is flush with indicator level or plug, see Chapter Two.

g. Perform *Pulley Alignment*.

PULLEY ALIGNMENT

CAUTION
Proper pulley/drive belt alignment is very important. A misaligned drive belt can be destroyed in a few hours of operation.

NOTE: *If proper pulley alignment cannot be achieved through adjustment and the use of the proper number of shims, inspect drive components as well as frame for possible damage.*

Check alignment whenever engine is installed or rapid belt wear is experienced.

Alignment (1970—1973 Models)

1. Remove drive belt.

2. Check that engine mount nuts are torqued to 33-35 ft.-lb. (4.6-4.8 mkg).

3. Using appropriate adjuster bar, check pulley offset as specified in **Table 3**. See **Figure 24**.

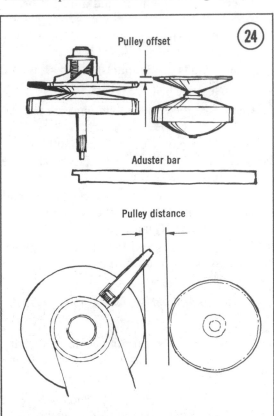

4. Check the distance between pulley rims (**Figure 24**). See **Table 3** for specifications.

5. If offset is greater than specified value, remove drive pulley and add shims to crankshaft.

CAUTION
Do not use more than 5 shims on crankshaft.

6. If offset is less than specified, install shims between chaincase and frame.

> NOTE: *On steel chaincases, shim can be cut in half to correct for a bent chaincase.*

> **CAUTION**
> *On aluminum chaincases, always use full length shims.*

7. If pulley distance is out of tolerance, loosen chaincase. Loosen driven pulley support, if necessary, and tighten or loosen hinge rod to move driven pulley to specified distance.

8. Tighten chaincase. Recheck alignment and distance.

9. Check brake operation and adjust if necessary.

10. Install drive belt.

Alignment (1974-1975 models)

1. Remove drive belt.

2. Check that the engine mount nuts are torqued to 22-30 ft.-lb. (2.9-4.1 mkg).

3. Place a piece of specified size simulator rod between driven pulley halves (**Figure 25**). See **Table 3** for simulator rod size.

4. Use a straight end or stretched rope and check that inner halves of drive and driven pulleys are aligned (**Figure 25**).

5. If drive pulley is too far in, remove pulley and add shims on crankshaft.

> **CAUTION**
> *Do not use more than 5 shims on crankshaft.*

6. If drive pulley is too far out, loosen chaincase and install necessary shims between frame and chaincase.

> NOTE: *On steel chaincases, shims can be cut in half to correct for a bent chaincase.*

> **CAUTION**
> *On aluminum chaincases always use full length shims.*

7. On T'NT F/A models with self-adjusting driven pulley, alignment takes place automatically during operation. Apply anti-seize lubricant to pulley shaft to ensure its free movement. Check that pulley retaining bolt is torqued to 25 ft.-lb. (3.5 mkg).

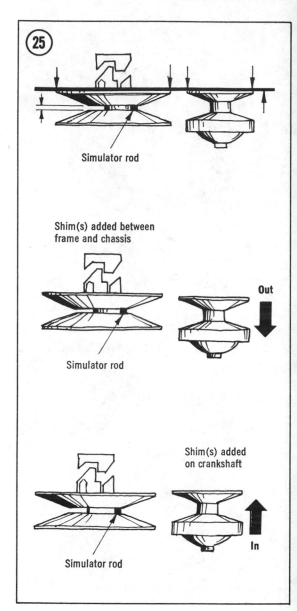

(25)

Simulator rod

Shim(s) added between frame and chassis

Simulator rod

Out

Shim(s) added on crankshaft

Simulator rod

In

8. Check distance between pulley rims. See **Table 3** for specifications.

9. If pulley distance is not as specified, loosen and adjust chaincase as necessary.

10. Check brake operation and adjust if necessary.

11. Install drive belt.

Alignment (1976 and Later Models)

1. Remove drive belt.

2. Check that engine mount nuts are torqued to 22-30 ft.-lb. (2.9-4.1 mkg).

3. Lay a 19 in. (48 cm) length of ⅜ in. square bar between pulley halves **(Figure 26)**.

4. Check pulley offset and distance as specified in **Table 3**.

5. On front mounted engines if pulley offset is out of tolerance, loosen engine support and adjust in required direction to obtain specified offset.

6. On center mounted engines, remove drive pulley and add shims to crankshaft.

> CAUTION
> *Do not use more than 5 shims on crankshaft.*

If drive pulley is too far out, loosen chaincase and install necessary shims between frame and chaincase.

7. If pulley distance is not as specified, loosen and adjust chaincase as necessary.

8. Check brake operation and adjust if necessary.

9. Install drive belt.

CHAINCASE, DRIVE CHAIN, AND SPROCKETS

Pressed Steel Chaincase
Assembly Removal/Installation

1. Remove driven pulley.

2. Release track tension (Chapter Two).

3. Place a drain pan beneath chaincase and pry out drive axle oil seal from chaincase with a small screwdriver **(Figure 27)**.

4. Disconnect brake cable.

> NOTE: *On 1970 models with 18 in. track, remove foot rest secured to frame and chaincase (Figure 28).*

5. Remove lower access plug **(Figure 28)** from chaincase and remove cotter pin and spacer securing lower sprocket.

6. Remove nut securing hinge rod to chaincase bracket **(Figure 29)**.

7. Remove nut securing lower chaincase bracket and remove bracket **(Figure 28)**.

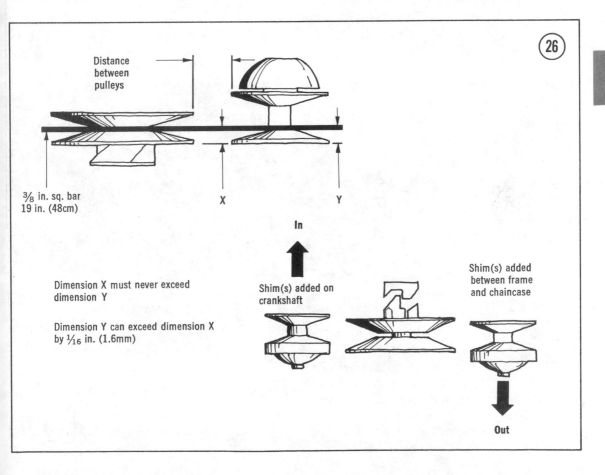

Distance between pulleys

26

7

⅜ in. sq. bar
19 in. (48cm)

X   Y

In

Dimension X must never exceed dimension Y

Dimension Y can exceed dimension X by ¹⁄₁₆ in. (1.6mm)

Shim(s) added on crankshaft

Shim(s) added between frame and chaincase

Out

8. Remove nuts and washers from "U" clamp securing chaincase to frame (**Figure 28**).

9. Note number of shims, if any, between chaincase and frame and remove shims.

10. Shift chaincase and disengage hinge rod.

11. Remove drive axle.

12. Using 2 large screwdrivers between chaincase and frame, pry chaincase assembly from machine.

13. Perform *Inspection and Repair*.

14. Installation is the reverse of these steps. Keep the following points in mind:

    a. Ensure that spacer is on drive axle before installing axle.

    NOTE: *Spacer is not installed on Elan models.*

    b. When installing oil seal on drive axle, ensure that approximately ⅟₁₆ in. (1.5mm)

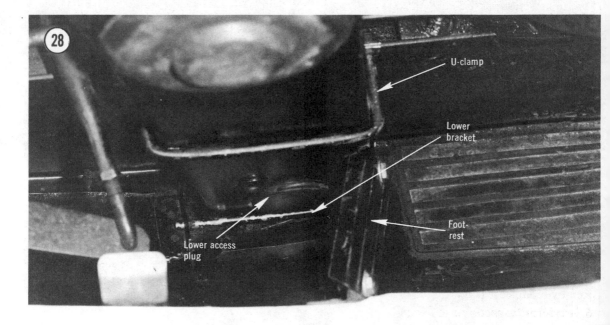

gap is present between end of chaincase flange and oil seal.

c. On 1970 models, adjust tensioner for ¼ in. (6.4mm) chain deflection measured through chaincase inspection hole (**Figure 22**).

d. Perform *Pulley Alignment*.

e. Perform *Brake Adjustment* and *Track Tension Adjustment* as outlined in Chapter Two.

f. Add approved chaincase oil until level is flush with chaincase plug. See Chapter Two.

Aluminum Chaincase (With Automatic Chain Tensioner) Removal/Installation

1. Remove driven pulley.

2. Release track tension (Chapter Two).

3. Pry out drive axle oil seal from chaincase with a small screwdriver (**Figure 27**).

4. Remove cotter pin and spacer securing lower sprocket (**Figure 30**). Remove lower sprocket and chain.

5. Remove bolts securing chaincase to frame (**Figure 31**). Note number of shims, if any, between chaincase and frame and remove shims. Remove chaincase (**Figure 32**).

6. Perform *Inspection and Repair*.

7. Installation is the reverse of these steps. Keep the following points in mind:

a. Ensure that the spacer is on the drive axle (**Figure 33**).

b. When installing oil seal on drive axle, ensure that approximately ¹⁄₁₆ in. (1.5mm) gap is present between end of chaincase flange and oil seal.

c. Perform *Pulley Alignment*.

d. Perform *Brake Adjustment* and *Track Tension Adjustment* as outlined in Chapter Two.

e. Use new O-ring on chaincase cover. Tighten cover bolts gradually and evenly. Torque bolts to 5 ft.-lb. (0.7 mkg).

f. Add approved chaincase oil until level is flush with indicator level or plug, see Chapter Two.

Aluminum Chaincase (With External Chain Tension Adjuster) Removal/Installation

1. Remove driven pulley.

2. Pry out drive axle oil seal from chaincase with a small screwdriver (**Figure 27**).

3. Release track tension (Chapter Two).

4. Remove bolt and washer securing lower sprocket and remove sprocket.

5. Remove bolt securing chaincase to frame and remove chaincase.

6. Perform *Inspection and Repair*.

7. Installation is the reverse of these steps. Keep the following points in mind:

a. Tighten tension adjuster bolt for ¼ in. (6.4mm) slack measured at driven pulley level (**Figure 23**).

b. Perform *Pulley Alignment*.

c. Perform *Track Tension Adjustment* as outlined in Chapter Two.

d. Use new O-ring on chaincase cover. Tighten bolts gradually and evenly. Torque bolts to 5 ft.-lb. (0.7 mkg).

e. Add approved chaincase oil as outlined in Chapter Two.

Inspection and Repair

1. Inspect chain for damaged or broken rollers.

2. Inspect sprocket teeth for wear. If a new drive chain is installed, replace both sprockets. A new chain will not match worn sprockets.

3. Examine chain tensioners and replace if contact surfaces are deeply worn.

4. To replace chain, sprockets, or tensioners, perform the following:

a. Remove cotter pin and castellated nut securing drive pulley to upper sprocket and remove drive pulley.

b. Remove bolt securing chain tensioner to chaincase and remove tensioner (**Figure 34**).

c. Inspect bearings on upper sprocket shaft and replace if damaged or worn.

d. If replacing upper sprocket oil seal ensure that oil seal sits flush with chaincase hub.

e. When installing lower sprocket ensure that longer flange on sprocket is toward track side of chaincase.

f. On models not equipped with self-adjusting drive pulley (**Table 3**), tighten nut securing driven pulley and upper sprocket then back off ⅙ turn. Install cotter pin (**Figure 20**).

> CAUTION
> *Failure to back off castellated nut ⅙ turn may result in damaged bearing on drive pulley shaft.*

BRAKES

Pivot Brake Assembly Removal/Installation

1. Remove drive belt.

2. Disconnect brake cable from handle plate.

3. Remove nut securing hinge rod to cross frame support (**Figure 35**).

4. Remove U-clamp and shims securing chaincase (**Figure 28**). Loosen lower bracket securing chaincase to frame.

5. Move chaincase and disengage hinge rod from cross support.

6. Remove nut securing hinge rod to chaincase and remove brake assembly with hinge rod and spring **(Figure 35)**.

7. Examine brake lining and replace if oil-soaked or worn to level of rivets.

8. Installation is the reverse of these steps. Keep the following points in mind:

    a. Perform *Pulley Alignment*.

    b. Adjust brake cable so brake is fully applied when brake lever is ¼ in. (6.4mm) from handlebar grip.

Drum Brake Removal/Installation

Refer to **Figure 36** for this procedure.

1. Remove drive belt.

2. Disconnect brake lever spring.

3. Remove bolt and cable lock bracket securing brake cable to brake lever.

4. Remove brake lever and brake assembly from machine.

5. Replace brake lining if oil-soaked or worn to level of rivets.

6. Installation is the reverse of these steps. Keep the following points in mind:

    a. Lightly lubricate all moving parts with light oil. Do not get oil on brake shoe of drum.

    b. Adjust brake cable so brake is fully applied when brake lever is 1 in. (25mm) from handlebar grip.

c. Check brake light operation and loosen and adjust brake light switch locknuts if necessary.

Regular Type Disc Brake Removal/Installation

Refer to **Figure 37** for this procedure.

1. Disconnect wires from brake light switch on models so equipped.

2. Remove bolt and nut securing cable to brake lever.

3. Remove locknut from cable housing and withdraw cable.

4. Remove bolts securing brake assembly to chaincase and remove brake assembly with return spring.

5. Check brake pad thickness and replace if less than ³⁄₁₆ in. (4.8mm) thick.

6. Installation is the reverse of these steps. Keep the following points in mind:

  a. Torque nuts securing brake assembly to brake support to 25 ft.-lb. (3.5 mkg).

b. Adjust brake cable so brake is fully applied when brake lever is 1 in. (25mm) from handlebar grip.

c. Check brake light operation and loosen and adjust brake light switch locknuts if necessary.

Heavy Duty Disc Brake Removal/Installation

1. Disconnect brake cable from brake lever. Disconnect brake light switch spring.

2. Remove bolts securing brake assembly to brake support bracket and remove brake assembly.

3. Inspect brake pads and replace if worn level with rivets.

4. Installation is the reverse of these steps. Keep the following points in mind:

  a. Tighten castellated adjuster nut until disc/pad friction is just felt. Screw in small adjusting screw until pads are parallel and apply equal pressure on disc. Lock small adjusting screw with jam nut.

b. Back off castellated nut slightly and secure with hair pin keeper.

c. Tighten small cone nut then back off one turn.

d. Adjust brake cable for 1 in. (25mm) gap between brake lever and handlebar grip when brake is fully applied.

e. Check operation of brake light and loosen and adjust light switch locknuts if necessary.

Self-Adjusting Disc Brake
(Non-Bombardier Type)
Removal/Installation

Refer to **Figure 38** for this procedure.

1. Disconnect brake cable.

2. Disconnect brake light switch electrical junction block.

3. Remove locknut securing cable housing and pull out housing.

4. Remove bolts securing brake assembly and remove complete assembly.

5. Inspect brake pads and replace if less than ⅛ in. (3.2mm) thick.

6. If necessary to replace pads perform the following:

a. Remove cotter pin securing retaining pin and remove retaining pin.

b. Slip strips of thin, stiff cardboard between pawls and ratchet wheels. Screw ratchet wheel up against stop nut.

c. Disengage pawls from brake pads and brake lever and remove pads.

d. Lightly lubricate adjusting screw threads with graphite base lubricant.

e. Lightly grease mating surfaces of pawls with low temperature grease.

f. Install pawls and position brake lever on adjusting screw stud so brake lever tab engages slot of adjusting pawl.

g. Apply low-temperature grease on cam recess of brake lever and install sliding pad assembly over adjusting screw stud so sliding pad tab engages slot of backstop pawl.

38
7

h. Install retaining pin and secure with new cotter pin.

7. Installation is the reverse of these steps. Keep the following points in mind:

a. With brake spring disconnected and switch tab rotated away from brake light switch, press brake lever lightly until free play is taken up. Measure and record distance between brake lever and brake light switch bracket. This is neutral position.

b. Secure brake cable housing to bracket, making sure adjusting nuts are halfway on housing threads.

c. Connect brake cable to brake lever in neutral position.

d. Connect brake lever spring and check neutral position. Readjust if necessary with adjusting nuts on cable housing.

e. Apply brake repeatedly until no more clicks are heard. Brakes must apply fully before brake lever is ½ in. (13mm) from handlebar grip.

f. Check operation of brake light and loosen and adjust light switch locknuts if necessary.

Self-Adjusting Disc Brake (Bombardier Type) Removal/Installation

Refer to **Figure 39** for this procedure.

1. Disconnect brake cable and brake light switch.

2. On models with floating caliper type brake, remove bolts securing brake support to chaincase and slide caliper assembly from brake support.

3. On models with floating disc type brake, remove bolts securing brake bracket to chaincase and remove caliper assembly.

4. Inspect brake pads and replace if oil-soaked or less than ⅛ in. (3.20mm) thick.

5. Installation is the reverse of these steps. Keep the following points in mind:

a. Apply brake repeatedly until no more clicks are heard.

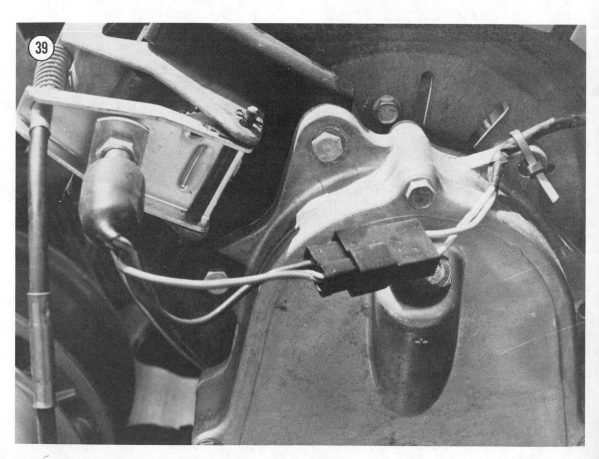

b. Rotate cable adjusting nut until no free play exists between brake lever and brake housing.

c. Measure gap between brake lever and caliper. Gap should be $2 \pm \frac{1}{8}$ in. (50 ± 3mm) on floating caliper type and $1\frac{1}{2} \pm \frac{1}{8}$ in. (38 ± 3mm) on floating disc type (**Figure 40**).

NOTE: *On floating caliper type it may be necessary to move brake light switch support to achieve recommended gap between lever and caliper housing.*

d. On floating caliper models, torque nut securing caliper assembly to 14-17 ft.-lb. (1.9-2.4 mkg).

e. Check operation of brake light and loosen and adjust light switch locknuts if necessary.

7

CHAPTER EIGHT

FRONT SUSPENSION AND STEERING

The front suspension and steering consist of spring mounted skis on spindles connected to the steering column by tie rods.

All machines except T'NT R/V models are equipped with multi-leaf springs. T'NT R/V models use a mono-leaf spring.

Ski legs (spindles) are mounted in replaceable bushings. Ski runner shoes are also replaceable.

This chapter includes removal and installation procedures for typical steering and ski components.

SKIS

The following procedures are typical for most models. Special model details, where applicable, are noted. During removal and disassembly always note and record location of bolts of different sizes and lengths as well as shims, spacers, and lockwashers (if any) to aid assembly and installation.

Removal/Installation

1. Raise front of machine off the ground and block up securely.

2. Remove nut from ski spring coupler and unscrew bolt from coupler (**Figure 1**).

> CAUTION
> *After removing nut do not attempt to drive bolt from coupler. Bolt must be*

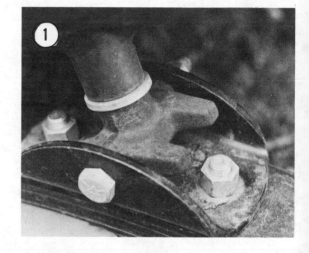

unscrewed or damage to bolt and/or coupler will occur.

NOTE: *On models where spring coupler pivots directly on ski leg (spindle), clamp spring leaves together with Vise Grip pliers and remove bolts and nuts securing spring coupler to springs.*

3. Remove ski assembly from machine.

4. Inspect ski runner shoes. Replace runner shoes if worn more than ½ of their thickness.

> WARNING
> *Ski runner shoes are under tension. Remove runner shoes carefully or injury may result.*

5. Installation is the reverse of these steps. Keep the following points in mind:

   a. When installing spring couplers with threaded holes for coupler bolts, ensure that threaded holes are on the inside of the machine.

   b. Torque coupler bolts to 46-50 ft.-lb. (6.4-6.8 mkg), then torque locknut to 44-55 ft.-lb. (6.1-7.6 mkg). See **Table 1**.

Table 1   SKI TORQUE SPECIFICATIONS

Components	Torque Ft.-lb.	Mkg
Spring coupler to leaf spring*	35-40	4.8-5.5
Runner shoe		
Elan 294SS and 300SS	4-5	0.6-0.7
All other models	9-12	1.2-1.7
Ski coupler		
Bolt (all models except T'NT R/V)	46-50	6.4-6.9
Bolt (T'NT R/V)	25	3.5
Nut	44-55	6.1-7.6
Shock absorber	33-35	4.6-4.8

* Tighten to specified torque then loosen and retorque to specified value.

   c. Torque bolts securing ski coupler to spring to 35-40 ft.-lb. (4.8-5.5 mkg).

   d. Ensure that ski pivots freely on ski leg. Lightly lubricate ski coupler bolt with oil.

   e. Perform *Ski Alignment*.

Disassembly/Assembly

1. Release Vise Grip pliers if used during ski removal.

2. On models so equipped, remove bolts securing shock absorber, and remove shock absorber (**Figure 2**).

3. Remove cotter pins securing retaining pins on front and rear of main leaf (**Figure 3**).

4. Using a hammer and punch, gently tap spring retaining pins from ski, and remove springs.

5. Remove spring slide cushion from front ski bracket.

6. If further spring disassembly is desired, remove bolts and nuts securing spring coupler to spring and remove coupler.

7. If ski runner shoe is worn to less than ½ its original thickness, remove nuts securing shoe to ski and remove shoe.

WARNING
Ski runner shoes are under tension. Remove runner shoes carefully or injury may result.

8. Assembly is the reverse of these steps. Keep the following points in mind:

   a. To aid leaf spring assembly cross leaf springs and temporarily install one bolt and nut to hold leaves together. Align springs parallel to each other and install other bolt and nut. Use *new* elastic locknuts or *new* tab locks on coupler bolts. Torque

8

bolts securing coupler to spring to 35-40 ft.-lb. (4.8-5.5 mkg).

b. Torque nuts securing runner shoes and shock absorbers as specified in **Table 1**.

c. Insert front and rear spring retaining pins from opposite sides. On left ski insert front pin from left and rear pin from right. On right ski insert front pin from right and rear pin from left. Use *new* cotter pins to secure retaining pins.

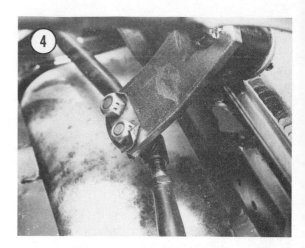

STEERING

The following procedures are typical for most models. Special model details, where applicable, are noted. During removal always note and record location of bolts of different sizes and lengths as well as shims, spacers, and lockwashers (if any) to aid installation.

Mid-Engine Model Steering Column Removal/Installation

1. Remove console.

2. On Elan models, disconnect throttle and brake cables and remove cable housings from handlebar. On Olympique models, disconnect brake cable and housing at brake assembly brake lever.

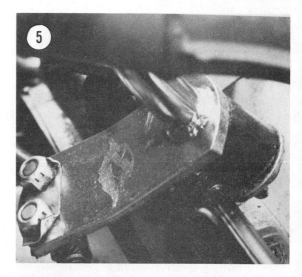

3. On models so equipped remove dimmer and cut-out buttons from handlebar.

4. On Elan models remove cotter pin, with washer and spring, securing upper tie rod end to steering column. Disengage tie rod end from steering column.

5. On other models remove nuts securing tie rod ends to steering column and disconnect tie rod ends (**Figure 4**).

6. Using a small punch and hammer, drive out pin securing steering column (**Figure 5**). Remove shims (if any) and washer.

7. Remove U-clamp (**Figure 6**) securing steering column to upper column and remove steering column.

> NOTE: *Do not remove steering column bushing unless bushing is to be replaced.*

8. Inspect tie rod ends for excessive wear and replace if necessary. Tie rod ends attached to steering column have left-hand threads.

9. Installation is the reverse of these steps. Keep the following points in mind:

   a. Adjust steering column free play by adding or removing 0.025 in. (0.64mm) shims between steering column bushing and washer before installing pin.

   b. Tighten components to torque values specified in **Table 2**.

   c. Perform *Ski Alignment*.

Table 2   STEERING TORQUE SPECIFICATIONS

Components	Torque	
	Ft.-lb.	Mkg
Steering arm		
1970-1973 models		
Bolt	45-50	6.2-6.9
Nut	55-60	7.6-8.3
1974 and later models	18-23	2.5-3.2
Tie rod end	18-23	2.5-3.2
Handlebar	28-35	3.8-4.8

Front-Engine Model Steering Column Removal/Installation

1. Remove console if so equipped.

2. Disconnect throttle cable from lever and remove circlip and throttle lever housing.

3. Remove dimmer and kill button from handlebar.

4. On all but T'NT R/V models remove bolt securing handlebar to steering column and remove handlebar.

5. Remove nuts securing tie rod ends to steering column and disconnect tie rod ends (**Figure 4**).

6. Remove nuts securing steering column to upper column (**Figure 7**).

   NOTE: *On some models it may be necessary to remove locking pin and clevis pin and raise driven pulley support (Figure 8) to gain access to tie rod ends.*

7. Using a small punch and hammer, drive out pin securing steering column (**Figure 5**). Remove shims (if any) and washer. Remove steering column.

   NOTE: *Do not remove steering column bushing unless bushing is to be replaced.*

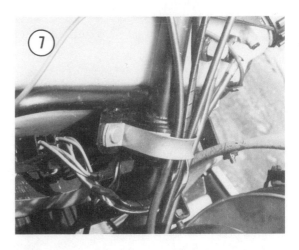

8. Inspect tie rod ends for excessive wear or looseness and replace if necessary.

9. Installation is the reverse of these steps. Keep the following points in mind:

   a. Tie rod ends attached to steering column have left-hand threads. Ensure that tie rod end joint runs parallel to horizontal line of steering arm.

   b. If replacing tie rod end ensure that at least half of threads are screwed into tie rod.

   c. Hold tie rod end with wrench while tightening tie rod locknut.

   d. Tighten components to torque values specified in **Table 2**.

   e. Adjust steering column free play by adding or removing 0.025 in. (0.64mm) shims between steering column bushing and washer before installing pin.

   f. Perform *Ski Alignment*.

8

**Ski Leg and Steering
Arm Removal/Installation**

1. Perform *Ski Removal*.

2. Remove nuts securing tie rod ends to steering arms and disconnect tie rod ends (**Figure 9**). On Elan models, remove cotter pin and washer and disengage tie rod from steering arm (**Figure 10**).

3. Remove bolts or nuts securing steering arms to ski legs. Remove arms with spacers, washers, and springs from ski leg spines. If steering arms are difficult to disengage from ski legs perform the following:

   a. Raise front of machine.

   b. Loosen steering arm bolt 3 or 4 turns or loosen steering arm nut until flush with ski leg.

   c. Gently tap on bolt or ski leg end with a soft faced hammer or a hammer and block of wood to disengage splines.

4. Remove upper ski leg bushing and remove ski leg from machine. Remove lower ski leg bushing if necessary.

5. Installation is the reverse of these steps. Keep the following points in mind:

   a. Ensure that tie rod end joints run parallel to horizontal line of steering arm.

   b. Tighten components to torque values specified in **Table 2**.

   c. Perform *Ski Alignment*.

SKI ALIGNMENT

Ski alignment should be performed whenever steering difficulties are experienced or when repair work has been performed on ski or steering components.

1. Position snowmobile on level ground and measure distance between ski at front and rear leaf springs (**Figure 11**). Front dimension should be ⅛ in. (3.2mm) more than rear on all models except 1973 T'NT F/A which is ¼ in. (6.4mm). Ensure that handlebar is in horizontal position.

2. When measuring ski toe out manually, close front of skis to take up all mechanical slack in steering mechanism.

3. If adjustment is necessary, loosen locknuts on tie rod ends and turn tie rods to increase or decrease ski toe-out.

4. Tighten locknuts, manually close front of skis and recheck measurement. Readjust if necessary.

5. On models equipped with steering travel adjustment (**Figure 12**), turn handlebar fully right until gap of ⅛ in. (3.2mm) exists between lower nut of left tie rod ball joint and bottom plate. Adjust stopper bolt on right side of reinforcing cross member so it just touches right steering arm. Repeat for stopper on left side.

Stopper bolt

CHAPTER NINE

REAR SUSPENSION AND TRACK

Ski-Doo snowmobiles are equipped with either a bogie or slide rail rear suspension.

Elan models are equipped with 3 sets of bogie wheels, a 4-wheel set in the front and 3-wheel sets in the center and rear. All other models use 4-wheel sets in the front, center, and rear locations.

Three basic types of slide suspensions are utilized: a ground leveler, high performance, and torque reaction. See **Table 1** for model application.

Table 1   SLIDE SUSPENSION MODEL APPLICATION

Model	Suspension
Olympique 1970-1974 T'NT F/C 1970-1973 Elan 294 SS 1974 Elan 300 SS 1975	Ground leveller
T'NT F/A 1973-1974	High performance
All other models	Torque reaction

This chapter includes removal and installation procedures for bogie and slide suspensions, track, rear axle and drive axle. Refer to Chapter Two for suspension and track adjustments and Chapter Three for *Track Wear Analysis*.

BOGIE WHEEL SUSPENSION

1. Raise rear of snowmobile off ground and block up securely.

2. Using link plate spring lever or locally fabricated equivalent, unhook link plate springs to release track tension (**Figure 1**).

3. Start with center bogie wheel set and remove bolts and lockwashers securing cross shaft to frame (**Figure 2**).

NOTE: *When removing second bolt from cross shaft, wedge a screwdriver blade between shaft and support to prevent cross shaft from turning.*

Remove bogie wheel set.

4. Remove front and rear bogie wheel sets.

NOTE: *Springs on bogie wheel assemblies may vary depending on installation location. Mark the location of each bogie wheel set to make sure each set is installed in the proper location.*

5. Refer bogie wheel assembly repair to an authorized dealer.

6. Installation is the reverse of these steps. Keep the following points in mind:

a. On bogie wheel sets with single springs, position wheel set with wider wheel support to front of snowmobile.

b. Grease each bogie wheel until new grease appears then wipe off excess.

c. On models with 3-position anchor for link plate spring, locate spring in middle position (**Figure 1**).

d. Perform *Track Tension Adjustment* as outlined in Chapter Two.

SLIDE SUSPENSION

Refer to **Table 1** for slide suspension model application.

Ground Leveller Suspension
Removal/Installation

1. Raise rear of snowmobile off ground and block up securely.

2. Loosen spring adjuster bolt and track tension adjuster bolt to loosen track tension (**Figure 3**).

3. On 1970 models remove capscrews securing reinforcing cross shaft and remove cross shaft.

4. Use link plate spring lever or locally fabricated equivalent and unhook link plate springs (**Figure 1**).

5. Remove bolt securing link plate to frame (**Figure 4**).

6. On 1970 models, remove capscrews and washers securing 4 cross shafts to frame. It may be necessary to hold one end of cross shaft with Vise Grip pliers to remove capscrew from other end.

9

7. On other models remove 6 bolts securing side members to frame (**Figure 5**). Remove suspension.

8. Refer required suspension component repair to an authorized dealer.

9. Installation is the reverse of these steps. Keep the following points in mind:

    a. To ease suspension installation, apply downward pressure on front cross support and collapse suspension. Tie front cross support to front runner tube with wire to keep suspension collapsed.

    b. Grease front runner tube wheels and rear cross support wheels with low-temperature grease. Wipe off excess.

    c. Perform *Track Tension Adjustment* as outlined in Chapter Two.

High Performance Suspension Removal/Installation

1. Raise rear of snowmobile off ground and block up securely.

2. Loosen adjuster bolts on inner side of rear idler wheels to release track tension (**Figure 6**).

3. Loosen nuts on spring adjuster bolts to release front and rear spring tension.

4. Remove upper idler wheel assembly and withdraw suspension assembly.

5. Refer required suspension component repair to an authorized dealer.

6. Installation is the reverse of these steps. Keep the following points in mind:

    a. Ensure that cups are positioned over front and rear cross shaft end before locating arms in frame.

b. Torque bolts securing front and rear arms to frame to 28-35 ft.-lb. (3.9-4.8 mkg).

c. Torque bolts securing upper idler assembly to 28-33 ft.-lb. (3.9-4.4 mkg).

d. Perform *Track Tension Adjustment* as outlined in Chapter Two.

Torque Reaction Suspension
Removal/Installation

1. Raise rear of snowmobile off ground and block up securely.

2. Loosen adjuster bolts on inner side of rear idler wheels to release track tension (**Figure 7**).

3. Position adjustment cams at lowest elevation (**Figure 8**).

4. Disconnect stopper strap (**Figure 9**).

5. Apply downward pressure on seat and detach shock absorber (**Figure 10**).

6. Remove 4 bolts securing cross shafts and suspension to frame, and withdraw suspension.

> NOTE: *To aid removal of bolts from cross shafts, wedge the blade of a screwdriver between cross shaft and suspension arm.*

7. Refer suspension component repair to an authorized dealer.

8. Installation is the reverse of these steps. Keep the following points in mind:

a. Torque bolts securing front and rear arms to frame to 28-35 ft.-lb. (3.9-4.8 mkg).

b. Lower machine to ground and press down on seat to connect shock absorber and stopper strap.

> NOTE: *Stopper strap is provided with 4 adjustment holes. The second hole (from end) provides maximum traction and*

9

steering efficiency for most snow conditions. Using 1st hole shifts weight toward rear of machine which increases traction but decreases steering efficiency. The 3rd or 4th hole decreases traction and increases steering efficiency and effort.

   c. Perform *Track Tension Adjustment* as outlined in Chapter Two.

REAR AXLE

Removal/Installation

1. Raise rear of snowmobile off ground and block up securely.

2. Remove locknuts and retainer washers securing link plate springs (**Figure 2**).

3. Using link plate spring lever or locally fabricated equivalent, unhook link plate springs (**Figure 1**).

4. On 1970 models equipped with reinforcing cross shaft, remove bolts securing shaft and remove shaft.

5. Remove track adjuster bolts, eye bolts, link plate springs, hardener washers, and adjuster sleeves.

6. Remove rear axle assembly.

7. Perform *Inspection*. Refer necessary repair to an authorized dealer.

8. Installation is the reverse of these steps. Keep the following points in mind:

   a. Ensure that spring anchors on link plates are up.

   b. On models equipped with 3-position spring anchors, hook link spring in middle position.

   c. Perform *Track Tension Adjustment* as outlined in Chapter Two.

Inspection

1. Examine sprockets for worn teeth, cuts, distortion, or other damage. Replace if necessary.

2. Inspect all oil seals for evidence of leaking or damage and replace if necessary.

3. Inspect bearings for freedom of movement and free play. If play is excessive or ball bearings are pitted or damaged, replace bearings.

4. Inspect other components including threaded parts, for damage, distortion, or excessive wear. Replace as necessary.

DRIVE AXLE

Removal/Installation

1. Remove rear suspension.

2. Remove chaincase as outlined in Chapter Seven.

3. On electric start models, remove battery cover, battery and battery platform (except Elan models).

4. On models equipped with speedometer, remove angle drive unit and coupling cable (**Figure 11**).

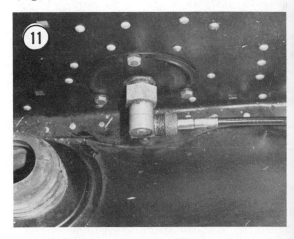

5. Tip snowmobile on its side and remove 3 capscrews securing end bearing housing (**Figure 12**) to frame. It may be necessary to pry housing from frame with 2 large screwdrivers.

6. Disengage sprocket teeth from track, pull drive axle towards end bearing side of frame and remove drive axle assembly (**Figure 13**). Do not lose spacer or shim (if so equipped) located between bearing and lower chaincase sprocket.

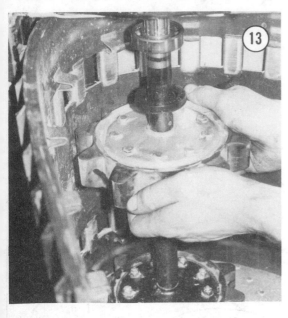

7. Perform *Inspection*. Refer necessary repairs to an authorized dealer.

8. Installation is the reverse of these steps. Keep the following points in mind:

    a. On speedometer equipped models, if *new* drive axle is installed, insert speedometer drive into axle flush with axle end (**Figure 14**).

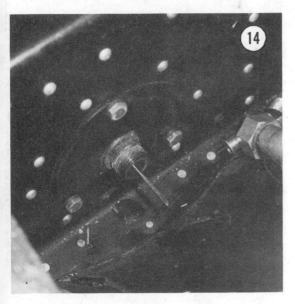

    b. Install chaincase as outlined in Chapter Seven.

    c. Perform *Track Tension Adjustment* as outlined in Chapter Two.

Inspection

1. Examine sprockets for worn teeth, cuts, distortion, or other damage. Replace if necessary.

2. Inspect all oil seals for evidence of leaking or damage and replace if necessary.

3. Inspect bearings for freedom of movement and free play. If play is excessive or ball bearings are pitted or damaged, replace bearings.

4. Inspect splines for cracks or twisting and excessive wear. If splines are damaged, axle must be replaced.

5. Inspect other components, including threaded parts, for damage, distortion, or excessive wear. Replace as necessary.

TRACK

Removal/Installation

1. Raise rear of snowmobile off ground and block up securely.

2. Remove rear suspension.

3. Remove rear axle.

4. Remove drive axle and withdraw track from machine.

5. Perform *Inspection*. Refer to *Track Wear Analysis* in Chapter Three.

6. Installation is the reverse of these steps. Keep the following points in mind:

    a. Ensure that right angle of track rib is toward front of machine.

    b. Perform *Track Tension Adjustment* as outlined in Chapter Two.

Inspection

If abnormal wear or damage is evident, refer to *Track Wear Analysis* in Chapter Three.

1. Inspect track for cuts and abnormal wear.

2. Examine track rods. Replace track if excessive damage is evident and rods are broken.

3. Inspect track for missing or damaged inserts. Have an authorized dealer replace track inserts if necessary.

9

CHAPTER TEN

LIQUID COOLING SYSTEM

Certain 1978 and later Blizzard and Everest models are equipped with a liquid cooling system. The cooling system consists of a water pump, coolant tank, thermostat, and tunnel mounted radiators. Refer to **Figure 1** for a typical liquid cooling system.

The thermostat maintains uniform engine temperatures throughout the engine's operation range.

The pressure cap maintains the cooling system under pressure to achieve a higher potential coolant boiling point. Coolant is a 60/40 mixture of ethylene glycol anti-freeze and water. The coolant recovery tank holds any possible system overflow. Coolant captured in the recovery tank is siphoned back into the cooling system when engine cools. See **Table 1** for cooling system specifications.

COOLING SYSTEM PRESSURE TESTING

Special pressure testing tools and adapters are required for system pressure tests. For this reason, have an authorized dealer perform any necessary cooling system tests.

DRAINING AND FILLING COOLING SYSTEM

Drain and refill cooling system at least every two years.

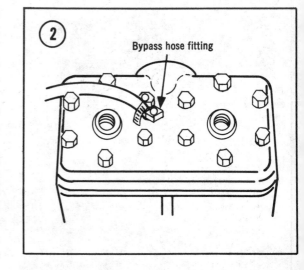

1. Remove coolant tank pressure cap and disconnect bypass hose from cylinder head fitting (**Figure 2**).

2. Route bypass hose into a clean container if coolant is to be kept. Block off bypass fitting and keep bypass hose as low as possible to drain the system.

3. Cover filler neck with your hand and blow through tank vent tube to completely drain the system (**Figure 3**). Elevate rear of snowmobile to help drain radiators.

4. Rinse engine and engine compartment with clean water.

5. Position machine on a level surface.

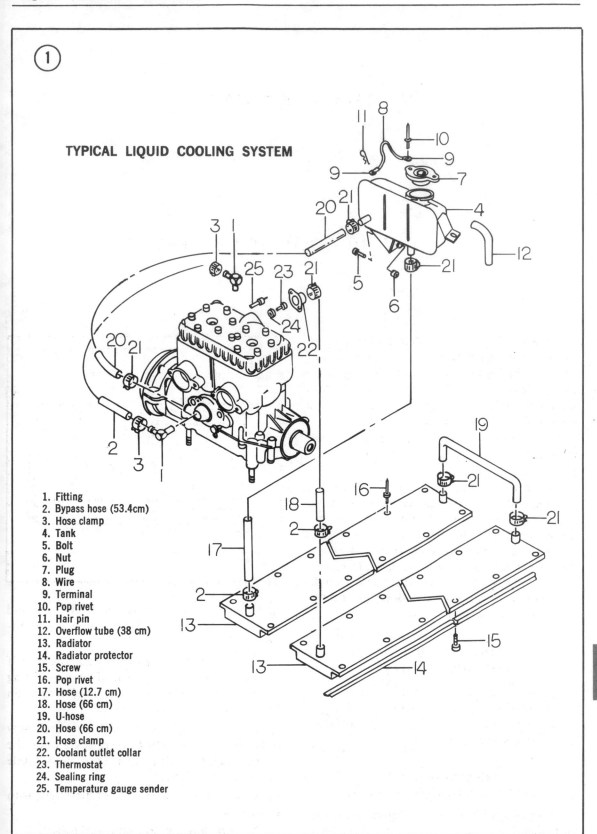

TYPICAL LIQUID COOLING SYSTEM

1. Fitting
2. Bypass hose (53.4cm)
3. Hose clamp
4. Tank
5. Bolt
6. Nut
7. Plug
8. Wire
9. Terminal
10. Pop rivet
11. Hair pin
12. Overflow tube (38 cm)
13. Radiator
14. Radiator protector
15. Screw
16. Pop rivet
17. Hose (12.7 cm)
18. Hose (66 cm)
19. U-hose
20. Hose (66 cm)
21. Hose clamp
22. Coolant outlet collar
23. Thermostat
24. Sealing ring
25. Temperature gauge sender

10

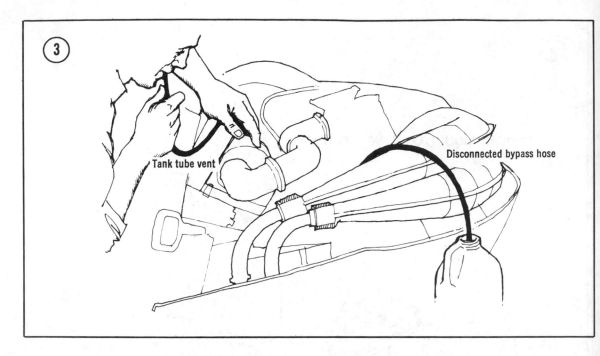

Tank tube vent

Disconnected bypass hose

Table 1   COOLING SYSTEM SPECIFICATIONS

| Engine | Liter | Coolant Capacity* | |
		U.S. Gal.	Imp. Gal.
354	2.5	0.6	0.5
444	5	1.2	1.0
Pressure cap		13 psi	
Coolant mixture ratio		60% anti-freeze, 40% water	
Thermostat opening temperature		110°F (43°C)	

*Coolant capacities are approximate. After cooling system is bled, fill until coolant level is 1 in. (25mm) below filler neck.

6. Keep bypass hose near fitting on cylinder head and fill coolant tank with proper mixture of anti-freeze and water.

7. Cover filler neck with your hand and blow through tank vent tube until coolant comes out the bypass hose and the fitting on the cylinder head (**Figure 4**). Keep coolant tank full while purging the system of air.

8. Connect bypass hose and fill coolant tank until level is 1 in. (25mm) below filler neck. Refer to **Table 1** for approximate coolant capacities.

9. Check all hose connections for leaks. Install filler cap.

10. Block up rear of machine to clear track off the ground.

11. Start engine and warm up to operating temperature. Check entire cooling system for leaks.

12. Shut off engine and let cool. Recheck coolant level.

THERMOSTAT REMOVAL/INSTALLATION

Refer to **Figure 1** for this procedure.

1. Drain cooling system.

2. Remove bolts securing thermostat housing and remove housing. Lift out thermostat. If engine has been running too cold or overheating, replace thermostat.

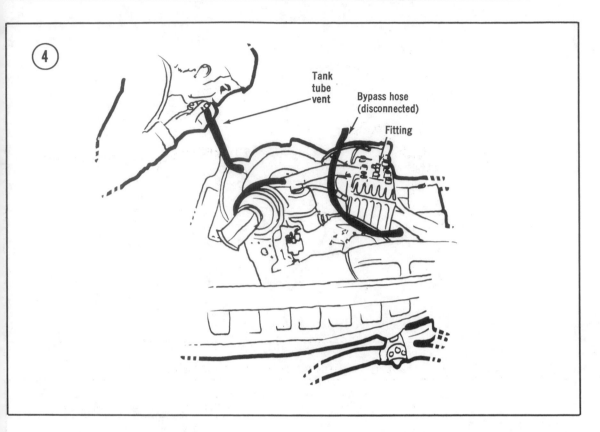

④

Tank
tube
vent

Bypass hose
(disconnected)

Fitting

3. Installation is the reverse of these steps. Use a new gasket on thermostat housing. Fill cooling system as outlined under *Draining and Filling Cooling System*.

WATER PUMP REMOVAL/INSTALLATION

Refer to **Figure 5** for this procedure.

1. Drain cooling system.

2. Loosen clamps securing coolant hoses to water pump housing.

3. Remove bolts and O-ring gaskets securing pump housing and remove housing. Remove and discard pump housing gasket.

4. Remove locking nut and washer securing pump impeller to pump shaft and remove impeller.

5. If pump shaft, bearings, and seal removal is desired, perform *Rotary Valve Removal* as outlined in Chapter Four. Refer shaft bearing and seal replacement to a dealer.

6. Installation is the reverse of these steps. Keep the following points in mind:

a. Install a new pump housing gasket.

b. Apply Loctite Lock'N'Seal to bolts securing pump housing.

c. Secure coolant hoses and fill cooling system as outlined in *Draining and Filling Cooling System*.

RADIATOR REMOVAL/INSTALLATION

Refer to **Figure 1** for this procedure.

1. Drain cooling system.

2. Refer to Chapter Nine and perform *Torque Reaction Suspension Removal/Installation*.

3. Remove screws securing radiator protector strips and remove strips.

4. Disconnect radiator hoses.

5. Using a cold chisel, gently remove rivets securing radiators.

6. Installation is the reverse of these steps. Pop rivet radiators to tunnel from the top. Refer radiator repair to an authorized dealer. Fill cooling system as outlined under *Draining and Filling Cooling System*.

10

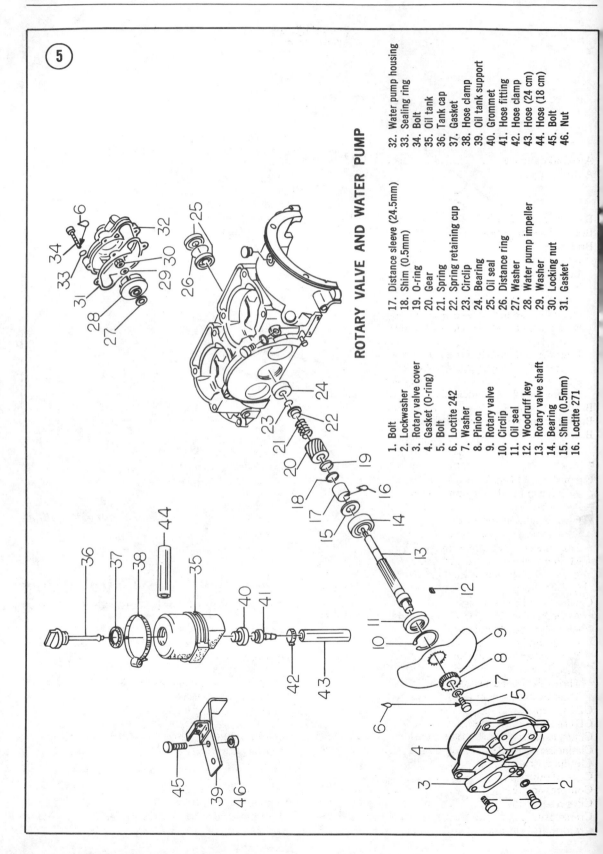

ROTARY VALVE AND WATER PUMP

1. Bolt
2. Lockwasher
3. Rotary valve cover
4. Gasket (O-ring)
5. Bolt
6. Loctite 242
7. Washer
8. Pinion
9. Rotary valve
10. Circlip
11. Oil seal
12. Woodruff key
13. Rotary valve shaft
14. Bearing
15. Shim (0.5mm)
16. Loctite 271

17. Distance sleeve (24.5mm)
18. Shim (0.5mm)
19. O-ring
20. Gear
21. Spring
22. Spring retaining cup
23. Circlip
24. Bearing
25. Oil seal
26. Distance ring
27. Washer
28. Water pump impeller
29. Washer
30. Locking nut
31. Gasket

32. Water pump housing
33. Sealing ring
34. Bolt
35. Oil tank
36. Tank cap
37. Gasket
38. Hose clamp
39. Oil tank support
40. Grommet
41. Hose fitting
42. Hose clamp
43. Hose (24 cm)
44. Hose (18 cm)
45. Bolt
46. Nut

INDEX

11

11

NOTES

1970 OLYMPIQUE 335E

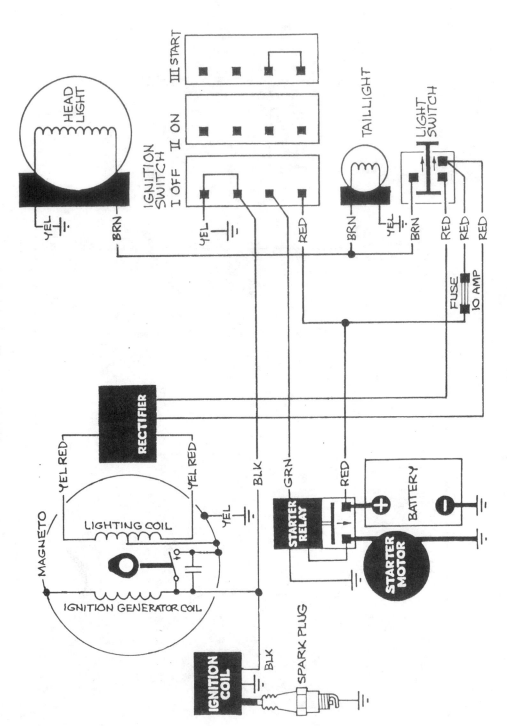

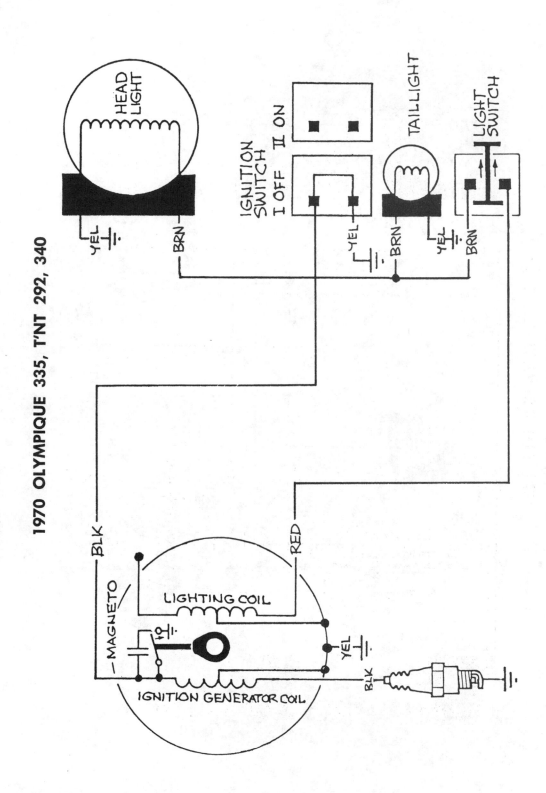

1970 OLYMPIQUE 335, T'NT 292, 340

HEAD LIGHT

YEL

BRN

IGNITION SWITCH
I OFF   II ON

YEL

TAILLIGHT

BRN

YEL

LIGHT SWITCH

BRN

BLK

RED

MAGNETO

LIGHTING COIL

YEL

BLK

IGNITION GENERATOR COIL

1970 T'NT 399, OLYMPIQUE 399
1971 T'NT 440, OLYMPIQUE 399

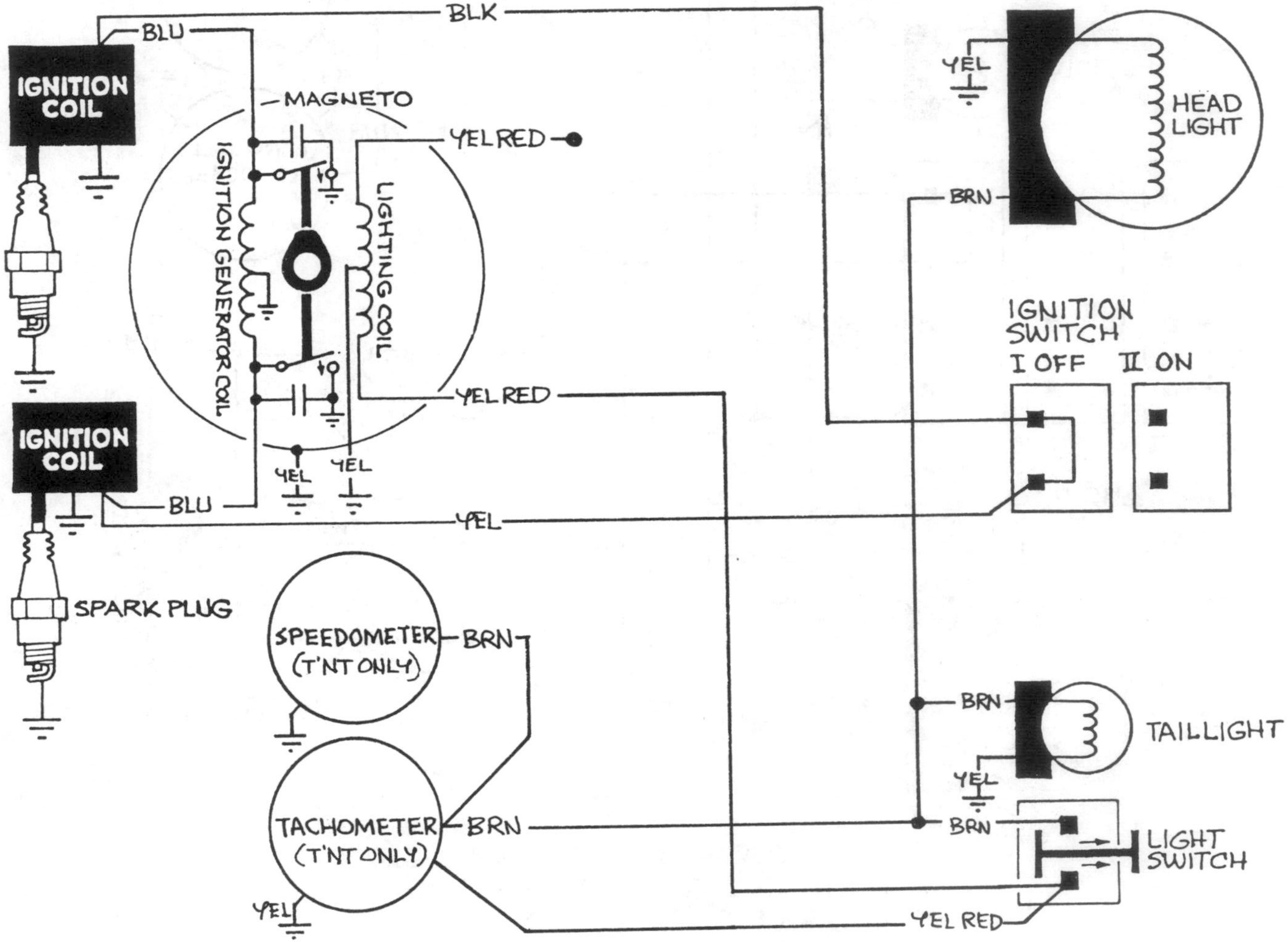

HEAD LIGHT

YEL

BRN

IGNITION SWITCH
I OFF   II ON

TAILLIGHT

BRN

YEL

LIGHT SWITCH

BRN

YEL RED

MAGNETO

YEL RED

LIGHTING COIL

YEL RED

YEL

BLK

YEL   YEL

YEL

YEL

IGNITION GENERATOR COIL

SPEEDOMETER
(T'NT ONLY)
BRN

TACHOMETER
(T'NT ONLY)
BRN

YEL

BLU

BLU

IGNITION COIL

IGNITION COIL

SPARK PLUG

12

1971 ELAN 250, T'NT 292-340, OLYMPIQUE 300-350

1972 ELAN 250, OLYMPIQUE 300-350

1971 OLYMPIQUE 335E, 399E, ELAN 250E

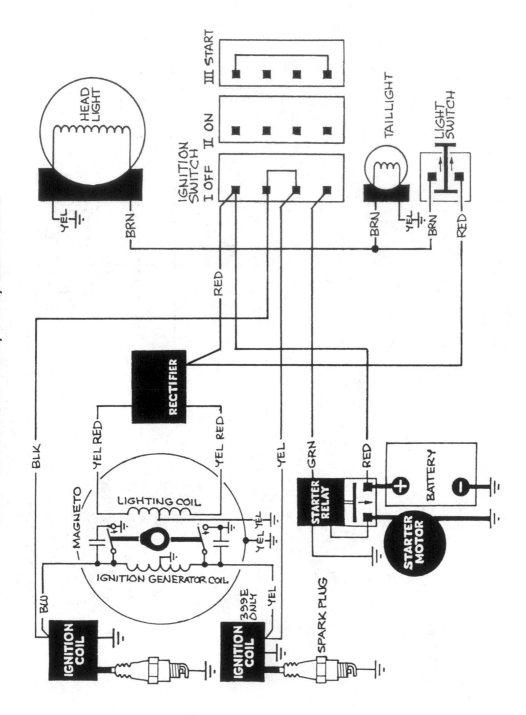

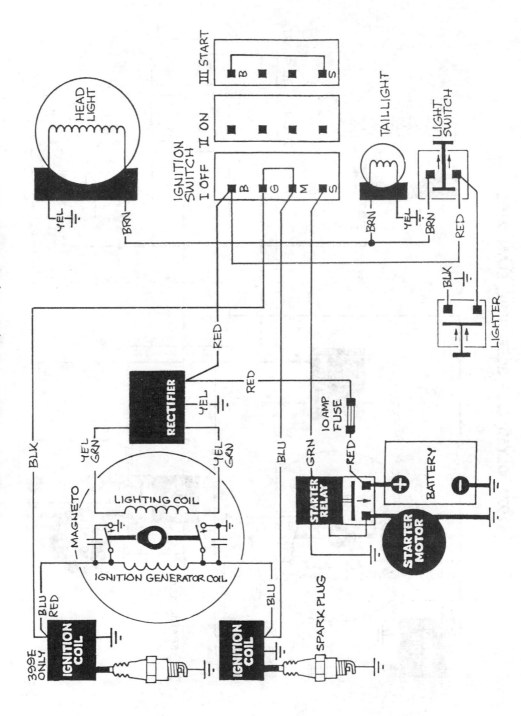

1972 OLYMPIQUE 335E, 399E, ELAN 250E

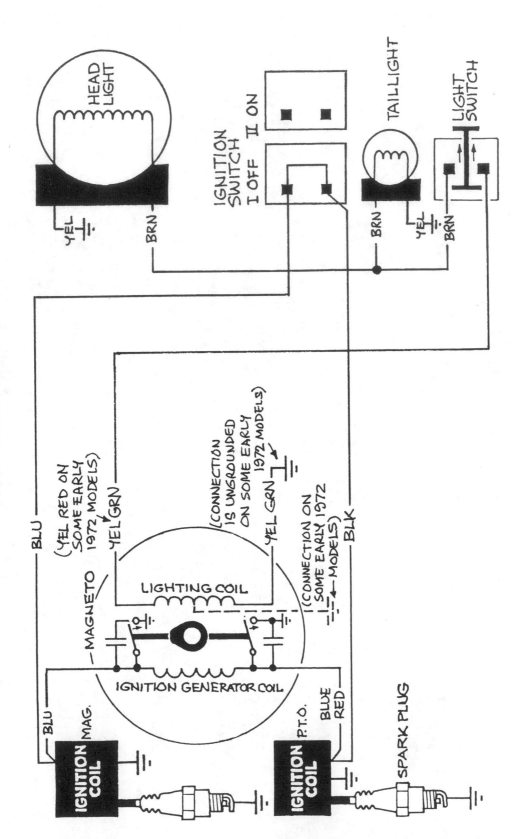

1972 OLYMPIQUE 399

12

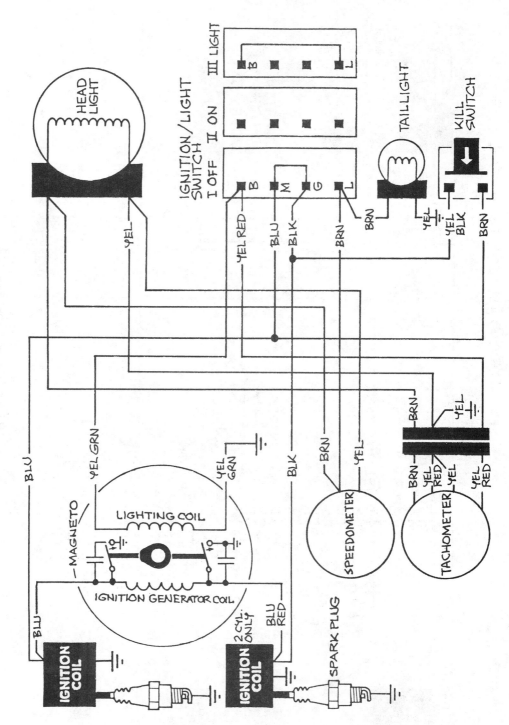

1972 T'NT 292, 340, 440

1973 ELAN 250E, OLYMPIQUE 340E-400E

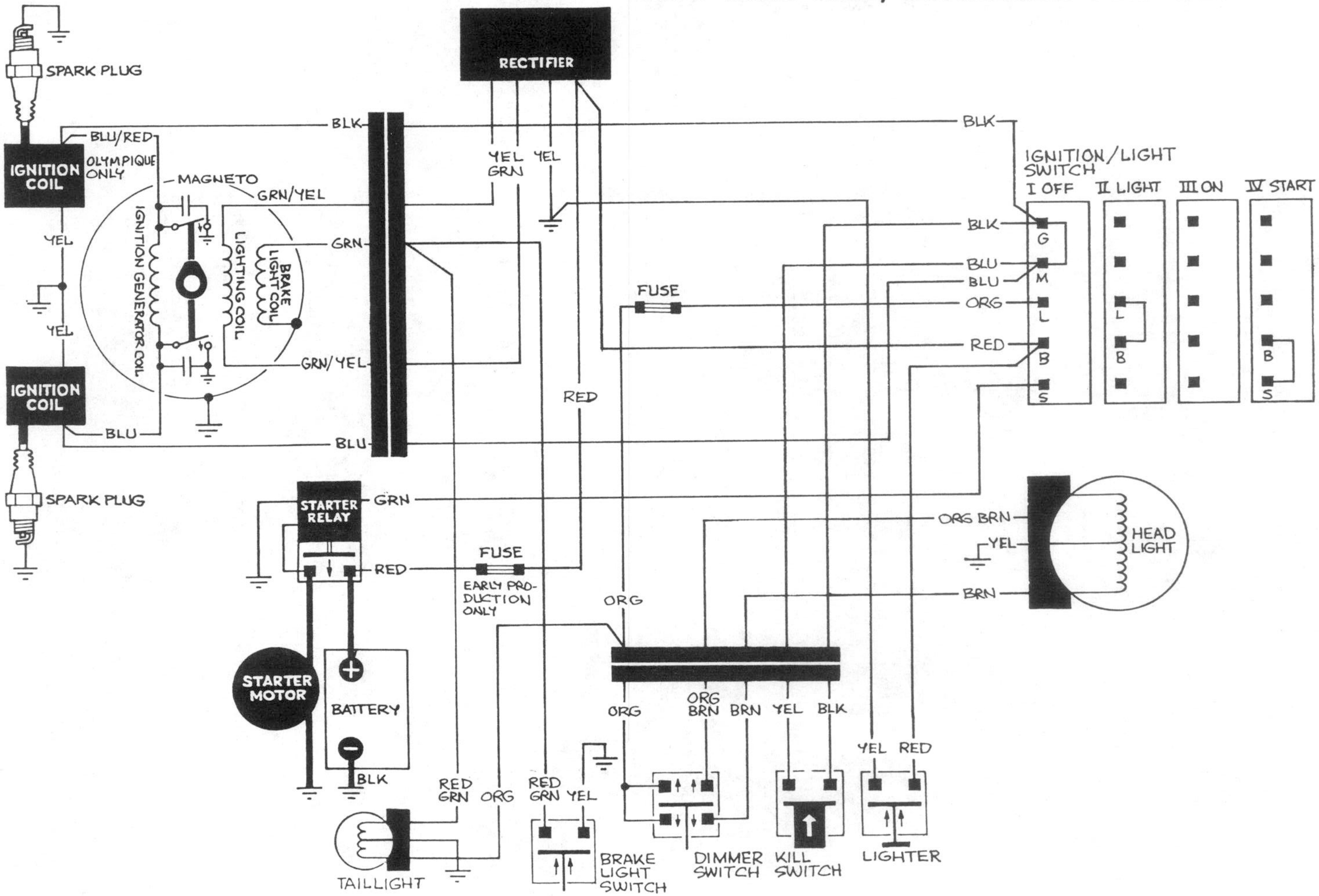

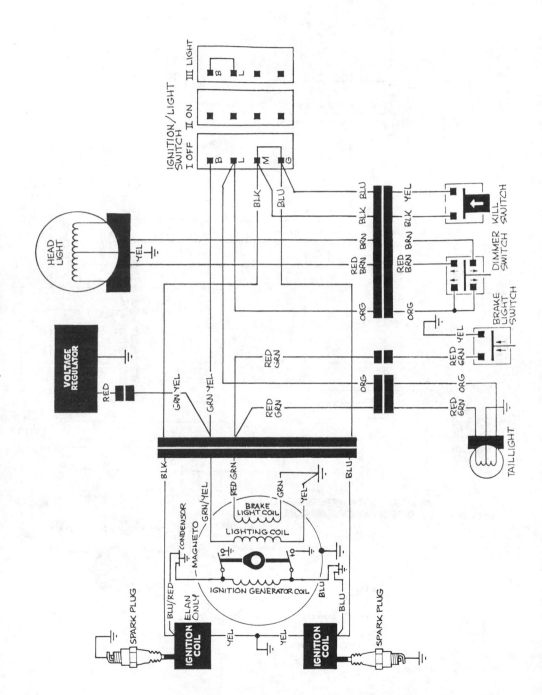

1973 ELAN 250T-250SS, OLYMPIQUE 300-335

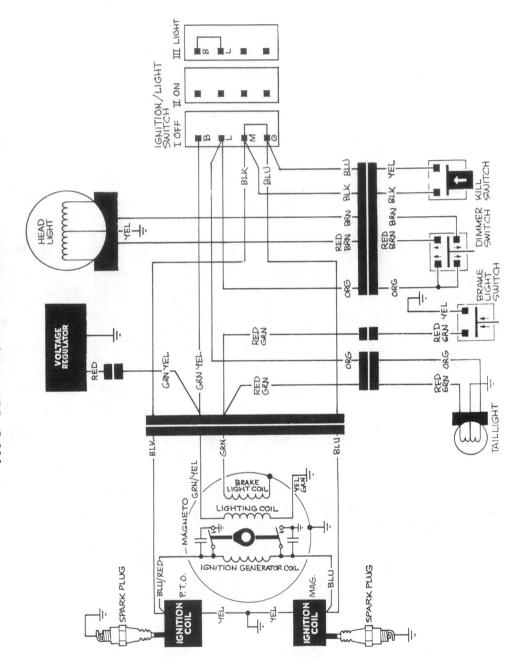

1973 OLYMPIQUE 340-400-440

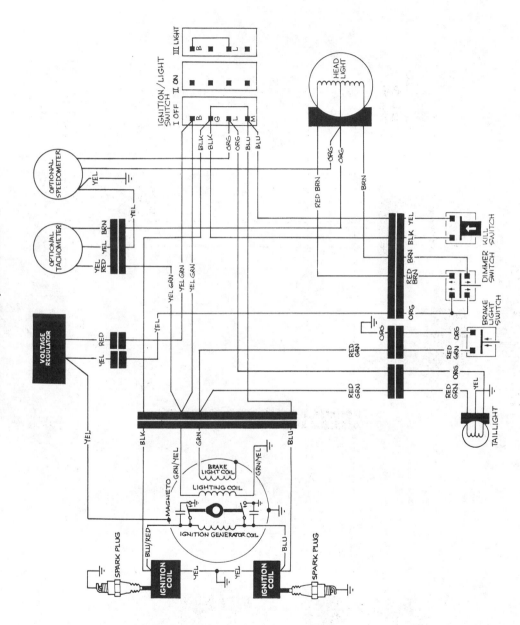

1973 T'NT 294, 340-440

1973 T'NT 340 F/A

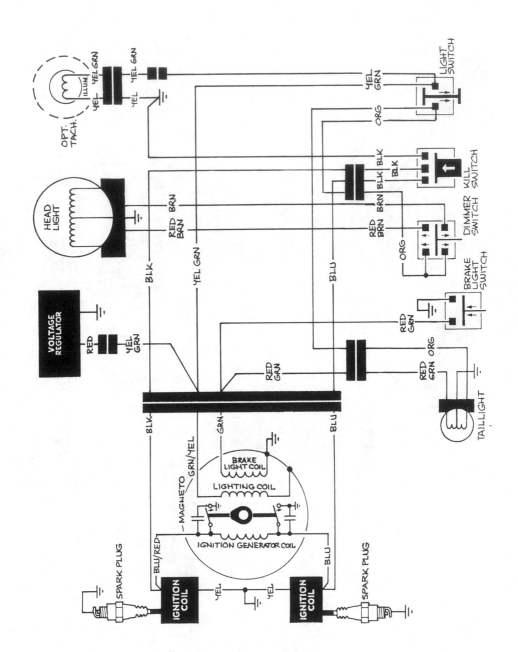

1973 T'NT 400 F/A

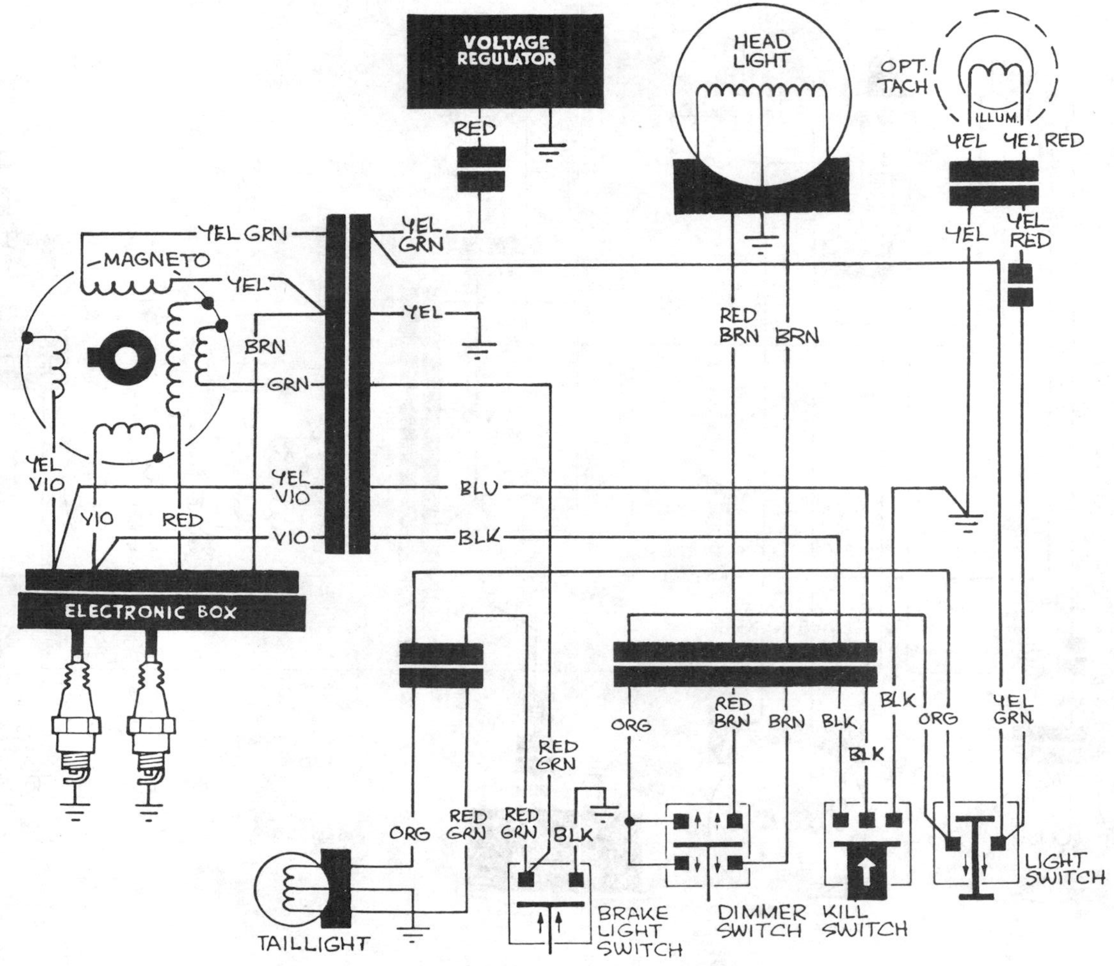

OPT. TACH

YEL YEL RED

YEL RED

YEL

ILLUM

HEAD LIGHT

RED BRN

BRN

RED BRN

VOLTAGE REGULATOR

RED

YEL GRN

YEL

BLU

BLK

YEL GRN

MAGNETO

YEL

BRN

GRN

YEL VIO

VIO

YEL VIO

RED

VIO

ELECTRONIC BOX

LIGHT SWITCH

YEL GRN

ORG

BLK

BLK

BLK

KILL SWITCH

BRN

RED BRN

ORG

DIMMER SWITCH

BRAKE LIGHT SWITCH

RED GRN

BLK

RED GRN

RED GRN

ORG

TAILLIGHT

ELAN 250 (1974)

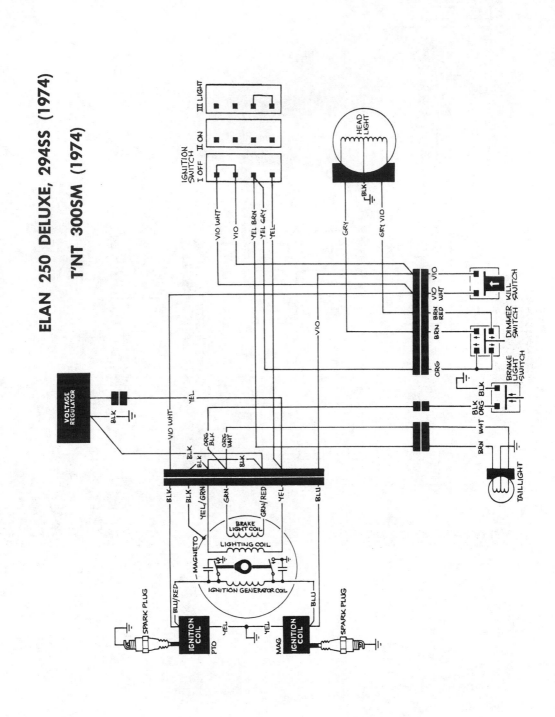

ELAN 250 DELUXE, 294SS (1974)
T'NT 300SM (1974)

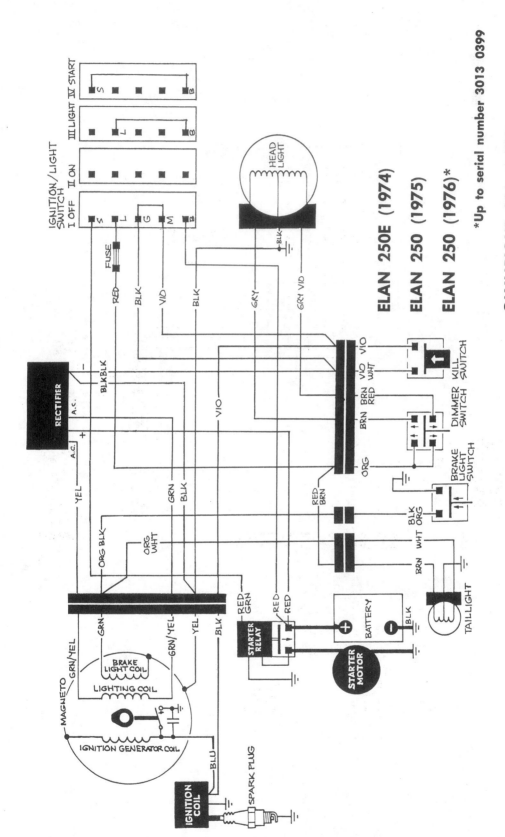

ELAN 250E (1974)

ELAN 250 (1975)

ELAN 250 (1976)*

OLYMPIQUE 300 (1974)

*Up to serial number 3013 0399

OLYMPIQUE 300 (1974)

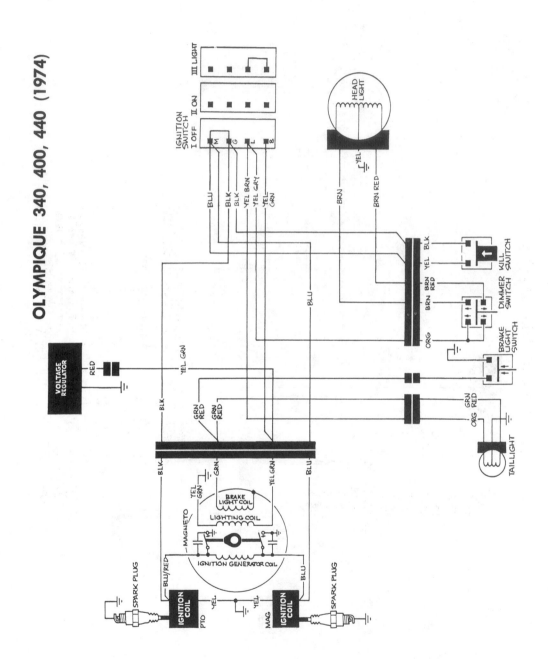

OLYMPIQUE 340, 400, 440 (1974)

OLYMPIQUE 340E, 440E (1974)

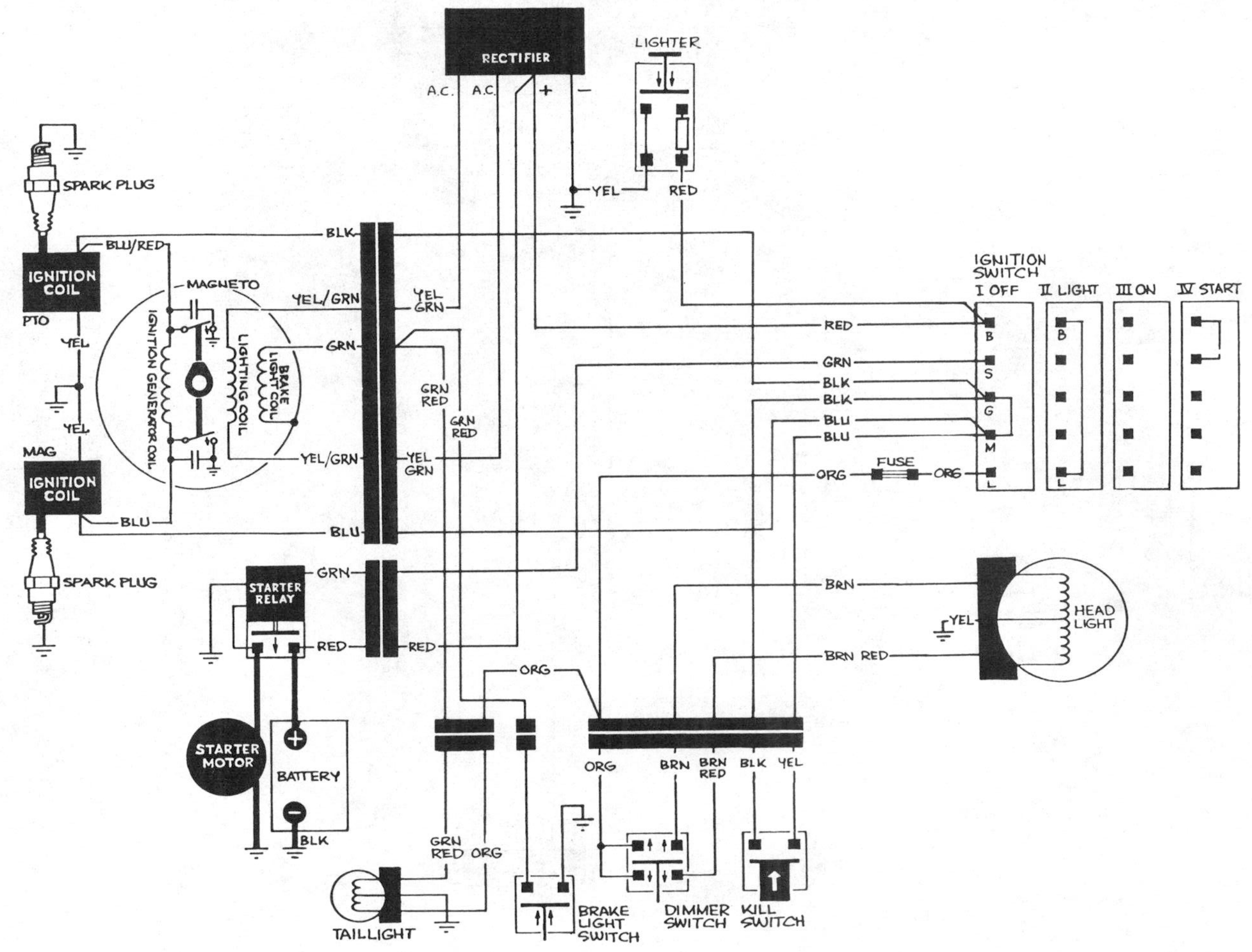

T'NT 340SE, 440SE (1974)

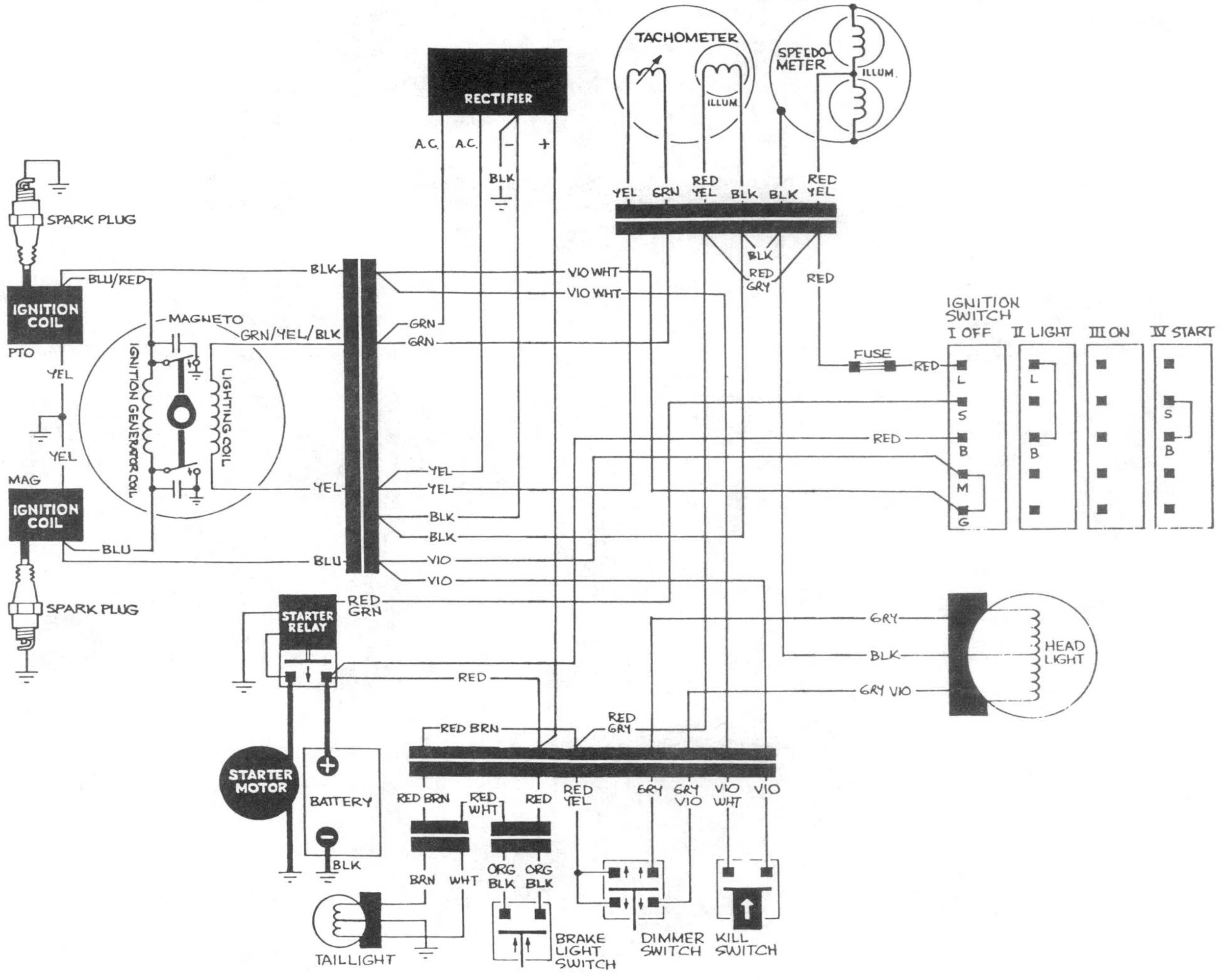

IGNITION SWITCH

IV START — S B

III ON

II LIGHT — L B

I OFF — L S B M G

FUSE

RED

RED

SPEEDO METER — ILLUM

TACHOMETER — ILLUM

RED YEL
RED BLK BLK YEL
YEL GRN YEL
RED YEL

BLK
RED GRY

RED

HEAD LIGHT

GRY
BLK
GRY VIO

VIO
VIO WHT

KILL SWITCH

GRY GRY VIO
VIO

DIMMER SWITCH

RED GRY

BRAKE LIGHT SWITCH

RED YEL

RECTIFIER
+ −
BLK
A.C. A.C.

VIO WHT
VIO WHT

GRN
GRN

YEL
YEL

BLK
BLK

VIO
VIO

RED

RED RED BRN

ORG ORG
ORG ORG
BLK BLK

RED BRN RED WHT

RED BRN BRN WHT

TAILLIGHT

BLK

RED
RED GRN

MAGNETO

GRN/YEL/BLK

YEL
YEL

BLU

STARTER RELAY

BATTERY
+ −

BLK

STARTER MOTOR

LIGHTING COIL

IGNITION GENERATOR COIL

BLK

BLU/RED

SPARK PLUG

IGNITION COIL
PTO

YEL

YEL

IGNITION COIL
MAG

SPARK PLUG

BLU

12

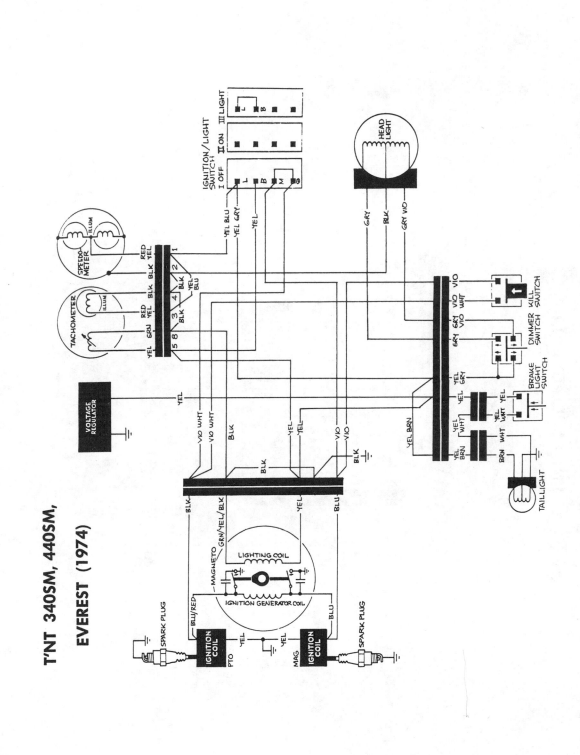

T'NT 340SM, 440SM,
EVEREST (1974)

T'NT F/A 340, 400, 440 (1974)

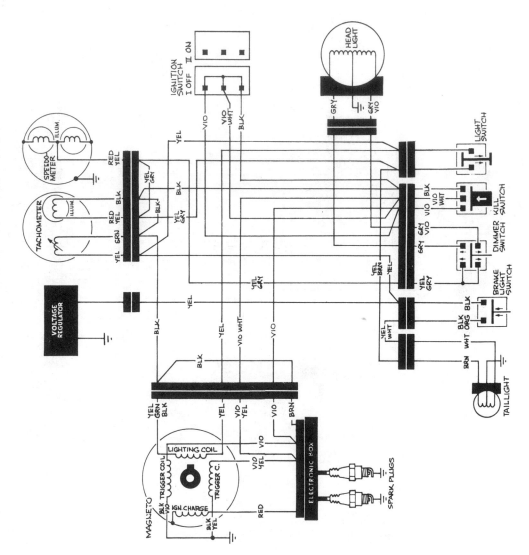

ELAN 250 DELUXE, 300SS (1975)
ELAN 250 DELUXE (1976-1977)

OLYMPIQUE 300, 340 (1975-1977)

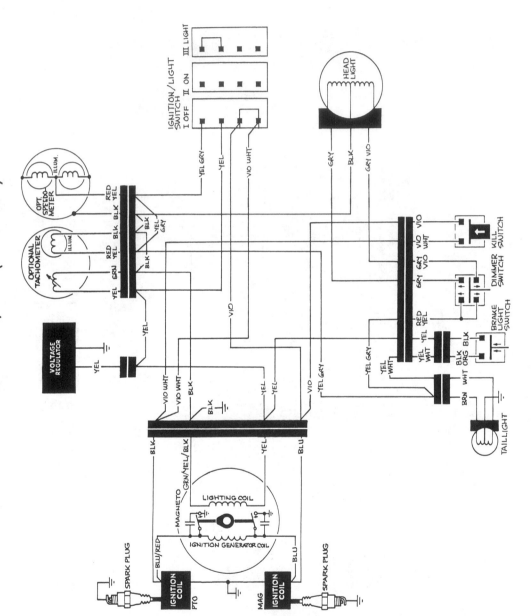

OLYMPIQUE 300E, 340E (1975-1977)

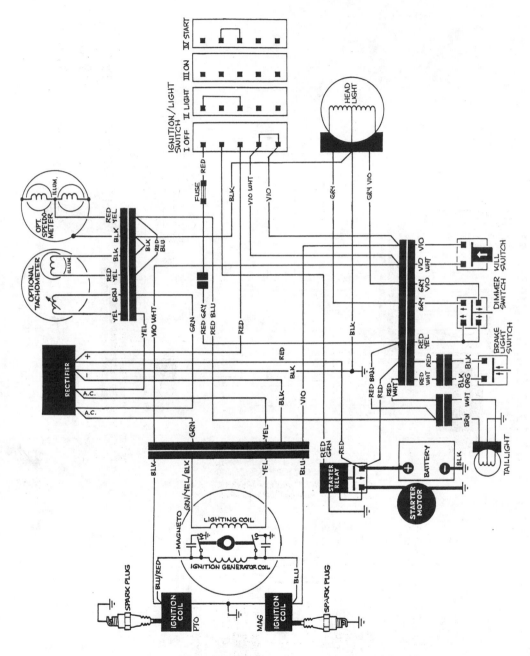

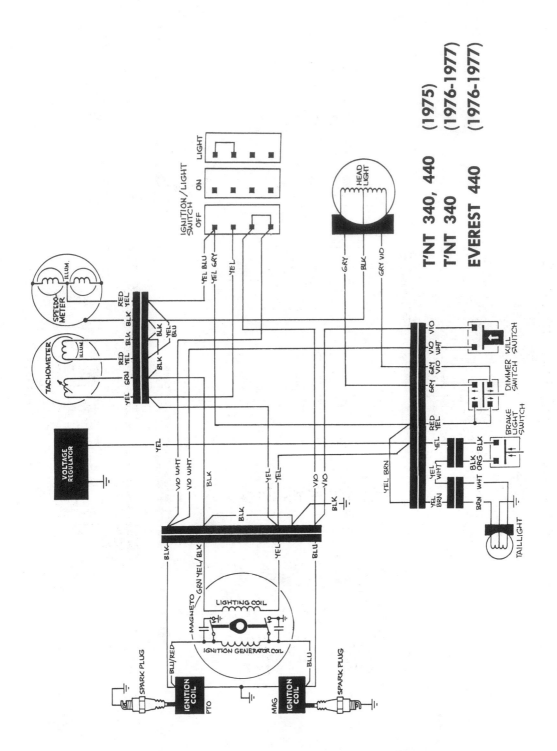

T'NT 340, 440 (1975)
T'NT 340 (1976-1977)
EVEREST 440 (1976-1977)

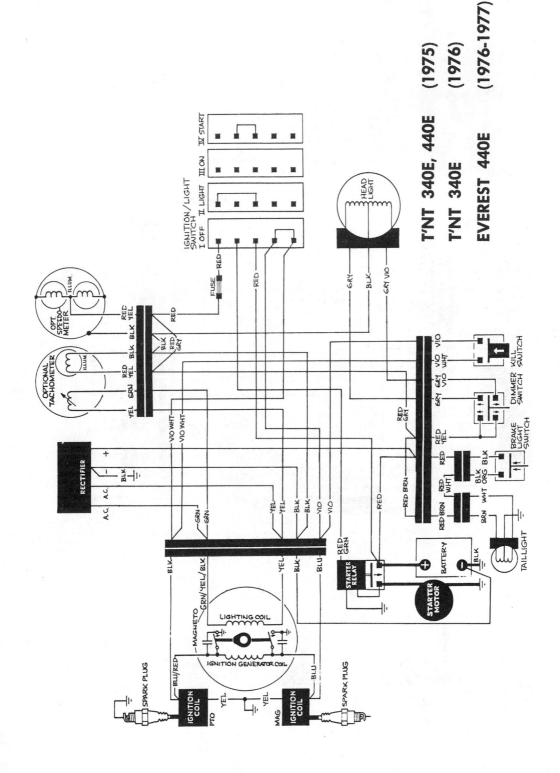

T'NT 340E, 440E (1975)

T'NT 340E (1976)

EVEREST 440E (1976-1977)

T'NT EVEREST 440 (1975)

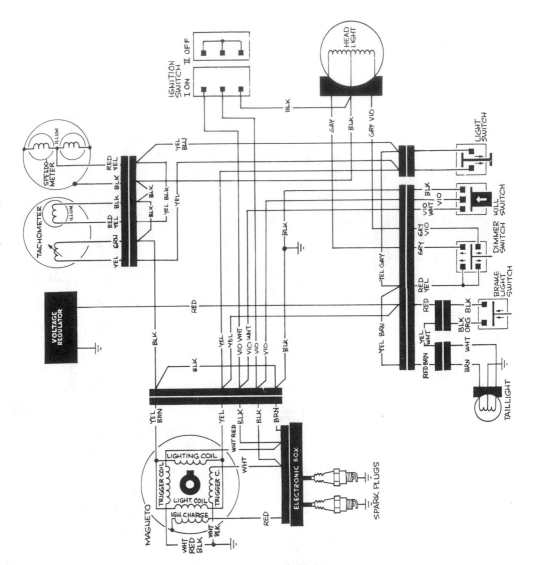

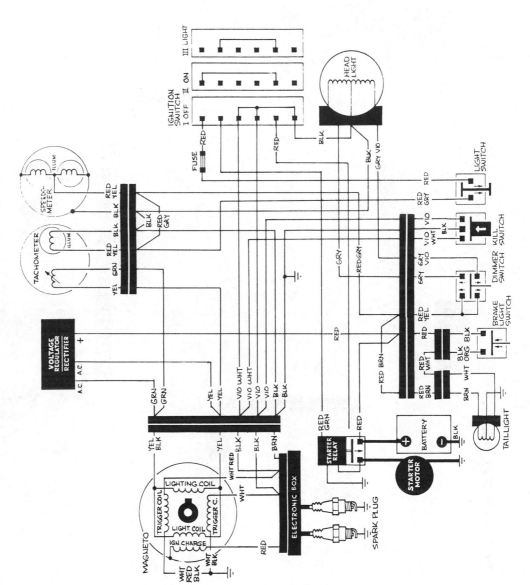

T'NT EVEREST 440E (1975)

T'NT F/A 340, 440 (1975)

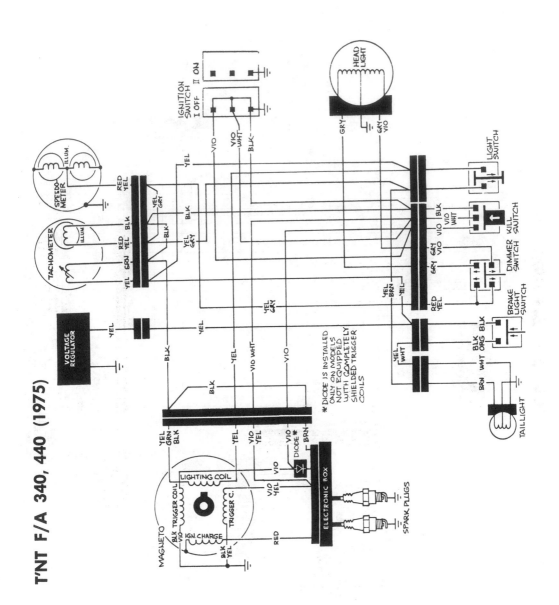

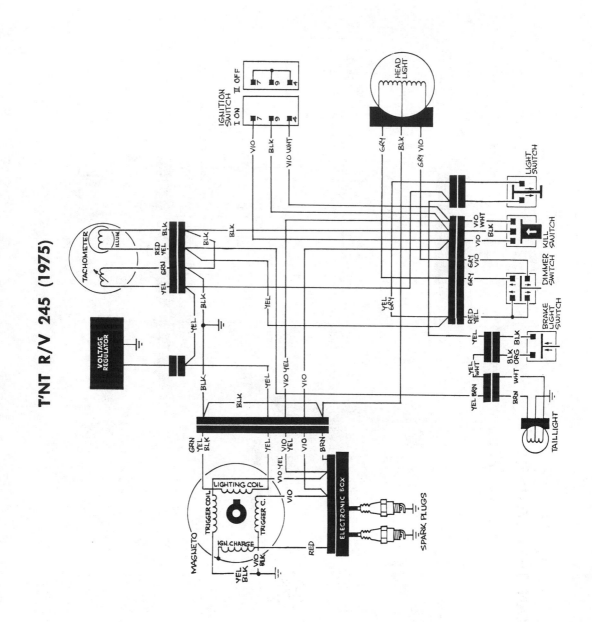

T'NT R/V 245 (1975)

ELAN 250 (1976-1977)

After serial number 3013 03999

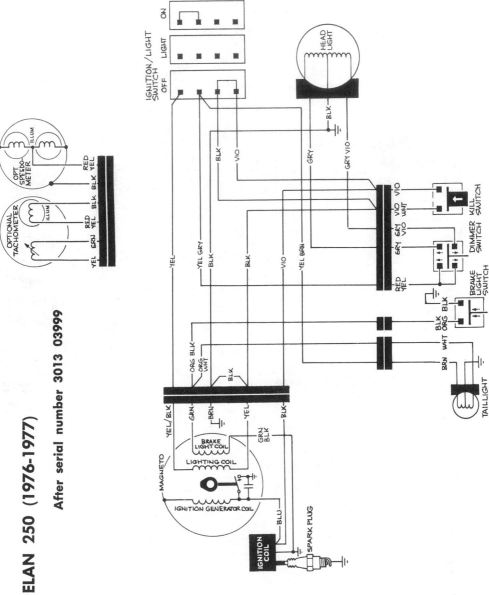

12

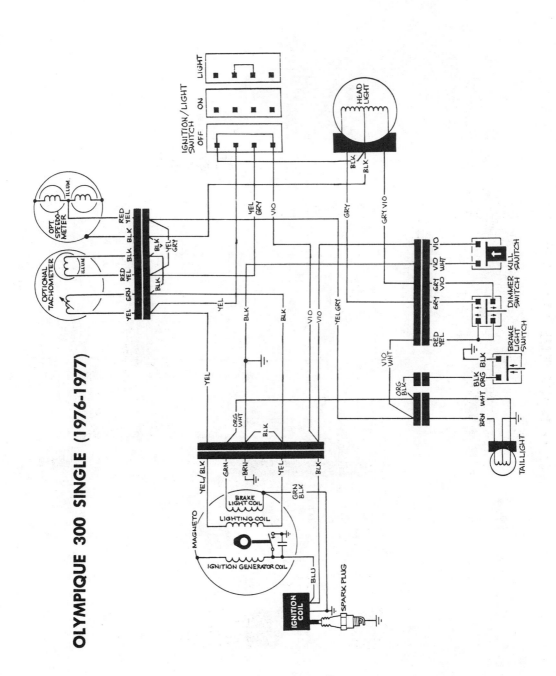

OLYMPIQUE 300 SINGLE (1976-1977)

OLYMPIQUE PLUS 440 (1976)

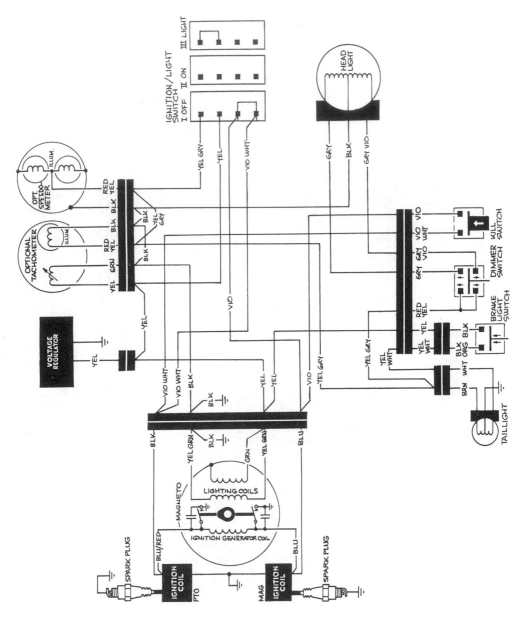

T'NT R/V 250, 350 (1976-1977)

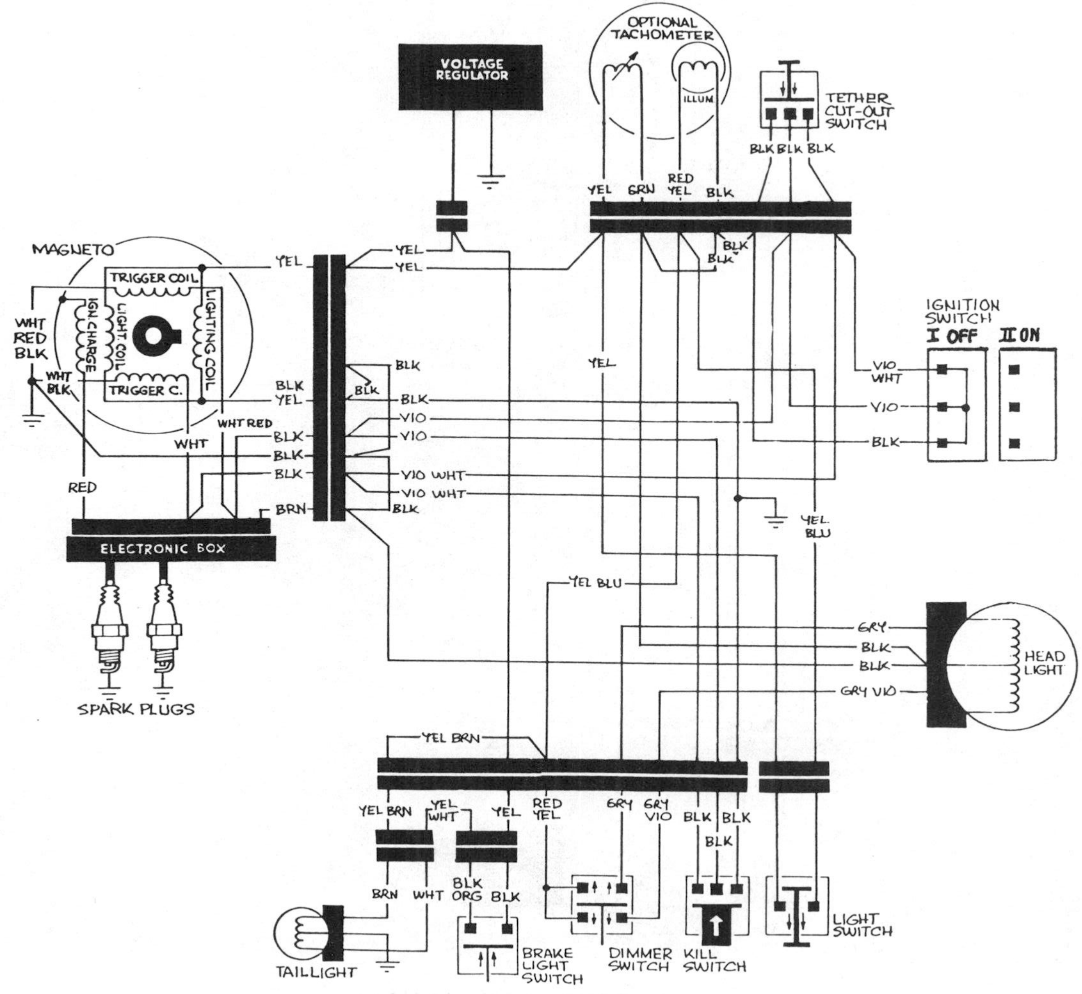

BLIZZARD 6500 (1978)

CITATION (1978-1979)

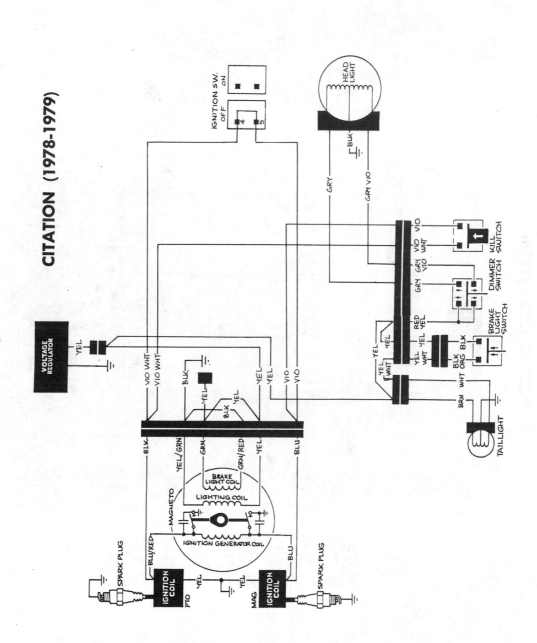

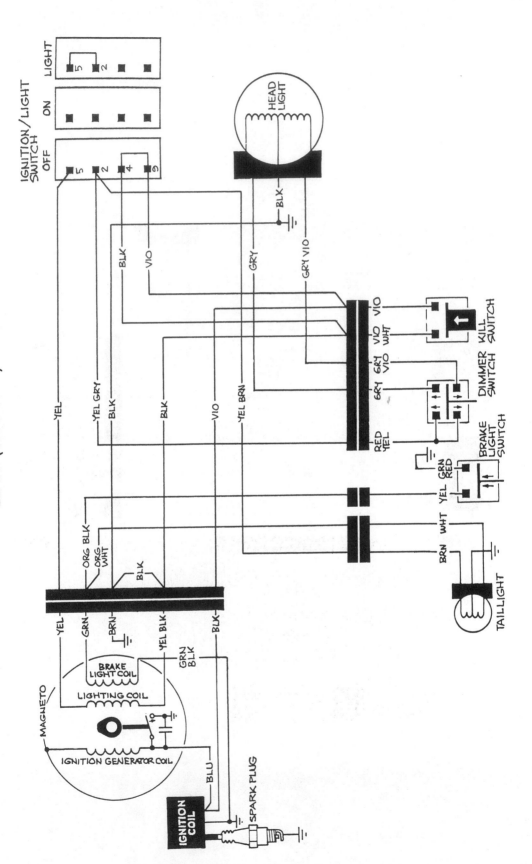

ELAN (1978-1979)

12

ELAN 250 DELUXE (1978-1979)

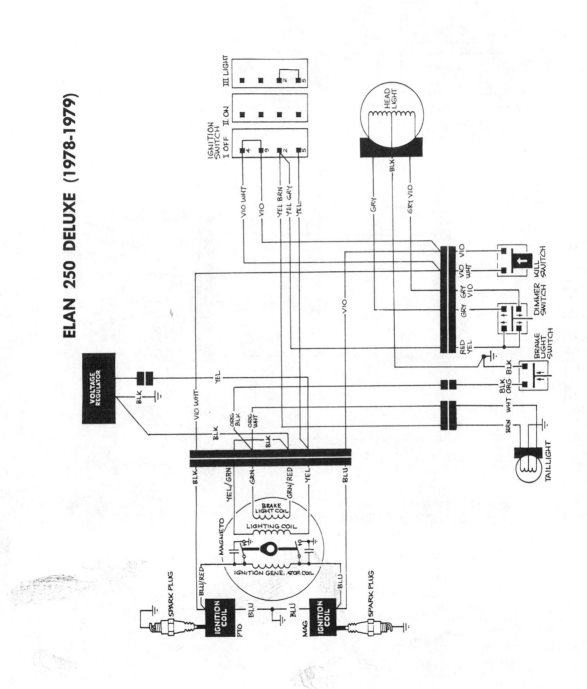

EVEREST 440E (1978-1979)

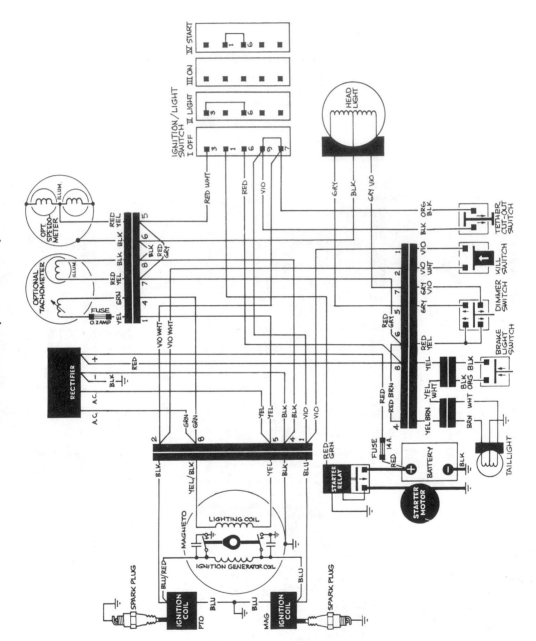

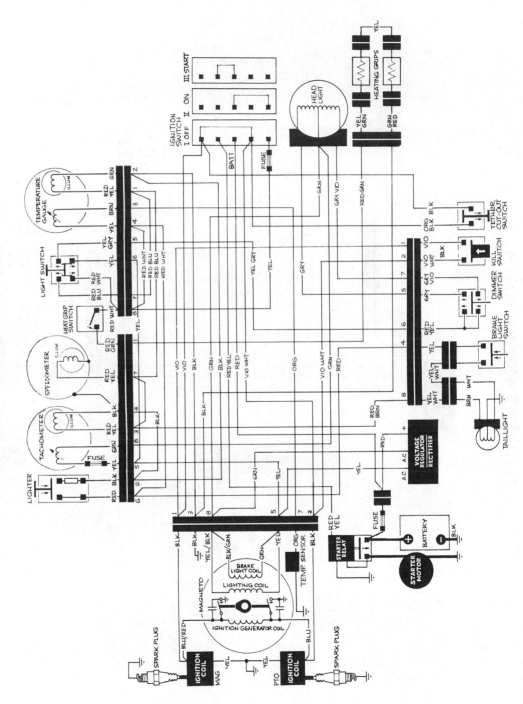

EVEREST 444LC (1978-1979)

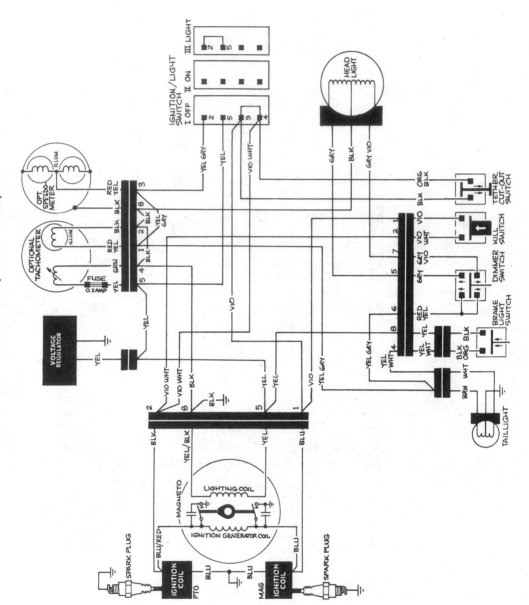

OLYMPIQUE 300-340 (1978-1979)

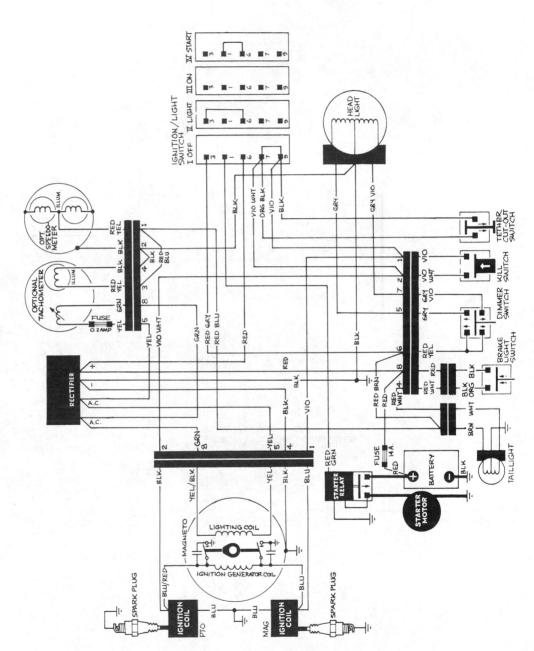

OLYMPIQUE 340E (1978-1979)

RV 340 (1978)

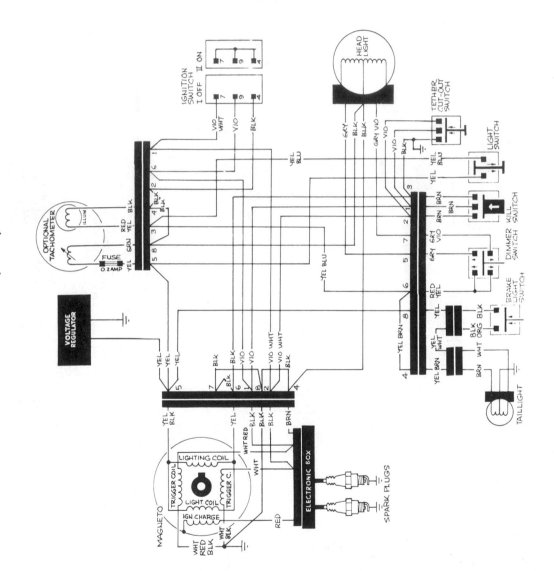

TN'T F/A 340; T'NT F/C 440 (1978)
EVEREST 340-440 (1978-1979)

411016